The Oxf
French

Edited by
Marie-Hélène Corréard
and Mary O'Neill

Oxford   New York
OXFORD UNIVERSITY PRESS
1997

Oxford University Press, Great Clarendon Street, Oxford OX2 6DP

Oxford New York
Athens Auckland Bangkok Bogota Bombay
Buenos Aires Calcutta Cape Town Dar es Salaam
Delhi Florence Hong Kong Istanbul Karachi
Kuala Lumpur Madras Madrid Melbourne
Mexico City Nairobi Paris Singapore
Taipei Tokyo Toronto Warsaw

and associated companies in
Berlin Ibadan

Oxford is a trade mark of Oxford University Press

© Oxford University Press, 1997

First published 1997

British Library Cataloguing in Publication Data
Data available

Library of Congress Cataloging in Publication Data
Data available
ISBN 0–19–864527–9

10   9   8   7   6   5   4   3   2   1

Typeset by Latimer Trend & Company Ltd.
Printed in Great Britain by
The Bath Press

Contents

The Oxford Starter French Dictionary

Chief Editor
Marie-Hélène Corréard

Associate Editor
Mary O'Neill

Editors
Gearóid Cronin
Françoise de Peretti
Natalie Pomier

Lexical usage notes
Henri Béjoint
Richard Wakely

Data-capture
Alison Curr
Diane Diffley

Administration
Isabelle Lemoine

Proofreading
Alison Curr
Isabelle Lemoine

North American English
Tim Horner
Carol Petersen

Dictionary know-how
Glossary of grammatical terms
Martyn Bird

Design
Information Design Unit
Jane Stevenson

Introduction

The *Oxford Starter French Dictionary* represents a major departure from traditional bilingual dictionaries on several fronts. It has been specially designed for beginners and is not simply a scaled-down version of a larger dictionary. It approaches the specific needs of the English-speaking learner of French from a very different angle.

It looks different

The dictionary page is refreshingly uncluttered with streamlined typeface and symbols providing a consistent structure for the information both in English and French. Subdivisions of text are clearly indicated using bullet points and Arabic numerals. The move from one language to the other is explicitly indicated in = signs. Points of basic grammar are reinforced using the ! sign and colloquial usage is marked for French.

It provides essential information in a new way

Every effort has been made to approach the foreign language from the point of view of the beginner who may be unfamiliar with the conventions of the more traditional bilingual dictionary.

The only abbreviations you will find are those which are entirely self-explanatory as headwords in the wordlist. Parts of speech, gender labels, and grammatical terms are all given in full with a glossary providing explanations and examples of different parts of speech in use. More complex grammatical issues are dealt with in short notes at appropriate points in the text or in the more detailed boxed grammar notes.

Entries which present similar problems—pronouns, negatives, etc.—are treated in parallel, reinforcing the idea of language as an ordered, coherent structure. Sets of words which behave in a similar way are also treated in a consistent manner and the user is encouraged to cross-refer to different parts of the dictionary, whether it be to consult verb tables, a phrasal verb block or usage notes dealing with *games and sports, days of the week* or *languages and nationalities*.

The language used in examples and in sense indicators (or signposts to the correct translation) is carefully screened and reflects current English and French as it is based on up-to-date corpus information.

Both varieties of English—British and American—are covered and clearly labelled on the English–French side, while users on both sides of the Atlantic will recognize the appropriate English-language equivalent for items in the French–English part of the dictionary.

The two sides of the dictionary have distinct functions

Each side of the dictionary is shaped by its specific function. The French–English side is designed to capitalize on what English speakers know about their language, hence the more streamlined presentation of English-language information. From irregular verb forms to common idiomatic usage such as might be encountered in the media, the *Oxford Starter French Dictionary* provides generous coverage of those aspects of French which are less easy to decode for English speakers. Irregular verbs, adjectives and plurals are all featured in the wordlist, referring the user to the base form with the translations. Colloquial usage is indicated by means of symbols which are explained at the bottom of the page, alerting users to the issue of register in the foreign language.

The English–French side is longer, providing the user going into the foreign language with maximum guidance in the form of detailed coverage of essential grammar, clear signposts to the correct translation for a particular context and lots of examples.

The *Oxford Starter French Dictionary* is unique as an accessible and user-friendly introduction to the French language. It has been designed to deal with the perennial problems of language learning and language teaching in a radically different way.

The structure of French–English entries

headword ······ **bête**
1 *adjective*
numbers indicating ···· = stupid, silly
grammatical ····· **2** *noun, feminine*
categories une bête = an animal ···························· translation clearly
indicated by =

champion/championne *noun,*
masculine/feminine
un champion/une championne = a ·········· feminine form of
champion headword

abbreviation ······ **DOM-TOM** *noun, masculine plural*
(*abbreviation of* **départements et**
territoires d'outre-mer)
explanatory gloss ······ *French overseas departments and*
territories

eau *noun, feminine* ····························· part of speech plus
(*plural*) **eaux** gender
l'eau = water
compounds ······ **l'eau gazeuse** = fizzy water, sparkling
presented in water
block at end **l'eau minérale** = mineral water
of entry **l'eau potable** = drinking water

··························· number of verb
informer *verb* 1 conjugation pattern
1 (**!** + *avoir*) ···························
= to inform
2 s'informer (**!** + *être*) ···················· information
• s'informer = to keep oneself informed on correct
• s'informer de = to enquire about grammatical usage

pleut ▶ **pleuvoir** ····························· cross-reference to
headword

rattraper *verb* 1
bullet points ······ • = to catch up with
indicating a **rattraper un concurrent** = to catch up
separate sense of with a competitor ···························· examples
the headword • = to make up for
rattraper le temps perdu = to make up
for lost time
• = to recapture, to catch

symbol drawing ··············
attention to **zut×** *exclamation*
register = blast!
= oh dear!

The structure of English–French entries

headword ····· **circus** *noun*
a circus = un cirque ··· gender of French
nouns made clear

delicious *adjective*
= délicieux/délicieuse ···································· feminine form of
adjectives made
clear

part of speech ····················
made clear

fed up *adjective*
to be fed up = en avoir marre**×** ························· symbol drawing
attention to
register

fire

numbers indicating ····· **1** *noun*
grammatical
categories
fire = le feu ·· indicators which
a fire *(for heat)* = un feu ·· spell out the
(causing damage) = un incendie different senses
to catch fire = prendre feu of the headword
to be on fire = être en feu

2 *verb*
bullet points ······ • *(to shoot)* = tirer
indicating a ·········· • *(to dismiss)* = renvoyer
separate sense
of the headword

fireman *noun* ▶ **315**│ ································· page number
a fireman = un pompier cross-reference
separate entries ····· **fire station** *noun* to a usage note
for compounds
a fire station = une caserne de pompiers

····································· translation clearly
···: indicated by =

kick *verb*
to kick someone = donner un coup de
pied à quelqu'un
he kicked the ball = il a donné un coup de
pied dans le ballon

phrasal verbs ······ **kick off** = donner le coup d'envoi
presented in ········ **kick out**
independent
blocks
to kick someone out = mettre
quelqu'un à la porte

need *verb*
• *(to have to)* ··· basic structure to
you don't need to ask permission = tu use as a model
n'es pas obligé de demander la
permission
they'll need to come early = il va falloir
qu'ils viennent de bonne heure

information ·········· **!** *Note that the subjunctive is used after*
on correct *falloir que.*
grammatical usage

• *(to want)* = avoir besoin de
they need [money│help│friends...] = ils ont
besoin [d'argent│d'aide│d'amis...]
example indicating ······ we need to see the doctor = nous avons
generative besoin de voir le médecin
structure everything you need = tout ce qu'il
vous faut

How to use the dictionary

Where to look for a word

The dictionary is divided into two sections: French into English and English into French. What you need to decide first of all is whether you are trying to work out the meaning of something in French or to translate something into French. Then you know which section of the dictionary to consult to find the word or words you want.

How to use the information given in the dictionary

Once you have found the dictionary entry for the word you want, scan the whole entry if it's a short one to find the sense which is closest to the one you need. If you find that the entry is long and quite complex first identify the part of speech of the word you want to translate.

---

breton/bretonne
1 *adjective*
  = Breton
2 breton *noun, masculine*
  le breton = Breton

drink
1 *verb*
  = boire
2 *noun*
  a drink = une boisson
  a drink of water = un verre d'eau

If you need help in finding out what part of speech you are dealing with, have a look at the glossary of grammatical terms on p. x.

Once you've found the right grammatical category, check the range of senses covered within each category as before to find the one you want.

---

broche *noun, feminine*
• (*an ornament*)
  une broche = a brooch, a pin
• (*for cooking*)
  une broche = a spit

go off
• (*to explode*) = exploser
• (*to ring*) (*if it's an alarm clock*) = sonner
  (*if it's an alarm*) = se déclencher
  (**!** + *être*)
• (*to leave*) = partir (**!** + *être*)
• **the milk will go off** = le lait va tourner
• (*to be switched off*) = s'éteindre
  (**!** + *être*)

Understanding French

A very important factor in understanding the French word is to know whether it is masculine or feminine. Since this will determine the form of the adjective, determiner or pronoun to be used, it is worth looking out for clues to the gender of the word. This might very well affect the shape of the word or words you are dealing with.

---

brocanteur/brocanteuse *noun,*
masculine/feminine
  un brocanteur/une brocanteuse = a bric-à-
    brac dealer

The same applies to number, whether a word is singular or plural.

---

actualité
1 *noun, feminine*
  l'actualité = current affairs, current events
2 actualités *noun, feminine plural*
  les actualités = the news

Irregular or 'unrecognizable' forms of verbs, nouns, adjectives and pronouns have their own place in the wordlist with a handy cross-reference to the main entry where the information is presented.

plu
- ▶ **plaire** ⑤⑨
- ▶ **pleuvoir** ③③

Translating into French

In order to translate into the foreign language, you need full guidance on how to write and speak correctly in French. All the information which is necessary to get it right will be found in the dictionary in the English to French section.

cool *adjective*
- *(fresh, not hot)* = frais/fraîche
  a cool drink = une boisson fraîche
  it's much cooler today = il fait beaucoup
    plus frais aujourd'hui
- *(calm)* = calme
- *(fashionable)* = branché/branchée✱
- *(relaxed)* = décontracté/décontractée
cool down
- *(to get colder)* = refroidir
- *(to calm down)* = se calmer (**!** + *être*)

You will find additional information on points of basic French grammar such as the use of *être* when forming the past tense of certain verbs and the obligatory use of the *subjunctive* in a range of contexts. These notes are designed to help you to produce correct French in areas where it is all too easy to forget certain important grammatical rules.

pity
1 *noun*
- **pity** = la pitié
- *(when expressing regret)*
  what a pity! = quel dommage!
  it's a pity you can't come = c'est
    dommage que tu ne puisses pas venir
  ! *Note that the subjunctive is used after* c'est dommage que.

drown *verb*
= se noyer (**!** + *être*)

If you are unable to translate an English word into French because you can't find it in the wordlist, try to use another word with the same or a similar sense or choose another form of wording which will enable you to find what you're looking for.

You want to translate *to defend yourself* but only have the translation for *defend*. You could try *fight back* as an alternative which gives *se défendre* as the translation. Instead of saying *I'd like a chance to travel*, try *I'd like an opportunity to travel* and so on.

defend *verb*
= défendre

fight back = se défendre (**!** + *être*)

A very useful feature of this dictionary are the boxed usage notes which cover sets of related words based on topics such as *countries, cities, and continents, days of the week*, and *nationalities*. At the entry for Chinese, you'll see a number which refers you to the page with a note dealing with languages and nationalities. The information there is relevant for all other words of this kind in the dictionary.

Chinese ▶ 275|
1 *adjective*
= chinois/chinoise
2 *noun*
- *(the people)*
  the Chinese = les Chinois (*masculine plural*)
- *(the language)*
  Chinese = le chinois

Glossary of grammatical terms

This section explains the basic terms that are used in this dictionary to help you to find the information that you need. The numbers in brackets refer to the appropriate exercises in the Dictionary know-how section p. 171.

Adjective (1, 14) An adjective is used to add extra information to a noun—*a **worried** farmer, a **black** cat, a **thick** book*. In French: *un fermier **inquiet**, un chat **noir**, un livre **épais***. Note that in English, the adjective usually comes before the noun, whereas in French it usually comes after the noun.

Sometimes, of course, the adjective is separated from its noun:

*Your garden is **beautiful**.*

*Votre jardin est **beau**.*

Adverb (5, 16) An adverb is used to add extra information to a verb, an adjective or another adverb—*to walk **slowly**, **extremely** satisfied, **quite** often*. In French: *marcher **lentement**, **extrêmement** satisfait, **assez** souvent*.

Agreement There are two kinds of agreement in French which you must be careful about.

The first is the agreement of nouns and adjectives. All nouns in French have a gender, and most can also be either singular or plural. Any adjective which describes a noun must 'agree' with it in both gender (masculine or feminine) and number (singular or plural). In other words, the adjective must also be masculine or feminine, singular or plural: *un garçon intelligent, une fille intelligente, deux garçons intelligents, deux filles intelligentes*.

The other kind of agreement is that between a verb and its subject. You must always ensure that the ending of the verb is the one which matches the subject. If the subject is a pronoun, this is fairly straightforward since we usually learn the various forms of a verb together with the appropriate pronoun: *je vais, tu vas, il/elle va, nous allons, vous allez, ils/elles vont*.

If the subject of the verb is a noun, or a pronoun like *moi, toi* etc, you have to be more careful to get the form of the verb right.

Pierre et son ami vont au cinéma.
*(Pierre + son ami = **ils**)*

La banque ouvre à neuf heures.
*(la banque = **elle**)*

Hélène et moi avons deux enfants.
*(Hélène + moi = **nous**)*

C'est toi qui as acheté ces carottes?
*(c'est toi qui = **tu**)*

Auxiliary verbs An auxiliary verb is a verb which is combined with another verb in order to form the so-called compound tenses of that verb (the main compound

tenses in French are the perfect, the pluperfect and the future perfect). There are two auxiliary verbs in French, *avoir* and *être*, and each is used with a particular group of verbs.

The auxiliary verb *être* is used first of all to form the compound tenses of all reflexive verbs:

*Vous vous **êtes** levé à quelle heure?*
(What time did you get up?)

*Je m'**étais** couché tard.*
(I had gone to bed late).

It is also used to form the compound tenses of a small group of verbs. These verbs are:

aller	to go
arriver	to arrive
descendre	to go/come down
entrer	to enter
monter	to go/come up
mourir	to die
naître	to be born
partir	to leave, to set out
passer	to go past, to drop in on
rester	to remain, to stay
retourner	to return
sortir	to go/come out
tomber	to fall
venir	to come

il est allé au marché.
(he went to the market.)

je suis descendu.
(I went down.)

The auxiliary verb *avoir* is used to form the compound tenses of all other verbs:

j'ai fait le ménage.
(I've done the housework.)

elle a fini son travail.
(she has finished her work.)

nous avions déjà mangé.
(we had already eaten.)

Comparative The comparative, as its name indicates, is the form of the adjective or adverb which enables us to compare two or more nouns or pronouns. In English, this is usually done by putting *more, less* or *as* before the appropriate adjective or adverb:

*Anne is **more** sensitive (than her sister).*
*Louise is **less** tired (than Jacqueline).*
*Léa is **as** intelligent (as Louise).*

In French, the equivalent comparatives are *plus, moins* and *aussi*:

*Anne est **plus** sensible (que sa sœur).*
*Louise est **moins** fatiguée (que Jacqueline).*
*Léa est **aussi** intelligente (que Louise).*

Note that the French for both *than* and *as* is *que*.

In English, a few adjectives have an irregular comparative form (*good*/**better**, *bad*/**worse**, *little*/**less**, *much* or *many*/**more**) and some shorter English adjectives have a special comparative form ending in *-er* (for example, *bigger*, *smaller*, *happier*, *slower*). In French, there are only three adjectives with a special form: *bon*/**meilleur** (*good*/*better*); *mauvais*/**pire** (*bad*/*worse*); *petit*/**moindre** (*small*/*less*). However, note that *plus petit* is used instead of *moindre* when referring to size: *ma voiture est **plus petite** que la tienne* (*my car is smaller than yours*). The only irregular form which is always used is *meilleur*—don't forget that, like all comparative adjectives, it must agree with its noun: *une **meilleure** chanson* (*a better song*), *de **meilleurs** chanteurs* (*better singers*).

The comparative of adverbs is formed in much the same way:

> *Paul walks **more** slowly (than his brother).*
> *Peter speaks **less** quickly (than Paul).*
> *Paul goes to Paris **as** often (as Peter).*
>
> *Paul marche **plus** lentement (que son frère).*
> *Peter parle **moins** vite (que Paul).*
> *Paul va à Paris **aussi** souvent (que Peter).*

In both English and French, there are four irregular forms: *beaucoup*/**plus** (*much* or *a lot*/**more**); *bien*/**mieux** (*well*/**better**); *peu*/**moins** (*little*/**less**); *mal*/**pis** or *plus mal* (*badly*/**worse**). However, *pis* is only found in a few fixed expressions and the usual comparative of *mal* is *plus mal*: *je chante **plus mal** que lui* (*I sing worse than he does*).

Conditional A conditional sentence is one in which the statement contained in the main clause can only be fulfilled if the condition stated in the subordinate clause is also fulfilled. This condition is usually introduced by *if* in English and by *si* in French.

> *If it's fine tomorrow, we'll go to the beach.*
> *I would be surprised if he came today.*
>
> *S'il fait beau demain, nous irons à la plage.*
> *Je serais surpris s'il venait aujourd'hui.*

Conjunction (14) A conjunction can be either (i) a word like *and* or *but* which is used to join words or simple sentences together, or (ii) a word like *when*, *although*, *if*, *where*, which is used to form a complex sentence. Look at these examples:

> (i) *John **and** Sarah*
> *Tired **but** happy*
> *They came down the steps **and** got into the car.*
>
> *Sophie **et** Pierre*
> *Fatigué **mais** heureux*
> *Ils ont descendu les marches **et** sont montés dans la voiture.*

> (ii) ***Although** he doesn't like the rain, he agreed to go for a walk.*
> *He was about to go to bed **when** he heard the noise of an aircraft.*
>
> ***Bien qu'**il n'aime pas la pluie, il a accepté de faire une promenade.*
> *Il était sur le point de se coucher, **quand** il a entendu le bruit d'un avion.*

Determiner (16) A determiner is used before a noun in order to identify more precisely what is being referred to. Here are some examples of determiners in English: *a car*, *the car*, *my car*, *this car*, *these cars*, *some cars*. Examples of French determiners are: ***une** voiture*, ***la** voiture*, ***ma** voiture*, ***cette** voiture*, ***ces** voitures*, ***certaines** voitures*.

Exclamation An exclamation is a word or phrase conveying a reaction such as surprise, shock, disapproval, indignation, amusement etc. In both English and French, it is usually followed by an exclamation mark.

> *Well, well!*
> *What!*
>
> *Ça alors!*
> *Quoi!*

Feminine (10, 13, 19) ▶ Gender

Gender (2, 10, 13, 19) You will see when using the French–English half of this dictionary that some French words are marked (*noun, masculine*) or (*noun, feminine*). Unlike English nouns, every French noun has a gender—it is either masculine or feminine. For example, the French words for *office*, *pen*, *tree*, *roof* are masculine (*un bureau*, *un stylo*, *un arbre*, *un toit*), and the words for *car*, *table*, *house*, *photo* are feminine (*une voiture*, *une table*, *une maison*, *une photo*). When looking up a noun in the dictionary, it is important to note whether the French word is masculine or feminine, because this will determine the form of most adjectives and determiners which go with it—*un grand arbre*, but *une grande maison*.

Imperative The imperative is the form of the verb which we use when we want to order someone to do something. In English, there are two imperatives: for example, *leave* and *let's leave*. In French, there are three in order to allow for the *tu* and *vous* forms of the verb: for example, *pars* (*tu* form), *partons*, *partez* (*vous* form).

Indicative ▶ Subjunctive

Infinitive The infinitive is a form of the verb which has no indication of person or tense. In English, it is often preceded by *to*: *to walk*, *to run*, *to read*, *to receive*. In French, the infinitive ends in *-er*, *-ir*, *-re* or *-oir*: *marcher*, *courir*, *écrire*, *recevoir*. The infinitive is the form you will find at the beginning of verb entries in this and other dictionaries.

Masculine (10) ▶ Gender

Noun (1, 16, 17) A noun is used to identify a person, an animal, an object, an idea or an emotion—*farmer, cat, book, suggestion, happiness* are all nouns. It can also be the name of an individual, a company or an institution—*Emma, Peter, Robertson's, Parliament* are nouns. Equivalent French nouns are *fermier, chat, livre, suggestion, bonheur, Sophie, Pierre, Boulangerie Fauré, Conseil d'État.*

Number (16) As in English, most nouns in French may be singular or plural and change their ending accordingly (usually by adding '-s' in the plural: *a tree, two tree**s***; *un arbre, deux arbre**s***). Unlike English, however, adjectives in French may also be singular or plural and in most cases change their ending in order to agree with the noun they describe: *un grand arbre, deux grand**s** arbre**s**.*

In the French–English half of this dictionary, when a noun has an irregular plural, the plural form is given after the noun. A noun which doesn't change in the plural has the warning (**!** *never changes*).

Object (6) The object of a sentence is the word or group of words which is immediately affected by the action indicated by the verb. So, in the sentence *The dog chewed the bone, dog* is the subject, *chewed* is the verb and ***bone*** is the object. Similarly, in the sentence *Le chien a rongé l'os, chien* is the subject, *a rongé* is the verb and *os* is the object.

There may be two kinds of object in a sentence, a direct object and an indirect object. In the examples above, *bone* and *os* are strictly direct objects. However, in the sentence *John gave the dog a bone, John* is the subject, *gave* is the verb, *bone* is the direct object and *dog* is the indirect object. Similarly, in the French sentence *Jean a donné un os au chien, Jean* is the subject, *a donné* is the verb, *os* is the direct object and *chien* is the indirect object. So, in general terms, the indirect object indicates the person or thing which 'benefits' from the action of the verb upon the direct object.

Phrasal verb (15) A phrasal verb is a verb combined with a preposition or an adverb and having a particular meaning. For example, *to **run away***, meaning to flee, or *to **see to** something*, meaning to ensure that something is done.

Phrasal verbs don't exist in French and you therefore need to use your dictionary carefully in order to select the correct translation. If you look up *to run away* for

example, you will see that phrasal verbs are listed after all the other meanings of the word *run*, and in alphabetical order of the following adverb or preposition.

Plural ▶ Number

Preposition (11) A preposition is a word, such as *under, beside, across, in*, which is usually followed by a noun: *under the table, beside the road, in the garden*; ***sous** la table, **au bord de** la route, **dans** le jardin.* Most preposition + noun groups indicate movement

> he ran **towards the house**
> il a couru **vers la maison**

position

> your books are **on the table**
> vos livres sont **sur la table**

or time

> I'll be there **at 4 o'clock**
> je serai là **à six heures**.

Pronoun (3, 14) A pronoun is used instead of a noun in order to avoid repeating it unnecessarily. English pronouns are *I, me, you, he, him, she, her, it, we, us, they, them, mine, yours, his, hers, ours, theirs, this, that, these* and *those*. Equivalent French pronouns are: *je, me, tu, te, il, le, elle, la, nous, vous, ils, les, elles, leur, lui, le mien, la mienne, les miens, les miennes* etc, *ceci, cela, celui, celle, ceux, celles.* All of these are labelled as pronouns in this dictionary. However, some of the English pronouns (but *not* their French equivalents) can also be used as determiners and you must be careful not to confuse them. Compare these sentences:

> He lent me **his** book. (determiner)
> He lent me **his**. (pronoun)

> **These** ideas are important. (determiner)
> **These** are important. (pronoun)

> **Those** people have just arrived. (determiner)
> **Those** have just arrived. (pronoun)

Now look at the French equivalents:

> Il m'a prêté **son** livre. (determiner)
> Il m'a prêté **le sien**. (pronoun)

> **Ces** idées-ci sont importantes. (determiner)
> **Celles**-ci sont importantes. (pronoun)

> **Ces** gens-là viennent d'arriver. (determiner)
> **Ceux**-là viennent d'arriver. (pronoun)

Reflexive verb (24) A reflexive verb is one whose action is 'reflected back' upon the subject of the verb. In English, this is indicated by the use of reflexive pronouns such as *myself, yourself, herself, themselves, each other* etc. For example:

> When he hurts **himself**, he cries.
> We speak to **each other** every day.

In French, this reflexive action is conveyed by the use of the pronouns *me*, *te*, *se*, *nous* or *vous*:

> Quand il **se** fait mal, il pleure.
> Nous **nous** parlons tous les jours.

Here are the full present tense forms of the reflexive verb *se baigner* (*to go for a swim*):

je **me** baigne	nous **nous** baignons
tu **te** baignes	vous **vous** baignez
il **se** baigne	ils **se** baignent
elle **se** baigne	elles **se** baignent

Remember that many reflexive verbs in French have English equivalents which are not reflexive. Other examples are *se souvenir de* (*to remember*), *se laver* (*to wash*).

Singular ▶ Number

Subject (6) The subject of a sentence is the word or group of words which performs the action indicated by the verb. So, in the sentence *John coughed*, John is the subject of the verb *coughed*. Of course, the verb doesn't necessarily express an action as such. For example, in the sentence *John is tall*, John is the subject of the verb *is*. In the French sentence *Jean a toussé*, Jean is similarly the subject of the verb *a toussé*, and in the sentence *Jean est grand*, Jean is the subject of the verb *est*.

Subjunctive The subjunctive is a special form of some tenses of the verb, which in French is mostly used to express doubt and possibility, rather than fact or certainty. It is also used when expressing an emotional reaction to something. This form of the verb is much more widely used in French than in English, where it has almost disappeared, and you will find a fuller explanation and examples on p. 291. Note that the usual form of the various tenses of a verb is known as the indicative because it 'indicates' fact or certainty.

Superlative The superlative is the form of the adjective or adverb which is used to express the highest or lowest degree. In English, the adjective or adverb is usually preceded by *most* or *least*, **most** *important*, **least** *important*, **most** *carefully*, **least** *carefully*. Some adjectives and adverbs (usually of one syllable) have their own form: *best*, *worst*, *biggest*, *smallest*, *fastest*, *slowest* etc. In French, the superlative adjective (which must agree with its noun) is usually formed by putting *le plus*, *la plus*, *les plus*, *le moins*, *la moins* or *les moins* before the adjective: *le livre* **le plus** *long*, *le livre* **le moins** *long*, *la question* **la plus** *importante*, *la question* **la moins** *importante*, *les avions* **les plus** *rapides*, *les avions* **les moins** *rapides*. The superlative adverb is usually preceded by *le plus* or *le moins*: **le plus** *vite*, **le moins** *vite*, **le plus** *soigneusement*, **le moins** *soigneusement*.

Some French adjectives and adverbs have their own form of the superlative, for example:

bon/bonne	**le meilleur/la meilleure**
mauvais/mauvaise	**le pire/la pire**
bien	**le mieux**
mal	**le plus mal**

Tense The tense is the particular form of the verb which tells us the approximate time when the action of the verb takes place:

Present tense
He **is telephoning** all his friends.
Il téléphone à tous ses amis.

Future tense
He will telephone all his friends.
Il téléphonera à tous ses amis.

The main past and future tenses used in French are:

Past tenses	(i) Imperfect
	(ii) Present perfect (or Perfect)
	(iii) Past perfect (or Pluperfect)
Future tenses	(iv) Future (simple)
	(v) Future perfect

For example:

(i) Il **téléphonait** souvent à tous ses amis.
(He often used to telephone all his friends.)

(ii) Hier, il **a téléphoné** à tous ses amis.
(Yesterday he telephoned all his friends.)

(iii) Il **avait** déjà **téléphoné** à tous ses amis.
(He had already telephoned all his friends.)

(iv) Demain, il **téléphonera** à tous ses amis.
(Tomorrow he will telephone all his friends.)

(v) Avant 6 heures il **aura téléphoné** à tous ses amis.
(By 6 o'clock he will have telephoned all his friends.)

Verb (4, 12, 16) The verb propels the sentence along, telling us what is happening. Look at these examples:

> Paul **carried** the boxes upstairs to the attic.
> The storm **did** a lot of damage.

> Paul **a monté** les cartons au grenier.
> La tempête **a fait** beaucoup de dégâts.

Sometimes, of course, the verb doesn't describe an action, but rather a state of affairs:

> Paul **has** a back problem.
> He **is** often ill.
> The damage **appears** less serious than we expected.

> Paul **a** un problème de dos.
> Il **est** souvent malade.
> Les dégâts **semblent** moins importants que prévu.

A guide to French pronunciation

While phonetics have not been given for entries in the present dictionary, a simplified, user-friendly table summarizing the main features of French pronunciation and spelling follows.

This table is designed
(a) to help English speakers to bridge the gap between the sound systems of English and French
(b) to connect French sounds to the most frequent written representations of those sounds, illustrating the link by means of examples from basic French vocabulary.

Learners will find in it a useful point of departure for a more advanced study of French phonetics at a later stage. It is not, however, meant to take the place of either a human model—a teacher, for example—or a recording of the same sounds produced by a native speaker.

The table is subdivided into three main categories of phonetic sounds: *vowels*, *semi-vowels*, and *consonants*. The French sounds are presented in order of increasing complexity when compared with the English sound system. In many cases, the sounds are broadly similar, if not actually the same. In others, however, it is only possible in the present format to give an approximation in English terms of the French sound. This is indicated by the symbol ≈. This is particularly true of the French vowels which are nasalized (represented by ɛ̃, ɑ̃, ɔ̃, and œ̃ in the International Phonetic Alphabet) and those which require a marked degree of lip-rounding (represented by ø, œ, y, and ɥ).

A major distinguishing feature of written French is the mute h, as in **homme**, **hôtel**. It functions in the same way as a vowel and spelling or pronunciation adjust accordingly l'homme, cet homme, les hommes [lezɔm]. We have systematically included the mute h in the column dealing with French spelling forms while notes throughout the dictionary text regularly draw users' attention to this important feature.

M. O'N.

Vowels

phonetic symbol	sounds like English	written in French as	examples
a	c*a*t, fl*a*t	a, à, ha-	acheter, basse, patte, à, voilà, hameau (*note also* femme)
ɑ	*ar*m, c*ar*	â, as	âgé, gâteau, pâte, bas, las
e	h*ay*, tr*ay* but *shorter*	-er, -es, -ez, -é, -ée, é-, hé-	aller, des, nez, âgé, année, étage, hélas
ɛ	p*e*t, thr*ea*t	è-, ê-, e-, ai, -ais, ait, -ei-, aî-, -ê-, -et	règle, très, être, bête, elle, cet, aide, faible, français, lait, était, pleine, connaître, Noël, secret
i	tr*ea*t, fl*ee*t	i, -ie, -is, î-, hi, y, -ï	il, immeuble, libre, pile, vie, pris, île, hibou, elle y va, type, maïs
o	h*or*se, c*our*se	au, eau, aux, eaux, o, os, ô, hô-	aussi, gauche, tuyau, beau, château, chevaux, eaux, chose, orage, loto, gros, côte, hôtel (*note also* trop)
ɔ	h*o*t, wh*a*t	o-, ho-, hô-	objet, dommage, randonnée, botte, horaire, hôpital
u	h*oo*t, fl*u*te	ou, où, -oû-, -oo-, hou-, -oux	ouvrir, trou, mourir, amour, où, goûter, football, houx, roux (*note also* août)

Vowels

phonetic symbol	sounds like English	written in French as	examples
ə	ago, gather (*British English*)	e (*silent at the end of words and may even be left out*)	mère, elle, j'aime, même, premier, grenouille, menu, le, ne, de, petit, fera, chemin, médecin
ø	*purr*, h*er* but *shorter*	eu, eux	Europe, peu, neveu, bleu, chanteuse, heureux, cheveux, yeux
œ	≈ f*un*, s*on*	eu, œu-, heu-, œ	peur, déjeuner, meuble, humeur, fauteuil, œuf, sœur, heure, œil
y	*ee* but with *rounded lips*	u, û, hu	une, utile, rue, vendu, mûr, sûr, humeur, hurler (*note also* eu)
ɛ̃	*an*/*am* + *nasal twang*	in, im, ain, -ein, -yn, ym, -en, -aim, hein	intéressant, matin, imbécile, train, copain, plein, peindre, syndicat, sympa, italien, rien, faim, hein
ɑ̃	*awn*/*alm* + *nasal twang*	an, -ant, en, em-, -ent, am-	an, chanter, chant, entrer, ennui, empêcher, tempête, souvent, rampe (*note also* temps, paon, banc, sang *and* champ)
ɔ̃	*on* + *nasal twang*	on, om, hon-	onze, bon, montrer, jambon, ombre, sombre, tromper, honte
œ̃	f*un*, s*on* + *nasal twang*	un, -um	un, brun, lundi, parfum

Semi-Vowels

phonetic symbol	sounds like English	written in French as	examples
j	*yes*, pla*y*er	-i-, y, -il, -ill-	bien, ciel, tiède, il y a, yaourt, payer, soleil, travail, feuille, fille, billet
w	≈ *was*	oi, -oî-, ou, -oê-, w-	oiseau, voir, besoin, quoi, oui, jouet, boîte, poêle, K-way
ɥ	≈ *we*, *tweet* but with *rounded lips*	-ui-, hui, -uî-, huî-	nuit, lui, aujourd'hui, huit, huître

Consonants

phonetic symbol	sounds like English	written in French as	examples
b	as English	b, -bb-	bain, robe, abbaye
d	as English	d, -dd-	devoir, aide, addition
f	as English	f, -ff-, ph	fête, neuf, affaires, photo, téléphone
k	as English	c, qu-, -q, -cc-, k, -ck-, -ch-	café, sac, quartier, marquer, coq, occupé, kilomètre, kayak, ticket, orchestre
l	as English	l, -ll-	lettre, pile, mal, ville, salle
m	as English	m, -mm-	mère, madame, femme, sommeil
n	as English	n, -nn-	non, animal, panne, donner
p	as English	p, -pp-, -bs-	pomme, chapeau, hop, appuyer, observer
s	as English	s, -ss-, c, ç-, sc-	son, festival, assiette, poisson, chasse, cette, tracer, cil, garçon, ça, reçu, scène, piscine (*note also* six, dix)
t	as English	t, -tt-, th	tour, auto, patte, thé, bibliothèque
v	as English	v, w	venir, lever, grave, wagon, W-C
z	as English	-s-, z, -x-	maison, loisirs, brise, zoo, bizarre, dix-huit, sixième
g	as English	g, gu-, -gg-	goût, bagarre, gai, guitare, blague, aggressif
ʒ	lei*s*ure, sei*z*ure	j, g-, ge-	j'ai, jeune, déjeuner, plage, geler, gifler, gîte, nageons
ʃ	ra*sh*, *sh*oe	ch, sh	château, achats, riche, poche, short
ɲ	*n*ew, o*ni*on	gn	ignorer, vignoble, soigner, champignon (*note also* oignon)
ŋ	si*ng*, wro*ng*	-ng	camping, parking
ʀ	≈ a very soft lo*ch* sound produced at the *back* of the throat	r, -rr-, rh-	rouge, partir, arrêter, marre, rhume

a ▶ avoir 8

à *preposition*
(**!** à + le *becomes* au; à + les *becomes* aux)

> **!** *You will find translations for phrases with* à *such as* à côté de, à l'étranger, penser à, *etc. under the entries* côté, étranger, penser, *etc.*

- (*showing destination*) = to
  se rendre [à Nice | à l'école | aux courses ...]
    = to go [to Nice | to school | to the races ...]
- (*showing location*) = in
  = at
  = on
  habiter [à la campagne | au Portugal | aux États-Unis ...] = to live [in the country | in Portugal | in the United States ...]
- (*in a description*) = with
  la maison aux volets verts = the house with the green shutters
- (*showing ownership*)
  le livre est [à moi | à eux | à Isabelle ...] = the book is [mine | theirs | Isabelle's ...]
- (*indicating a time, a speed, a price*) = at
  à minuit = at midnight
  un timbre à trois francs = a three-franc stamp
- (*meaning during a period of time*) = in
  au printemps = in (the) spring
- (*indicating a distance*)
  à cinq kilomètres = five kilometres away
- (*showing how something is done*)
  écrire au crayon = to write in pencil
  à pied = on foot

abandonner *verb* 1
- = to abandon
- = to give up

abeille *noun, feminine*
  une abeille = a bee

abîmer *verb* 1
1 (**!** + *avoir*)
  = to damage, to spoil
2 s'abîmer (**!** + *être*)
  s'abîmer = to get damaged

abonné/abonnée *noun, masculine/feminine*
  un abonné/une abonnée = a subscriber

abonnement *noun, masculine*
  un abonnement = a subscription

abonner: **s'abonner à** *verb* 1 (**!** + *être*)
  s'abonner à = to subscribe to

abord: **d'abord** *adverb*
  d'abord = first, at first
  tout d'abord = first of all

abri *noun, masculine*
  un abri = (a) shelter

abricot *noun, masculine*
  un abricot = an apricot

abriter *verb* 1
1 (**!** + *avoir*)
  = to shelter
2 s'abriter (**!** + *être*)
  s'abriter = to shelter, to take shelter

absent/absente *adjective*
  = absent, missing

absolument *adverb*
  = absolutely

accélérer *verb* 14
  = to accelerate

accepter *verb* 1
- = to accept
- = to agree to

accès *noun, masculine* (**!** *never changes*)
  l'accès = access
  'accès interdit' = 'no entrance', 'do not enter'

accident *noun, masculine*
  un accident = an accident

accompagner *verb* 1
- = to accompany, to go with
- = to take

accomplir *verb* 3
  = to carry out, to accomplish

accord *noun, masculine*
- **un accord** = an agreement
- **d'accord!** = OK!, all right!
  je suis d'accord avec toi = I agree with you

accorder *verb* 1
  = to give, to grant

accotement *noun, masculine*
  un accotement = a verge, a shoulder
  accotement non stabilisé = soft verge, soft shoulder

accroc *noun, masculine*
  un accroc (*in material*) = a tear, a rip

accrocher *verb* 1
1 (**!** + *avoir*)
  = to hang
2 s'accrocher (**!** + *être*)
  s'accrocher = to hang on, to cling
  accroche-toi à la branche = hang on to the branch

accueil *noun, masculine*
  un accueil = a welcome, a reception
  ils nous ont fait bon accueil = they made us welcome, they made us feel at home
  la famille d'accueil = the host family

accueillir verb 27
- (*if it's a host*) = to welcome
- (*if it's a stadium, a hotel*) = to accommodate

achat noun, masculine
un achat = a purchase
faire des achats = to do some shopping

acheter verb 18
= to buy

acheteur/acheteuse noun, masculine/feminine
un acheteur/une acheteuse = a buyer, a purchaser

acteur/actrice noun, masculine/feminine
un acteur/une actrice = an actor/an actress

actif/active adjective
= active

activité noun, feminine
une activité = an activity

actrice ▶ acteur

actualité
1 noun, feminine
l'actualité = current affairs, current events
2 **actualités** noun, feminine plural
les actualités = the news

actuel/actuelle adjective
= present, current

actuellement adverb
= currently, at the moment

addition noun, feminine
- (*in a restaurant, a café*)
l'addition = the bill, the check
- (*in arithmetic*)
une addition = an addition

additionner verb 1
= to add

adhérent/adhérente noun, masculine/feminine
un adhérent/une adhérente = a member

adhésion noun, feminine
l'adhésion = membership

adieu noun, masculine
(*plural*) **adieux**
= goodbye, farewell
faire ses adieux = to say goodbye

adjectif noun, masculine
un adjectif = an adjective

admettre verb 60
- = to admit
- = to allow
- être admis à un examen = to pass an exam, to pass a test
- admettons qu'il vienne = (let's) suppose he comes

admis/admise ▶ admettre 60

admission noun, feminine
l'admission = admission

adolescent/adolescente noun, masculine/feminine
un adolescent/une adolescente = a teenager, an adolescent

adorer verb 1
= to love, to adore

adresse noun, feminine
une adresse = an address
changer d'adresse = to move

adresser verb 1
1 (! + *avoir*)
- = to send
- = to address
2 **s'adresser** (! + *être*)
- s'adresser à un employé = to talk to an employee
- s'adresser à la banque = to contact the bank

adroit/adroite adjective
- = skil(l)ful
- = clever, smart

adversaire noun, masculine/feminine
un adversaire/une adversaire = an opponent

aérer verb 14
= to air

aérien/aérienne adjective
= air

aérobic noun, masculine
l'aérobic = aerobics

aérogare noun, feminine
une aérogare = an air terminal

aéroglisseur noun, masculine
un aéroglisseur = a hovercraft

aéroport noun, masculine
un aéroport = an airport

affaire
1 noun, feminine
une affaire = a bargain
2 **affaires** noun, feminine plural
- les affaires = business
- mes affaires = my things, my belongings

affairer: s'affairer verb 1 (! + *être*)
s'affairer = to bustle about, to hurry around

affectueusement adverb
= affectionately
(*ending a letter*) = love

affectueux/affectueuse adjective
= affectionate

affiche noun, feminine
une affiche = a poster
= a notice

afficher verb 1
- = to put up, to hang up
- = to display
  afficher complet = to be fully booked

affoler verb 1
1 (! + avoir)
  = to throw into a panic
2 s'affoler (! + être)
  s'affoler = to get into a panic

affreux/affreuse adjective
  = awful

afin
1 afin de preposition
  afin de = in order to
2 afin que conjunction
  afin que = so that

africain/africaine adjective
  = African

Afrique noun, feminine
  l'Afrique = Africa

agacer verb 12
  = to annoy, to irritate

âge noun, masculine
  l'âge = age
  quel âge as-tu? = how old are you?

âgé/âgée adjective
- = old, elderly
- **être âgé de 18 ans** = to be 18 years old

agence noun, feminine
  une agence = an agency
  une agence immobilière = an estate
  agent's, a real estate agency
  une agence de voyages = a travel
  agency

agenda noun, masculine
  un agenda = a diary, a date book

agent noun, masculine
  un agent = an agent
  un agent de la circulation = a traffic
  policeman
  un agent de police = a policeman, a
  police officer

agglomération noun, feminine
  une agglomération = a town
  = a village

agile adjective
  = agile

agir verb 3
1 (! + avoir)
  = to act
2 s'agir de (! + être)
  s'agir de = to be about
  de quoi s'agit-il? = what's it about?

agitation noun, feminine
- **l'agitation** = (the) bustle
- **l'agitation** = (the) excitement

agité/agitée adjective
  (describing the sea) = rough, choppy

agiter verb 1
1 (! + avoir)
- **agiter un mouchoir** = to wave a
  handkerchief
- **agiter un flacon** = to shake a bottle
2 s'agiter (! + être)
- **s'agiter** = to fidget
- **s'agiter** = to become restless

agneau noun, masculine
(plural) **agneaux**
- (the animal)
  un agneau = a lamb
- (the meat)
  l'agneau = lamb

agréable adjective
  = pleasant

agressif/agressive adjective
  = aggressive

agression noun, feminine
- **une agression** = an attack
- **une agression** = a mugging

agricole adjective
  = agricultural

agriculteur/agricultrice noun,
masculine/feminine
  un agriculteur/une agricultrice = a farmer

ai ▶ **avoir** 8

aide
1 noun, feminine
  l'aide = help
  = assistance
2 noun, masculine/feminine
  un aide/une aide = an assistant

aider verb 1
1 (! + avoir)
  = to help
2 s'aider de (! + être)
  s'aider de = to use

aïe exclamation
  = ouch!

aigle noun, masculine
  un aigle = an eagle

aigre adjective
- (tasting unpleasant) = sour
- (sounding unpleasant) = sharp

aiguille noun, feminine
- **une aiguille** = a needle
  une aiguille à tricoter = a knitting needle
- **les aiguilles d'une montre** = the hands on
  a watch

ail noun, masculine
  l'ail = garlic

aile noun, feminine
  une aile = a wing

aille ▶ **aller 1** 9

ailleurs
1 *adverb*
ailleurs = elsewhere, somewhere else
2 d'ailleurs = besides

aimable *adjective*
= kind, friendly

aimer *verb* [1]
• = to love
aimer ses enfants = to love one's children
• = to like, to be fond of
j'aime mieux le vin = I prefer wine

aîné/aînée *adjective*
= eldest, oldest
= elder, older

ainsi
1 *adverb*
• = in this way
et ainsi de suite = and so on
• = so
ainsi tu t'en vas? = so you're leaving?
2 ainsi que = and, as well as

air *noun, masculine*
• l'air = (the) air
en plein air = in the open (air), outdoors
allons prendre l'air = let's go and get some
  fresh air
• de l'air = a wind, a breeze
• (*appearance*)
un air = a look
avoir l'air heureux = to look happy
il n'a pas l'air de comprendre = he doesn't
  seem to understand
• (*for a song*)
un air = a tune

aire *noun, feminine*
une aire = an area
une aire de jeux = a playground
une aire de loisirs = a recreation area

aise: à l'aise *adverb*
à l'aise = at ease

ajouter *verb* [1]
1 (**!** + *avoir*)
= to add
2 s'ajouter à (**!** + *être*)
s'ajouter à = to be added to

alarme *noun, feminine*
donner l'alarme = to raise the alarm

album *noun, masculine*
un album = an album
un album à colorier = a colo(u)ring book

alcool *noun, masculine*
l'alcool = alcohol
sans alcool = nonalcoholic, alcohol-free

alcoolisé/alcoolisée *adjective*
= alcoholic

alcootest *noun, masculine*
un alcootest = a Breathalyzer® test

algèbre *noun, feminine*
l'algèbre = algebra

Alger *noun*
= Algiers

Algérie *noun, feminine*
l'Algérie = Algeria

algérien/algérienne *adjective*
= Algerian

aliment *noun, masculine*
un aliment = a food

alimentation *noun, feminine*
• (*the foods usually eaten*)
une alimentation saine = a healthy diet
• (*food retailing*)
un magasin d'alimentation = a grocery
  store

allais ▶ **aller 1** [9]

allée
1 *noun, feminine*
une allée = a path
(*wider*) = an avenue
(*leading to a garage*) = a drive, a driveway
2 allées *noun, feminine plural*
leurs allées et venues = their comings
  and goings

Allemagne *noun, feminine*
l'Allemagne = Germany

allemand/allemande
1 *adjective*
= German
2 allemand *noun, masculine*
l'allemand = German

aller
1 *verb* [9] (**!** + *être*)
• = to go
où vas-tu? = where are you going?
il faut que j'aille les voir = I must go and
  see them
allons-y! = let's go!
• (*when talking about the near future*) = to be
  going to
= to be about to
attention, tu vas tomber! = careful, you're
  going to fall!
j'allais partir quand il est arrivé = I was
  about to leave when he arrived
• (*when talking about health, business*)
comment vas-tu?, comment allez-vous?
  = how are you?
je vais bien = I'm fine
qu'est-ce qui ne va pas? = what's the
  matter?
  ! *For more examples, see* ça.

• (*to be flattering or convenient*) = to suit, to
  be good for
le rouge te va bien = red suits you, red is
  right for you
• (*to be of the right size*) = to fit
son costume ne lui va plus = his suit
  doesn't fit him any more
• (*when urging or encouraging*)
allons, taisez-vous! = come on, be quiet!
allez-y, tirez! = go on, pull!

2 s'en aller verb (**!** + être)
* (if it's a person)
s'en aller = to leave, to be off, to go (away)
va-t'en!, allez-vous-en! = go away!
* (if it's a stain)
s'en aller = to come out
3 noun, masculine
un aller simple = a single (ticket), a one-way ticket
un aller retour = a return ticket, a round trip ticket

allô exclamation
allô! = hello!

allonger verb 13
1 (**!** + avoir)
* = to lengthen
* = to stretch out
2 s'allonger (**!** + être)
* s'allonger = to lie down
* s'allonger = to get longer

allumer verb 1
* = to light
* = to turn on

allumette noun, feminine
une allumette = a match

allure noun, feminine
* l'allure = the speed
= the pace
à toute allure = at top speed
* une allure = an appearance
= a look

alors
1 adverb
* = so
et alors? = so what?
* = then
alors je prendrai le bleu = I'll take the blue one then, OK I'll take the blue one
* ça alors! = my goodness!, oh dear!
2 alors que = while
= even though

alouette noun, feminine
une alouette = a lark

alpinisme noun, masculine
l'alpinisme = climbing, mountaineering

alpiniste noun, masculine/feminine
un alpiniste/une alpiniste = a mountain-climber

altitude noun, feminine
l'altitude = the altitude
= the height

amande noun, feminine
une amande = an almond

amateur noun, masculine
* (a keen person)
un amateur = an enthusiast
* (not a professional)
un amateur = an amateur

ambassade noun, feminine
une ambassade = an embassy

ambiance noun, feminine
l'ambiance = the atmosphere
il y a de l'ambiance = it's pretty lively

ambition noun, feminine
l'ambition = ambition

âme noun, feminine
une âme = a soul

amélioration noun, feminine
une amélioration = an improvement

améliorer verb 1
= to improve

aménagé/aménagée adjective
* = fully-equipped
* = converted

aménager verb 13
* = to equip
= to fit out
* = to convert
aménager une grange = to convert a barn

amende noun, feminine
une amende = a fine

amener verb 16
= to bring
amenez vos amis = bring your friends

amer/amère adjective
= bitter

américain/américaine
1 adjective
= American
2 américain noun, masculine
l'américain = American English

Amérique noun, feminine
l'Amérique = America
l'Amérique du Nord = North America

ami/amie noun, masculine/feminine
un ami/une amie = a (male) friend/a (female) friend
un petit ami/une petite amie = a boyfriend/a girlfriend

amical/amicale adjective
(plural) **amicaux/amicales**
= friendly

amicalement adverb
* = in a friendly way
* (ending a letter) = best wishes

amitié noun, feminine
* l'amitié = friendship
* (ending a letter)
amitiés = kindest regards, fondly

amour noun, masculine
l'amour = love

amoureux/amoureuse adjective
= in love

ampoule noun, feminine
* (for lighting)
  une ampoule = a light bulb
* (on the skin)
  une ampoule = a blister

amusant/amusante adjective
= entertaining
= funny

amuser verb ①
1 (**!** + avoir)
= to amuse
2 s'amuser (**!** + être)
s'amuser = to enjoy oneself
= to have fun

an noun, masculine
un an = one year
avoir seize ans = to be sixteen years old

ananas noun, masculine (**!** never changes)
un ananas = a pineapple

ancêtre noun, masculine/feminine
un ancêtre/une ancêtre = an ancestor

anchois noun, masculine (**!** never changes)
un anchois = an anchovy

ancien/ancienne adjective
* (if placed before the noun) = former
  l'ancienne mairie = the former town hall
* (if placed after the noun) = old
  = antique

âne noun, masculine
un âne = a donkey

ange noun, masculine
un ange = an angel

angine noun, feminine
une angine = a throat infection, tonsillitis

anglais/anglaise
1 adjective
= English
2 anglais noun, masculine
l'anglais = English

Anglais/Anglaise noun, masculine/feminine
un Anglais/une Anglaise = an Englishman/an Englishwoman
les Anglais = the English

angle noun, masculine
* **un angle** = an angle
* **un angle** = a corner
  le magasin qui fait l'angle = the shop on the corner

Angleterre noun, feminine
l'Angleterre = England

animal noun, masculine
(plural) **animaux**
un animal = an animal
un animal de compagnie = a pet

animé/animée adjective
= lively

anneau noun, masculine
(plural) **anneaux**
un anneau = a ring

année noun, feminine
une année = a year
Bonne année! = Happy New Year!
les années 60 = the sixties

anniversaire noun, masculine
un anniversaire (of one's birth) = a birthday
(of an event) = an anniversary
Joyeux anniversaire! = Happy birthday!

annonce noun, feminine
* **une annonce** = an advertisement
  les petites annonces = classified advertisements
* **une annonce** = an announcement

annoncer verb ⑫
1 (**!** + avoir)
= to announce
2 s'annoncer (**!** + être)
ça s'annonce bien = it looks promising

annuaire noun, masculine
un annuaire (téléphonique) = a telephone directory, a phone book
l'annuaire électronique = the electronic telephone directory on Minitel

annuler verb ①
= to cancel

antigel noun, masculine
l'antigel = antifreeze

antillais/antillaise adjective
= West Indian

Antilles noun, feminine plural
les Antilles = the West Indies

antipathique adjective
= unpleasant

antivol noun, masculine
un antivol = an antitheft device

anxieux/anxieuse adjective
= anxious

août noun, masculine
août = August

apercevoir verb ⑤
1 (**!** + avoir)
= to catch sight of
= to see
2 s'apercevoir (**!** + être)
s'apercevoir que = to realize that
= to notice that

aperçu/aperçue
1 ▶ apercevoir ⑤
2 aperçu noun, masculine
un aperçu = a general idea

aplatir verb ③
= to flatten

appareil noun, masculine
• **un appareil** = a device, a gadget
   = an appliance
• **un appareil** = a telephone
   Victor à l'appareil = (this is) Victor
   speaking
• **un appareil** = an aeroplane, an airplane
• **un appareil** (photo) = a camera

apparence noun, feminine
   l'apparence = appearance

appartement noun, masculine
   un appartement = a flat, an apartment

appartenir verb 36
   appartenir à = to belong to
   à qui appartiennent les clés? = whose keys
   are they?

appel noun, masculine
• (in order to attract attention)
   un appel = a call
• (at school)
   l'appel = registration
   faire l'appel = to take the register, to call
   the roll

appeler verb 19
1 (! + avoir)
• = to call
• = to phone
2 s'appeler (! + être)
   s'appeler = to be called
   comment t'appelles-tu? = what's your
   name?

appendicite noun, feminine
   l'appendicite = appendicitis

appétissant/appétissante adjective
   = appetizing

appétit noun, masculine
   l'appétit = appetite
   bon appétit! = enjoy your meal!

applaudir verb 3
   = to applaud, to clap

applaudissements noun, masculine
plural
   des applaudissements = applause

appliquer verb 1
1 (! + avoir)
• (on the skin, on a surface) = to apply
• (to enforce) = to implement
2 s'appliquer (! + être)
• (to do one's best)
   s'appliquer = to apply oneself
• (to be relevant)
   s'appliquer = to apply

apporter verb 1
   = to bring

apprécier verb 2
   = to like, to appreciate

apprendre verb 52
• (to get knowledge) = to learn
   ils ont appris à lire = they've learned to
   read
• (to give lessons) = to teach
   elle m'apprenait à conduire = she was
   teaching me to drive
   ça t'apprendra! = that'll teach you!
• (to receive information) = to hear
   j'ai appris qu'elle était partie = I heard that
   she'd left
• (to give information) = to tell

apprentissage noun, masculine
• **l'apprentissage** = training
• **l'apprentissage du russe** = learning
   Russian

appris/apprise ▶ **apprendre** 52

approcher verb 1
1 (! + avoir)
• = to get nearer, to get closer
• = to bring nearer, to bring closer
2 approcher de (! + avoir)
   approcher de = to be getting close to
3 s'approcher de (! + être)
   s'approcher de = to go closer to
   = to come closer to

approuver verb 1
   = to approve of

approximativement adverb
   = approximately

appuyer verb 22
1 (! + avoir)
• = to press, to push
• = to rest
• = to lean
2 s'appuyer (! + être)
   s'appuyer = to lean

après
1 preposition
   = after
2 adverb
   = afterward(s), after
   = later
3 d'après
   d'après moi = in my opinion
   d'après [lui | eux | le journal ...] = according
   to [him | them | the newspaper ...]

après-demain adverb
   = the day after tomorrow

après-midi noun, masculine or feminine
(! never changes)
   un or **une après-midi** = an afternoon

après-vente adjective (! never changes)
   le service après-vente = after-sales service

aquarium noun, masculine
   un aquarium = an aquarium, a fish tank

arabe
1 adjective
   = Arab
   = Arabic

2 *noun, masculine*
l'arabe = Arabic

Arabe *noun, masculine|feminine*
un Arabe/une Arabe = an Arab

araignée *noun, feminine*
une araignée = a spider

arbitre *noun, masculine*
un arbitre = a referee

arbre *noun, masculine*
un arbre = a tree
un arbre de Noël = a Christmas tree

arc *noun, masculine*
un arc (*a weapon*) = a bow

arc-en-ciel *noun, masculine*
(*plural*) **arcs-en-ciel**
un arc-en-ciel = a rainbow

arche *noun, feminine*
une arche = an arch

ardoise *noun, feminine*
l'ardoise = slate

arête *noun, feminine*
• (*in a fish*)
une arête = a fishbone
• (*of a mountain*)
l'arête = the ridge

argent *noun, masculine*
• (*metal*)
l'argent = silver
• (*currency*)
l'argent = money
l'argent liquide = cash
l'argent de poche = pocket money,
spending money

argot *noun, masculine*
l'argot = slang

arme *noun, feminine*
une arme = a weapon
une arme à feu = a firearm

armée *noun, feminine*
une armée = an army

armoire *noun, feminine*
une armoire = a wardrobe, a closet
une armoire à pharmacie = a medicine
cupboard, a medicine cabinet

arracher *verb* [1]
• = to pull out
= to tear out
• = to snatch

arranger *verb* [13]
1 (**!** + *avoir*)
• = to arrange
• = to fix, to repair
• = to tidy, to clean up
• = to suit
ça m'arrange d'y aller avec eux = it suits
me to go with them

2 s'arranger (**!** + *être*)
• s'arranger = to improve
le temps s'est arrangé = the weather has
improved
• s'arranger = to sort itself out, to work out
• s'arranger = to come to an agreement

arrestation *noun, feminine*
une arrestation = an arrest

arrêt *noun, masculine*
un arrêt = a stop
un arrêt d'autobus = a bus stop

arrêter *verb* [1]
1 (**!** + *avoir*)
• = to stop
arrête de crier = stop shouting
arrête! = stop it!
• = to arrest
2 s'arrêter (**!** + *être*)
s'arrêter = to stop

arrhes *noun, feminine plural*
des arrhes = a deposit

arrière
1 *adjective*
= back
= rear
2 *noun, masculine*
• (*the rear part*)
l'arrière = the back
• (*in sport*)
un arrière = a fullback
= a defender
3 en arrière *adverb*
• = backward(s)
se pencher en arrière = to lean back
• = behind
rester en arrière = to stay behind

arrivée *noun, feminine*
• (*of a plane, a passenger*)
une arrivée = an arrival
aller chercher un ami à l'arrivée du train
= to meet a friend off the train, to meet
a friend from the train
• (*of a race*)
l'arrivée = the finish

arriver *verb* [1] (**!** + *être*)
• = to arrive
• = to come
j'arrive! = I'm coming!
ils sont arrivés en courant = they came up
running, they ran up
• = to reach
• arriver à faire = to manage to do, to
succeed in doing
je n'y arrive pas = I can't manage it, I can't
do it
• = to happen
c'est arrivé à mon frère = it happened to
my brother
que t'est-il arrivé? = what happened to
you?
il m'arrive d'oublier = I sometimes forget

arrondir verb 3
  arrondir un chiffre = to round off a figure

arrondissement noun, masculine
  un arrondissement = an arrondissement, a
   district

arroser verb 1
  = to water
  = to spray

arrosoir noun, masculine
  un arrosoir = a watering can

art noun, masculine
  l'art = art
  les arts ménagers = home economics

artichaut noun, masculine
  un artichaut = an artichoke

article noun, masculine
• (in grammar)
  un article = an article
• (in a shop)
  un article = an item
  des articles de sport = sports equipment
  des articles de toilette = toiletries

artificiel/artificielle adjective
  = artificial
  = man-made

artisan noun, masculine
  un artisan = a craftsman

artisanal/artisanale adjective
(plural) **artisanaux/artisanales**
  une méthode artisanale = a traditional
   method
  de fabrication artisanale = hand-crafted,
   hand-made
  = home-made

artisanat noun, masculine
  l'artisanat = the craft industry
  magasin d'artisanat = arts and crafts shop

artiste noun, masculine/feminine
  un artiste/une artiste = an artist
  (in films, plays) = an actor/an actress
  un artiste peintre = a painter

as¹ ▶ **avoir** 8

as² noun, masculine (**!** never changes)
  un as = an ace

ascenseur noun, masculine
  un ascenseur = a lift, an elevator

ascension noun, feminine
  une ascension = an ascent

Ascension noun, feminine
  l'Ascension = Ascension

asiatique adjective
  = from the Far East, Asian

Asie noun, feminine
  l'Asie = Asia

asperge noun, feminine
  des asperges = asparagus

asphyxier: **s'asphyxier** verb 2
(**!** + être)
  s'asphyxier = to suffocate

aspirateur noun, masculine
  un aspirateur = a vacuum cleaner

assassin noun, masculine
  un assassin = a murderer

assassinat noun, masculine
  un assassinat = a murder

assassiner verb 1
  = to murder

asseoir: **s'asseoir** verb 34 (**!** + être)
  s'asseoir = to sit (down)
  (in bed) = to sit up

assez adverb
  = enough
  = quite, pretty

assiette noun, feminine
  une assiette = a plate
  une assiette anglaise = assorted cold
   meats, cold cuts

assis/assise
1 ▶ asseoir 34
2 adjective
  = seated

assister verb 1
• assister à = to attend, to be at
• assister à = to witness

association noun, feminine
  une association sportive = a sports
   association, a (sports) club

assorti/assortie adjective
• = matching
• = assorted

assurance noun, feminine
• (a feeling)
  l'assurance = (self-)confidence
• (against accidents)
  une assurance = insurance
  l'assurance maladie = health insurance
  l'assurance au tiers = third-party
   insurance
  l'assurance tous risques
   = comprehensive insurance

assuré/assurée
1 adjective
• = confident
• = certain
2 noun, masculine/feminine
  l'assuré/l'assurée = the insured party

assurer verb 1
1 (**!** + avoir)
• (to tell confidently) = to assure
  il m'a assuré que c'était vrai = he assured
   me that it was true
• (against accidents) = to insure
2 s'assurer (**!** + être)
• s'assurer = to take out insurance
• s'assurer que = to make sure that

astrologue noun, masculine|feminine
un astrologue/une astrologue = an astrologer

astronaute noun, masculine|feminine
un astronaute/une astronaute = an astronaut

astuce noun, feminine
• une astuce = a trick
• l'astuce = cleverness
= shrewdness

astucieux/astucieuse adjective
= clever, smart
= shrewd

atelier noun, masculine
un atelier (for a craftsman) = a workshop
(for a painter) = a studio

athlétisme noun, masculine
l'athlétisme = athletics

Atlantique noun, masculine
l'(océan) Atlantique = the Atlantic (Ocean)

atout noun, masculine
• (at cards)
un atout = a trump
atout trèfle! = clubs are trumps!
• (in life)
un atout = an asset, an advantage

attacher verb 1
1 (! + avoir)
= to tie
= to fasten
2 s'attacher à (! + être)
s'attacher à = to become attached to

attaquer verb 1
1 (! + avoir)
= to attack
2 s'attaquer à (! + être)
s'attaquer à = to attack

atteindre verb 55
• = to reach
• = to hit
• être atteint d'une maladie = to suffer from a disease

atteint/atteinte ▶ atteindre 55

attendre verb 6
1 (! + avoir)
• = to wait
= to wait (for)
• = to expect
j'attends une visite = I'm expecting a visit
2 s'attendre à (! + être)
s'attendre à = to expect
il fallait s'y attendre = it was to be expected

attendu/attendue ▶ attendre 6

attentat noun, masculine
un attentat (on a person) = an assassination attempt
(on a group, a building) = an attack

attente noun, feminine
l'attente = wait(ing)

attention noun, feminine
l'attention = attention
faire attention (to take care) = to be careful
(to concentrate) = to pay attention
attention! = careful!, watch out!
attention à la marche! = mind the step!, watch the step!

attentivement adverb
= attentively

atterrir verb 3
= to land

atterrissage noun, masculine
un atterrissage = a landing

attirer verb 1
1 (! + avoir)
= to attract
2 s'attirer (! + être)
s'attirer des ennuis = to get into trouble

attraction noun, feminine
• l'attraction = attraction
• des attractions = entertainment
un parc d'attractions = an amusement park

attraper verb 1
= to catch

au ▶ à

auberge noun, feminine
une auberge = an inn
une auberge de jeunesse = a youth hostel

aucun/aucune
1 adjective
= no, not any
en aucun cas = under no circumstances
aucune idée! = I've no idea!
2 pronoun
= none, not any
aucun d'entre nous = none of us
aucune des deux = neither of them

audace noun, feminine
l'audace (bravery) = boldness
(guts) = audacity, nerve

audacieux/audacieuse adjective
= bold

au-delà de preposition
= beyond
= over

au-dessous de preposition
= below
= under

au-dessus de preposition
= above
= over

auditeur/auditrice noun, masculine|feminine
un auditeur/une auditrice = a listener

A

augmenter verb [1]
= to increase

aujourd'hui adverb
* = today
* = nowadays

aurai ▶ avoir [8]

aussi
1 adverb
* = also, as well
= too
eux aussi ont faim = they are hungry too
* = so
je ne savais pas que c'était aussi cher = I
didn't know it was so expensive
il n'avait jamais vu un aussi gros chien
= he'd never seen such a large dog
* = as
aussi [riche | vieux | petit ...] que = as [rich |
old | small ...] as
2 conjunction
= so, consequently
aussi sommes-nous partis = (and) so we
left

aussitôt
1 adverb
= immediately, right away
2 aussitôt que = as soon as

Australie noun, feminine
l'Australie = Australia

australien/australienne adjective
= Australian

autant adverb
1 autant que = as much as
il gagne autant que toi = he earns as much
as you
2 autant de = as much
= as many
autant de [valeur | patience | temps ...] que
= as much [value | patience | time ...] as
autant de [fautes | lettres | soucis ...] que = as
many [mistakes | letters | worries ...] as

auteur noun, masculine
l'auteur (of a book) = the author
(of a song) = the composer

auto noun, feminine
une auto = a car

autobus noun, masculine (**!** never
changes)
un autobus = a bus

autocar noun, masculine
un autocar = a coach, a bus

autocollant/autocollante
1 adjective
= self-adhesive
2 autocollant noun, masculine
un autocollant = a sticker

auto-école noun, feminine
(plural) **auto-écoles**
une auto-école = a driving school

automne noun, masculine
l'automne = autumn, fall

automobile noun, feminine
une automobile = a (motor)car, an
automobile

automobiliste noun, masculine/feminine
un automobiliste/une automobiliste = a
motorist

autoritaire adjective
= authoritarian

autoroute noun, feminine
une autoroute = a motorway, a highway

auto-stop noun, masculine
l'auto-stop = hitchhiking
faire de l'auto-stop = to hitchhike

autour de preposition
= around

autre
1 determiner
= other
l'autre jour = the other day
rien d'autre = nothing else
2 d'autre part = besides
= on the other hand

autrefois adverb
= in the past
= before

autrement adverb
* = in a different way, differently
autrement dit = in other words
* (if not) = otherwise
autrement il ne viendra pas = otherwise he
won't come

Autriche noun, feminine
l'Autriche = Austria

autrichien/autrichienne adjective
= Austrian

autruche noun, feminine
une autruche = an ostrich

aux ▶ à

avais ▶ avoir [8]

avaler verb [1]
= to swallow

avance
1 noun, feminine
* (of an army)
l'avance = the advance
* (on a competitor)
une avance = a lead
* (money)
une avance = an advance
2 à l'avance = in advance
3 d'avance
* payer d'avance = to pay in advance
* avoir cinq minutes d'avance = to be five
minutes early

avoir verb 8

present	imperfect	future	past participle
j'ai	j'avais	j'aurai	eu / eue
tu as	tu avais	tu auras	
il / elle a	ill / elle avait	il / elle aura	
nous avons	nous avions	nous aurons	
vous avez	vous aviez	vous aurez	
ils / elles ont	ils / elles avaient	ils / elles auront	

● **1 avoir** functions as an ordinary verb:
= to have (got)
ils **ont** un chien = *they have a dog*

● = to get
réussir à **avoir** des billets = *to manage to get tickets*

2 avoir is used as an auxiliary verb to conjugate most other verbs, except all reflexive verbs and those verbs labelled (**!** + *être*):
elle **a** bu son lait = *she drank her milk*
ils **auraient** aimé te voir = *they would have liked to see you*

3 avoir is used in the phrase **il y a**:
il y **a** = *there is* or *there are*
il y **aura** = *there will be*

4 avoir is used in expressions like **avoir faim**, **avoir soif**, **avoir l'air**, **avoir besoin de** etc. You will find translations at **faim**, **soif**, **air**, **besoin** etc.

---

4 en avance
arriver en avance = to arrive early
être en avance sur les autres = to be ahead of the others

avancer verb 12
1 (**!** + *avoir*)
• = to move forward
avancer d'un mètre = to move forward one metre
• = to make progress
avancer lentement = to make slow progress
• = to be fast
ta montre avance de cinq minutes = your watch is five minutes fast
• = to bring forward
avancer une réunion = to bring a meeting forward, to push a meeting up
• = to lend
avancer de l'argent à un ami = to lend money to a friend
2 s'avancer (**!** + *être*)
s'avancer = to move forward
il s'est avancé vers la table = he moved toward(s) the table

avant
1 *noun, masculine*
• (*the front part*)
l'avant = the front

• (*in sport*)
un avant = a forward
2 *adjective* (**!** *never changes*)
= front
les roues avant = the front wheels
3 *preposition*
= before
juste avant de partir = just before leaving
4 *adverb*
= before
= first
que faisait-il avant? = what was he doing before?
la semaine d'avant = the week before
la dame était avant = the lady was first
5 en avant = forward(s)
• se pencher en avant = to lean forward(s)
• partir en avant = to go (on) ahead

avantage *noun, masculine*
un avantage = an advantage

avant-hier *adverb*
= the day before yesterday

avare *adjective*
= mean, miserly

avec *preposition*
= with

avenir *noun, masculine*
l'avenir = the future
à l'avenir = in (the) future

✗ in informal situations

aventure *noun, feminine*
une aventure = an adventure
partir à l'aventure = to set off in search of
adventure

aventurier/aventurière *noun,*
masculine/feminine
un aventurier/une aventurière = an
adventurer

averse *noun, feminine*
une averse = a shower, a downpour

avertir *verb* 3
• = to warn
• = to inform

aveugle *adjective*
= blind

avez ▶ **avoir** 8

avion *noun, masculine*
un avion = an aeroplane, an airplane
un avion = a jet (plane)

aviron *noun, masculine*
• l'aviron = rowing
• un aviron = an oar

avis *noun, masculine* (! *never changes*)
• (*a belief*)
un avis = an opinion
changer d'avis = to change one's mind
• (*an announcement*)
un avis = a notice, a sign

avocat¹ *noun, masculine*
un avocat = an avocado

avocat²/avocate *noun,*
masculine/feminine
un avocat/une avocate = a lawyer
= a barrister, an attorney

avoir *verb* 8
▶ *See the boxed note.*

avons ▶ **avoir** 8

avouer *verb* 1
= to confess

avril *noun, masculine*
avril = April

ayant ▶ **avoir** 8

baby-foot *noun, masculine* (! *never*
changes)
le baby-foot = table football

bac×, baccalauréat *noun, masculine*
le baccalauréat = the baccalaureate (*a*
school-leaving diploma taken at 17–18)

badaud *noun, masculine*
un badaud = an onlooker

bagage *noun, masculine*
un bagage = a piece of luggage

bagarre *noun, feminine*
une bagarre = a fight

bagarrer: se bagarrer *verb* 1 (! + *être*)
se bagarrer = to fight

bague *noun, feminine*
une bague = a ring

baguette *noun, feminine*
• (*bread*)
une baguette = a baguette, a French stick,
French bread
• (*a thin piece of wood*)
une baguette = a stick
une baguette magique = a magic wand

baie *noun, feminine*
• (*on the coast*)
une baie = a bay
• (*fruit*)
une baie = a berry

baignade *noun, feminine*
la baignade = swimming

baigner: se baigner *verb* 1 (! + *être*)
se baigner = to go for a swim

baignoire *noun, feminine*
une baignoire = a bathtub

bâiller *verb* 1
= to yawn

bain *noun, masculine*
• (*at home*)
un bain = a bath
prendre un bain = to have a bath, to take a
bath
• (*at the swimming pool*)
le grand bain = the (main) pool
le petit bain = the shallow pool, the
learners' pool

baiser *noun, masculine*
un baiser = a kiss

baisser *verb* 1
1 (! + *avoir*)
• = to lower
baisser le store = to lower the blinds
• = to drop
la température a baissé = the temperature
has dropped
2 se baisser (! + *être*)
se baisser = to bend down, to reach down

bal *noun, masculine*
un bal = a dance, a ball

balade *noun, feminine*
une balade (*on foot*) = a walk, a stroll
(*by car*) = a drive
(*on a bicycle*) = a ride

B

balader: **se balader** verb [1] (**!** + être)
  se balader (on foot) = to go for a walk
  (by car) = to go for a drive
  (on a bicycle) = to go for a ride

baladeur noun, masculine
  un baladeur = a walkman®

balai noun, masculine
  un balai = a broom

balance noun, feminine
  une balance = scales

Balance noun, feminine
  la Balance = Libra

balançoire noun, feminine
  une balançoire = a swing
  = a see-saw

balayer verb [21]
  = to sweep

balcon noun, masculine
  un balcon = a balcony

baleine noun, feminine
  une baleine = a whale

balle noun, feminine
• (for playing)
  une balle = a (small) ball
• (for a gun)
  une balle = a bullet

ballerine noun, feminine
• (a person)
  une ballerine = a ballerina
• (footwear)
  une ballerine (for dancing) = a ballet
    pump, a ballet slipper
  (for walking) = a flat pump, a slipper

ballon noun, masculine
  un ballon = a (large) ball

bambou noun, masculine
  le bambou = bamboo

banal/**banale** adjective
  = commonplace, ordinary

banane noun, feminine
• **une banane** = a banana
• **une banane** = a bum bag, a fanny pack

banc noun, masculine
  un banc = a bench

bancaire adjective
  = bank, banking

bande noun, feminine
• (of people)
  une bande = a group, a bunch
• (with sound)
  une bande = a tape
• (something long and narrow)
  une bande = a strip
  une bande dessinée = a comic strip

bandeau noun, masculine
(plural) **bandeaux**
  un bandeau (holding the hair) = a
    hairband, a headband
  (over the eyes) = a blindfold

banlieue noun, feminine
  la banlieue = the suburbs

banque noun, feminine
  une banque = a bank

banquette noun, feminine
  une banquette = a seat

banquier noun, masculine
  un banquier = a banker

baptême noun, masculine
  un baptême = a christening

bar noun, masculine
  un bar = a bar

barbant/**barbante✗** adjective
  = boring

barbare noun, masculine/feminine
  un barbare/une barbare = a barbarian

barbe noun, feminine
• **une barbe** = a beard
• **quelle barbe✗**! = what a bore!
  la barbe à papa = candyfloss, cotton
  candy

barber: **se barber✗** [1] (**!** + être)
  se barber = to be bored

barboter verb [1]
  = to paddle

barbu noun, masculine
  un barbu = a bearded man

barque noun, feminine
  une barque = a (small) boat

barrage noun, masculine
• (on a river)
  un barrage = a dam
• (on a road)
  un barrage de police = a police roadblock

barre noun, feminine
• (of metal, chocolate)
  une barre = a bar
• (a line)
  une barre = a stroke, a mark
• (on a ship)
  la barre = the tiller, the helm

barreau noun, masculine
(plural) **barreaux**
  un barreau (on a cage) = a bar

barrer verb [1]
• = to cross out
• = to block

barrière noun, feminine
• (enclosing an area)
  une barrière = a fence

- (*an obstacle*)
  une barrière = a barrier

bar-tabac *noun, masculine*
(*plural*) **bars-tabac**
  un bar-tabac = a café (*also selling stamps and cigarettes*)

bas/basse
1 *adjective*
  = low
2 bas *adverb*
- = low
  voir plus bas = see below
- = quietly
  parler tout bas = to speak in a whisper
3 bas *noun, masculine* (**!** *never changes*)
- (*the lower part*)
  le bas = the bottom
  en bas = downstairs
  à bas les patrons! = down with bosses!
- (*a garment*)
  un bas = a stocking

basculer *verb* 1
- (*to fall over*) = to topple over
- (*to tilt*) = to tip up

basilic *noun, masculine*
  le basilic = basil

basket
1 *noun, masculine*
  le basket = basketball
2 *noun, feminine*
  des baskets = trainers, sneakers

basse ▶ bas 1

bassin *noun, masculine*
  un bassin = a pool

bataille *noun, feminine*
  une bataille = a battle
  la bataille navale = battleships

bateau *noun, masculine*
(*plural*) **bateaux**
  un bateau = a boat
  faire du bateau = to go boating
  = to go sailing

bateau-mouche *noun, masculine*
(*plural*) **bateaux-mouches**
  un bateau-mouche *a large river boat for sightseeing*

bâtiment *noun, masculine*
  un bâtiment = a building

bâtir *verb* 3
  = to build

bâton *noun, masculine*
  un bâton = a stick

batterie *noun, feminine*
- (*in a car*)
  la batterie = the battery
- (*in a band*)
  la batterie = the percussion, the drums

battre *verb* 61
1 (**!** + *avoir*)
  = to beat
  battre un record = to break a record
- **le cœur battant** = with a beating heart
- **battre des mains** = to clap
2 se battre (**!** + *être*)
  se battre = to fight

battu/battue ▶ battre 61

baudruche *noun, feminine*
  un ballon en baudruche = a balloon

bavard/bavarde *adjective*
  = talkative

bavarder *verb* 1
  = to chat

bazar *noun, masculine*
  un bazar (*a shop*) = a general store

BD *noun, feminine*
  une BD = a comic strip

beau/belle *adjective*
(*plural*) **beaux/belles**

> **!** **bel** *is used instead of* **beau** *before masculine nouns beginning with a vowel or a mute h. The plural of* **bel** *is* **beaux**.

  = beautiful, handsome
  = fine
  il fait beau = the weather is fine

beaucoup *adverb*
  = a lot
  = much
  c'est beaucoup trop = it's far too much
  beaucoup de [patience | temps | livres ...] = a lot of [patience | time | books ...]
  il ne me reste plus beaucoup d'argent = I haven't got much money left

beau-frère *noun, masculine*
(*plural*) **beaux-frères**
  un beau-frère = a brother-in-law

beau-père *noun, masculine*
(*plural*) **beaux-pères**
  un beau-père = a father-in-law
  = a stepfather

beauté *noun, feminine*
  la beauté = beauty

beaux-arts *noun, masculine plural*
  les beaux-arts = fine arts

bébé *noun, masculine*
  un bébé = a baby

bec *noun, masculine*
  un bec = a beak

bêche *noun, feminine*
  une bêche = a spade, a shovel

beignet *noun, masculine*
  un beignet = a fritter
  = a doughnut, a donut

bel ▶ **beau**

belge *adjective*
= Belgian

Belgique *noun, feminine*
la Belgique = Belgium

Bélier *noun, masculine*
le Bélier = Aries

belle ▶ **beau**

belle-fille *noun, feminine*
(*plural*) **belles-filles**
une belle-fille = a daughter-in-law

belle-mère *noun, feminine*
(*plural*) **belles-mères**
une belle-mère = a mother-in-law
= a stepmother

belle-sœur *noun, feminine*
(*plural*) **belles-sœurs**
une belle-sœur = a sister-in-law

bénéfice *noun, masculine*
faire un bénéfice = to make a profit

béquille *noun, feminine*
une béquille = a crutch

berceau *noun, masculine*
(*plural*) **berceaux**
un berceau = a cradle

bercer *verb* 12
= to rock

berge *noun, feminine*
la berge (de la rivière) = the (river)bank

berger/bergère *noun,*
masculine/feminine
un berger/une bergère = a shepherd/a
shepherdess
un berger allemand = a German
shepherd dog, an Alsatian

bermuda *noun, masculine*
un bermuda = bermuda shorts

besoin *noun, masculine*
un besoin = a need
avoir besoin d'argent = to need money

bête
1 *adjective*
= stupid, silly
2 *noun, feminine*
une bête = an animal

bêtise *noun, feminine*
• la bêtise = stupidity
• faire une bêtise = to do something silly
dire des bêtises = to talk nonsense

béton *noun, masculine*
le béton = concrete

betterave *noun, feminine*
une betterave = a beetroot, a beet

beurre *noun, masculine*
le beurre = butter

bibelot *noun, masculine*
un bibelot = an ornament

biberon *noun, masculine*
un biberon = a (baby's) bottle, a (nursing)
bottle

bibliothèque *noun, feminine*
une bibliothèque (*a room or a building*) = a
library
(*a piece of furniture*) = a bookcase

bic® *noun, masculine*
un bic = a biro®, a ballpoint pen

bicyclette *noun, feminine*
• (*the equipment*)
une bicyclette = a bicycle
• (*the sport*)
faire de la bicyclette = to cycle, to go
cycling

bidon
1 *adjective*✖ (**!** *never changes*)
= bogus, phoney
2 *noun, masculine*
un bidon = a can
= a drum

bidonville *noun, masculine*
un bidonville = a shanty town

bien
1 *adjective* (**!** *never changes*)
• = good
2 *adverb*
• = well
ils vont bien = they're well
ça s'est bien passé = it went well
c'est bien fait pour lui! = it serves him
right!
• = very
c'est bien triste = it's very sad
je l'espère bien = I very much hope so, I
hope so
• = exactly
• = definitely
c'est bien ce que je pensais = that's
(exactly) what I thought
la voiture rouge est bien à eux = the red
car is definitely theirs
je te l'avais bien dit! = I told you so!
3 *noun, masculine*
le bien = good
c'est pour ton bien = it's for your own good
4 bien sûr = of course
5 bien entendu = naturally

bientôt *adverb*
= soon

bienvenu/bienvenue *adjective*
= welcome

bière *noun, feminine*
la bière = beer
la bière (à la) pression = draught beer,
draft beer

✖ in informal situations

la bière blonde = lager, light beer
la bière brune = stout

bifteck *noun, masculine*
  le bifteck = steak

bifurquer *verb* [1]
• (*if it's a road*) = to fork
• (*if it's a driver*) = to turn off

bijou *noun, masculine*
(*plural*) **bijoux**
  un bijou = a piece of jewellery, a piece of jewelry

bijouterie *noun, feminine*
  une bijouterie = a jeweller's, a jewellery shop, a jewelry store

bijoutier/bijoutière *noun, masculine/feminine*
  un bijoutier/une bijoutière = a jeweller, a jeweler

bilingue *adjective*
  = bilingual

billard *noun, masculine*
  le billard = billiards
le billard américain = pool
le billard anglais = snooker

bille *noun, feminine*
  une bille = a marble

billet *noun, masculine*
• (*on a train, at the theatre*)
  un billet = a ticket
• (*money*)
  un billet (de banque) = a (bank)note, a bill

biscotte *noun, feminine*
  une biscotte ≈ a rusk

bise* *noun, feminine*
  une bise* = a kiss

bisou* *noun, masculine*
  un bisou* = a kiss

bissextile *adjective*
  une année bissextile = a leap year

bistro(t)* *noun, masculine*
  un bistro(t)* = a bistro, a café

bizarre *adjective*
  = strange, peculiar

blague* *noun, feminine*
• une blague* = a funny story
• (*a piece of mischief*)
  une blague* = a trick
  faire une blague* à un ami = to play a trick on a friend

blanc/blanche
1 *adjective*
• = white
• = blank
2 blanc *noun, masculine*
  un blanc (*a space*) = a blank
un blanc d'œuf = an egg white

du blanc de poulet = a piece of chicken breast

blanchisserie *noun, feminine*
  une blanchisserie = a laundry, a dry cleaner's

blé *noun, masculine*
  le blé = wheat, corn

blessé/blessée
1 *adjective*
  = injured
  = wounded
2 *noun, masculine/feminine*
  un blessé/une blessée = an injured person
  = a casualty

blesser *verb* [1]
1 (**!** + *avoir*)
  = to hurt
  = to wound
2 se blesser (**!** + *être*)
  se blesser = to hurt oneself
  elle s'est blessée à la jambe = she hurt her leg

blessure *noun, feminine*
  une blessure = an injury
  = a wound

bleu/bleue
1 *adjective*
  = blue
  bleu marine = navy blue
2 bleu *noun, masculine*
  un bleu = a bruise

bloc
1 *noun, masculine*
  (*for writing*)
  un bloc = a notepad
2 à bloc = completely
  vissé à bloc = tightly screwed
  gonflé à bloc = fully inflated

blond/blonde *adjective*
  (*describing hair*) = blonde, blond
  (*describing tobacco*) = light, Virginia

bloquer *verb* [1]
1 (**!** + *avoir*)
• = to block
• = to jam
• bloquer les salaires = to freeze wages
2 se bloquer (**!** + *être*)
  se bloquer = to jam

blouse *noun, feminine*
• (*worn for protection*)
  une blouse = an overall
• (*a kind of shirt*)
  une blouse = a blouse

blouson *noun, masculine*
  un blouson = a blouson, a jacket

bobo* *noun, masculine*
  ce n'est qu'un bobo* = it's only a scratch

bocal *noun, masculine*
(*plural*) **bocaux**
  un bocal = a jar

bœuf *noun, masculine*
• (*the animal*)
  un bœuf = an ox
• (*the meat*)
  le bœuf = beef

boire *verb* 51
  = to drink

bois
1 ▶ **boire** 51
2 *noun, masculine* (! *never changes*)
• (*timber*)
  le bois = wood
• (*a place*)
  un bois = a wood

boisson *noun, feminine*
  une boisson = a drink

boîte *noun, feminine*
  une boîte = a box
une boîte de conserve = a tin, a can
une boîte aux lettres = a postbox, a
  mailbox
  = a letter box, a mailbox
une boîte de nuit = a nightclub
une boîte de vitesses = a gearbox

boiter *verb* 1
  = to limp

boiteux/boiteuse *adjective*
  = lame

bol *noun, masculine*
  un bol = a bowl

bombe *noun, feminine*
• (*a weapon*)
  une bombe = a bomb
• (*an aerosol*)
  une bombe = a spray

bon/bonne¹
1 *adjective*
• = good
• = right
  la bonne réponse = the right answer
• = valid
  le billet est encore bon = the ticket is still
  valid
• bon anniversaire! = happy birthday!
  bonne journée! = have a nice day
2 bon *adverb*
  il fait bon dehors = it's nice outside
  sentir bon = to smell nice
3 bon *noun, masculine*
  un bon = a coupon
  = a voucher
4 bon *exclamation*
  bon! = right!
  ah bon? = really?

bon marché = cheap
le bon sens = common sense

bonbon *noun, masculine*
  un bonbon = a sweet, a candy

bonbonne *noun, feminine*
  une bonbonne (*for wine*) = a demijohn
  (*for gas*) = a cylinder

bond *noun, masculine*
  un bond = a leap

bondé/bondée *adjective*
  = packed

bondir *verb* 3
  = to leap

bonhomme✗ *noun, masculine*
(*plural*) **bonshommes**
  un bonhomme✗ = a chap, a guy, a fellow
un bonhomme de neige = a snowman

bonjour *noun, masculine*
  bonjour! = hello!, good morning!, good
  afternoon!

bonne² *noun, feminine*
  une bonne = a maid

bonnet *noun, masculine*
  un bonnet = a cap, a hat

bonsoir *noun, masculine*
  bonsoir = good evening!, good night!

bonté *noun, feminine*
  la bonté = kindness

bord
1 *noun, masculine*
  le bord (*of a bed, a cliff*) = the edge
  (*of a road*) = the side
  (*of a river*) = the bank
  des vacances au bord de la mer = seaside
  holidays, a seaside vacation
2 à bord = on board, aboard

bordeaux
1 *adjective* (! *never changes*)
  = burgundy
2 *noun, masculine* (! *never changes*)
  le Bordeaux = Bordeaux wine

bordure *noun, feminine*
  la bordure (*the limit*) = the edge
  (*ornamental*) = the border

bosse *noun, feminine*
  une bosse (*on the head*) = a lump
  (*on the back*) = a hump
  (*on a car*) = a dent

botte *noun, feminine*
• (*footwear*)
  une botte = a boot
• (*a bundle*)
  une botte = a bunch

bouc *noun, masculine*
• (*an animal*)
  un bouc = a billy goat

✗ in informal situations

- (*a beard*)
  un bouc = a goatee

bouche *noun, feminine*
  la bouche = the mouth
une bouche de métro = a tube entrance,
  a subway entrance

bouchée *noun, feminine*
  une bouchée = a mouthful

boucher¹ *verb* 1
- = to plug
  = to fill up
- = to block
  = to clog up
- = to cork

boucher²/bouchère *noun,*
masculine/feminine
  le boucher/la bouchère = the butcher

boucherie *noun, feminine*
  une boucherie = a butcher's (shop)

bouchon *noun, masculine*
- (*on a bottle*)
  un bouchon = a cork
  = a top
- (*on the road*)
  un bouchon = a traffic jam

boucle *noun, feminine*
- (*on a belt*)
  une boucle = a buckle
- (*of hair*)
  une boucle = a curl
- (*a curved shape*)
  une boucle = a loop
une boucle d'oreille = an earring

bouclé/bouclée *adjective*
  = curly

boucler *verb* 1
- = to buckle
- = to fasten

boudin *noun, masculine*
  le boudin = black pudding, blood pudding

boue *noun, feminine*
  la boue = mud

bouffer✗ *verb* 1
  = to eat

bouger *verb* 13
  = to move

bougie *noun, feminine*
- (*for lighting*)
  une bougie = a candle
- (*in an engine*)
  une bougie = a sparking plug, a spark
  plug

bouillir *verb* 31
  = to boil

bouilloire *noun, feminine*
  une bouilloire = a kettle

bouillotte *noun, feminine*
  une bouillotte = a hot-water bottle

boulanger/boulangère *noun,*
masculine/feminine
  un boulanger/une boulangère = a baker

boulangerie *noun, feminine*
  une boulangerie = a baker's (shop)

boule *noun, feminine*
- (*a shape*)
  une boule = a ball
  une boule de neige = a snowball
- (*in games*)
  une boule = a bowl
  = a boule

boulevard *noun, masculine*
  un boulevard = an avenue

boulot✗ *noun, masculine*
- **le boulot✗** = work
- **un boulot✗** = a job

boum✗ *noun, feminine*
  une boum✗ = a party

bouquet *noun, masculine*
  un bouquet = a bunch

bouquin✗ *noun, masculine*
  un bouquin✗ = a book

bourgeon *noun, masculine*
  un bourgeon = a bud

bousculer *verb* 1
- = to bump into
  = to jostle
- = to rush
  ne me bouscule pas = don't rush me

boussole *noun, feminine*
  une boussole = a compass

bout *noun, masculine*
- **un bout** = a piece
- **le bout** = the end
  = the tip

bouteille *noun, feminine*
  une bouteille = a bottle
  une bouteille de gaz = a gas cylinder

boutique *noun, feminine*
  une boutique = a shop

bouton *noun, masculine*
- (*on a coat, for a doorbell*)
  un bouton = a button
- (*on the skin*)
  un bouton = a spot, a pimple
- (*on an appliance*)
  un bouton = a switch
- (*on a plant*)
  un bouton = a bud

boxe *noun, feminine*
  la boxe = boxing

bracelet *noun, masculine*
  un bracelet = a bracelet
  = a bangle

B

un bracelet de montre = a watchstrap, a watchband

branche *noun, feminine*
- (*on a tree*)
  une branche = a branch
- (*an area of work, study*)
  une branche = a field

branché/branchée* *adjective*
= trendy, cool

brancher *verb* 1
= to plug in
= to connect

braquer *verb* 1
- **braquer un revolver sur quelqu'un** = to aim a gun at someone
- **braquer le volant à gauche** = to turn the wheel hard (to the) left

bras *noun, masculine* (! *never changes*)
un bras = an arm
en bras de chemise = in one's shirtsleeves

brasserie *noun, feminine*
- (*for meals*)
  une brasserie = a brasserie, a café
- (*a factory*)
  une brasserie = a brewery

bravo *exclamation*
= bravo!, well done!

brebis *noun, feminine* (! *never changes*)
une brebis = a ewe

bref/brève
1 *adjective*
= brief, short
2 (en) bref *adverb*
= in short

Bretagne *noun, feminine*
la Bretagne = Brittany

breton/bretonne
1 *adjective*
= Breton
2 breton *noun, masculine*
le breton = Breton

brève ▶ bref 1

brevet *noun, masculine*
un brevet (*a qualification*) = a certificate
un brevet des collèges = a certificate of general education
un brevet de pilote = a pilot's licence

bricolage *noun, masculine*
le bricolage = DIY, do-it-yourself

brillant/brillante *adjective*
- = shiny
- = brilliant

briller *verb* 1
= to shine

brin *noun, masculine*
un brin (*of parsley, mimosa*) = a sprig
(*of grass*) = a blade

brioche *noun, feminine*
une brioche = a brioche, a (sweet) bun

briquet *noun, masculine*
un briquet = a cigarette lighter

britannique *adjective*
= British

brocante *noun, feminine*
une brocante = a flea market

brocanteur/brocanteuse *noun, masculine/feminine*
un brocanteur/une brocanteuse = a bric-à-brac dealer

broche *noun, feminine*
- (*an ornament*)
  une broche = a brooch, a pin
- (*for cooking*)
  une broche = a spit

brochette *noun, feminine*
une brochette = a kebab, a brochette

brochure *noun, feminine*
une brochure = a brochure

broder *verb* 1
= to embroider

bronzage *noun, masculine*
un bronzage = a (sun)tan

bronzé/bronzée *adjective*
= tanned, brown

bronzer *verb* 1
= to get a tan, to go brown

brosse *noun, feminine*
une brosse = a brush
avoir les cheveux (taillés) en brosse = to have a crew cut
une brosse à dents = a toothbrush

brosser *verb* 1
= to brush

brouillard *noun, masculine*
le brouillard = fog

brouillé/brouillée *adjective*
= jumbled, mixed up

brouillon *noun, masculine*
un brouillon = a rough draft

broussailles *noun, feminine plural*
les broussailles = the undergrowth

brugnon *noun, masculine*
un brugnon = a nectarine

bruit *noun, masculine*
le bruit = noise

brûlant/brûlante *adjective*
= burning hot

---

brûlé noun, masculine
ça sent le brûlé = there's a smell of burning

brûler verb 1
1 (! + avoir)
• = to burn
• brûler un feu (rouge) = to jump the lights, to run the lights
2 se brûler (! + être)
se brûler = to burn oneself

brume noun, feminine
la brume = mist

brumeux/brumeuse adjective
= misty

brun/brune adjective
• = brown, dark
• = dark-haired

brunir verb 3
= to tan

brusque adjective
• = abrupt
• = sudden

Bruxelles noun
= Brussels

bruyant/bruyante adjective
= noisy

bu/bue ▶ boire 51

bûche noun, feminine
une bûche = a log

buffet noun, masculine
• (a piece of furniture)
un buffet = a sideboard
• (a meal, a place)
un buffet = a buffet

buisson noun, masculine
un buisson = a bush
= a shrub

buissonnière adjective, feminine
faire l'école buissonnière = to play truant, to play hooky

bulle noun, feminine
• (of soap)
une bulle = a bubble
faire des bulles = to blow bubbles
• (in a cartoon)
une bulle = a speech bubble

bulletin noun, masculine
un bulletin = a report
= a form
= a certificate
un bulletin météorologique = a weather report
un bulletin scolaire = a school report, a report card

bureau noun, masculine
(plural) **bureaux**

• (a piece of furniture)
un bureau = a desk
• (a room)
un bureau = an office
le bureau de poste = the post office
le bureau des renseignements = the information office, the information desk

bus noun, masculine (! never changes)
un bus = a bus

but noun, masculine
• (what one has in mind)
un but = a goal
= an aim, a purpose
= an intention
dans le but de = with the intention of
• (in football)
un but = a goal

buvable adjective
= drinkable
(on a medicine label) = to be taken orally

buveur/buveuse noun, masculine/feminine
un buveur/une buveuse = a drinker

Cc

c' ▶ ce

ça pronoun
• = this
= that
donne-moi ça = give me that
ça, c'est bizarre = that's strange
• = it
ça ne fait rien = it doesn't matter
c'est ça! = that's right!, that's it!
c'est pour ça que ... = that's why ...
et avec ça? = anything else?
• où ça? = where?
• comment ça va? = how are you?
ça va mal = things are bad
ça y est, j'ai fini = that's it, I've finished

cabane noun, feminine
une cabane = a hut, a shack

cabillaud noun, masculine
le cabillaud = cod

cabine noun, feminine
une cabine (for sleeping) = a cabin
(for changing) = a cubicle, a changing room
une cabine d'essayage = a fitting room
une cabine téléphonique = a telephone box, a telephone booth

cabinet noun, masculine
- (a place of work)
  un cabinet = an office
  (for a doctor) = a surgery, an office
- (a W.C.)
  le cabinet, les cabinets = the toilet, the bathroom
un cabinet de toilette = washing facilities

câble noun, masculine
  un câble = a cable

cacahuète noun, feminine
  une cacahuète = a peanut

cacao noun, masculine
  le cacao = cocoa

cache-cache noun, masculine (**!** never changes)
  jouer à cache-cache = to play hide and seek

cacher verb [1]
  = to hide

cachet noun, masculine
- (a medicine)
  un cachet = a tablet, a pill
- (on a form)
  un cachet = a stamp

cachette noun, feminine
  une cachette = a hiding place
  en cachette = secretly

c-à-d conjunction
(abbreviation of **c'est-à-dire**)
  c-à-d = i.e.

cadeau noun, masculine
(plural) **cadeaux**
  un cadeau = a present, a gift

cadet/cadette adjective
  = younger, youngest

cadre noun, masculine
- (for a picture)
  un cadre = a frame
- (an employee)
  un cadre = an executive
- (the space around a person or a thing)
  le cadre = the surroundings

cafard noun, masculine
- un cafard = a cockroach
- avoir le cafard = to feel down, to feel blue

café noun, masculine
- (a product)
  le café = coffee
- (a place)
  un café = a café, a diner
un café crème = an espresso with milk
un café au lait = a coffee with milk

cafetière noun, feminine
  une cafetière = a coffee maker

cage noun, feminine
  une cage = a cage

cahier noun, masculine
  un cahier = an exercise book
un cahier de brouillon = a rough book, a notebook
un cahier de textes = a homework notebook

caillou noun, masculine
(plural) **cailloux**
  un caillou = a stone

Caire noun, masculine
  le Caire = Cairo

caisse noun, feminine
- (for goods)
  une caisse = a crate
- (for money)
  une caisse = a till, a cash register
- (where you pay in a shop)
  la caisse = the cash desk
  = the checkout

calcul noun, masculine
- (the study of numbers)
  le calcul = arithmetic
- (an operation)
  un calcul = a calculation

calculatrice noun, feminine
  une calculatrice = a (pocket) calculator

calculer verb [1]
  = to calculate, to work out

calé/calée* adjective
  = clever

caleçon noun, masculine
  un caleçon (for men) = boxer shorts
  (for women) = leggings
un caleçon long = long johns

calendrier noun, masculine
  un calendrier = a calendar

caler verb [1]
- (in order to fix in a position) = to wedge
- (when driving) = to stall

calmant noun, masculine
  un calmant = a sedative

calmar noun, masculine
  un calmar = a squid

calme
1 adjective
  = calm, quiet
2 noun, masculine
  le calme = peace (and quiet)

calmer verb [1]
1 (**!** + avoir)
  = to calm (down)
2 se calmer (**!** + être)
  se calmer = to calm down

camarade noun, masculine/feminine
  un camarade/une camarade = a friend

---

cambriolage noun, masculine
un cambriolage = a burglary

cambrioler verb [1]
= to burgle

caméra noun, feminine
une caméra = a (cine-)camera, a movie
camera

caméscope® noun, masculine
un caméscope = a camcorder

camion noun, masculine
un camion = a lorry, a truck

camionnette noun, feminine
une camionnette = a van

campagne noun, feminine
• (the area around towns)
la campagne = the country
= the countryside
• (for an election, in war)
une campagne = a campaign

camper verb [1]
= to camp

campeur/campeuse noun,
masculine/feminine
un campeur/une campeuse = a camper

camping noun, masculine
• (the activity)
le camping = camping
• (the place)
un camping = a campsite, a campground

camping-car noun, masculine
(plural) **camping-cars**
un camping-car = a camper-van, an RV

Canada noun, masculine
le Canada = Canada

canadien/canadienne adjective
= Canadian

canal noun, masculine
(plural) **canaux**
• (a waterway)
un canal = a canal
• (in telecommunications)
un canal = a channel

canapé noun, masculine
un canapé = a settee, a sofa

canard noun, masculine
un canard = a duck

Cancer noun, masculine
le Cancer = Cancer

candidat/candidate noun,
masculine/feminine
un candidat/une candidate (in an
examination, an election) = a candidate
(for a job) = an applicant

caniche noun, masculine
un caniche = a poodle

canif noun, masculine
un canif = a penknife, a pocketknife

canne noun, feminine
une canne = a (walking) stick, a cane
une canne à pêche = a fishing rod

canoë noun, masculine
• (the equipment)
un canoë = a (Canadian) canoe
• (the sport)
le canoë = canoeing

canot noun, masculine
un canot = a (small) boat, a dinghy
un canot de sauvetage = a lifeboat

cantine noun, feminine
une cantine = a canteen

caoutchouc noun, masculine
le caoutchouc = rubber

CAP noun, masculine ▶ **certificat**

capitaine noun, masculine
un capitaine = a captain

capitale noun, feminine
• (a town)
une capitale = a capital (city)
• (a letter)
une capitale = a capital

capot noun, masculine
le capot = the bonnet, the hood

Capricorne noun, masculine
le Capricorne = Capricorn

capuchon noun, masculine
• (for the head)
un capuchon = a hood
• (for a pen)
un capuchon = a cap

car
1 noun, masculine
un car = a coach, a bus
2 conjunction
car = because, for

caractère noun, masculine
• (a personality)
un caractère = a character, a nature
• (in writing)
un caractère = a letter

Caraïbes noun, feminine plural
les Caraïbes = the Caribbean islands

carambolage noun, masculine
un carambolage = a pile-up

caramel noun, masculine
• (on ice cream, custard)
le caramel = caramel
• (a sweet)
un caramel = a toffee

caravane noun, feminine
une caravane = a caravan, a trailer

carburateur noun, masculine
le carburateur = the carburettor

caresser verb [1]
= to stroke

carnet noun, masculine
• (in which to write)
un carnet = a notebook
• (a set of tickets, stamps)
un carnet = a book
un carnet d'adresses = an address book
un carnet de chèques = a cheque book,
a checkbook

carotte noun, feminine
une carotte = a carrot

carré/carrée adjective
= square

carreau noun, masculine
(plural) **carreaux**
• (on a window)
un carreau = a window pane
• (on the wall, the floor)
un carreau = a tile
du tissu à carreaux = check(ed) material,
chequered material
• (at cards)
carreau = diamonds

carrefour noun, masculine
le carrefour = the crossroads

carrière noun, feminine
• (a profession)
une carrière = a career
• (a place)
une carrière = a quarry

carrosserie noun, feminine
la carrosserie = bodywork

cartable noun, masculine
un cartable = a satchel, a schoolbag
= a briefcase

carte noun, feminine
• (in games)
une carte = a card
• (of a country)
une carte = a map
• (in a restaurant)
la carte = the menu
une carte bleue = a credit card
une carte grise = a logbook
une carte d'identité = an ID card
une carte orange = a season ticket (in the
Paris area)
une carte postale = a postcard
une carte à puce = a smart card
une carte de visite = a visiting card
= a business card
une carte de vœux = a greeting(s) card

carton noun, masculine
• (the substance)
le carton = cardboard
• (a container)
un carton = a cardboard box

cas noun, masculine (**!** never changes)
un cas = a case

case noun, feminine
une case = a box

casier noun, masculine
un casier (for messages) = a pigeonhole
(for keeping things organized) = a locker

casque noun, masculine
• (for protection)
un casque = a helmet
= a hard hat
• (for listening to music)
un casque = headphones

casquette noun, feminine
une casquette = a cap

casse-croûte noun, masculine (**!** never
changes)
un casse-croûte = a snack

casser verb [1]
1 (**!** + avoir)
= to break
2 se casser (**!** + être)
se casser = to break
je me suis cassé le poignet = I broke my
wrist

casserole noun, feminine
une casserole = a saucepan, a pan

cassis noun, masculine (**!** never changes)
le cassis = blackcurrants

catastrophe noun, feminine
une catastrophe = a disaster

catch noun, masculine
le catch = wrestling

catéchisme noun, masculine
le catéchisme = catechism

catégorie noun, feminine
une catégorie = a category

cauchemar noun, masculine
un cauchemar = a nightmare

cause noun, feminine
la cause = the cause
à cause de = because of

causer verb [1]
• = to cause
causer un accident = to cause an accident
• **✕** = to chat, to talk

caution noun, feminine
une caution = a deposit

cave noun, feminine
une cave = a cellar

✕ in informal situations

ce¹/cette *adjective*
(*plural*) **ces**

> **!** cet *is used instead of* ce *before a masculine noun beginning with a vowel or a mute h. The plural of* cet *is* ces.

= this, that
ce livre(-ci) = this book
cet oiseau(-là) = that bird
ces enfants = these children, those children

ce² *pronoun* (**c'** *before e*)
- (*when the verb* être *is in the singular*)
c'est un cadeau = it's a present
ce serait dommage = it would be a shame
qui est-ce? = who is it?
qu'est-ce que c'est? = what is it?
c'est moi qui l'ai cassé = I was the one who broke it
- (*when the verb* être *is in the plural*)
ce sont des insectes = they're insects
ce sont des détails sans importance = these are unimportant details
- voilà ce que j'ai dit = that's what I said
prenez ce dont vous avez besoin = take what you need
c'est ce qui les inquiète = that's what worries them
ce qui m'ennuie le plus, c'est qu'il faudra se lever tôt = what bothers me most is that we'll have to get up early
il est venu, ce qui est étonnant = he came, which is surprising

> **!** Look up the verb être *for translations of* est-ce que.

ceci *pronoun*
= this

céder *verb* 14
- = to give up
- = to give in
céder le passage = to give way, to yield
- = to collapse

cédille *noun, feminine*
une cédille = a cedilla

CEE *noun, feminine* ▶ **communauté**

ceinture *noun, feminine*
une ceinture = a belt
une ceinture de sécurité = a seatbelt

cela *pronoun*
= it, that

célèbre *adjective*
= famous

célébrer *verb* 14
= to celebrate

céleri *noun, masculine*
le céleri = celery

célibataire
1 *adjective*
= single

2 *noun, masculine/feminine*
un célibataire/une célibataire = a single man/woman

celle ▶ **celui**

celle-ci ▶ **celui-ci**

celle-là ▶ **celui-là**

celles-ci ▶ **celui-ci**

celles-là ▶ **celui-là**

celui/celle *pronoun*
(*plural*) **ceux/celles**
celui/celle = the one
ceux/celles = the ones
= those
celle de ma sœur = my sister's

celui-ci/celle-ci *pronoun*
(*plural*) **ceux-ci/celles-ci**
celui-ci/celle-ci = this one
ceux-ci/celles-ci = these

celui-là/celle-là *pronoun*
(*plural*) **ceux-là/celles-là**
celui-là/celle-là = that one
ceux-là/celles-là = those

cendre *noun, feminine*
la cendre = ash

cendrier *noun, masculine*
un cendrier = an ashtray

Cendrillon *noun, feminine*
Cendrillon = Cinderella

censé/censée *adjective*
être censé = to be meant to

cent *number*
= hundred
pour cent = per cent

centaine *noun, feminine*
une centaine = about a hundred

centième *number*
= hundredth

centime *noun, masculine*
un centime = a centime

centimètre *noun, masculine*
- (*a unit of length*)
un centimètre = a centimetre, a centimeter
- (*a measuring device*)
un centimètre = a tape measure

central/centrale¹
(*plural*) **centraux/centrales**
1 *adjective*
= central
2 central *noun, masculine*
le central (téléphonique) = the (telephone) exchange

centrale² *noun, feminine*
une centrale = a power station

centre noun, masculine
le centre = the centre, the center
un centre aéré = a children's outdoor
activity centre
un centre commercial = a shopping
centre, a shopping mall

centre-ville noun, masculine
(plural) **centres-villes**
le centre-ville = the town centre, the town
center

cependant conjunction
= however

cercle noun, masculine
un cercle = a circle

cercueil noun, masculine
un cercueil = a coffin

céréale noun, feminine
une céréale = a cereal, a grain

cérémonie noun, feminine
une cérémonie = a ceremony

cerf noun, masculine
un cerf = a stag

cerf-volant noun, masculine
(plural) **cerfs-volants**
un cerf-volant = a kite

cerise noun, feminine
une cerise = a cherry

cerisier noun, masculine
un cerisier = a cherry tree

certain/certaine
1 adjective
= certain, sure
2 determiner
= some
3 **certains/certaines** pronoun, plural
= some
certains d'entre vous = some of you

certainement adverb
= most probably
= certainly

certificat noun, masculine
un certificat = a certificate
un certificat d'aptitude
professionnelle, un CAP = a
vocational training qualification
un certificat médical = a doctor's
certificate
un certificat de naissance = a birth
certificate

cerveau noun, masculine
(plural) **cerveaux**
le cerveau = the brain

cervelle noun, feminine
la cervelle = the brain

✗ in informal situations

ces ▶ ce¹

CES noun, masculine ▶ **collège**

cesser verb ⓵
= to stop

c'est-à-dire adverb
= that is (to say)

cet ▶ ce¹

CET noun, masculine ▶ **collège**

cette ▶ ce¹

ceux ▶ celui

chacun/chacune pronoun
• = each (one)
chacun d'entre vous = each one of you
• = everybody

chahut noun, masculine
du chahut = a racket

chaîne noun, feminine
• (linked metal rings)
une chaîne = a chain
• (on television)
une chaîne = a channel
• (in a factory)
la chaîne = the assembly line
une chaîne hi-fi = a hi-fi system
une chaîne laser = a CD system
une chaîne de montagnes
= a mountain range

chair noun, feminine
la chair = flesh
la chair de poule = goose pimples, goose
bumps

chaise noun, feminine
une chaise = a chair
une chaise longue = a deckchair

chaleur noun, feminine
la chaleur = heat, warmth

chambre noun, feminine
une chambre = a room, a bedroom
une chambre pour une personne
= a single room
une chambre pour deux personnes
= a double room
une chambre d'hôte = a room in a B & B
'chambres d'hôte' = 'bed and breakfast'

chameau noun, masculine
(plural) **chameaux**
un chameau = a camel

champ
1 noun, masculine
un champ = a field
2 à tout bout de champ✗ = all the time

champignon noun, masculine
un champignon = a mushroom

champion/championne noun,
masculine/feminine
un champion/une championne
= a champion

championnat *noun, masculine*
un championnat = a championship

chance *noun, feminine*
- (*good fortune*)
la chance = luck
- (*possibility*)
avoir des chances de gagner = to stand a chance of winning

change *noun, masculine*
le taux de change = the exchange rate

changement *noun, masculine*
un changement = a change

changer *verb* 13
= to change
changer d'avis = to change one's mind
changer d'adresse = to move

chanson *noun, feminine*
une chanson = a song

chant *noun, masculine*
un chant = a song

chanter *verb* 1
= to sing

chanteur/chanteuse *noun, masculine/feminine*
un chanteur/une chanteuse = a singer

chantier *noun, masculine*
un chantier = a building site

chantilly *noun, feminine* (**!** *never changes*)
la chantilly = whipped cream

chapeau *noun, masculine*
(*plural*) **chapeaux**
- un chapeau = a hat
- (*when praising*)**�✶**
chapeau**✶**! = well done!, good job!
un chapeau melon = a bowler hat, a derby hat

chapitre *noun, masculine*
un chapitre = a chapter

chaque *determiner*
= each, every

char *noun, masculine*
- (*in a carnival*)
un char = a float
- (*a military vehicle*)
un char = a tank

charcuterie *noun, feminine*
- (*a shop*)
une charcuterie = a pork butcher's
- (*a type of food*)
la charcuterie = cooked pork meats

charcutier/charcutière *noun, masculine/feminine*
un charcutier/une charcutière = a pork butcher

charger *verb* 13
1 (**!** + *avoir*)

- = to load
charger un camion de légumes = to load a truck with vegetables
- = to ask
charger quelqu'un [de poster une lettre | d'arroser les plantes | de transmettre un message ...] = to ask someone [to post a letter | to water the plants | to pass on a message ...]
- ils sont chargés de surveiller les enfants = they're responsible for looking after the children
2 se charger (**!** + *être*)
se charger d'une tâche = to take responsibility for a job, to see to a job
je me charge de le leur dire = I'll tell them

chariot *noun, masculine*
un chariot = a trolley, a cart

charité *noun, feminine*
la charité = charity

charmant/charmante *adjective*
= charming

chasse *noun, feminine*
la chasse = hunting
la chasse d'eau = the (toilet) flush

chasse-neige *noun, masculine* (**!** *never changes*)
un chasse-neige = a snowplough, a snowplow

chasser *verb* 1
- = to hunt
- = to shoot
- = to drive away

chasseur *noun, masculine*
un chasseur = a hunter

chat *noun, masculine*
un chat = a cat

châtaigne *noun, feminine*
une châtaigne = a (sweet) chestnut

châtain *adjective*
= brown

château *noun, masculine*
(*plural*) **châteaux**
un château = a castle
un château fort = a fortified castle

chaton *noun, masculine*
un chaton = a kitten

chatte *noun, feminine*
une chatte = a (female) cat

chaud/chaude
1 *adjective*
= hot, warm
2 chaud *adverb*
il fait chaud ici = it's hot in here
3 chaud *noun, masculine*
avoir chaud = to be hot

chaudière *noun, feminine*
une chaudière = a boiler

chauffage noun, masculine
le chauffage = the heating

chauffard✗ noun, masculine
un chauffard✗ = a reckless driver

chauffer verb 1
• = to heat
• = to overheat
le moteur chauffe = the engine is overheating
• = to give out heat, to give off heat
le poêle chauffe bien = the stove gives out a lot of heat
le soleil chauffe aujourd'hui = the sun is hot today

chauffeur noun, masculine
un chauffeur = a driver

chaumière noun, feminine
une chaumière = a thatched cottage

chaussée noun, feminine
la chaussée = the road, the highway
'chaussée déformée' = 'uneven road surface'

chausser verb 1
chausser du 39 = to take a size 39 (in shoes), to take a size 6

chaussette noun, feminine
une chaussette = a sock

chausson noun, masculine
• (footwear)
un chausson = a slipper
• (a cake)
un chausson = a turnover

chaussure noun, feminine
une chaussure = a shoe
des chaussures de ski = ski boots

chauve adjective
= bald

chauve-souris noun, feminine
(plural) **chauves-souris**
une chauve-souris = a bat

chef
1 noun, masculine
• (the person in charge)
le chef = the leader
• (in a restaurant)
un chef (cuisinier) = a chef
2 en chef
l'ingénieur en chef = the chief engineer
un chef d'entreprise = a company manager
un chef d'État = a head of state
un chef de gare = a station master
un chef d'orchestre = a conductor

chef-d'œuvre noun, masculine
(plural) **chefs-d'œuvre**
un chef-d'œuvre = a masterpiece

chemin noun, masculine
• un chemin = a country lane, a path
• le chemin = the way
le chemin de fer = the railway, the railroad

cheminée noun, feminine
une cheminée = a chimney
= a fireplace
= a mantelpiece, a mantel

chemise noun, feminine
une chemise = a shirt

chemisier noun, masculine
un chemisier = a blouse

chêne noun, masculine
un chêne = an oak (tree)

chenille noun, feminine
une chenille = a caterpillar

chèque noun, masculine
un chèque = a cheque, a check
un chèque sans provision = a bad cheque, a dud check

chèque-voyage noun, masculine
(plural) **chèques-voyage**
un chèque-voyage = a traveller's cheque, a traveler's check

chéquier noun, masculine
un chéquier = a cheque book, a checkbook

cher/chère adjective
• = dear
• = expensive

chercher verb 1
• = to look for
• aller chercher de l'eau = to go and get some water

chère ▶ cher

chéri/chérie noun, masculine|feminine
(mon) chéri/(ma) chérie = (my) darling

cheval noun, masculine
(plural) **chevaux**
• (an animal)
un cheval = a horse
monter à cheval = to ride (a horse)
• (the sport)
le cheval = horseriding, horseback riding
• (meat)
le cheval = horsemeat

chevalier noun, masculine
un chevalier = a knight

chevet noun, masculine
une lampe de chevet = a bedside lamp

cheveu noun, masculine
(plural) **cheveux**
les cheveux = hair

cheville noun, feminine
une cheville = an ankle

✗ in informal situations

chèvre noun, feminine
une chèvre = a goat

chez preposition
- = at
  je serai chez moi = I'll be at home
  il est chez eux ce matin? = is he at their
  place this morning?
- = to
  aller chez le dentiste = to go to the
  dentist's

chic adjective
- (elegant) = chic, smart
- (kind, obliging)✸ = nice

chien noun, masculine
- un chien = a dog
  un chien d'aveugle = a guide dog
- il fait un temps de chien✸ = the weather is
  awful

chienne noun, feminine
une chienne = a female dog, a bitch

chiffon noun, masculine
un chiffon = a rag, a cloth
un chiffon (à poussière) = a duster, a dust
cloth

chiffre noun, masculine
un chiffre = a figure

chignon noun, masculine
un chignon = a bun, a chignon

chimie noun, feminine
la chimie = chemistry

chimique adjective
= chemical

chinois/chinoise
1 adjective
= Chinese
2 chinois noun, masculine
le chinois = Chinese

chiot noun, masculine
un chiot = a puppy

chips noun, feminine (! never changes)
une chips = a crisp, a (potato) chip

chirurgien noun, masculine
un chirurgien = a surgeon

choc noun, masculine
un choc = a shock

chocolat noun, masculine
le chocolat = chocolate

choisir verb ③
= to choose

choix noun, masculine (! never changes)
un choix = a choice
des produits de choix = choice products
de premier choix = top quality

chômage noun, masculine
le chômage = unemployment
être au chômage = to be unemployed

chômeur/chômeuse noun,
masculine/feminine
un chômeur/une chômeuse = an
unemployed man/woman

choquer verb ①
= to shock

chorale noun, feminine
une chorale = a choir

chose noun, feminine
une chose = a thing
quelque chose = something
= anything
pas grand chose = not much

chou noun, masculine
(plural) **choux**
- (a vegetable)
  un chou = a cabbage
- (a cake)
  un chou = a choux bun, a pastry shell
- (a person)
  mon chou = my darling
un chou de Bruxelles = a Brussels sprout
un chou à la crème = a cream puff

choucroute noun, feminine
la choucroute = sauerkraut

chouette
1 adjective✸
= nice, great
2 noun, feminine
une chouette = an owl

chou-fleur noun, masculine
(plural) **choux-fleurs**
un chou-fleur = a cauliflower

chronométrer verb ⑭
= to time

chrysanthème noun, masculine
un chrysanthème = a chrysanthemum

chuchoter verb ①
= to whisper

chut exclamation
chut! = shh!, hush!

chute noun, feminine
une chute = a fall

cicatrice noun, feminine
une cicatrice = a scar

ci-contre adverb
= opposite

ci-dessous adverb
= below

ci-dessus adverb
= above

cidre noun, masculine
le cidre = cider, hard cider

ciel noun, masculine
- le ciel = the sky
- le ciel = heaven

cieux *noun, masculine plural*
les cieux = heaven

cigale *noun, feminine*
une cigale = a cicada

ci-joint/ci-jointe *adjective*
= enclosed

cil *noun, masculine*
un cil = an eyelash

cime *noun, feminine*
la cime = the top

cimetière *noun, masculine*
un cimetière = a graveyard, a cemetery

ciné* *noun, masculine*
le ciné* = the pictures, the movies

cinéma *noun, masculine*
• un cinéma = a cinema, a movie theater
• le cinéma = the cinema, the movies

cinglé/cinglée* *adjective*
= mad, crazy

cinq *number*
= five

cinquantaine *noun, feminine*
une cinquantaine = about fifty

cinquante *number*
= fifty

cinquième
1 *number*
= fifth
2 *noun, feminine*
la cinquième = *the class for secondary
school students aged 12 to 13*

cirage *noun, masculine*
le cirage = shoe polish

circuit *noun, masculine*
• (*visiting several places*)
un circuit = a tour
• (*in a race*)
un circuit = a circuit

circulation *noun, feminine*
la circulation = the traffic

circuler *verb* 1
• = to move
• = to run
ce train ne circule pas le dimanche = this
train doesn't run on Sundays
• = to circulate

cirque *noun, masculine*
le cirque = the circus

ciseaux *noun, masculine plural*
des ciseaux = scissors

citadelle *noun, feminine*
une citadelle = a fortress

cité *noun, feminine*
• une cité = a city, a town
• une cité = a housing estate, a housing
development
une cité universitaire = student halls of
residence, dormitories

citoyen/citoyenne *noun,
masculine/feminine*
un citoyen/une citoyenne = a citizen

citron *noun, masculine*
un citron = a lemon
un citron pressé = a freshly squeezed
lemonade

citronnade *noun, feminine*
la citronnade = lemon squash, (still)
lemonade

clair/claire
1 *adjective*
• = clear
• = light
2 clair *noun, masculine*
le clair de lune = moonlight

claqué/claquée* *adjective*
= exhausted

claquer *verb* 1
• = to slam
claquer la porte = to slam the door
• = to bang
une porte claquait = a door was banging
• faire claquer ses doigts = to snap one's
fingers
il claque des dents = his teeth are
chattering

claquettes *noun, feminine plural*
les claquettes = tap dancing

clarinette *noun, feminine*
une clarinette = a clarinet

classe *noun, feminine*
• (*a room*)
une (salle de) classe = a classroom
aller en classe = to go to school
• (*a category*)
une classe = a class
un billet de première classe = a first-class
ticket
une classe de mer = a seaside trip (*with a
school*)
une classe de neige = a skiing trip (*with
a school*)
une classe verte = a field trip (*with a
school*)

classeur *noun, masculine*
un classeur = a folder

clavier *noun, masculine*
un clavier = a keyboard

clé *noun, feminine*
• (*for a lock*)
une clé = a key
fermer à clé = to lock

---

* in informal situations

- (*a tool*)
  une clé = a spanner, a wrench
- **le mot(-)clé** = the key word

clef ▶ clé

client/cliente *noun, masculine/feminine*
  un client/une cliente = a customer, a client

clignotant *noun, masculine*
  un clignotant = an indicator, a turn signal

climat *noun, masculine*
  le climat = the climate

climatisation *noun, feminine*
  la climatisation = air-conditioning

clinique *noun, feminine*
  une clinique = a (private) clinic

clochard/clocharde *noun,*
masculine/feminine
  un clochard/une clocharde = a tramp, a
  bum

cloche *noun, feminine*
- **une cloche** = a bell
- **une cloche✱** = an idiot

cloche-pied: **à cloche-pied** *adverb*
  sauter à cloche-pied = to hop

clocher *noun, masculine*
  un clocher = a steeple
  = a church tower, a bell tower

clochette *noun, feminine*
  une clochette = a small bell

cloison *noun, feminine*
  une cloison = a partition

cloque *noun, feminine*
  une cloque = a blister

clos/close *adjective*
- = enclosed
- = closed

clôture *noun, feminine*
  une clôture = a fence

clou
1 *noun, masculine*
  un clou = a nail
2 clous *noun, masculine plural*
  les clous = the pedestrian crossing, the
  crosswalk

clouer *verb* 1
  = to nail (down)

clouté *adjective, masculine*
  un passage clouté = a pedestrian crossing,
  a crosswalk

clown *noun, masculine*
  un clown = a clown
  faire le clown = to clown around

club *noun, masculine*
  un club = a club

cobaye *noun, masculine*
  un cobaye = a guinea pig

coca *noun, masculine*
  un coca = a Coke®, a Coca-Cola®

cocher *verb* 1
  = to tick, to check (off)

cochon *noun, masculine*
  un cochon = a pig
un cochon d'Inde = a guinea pig

coco *noun, masculine*
  une noix de coco = a coconut

cocotier *noun, masculine*
  un cocotier = a coconut tree

code
1 *noun, masculine*
  un code = a code
2 codes *noun, masculine plural*
  les codes = dipped headlights, dimmed
  headlights
  se mettre en codes = to dip one's
  headlights, to dim one's headlights
un code confidentiel (d'identification)
  = a personal identification number
un code postal = a postcode, a zip code
le code de la route = the highway code,
  the rules of the road

cœur
1 *noun, masculine*
- **le cœur** = the heart
  avoir mal au cœur = to feel sick, to feel
  nauseous
  avoir bon cœur = to be kind-hearted
- (*at cards*)
  cœur = hearts
2 par cœur = by heart

coffre *noun, masculine*
- **un coffre** (*for storage*) = a chest, a trunk
  (*for valuables*) = a safe
- (*in a car*)
  le coffre = the boot, the trunk

coffre-fort *noun, masculine*
(*plural*) **coffres-forts**
  un coffre-fort = a safe

cognac *noun, masculine*
  le cognac = brandy

coiffer: **se coiffer** *verb* 1 (**!** + *être*)
  se coiffer = to do one's hair

coiffeur/coiffeuse *noun,*
masculine/feminine
  un coiffeur/une coiffeuse = a hairdresser, a
  hairstylist

coin *noun, masculine*
- (*an angle*)
  un coin = a corner
  au coin de la rue = on the corner of the
  street
  au coin du feu = by the fire
- (*a place*)
  un coin = a spot
  un petit coin tranquille = a nice quiet spot

- (*the surrounding area*)
  le coin = the neighbo(u)rhood
  le café du coin = the local café
  dans le coin = in the area

coincer *verb* 12
= to jam, to wedge

col *noun, masculine*
- (*on a garment*)
  un col = a collar
  un col roulé = a polo neck, a turtleneck
- (*in the mountain*)
  un col = a pass

colère *noun, feminine*
la colère = anger

coléreux/coléreuse *adjective*
= quick-tempered, short-tempered

colique *noun, feminine*
la colique = diarrh(o)ea

colis *noun, masculine* (**!** *never changes*)
un colis = a parcel, a package

collant/collante
1 *adjective*
= sticky
2 collant *noun, masculine*
un collant = (a pair of) tights, pantyhose

colle *noun, feminine*
la colle = glue

collectionner *verb* 1
= to collect

collège *noun, masculine*
un collège (d'enseignement secondaire),
un CES = a secondary school, ≈ a junior
high school (*for students aged 11 to 14*)
**un collège d'enseignement technique, un
CET** = a technical secondary school (*for
students aged 11 to 14*)

collègue *noun, masculine/feminine*
un collègue/une collègue = a colleague

coller *verb* 1
- = to stick, to glue
- (*in an examination*)**✗**
  se faire coller✗ à un examen = to fail an
  examination

collier *noun, masculine*
un collier (*on a person*) = a necklace
(*on an animal*) = a collar

colline *noun, feminine*
une colline = a hill

colonie *noun, feminine*
une colonie = a colony
une colonie de vacances = a holiday
camp, a summer camp (*for children*)

colonne *noun, feminine*
une colonne = a column

colorier *verb* 2
= to colo(u)r

coloris *noun, masculine* (**!** *never changes*)
un coloris = a colo(u)r

combien
1 *adverb*
combien (de) = how much, how many
2 *noun* (**!** *never changes*)
le combien sommes-nous? = what's the
date today?
du combien chaussez-vous? = what size
shoe do you take?

combinaison *noun, feminine*
une combinaison (*a fashion garment*) = a
jumpsuit
(*protective clothing*) = overalls, coveralls
une combinaison de plongée = a
wetsuit
une combinaison de ski = a ski-suit

combiné *noun, masculine*
le combiné = the handset, the receiver

comédie *noun, feminine*
- (*a play*)
  une comédie = a comedy
- (*pretence*)
  de la comédie = an act

comédien/comédienne *noun,
masculine/feminine*
un comédien/une comédienne = an
actor/an actress

comestible *adjective*
= edible

comique *adjective*
- = comic
- = funny

commandant *noun, masculine*
le commandant = the major
le commandant de bord = the captain

commande *noun, feminine*
- (*for goods*)
  une commande = an order
- (*a device*)
  une commande = a control
  être aux commandes = to be at the
  controls

commander *verb* 1
- (*in a restaurant*) = to order
- (*in a group*) = to be in command

comme
1 *adverb*
comme c'est beau! = it's so beautiful!
2 *conjunction*
- = like
  il conduit comme un fou = he drives like a
  maniac
- = as
  comme toujours = as always
  gros comme mon poing = as big as my fist

✗ in informal situations

- = as, since
  comme il pleuvait, je ne suis pas sorti = as it was raining I didn't go out
- = as a
  travailler comme serveuse = to work as a waitress
  comme ci comme ça✗ = so so
3 comme il faut = properly, correctly

commencer verb 12
= to start, to begin

comment adverb
- = how
  comment allez-vous? = how are you?
- = what
  comment s'appelle-t-il? = what's his name?
  comment trouves-tu leur jardin? = what do you think of their garden?
  c'est comment? = what's it like?
- (when asking someone to repeat)
  comment? = sorry?, pardon?, excuse me?

commentaire noun, masculine
- (on a text, on a match)
  un commentaire = a commentary
- (a remark)
  un commentaire = a comment

commerçant/commerçante noun, masculine/feminine
  un commerçant/une commerçante = a shopkeeper

commerce noun, masculine
- (a place)
  un commerce = a shop, a store
- (an activity)
  le commerce = trade

commettre verb 60
  commettre un meurtre = to commit a murder
  commettre une erreur = to make a mistake

commis/commise ▶ **commettre** 60

commissariat noun, masculine
  le commissariat (de police) = the police station

commode
1 adjective
  = convenient, handy
2 noun, feminine
  une commode = a chest of drawers, a dresser

commun/commune adjective
  = common

communauté noun, feminine
  une communauté = a community
la Communauté Européenne, la CE
  = the European Community, the EC

communication noun, feminine
  une communication (téléphonique) = a (phone) call

communiquer verb 1
  = to communicate

compagne noun, feminine
  une compagne = a (female) companion

compagnie noun, feminine
- (a firm, a group of actors)
  une compagnie = a company
- (the presence of other people)
  la compagnie = company
une compagnie aérienne = an airline

compagnon noun, masculine
  un compagnon = a (male) companion

comparaison noun, feminine
  une comparaison = a comparison

comparer verb 1
  = to compare

compartiment noun, masculine
  un compartiment = a compartment

compétition noun, feminine
- **la compétition** = competition, rivalry
- **une compétition (sportive)** = a sporting event

complet/complète adjective
- = complete
- = full

compliment noun, masculine
  un compliment = a compliment
  tous mes compliments! = congratulations!

compliqué/compliquée adjective
  = complicated

comporter verb 1
1 (! + avoir)
  = to consist of
2 se comporter (! + être)
  se comporter = to behave

composer verb 1
1 (! + avoir)
- = to dial
  composer un numéro = to dial a number
- = to put together
  composer un menu = to put a menu together
- = to make up
  les joueurs qui composent l'équipe = the players who make up the team
  composé de = made up of
- = to compose
  qui a composé la musique du film? = who composed the score for the film?
2 se composer de (! + être)
  se composer de = to be made up of

compositeur/compositrice noun, masculine/feminine
  un compositeur/une compositrice = a composer

composter verb 1
  = to punch

C

compote noun, feminine
la compote de pommes = stewed apple

comprendre verb 52
1 (**!** + avoir)
• = to understand
• = to include
2 se comprendre (**!** + être)
• se comprendre = to understand each
  other
• se comprendre = to be understandable

comprimé noun, masculine
un comprimé = a tablet, a pill

compris/comprise
1 ▶ comprendre 52
2 adjective
= included
3 y compris = including

compte noun, masculine
• (in a bank, a post office)
  un compte = an account
• se rendre compte = to realize
• tenir compte de = to take into account
• travailler à son compte = to be self-
  employed

compter verb 1
• = to count
• = to intend
• compter sur = to count on

comptoir noun, masculine
le comptoir (in a shop) = the counter
(in a café) = the bar, the counter

con noun, masculine
un con = a stupid jerk

concerner verb 1
• = to concern
• = to affect

concessionnaire noun, masculine/
feminine
un concessionnaire/une concessionnaire
= a distributor, an agent

concierge noun, masculine/feminine
un concierge/une concierge = a caretaker,
a superintendent

concombre noun, masculine
un concombre = a cucumber

concours noun, masculine (**!** never
changes)
• (a game, an event)
  un concours = a competition, a contest
• (an examination)
  un concours = a competitive examination

concurrence noun, feminine
la concurrence = competition

concurrent/concurrente noun,
masculine/feminine
un concurrent/une concurrente = a
competitor

condamner verb 1
• (to declare someone guilty) = to convict
• (to punish) = to sentence
  être condamné à une amende = to be fined

condition noun, feminine
une condition = a condition
à condition de, à condition que = provided
(that), on condition that

condoléances noun, feminine plural
des condoléances = condolences

conducteur/conductrice noun,
masculine/feminine
un conducteur/une conductrice = a driver

conduire verb 62
1 (**!** + avoir)
• = to drive
• = to lead
  le sentier conduit au village = the path
  leads to the village
2 se conduire (**!** + être)
  se conduire = to behave

conduite noun, feminine
ta conduite = your behavio(u)r
= your conduct

confection noun, feminine
la confection = ready-to-wear clothes

confiance noun, feminine
• (in someone's honesty)
  la confiance = trust
  faire confiance = to trust
• (in someone's ability)
  la confiance = confidence
  la confiance en soi = (self-)confidence

confier verb 2
1 (**!** + avoir)
= to entrust
2 se confier (**!** + être)
  se confier à quelqu'un = to confide in
  someone

confiserie noun, feminine
une confiserie = a sweet shop, a candy
store

confisquer verb 1
= to confiscate

confiture noun, feminine
la confiture = jam, jelly
la confiture d'orange = marmalade

confort noun, masculine
le confort = comfort

confortable adjective
= comfortable

congé noun, masculine
un congé = a holiday, a vacation
être en congé = to be on holiday, to be on
vacation
un congé de maladie = sick leave

✗ in informal situations   **☛** may be considered offensive

congélateur *noun, masculine*
un congélateur = a freezer

conjuguer *verb* 1
= to conjugate

connaissance *noun, feminine*
• la connaissance = knowledge
• une connaissance = an acquaintance
j'ai fait la connaissance de leur fils = I met
    their son
• perdre connaissance = to lose
    consciousness
sans connaissance = unconscious

connaître *verb* 63
1 (**!** + *avoir*)
= to know
2 se connaître (**!** + *être*)
• se connaître = to know each other
• se connaître = to know oneself
3 s'y connaître en (**!** + *être*)
s'y connaître en = to know about
tu t'y connais en voitures? = do you know
    about cars?

connu/connue
1 ▶ connaître 63
2 *adjective*
= well-known

consciencieux/consciencieuse
adjective
= conscientious

conseil *noun, masculine*
• (*an opinion*)
un conseil = a piece of advice
des conseils = advice
• (*a group of people*)
un conseil = a council
un conseil de classe = a staff meeting
(*for those teaching a given class*)
le conseil municipal = the town council

conseiller¹ *verb* 1
• = to advise
• = to recommend

conseiller²/conseillère *noun,*
masculine/feminine
• (*an expert*)
un conseiller/une conseillère = an adviser,
    a consultant
• (*an elected member*)
un conseiller/une conseillère = a
    councillor
un conseiller d'éducation = a
supervisor
un conseiller municipal = a town
councillor
un conseiller d'orientation = a careers
adviser

conservatoire *noun, masculine*
un conservatoire = an academy, a
    conservatory

conserve *noun, feminine*
les conserves (*in tins*) = canned food

(*in jars*) = preserves
une boîte de conserve = a can (of food)

conserver *verb* 1
• = to keep
• = to preserve

consigne *noun, feminine*
• la consigne = the left luggage office
• la consigne = orders, instructions
la consigne automatique = the left
luggage lockers, the baggage lockers

consoler *verb* 1
= to comfort
= to console

consommateur/consommatrice
noun, masculine/feminine
un consommateur/une consommatrice (*of
    goods, services*) = a consumer
(*in a café*) = a customer

consommation *noun, feminine*
• (*in a café*)
une consommation = a drink
• (*of gas, food*)
la consommation = consumption

consommer *verb* 1
= to consume

constater *verb* 1
= to notice

construire *verb* 62
= to build

construit ▶ construire 62

consulat *noun, masculine*
un consulat = a consulate

consulter *verb* 1
= to consult

contacter *verb* 1
= to contact, to get in touch with

contagieux/contagieuse *adjective*
= contagious

conte *noun, masculine*
un conte = a story, a tale
un conte de fées = a fairy tale

contenir *verb* 36
• = to contain
• = to hold

content/contente *adjective*
= happy, pleased, glad
il est content de te voir = he's happy to see
you

contenu/contenue
1 ▶ contenir 36
2 contenu *noun, masculine*
le contenu = the contents

continuellement *adverb*
= continuously

continuer *verb* 1
= to continue

contourner verb ①
= to go (a)round
= to bypass

contraire adjective
= opposite

contrarier verb ②
= to upset

contravention noun, feminine
une contravention = a fine

contre
1 preposition
= against
2 noun, masculine
le pour et le contre = the pros and cons
3 par contre = on the other hand

contrebande noun, feminine
la contrebande = smuggling
des produits de contrebande = smuggled
goods

contrebasse noun, feminine
une contrebasse = a double bass, an
upright bass

contribuer verb ①
contribuer à = to contribute to

contrôle noun, masculine
• (a way of checking)
un contrôle = a check
= an inspection
(in class) = a test
un contrôle de qualité = a quality check
un contrôle des billets = a ticket
inspection
• (over a vehicle)
le contrôle = control
le contrôle (continu) des
connaissances = (continuous)
assessment

contrôler verb ①
= to check
= to inspect

contrôleur/contrôleuse noun,
masculine/feminine
un contrôleur/une contrôleuse = an
inspector

convaincre verb ⑤⑦
= to convince
= to persuade

convaincu/convaincue ▶
convaincre ⑤⑦

convenable adjective
• = suitable
• = proper

convenir verb �
convenir à = to suit
= to be suitable for

✗ in informal situations

convenu/convenue ▶ **convenir** ㊱

convoi noun, masculine
un convoi = a convoy

convoquer verb ①
= to summon
= to send for

copain noun, masculine
mon copain = my friend
= my boyfriend

copie noun, feminine
• (of a letter, a painting)
une copie = a copy
• (a piece of schoolwork)
une copie = a paper

copier verb ②
= to copy

copine noun, feminine
ma copine = my friend
= my girlfriend

coq noun, masculine
un coq = a cock, a rooster

coquillage noun, masculine
• un coquillage = a shell
• les coquillages = shellfish

coquille noun, feminine
une coquille = a shell
une coquille Saint-Jacques = a scallop

cor noun, masculine
un cor = a horn

corbeau noun, masculine
(plural) **corbeaux**
un corbeau = a crow

corbeille noun, feminine
une corbeille = a basket
une corbeille à papier = a wastepaper
basket

corde noun, feminine
• une corde = a rope
• (on a violin, a bow, a racket)
une corde = a string
une corde à sauter = a skipping rope, a
jumprope

corne noun, feminine
une corne = a horn

cornet noun, masculine
• (for ice cream)
un cornet = a cornet
• (for fries, sweets)
un cornet = a bag

Cornouailles noun, feminine
la Cornouailles = Cornwall

corps noun, masculine (**!** never changes)
le corps = the body

correct/correcte adjective
• = correct

* = proper
* = polite

correspondance *noun, feminine*
* (*when travelling*)
  une correspondance = a connection
* (*when writing letters*)
  la correspondance = correspondence

correspondant/correspondante
noun, masculine/feminine
  un correspondant/une correspondante = a
  penfriend, a penpal

correspondre *verb* 6
* = to write
* **correspondre à** = to correspond to, to
  match

corrigé *noun, masculine*
  le corrigé = the correct version

corriger *verb* 13
* = to correct
* = to mark, to grade

Corse *noun, feminine*
  la Corse = Corsica

cortège *noun, masculine*
  un cortège = a procession

corvée *noun, feminine*
  une corvée = a chore

costaud* *adjective*
  = strong, sturdy

costume *noun, masculine*
* (*a man's outfit*)
  un costume = a suit
* (*worn by actors*)
  un costume = a costume

côte
1 *noun, feminine*
* (*by the sea*)
  la côte = the coast
* (*an incline*)
  une côte = a hill
  = a slope
* (*in the body*)
  une côte = a rib
2 côte à côte = side by side

côté
1 *noun, masculine*
  un côté = a side
2 à côté = nearby
  j'habite à côté = I live nearby
  la maison d'à côté = the house next door
3 à côté de = next to

Côte-d'Ivoire *noun, feminine*
  la Côte-d'Ivoire = the Ivory Coast

côtelette *noun, feminine*
  une côtelette = a chop, a cutlet

cotisation *noun, feminine*
  une cotisation = a subscription

coton *noun, masculine*
* (*a natural fibre*)
  le coton = cotton
* (*fluffy wadding*)
  le coton (hydrophile) = cotton wool,
  (absorbent) cotton

cou *noun, masculine*
  le cou = the neck

couche *noun, feminine*
* (*a thickness*)
  une couche = a layer
* (*on a baby*)
  une couche = a nappy, a diaper

coucher
1 *verb* 1 (**!** + *avoir*)
* = to put to bed
* = to sleep
2 se coucher *verb* 1 (**!** + *être*)
* **se coucher** = to go to bed
  ils sont couchés = they're in bed
* **se coucher** = to lie (down)
* **se coucher** = to set, to go down
  le soleil se couche vers 8 heures = the sun
  sets at about 8 o'clock
3 *noun, masculine*
  le coucher du soleil = sunset

couchette *noun, feminine*
  une couchette = a couchette, a berth

coucou *exclamation*
  coucou! = peekaboo!

coude *noun, masculine*
  un coude = an elbow

coudre *verb* 66
  = to sew

couette *noun, feminine*
* (*on a bed*)
  une couette = a duvet, a comforter
* (*a hairstyle*)
  des couettes = bunches, pigtails

couler *verb* 1
  = to flow

couleur *noun, feminine*
  une couleur = a colo(u)r

couloir *noun, masculine*
  un couloir = a corridor, a hallway
  = a passage

coup *noun, masculine*

> **!** *For translations of phrases such as* coup
> de foudre, coup de fil, coup de soleil *etc*
> *look up the entries at* foudre, fil, soleil *etc.*

* (*a hard hit*)
  un coup = a blow
  donner un coup de [pied | poing | couteau ...]
  à quelqu'un = [to kick | to punch | to stab ...]
  someone
  à coups de marteau = with a hammer

- (a loud noise)
  un coup = a knock
  frapper trois coups à la porte = to knock
    three times on the door
- (the firing of a gun)
  un coup de [feu | fusil | revolver ...] = a shot
  tué d'un coup de fusil = shot dead
- (an attempt, an occasion)
  du premier coup = first time
  à chaque coup = every time
  ce coup-ci = this time
  sur le coup = at the time
  = instantly
  tout d'un coup, tout à coup = suddenly, all
    of a sudden

coupable
1 *adjective*
  = guilty
2 *noun, masculine|feminine*
  un coupable/une coupable = a culprit

coupe *noun, feminine*
- (a trophy)
  une coupe = a cup
- (at the hairdresser's)
  une coupe = a haircut
- (a container)
  une coupe = a bowl

couper *verb* 1
1 (! + *avoir*)
  = to cut off
2 **se couper** (! + *être*)
  se couper = to cut oneself
  se couper le doigt = to cut one's finger

cour *noun, feminine*
- (an enclosed area)
  une cour = a yard
  = a courtyard
  = a farmyard
- (a play area at school)
  une cour (de récréation) = a playground, a
    schoolyard
- (for royalty, trials)
  la cour = the court

courageux/courageuse *adjective*
  = courageous, brave

couramment *adverb*
- = fluently
- = widely

courant
1 ▶ **courir** 26
2 *noun, masculine*
  un courant = a current
3 **au courant**
  être au courant de ce qui se passe = to
    know what's going on
  je vous tiendrai au courant = I'll keep you
    informed
un courant d'air = a draught, a draft

✖ in informal situations

coureur/coureuse *noun, masculine|
feminine*
  un coureur/une coureuse = a runner
un coureur cycliste = a racing cyclist

courir *verb* 26
- = to run
- = to race
- = to rush

couronne *noun, feminine*
- (on a king's head)
  une couronne = a crown
- (on a grave)
  une couronne = a wreath

courrier *noun, masculine*
  le courrier = the post, the mail
  = letters
  par retour du courrier = by return (post),
    by return mail
le courrier du cœur = the problem page,
  the advice column

cours *noun, masculine* (! *never changes*)
- (a teaching session)
  un cours = a lesson, a class
  faire cours = to teach
- (a series of lessons)
  un cours = a course
- (on the foreign exchange)
  le cours du dollar = the (exchange) rate for
    the dollar
- **au cours de la journée** = during the course
    of the day
  en cours de route = along the way
un cours d'eau = a waterway
un cours du soir = an evening class

course
1 *noun, feminine*
- (a competition)
  une course = a race
- (some business to attend to)
  une course = an errand
2 **courses** *noun, feminine plural*
  des courses = shopping

coursier/coursière *noun, masculine|
feminine*
  un coursier/une coursière = a messenger, a
    dispatch rider

court/courte *adjective*
  = short
  de courte durée = short-lived

couru/courue ▶ **courir** 26

cousin/cousine *noun,
masculine|feminine*
  un cousin/une cousine = a cousin

coussin *noun, masculine*
  un coussin = a cushion

cousu/cousue ▶ **coudre** 66

coût *noun, masculine*
  le coût = the cost

couteau *noun, masculine*
(*plural*) **couteaux**
  un couteau = a knife

coûter verb [1]
= to cost

coûteux/coûteuse adjective
= costly

coutume noun, feminine
une coutume = a custom

couture noun, feminine
• (an activity)
la couture = sewing
• (in a garment)
une couture = a seam

couvercle noun, masculine
un couvercle = a lid

couvert¹ noun, masculine
un couvert = a place setting
mettre le couvert = to set the table

couvert²/couverte ▶ couvrir [32]

couverture noun, feminine
• (on a bed)
une couverture = a blanket
• (on a book)
une couverture = a cover

couvrir verb [32]
= to cover

crabe noun, masculine
un crabe = a crab

cracher verb [1]
• = to spit
• = to spit out

craie noun, feminine
la craie = chalk

craindre verb [54]
• = to fear, to be afraid
ne craignez rien = don't be afraid
• = to be sensitive to

craint/crainte¹ ▶ craindre [54]

crainte¹ noun, feminine
la crainte = fear

cramoisi/cramoisie adjective
= crimson

crampe noun, feminine
une crampe = a cramp

crâne noun, masculine
le crâne = the skull

crapaud noun, masculine
un crapaud = a toad

craquer verb [1]
• = to break
• = to creak
• (emotionally)✗ = to crack up

cravate noun, feminine
une cravate = a tie

crayon noun, masculine
un crayon = a pencil

un crayon à bille = a ballpoint pen
un crayon de couleur = a colo(u)red
pencil
un crayon feutre = a felt-tip pen

crèche noun, feminine
• (for babies)
une crèche = a day-nursery, a nursery
• (a Christmas scene)
une crèche = a crib, a crèche

crédit noun, masculine
le crédit = credit
acheter à crédit = to buy on credit
'la maison ne fait pas de crédit' = 'no
credit'

créer verb [11]
• = to create
• = to set up, to found

crème
1 noun, feminine
la crème = cream
2 noun, masculine
un crème = an espresso with milk

crémerie noun, feminine
une crémerie = a cheese shop, a cheese
store

crêpe noun, feminine
une crêpe = a pancake

crêperie noun, feminine
une crêperie = a pancake restaurant

cresson noun, masculine
le cresson = watercress

crête noun, feminine
• (of a hill, a wave)
la crête = the crest
• (of a roof)
la crête = the ridge
• (on a bird)
la crête = the comb

creuser verb [1]
• = to dig
• l'exercice, ça creuse✗! = exercise gives you
an appetite!

creux/creuse adjective
= hollow

crevaison noun, feminine
une crevaison = a puncture

crevant/crevante✗ adjective
• = exhausting
• = hilarious

crevé/crevée✗ adjective
• = exhausted
• = flat, punctured

crever verb [16]
• = to have a puncture
• = to burst
= to puncture
• = to die
un chat crevé = a dead cat

- (*to exhaust*)✱ = to wear out
la course m'a crevé✱ = the race wore me out

crevette *noun, feminine*
une crevette grise = a shrimp
une crevette rose = a prawn

cri *noun, masculine*
- (*by a person*)
un cri = a cry, a shout
= a scream
pousser un cri = to scream
- (*by an animal*)
un cri = a cry
= a call

crier *verb* 2
= to shout
= to scream

crime *noun, masculine*
un crime (*a criminal action*) = a crime
(*an unlawful killing*) = a murder

criminel/criminelle
1 *adjective*
= criminal
2 *noun, masculine/feminine*
un criminel/une criminelle = a criminal
= a murderer

crise *noun, feminine*
- (*a difficult situation*)
une crise = a crisis
- (*an outburst*)
une crise = a fit
- (*a sudden illness*)
une crise = an attack
une crise cardiaque = a heart attack

critiquer *verb* 1
= to criticize

crochet *noun, masculine*
- (*a piece of bent metal*)
un crochet = a hook
- (*on a journey*)
un crochet = a detour

croire *verb* 53
1 (**!** + *avoir*)
- = to believe
je te crois = I believe you
- = to think
je ne crois pas = I don't think so
2 se croire (**!** + *être*)
il se croit malin = he thinks he's smart

croisement *noun, masculine*
un croisement = a junction, an intersection

croiser *verb* 1
1 (**!** + *avoir*)

- = to cross
les jambes croisées = legs crossed
les bras croisés = arms folded
- = to pass
croiser une voiture = to pass a car (coming the other way)
2 se croiser (**!** + *être*)
- se croiser = to cross
- se croiser = to pass each other

croisière *noun, feminine*
une croisière = a cruise

croissance *noun, feminine*
la croissance = growth

croissant *noun, masculine*
- (*a pastry*)
un croissant = a croissant
- (*a shape*)
un croissant = a crescent

croix *noun, feminine* (**!** *never changes*)
une croix = a cross

croque-monsieur *noun, masculine*
(**!** *never changes*)
un croque-monsieur = a grilled ham and cheese sandwich

crotte *noun, feminine*
de la crotte de chien = dog mess, dog poop

croûte *noun, feminine*
- (*on bread*)
la croûte = the crust
- (*on cheese*)
la croûte = the rind
- (*on the skin*)
une croûte = a scab

croûton *noun, masculine*
un croûton = a crouton

CRS *noun, masculine* (**!** *never changes*)
un CRS *a member of the French riot police*

cru/crue
1 ▶ **croire** 53
2 *adjective*
= raw

crudités *noun, feminine plural*
des crudités = raw vegetables

cruel/cruelle *adjective*
= cruel

cueillir *verb* 27
= to pick

cuiller, **cuillère** *noun, feminine*
une cuiller, une cuillère = a spoon
une cuillère à café, une petite cuillère = a teaspoon
une cuillère à soupe = a soup spoon

✱ in informal situations   ● may be considered offensive

cuillerée *noun, feminine*
une cuillerée = a spoonful

cuir *noun, masculine*
le cuir = leather

cuire *verb* 62
= to cook
= to bake

cuisine *noun, feminine*
• (*a room*)
une cuisine = a kitchen
• (*the preparation of food*)
la cuisine = cooking

cuisinier/cuisinière¹ *noun,*
masculine/feminine
un cuisinier/une cuisinière = a cook

cuisinière² *noun, feminine*
une cuisinière = a cooker, a stove, a range

cuisse *noun, feminine*
une cuisse = a thigh
des cuisses de grenouille = frog's legs

cuit/cuite ▶ cuire 62

cul *noun, masculine*
le cul = the arse, the ass

culot× *noun, masculine*
le culot× = cheek, nerve

culotte *noun, feminine*
une culotte = pants, panties, knickers

cultiver *verb* 1
• = to cultivate
• = to grow

cure *noun, feminine*
une cure = a course of treatment (*in a spa*)

curé *noun, masculine*
un curé = a (parish) priest

curieux/curieuse
1 *adjective*
• = inquisitive
• = odd, strange
2 curieux *noun, masculine plural*
les curieux = onlookers

curiosité *noun, feminine*
la curiosité = curiosity

cuvette *noun, feminine*
une cuvette = a bowl

CV *noun, masculine*
• (*personal details*)
un CV = a CV, a résumé
• (*a unit of power*)
un CV = one HP

cyclable *adjective*
une piste cyclable = a cycle lane

cycliste *noun, masculine/feminine*
un cycliste/une cycliste = a cyclist

cygne *noun, masculine*
un cygne = a swan

cyprès *noun, masculine* (! *never changes*)
un cyprès = a cypress

Dd

d' ▶ de

dactylo *noun, masculine/feminine*
un dactylo/une dactylo = a typist

daim *noun, masculine*
• (*an animal*)
un daim = a deer
• (*a type of leather*)
le daim = suede

dame
1 *noun, feminine*
une dame = a lady
2 dames *noun, feminine plural*
les dames = draughts, checkers

Danemark *noun, masculine*
le Danemark = Denmark

danger *noun, masculine*
le danger = danger
'danger de noyade' = 'unsafe for swimming'

dangereux/dangereuse *adjective*
= dangerous

danois/danoise
1 *adjective*
= Danish
2 danois *noun, masculine*
le danois = Danish

dans *preposition*
• = in
vivre dans une ville = to live in a town
être dans les affaires = to be in business
aller dans la bonne direction = to go in the right direction
dans une semaine = in a week's time
• = into
entrer dans une maison = to go into a house
sortir dans le jardin = to go out into the garden
• = on
être dans un train = to be on a train
monter dans un avion = to get on a plane
dans l'ensemble = on the whole
• = through
fouiller dans un sac = to rummage through a bag
• = out of
prendre un verre dans un placard = to take a glass out of a cupboard

danse *noun, feminine*
• la danse = dancing
• une danse = a dance
la danse classique = ballet dancing

danser *verb* 1
= to dance

danseur/danseuse *noun,*
masculine/feminine
un danseur/une danseuse = a dancer

date *noun, feminine*
la date = the date
'date limite de consommation' = 'use-by
date'

dater *verb* 1
= to date
dater de = to date from

datte *noun, feminine*
une datte = a date

daube *noun, feminine*
la daube beef stew cooked in wine

dauphin *noun, masculine*
un dauphin = a dolphin

davantage *adverb*
• = more
• = longer

de (**d'** *before vowel or mute h;* de + le
becomes du; de + les *becomes* des)

> ! *You will find translations for phrases with*
> de *such as* d'abord, pomme de terre,
> chemin de fer *etc under the words* abord,
> pomme, chemin, *etc.*

1 *preposition*
• = of
un verre d'eau = a glass of water
la voiture de mon père = my father's car
• = from
le paquet vient de Paris = the package
comes from Paris
du matin au soir = from morning till night
• = by
un tableau de Picasso = a painting by
Picasso
il était suivi de son chien = he was
followed by his dog
• = about
elle parle des voisins = she's talking about
the neighbo(u)rs
de quoi s'agit-il? = what's it about?
• = than
plus de trois heures après mon arrivée
= more than three hours after I'd
arrived
moins de dix pour cent = less than ten per
cent
2 *determiner*
= some
= any
voulez-vous de la bière? = would you like
some beer?
il n'a pas de monnaie = he hasn't got any
change
as-tu des courses à faire? = have you got
any shopping to do?

dé *noun, masculine*
• (*in games*)
un dé = a dice
• (*in sewing*)
un dé = a thimble

déballer *verb* 1
• = to unpack
• = to display

débarquer *verb* 1
• = to disembark, to get off
• = to unload

débarras *noun, masculine* (! *never
changes*)
• (*a room*)
un débarras = a junk room
• bon débarras! = good riddance!

débarrasser *verb* 1
1 (! + *avoir*)
• = to clear (out)
débarrasser (la table) = to clear the table
débarrasser une pièce = to clear out a
room
• = to rid
je vous débarrasse de votre manteau?
= shall I take your coat?
2 se débarrasser de (! + *être*)
se débarrasser de = to get rid of

débattre: **se débattre** *verb* 61 (! + *être*)
se débattre = to struggle

déborder *verb* 1
= to overflow

débouché *noun, masculine*
un débouché = an opening

déboucher *verb* 1
• = to open
déboucher une bouteille = to open a bottle
• = to unblock, to unclog
déboucher un évier = to unblock a sink
• = to lead to
le sentier débouche sur une route = the
path leads to a road
• = to come out
la voiture a débouché d'une petite rue
= the car came out of a side street

debout *adverb*
• = standing
se mettre debout = to stand up
rester debout = to stand
• = upright
mets la caisse debout = stand the crate in
an upright position
• = up
être debout à six heures du matin = to be
up at six in the morning
debout! = get up!

déboutonner *verb* 1
= to unbutton

débraillé/débraillée *adjective*
= dishevelled

débrancher verb [1]
= to unplug

débrayer verb [21]
= to put the clutch in

débris noun, masculine (! never changes)
• (of glass, china)
un débris = a fragment
• (of car, plane)
un débris = a piece of wreckage

débrouiller verb [1]
1 (! + avoir)
• = to unscramble
• = to disentangle
2 se débrouiller (! + être)
• se débrouiller = to manage
se débrouiller pour avoir des billets = to manage to get tickets
• se débrouiller = to get by
se débrouiller en anglais = to get by in English

début noun, masculine
le début = the beginning
au début = at the beginning
début avril = at the beginning of April, in early April

débutant/débutante noun, masculine/feminine
un débutant/une débutante = a beginner

décacheter verb [20]
= to unseal

décaféiné/décaféinée adjective
= decaffeinated

décalage noun, masculine
le décalage horaire = the time difference
= jet lag

décapsuleur noun, masculine
un décapsuleur = a bottle-opener

décéder verb [14]
= to die
être décédé = to be dead

décembre noun, masculine
décembre = December

déception noun, feminine
une déception = a disappointment

décès noun, masculine (! never changes)
un décès = a death

décevant/décevante adjective
= disappointing

décevoir verb [5]
= to disappoint

déchaîner: se déchaîner verb [1]
(! + être)
se déchaîner = to go wild

décharger verb [13]
= to unload

déchets noun, masculine plural
les déchets = waste

déchiffrer verb [1]
= to decipher
= to decode

déchirer verb [1]
1 (! + avoir)
= to tear (up)
2 se déchirer (! + être)
se déchirer = to tear

décidément adverb
= really

décider verb [1]
1 (! + avoir)
• = to decide
elle a décidé de les inviter = she's decided to invite them
c'est décidé = it's settled
• = to persuade
j'ai décidé mes amis à venir = I persuaded my friends to come
2 se décider (! + être)
se décider = to make up one's mind

déclarer verb [1]
1 (! + avoir)
• = to declare
rien à déclarer = nothing to declare
• = to report
déclarer un vol = to report a theft
2 se déclarer (! + être)
se déclarer = to break out
un incendie s'est déclaré = a fire broke out

déclencher verb [1]
= to set off
= to trigger

décollage noun, masculine
le décollage = take-off

décoller verb [1]
1 (! + avoir)
• = to peel off
décoller une étiquette = to peel off a label
• = to take off
l'avion va décoller = the plane is about to take off
2 se décoller (! + être)
se décoller = to come off

décolleté/décolletée adjective
= low-cut

décolorer verb [1]
• = to bleach
• = to cause to fade

décombres noun, masculine plural
les décombres = the rubble

décongeler verb [17]
= to defrost

décontracté/décontractée adjective
• = relaxed, laid-back
• = casual

décorer verb 1
= to decorate

découper verb 1
= to cut out
= to cut up
= to carve

décourager verb 13
= to discourage

découvert/découverte[1]
▶ **découvrir** 32

découverte[2] noun, feminine
une découverte = a discovery

découvrir verb 32
• = to discover
• = to uncover

décrire verb 42
= to describe

décrocher verb 1
• (to remove from its hook) = to take down
  décrocher le téléphone = to pick up the
  receiver
  = to take the phone off the hook
• (in a competition, an exam)✶ = to pass
  = to get
  décrocher✶ son permis = to pass one's
  driving test

déçu/déçue ▶ **décevoir** 5

dedans adverb
= inside

défaire verb 10
1 (! + avoir)
  = to undo
  défaire sa valise = to unpack one's
  suitcase
2 se défaire (! + être)
  se défaire = to come undone

défaut noun, masculine
un défaut = a fault

défavorisé/défavorisée adjective
• = underprivileged
• = disadvantaged

défectueux/défectueuse adjective
= faulty

défendre verb 6
1 (! + avoir)
• = to forbid
  je vous défends de sortir = I forbid you to
  go out
  c'est défendu = it's forbidden, it's not
  allowed
• = to defend
2 se défendre (! + être)
  se défendre = to defend oneself

défendu/défendue ▶ **défendre** 6

défense noun, feminine
• (an order)
  'défense de fumer' = 'no smoking'
• (against an attack, an accusation)
  la défense = the defence, the defense
  prendre la défense d'un ami = to stand up
  for a friend
  sans défense = helpless, defenceless,
  defenseless
• (of an elephant, a walrus)
  une défense = a tusk

défilé noun, masculine
• (a military display)
  un défilé = a parade
• (people filing past)
  un défilé = a procession
  = a march
• (a constant flow of people)
  un défilé de visiteurs = a stream of visitors

défiler verb 1
= to march past

défoncer verb 12
  défoncer une porte = to break down a
  door

déformé/déformée adjective
= distorted
= misshapen
  'chaussée déformée' = 'uneven road
  surface'

dégager verb 13
1 (! + avoir)
• = to clear
  ciel dégagé = clear sky
• = to free
• = to give off
  dégager de la chaleur = to give off heat
2 se dégager (! + être)
• se dégager = to clear
  le temps s'est dégagé = the weather has
  cleared
• se dégager (de) = to free oneself (from)

dégâts noun, masculine plural
les dégâts = the damage

dégonfler verb 1
1 (! + avoir)
• = to deflate, to let down
2 se dégonfler (! + être)
• se dégonfler = to deflate, to go down
• (when faced with a challenge)✶
  se dégonfler✶ = to lose one's nerve, to
  chicken out

dégoûtant/dégoûtante adjective
• = filthy
• = disgusting

degré noun, masculine
• (a unit of measurement)
  un degré = one degree

✶ in informal situations

- (*a level*)
  l'enseignement du second degré
  = secondary education, high school
  education (*for students aged 11 to 18*)

dégringoler * *verb* 1
= to take a tumble
= to tumble down

déguiser *verb* 1
1 (! + *avoir*)
= to disguise
2 se déguiser (! + *être*)
- **se déguiser** = to disguise oneself
- **se déguiser** = to dress up

dégustation *noun, feminine*
une dégustation de vin = a wine tasting

déguster *verb* 1
- = to taste, to sample
- = to enjoy

dehors *adverb*
= outside

déjà *adverb*
= already

déjeuner
1 *noun, masculine*
- (*in the middle of the day*)
  le déjeuner = lunch
- (*in the morning*)
  le (petit) déjeuner = breakfast
2 *verb*
- = to have lunch
- = to have breakfast

delà: au delà de *preposition*
au delà de = beyond

délabré/délabrée *adjective*
= dilapidated

délai *noun, masculine*
- (*time allowed*)
  dans un délai de 24 heures = within 24
  hours
  sans délai = immediately
  mardi, dernier délai = Tuesday at the latest
- (*additional time*)
  un délai = an extension

délasser *verb* 1
= to refresh
= to relax

délicieux/délicieuse *adjective*
= delicious

délit *noun, masculine*
un délit = an offence, an offense

délivrer *verb* 1
- = to free
  délivrer un prisonnier = to free a prisoner
- = to issue
  délivrer un passeport = to issue a passport

deltaplane *noun, masculine*
- (*the equipment*)
  un deltaplane = a hang-glider

- (*the sport*)
  le deltaplane = hang-gliding

demain *adverb*
= tomorrow
à demain = see you tomorrow

demande *noun, feminine*
- **une demande** = an application
  = a request
  faire une demande de prêt = to apply for a
  loan
  'demandes d'emploi' = 'jobs wanted'
- (*in business*)
  l'offre et la demande = supply and
  demand

demander *verb* 1
1 (! + *avoir*)
- = to ask (for)
  elle a demandé de l'argent à ses parents
  = she's asked her parents for money
- = to require
  ça demande trop d'efforts = it requires too
  much effort
2 se demander (! + *être*)
  se demander = to wonder

démarrer *verb* 1
- (*if it's a vehicle*) = to pull away
- (*if it's a driver*) = to drive off

démarreur *noun, masculine*
le démarreur = the starter

déménagement *noun, masculine*
- (*going to live elsewhere*)
  un déménagement = a move
- (*transporting furniture*)
  un déménagement = a removal

déménager *verb* 13
= to move (house)

demeurer *verb* 1
- = to live
- = to remain

demi/demie[1]
1 *adjective*
- **demi-** (! *comes before the noun, never
  changes*)
  = half
  = semi
  une demi-heure = half an hour
  un demi-tarif = a half-price ticket
  une demi-finale = a semi-final
- **et demi/et demie** (! *comes after the noun,
  never plural*)
  = and a half
  deux et demi = two and a half
  à cinq heures et demie = at half past five,
  at five-thirty
2 demi *noun, masculine*
- (*a drink*)
  un demi = a glass of beer
- (*in rugby*)
  un demi de mêlée = a scrum half
3 à demi = half
  à demi éveillé = half awake

D

demie² *noun, feminine*
  la demie = half past
  il est déjà la demie = it's already half past

demi-frère *noun, masculine*
  (*plural*) **demi-frères**
  un demi-frère = a stepbrother, a half-brother

demi-pension *noun, feminine*
  la demi-pension = half board, accommodation with one meal only

demi-sœur *noun, feminine*
  (*plural*) **demi-sœurs**
  une demi-sœur = a stepsister, a half-sister

démissionner *verb* 1
  = to resign

demi-tour *noun, masculine*
  (*plural*) **demi-tours**
  un demi-tour = a half-turn
  faire demi-tour = to turn back

démodé/démodée *adjective*
  = old-fashioned

demoiselle *noun, feminine*
  une demoiselle = a young lady
  une demoiselle d'honneur = a bridesmaid

démolir *verb* 3
  = to demolish

démonter *verb* 1
• = to take apart, to dismantle
• = to remove, to take off

démontrer *verb* 1
  = to demonstrate

denrée *noun, feminine*
  une denrée = a product

dent *noun, feminine*
  une dent = a tooth
  avoir mal aux dents = to have (a) toothache

dentelle *noun, feminine*
  la dentelle = lace

dentifrice *noun, masculine*
  le dentifrice = toothpaste

dentiste *noun, masculine/feminine*
  un dentiste/une dentiste = a dentist

dépannage *noun, masculine*
  'service de dépannage' = 'breakdown service', 'emergency service'

dépanner *verb* 1
• = to fix, to repair
• (*if someone's in difficulty*)✖ = to help out

dépanneur/dépanneuse¹ *noun, masculine/feminine*
  un dépanneur/une dépanneuse = an engineer

dépanneuse² *noun, feminine*
  une dépanneuse = a breakdown truck, a tow truck

dépareillé/dépareillée *adjective*
  = odd

départ *noun, masculine*
• (*the act of leaving*)
  le départ = the departure
• (*the beginning*)
  le départ = the start
  au départ = at first

département *noun, masculine*
  un département = a department (*an administrative district*)

dépasser *verb* 1
• = to overtake, to pass
• = to exceed
  elle le dépasse de 5 centimètres = she's 5 centimetres taller than him
• = to be ahead of, to outstrip
• = to stick out
• = to pass, to go past
  nous avons dépassé l'école = we've gone past the school

dépêcher: se dépêcher *verb* 1
(**!** + *être*)
  se dépêcher = to hurry up
  dépêchez-vous! = hurry up!

dépendre *verb* 6
  dépendre de = to depend on
  ça dépendra du temps = it'll depend on the weather
  ça dépend! = it depends!

dépense *noun, feminine*
  la dépense du ménage = the household expenditure
  faire une dépense = to spend some money

dépenser *verb* 1
  = to spend (money)

déplacer *verb* 12
1 (**!** + *avoir*)
  = to move
2 se déplacer (**!** + *être*)
• se déplacer = to move
• se déplacer = to travel

dépliant *noun, masculine*
  un dépliant = a leaflet

déplier *verb* 2
  = to unfold

déposer *verb* 1
1 (**!** + *avoir*)
• déposer des ordures = to dump rubbish, to dump garbage
• déposer une gerbe = to lay a wreath
• déposer de l'argent sur un compte = to deposit money in an account
• déposer une valise à la consigne automatique = to leave a suitcase in a left-luggage locker

---

✖ in informal situations

- **déposer un passager** = to drop a passenger off
- **déposer une plainte** = to lodge a complaint, to make a complaint
- **une marque déposée** = a registered trademark

2 se déposer (**!** + *être*)
  se déposer = to settle
  = to collect

dépositaire *noun, masculine|feminine*
  un dépositaire/une dépositaire = an agent, a representative
  un dépositaire de journaux = a newsagent, a newsdealer

dépôt *noun, masculine*
- (*for goods*)
  un dépôt = a warehouse
- (*in a shop*)
  faire dépôt de gaz = to sell bottled gas
- (*in a bottle*)
  un dépôt = a deposit, a residue

déprime* *noun, feminine*
  la déprime* = depression

déprimer *verb* ①
- (*to cause sadness*) = to depress
- (*to feel sadness*)***** = to be depressed

déprogrammer *verb* ①
  = to cancel

depuis
1 *preposition*
- = since
  depuis lundi = since Monday
  depuis quand est-il à Paris? = how long has he been in Paris?
- = for
  depuis un an = for a year
  je le connais depuis longtemps = I've known him for a long time
  il pleuvait depuis trois jours = it had been raining for three days
  depuis combien de temps le sais-tu? = how long have you known?
2 *adverb*
  = since
  je n'ai pas de nouvelles depuis = since then I haven't heard any news
3 depuis que = since, ever since

député *noun, masculine*
  un député = a Member of the National Assembly
  un député européen = a member of the European Parliament, a Euro-MP

dérailler *verb* ①
  = to be derailed

déranger *verb* ⑬
1 (**!** + *avoir*)
- = to bother, to disturb
  excusez-moi de vous déranger = I'm sorry to bother you
  ça vous dérange si je mets la radio? = do you mind if I turn the radio on?
- = to disturb, to upset, to mess up

2 se déranger (**!** + *être*)
- **se déranger** = to get up
  = to move
- **se déranger** = to put oneself out

déraper *verb* ①
  = to skid

dériveur *noun, masculine*
  un dériveur = a dinghy

dernier/dernière
1 *adjective*
  = last
  = latest
  au dernier étage = on the top floor
2 *noun, masculine|feminine*
- **le dernier/la dernière** = the last one
  c'est le dernier qui me reste = it's my last one
  arriver le dernier = to arrive last
  être le dernier de la classe = to be bottom of the class, to be last in the class
- **ce dernier/cette dernière** = the latter
3 en dernier = lastly
  = last

dernièrement *adverb*
  = recently, lately

derrière
1 *preposition*
  = behind
2 *adverb*
  = behind
  = at the back, in the back
3 *noun, masculine*
- (*the rear*)
  le derrière = the back
  la porte de derrière = the back door
- (*part of the body*)*****
  le derrière* = the behind, the backside

des ▶ de

dès
1 *preposition*
  = from
  dès ce soir = from tonight
  dès mon arrivée = as soon as I arrive(d)
2 dès que = as soon as

désagréable *adjective*
  = unpleasant

désastre *noun, masculine*
  un désastre = a disaster

descendre *verb* ⑥
1 (**!** + *être*)
- = to go down, to come down
  il est descendu au village = he's gone down to the village
  tu es descendu à pied? = did you walk down?
  nous sommes descendus en courant = we ran down
- = to go downstairs, to come downstairs
- = to get off
  je descendrai à la prochaine gare = I'll get off at the next station

D

• (*other uses*)
descendre dans un hôtel = to stop (off) at a hotel
2 (**!** + *avoir*)
• = to go down
descendre la rue = to go down the street
il a descendu l'escalier en courant = he ran down the stairs
• = to take down, to bring down
je dois descendre mes bagages = I must take my luggage down
peux-tu me descendre mes lunettes? = can you bring my glasses down to me?

descente *noun, feminine*
• (*a steep surface*)
une descente = a slope
• (*in a plane*)
la descente = the descent
• (*in a skiing competition*)
la descente = the downhill event

désert/déserte
1 *adjective*
= deserted
2 désert *noun, masculine*
le désert = the desert

désespéré/désespérée *adjective*
(*describing a person*) = in despair
(*describing a situation*) = hopeless

désespoir *noun, masculine*
le désespoir = despair
être au désespoir = to be in despair

déshabiller *verb* 1
1 (**!** + *avoir*)
= to undress
2 se déshabiller (**!** + *être*)
se déshabiller = to get undressed

désigner *verb* 1
• = to point out
• = to choose, to designate

désirer *verb* 1
= to want
que désirez-vous? = what would you like?

désobéir *verb* 3
• = to be disobedient
• = to disobey
désobéir à son père = to disobey one's father

désobéissant/désobéissante *adjective*
= disobedient

désolé/désolée *adjective*
je suis désolé = I'm sorry

désordre *noun, masculine*
• (*in a room*)
le désordre = untidiness, messiness
quel désordre! = what a mess!
être en désordre = to be untidy
mettre du désordre dans une pièce = to make a room untidy, to make a room messy

• (*unrest*)
le désordre = disorder

désormais *adverb*
= from now on
= from then on

dessert *noun, masculine*
un dessert = a dessert

dessin *noun, masculine*
• (*a picture*)
un dessin = a drawing
• (*a subject*)
le dessin = art, drawing
= design
un dessin animé = a cartoon (film)

dessinateur/dessinatrice *noun, masculine/feminine*
un dessinateur/une dessinatrice = a draughtsman, a draftsman
= an illustrator
= a designer

dessiner *verb* 1
= to draw

dessous
1 *adverb*
= underneath
2 *noun, masculine* (**!** *never changes*)
le dessous = the underside
= the bottom
le drap de dessous = the bottom sheet
les voisins du dessous = the people who live (on the floor) below
3 en dessous = underneath
la taille en dessous = the next size down, the smaller size
4 en dessous de = below
en dessous de la moyenne = below average

dessus
1 *adverb*
= on top
écris ton nom dessus = write your name on it
2 *noun, masculine* (**!** *never changes*)
le dessus = the top
le drap de dessus = the top sheet
les voisins du dessus = the people who live (on the floor) above

destinataire *noun, masculine/feminine*
le destinataire/la destinataire = the addressee

destination
1 *noun, feminine*
une destination = a destination
2 à destination de = bound for
vol 802 à destination de Nice = flight 802 to Nice

détacher *verb* 1
1 (**!** + *avoir*)
• = to undo
= to untie
= to unfasten
• = to tear off, to detach

2 se détacher (**!** + *être*)
* se détacher = to come undone
* se détacher = to come off

détail *noun, masculine*
* (*a minor point*)
  un détail = a detail
  des détails supplémentaires = extra
    information
* (*selling direct to the public*)
  le détail = retail

détendre *verb* 6
1 (**!** + *avoir*)
* = to relax
* = to be relaxing
2 se détendre (**!** + *être*)
  se détendre = to relax

détenu/détenue *noun,*
masculine/feminine
  un détenu/une détenue = a prisoner

détester *verb* 1
  = to detest, to hate

détraquer *verb* 1
  = to damage

détresse *noun, feminine*
  la détresse = distress

détroit *noun, masculine*
  un détroit = a strait

détruire *verb* 62
  = to destroy

dette *noun, feminine*
  une dette = a debt

deuil *noun, masculine*
* un deuil = a bereavement
* le deuil = mourning

deux *number*
  = two
  ils iront tous les deux = both of them will
    go

deuxième *number*
  = second

deux-roues *noun, masculine* (**!** *never*
changes)
  un deux-roues = a two-wheeler

devant
1 *preposition*
* = in front of
  le livre est devant toi = the book is in front
    of you
* = ahead of
  Paul était loin devant nous = Paul was (a
    long) way ahead of us
* = outside
  attends-moi devant la bibliothèque = wait
    for me outside the library
* = past
  passer devant un magasin = to walk past
    a shop

2 *adverb*
  = in front
  = at the front
3 *noun, masculine*
  le devant = the front
  la fenêtre de devant = the front window

devenir *verb* 36 (**!** + *être*)
  = to become

déviation *noun, feminine*
  une déviation = a diversion, a detour

deviner *verb* 1
  = to guess

devinette *noun, feminine*
  une devinette = a riddle

devis *noun, masculine* (**!** *never changes*)
  un devis = an estimate

devise *noun, feminine*
* (*money*)
  une devise = a currency
* (*a short saying*)
  une devise = a motto

devoir
1 *noun, masculine*
* (*work set by a teacher*)
  un devoir = a piece of homework, an
    assignment
  faire ses devoirs = to do one's homework
* (*responsibility*)
  le devoir = duty
  faire son devoir = to do one's duty
2 *verb* 44
* = to owe
  devoir de l'argent à un ami = to owe a
    friend money
  je leur dois des excuses = I owe them an
    apology
* (*to be obliged to*) = to have to
  je dois aller travailler = I have to go to
    work, I must go to work
  tu aurais dû téléphoner = you should have
    phoned
  vous devriez les remercier = you ought to
    thank them
* (*meaning that something is likely*) = must
  il doit être arrivé = he must have arrived
  elle devait avoir 11 ans = she must have
    been 11
  ils ont dû oublier = they must have
    forgotten
* (*meaning that something is certain or
  expected*)
  cela devait arriver = it was bound to
    happen
  le train doit partir vers neuf heures = the
    train is due to leave at about nine
    o'clock

devrai ▶ **devoir 2** 44

diabétique *adjective*
  = diabetic

diabolo menthe noun, masculine
(plural) **diabolos menthe**
  un diabolo menthe = a mint cordial and
  lemonade, a mint cordial and soda

diamètre noun, masculine
  le diamètre = the diameter

diapositive noun, feminine
  une diapositive = a slide

diarrhée noun, feminine
  la diarrhée = diarrh(o)ea

dictée noun, feminine
  une dictée = a dictation

dicter verb 1
  = to dictate

dictionnaire noun, masculine
  un dictionnaire = a dictionary

diète noun, feminine
  être à la diète = to be on a restricted diet

diététicien/diététicienne noun,
masculine/feminine
  un diététicien/une diététicienne = a
  dietician

dieu noun, masculine
(plural) **dieux**
  un dieu = a god
  mon Dieu! = my God!

différence noun, feminine
  une différence = a difference
  à la différence des animaux = unlike
  animals

difficile adjective
• = difficult
• = fussy

difficulté noun, feminine
  une difficulté = a difficulty

difforme adjective
  = deformed

diffuser verb 1
  (on radio) = to broadcast

dimanche noun, masculine
  dimanche = Sunday

dinde noun, feminine
  une dinde = a turkey

dîner
1 noun, masculine
  le dîner = dinner
  à l'heure du dîner = at dinner time
2 verb 1
  = to have dinner

dingue✗ adjective
  = crazy

✗ in informal situations

diplôme noun, masculine
  un diplôme = a diploma
  = a qualification

dire verb 40
1 (**!** + avoir)
• = to say
  on dit que l'usine va fermer = they say the
  factory is going to close down
• = to tell
  dire des mensonges = to tell lies
  dites-leur de venir = tell them to come
• = to think
  qu'est-ce que tu en dis? = what do you
  think?
  on ne dirait pas qu'elle a 20 ans = you
  wouldn't think she was 20, she doesn't
  look 20
  on dirait qu'il va pleuvoir = it looks like
  rain
• vouloir dire = to mean
  qu'est-ce que ça veut dire? = what does it
  mean?
• ça ne me dit rien = it doesn't appeal to me,
  I don't feel like it
  = it doesn't mean anything to me, it
  doesn't ring a bell
2 se dire (**!** + être)
• se dire = to tell oneself
• se dire = to claim to be
  il se dit médecin = he claims to be a doctor
• ça ne se dit pas = you can't say that

direct/directe
1 adjective
  = direct
2 direct noun, masculine
• (a train)
  un direct = an express (train)
• (on radio, TV)
  le direct = live broadcasting
  en direct de Rome = live from Rome

directement adverb
• = straight
• = directly

directeur/directrice noun,
masculine/feminine
• (in a school)
  le directeur/la directrice = the headteacher,
  the principal
• (in an organization, a business)
  un directeur/une directrice = a director
  = a manager

direction noun, feminine
• (when moving)
  une direction = a direction
  dans quelle direction? = which way?
  en direction de Calais = toward(s) Calais
• (in an organization)
  la direction = (the) management
• (on a car)
  la direction = the steering

directrice ▶ directeur

diriger verb 13
1 (! + avoir)
- diriger une affaire = to manage a business, to run a business
- diriger une opération = to direct an operation
- diriger un orchestre = to conduct an orchestra
2 se diriger (! + être)
- se diriger vers Paris = to make for Paris, to head toward(s) Paris
- se diriger dans le noir = to find one's way in the dark

disco noun, masculine
le disco = disco music

discothèque noun, feminine
- (a library)
une discothèque = a record library
- (a nightclub)
une discothèque = a disco(theque)

discours noun, masculine (! never changes)
un discours = a speech

discuter verb 1
- = to chat, to talk
- = to argue
- discuter de = to discuss

disparaître verb 63
- = to disappear
- = to die

disparition noun, feminine
la disparition = the disappearance

disparu/disparue ▶ disparaître 63

disponible adjective
= available

disposer verb 1
1 (! + avoir)
- = to arrange, to position
- disposer de = to have (at one's disposal)
2 se disposer (! + être)
se disposer à partir = to prepare to leave, to be about to leave

dispute noun, feminine
une dispute = an argument, a quarrel

disputer: se disputer verb 1 (! + être)
se disputer = to argue, to quarrel

disque noun, masculine
- (in music)
un disque = a record, an LP
un disque compact = a compact disc
- (in sport)
le disque = the discus

disquette noun, feminine
une disquette = a diskette, a floppy disk

dissimuler verb 1
= to conceal, to hide

distance noun, feminine
la distance = distance
à une distance de 25 kilomètres = 25 kilometres away
la ville est à quelle distance? = how far is the town?
commande à distance = remote control

distingué/distinguée adjective
= distinguished

distraction noun, feminine
- (leisure activity)
une distraction = entertainment
- (lack of concentration)
la distraction = absent-mindedness

distraire verb 58
1 (! + avoir)
- = to entertain, to amuse
- = to distract
2 se distraire (! + être)
se distraire = to amuse oneself

distrait/distraite
1 ▶ distraire 58
2 adjective
= absent-minded

distribuer verb 1
= to give out, to distribute
distribuer le courrier = to deliver the mail
distribuer les cartes = to deal

distributeur noun, masculine
un distributeur automatique de billets = a cash dispenser

divan noun, masculine
un divan = a sofa

divers/diverse adjective
- = various
- = miscellaneous

diviser verb 1
= to divide

divorcé/divorcée noun, masculine/feminine
un divorcé/une divorcée = a divorcee

divorcer verb 12
= to get divorced

dix number
= ten

dix-huit number
= eighteen

dix-huitième number
= eighteenth

dixième number
= tenth

dix-neuf number
= nineteen

dix-neuvième number
= nineteenth

D

dix-sept *number*
= seventeen

dix-septième *number*
= seventeenth

dizaine *noun, feminine*
une dizaine = about ten
= ten

docteur *noun, masculine*
un docteur = a doctor

documentaire *noun, masculine*
un documentaire = a documentary

documentation *noun, feminine*
de la documentation = brochures,
literature

dodo✗ *noun, masculine*
au dodo✗! = beddy-byes!, bed time!

doigt *noun, masculine*
• (*on the hand*)
un doigt = a finger
montrer du doigt = to point at
un doigt de pied = a toe
• (*small amount*)
un doigt de vin = a drop of wine

dois ▶ devoir 2 [44]

doive ▶ devoir 2 [44]

domestique
1 *adjective*
= domestic
2 *noun, masculine/feminine*
un domestique/une domestique = a
servant

domicile
1 *noun, masculine*
un domicile = a (place of) residence
2 à domicile
travailler à domicile = to work from home
livrer à domicile = to deliver, to do home
deliveries

domicilié/domiciliée *adjective*
être domicilié à Londres = to live in
London

dominer *verb* [1]
1 (**!** + *avoir*)
• = to dominate
• = to tower over
le monument dominait le village = the
monument towered over the village
• = to control
dominer sa peur = to overcome one's fear
• = to be predominant
2 se dominer (**!** + *être*)
se dominer = to control oneself

domino *noun, masculine*
un domino = a domino

dommage *noun, masculine*
• (*in expressions of regret*)
(quel) dommage! = what a pity!, what a
shame!
• (*harm*)
un dommage = damage
des dommages et intérêts = damages

DOM-TOM *noun, masculine plural*
(*abbreviation of* **départements et**
territoires d'outre-mer)
French overseas departments and territories

don *noun, masculine*
• (*talent*)
un don = a gift
• (*something given*)
un don = a donation

donc *conjunction*
= so, therefore
il est malade, donc il restera au lit = he's
unwell, so he'll stay in bed
taisez-vous donc! = be quiet, will you?
sers-toi donc! = do help yourself!

donjon *noun, masculine*
un donjon = a keep

donner *verb* [1]
• = to give
donner un jouet à un enfant = to give a
child a toy
donner des coups à un animal = to hit an
animal
• donner une veste à nettoyer = to take a
jacket to be dry-cleaned
• donner sur = to overlook
la chambre donne sur la baie = the
bedroom overlooks the bay

dont *pronoun*
• = whose
voici le chauffeur dont la voiture a pris feu
= this is the driver whose car caught
fire
• = of which
= of whom
c'est le dessin dont il est si fier = it's the
drawing of which he's so proud
ils ont cinq fils, dont deux sont étudiants
= they've got five sons, two of whom are
students
j'ai lu le livre dont tu m'avais parlé = I read
the book that you'd told me about
il a pris les outils dont il avait besoin = he's
taken the tools that he needed
le pays dont elle vient = the country she
comes from
la façon dont il parle = the way he talks
c'est tout ce dont je me souviens = that's
all I can remember

doré/dorée *adjective*
= gilt
= golden
= gold

dormir *verb* [30]
= to sleep

D

dortoir noun, masculine
  un dortoir = a dormitory

dos noun, masculine (**!** never changes)
  le dos = the back
  avoir mal au dos = to have (a) backache
  je l'ai vu de dos = I saw him from behind

dose noun, feminine
  une dose = a dose

dossier noun, masculine
• (part of a seat)
  le dossier = the back(rest)
• (documents)
  un dossier = a file

douane noun, feminine
  la douane = the customs

douanier/douanière noun,
masculine/feminine
  un douanier/une douanière = a customs
  officer

double
1 adjective
  = double
2 noun, masculine
• (a quantity)
  payer le double = to pay twice as much
  le double de la taille normale = twice the
  normal size
• (a duplicate)
  un double = a copy
  le double des clés = a spare set of keys

doubler verb [1]
• (to increase twofold) = to double
• (in a car) = to overtake, to pass
• (for a film) = to dub
• (in dressmaking) = to line

douce ▶ doux

doucement adverb
• = gently
• = softly
• = slowly

douche noun, feminine
  une douche = a shower

doucher: se doucher verb [1] (**!** + être)
  se doucher = to take a shower

doué/douée adjective
  = gifted, talented

douleur noun, feminine
• une douleur = a pain
• la douleur = grief

douloureux/douloureuse adjective
  = painful

doute
1 noun, masculine
  le doute = doubt
  ça ne fait aucun doute = there's no doubt
  about it
2 sans doute = probably

Douvres noun
  = Dover

doux/douce
1 adjective
• = soft
  une voix douce = a soft voice
• = mild
  un temps doux = mild weather
• = gentle
  une pente douce = a gentle slope
2 doux adverb
  doux = mild
  il fait doux aujourd'hui = it's mild today

douzaine noun, feminine
  une douzaine = a dozen
  = about twelve

douze number
  = twelve

douzième number
  = twelfth

dragée noun, feminine
  une dragée = a sugared almond

draguer✶ verb [1]
  = to chat up, to come on to

drap noun, masculine
  un drap = a sheet

drapeau noun, masculine
(plural) **drapeaux**
  un drapeau = a flag

dresser verb [1]
1 (**!** + avoir)
• = to train
  dresser un animal = to train an animal
• = to put up
  dresser une tente = to put up a tent
• = to raise
  dresser la tête = to raise one's head
  dresser l'oreille = to prick up one's ears
2 se dresser (**!** + être)
  se dresser = to stand (up)

drogue noun, feminine
  la drogue = drugs

drogué/droguée noun,
masculine/feminine
  un drogué/une droguée = a drug addict

droguer: se droguer verb [1] (**!** + être)
  se droguer = to take drugs

droguerie noun, feminine
  une droguerie = a hardware shop, a
  hardware store

droguiste noun, masculine/feminine
  un droguiste/une droguiste = a hardware
  dealer, an ironmonger

droit/droite[1]

1 *adjective*
- = straight
  = upright
- = right
  du côté droit = on the right-hand side
2 droit *adverb*
  = straight
  continuez tout droit = carry straight on
3 droit *noun, masculine*
- (*something one is entitled to*)
  un droit = a right
  avoir le droit d'aller où l'on veut = to have
    the right to go wherever one wants
  = to be allowed to go wherever one wants
- (*money that has to be paid*)
  un droit = a fee
  = a tax
- (*a course of study*)
  le droit = law
les droits de douane = customs duties

droite[2] *noun, feminine*
  la droite = the right

droitier/droitière *noun,*
masculine/feminine
  un droitier/une droitière = a right-handed
    person

drôle *adjective*
  = funny

du ▶ de

dû/due ▶ devoir 2 [44]

duc *noun, masculine*
  un duc = a duke

dur/dure

1 *adjective*
  = hard, tough
  = harsh
2 dur *adverb*
  travailler dur = to work hard

durée *noun, feminine*
- (*of a reign, of a course*)
  la durée = the length
  = the duration
  un séjour de courte durée = a short stay
- (*of a cassette*)
  la durée = the playing time
- (*of a battery*)
  la durée = the life
  pile longue durée = long-life battery

durer *verb* [1]
  = to last

duvet *noun, masculine*
- (*for sleeping in*)
  un duvet = a sleeping bag
- (*feathers*)
  le duvet = down

dynamique *adjective*
  = dynamic

Ee

eau *noun, feminine*
(*plural*) **eaux**
  l'eau = water
l'eau gazeuse = fizzy water, sparkling
  water
l'eau minérale = mineral water
l'eau potable = drinking water

eau-de-vie *noun, feminine*
(*plural*) **eaux-de-vie**
  l'eau-de-vie = brandy

éboueur *noun, masculine*
  un éboueur = a dustman, a garbage
    collector

éboulement *noun, masculine*
  un éboulement (de rochers) = a rockfall

écarlate *adjective*
  = scarlet

écarter *verb* [1]
1 (**!** + *avoir*)
- (*to open*) = to spread
  = to part
- (*to remove*) = to push aside
  = to move away
2 s'écarter (**!** + *être*)
  s'écarter = to move out of the way
  = to move away

échafaudage *noun, masculine*
  un échafaudage = scaffolding

échalote *noun, feminine*
  une échalote = a shallot

échange
1 *noun, masculine*
  un échange = an exchange
  faire un échange = to swap
2 en échange (de) = in exchange (for), in
  return (for)

échanger *verb* [13]
  = to exchange

échangeur *noun, masculine*
  un échangeur = an interchange, a clover
    junction

échapper: s'échapper *verb* [1]
(**!** + *être*)
  s'échapper = to escape

écharpe *noun, feminine*
  une écharpe = a scarf

échasse *noun, feminine*
  une échasse = a stilt

échauffer: s'échauffer *verb* [1]
(**!** + *être*)
  s'échauffer = to warm up

échec
1 *noun, masculine*
un échec = a failure
2 échecs *noun, masculine plural*
les échecs = chess

échelle *noun, feminine*
• (*a piece of equipment*)
une échelle = a ladder
faire la courte échelle à Roger = to give
Roger a leg-up
• (*on a map*)
l'échelle = the scale

échiquier *noun, masculine*
un échiquier = a chessboard

échouer *verb* 1
1 (**!** + *avoir*)
= to fail
échouer à un examen = to fail an
examination
2 s'échouer (**!** + *être*)
s'échouer = to run aground

éclair *noun, masculine*
• (*in the sky*)
un éclair = a flash of lightning
• (*a cake*)
un éclair = an eclair

éclairage *noun, masculine*
l'éclairage = the lighting

éclaircie *noun, feminine*
une éclaircie = a sunny spell

éclairer *verb* 1
1 (**!** + *avoir*)
• = to light
• = to give light
2 s'éclairer (**!** + *être*)
s'éclairer (*if it's a face, a screen*) = to light
up

éclater *verb* 1
(*if it's a tyre, a pipe*) = to burst
(*if it's a bomb*) = to explode
(*if it's a storm*) = to break
(*if it's war*) = to break out
éclater de rire = to burst out laughing

école *noun, feminine*
une école = a school
une école libre = an independent school
une école maternelle = a nursery school
(*for children aged 2 to 6*)
une école primaire = a primary school
(*for children aged 6 to 11*)
une école secondaire = a secondary
school (*for students aged 11 to 18*)
une école publique = a state school
(*in the US*) = a public school

écolier/écolière *noun,*
masculine/feminine
un écolier/une écolière = a schoolboy/a
schoolgirl

écologie *noun, feminine*
l'écologie = ecology

écologiste *noun, masculine/feminine*
• (*a scientist*)
un écologiste/une écologiste = an
ecologist
• (*a person who is against pollution*)
un écologiste/une écologiste = an
environmentalist

économe *adjective*
= thrifty

économie *noun, feminine*
une économie = a saving
faire des économies = to save up, to save
money

écorce *noun, feminine*
l'écorce (*on a tree*) = the bark
(*on an orange*) = the peel

écossais/écossaise *adjective*
• = Scottish
• une veste écossaise = a tartan jacket, a
plaid jacket

Écosse *noun, feminine*
l'Écosse = Scotland

écouter *verb* 1
= to listen to
écouter un disque = to listen to a record

écran *noun, masculine*
• (*on a television set*)
un écran = a screen
• (*protection from the sun*)
une crème écran total = a sun block

écraser *verb* 1
1 (**!** + *avoir*)
• = to crush
• = to run over
se faire écraser = to get run over
2 s'écraser (**!** + *être*)
s'écraser = to crash

écrevisse *noun, feminine*
une écrevisse = a crayfish, a crawfish

écrire *verb* 42
1 (**!** + *avoir*)
= to write
2 s'écrire (**!** + *être*)
• s'écrire = to write (to each other)
• s'écrire = to be spelled

écriture *noun, feminine*
• (*the activity*)
l'écriture = writing
• (*the way one writes*)
ton écriture = your handwriting

écrivain *noun, masculine*
un écrivain = a writer

écrou *noun, masculine*
un écrou = a nut

écrouler: s'écrouler *verb* 1 (**!** + *être*)
s'écrouler = to collapse

écurie *noun, feminine*
une écurie = a stable

E

écusson noun, masculine
un écusson (on a garment) = a (cloth) badge

éducation noun, feminine
• (teaching)
l'éducation = education
• (politeness)
l'éducation = manners
l'éducation physique = PE, physical education

effacer verb 12
= to erase
= to delete
effacer le tableau = to wipe the board, to erase the board

effet
1 noun, masculine
• (result)
un effet = an effect
n'avoir aucun effet = to have no effect
faire de l'effet = to be effective
• (impact)
un effet = an impression
faire bon effet = to make a good impression
ça m'a fait un drôle d'effet = it made me feel strange
2 en effet = indeed

efficace adjective
• = effective
• = efficient

effondrer: **s'effondrer** verb 1 (! + être)
s'effondrer = to collapse

effort noun, masculine
un effort = an effort

effrayant/effrayante adjective
= frightening

effrayer verb 21
= to frighten, to scare

effronté/effrontée adjective
= cheeky

égal/égale adjective
(plural) **égaux/égales**
= equal
ça m'est égal = I don't mind either way
= I don't care

égaler verb 1
= to be equal to

égalité noun, feminine
l'égalité = equality

égarer verb 1
1 (! + avoir)
= to lose
2 s'égarer (! + être)
s'égarer = to get lost

église noun, feminine
une église = a church

égoïste adjective
= selfish

eh bien exclamation
eh bien! = well!

électricien/électricienne noun, masculine/feminine
un électricien/une électricienne = an electrician

électroménager
1 adjective, masculine
un appareil électroménager = an electrical household appliance
2 noun, masculine
l'électroménager = electrical household appliances

électrophone noun, masculine
un électrophone = a record player

élégant/élégante adjective
= elegant

éléphant noun, masculine
un éléphant = an elephant

élève noun, masculine/feminine
un élève/une élève = a pupil, a student

élevé/élevée adjective
• = high
• bien élevé = well brought-up, well-mannered
mal élevé = ill-mannered

élever verb 16
1 (! + avoir)
• (if it's children) = to bring up, to raise
• (if it's animals) = to breed
• (if it's a wall, a statue) = to erect, to raise
2 s'élever (! + être)
• s'élever = to rise
• s'élever à 500 francs = to add up to 500 francs

éliminer verb 1
• = to eliminate
= to knock out, to eliminate
être éliminé en quart de finale = to be knocked out in the quarter final
• = to rule out

elle pronoun, feminine
(plural) **elles**
• = she
= it
elles n'ont rien dit = they said nothing
elle est cassée = it's broken
• = her
à cause d'elle = because of her
la valise bleue est à elle = the blue suitcase is hers
c'est à elle de jouer = it's her turn to play
les livres sont pour elles = the books are for them

elle-même *pronoun, feminine*
(*plural*) **elles-mêmes**
  = herself
  = itself
  elles-mêmes = themselves

elles ▶ elle

éloigné/**éloignée** *adjective*
  = distant
  éloigné de = far from

éloigner: **s'éloigner** *verb* 1 (! + *être*)
  s'éloigner = to move away

Élysée *noun, masculine*
  (**le palais de**) **l'Élysée** = the Élysée palace
  (*the official residence of the French President*)

emballage *noun, masculine*
  l'emballage = the packaging
  = the wrapping

embarquer *verb* 1
1 (! + *avoir*)
• = to load
• = to board
2 s'embarquer (! + *être*)
  s'embarquer = to board

embêtant/**embêtante** *adjective*
  = annoying

embêter *verb* 1
1 (! + *avoir*)
• = to annoy
  = to pester
• **ça m'embête d'y aller** = I don't really want to go
2 s'embêter (! + *être*)
  s'embêter = to be bored

emblée: **d'emblée** *adverb*
  d'emblée = right away, straightaway

embouteillage *noun, masculine*
  un embouteillage = a traffic jam

embrasser *verb* 1
1 (! + *avoir*)
  = to kiss
2 s'embrasser (! + *être*)
  s'embrasser = to kiss (each other)

embrayage *noun, masculine*
  l'embrayage = the clutch

émeute *noun, feminine*
  une émeute = a riot

émigrer *verb* 1
  = to emigrate

émission *noun, feminine*
  une émission = a broadcast, a program(me)

emménager *verb* 13
  = to move in

emmener *verb* 16
  = to take
  = to take away

empêcher *verb* 1
1 (! + *avoir*)
• = to prevent
  empêcher un enfant de sortir = to prevent a child from going out, to stop a child from going out
• (**il**) **n'empêche que** = all the same, nevertheless
2 s'empêcher (! + *être*)
  je n'ai pas pu m'empêcher de rire = I couldn't help laughing

empiffrer: **s'empiffrer*** *verb* 1
(! + *être*)
  s'empiffrer = to stuff oneself

emplacement *noun, masculine*
  un emplacement (*for a building*) = a site
  (*for a tent*) = a pitch
  (*for a vehicle*) = a parking space

emploi *noun, masculine*
• (*a post*)
  un emploi = a job
• (*the job market*)
  l'emploi = employment
• (*of a word, a product*)
  l'emploi = the use
  un emploi du temps = a timetable

employé/**employée** *noun,*
masculine/feminine
  un employé/**une employée** = an employee
  un employé de banque = a bank clerk
  un employé de bureau = an office worker

employer *verb* 23
• = to employ
• = to use

empoisonné/**empoisonnée**
adjective
  = poisoned

emporter *verb* 1
1 (! + *avoir*)
• = to take
  emporte un parapluie = take an umbrella
• = to take away
  'plats à emporter' = 'take away food', 'food to go'
• = to sweep away
  le pont a été emporté = the bridge has been swept away
• **l'emporter** = to win
  l'emporter sur = to get the better of, to beat
2 s'emporter (! + *être*)
  s'emporter = to lose one's temper

empreinte *noun, feminine*
  une empreinte (*left by a foot*) = a footprint
  les empreintes digitales = fingerprints

emprunter *verb* 1
  = to borrow
  emprunter de l'argent à la banque = to borrow money from the bank

E

en

> ! You will find translations for phrases with en such as en train de, s'en aller etc at the entries train, aller, etc.

1 preposition
* = in
  vivre en France = to live in France
  en mai = in May
  faire le trajet en deux heures = to do the journey in two hours
* = to
  = into
  aller en Espagne = to go to Spain
  aller en ville = to go into town
  monter en voiture = to get into the car
* = by
  voyager en [train | bateau | voiture …] = to travel by [train | boat | car …]
* = made of
  c'est en bois = it's (made of) wood
  une chaîne en or = a gold chain
* (showing that two things are done at the same time) = while
  chanter en travaillant = to sing while working
  j'ai lu le journal en attendant = I read the paper while I was waiting
* (showing the manner in which something is done)
  sortir en courant = to run out
  se réveiller en pleurant = to wake up crying
  j'ai fini le travail en me levant tous les jours à six heures = I finished the work by getting up at six every day
* (showing the circumstances in which something occurs)
  il est tombé en traversant la rue = he fell as he was crossing the street
  tu t'es trompé en mesurant la pièce = you made a mistake when you measured the room

2 pronoun
* = of it
  = of them
  il en boit beaucoup = he drinks a lot of it
  il y en a quatre = there are four (of them)
  combien en voulez-vous? (if it's cheese) = how much (of it) would you like?
  (if it's cakes) = how many (of them) would you like?
  je m'en souviens = I remember
* = some/any
  encore un peu de thé? il en reste = a little more tea? there's some left
  des roses? il n'y en a plus = roses? there aren't any left
* (representing a place)
  j'en arrive à l'instant = I've just got back from there

enchanter verb 1
= to delight
enchanté (de faire votre connaissance) = pleased to meet you

enchères noun, feminine plural
une vente aux enchères = an auction

encombré/encombrée adjective
(describing a street) = congested
(describing a room, a cupboard) = cluttered

encombrement noun, masculine
l'encombrement (on the road) = traffic congestion

encore adverb
* = still
  tu es encore jeune = you're still young
* = again
  il a encore écrit = he's written again
* = more
  = another
  tu veux encore un peu de thé? = would you like some more tea?
  essaie encore une fois = try again
  encore un gâteau? = another cake?
* pas encore = not yet
  elle n'est pas encore arrivée = she hasn't arrived yet
* encore plus = even more
  c'est encore plus cher = it's even more expensive
  il fait encore plus chaud ici = it's even hotter here

encourager verb 13
= to encourage

encre noun, feminine
l'encre = ink

endormi/endormie adjective
= asleep

endormir verb 30
1 (! + avoir)
= to put to sleep
la télévision m'endort = television puts me to sleep
2 s'endormir (! + être)
s'endormir = to fall asleep
= to get to sleep

endroit noun, masculine
* (a spot)
  un endroit = a place
  au bon endroit = in the right place
  par endroits = in places
  à quel endroit? = where?
* (a side)
  l'endroit = the right side
  à l'endroit = the right way round, the right way around

énergie noun, feminine
l'énergie = energy

énergique adjective
= energetic

énervé/énervée adjective
= irritable
= on edge

énerver verb [1]
1 (**!** + avoir)
= to irritate
ça m'énerve = it irritates me, it gets on my nerves
2 s'énerver (**!** + être)
s'énerver = to get irritable, to get annoyed

enfance noun, feminine
l'enfance = childhood

enfant noun, masculine/feminine
un enfant/une enfant = a child

enfer noun, masculine
l'enfer = Hell
un bruit d'enfer = a hell of a noise

enfermer verb [1]
1 (**!** + avoir)
= to lock up
2 s'enfermer (**!** + être)
s'enfermer = to lock oneself in

enfin adverb
• = finally
• = at last
• **mais enfin, cesse de crier!** = for heaven's sake, stop shouting!

enflammer: **s'enflammer** verb [1]
(**!** + être)
s'enflammer = to go up in flames
= to catch fire

enfler verb [1]
= to swell (up)

enfoncer verb [12]
1 (**!** + avoir)
• = to push in
enfoncer un clou = to drive a nail in
enfoncer une épingle = to stick a pin in
enfoncer ses mains dans ses poches = to dig one's hands into one's pockets
• **enfoncer une porte** = to break down a door
2 s'enfoncer (**!** + être)
• **s'enfoncer** = to sink
s'enfoncer dans la boue = to sink in the mud
s'enfoncer dans un fauteuil = to sink back into an armchair
• **s'enfoncer une épine dans le doigt** = to get a thorn in one's finger

enfreindre verb [55]
enfreindre le règlement = to break the rules

enfuir: **s'enfuir** verb [29] (**!** + être)
s'enfuir = to run away
= to escape

engin noun, masculine
• **un engin** = a device
• **un engin** = a vehicle

engorger verb [13]
= to block
= to clog up

enlever verb [16]
1 (**!** + avoir)
• = to remove
• = to kidnap
2 s'enlever (**!** + être)
s'enlever = to come off

enneigé/enneigée adjective
= covered in snow

ennui noun, masculine
• **un ennui** = a problem
• **l'ennui** = boredom

ennuyer verb [22]
1 (**!** + avoir)
• = to bore
• = to bother
= to annoy
ça t'ennuie qu'il vienne? = do you mind if he comes?
2 s'ennuyer (**!** + être)
s'ennuyer = to be bored

ennuyeux/ennuyeuse adjective
• = boring
= tedious
• = annoying

énorme adjective
= huge, enormous

énormément adverb
= tremendously, immensely

enquête noun, feminine
• (into a crime)
une enquête = an inquiry, an investigation
• (on opinions, lifestyles)
une enquête = a survey

enquêteur/enquêtrice noun, masculine/feminine
un enquêteur/une enquêtrice = an investigator

enregistrement noun, masculine
• (for sound)
un enregistrement = a recording
• (for air passengers)
l'enregistrement = checking-in

enregistrer verb [1]
• (if it's sound, statistics) = to record
• (if it's luggage) = to register
(at an airport) = to check in

enrhumer: **s'enrhumer** verb [1]
(**!** + être)
s'enrhumer = to catch a cold
être enrhumé = to have a cold

enseignant/enseignante noun, masculine/feminine
un enseignant/une enseignante = a teacher

enseigne noun, feminine
une enseigne = a sign

E

enseignement *noun, masculine*
• (*as a career*)
  l'enseignement = teaching
• (*a system*)
  l'enseignement = education
l'enseignement par correspondance
  = correspondence courses

ensemble
1 *adverb*
  = together
2 *noun, masculine*
• (*clothes*)
  un ensemble = an outfit
  = a lady's suit
• (*the entirety*)
  l'ensemble = the whole
  = all
  une vue d'ensemble = an overall view
• (*a collection*)
  un ensemble = a set
  = a group
  un grand ensemble = a high-density
    housing complex, a high-rise housing
    complex
3 dans l'ensemble = on the whole

ensoleillé/ensoleillée *adjective*
  = sunny

ensuite *adverb*
  = then
  = later
  = next

entendre *verb* 6
1 (**!** + *avoir*)
  = to hear
  j'ai entendu dire qu'il était de retour = I've
    heard that he's back
  as-tu entendu parler de ce film? = have
    you heard about this film?
2 s'entendre (**!** + *être*)
  s'entendre = to get on, to get along
  elles s'entendent bien = they get on well,
    they get along well

entendu/entendue
1 ▶ **entendre** 6
2 *adjective*
  = agreed
  entendu! = OK then!
3 bien entendu = of course

enterrement *noun, masculine*
  un enterrement = a funeral

enterrer *verb* 1
  = to bury

enthousiasmer *verb* 1
1 (**!** + *avoir*)
  = to fill with enthusiasm
2 s'enthousiasmer (**!** + *être*)
  s'enthousiasmer = to get enthusiastic

enthousiaste *adjective*
  = enthusiastic

entier/entière *adjective*
  = whole, entire

entourer *verb* 1
• = to surround
  des collines entourent la ville = the town
    is surrounded by hills
  un jardin entouré d'une haie = a garden
    surrounded by a hedge
• = to circle
  entourer une date en rouge = to circle a
    date in red
• **entourer son doigt d'un mouchoir** = to put
  a handkerchief round one's finger

entracte *noun, masculine*
  un entracte = an interval, an intermission

entraînement *noun, masculine*
  l'entraînement (*for an athlete*) = training
  (*for a musician*) = practice

entraîner *verb* 1
1 (**!** + *avoir*)
• = to lead to
  entraîner des problèmes = to lead to
    problems, to cause problems
• = to drag along
  entraîner un ami à la plage = to drag a
    friend along to the beach
• = to coach, to train
  entraîner une équipe = to coach a team
2 s'entraîner (**!** + *être*)
  s'entraîner = to train
  = to practise, to practice

entraîneur *noun, masculine*
  un entraîneur = a coach

entre *preposition*
  = between
  l'un d'entre eux = one of them

entrée *noun, feminine*
• (*way in*)
  l'entrée = the entrance
  = the (entrance) hall
• (*access*)
  l'entrée = entry
  = admission
  'entrée interdite' = 'no entry', 'do not
    enter'
  'entrée gratuite' = 'free admission'
• (*on a menu*)
  une entrée = a starter, an appetizer

entreprise *noun, feminine*
  une entreprise = a firm
  = a company

entrer *verb* 1 (**!** + *être*)
  = to enter, to go in
  = to enter, to come in
  entrez! = come in!
  entrer dans la cuisine = to go into the
    kitchen
  = to come into the kitchen

entretien *noun, masculine*
• **un entretien** (*a conversation*) = a
  discussion
  (*for a job*) = an interview

- l'entretien (*of a house, a garden*) = the upkeep, the maintenance
  (*of clothes, furniture*) = the care

enveloppe *noun, feminine*
une enveloppe = an envelope

envelopper *verb* 1
= to wrap

envers
1 *preposition*
= toward, towards, to
2 *noun, masculine* (**!** *never changes*)
l'envers = the back
= the wrong side
= the reverse
3 à l'envers = the wrong way

envie *noun, feminine*
une envie = a desire
avoir envie de pleurer = to want to cry, to feel like crying

environ *adverb*
= about

environs *noun, masculine plural*
les environs = the surrounding area

envoler: **s'envoler** *verb* 1 (**!** + *être*)
s'envoler (*if it's a bird*) = to fly away
(*if it's a plane*) = to take off

envoyer *verb* 24
- = to send
- = to throw

épais/épaisse *adjective*
= thick

épaule *noun, feminine*
une épaule = a shoulder

épeler *verb* 19
= to spell

épice *noun, feminine*
une épice = a spice

épicerie *noun, feminine*
une épicerie = a grocer's, a grocery store

épicier/épicière *noun,*
masculine/feminine
un épicier/une épicière = a grocer

épinards *noun, masculine plural*
des épinards = spinach

épine *noun, feminine*
une épine = a thorn

épingle *noun, feminine*
une épingle = a pin
une épingle à nourrice, une épingle
de sûreté = a safety pin

épisode *noun, masculine*
un épisode = an episode
un roman à épisodes = a serialized novel

éplucher *verb* 1
= to peel

épluchure *noun, feminine*
des épluchures = peelings

éponge *noun, feminine*
- (*a type of material*)
  l'éponge = (terry-)towelling, terrycloth
- (*a sea creature*)
  une éponge = a sponge

époque *noun, feminine*
une époque = a period, an era
à notre époque = nowadays, in our times
à l'époque = at the time

épouse *noun, feminine*
une épouse = a wife

épouser *verb* 1
= to marry

épouvantable *adjective*
= dreadful

épouvante *noun, feminine*
l'épouvante = terror
= horror
un film d'épouvante = a horror film, a horror movie

époux (**!** *never changes*)
1 *noun, masculine singular*
un époux = a husband
2 *noun, masculine plural*
les époux = the (married) couple
les jeunes époux = the newly weds

épreuve *noun, feminine*
une épreuve (*at school*) = an examination
(*in sport*) = an event

éprouver *verb* 1
= to feel

EPS *noun, feminine* (**!** *never changes*)
l'EPS = PE

épuisé/épuisée *adjective*
= exhausted

équateur *noun, masculine*
l'équateur = the equator

équilibre *noun, masculine*
l'équilibre = balance
perdre l'équilibre = to lose one's balance
en équilibre = balanced

équilibrer *verb* 1
= to balance

équipage *noun, masculine*
un équipage = a crew

équipe *noun, feminine*
- (*of players, workers*)
  une équipe = a team
- (*in a factory*)
  l'équipe de nuit = the night shift

équipement *noun, masculine*
l'équipement = the equipment

équitation *noun, feminine*
l'équitation = (horse-)riding

E

erreur *noun, feminine*
une erreur = a mistake

es ▶ **être** 7

escalade *noun, feminine*
l'escalade = rock climbing

escalader *verb* 1
= to climb

escalier *noun, masculine*
• un escalier = a staircase
= (a flight of) stairs
• les escaliers = the stairs
un escalier roulant = an escalator

escargot *noun, masculine*
un escargot = a snail

esclave *noun, masculine|feminine*
un esclave/une esclave = a slave

escrime *noun, feminine*
l'escrime = fencing

escroc *noun, masculine*
un escroc = a crook

espace *noun, masculine*
• l'espace = space
• un espace = a space, a gap
un espace vert = an open space, a green
area, a park

Espagne *noun, feminine*
l'Espagne = Spain

espagnol/espagnole
1 *adjective*
= Spanish
2 espagnol *noun, masculine*
l'espagnol = Spanish

espèce *noun, feminine*
• (*a sort*)
une espèce de roue = a kind of wheel
• (*a group of animals or plants*)
une espèce = a species

espérer *verb* 14
= to hope (for)

espionnage *noun, masculine*
l'espionnage = espionage, spying

esquimau/esquimaude
(*plural*) **esquimaux/esquimaudes**
1 *adjective*
= Eskimo
2 esquimau® *noun, masculine*
un esquimau = a choc-ice, an ice cream
bar

essayer *verb* 21
• = to try
essayer d'ouvrir la porte = to try to open
the door
• = to try on
essayer un chapeau = to try on a hat

essence *noun, feminine*
l'essence = petrol, gas(oline)

l'essence sans plomb = unleaded petrol,
unleaded gas

essorage *noun, masculine*
l'essorage = spinning

essuie-glace *noun, masculine*
(*plural*) **essuie-glaces**
un essuie-glace = a windscreen wiper, a
windshield wiper

essuyer *verb* 22
1 (**!** + *avoir*)
• = to dry
• = to wipe (up)
2 s'essuyer (**!** + *être*)
s'essuyer = to wipe oneself
= to dry oneself
s'essuyer les mains = to wipe one's hands

est¹ ▶ **être** 7

est²
1 *noun, masculine*
l'est = the east
2 *adjective* (**!** *never changes*)
= east
= eastern

est-ce que ▶ **être** 7

estivant/estivante *noun,*
masculine|feminine
un estivant/une estivante = a summer
visitor

estomac *noun, masculine*
l'estomac = the stomach

et *conjunction*
= and
et avec ceci? = anything else?

étage *noun, masculine*
un étage = a floor, a story
habiter au premier étage (*in Britain*) = to
live on the first floor
(*in the US*) = to live on the second floor
à l'étage = upstairs

étagère *noun, feminine*
une étagère (*a flat piece of wood, glass*)
= a shelf
(*a piece of furniture*) = a bookshelf

étais ▶ **être** 7

étaler *verb* 1
= to spread (out)

étang *noun, masculine*
un étang = a pond

étant ▶ **être** 7

étape *noun, feminine*
• (*a place*)
une étape = a stop
faire étape à Nice = to stop in Nice
• (*part of a journey*)
une étape = a stage
(*in a race*) = a leg

état noun, masculine
un état = a state

États-Unis noun, masculine plural
les États-Unis = the United States

été
1 ▶ être [7]
2 noun, masculine
l'été = summer

éteindre verb [55]
1 (! + avoir)
• = to put out
• = to switch off, to turn off
2 s'éteindre (! + être)
• s'éteindre = to go out
• s'éteindre = to go off

éteint/éteinte ▶ éteindre [55]

étendre verb [6]
1 (! + avoir)
• (to put down flat)
étendre une nappe = to spread out a tablecloth
• (to put out to dry)
étendre le linge = to hang out the washing, to hang out the laundry
2 s'étendre (! + être)
• (if it's a person)
s'étendre = to lie down
• (if it's land)
s'étendre = to stretch
• (if it's a conflict)
s'étendre = to spread

étendu/étendue¹
1 ▶ étendre [6]
2 adjective
= extensive

étendue² noun, feminine
• (of land, water)
une étendue = an expanse
= a stretch
• (of a disaster)
l'étendue = the scale, the size

éternuer verb [1]
= to sneeze

êtes ▶ être [7]

étiquette noun, feminine
une étiquette = a label
= a tag

étirer: **s'étirer** verb [1] (! + être)
s'étirer = to stretch

étoile noun, feminine
une étoile = a star

étonnant/étonnante adjective
= surprising
= amazing

étonner verb [1]
1 (! + avoir)
= to surprise
2 s'étonner (! + être)
s'étonner = to be surprised

étouffant/étouffante adjective
= stifling

étouffer verb [1]
1 (! + avoir)
• = to smother
• = to suffocate
on étouffe ici! = it's stifling in here!
2 s'étouffer (! + être)
s'étouffer = to choke

étourdi/étourdie adjective
= scatterbrained

étrange adjective
= strange

étranger/étrangère
1 adjective
= foreign
2 noun, masculine/feminine
un étranger/une étrangère (from another country) = a foreigner
(an unknown person) = a stranger
3 à l'étranger = abroad

être verb [7] (! + avoir)
▶ 64 | See the boxed note.

étroit/étroite adjective
= narrow

étude
1 noun, feminine
• (an activity)
l'étude = study
• (a room in a school)
l'étude = the study room, the study hall
• (on the school timetable)
'étude' = 'private study', 'study hall'
2 études noun, feminine plural
les études = studies, higher education
faire des études = to study, to be a student

étudiant/étudiante noun,
masculine/feminine
un étudiant/une étudiante = a student

étudier verb [2]
• = to study
• = to examine

étui noun, masculine
un étui = a case
un étui à lunettes = a glasses case

eu/eue ▶ avoir [8]

eurochèque noun, masculine
un eurochèque = a Eurocheque

Europe noun, feminine
l'Europe = Europe

européen/européenne adjective
= European

eux pronoun
• = them
à cause d'eux = because of them

E

être *verb* 7

present	imperfect	future	past participle
je suis	j'étais	je serai	été
tu es	tu étais	tu seras	
il / elle est	il / elle était	il / elle sera	
nous sommes	nous étions	nous serons	
vous êtes	vous étiez	vous serez	
ils / elles sont	ils / elles étaient	ils / elles seront	

1 être functions as an ordinary verb:

● (*showing a quality or state*) = to be

je **suis** fatigué	= I'm tired
le ciel **est** bleu	= the sky is blue
elle **est** fatiguée	= she is tired
sois sage!	= be good!
ils **ont été** malades	= they've been ill

● (*showing ownership*)

la maison **est** à Pierre	= the house belongs to Pierre, the house is Pierre's
à qui **sont** ces gants?	= who do these gloves belong to, whose gloves are they?
ils **sont** à moi	= they belong to me, they're mine

2 être is used as an auxiliary verb to conjugate some verbs, notably reflexive verbs and a few others, all of which are labelled (**!** + *être*):

je **suis** né en Italie	= I was born in Italy
elle n'**est** pas encore rentrée	= she hasn't come home yet
ils **sont** partis	= they've left
tu t'**es** lavé les mains?	= did you wash your hands?

3 être is used to form questions in the phrase **est-ce que**:

est-ce que tu aimes le jazz?	= do you like jazz?
est-ce qu'il fait froid?	= is it cold?
est-ce que tu viendras?	= will you come?
est-ce qu'ils ont fini?	= have they finished?
est-ce que tu as de l'argent?	= have you got any money?

• (*indicating possession, turn*)
le chien est à eux = the dog is theirs
c'est à eux de jouer = it's their turn to play
• (*when used for emphasis*) = they
je suis resté, mais eux sont partis = I stayed but they left

eux-mêmes *pronoun*
= themselves

évaluer *verb* 1
• = to assess
• = to estimate
• = to value

évanouir: s'évanouir *verb* 3 (**!** + *être*)
s'évanouir = to faint

évasion *noun, feminine*
une évasion = an escape

événement *noun, masculine*
un événement = an event

éventail *noun, masculine*
un éventail = a fan

éventuellement *adverb*
• = possibly
• = if necessary

évidemment *adverb*
= obviously
= of course

évident/évidente *adjective*
= obvious

évier *noun, masculine*
un évier = a (kitchen) sink

éviter *verb* 1
= to avoid

exact/exacte *adjective*
• = correct
• = exact

✗ in informal situations

exactement *adverb*
= exactly

exagérer *verb* 14
= to exaggerate

examen *noun, masculine*
• *(for pupils, students)*
un examen = an examination, an exam, a test
passer un examen = to take an exam
réussir à un examen = to pass an exam
• *(by a doctor)*
un examen = an examination

examiner *verb* 1
= to examine

excursion *noun, feminine*
une excursion = an excursion, a trip
faire une excursion = to go on an excursion

excuse *noun, feminine*
• *(a reason)*
une excuse = an excuse
• *(when saying that one is sorry)*
des excuses = an apology
présenter des excuses = to apologize

excuser *verb* 1
1 (! + *avoir*)
= to excuse
excusez-moi *(when apologizing)* = I'm sorry
(when interrupting) = excuse me
2 s'excuser (! + *être*)
s'excuser = to apologize

exemple *noun, masculine*
un exemple = an example
par exemple = for example, for instance

exercer: s'exercer *verb* 12 (! + *être*)
s'exercer = to practise, to practice
s'exercer à sauter à la corde = to practise skipping

exercice *noun, masculine*
un exercice = an exercise

exiger *verb* 13
= to demand
= to require

expédier *verb* 2
= to send

expéditeur/expéditrice *noun, masculine/feminine*
un expéditeur/une expéditrice = a sender

expérience *noun, feminine*
• *(skill, knowledge)*
l'expérience = experience
• *(a test)*
une expérience = an experiment

expliquer *verb* 1
= to explain

explorateur/exploratrice *noun, masculine/feminine*
un explorateur/une exploratrice = an explorer

exploser *verb* 1
= to explode

exposer *verb* 1
• *(in a shop window)* = to display
• *(in a gallery)* = to exhibit
• *(to the sun, to a danger)* = to expose

exposition *noun, feminine*
une exposition = an exhibition

exprès *adverb*
= on purpose

express *noun, masculine* (! *never changes*)
un express = an express, a fast train

exprimer *verb* 1
= to express

extérieur/extérieure
1 *adjective*
= outside
2 extérieur *noun, masculine*
l'extérieur = the outside
à l'extérieur de la boîte = outside the box

externe
1 *adjective*
= external
2 *noun, masculine/feminine*
un externe/une externe = a day pupil, a day student

extra *adjective*
= first-class, great

extrait *noun, masculine*
un extrait = an extract

F

Ff

fabrication *noun, feminine*
la fabrication = manufacture

fabriquer *verb* 1
• = to make, to manufacture
• qu'est-ce que tu fabriques✗? = what are you up to?

façade *noun, feminine*
la façade = the front

face
1 *noun, feminine*
la face *(on a box)* = the side
(of a coin) = the heads side
pile ou face = heads or tails

2 de face = from the front
3 en face (de) = opposite

fâcher: **se fâcher** *verb* [1]
  se fâcher = to get angry

facile *adjective*
  = easy

facilement *adverb*
  = easily

façon *noun, feminine*
  une façon = a way
  la façon dont il parle = the way he talks
  de toute façon = anyway

façonner *verb* [1]
  = to shape, to mould

facteur/factrice *noun,*
masculine/feminine
  un facteur/une factrice = a postman/a
    postwoman, a mail carrier

facture *noun, feminine*
  une facture = a bill, an invoice

faible *adjective*
  = weak

faillir *verb* [28]
  j'ai failli y aller = I (very) nearly went, I
    almost went

faim *noun, feminine*
  la faim = hunger
  avoir faim = to be hungry

fainéant/fainéante *adjective*
  = lazy

faire *verb* [10]

  ! *You will find translations for phrases with*
  faire *such as* faire attention, faire le clown,
  faire pousser *etc under the words*
  attention, clown, pousser *etc.*

1 (! + *avoir*)
• = to make
  faire [un gâteau | un effort | une faute ...] = to
    make [a cake | an effort | a mistake ...]
• = to do
  faire [la vaisselle | ses devoirs | un travail ...]
    = to do [the dishes | one's homework | a job ...]
  que fait-il? (*for a living*) = what does he do?
  (*at this very moment*) = what's he doing?
• = to go
  faire [de l'escalade | du vélo | des courses ...]
    = to go [climbing | cycling | shopping ...]
• (*when talking about the weather*)
  il fait [chaud | gris | du vent ...] = it's [hot |
    overcast | windy ...]
  il faisait 30° à l'ombre = it was 30° in the
    shade
  il fera beau demain = the weather will be
    fine tomorrow

• (*when talking about a particular length of
  time*)
  ça fait deux heures que j'attends = I've
    been waiting for two hours
  ça fait longtemps qu'il est parti = he left a
    long time ago
• (*when talking about measurements*)
  faire 1,75 m = to be 1.75 m tall
  faire du 42 = to take a size 42
• (*to cause something to happen*)
  il m'a fait [tomber | manquer le train |
    travailler ...] = he made me [fall | miss the
    train | work ...]
• (*to get something done*)
  faire nettoyer une veste = to have a jacket
    cleaned
• (*some other uses*)
  ça ne fait rien = it doesn't matter
  qu'est-ce que ça peut bien te faire?
    = what's it to you?
  fais comme tu veux = do as you like
  faites comme chez vous = make yourself
    at home
2 se faire (! + *être*)
• (*to do something for oneself*)
  se faire = to make
  elle s'est fait du café = she made herself
    some coffee
  se faire des amis = to make friends
  se faire comprendre = to make oneself
    understood
• (*to get someone to do something for you*)
  se faire couper les cheveux = to have one's
    hair cut
  elle s'est fait faire une robe = she's had a
    dress made
• (*when something is done to you*)
  se faire [attraper | menacer | écraser ...] = to be
    [caught | threatened | run over ...]
• (*other uses*)
  ça ne se fait pas = it isn't the done thing,
    it isn't the thing to do
3 s'en faire (! + *être*)
  s'en faire = to worry
  ne t'en fais pas = don't worry

faire-part *noun, masculine* (! *never
changes*)
  un faire-part = an announcement card

fais ▶ faire [10]

faisable *adjective*
  = feasible
  c'est faisable = it can be done

faisais ▶ faire [10]

faisan *noun, masculine*
  un faisan = a pheasant

faisons ▶ faire [10]

fait/faite
1 ▶ faire [10]
2 *adjective*
• = done
  un travail bien fait = a job well done
  c'est bien fait pour lui! = it serves him
    right!

- **tout fait** = ready-made
  des rideaux tout faits = ready-made curtains, store-bought drapes
- **c'est fait pour nettoyer les vitres** = it's meant for cleaning windows

3 fait noun, masculine
un fait = a fact
4 au fait = by the way
5 en fait = in fact
un fait divers = a (short) news item

faites ▶ **faire** ⑩

falaise noun, feminine
une falaise = a cliff

falloir verb ⑤⓪
il faut une clé pour ouvrir la porte = you need a key to open the door
il me fallait de l'argent = I needed some money
allons, il faut partir = come on, we've got to go
il ne faut jamais arriver en retard = one must never be late
achète ce qu'il faut pour le jardin = buy whatever is necessary for the garden
il le fallait = it was necessary
il faudra que tu ailles au garage = you will have to go to the garage
il va falloir que vous le fassiez = you will have to do it

fallu ▶ **falloir** ⑤⓪

familial/familiale adjective
(plural) **familiaux/familiales**
= family

familier/familière adjective
= familiar

famille noun, feminine
une famille = a family
en famille = with the family
= as a family

fana* noun, masculine|feminine
un fana*/**une fana*** = a fanatic

fantastique adjective
= fantastic

fantôme noun, masculine
un fantôme = a ghost

farce noun, feminine
- (a trick)
  une farce = a practical joke
- (in cooking)
  la farce = the stuffing

farci/farcie adjective
= stuffed

fard noun, masculine
le fard = make-up

farfelu/farfelue* adjective
- = scatterbrained
- = eccentric

farine noun, feminine
la farine = flour

fasse ▶ **faire** ⑩

fatigant/fatigante adjective
= tiring

fatigue noun, feminine
la fatigue = tiredness

fatigué/fatiguée
= tired

fauché/fauchée* adjective
= broke

faudra ▶ **falloir** ⑤⓪

faune noun, feminine
la faune = wildlife

fausse ▶ **faux**

faut ▶ **falloir** ⑤⓪

faute noun, feminine
- (an error)
  une faute = a mistake
- (responsibility)
  c'est (de) ta faute = it's your fault

fauteuil noun, masculine
un fauteuil = an armchair
un fauteuil roulant = a wheelchair

faux/fausse
1 adjective
- (not right) = wrong
- (not genuine) = false
  = fake
2 faux adverb
chanter faux = to sing out of tune

favori/favorite adjective
= favo(u)rite

féculent noun, masculine
un féculent = a starchy food

fêlé/fêlée adjective
= cracked

félicitations noun, feminine plural
des félicitations = congratulations

femme noun, feminine
une femme = a woman
= a wife
une femme d'affaires = a business-woman
une femme de ménage = a cleaning lady

fenêtre noun, feminine
une fenêtre = a window

fente noun, feminine
une fente (for a coin) = a slot
(in a wall) = a crack
(in a mask) = a slit

fer noun, masculine
le fer = iron
un fer à repasser = an iron

F

ferai ▶ faire 50

férié/fériée *adjective*
un jour férié = a public holiday, a holiday

ferme *noun, feminine*
une ferme = a farm

fermer *verb* 1
= to close, to shut

fermeture *noun, feminine*
• (*of a shop*)
la fermeture = closing (down)
'fermeture annuelle' = 'annual closing'
• (*a device*)
une fermeture = a fastener
une fermeture éclair® = a zip(per)

fermier/fermière *noun, masculine/feminine*
un fermier/une fermière = a farmer

féroce *adjective*
= fierce

ferroviaire *adjective*
= rail, railroad

fesse *noun, feminine*
une fesse = a buttock

fête *noun, feminine*
• (*a special day in a country*)
une fête = a public holiday, a holiday
• (*a special day for a person*)
ma fête = my (saint's) name-day
bonne fête! = happy saint's day!
• (*an organized event*)
une fête = a festival
• (*at home*) = a celebration
= a party
faire une fête = to have a party
une fête foraine = a funfair, a carnival
la fête des Mères = Mother's day
(*celebrated in France on the last Sunday in May*)
la fête du travail = May Day

fêter *verb* 1
= to celebrate

feu *noun, masculine*
(*plural*) **feux**
• (*flames*)
un feu = a fire
mettre le feu à une maison = to set fire to a house
au feu! = fire!
en feu = on fire
• (*the flame from a match or a lighter*)
du feu = a light
demander du feu = to ask for a light
• (*on a car, in the street*)
un feu = a light
les feux = the traffic lights
un feu d'artifice = a fireworks display
les feux de détresse = hazard lights

les feux de signalisation, les feux tricolores = the traffic lights

feuille *noun, feminine*
• (*on a tree*)
une feuille = a leaf
• (*paper*)
une feuille = a sheet

feuilleter *verb* 20
= to flick through

feuilleton *noun, masculine*
un feuilleton = a serial
= a soap opera

feutre *noun, masculine*
un feutre = a felt-tip pen

fève *noun, feminine*
• une fève = a broad bean, a fava bean
• une fève = a lucky charm (*hidden in the galette des rois*)

février *noun, masculine*
février = February

fiançailles *noun, feminine plural*
des fiançailles = an engagement

fiancer: se fiancer *verb* 12 (**!** + *être*)
se fiancer = to get engaged

ficelle *noun, feminine*
• (*around a parcel*)
de la ficelle = string
• (*bread*)
une ficelle = a thin baguette

fiche *noun, feminine*
une fiche = a form
= card

ficher✶ *verb* 1
1 (**!** + *avoir*)
• = to do
il n'a rien fiché✶ *or* fichu✶ de la journée
= he's done nothing all day
• ficher✶ à la poubelle = to bin, to throw out
• fiche-moi la paix✶! = leave me alone!
2 se ficher✶ (**!** + *être*)
• se ficher de quelqu'un✶
(*to mock*) = to make fun of someone
(*to lack consideration*) = to mess someone around
• je m'en fiche✶ = I couldn't care less
je me fiche✶ de ce qu'on dit = I couldn't care less what people say

fichu/fichue✶
1 ▶ ficher 1
2 *adjective*
• = rotten, nasty
avoir un fichu✶ caractère = to have a nasty temper
• = done for
ma voiture est fichue✶ = my car's had it
s'il pleut c'est fichu✶ = if it rains that's the end of that
• être fichu✶ de faire = to be capable of doing

✶ in informal situations

fidèle *adjective*
= faithful

fier/fière *adjective*
= proud

fièvre *noun, feminine*
une fièvre = a fever
avoir de la fièvre = to have a temperature

fiévreux/fiévreuse *adjective*
= feverish

figue *noun, feminine*
une figue = a fig

figure *noun, feminine*
• la figure = the face
• une figure = a figure
= a diagram

figurer *verb* 1
1 (! + *avoir*)
= to appear, to feature
figurer sur une liste = to appear on a list
2 se figurer (! + *être*)
se figurer = to think, to imagine

fil *noun, masculine*
• (*for sewing*)
le fil = thread
• (*connecting a telephone*)
un fil = a wire
un coup de fil = a phone call
passe-moi un coup de fil = give me a call
le fil de fer = wire

file *noun, feminine*
• (*a row of people or cars*)
une file = a line
(*at a cinema, a bus stop, a store*)
une file d'attente = a queue, a line
• (*part of a road*)
une file = a lane

filer✗ *verb* 1
• (*if it's time*) = to fly by
• (*to leave*)✗ = to go off
• (*to escape*)✗ = to get away

filet *noun, masculine*
un filet = a net
un filet à provisions = a string bag

fille *noun, feminine*
une fille = a girl
= a daughter

fillette *noun, feminine*
une fillette = a little girl

filleul/filleule *noun, masculine/feminine*
un filleul/une filleule = a godson/a
goddaughter

film *noun, masculine*
un film = a film, a movie
un film d'animation = a cartoon (film)
un film policier = a detective film

fils *noun, masculine* (! *never changes*)
un fils = a son

fin[1] *noun, feminine*
la fin = the end
en fin de matinée = late in the morning
en fin de compte = in the end, finally

fin[2]**/fine** *adjective*
= thin
= slender
= fine

finalement *adverb*
= finally, in the end

finir *verb* 3
• = to finish
j'ai fini d'écrire = I've finished writing
• = to end
il a fini par avoir un accident = he ended
up having an accident
l'histoire finit bien = the story has a happy
ending

fioul *noun, masculine*
le fioul = fuel oil

firme *noun, feminine*
une firme = a firm

fixe *adjective*
un prix fixe = a fixed price
une résidence fixe = a permanent address
manger à heure fixe = to eat at a set time

flamme *noun, feminine*
une flamme = a flame

flan *noun, masculine*
un flan ≈ custard
= a custard tart, a custard flan

flâner *verb* 1
= to stroll

flaque *noun, feminine*
une flaque = a puddle

flèche *noun, feminine*
une flèche = an arrow

fléchette *noun, feminine*
une fléchette = a dart

fleur *noun, feminine*
une fleur = a flower

fleuriste *noun, masculine/feminine*
un fleuriste/une fleuriste = a florist

fleuve *noun, masculine*
un fleuve = a (large) river

flic✗ *noun, masculine*
un flic✗ = a cop, a policeman

flipper *noun, masculine*
le flipper (*the machine*) = the pinball
machine
(*the device in the machine*) = the flipper
(*the game*) = pinball

flocon *noun, masculine*
un flocon de neige = a snowflake

flotter *verb* 1
= to float

F

flotteur *noun, masculine*
un flotteur = a float

fluo *adjective* (! *never changes*)
= fluorescent

fluorescent/fluorescente *adjective*
= fluorescent

flûte *noun, feminine*
• (*an instrument*)
une flûte = a flute
une flûte à bec = a recorder
• (*bread*)
une flûte = a French stick, French bread

foie *noun, masculine*
le foie = (the) liver

foire *noun, feminine*
une foire = a fair
= a trade fair

fois
1 *noun, feminine* (! *never changes*)
encore une fois = one more time
une fois = once
deux fois = twice
trois fois = three times
une fois qu'il aura fini = once he's finished
une fois pour toutes = once and for all
2 à la fois = at the same time
= at once
3 des fois* = sometimes

folklorique *adjective*
= folk

folle ▶ fou

foncé/foncée *adjective*
= dark

foncer *verb* 12
foncer sur quelqu'un = to charge at
someone

fonctionnaire *noun, masculine/feminine*
un fonctionnaire/une fonctionnaire = a
civil servant

fonctionner *verb* 1
= to work

fond
1 *noun, masculine*
• (*the deepest part*)
le fond = the bottom
au fond du verre = at the bottom of the
glass
• (*the furthest part*)
le fond (*of a cupboard, a shop*) = the back
(*of a room, a yard*) = the far end
(*on a picture*) = the background
2 à fond
respirer à fond = to breathe deeply
appuyer à fond = to press hard

3 au fond, dans le fond
au fond, ce n'est pas bête = it's a rather
good idea
dans le fond, il a raison = he's right, really
un fond de teint = a foundation, a make-
up base

fonder *verb* 1
= to found

fondre *verb* 6
= to melt
faire fondre = to melt

fondu/fondue *adjective*
= melted

font ▶ faire 10

fontaine *noun, feminine*
une fontaine = a fountain

foot* *noun, masculine*
le foot* = football, soccer

football *noun, masculine*
le football = football, soccer

footing *noun, masculine*
le footing = jogging

force
1 *noun, feminine*
• (*energy*)
la force = strength
avoir de la force = to be strong
• (*violence*)
la force = force
de force = by force
2 à force de
réussir à force de travailler = to succeed by
dint of hard work
j'ai mal au bras à force d'écrire = I've done
so much writing that my arm hurts

forcer *verb* 12
1 (! + *avoir*)
= to force
forcer un enfant à manger = to force a
child to eat
2 se forcer (! + *être*)
se forcer = to force oneself

forêt *noun, feminine*
une forêt = a forest

forfaitaire *adjective*
= inclusive

forgeron *noun, masculine*
un forgeron = a blacksmith

formation *noun, feminine*
• (*the learning of skills*)
la formation = training
• (*the process of creating or developing*)
la formation = the formation

✗ in informal situations   **☞** may be considered offensive

forme *noun, feminine*
* (*an outline*)
  une forme = a shape
  = a form
  en forme de T = T-shaped
* (*a person's energy*)
  avoir la forme = to be in good form
  être en (pleine) forme = to be in (very) good form

former *verb* 1
* = to form
* = to train

formidable *adjective*
* = tremendous
* = great

formulaire *noun, masculine*
  un formulaire = a form

fort/forte
1 *adjective*
* (*not weak*) = strong
* (*not slim*) = stout
  = broad
* (*not soft*) = loud
* (*not slight*)
  de fortes pluies = heavy rain
  une forte chaleur = intense heat
  une forte pente = a steep slope
* (*gifted*)
  fort en = good at
  être fort en chimie = to be good at chemistry
2 fort *adverb*
* = hard
  taper fort = to hit hard
* = loudly
  parler fort = to speak loudly

fortement *adverb*
  = strongly
  = deeply

fortune *noun, feminine*
  une fortune = a fortune
  faire fortune = to make one's fortune

fossé *noun, masculine*
  un fossé = a ditch

fou/folle
1 *adjective*
  = mad, crazy
  être fou✶/folle✶ de quelqu'un = to be mad about someone
2 *noun, masculine|feminine*
  un fou/une folle = a madman/a madwoman

foudre *noun, feminine*
* **la foudre** = lightning
* **le coup de foudre** = love at first sight

fouiller *verb* 1
* = to search
* **fouiller dans un tiroir** = to rummage around in a drawer

foulard *noun, masculine*
  un foulard = a scarf

foule *noun, feminine*
  la foule = the crowd

fouler: se fouler *verb* 1 (**!** + *être*)
  se fouler la cheville = to sprain one's ankle

four *noun, masculine*
  un four = an oven
  faire cuire au four = to roast
  = to bake
  un four à micro-ondes = a microwave (oven)

fourche *noun, feminine*
  une fourche = a garden fork
  = a pitchfork

fourchette *noun, feminine*
  une fourchette = a fork

fourgonnette *noun, feminine*
  une fourgonnette = a (small) van

fourmi *noun, feminine*
  une fourmi = an ant

fournir *verb* 3
  = to provide, to supply

fourrer✶ *verb* 1
1 (**!** + *avoir*)
  = to shove, to put
  fourrer✶ des lettres dans un sac = to shove letters into a bag
2 se fourrer✶ (**!** + *être*)
  se fourrer = to put oneself

fourrure *noun, feminine*
  la fourrure = fur

foutre: se foutre de✶ *verb* 6 (**!** + *être*)
  se foutre de✶ = not to give a damn about
  je m'en fous✶ = I couldn't care less, I don't give a damn

foyer *noun, masculine*
* (*for a large group*)
  un foyer = a hostel
* (*where a family lives*)
  un foyer = a home
* (*in a fireplace*)
  le foyer = the hearth

fracture *noun, feminine*
  une fracture = a fracture

fragile *adjective*
  = fragile
  = delicate

fraîche ▶ frais 1

frais/fraîche
1 *adjective*
* = cool
  = chilled
  des boissons fraîches = cool drinks, cold drinks
  'servir frais' = 'serve chilled'

• = fresh
des légumes frais = fresh vegetables
des nouvelles fraîches = fresh news
2 frais *adverb*
• = cool
= chilly
il fait frais ce matin = it's cool this morning
= it's chilly this morning
3 frais *noun, masculine* (**!** *never changes*)
'**garder au frais**' = 'keep in a cool place'
prendre le frais = to take a breath of fresh air
4 frais *noun, masculine plural*
des frais = expenses

fraise *noun, feminine*
une fraise = a strawberry

framboise *noun, feminine*
une framboise = a raspberry

franc/franche
1 *adjective*
= frank
2 franc *noun, masculine*
un franc = one franc

français/française
1 *adjective*
= French
2 français *noun, masculine*
le français = French

Français/Française *noun, masculine/feminine*
un Français/une Française = a Frenchman/a Frenchwoman
les Français = the French

France *noun, feminine*
la France = France

franchement *adverb*
= frankly

franchir *verb* ③
• = to cross
franchir une frontière = to cross a border
• = to get over
franchir une clôture = to get over a fence
• = to cover
franchir dix kilomètres = to cover ten kilometres

francophone *adjective*
= French-speaking

frange *noun, feminine*
une frange = a fringe, bangs

frapper *verb* ①
• = to hit
• = to knock

fraternité *noun, feminine*
la fraternité = fraternity

frein *noun, masculine*
un frein = a brake
le frein à main = the handbrake
donner un coup de frein = to brake

✗ in informal situations

freiner *verb* ①
= to brake

fréquenter *verb* ①
• = to mix with, to associate with
fréquenter des voyous = to mix with hooligans
• = to go to
= to visit
= to attend

frère *noun, masculine*
un frère = a brother

frigidaire® *noun, masculine*
un frigidaire = a refrigerator

frigo✗ *noun, masculine*
un frigo✗ = a fridge

frimeur/frimeuse✗ *noun, masculine/feminine*
un frimeur✗/une frimeuse✗ = a show-off

fringues✗ *noun, feminine plural*
des fringues✗ = clothes

frire *verb* ③⑨
= to fry

frisé/frisée *adjective*
= curly

frisson *noun, masculine*
un frisson = a shiver
= a shudder

frit/frite *adjective*
= fried

frites *noun, feminine plural*
les frites = chips, French fries

froid/froide
1 *adjective*
= cold
2 froid *adverb*
il fait froid = it's cold
3 froid *noun, masculine*
le froid = the cold
avoir froid = to feel cold, to be cold
prendre froid = to catch (a) cold

fromage *noun, masculine*
le fromage = cheese
le fromage blanc ≈ fromage frais

front *noun, masculine*
le front = the forehead

frontière *noun, feminine*
une frontière = a border, a frontier

frotter *verb* ①
= to rub

fruit *noun, masculine*
un fruit = a piece of fruit
des fruits = fruit
des fruits de mer = seafood

fuir *verb* ②⑨
• (*if it's a person*) = to flee
• (*if it's a tap, a hose*) = to leak

fuite noun, feminine
• (of a person)
la fuite = the flight
= the escape
• (in a pipe, a hose)
une fuite = a leak

fumée noun, feminine
la fumée = smoke

fumer verb 1
= to smoke

fumeur/fumeuse noun,
masculine/feminine
un fumeur/une fumeuse = a smoker

funiculaire noun, masculine
un funiculaire = a funicular (railway)

fur: **au fur et à mesure** adverb
au fur et à mesure = as one goes along
au fur et à mesure que = as
au fur et à mesure qu'on fait des progrès
= as one improves

furieux/furieuse adjective
= furious, angry

fuseau noun, masculine
(plural) **fuseaux**
un fuseau = ski pants
un fuseau horaire = a time zone

fusée noun, feminine
une fusée = a rocket

fusil noun, masculine
un fusil = a (shot)gun
= a rifle
un coup de fusil = a shot

gâcher verb 1
= to waste
= to spoil

gaffe✗ noun, feminine
• une gaffe = a blunder
• faire gaffe✗ = to watch out

gagnant/gagnante
1 adjective
= winning
2 noun, masculine/feminine
un gagnant/une gagnante = a winner

gagner verb 1
• = to win
• = to earn
il gagne bien sa vie = he makes a good
living

• = to save
gagner du temps = to save time
gagner de la place = to make more room

gai/gaie adjective
= happy
= cheerful

gain noun, masculine
c'est un gain de temps = it saves time

gala noun, masculine
un gala = a gala, a gala event

galerie noun, feminine
• (a passage)
une galerie = a gallery
• (on a car)
la galerie = the roof rack
• **une galerie d'art** = an art gallery
une galerie marchande = a shopping
centre, a shopping mall

galet noun, masculine
un galet = a pebble

galette noun, feminine
une galette = a biscuit, a cookie
= a pancake
la galette des rois = the Twelfth Night
cake (eaten on the Epiphany)

Galles noun, plural
le pays de Galles = Wales

gallois/galloise
1 adjective
= Welsh
2 gallois noun, masculine
le gallois = Welsh

galop noun, masculine
un galop = a gallop
au galop = at a gallop

galoper verb 1
= to gallop

gamin/gamine✗ noun,
masculine/feminine
un gamin✗/une gamine✗ = a kid, a child

gamme noun, feminine
• (of products)
une gamme = a range
• (in music)
une gamme = a scale

gant noun, masculine
un gant = a glove
un gant de toilette ≈ a face flannel, a
wash cloth

garage noun, masculine
un garage = a garage
un garage à vélos = a bicycle shed

garagiste noun, masculine/feminine
un garagiste/une garagiste = a garage
owner
= a car mechanic

G

garantie noun, feminine
　une garantie = a guarantee
　= a warranty
　un bon de garantie = a guarantee

garçon noun, masculine
• un garçon = a boy
　= a young man
• un garçon (de café) = a waiter
　un garçon d'honneur = a best man
　un garçon manqué = a tomboy

garde
1 noun, feminine
• la garde (of a child) = the care
　(of a building) = guarding
• être de garde (if it's a doctor) = to be on call
　(if it's a pharmacist) = to be on duty
2 noun, masculine
　un garde = a guard
　un garde du corps = a bodyguard

garde-chasse noun, masculine
(plural) **gardes-chasses**
　un garde-chasse = a game warden
　= a gamekeeper

garde-fou noun, masculine
(plural) **garde-fous**
　un garde-fou = a parapet
　= a safeguard

garder verb 1
• = to keep (on)
• = to look after
• = to guard

gardien/gardienne noun,
masculine/feminine
　un gardien/une gardienne (in a prison) = a
　　warder, a guard
　(in a museum) = an attendant, a museum
　　security guard
　(on work premises) = a security guard
　(in an apartment block) = a caretaker, a
　　janitor
　un gardien de but = a goalkeeper
　une gardienne d'enfant = a childminder,
　　a day-care lady

gare
1 noun, feminine
　une gare = a railway station
2 exclamation
　gare à toi! = watch it!
　une gare maritime = a harbo(u)r station
　une gare routière = a coach station, a bus
　　station

garer verb 1
1 (! + avoir)
　= to park
2 se garer (! + être)
　se garer = to park
　= to pull over

garni/garnie adjective
　= served with vegetables

gars✗ noun, masculine (! never changes)
• un (petit) gars✗ = a (young) lad, a (young)
　guy
• un gars✗ = a chap, a guy

gas-oil noun, masculine
　le gas-oil = diesel oil, fuel oil

gaspiller verb 1
　= to waste

gâteau noun, masculine
(plural) **gâteaux**
　un gâteau = a cake
　le gâteau de riz = rice pudding
　un gâteau sec = a biscuit, a cookie

gâter verb 1
1 (! + avoir)
• = to spoil
　un enfant gâté = a spoiled child
2 se gâter (! + être)
• (if it's fruit)
　se gâter = to go bad
• (if it's the weather)
　se gâter = to take a turn for the worse

gauche
1 adjective
• = left
• = awkward
　= clumsy
2 noun, feminine
　la gauche = the left
　tournez à gauche = turn left
　conduire à gauche = to drive on the left-
　　hand side

gaucher/gauchère adjective
　= left-handed

gaufre noun, feminine
　une gaufre = a waffle

Gaulois/Gauloise noun,
masculine/feminine
　un Gaulois/une Gauloise = a Gaul

gaz noun, masculine (! never changes)
　le gaz = gas
　se chauffer au gaz = to have gas heating
　le gaz carbonique = carbon dioxide
　le gaz de ville = mains gas

gazeux/gazeuse adjective
　= fizzy, sparkling
　une boisson gazeuse = a fizzy drink

gazon noun, masculine
　le gazon = grass, lawn

géant/géante
1 adjective
　= huge
2 noun, masculine/feminine
　un géant/une géante = a giant/a giantess

gel noun, masculine
• (in winter)
　le gel = frost

✗ in informal situations

- (*for hair*)
  un gel coiffant = a styling gel

gelé/gelée¹ *adjective*
= frozen

gelée² *noun, feminine*
- (*on the ground*)
  la gelée = frost
- (*in cooking*)
  la gelée de groseilles = redcurrant jelly

geler *verb* 17
1 (**!** + *avoir*)
= to freeze
il gèle = it's freezing
2 se geler✶ (**!** + *être*)
se geler✶ = to be freezing

gélule *noun, feminine*
une gélule = a capsule

Gémeaux *noun, masculine plural*
les Gémeaux = Gemini

gémir *verb* 3
= to moan
= to whimper

gênant/gênante *adjective*
= embarrassing

gendarme *noun, masculine*
un gendarme = a gendarme, a French
  policeman

gendarmerie *noun, feminine*
- **la gendarmerie (nationale)** = the
  gendarmerie
- **une gendarmerie** ≈ a police station

gendre *noun, masculine*
un gendre = a son-in-law

généalogique *adjective*
un arbre généalogique = a family tree

gêner *verb* 1
1 (**!** + *avoir*)
- = to disturb
- = to bother
  ça te gêne si j'allume? = do you mind if
  I switch the light on?
- = to be in the way
- = to embarrass
2 se gêner (**!** + *être*)
- **se gêner** = to get in each other's way
- **ne te gêne pas pour moi** = don't mind me

général/générale
(*plural*) **généraux/générales**
1 *adjective*
- = general
  de l'avis général = in most people's
  opinion
  dans l'intérêt général = in the public
  interest
- **en général** = generally
- = usually
2 général *noun, masculine*
un général = a general

généralement *adverb*
= generally
= normally

généraliste *adjective*
- = non-specialized
- **un médecin généraliste** = a general
  practitioner, a GP, a family doctor

généreux/généreuse *adjective*
= generous

génétique *adjective*
= genetic

Genève *noun*
= Geneva

génial/géniale✶ *adjective*
(*plural*) **géniaux/géniales**
= brilliant

génie *noun, masculine*
le génie = genius
une idée de génie = a brainwave

genou *noun, masculine*
(*plural*) **genoux**
un genou = a knee
être sur les genoux de sa mère = to be on
  one's mother's lap
à genoux = on one's knees
se mettre à genoux = to kneel down

genre *noun, masculine*
- (*a type*)
  un genre = a kind
  ce genre de travail = this kind of work
  un peu dans le genre de ta robe = a little
  bit like your dress
- (*a look*)
  avoir un drôle de genre = to look a bit
  shady
  pour se donner un genre = to make
  oneself look different
- (*in grammar*)
  le genre = gender
- (*in literature, cinema*)
  un genre = a genre

gens *noun, masculine plural*
les gens = people

gentil/gentille *adjective*
= kind, nice

gentillesse *noun, feminine*
la gentillesse = kindness

gentiment *adverb*
= nicely, kindly

géographie *noun, feminine*
la géographie = geography

gérant/gérante *noun,*
masculine/feminine
- (*in a shop*)
  un gérant/une gérante = a manager
- (*for a property*)
  un gérant/une gérante = a managing
  agent

G

gerboise *noun, feminine*
une gerboise = a gerbil

germain/germaine *adjective*
un cousin germain = a first cousin

geste *noun, masculine*
un geste = a movement
= a gesture

gibier *noun, masculine*
le gibier = game

gifle *noun, feminine*
une gifle = a slap in the face

gigantesque *adjective*
= huge, gigantic

gigot *noun, masculine*
un gigot d'agneau = a leg of lamb

gilet *noun, masculine*
• un gilet = a cardigan
• un gilet = a waistcoat, a vest
un gilet de sauvetage = a lifejacket

girafe *noun, feminine*
une girafe = a giraffe

gîte *noun, masculine*
un gîte rural = a self-catering cottage

givrant *adjective, masculine*
du brouillard givrant = freezing fog

givre *noun, masculine*
le givre = frost

glace *noun, feminine*
• (*frozen water*)
la glace = ice
• (*a confection*)
la glace = ice cream
une glace à la vanille = a vanilla ice cream
• (*a looking glass*)
une glace = a mirror

glacé/glacée *adjective*
• = ice-cold
= frozen
• = glossy

glaçon *noun, masculine*
un glaçon = an ice cube

glisser *verb* 1
1 (! + *avoir*)
• = to slip
= to slide
• = to be slippery
2 se glisser (! + *être*)
se glisser dans = to slip into
= to sneak into
= to creep into

globe *noun, masculine*
le globe (terrestre) = the globe, the Earth

gloire *noun, feminine*
la gloire = glory, fame

goal *noun, masculine*
un goal = a goalkeeper

gogo : **à gogo✗** *adverb*
à gogo✗ = galore

golfe *noun, masculine*
un golfe = a gulf

gomme *noun, feminine*
• une gomme = a rubber, an eraser
• la gomme = gum

gonflé/gonflée *adjective*
• = inflated
• = swollen
• être gonflé✗ = to have a nerve
= to have guts

gonfler *verb* 1
• = to inflate
• = to swell (up)

gorge *noun, feminine*
la gorge = the throat
avoir mal à la gorge = to have a sore throat
avoir la gorge serrée = to have a lump in
one's throat

gorgée *noun, feminine*
une gorgée = a sip
= a gulp

gorille *noun, masculine*
• un gorille = a gorilla
• un gorille✗ = a bodyguard

gosse✗ *noun, masculine|feminine*
un gosse✗/une gosse✗ = a kid, a child

goudron *noun, masculine*
le goudron = tar

goudronner *verb* 1
= to tarmac, to blacktop

gourde *noun, feminine*
une gourde = a gourd
= a flask

gourmand/gourmande *adjective*
être gourmand = to be fond of good food
(*to like sweet things*) = to have a sweet
tooth

goût *noun, masculine*
le goût = taste

goûter
1 *verb* 1
= to taste
2 *noun, masculine*
• le goûter = an afternoon snack
• un goûter = a children's party

goutte *noun, feminine*
une goutte = a drop
goutte à goutte = drop by drop

grâce
1 *noun, feminine*
la grâce = grace
2 grâce à = thanks to

✗ in informal situations

gradins noun, masculine plural
les gradins = the terraces, the bleachers

graine noun, feminine
une graine = a seed

graisse noun, feminine
la graisse (in food) = fat
(for machinery) = grease

graisser verb [1]
= to grease
= to lubricate

grammaire noun, feminine
la grammaire = grammar

gramme noun, masculine
un gramme = a gram

grand/grande
1 adjective
• = tall
= big, large
= long
Théo est grand = Théo is tall
un grand jardin = a large garden
un grand voyage = a long journey
il n'y avait pas grand monde = there
weren't many people
faire de grands gestes = to wave one's
arms around
• = great
un grand homme = a great man
un train à grande vitesse = a high-speed
train
2 **grand** adverb
= wide
grand ouvert = wide open
voir grand = to think big
le grand bassin = the main pool
un grand magasin = a department store
le grand public = the general public
une grande personne = a grown-up
une grande surface = a supermarket
les grandes lignes = main train routes
les grandes vacances = the summer
holidays, the summer vacation

grand-chose pronoun
pas grand-chose = not much, not a lot
ça ne sert pas à grand-chose = it's not
much use

Grande-Bretagne noun, feminine
la Grande-Bretagne = Great Britain

grandir verb [3]
= to grow

grand-mère noun, feminine
(plural) **grands-mères**
une grand-mère = a grandmother

grand-père noun, masculine
(plural) **grands-pères**
un grand-père = a grandfather

grands-parents noun, masculine plural
des grands-parents = grandparents

grange noun, feminine
une grange = a barn

granulé noun, masculine
un granulé = a granule

graphique
1 adjective
= graphic
2 noun, masculine
un graphique = a graph

grappe noun, feminine
une grappe = a bunch
= a cluster

gras/grasse
1 adjective
• = greasy
= fatty
• = fat
• (if it's a letter) = bold
2 **gras** noun, masculine (**!** never changes)
le gras (on meat) = fat

gratin noun, masculine
un gratin = a gratin (a dish topped with
browned cheese and breadcrumbs)
un gratin de pommes de terre = potatoes
au gratin

gratis
1 adjective (**!** never changes)
= free
2 adverb
= free, for free

gratter verb [1]
1 (**!** + avoir)
• = to scratch
= to scrape (off)
• ça me gratte partout = I'm itching all over
2 **se gratter** (**!** + être)
se gratter = to scratch

gratuit/gratuite adjective
= free

gratuitement adverb
= free, for free
travailler gratuitement = to work for
nothing

grave adjective
• = serious
• = grave, solemn
• une voix grave = a deep voice

gravement adverb
• = seriously
• = gravely, solemnly

gravier noun, masculine
du gravier = gravel

gravillon noun, masculine
un gravillon = a bit of grit, some grit

grec/grecque
1 adjective
= Greek
2 **grec** noun, masculine
le grec = Greek

G

Grèce noun, feminine
la Grèce = Greece

grecque ▶ grec 1

grêle noun, feminine
la grêle = hail
il tombe de la grêle = it's hailing

grêlon noun, masculine
un grêlon = a hailstone

grelotter verb 1
= to shiver

grenier noun, masculine
un grenier = an attic, a loft

grenouille noun, feminine
une grenouille = a frog

grève noun, feminine
• (at work)
une grève = a strike
faire grève = to go on strike
• (by the sea)
la grève = the shore
une grève de la faim = a hunger strike

griffe noun, feminine
une griffe = a claw

griffer verb 1
= to scratch

grignoter verb 1
= to nibble

grillade noun, feminine
une grillade = grilled meat

grillage noun, masculine
le grillage = wire netting

grille noun, feminine
• (in a garden)
une grille = a gate
• (for a crossword)
une grille = a grid

grille-pain noun, masculine (**!** never changes)
un grille-pain = a toaster

griller verb 1
• (in cooking)
(faire) griller = to grill
= to toast
• griller✗ un feu = to go through a red light

grimace noun, feminine
une grimace = a (funny) face
faire des grimaces = to make faces
faire la grimace devant un plat = to turn one's nose up at a dish

grimper verb 1
= to climb

grippe noun, feminine
la grippe = flu

──────────
✗ in informal situations

gris/grise adjective
• = grey, gray
• = dull, dreary
un temps gris = dull weather

grive noun, feminine
une grive = a thrush

grognon adjective
= grumpy, grouchy

gros/grosse
1 adjective
• = big
• = heavy
un gros fumeur = a heavy smoker
2 gros adverb
• écrire gros = to write in big letters
• perdre gros = to lose a lot
3 gros noun, masculine (**!** never changes)
• le gros du travail = the bulk of the work
• le prix de gros = the wholesale price
4 en gros
• en gros = roughly
• en gros = wholesale
• en gros = in big letters
le gros lot = the first prize
un gros mot = a swearword
les gros titres = the headlines

groseille noun, feminine
une groseille = a redcurrant
une groseille à maquereau = a gooseberry

grosse ▶ gros 1

grossier/grossière adjective
• = rude
• = coarse

grotte noun, feminine
une grotte = a cave
= a grotto

groupe noun, masculine
un groupe = a group
un groupe scolaire = a school

guépard noun, masculine
un guépard = a cheetah

guêpe noun, feminine
une guêpe = a wasp

guère adverb
= hardly
il n'avait guère le choix = he didn't really have a choice

guérir verb 3
= to cure
= to heal
= to recover

guerre noun, feminine
une guerre = a war

guetter verb 1
= to watch
= to watch out for

gueule *noun, feminine*
　une gueule = a mouth
　avoir une grande gueule✱ = to have a big
　　mouth

gui *noun, masculine*
　le gui = mistletoe

guichet *noun, masculine*
　un guichet (*in a bank, a post office*) = a
　　counter
　= a window
　(*in a museum, a station*) = a ticket office
　(*in a theatre, a cinema*) = a box office
un guichet automatique = an automatic
　cash dispenser

guide *noun, masculine*
　un guide = a guide

guidon *noun, masculine*
　le guidon = the handlebars

guignol *noun, masculine*
　un guignol = a puppet show

guillemets *noun, masculine plural*
　des guillemets = inverted commas
　= quotation marks

guitare *noun, feminine*
　une guitare = a guitar

gym✱ *noun, feminine*
• (*at school*)
　la gym✱ = physical education
• (*as a sport*)
　la gym✱ = gymnastics

gymnase *noun, masculine*
　un gymnase = a gymnasium

gymnastique *noun, feminine*
　la gymnastique (*the sport*) = gymnastics
　(*to keep fit*) = exercise

habile *adjective*
　= clever
　= skil(l)ful

habiller *verb* ⊡
1 (**!** + *avoir*)
　= to dress
2 s'habiller (**!** + *être*)
　s'habiller = to get dressed
　= to dress up

habitant/habitante *noun,*
masculine/feminine
　un habitant/une habitante = an inhabitant

habiter *verb* ⊡
　= to live (in)
　habiter la campagne = to live in the
　　country
　habiter à Paris = to live in Paris

habitude
1 *noun, feminine*
　une habitude = a habit
　avoir l'habitude de se lever tôt = to be in
　　the habit of getting up early
　= to be used to getting up early
　avoir l'habitude des enfants = to be used
　　to children
2 d'habitude = usually
　comme d'habitude = as usual

habituel/habituelle *adjective*
　= usual

haché/hachée *adjective*
　= minced
　= chopped

hachis *noun, masculine* (**!** *never changes*)
　le hachis = mince, ground meat
le hachis Parmentier = shepherd's pie

haie *noun, feminine*
　une haie = a hedge

haleine *noun, feminine*
　l'haleine = the breath
　hors d'haleine = out of breath

halte *noun, feminine*
　une halte (*a pause*) = a stop
　(*a place*) = a stopping place
　faire halte = to stop

haltérophilie *noun, feminine*
　l'haltérophilie = weightlifting

hameau *noun, masculine*
(*plural*) **hameaux**
　un hameau = a hamlet

hameçon *noun, masculine*
　un hameçon = a fish-hook

hanche *noun, feminine*
　une hanche = a hip

handicapé/handicapée
1 *adjective*
　= handicapped
2 *noun, masculine/feminine*
　un handicapé/une handicapée = a
　　handicapped person

hanté/hantée *adjective*
　= haunted

hareng *noun, masculine*
　un hareng = a herring

haricot *noun, masculine*
　un haricot = a bean
　les haricots verts = French beans

hasard *noun, masculine*
　le hasard = chance
　un hasard = a coincidence

H

hâte *noun, feminine*
• la hâte = haste
à la hâte = hastily
• j'ai hâte de partir = I can't wait to leave

hausse *noun, feminine*
une hausse = a rise, an increase

hausser *verb* 1
= to raise
hausser les épaules = to shrug one's
shoulders

haut/haute
1 *adjective*
• = high
= tall
• à haute voix = aloud
= loudly
2 haut *adverb*
• = high
haut les mains! = hands up!
• = loud(ly)
tout haut = aloud
3 haut *noun, masculine*
• le haut = the top
les pièces du haut = the upstairs rooms
• faire 15 mètres de haut = to be 15 metres
high
4 en haut = at the top
= upstairs

hauteur *noun, masculine*
la hauteur = the height

Haye *noun, feminine*
la Haye = the Hague

hebdomadaire *adjective*
= weekly

hébergement *noun, masculine*
l'hébergement = accommodation, lodging

héberger *verb* 13
= to put up

hein* *exclamation*
• hein*? = what?
• tu n'iras pas, hein*? = you won't go, will
you?

hélas *exclamation*
hélas! = unfortunately!

hélice *noun, feminine*
une hélice = a propeller

hélicoptère *noun, masculine*
un hélicoptère = a helicopter

herbe *noun, feminine*
• de l'herbe = grass
• une herbe = a(n) herb
• une mauvaise herbe = a weed

hérisson *noun, masculine*
un hérisson = a hedgehog

héritage *noun, masculine*
un héritage = an inheritance

hériter *verb* 1
= to inherit

héritier/héritière *noun,*
masculine/feminine
un héritier/une héritière = an heir/an
heiress

héros *noun, masculine* (! *never changes*)
un héros = a hero

hésiter *verb* 1
= to hesitate

heure *noun, feminine*
• l'heure = the time
quelle heure est-il? = what time is it?
il est huit heures = it's eight o'clock
il est huit heures dix = it's ten past eight
il est huit heures moins dix = it's ten to
eight
l'heure du déjeuner = lunchtime
être à l'heure = to be on time
de bonne heure = early
mettre sa montre à l'heure = to set one's
watch
• une heure = an hour
toutes les trois heures = every three hours
faire du 100 à l'heure* = to do 100 km per
hour
les heures d'affluence = peak times
les heures de pointe = the rush hour
les heures supplémentaires = overtime

heureuse ▶ heureux

heureusement *adverb*
= fortunately
= luckily

heureux/heureuse *adjective*
= happy

heurter *verb* 1
= to bump into
= to hit, to crash into

hibou *noun, masculine*
(*plural*) **hiboux**
un hibou = an owl

hier *adverb*
= yesterday
hier soir = yesterday evening

hippodrome *noun, masculine*
un hippodrome = a racecourse

hippopotame *noun, masculine*
un hippopotame = a hippopotamus

hirondelle *noun, feminine*
une hirondelle = a swallow

histoire *noun, feminine*
• l'histoire = history
• une histoire = a story
• faire des histoires* = to make trouble

---

* in informal situations

historique *adjective*
• = historic
• = historical

hit-parade *noun, masculine*
(*plural*) **hit-parades**
le hit-parade = the charts

hiver *noun, masculine*
l'hiver = winter

HLM *noun, masculine or feminine*
un(e) HLM ≈ a council flat, a low-rent
  apartment
= a block of council flats, a low-rent
  apartment building

hocher *verb* [1]
hocher la tête (*in agreement*) = to nod
(*to say no*) = to shake one's head

hollandais/hollandaise
1 *adjective*
= Dutch
2 hollandais *noun, masculine*
le hollandais = Dutch

Hollande *noun, feminine*
la Hollande = Holland

homard *noun, masculine*
un homard = a lobster

homme *noun, masculine*
un homme = a man
un homme d'affaires = a businessman

Hongrie *noun, feminine*
la Hongrie = Hungary

hongrois/hongroise
1 *adjective*
= Hungarian
2 hongrois *noun, masculine*
le hongrois = Hungarian

honnête *adjective*
= honest

honoraire
1 *adjective*
= honorary
2 honoraires *noun, masculine plural*
les honoraires = the fee(s)

honte *noun, feminine*
la honte = shame
avoir honte = to be ashamed

hôpital *noun, masculine*
(*plural*) **hôpitaux**
un hôpital = a hospital

hoquet *noun, masculine*
le hoquet = hiccoughs, hiccups

horaire *noun, masculine*
un horaire = a timetable
**les horaires à la carte, les horaires
libres** = flexitime, flextime

horizon *noun, masculine*
l'horizon = the horizon
à l'horizon = on the horizon

horizontal/horizontale *adjective*
(*plural*) **horizontaux/horizontales**
= horizontal, flat

horizontalement *adverb*
• = horizontally
• (*in a crossword*) = across

horloge *noun, feminine*
une horloge = a clock

horloger/horlogère *noun,
masculine/feminine*
un horloger/une horlogère = a
  watchmaker

horreur *noun, feminine*
• l'horreur = horror
quelle horreur! = how horrible!
= it's hideous!
• l'horreur = loathing
avoir horreur de laver la voiture = to loathe
  washing the car

horrible *adjective*
= awful, horrible

hors *preposition*
hors (de) = outside, out of
hors d'haleine = out of breath
hors jeu = offside
hors de prix = ridiculously expensive
hors (de) saison = out of season
'hors service' = 'out of order'
hors taxes, HT (*describing a shop*) = duty-
  free
(*describing a price*) = excluding tax
hors d'usage = worn out

hors-d'œuvre *noun, masculine* (**!** *never
changes*)
un hors-d'œuvre = a starter

hospitalité *noun, feminine*
l'hospitalité = hospitality

hôte
1 *noun, masculine*
un hôte = a host
2 *noun, masculine/feminine*
un hôte/une hôte = a guest

hôtel *noun, masculine*
un hôtel = a hotel
l'hôtel de ville = the town hall

hôtelier/hôtelière *noun,
masculine/feminine*
un hôtelier/une hôtelière = a hotel-keeper,
  a hotel manager

hôtesse *noun, feminine*
• (*a person who has guests*)
une hôtesse = a hostess
• (*a person who deals with customers*)
une hôtesse (*in a firm*) = a receptionist
(*on a train, a boat*) = a stewardess
une hôtesse d'accueil = a receptionist
une hôtesse de l'air = a flight attendant,
  an air hostess

H

houx *noun, masculine* (**!** *never changes*)
le houx = holly

HT ▶ hors

hublot *noun, masculine*
un hublot = a porthole

huile *noun, feminine*
l'huile = oil

huissier *noun, masculine*
un huissier (de justice) = a bailiff

huit *number*
= eight
huit jours = a week
= eight days
lundi en huit = a week on Monday

huitaine *noun, feminine*
une huitaine = about a week
= about eight

huitante *number*
= eighty

huitième *number*
= eighth

huître *noun, feminine*
une huître = an oyster

humain/humaine *adjective*
• = human
• = humane

humeur *noun, feminine*
une humeur = a mood
être de bonne humeur = to be in a good mood
être de mauvaise humeur = to be in a bad mood

humide *adjective*
= damp
= humid

hurlement *noun, masculine*
un hurlement = a howl

hurler *verb* 1
= to howl

hydroglisseur *noun, masculine*
un hydroglisseur = a hydrofoil

hydrophile *adjective*
= absorbent

hygiénique *adjective*
le papier hygiénique = toilet paper

hyper* *adverb*
= extremely

hypermarché *noun, masculine*
un hypermarché = a hypermarket, a large supermarket

I i

ici *adverb*
= here
venez par ici = come this way

idéal/idéale *adjective*
(*plural*) **idéaux/idéales**
= ideal

idée *noun, feminine*
une idée = an idea

identifier *verb* 2
= to identify

identité *noun, feminine*
l'identité = identity

idiot/idiote
1 *adjective*
= stupid
2 *noun, masculine/feminine*
un idiot/une idiote = an idiot

ignorer *verb* 1
• = not to know
j'ignore où il habite = I don't know where he lives
• = to ignore

il *pronoun, masculine*
1 (*referring to a person, an animal or a thing*)
= he
= it
ils = they
2 (*impersonal use*)
• = it
il fait froid = it's cold
il est facile d'obtenir des billets = it's easy to get tickets
• il y a = there is
= there are
il y a une fuite = there is a leak
• (*when talking about time*)
il y a une heure que j'attends = I've been waiting for an hour
il y a un an qu'il est parti = he left a year ago

île *noun, feminine*
une île = an island
les îles Anglo-Normandes = the Channel Islands

illégal/illégale *adjective*
(*plural*) **illégaux/illégales**
= illegal

illettré/illettrée *adjective*
= illiterate

illimité/illimitée *adjective*
= unlimited

✗ in informal situations

illisible *adjective*
• = illegible
• = unreadable

illuminé/illuminée *adjective*
= lit up
= illuminated

illustre *adjective*
= illustrious

illustré *noun, masculine*
un illustré = an illustrated magazine
= a comic, a comic book

illustrer *verb* [1]
= to illustrate

ils *pronoun, masculine plural*
= they

image *noun, feminine*
une image = a picture
= an image

imaginaire *adjective*
= imaginary

imaginer *verb* [1]
= to imagine

imbattable *adjective*
= unbeatable

imbécile *noun, masculine/feminine*
un imbécile/une imbécile = an idiot
faire l'imbécile = to be silly

imiter *verb* [1]
= to imitate

immatriculation *noun, feminine*
l'immatriculation = registration
= the registration number

immédiatement *adverb*
= immediately

immense *adjective*
= huge
= great

immeuble *noun, masculine*
un immeuble = a building
= a block of flats, an apartment block

immigré/immigrée *adjective*
= immigrant

immobile *adjective*
= still

immobilier *noun, masculine*
l'immobilier = property, real estate

impair/impaire *adjective*
les nombres impairs = odd numbers

imparfait/imparfaite
1 *adjective*
= imperfect
2 **imparfait** *noun, masculine*
l'imparfait = the imperfect (tense)

impasse *noun, feminine*
une impasse = a cul-de-sac, a dead end

impatienter: **s'impatienter** [1]
(**!** + *être*)
s'impatienter = to get impatient

imper✶ *noun, masculine*
un imper✶ = a mac, a raincoat

imperméable
1 *noun, masculine*
un imperméable = a raincoat
2 *adjective*
= waterproof

impoli/impolie *adjective*
= impolite, rude

important/importante *adjective*
= important
= considerable
= sizeable

importer *verb* [1]
• = to import
• = to be important
il importe de [faire | dire | savoir ...] = it's
important to [do | say | know ...]
n'importe
n'importe lequel = any
n'importe où = anywhere
n'importe quel = any
n'importe qui = anybody
n'importe quoi = anything

impôt *noun, masculine*
un impôt = a tax

impressionnant/impressionnante
adjective
= impressive

impressionner *verb* [1]
= to impress

imprévu/imprévue *adjective*
= unexpected

imprimé/imprimée
1 *adjective*
= printed
2 **imprimé** *noun, masculine*
• (*paper*)
un imprimé = a leaflet
• (*on material*)
un imprimé = a print

imprimer *verb* [1]
= to print

imprimeur *noun, masculine*
un imprimeur = a printer

improviser *verb* [1]
= to improvise

improviste: **à l'improviste** *adverb*
à l'improviste = unexpectedly

imprudence *noun, feminine*
• l'imprudence = recklessness
• faire une imprudence = to do something
reckless

imprudent/imprudente *adjective*
= reckless

inabordable *adjective*
- (*describing a price*) = prohibitive, unaffordable
- (*describing a person*) = unapproachable

inadmissible *adjective*
= unacceptable

inattendu/inattendue *adjective*
= unexpected

incapable *adjective*
= incompetent
être incapable de conduire = to be incapable of driving
= to be unable to drive

incendie *noun, masculine*
un incendie = a fire

incident *noun, masculine*
un incident = an incident

inclus/incluse *adjective*
- = including
- = enclosed

inconnu/inconnue
1 *adjective*
= unknown
2 *noun, masculine/feminine*
un inconnu/une inconnue = a stranger
= an unknown man/woman

inconvénient *noun, masculine*
un inconvénient = a drawback, a disadvantage
si vous n'y voyez pas d'inconvénient = if you have no objection

incroyable *adjective*
= unbelievable

incroyablement *adverb*
= incredibly

inculpé/inculpée *noun, masculine/feminine*
l'inculpé/l'inculpée = the accused

inculper *verb* 1
= to charge
on l'a inculpé de meurtre = he's been charged with murder

Inde *noun, feminine*
l'Inde = India

indemne *adjective*
= unharmed

indépendant/indépendante *adjective*
= independent

index *noun, masculine* (**!** *never changes*)
l'index = the index finger, the forefinger

indicateur *noun, masculine*
- (*a book giving information*)
un indicateur (*for trains*) = a timetable
(*for streets*) = a directory
- (*an instrument*)
un indicateur = a gauge

indicatif *noun, masculine*
- (*when making a phone call*)
l'indicatif = the dialling code, the area code
- (*of a radio or TV programme*)
l'indicatif = the signature tune, the theme music
- (*in grammar*)
l'indicatif = the indicative

indice *noun, masculine*
un indice = a sign, an indication
(*in a police inquiry*) = a clue

indien/indienne *adjective*
= Indian

indigestion *noun, feminine*
une indigestion = a stomach upset

indigner : s'indigner *verb* 1 (**!** + *être*)
s'indigner = to be indignant

indiquer *verb* 1
- (*with one's hand*) = to indicate, to point to
- (*to give information*) = to tell
pouvez-vous m'indiquer la banque la plus proche? = could you tell me where the nearest bank is?
je leur ai indiqué le moyen d'entrer sans payer = I told them how to get in for free
il m'a indiqué un bon restaurant = he recommended a good restaurant
indiquez votre nom et votre adresse = give your name and address
- (*to display information*) = to show
le village n'est pas indiqué sur la carte = the village isn't shown on the map
- (*to be a sign or a clue*) = to suggest
rien n'indique qu'il changera d'avis = there's nothing to suggest that he'll change his mind

individu *noun, masculine*
un individu = an individual
= a person

individuel/individuelle *adjective*
= individual

industrie *noun, feminine*
l'industrie = industry

industriel/industrielle *adjective*
= industrial

inédit/inédite *adjective*
- = (previously) unpublished
- = new

infect/infecte *adjective*
= horrible, revolting

infecter : s'infecter *verb* 1 (**!** + *être*)
s'infecter = to become infected, to go septic

inférieur/inférieure *adjective*
- = lower
- = inferior

infirme
1 *adjective*
= disabled
2 *noun, masculine|feminine*
un infirme/une infirme = a disabled person

infirmerie *noun, feminine*
l'infirmerie = the sick bay

infirmier/infirmière *noun,*
masculine|feminine
un infirmier/une infirmière = a nurse

inflammable *adjective*
= flammable

infliger *verb* 13
= to inflict

informaticien/informaticienne
noun, masculine|feminine
un informaticien/une informaticienne = a
computer scientist

informations *noun, feminine plural*
les informations = the news

informatique *noun, feminine*
l'informatique = computer science,
computing

informer *verb* 1
1 (**!** + *avoir*)
= to inform
2 **s'informer** (**!** + *être*)
• **s'informer** = to keep oneself informed
• **s'informer de** = to enquire about

ingénieur *noun, masculine*
un ingénieur = an engineer

ingrat/ingrate *adjective*
• (*not thankful*) = ungrateful
• (*not pretty*) = unattractive

inhabité/inhabitée *adjective*
= uninhabited

inhabituel/inhabituelle *adjective*
= unusual

inhumer *verb* 1
= to bury

initiale *noun, feminine*
une initiale = an initial

injure *noun, feminine*
une injure = an insult

injuste *adjective*
= unfair

inquiet/inquiète *adjective*
= worried, anxious

inquiéter *verb* 14
1 (**!** + *avoir*)
= to worry
2 **s'inquiéter** (**!** + *être*)
s'inquiéter = to worry

inquiétude *noun, feminine*
l'inquiétude = worry

inscrire *verb* 42
1 (**!** + *avoir*)
• = to enrol(l), to register
• = to write down
2 **s'inscrire** (**!** + *être*)
s'inscrire = to register
= to enrol

inscrit/inscrite ▶ **inscrire** 42

insecte *noun, masculine*
un insecte = an insect

insolation *noun, feminine*
une insolation = sunstroke

insolent/insolente *adjective*
= insolent, cheeky

insomniaque *adjective*
= insomniac, unable to sleep

inspecter *verb* 1
= to inspect

inspecteur/inspectrice *noun,*
masculine|feminine
un inspecteur/une inspectrice = an
inspector
un inspecteur de police = a detective
constable, a police detective

inspirer *verb* 1
1 (**!** + *avoir*)
• = to inspire
• = to breathe in
2 **s'inspirer de** (**!** + *être*)
s'inspirer de = to be inspired by, to draw
one's inspiration from

installation
1 *noun, feminine*
• (*the fact of fitting*)
l'installation = installing, putting in
• (*going to new premises*)
une installation = a move
2 **installations** *noun, feminine plural*
des installations = facilities
des installations sanitaires = toilets

installer *verb* 1
1 (**!** + *avoir*)
• (*to fit*) = to install, to put in
(*if it's gas, water, electricity*) = to connect
faire installer le téléphone = to have the
telephone connected
• (*to position*)
installer une tente sous un arbre = to put
up a tent under a tree
installer un invité dans un fauteuil = to sit
a guest in an armchair
2 **s'installer** (**!** + *être*)
s'installer dans une ville = to settle in a
town
s'installer près du feu = to sit by the fire

instant *noun, masculine*
un instant = a moment
à chaque instant = constantly

instinctivement *adverb*
= instinctively

I

instituteur/institutrice noun, masculine/feminine
  un instituteur/une institutrice = a (primary school) teacher

instruction noun, feminine
• des instructions = instructions
• l'instruction = education
l'instruction civique = social studies
l'instruction religieuse = religious education

instrument noun, masculine
  un instrument = an instrument
un instrument de musique = a musical instrument

insuffisant/insuffisante adjective
  = insufficient

insulter verb 1
  = to insult

insupportable adjective
  = unbearable

intelligent/intelligente adjective
  = intelligent, clever

intention noun, feminine
  une intention = an intention
  avoir l'intention de voyager = to intend to travel

interdire verb 40
  = to forbid
  elle nous a interdit de sortir = she forbade us to go out

interdit/interdite adjective
  = forbidden, not allowed
  'baignade interdite' = 'no swimming'

intéressant/intéressante adjective
  = interesting

intéresser verb 1
1 (! + avoir)
  = to interest
  ça ne m'intéresse pas = I'm not interested
2 s'intéresser (! + être)
  s'intéresser à = to be interested in

intérêt noun, masculine
  un intérêt = an interest

intérieur/intérieure
1 adjective
  = inside
  = inner
2 extérieur noun, masculine
  l'intérieur = the inside
  à l'intérieur de la boîte = inside the box

internat noun, masculine
  un internat = a boarding school

interne
1 adjective
  = internal

2 noun, masculine/feminine
  un interne/une interne (a pupil) = a boarder, a boarding student

interprète noun, masculine/feminine
  un interprète/une interprète = an interpreter

interro* noun, feminine
(abbreviation of **interrogation**)
  une interro* = a test

interrogation noun, feminine
• (in class)
  une interrogation = a test
  une interrogation écrite = a written test
• (in grammar)
  une interrogation = a question

interroger verb 13
• = to question
• = to test

interviewer verb 1
  = to interview

intituler verb 1
1 (! + avoir)
  = to call, to entitle
2 s'intituler (! + être)
  s'intituler = to be called

intoxication noun, feminine
  une intoxication alimentaire = food poisoning

introduire verb 62
1 (! + avoir)
  = to insert
2 s'introduire dans (! + être)
  s'introduire dans (to go in) = to enter

intrus/intruse noun, masculine/feminine
• (a person)
  un intrus/une intruse = an intruder
• (in a game)
  'cherchez l'intrus' = 'spot the odd one out', 'pick the one that doesn't fit'

inutile adjective
  = useless
  = pointless

inutilisable adjective
  = unusable

inventer verb 1
• = to invent
• = to think up

inverse noun, masculine
  l'inverse = the opposite

invité/invitée noun, masculine/feminine
  un invité/une invitée = a guest

inviter verb 1
  = to invite

irai ▶ aller 1 9

irlandais/irlandaise
1 adjective
  = Irish

---

* in informal situations

2 irlandais noun, masculine
l'irlandais = Irish

Irlande noun, feminine
l'Irlande = Ireland
la République d'Irlande = the Republic of
Ireland
l'Irlande du Nord = Northern Ireland

irriter verb 1
= to irritate

islamique adjective
= Islamic

isolé/isolée adjective
= isolated
= lonely

issue noun, feminine
une issue = an exit, a way out
une issue de secours = an emergency exit
'voie sans issue' = 'no through road'

Italie noun, feminine
l'Italie = Italy

italien/italienne
1 adjective
= Italian
2 italien noun, masculine
l'italien = Italian

italique noun, masculine
en italique(s) = in italics

itinéraire noun, masculine
un itinéraire = a route, an itinerary
'itinéraire bis' = 'alternative route'

ivoire noun, masculine
l'ivoire = ivory

ivre adjective
= drunk

ivresse noun, feminine
l'ivresse = drunkenness, intoxication

ivrogne noun, masculine/feminine
un ivrogne/une ivrogne = a drunkard

Jj

j' ▶ **je**

jadis adverb
= in the past, a long time ago

jaloux/jalouse adjective
= jealous

jamaïcain/jamaïcaine adjective
= Jamaican

Jamaïque noun, feminine
la Jamaïque = Jamaica

jamais adverb
• (at no time) = never
= ever
il n'écrit jamais = he never writes
plus jamais = never again
rien n'est jamais certain = nothing is ever
certain
• (at any other time) = ever
il fait plus froid que jamais = it's colder
than ever

jambe noun, feminine
une jambe = a leg

jambon noun, masculine
le jambon = ham

janvier noun, masculine
janvier = January

Japon noun, masculine
le Japon = Japan

japonais/japonaise
1 adjective
= Japanese
2 japonais noun, masculine
le japonais = Japanese

jardin noun, masculine
un jardin = a garden, a yard
faire son jardin = to work in one's garden
un jardin potager = a vegetable garden
un jardin public = a park
un jardin zoologique = a zoo

jardinage noun, masculine
le jardinage = gardening

jardinier/jardinière noun,
masculine/feminine
un jardinier/une jardinière = a gardener

jaune adjective
= yellow

javelot noun, masculine
un javelot = a javelin

J.-C. (abbreviation of **Jésus-Christ**)
avant J.-C. = BC
après J.-C. = AD

je (**j'** before vowel or mute h) pronoun
= I

jean noun, masculine
un jean = (a pair of) jeans

jetable adjective
= disposable

jeter verb 20
= to throw (away)

jeton noun, masculine
un jeton = a counter

jeu noun, masculine
(plural) **jeux**
• (the activity)
un jeu = a game
faire un jeu = to play a game

J

• (*the equipment*)
un jeu = a set
un jeu d'échecs = a chess set
un jeu de mots = a pun
le jeu de l'oie ≈ snakes and ladders, chutes and ladders
un jeu de société = a board game = a party game
un jeu télévisé = a game show
les jeux Olympiques = the Olympic Games

jeudi *noun, masculine*
jeudi = Thursday

jeun: **à jeun** *adverb*
être à jeun = to have had nothing to eat

jeune
1 *adjective*
= young
2 *noun, masculine*
un jeune = a youth, a lad
les jeunes = young people
une jeune fille = a girl
un jeune homme = a young man

jeunesse *noun, feminine*
• (*the young years*)
la jeunesse = youth
• (*young boys and girls*)
la jeunesse = young people

jf (*abbreviation of* **jeune fille**)
= young woman

jh (*abbreviation of* **jeune homme**)
= young man

Joconde *noun, feminine*
la Joconde = the Mona Lisa

joie *noun, feminine*
la joie = joy

joindre *verb* 56
1 (**!** + *avoir*)
• (*to add*) = to attach
= to enclose
• (*to link, to fasten*) = to join
= to put together
• (*to make contact*) = to get hold of
= to get in touch with
2 se joindre à (**!** + *être*)
se joindre à = to join

joli/jolie *adjective*
= pretty, attractive
= nice

jongler *verb* 1
= to juggle

jongleur/jongleuse *noun, masculine/feminine*
un jongleur/une jongleuse = a juggler

jonquille *noun, feminine*
une jonquille = a daffodil

joue *noun, feminine*
une joue = a cheek

jouer *verb* 1
• = to play
jouer à [cache-cache | la marelle | colin-maillard ...] = to play [hide-and-seek | hopscotch | blind man's buff ...]
jouer aux cartes = to play cards
à quoi jouez-vous? = what are you playing?
jouer de [la guitare | la flûte | la harpe ...] = to play [the guitar | the flute | the harp ...]
jouer du piano = to play the piano
de quoi joue-t-il? = what does he play?
• = to gamble
• **qu'est-ce qu'on joue au théâtre?** = what's on at the theatre?, what's showing at the theater?

jouet *noun, masculine*
un jouet = a toy

joueur/joueuse *noun, masculine/feminine*
un joueur/une joueuse (*in a game, in sport*) = a player
(*at the casino*) = a gambler
être mauvais joueur = to be a bad loser

jour *noun, masculine*
• (*24 hours*)
un jour = a day
tous les jours = every day
par jour = per day
un jour de congé = a day off
il y a quinze jours = a fortnight ago, two weeks ago
de nos jours = nowadays
• (*the light*)
le jour = daylight
il fait jour = it's daylight
en plein jour = in broad daylight
voyager de jour = to travel by day, to travel in the daytime
le jour de l'An = New Year's (Day)
un jour férié = a bank holiday, a legal holiday
le jour J = D-day
un jour ouvrable = a working day

journal *noun, masculine*
(*plural*) **journaux**
• (*a publication*)
un journal = a newspaper
• (*a private record*)
un journal (**intime**) = a diary
le journal télévisé = the TV news

journaliste *noun, masculine/feminine*
un journaliste/une journaliste = a journalist

journée *noun, feminine*
une journée = a day
dans la journée = during the day

joyeux/joyeuse *adjective*
= happy

juger *verb* 13
= to judge

juif/juive
1 *adjective*
= Jewish
2 *noun, masculine/feminine*
un juif/une juive = a Jew

juillet *noun, masculine*
juillet = July
le 14 juillet = Bastille Day

juin *noun, masculine*
juin = June

juive ▶ juif

jumeau/jumelle
(*plural*) **jumeaux/jumelles**
1 *adjective*
= twin
2 *noun, masculine/feminine*
un jumeau/une jumelle = a (male) twin/a (female) twin
des jumeaux/des jumelles = twins

jumelage *noun, masculine*
un jumelage = a (town) twinning

jumelé/jumelée *adjective*
= twinned
Oxford est jumelé avec Grenoble = the city of Oxford is twinned with Grenoble

jumelles *noun, feminine plural*
des jumelles = binoculars

jupe *noun, feminine*
une jupe = a skirt

jurer *verb* 1
= to swear

jus *noun, masculine* (**!** *never changes*)
• (*from fruit*)
du jus = juice
un jus de fruit = a fruit juice
• (*from a roast*)
le jus = the gravy

jusque (**jusqu'** *before vowel*)
1 *preposition*
• = as far as
aller jusqu'à Rome = to go as far as Rome
• = up to
= down to
de l'eau jusqu'à la taille = water up to the waist
se pencher jusqu'à terre = to bend down to the ground
• = until, till
jusqu'à lundi = until Monday
jusqu'à l'an 2000 = until the year 2000
jusqu'ici, jusqu'à présent = till now, up to now
2 jusqu'à ce que = until

juste
1 *adjective*
• = right, correct
une réponse juste = a correct answer
• = fair
ce n'est pas juste = it's not fair, it's unfair
• = tight
2 *adverb*
• **chanter juste** = to sing in tune
• **il est huit heures juste** = it's exactly eight o'clock
• **tout juste** = only just
il arrive juste = he's (only) just arrived
juste à temps = just in time
3 au juste = exactly

justement *adverb*
= exactly

kaki
1 *adjective* (**!** *never changes*)
= khaki
2 *noun, masculine*
un kaki = a persimmon

kangourou *noun, masculine*
un kangourou = a kangaroo

karting *noun, masculine*
le karting = go-karting

kayak *noun, masculine*
• (*the equipment*)
un kayak = a kayak
• (*the sport*)
le kayak = canoeing

kermesse *noun, feminine*
une kermesse = a fête, a festival

kilo, kilogramme *noun, masculine*
un kilo, un kilogramme = a kilo, a kilogram

kilomètre *noun, masculine*
un kilomètre = a kilometre, a kilometer

kiosque *noun, masculine*
un kiosque = a kiosk
un kiosque à journaux = a newspaper kiosk, a newsstand
un kiosque à musique = a bandstand

klaxon® *noun, masculine*
un klaxon = a (car) horn

klaxonner *verb* 1
= to sound one's horn, to honk the horn

KO adjective (**!** never changes)
(abbreviation of **knocked out**)
- = KO'ed
  mettre son adversaire KO = to KO one's
  opponent
- **je suis KO✗** = I'm exhausted

K-way® noun, masculine
  un K-way = a windcheater, a windbreaker

L1

l' ▶ **le**

la ▶ **le**

là adverb
- (indicating a place) = there
  j'habitais là = I used to live there
  passez par là = go that way
  c'est là qu'il est né = that's where he was
  born
  là où elle travaille = where she works
- (indicating a time) = then
  d'ici là j'aurai fini = by then, I'll have
  finished
  ce jour-là = that day
  en ce temps-là = in those days

là-bas adverb
  = over there

laboratoire noun, masculine
  un laboratoire = a laboratory

lac noun, masculine
  un lac = a lake

lacet noun, masculine
- (for shoes)
  un lacet = a lace
- (in a road)
  un lacet = a hairpin bend, a hairpin turn
  une route en lacets = a twisting road

lâcher verb 1
- (to stop holding) = to drop
  = to let go of
- (to collapse) = to give way
- (to stop working) = to fail

là-dedans adverb
  = in there

là-dessous adverb
  = under there, under it

là-dessus adverb
- (on a surface) = there, on it
- (on a subject) = about it

✗ in informal situations

là-haut adverb
  = up there
  = upstairs

laid/laide adjective
  = ugly

laine noun, feminine
  la laine = wool
  de laine, en laine = wool(l)en, wool

laisse noun, feminine
  une laisse = a leash

laisser verb 1
1 (**!** + avoir)
- = to leave
  laisser sa voiture à l'ombre = to leave one's
  car in the shade
  laissez-moi tranquille! = leave me alone!
- = to let
  laisser couler l'eau = to let the water run
  laisser tomber un verre = to drop a glass
2 se laisser (**!** + être)
- **se laisser influencer** = to allow oneself to
  be influenced
- **se laisser tomber sur le sable** = to flop
  down on the sand

lait noun, masculine
  le lait = milk
  le lait en poudre = powdered milk
  le lait solaire = suntan lotion

laitier/laitière
1 adjective
  les produits laitiers = dairy products
  une vache laitière = a dairy cow
2 noun, masculine/feminine
  un laitier/une laitière = a milkman/a
  milkwoman

laitue noun, feminine
  une laitue = a (head of) lettuce

lame noun, feminine
  une lame = a blade
  une lame de rasoir = a razor blade

lamentable adjective
  = pitiful
  = awful

lampadaire noun, masculine
  un lampadaire (in a house) = a standard
  lamp, a floor lamp
  (in the street) = a streetlamp, a streetlight

lampe noun, feminine
  une lampe = a lamp
  une lampe de chevet = a bedside lamp
  une lampe électrique = a torch, a
  flashlight
  une lampe de poche = a pocket torch, a
  flashlight

lancer verb 12
1 (**!** + avoir)
- = to throw
- = to launch
2 se lancer (**!** + être)

- (*to jump*)
  se lancer = to throw oneself
- (*to dare*)
  se lancer = to take the plunge
- (*to start*)
  se lancer dans les affaires = to go into business

langage *noun, masculine*
un langage = a language

langouste *noun, feminine*
une langouste = a rock lobster

langue *noun, feminine*
- la langue = the tongue
- une langue = a language
la langue maternelle = the mother tongue
les langues vivantes = modern languages

languir *verb* [3]
1 (**!** + *avoir*)
languir de revoir un ami = to be longing to see a friend
2 se languir de (**!** + *être*)
se languir de = to be pining for

lapin *noun, masculine*
- un lapin = a rabbit
- poser un lapin✱ à quelqu'un = to stand someone up

laquelle ▶ lequel

large
1 *adjective*
= wide
2 *noun, masculine*
- faire trois mètres de large = to be three metres wide
- le large = the open sea
  au large de la Bretagne = off the coast of Brittany

largement *adverb*
avoir largement le temps = to have plenty of time
c'est largement suffisant = it's more than enough

largeur *noun, feminine*
la largeur = the width

larme *noun, feminine*
une larme = a tear

las/lasse *adjective*
= tired, weary

lassant/lassante *adjective*
= tedious
= tiresome

lasser: **se lasser de** *verb* [1] (**!** + *être*)
se lasser de = to grow tired of

latin *noun, masculine*
le latin = Latin

laurier *noun, masculine*
le laurier = laurel
= bay
une feuille de laurier = a bay leaf

lavable *adjective*
= washable

lavabo *noun, masculine*
un lavabo = a washbasin, a wash-hand basin

lavage *noun, masculine*
le lavage = washing

lavande *noun, feminine*
la lavande = lavender

lave-linge *noun, masculine* (**!** *never changes*)
un lave-linge = a washing machine

laver *verb* [1]
1 (**!** + *avoir*)
= to wash
2 se laver (**!** + *être*)
se laver = to wash oneself
se laver les mains = to wash one's hands

laverie *noun, feminine*
une laverie (automatique) = a launderette, a laundromat

lave-vaisselle *noun, masculine* (**!** *never changes*)
un lave-vaisselle = a dishwasher

le/la (**l'** *before vowel or mute h*)
(*plural*) **les**
1 *determiner*
- = the
  la fenêtre de la cuisine = the kitchen window
  les Martin = the Martins
- (*not translated in some cases*)
  apprendre le russe = to learn Russian
  aimer le café = to like coffee
  les enfants aiment les animaux = children like animals
- = a
  20 francs le kilo = 20 francs a kilo
  cent kilomètres à l'heure = one hundred kilometres an hour
- (*used with nouns relating to a part of the body*)
  avoir les yeux bleus = to have blue eyes
  se casser la jambe = to break one's leg
  il m'a serré la main = he shook my hand
- (*used with a day of the week*)
  travailler le lundi = to work on Mondays
  tous les mardis = every Tuesday
2 *pronoun*
- (*referring to a person, an animal or a thing*)
  = him/her
  = it
  (*plural*) = them
  il l'a invitée = he invited her
  où les as-tu achetés? = where did you buy them?

L

- (*other cases*)
  comme vous le savez = as you know
  je te l'avais dit = I told you
  il ne peut pas te le dire = he can't tell you
  espérons-le! = let's hope so!

lécher *verb* ⓵
= to lick

leçon *noun, feminine*
une leçon = a lesson

lecteur/lectrice
1 *noun, masculine/feminine*
un lecteur/une lectrice = a reader
2 lecteur *noun, masculine*
un lecteur de cassettes = a cassette player
un lecteur laser = a CD player

lecture *noun, feminine*
la lecture = reading

légendaire *adjective*
= legendary

légende *noun, feminine*
- (*a story*)
  une légende = a legend
- (*on a picture, a cartoon*)
  la légende = the caption
- (*on a map*)
  la légende = the key

léger/légère *adjective*
- (*not heavy*) = light
- (*not serious*) = slight
- (*not strong*)
  un café léger = a weak coffee
  une cigarette légère = a mild cigarette
  un vent léger = a light wind

légèrement *adverb*
= slightly

légume *noun, masculine*
un légume = a vegetable

lendemain *noun, masculine*
le lendemain = the next day, the following day
le lendemain matin = the next morning
le lendemain de mon arrivée = the day after I arrived

lent/lente *adjective*
= slow

lentement *adverb*
= slowly

lentille *noun, feminine*
- (*food*)
  des lentilles = lentils
- (*optical device*)
  une lentille = a lens
  les lentilles de contact = contact lenses

lequel/laquelle *pronoun*
(*plural*) **lesquels/lesquelles**
- = which one

lequel d'entre eux a payé? = which one of them paid?
lesquelles veux-tu? = which ones do you want?
- = which
  la situation dans laquelle je me trouve = the situation in which I find myself

les ▶ le

lesquels/lesquelles ▶ lequel

lessive *noun, feminine*
la lessive = the washing, the laundry

lettre *noun, feminine*
une lettre = a letter
en toutes lettres = in full

leur
1 *determiner*
= their
leur jardin = their garden
leurs sacs = their bags
2 *pronoun* (! *never changes*)
= them
il leur a prêté sa voiture = he lent them his car
je la leur ai envoyée = I sent it to them
3 *pronoun*
le leur/la leur/les leurs = theirs

levée *noun, feminine*
une levée (*from a post-box*) = a collection

lever
1 *verb* ⓰ (! + *avoir*)
= to raise
levez les bras = raise your arms
lever le doigt (*in class*) ≈ to put up one's hand
2 se lever *verb* ⓰ (! + *être*)
- (*if it's a person*)
  se lever = to get up
  = to stand up
- (*if it's the sun, the wind*)
  se lever = to rise
3 *noun, masculine*
au lever = when one gets up
= on getting up
le lever du soleil = sunrise

lèvre *noun, feminine*
une lèvre = a lip

levure *noun, feminine*
la levure = yeast
la levure chimique = baking powder

lexique *noun, masculine*
un lexique = a vocabulary list

libérer *verb* ⓮
= to release, to free

liberté *noun, feminine*
la liberté = freedom

libraire *noun, masculine/feminine*
un libraire/une libraire = a bookseller

librairie *noun, feminine*
une librairie = a bookshop, a bookstore

libre *adjective*
• = free
ils sont libres d'y aller = they're free to go
'entrée libre' = 'admission free'
• = clear
la route est libre = the road is clear
• = vacant
une place libre = a vacant seat
• la ligne n'est pas libre = the line is
engaged, the line is busy

librement *adverb*
= freely

libre-service *noun, masculine*
(*plural*) **libres-services**
un libre-service = a self-service

licence *noun, feminine*
une licence (*a diploma*) = a degree

licencier *verb* 2
= to dismiss, to lay off
= to make redundant, to let go

lien *noun, masculine*
un lien = a tie
= a bond
= a link

lieu *noun, masculine*
(*plural*) **lieux**
1 un lieu = a place
un lieu de rencontre = a meeting place
votre lieu de naissance = your place of
birth
2 avoir lieu = to take place
3 au lieu de = instead of

lièvre *noun, masculine*
un lièvre = a hare

ligne *noun, feminine*
une ligne = a line

lilas *noun, masculine* (**!** *never changes*)
le lilas = lilac

limande *noun, feminine*
une limande (*a fish*) = a dab

limonade *noun, feminine*
la limonade = lemonade

linge *noun, masculine*
• (*sheets, towels*)
le linge (de maison) = (household) linen
le linge sale = dirty linen
• (*when being laundered*)
le linge = the washing, the laundry
avoir du linge à laver = to have some
washing to do

lion *noun, masculine*
un lion = a lion

Lion *noun, masculine*
le Lion = Leo

liquide *noun, masculine*
• un liquide = a liquid
• payer en liquide = to pay cash

lire[1] *verb* 41
= to read

lire[2] *noun, feminine*
la lire = the lira

lisse *adjective*
= smooth

liste *noun, feminine*
une liste = a list
une liste d'attente = a waiting list
être sur liste rouge = to be ex-directory, to
have an unlisted number

lit *noun, masculine*
un lit = a bed
un lit de camp = a camp bed
un grand lit = a double bed
des lits superposés = bunk beds

litre *noun, masculine*
un litre = a litre, a liter

littérature *noun, feminine*
la littérature = literature

littoral *noun, masculine*
(*plural*) **littoraux**
le littoral = the coast

livraison *noun, feminine*
une livraison = a delivery

livre
1 *noun, masculine*
un livre = a book
2 *noun, feminine*
une livre = a pound

livrer *verb* 1
= to deliver

livret *noun, masculine*
un livret = a booklet
un livret de famille = a family record
book (*of births, marriages and deaths*)
un livret scolaire = a school report book

local/locale
(*plural*) **locaux/locales**
1 *adjective*
= local
2 local *noun, masculine*
un local = a place

locataire *noun, masculine|feminine*
un locataire/une locataire = a tenant

location *noun, feminine*
la location (*of accommodation*) = renting
(*of equipment*) = hiring
(*of seats*) = booking, reservation
'location de voitures' = 'car hire', 'car
rental'

loge *noun, feminine*
• (*for a caretaker*)
une loge = a lodge

L

- *(for an actor)*
  une loge = a dressing room

logé/logée *adjective*
= housed
être logé et nourri = to have room and
  board

logement *noun, masculine*
- **un logement** = accommodation
  = a flat, an apartment
- **le logement** = housing

loger *verb* 13
1 (**!** + *avoir*)
- *(to provide accommodation)* = to house
  (for a short time) = to put up
- *(to have accommodation)* = to live
  (for a short time) = to stay
2 se loger (**!** + *être*)
trouver à se loger = to find somewhere to
  live

logique *adjective*
= logical

loi *noun, feminine*
une loi = a law

loin *adverb*
- = a long way, far (away)
  c'est trop loin = it's too far
  c'est encore loin? = is it much further?
- **de loin** = from a distance
- **au loin** = in the distance

lointain/lointaine *adjective*
= distant

loisir *noun, masculine plural*
- *(spare time)*
  le loisir = leisure
- *(activity)*
  un loisir = a leisure activity, a pastime

Londres *noun*
= London

long/longue
1 *adjective*
= long
2 long *noun, masculine*
faire deux mètres de long = to be two
  metres long
marcher de long en large = to pace up and
  down
3 le long de = along

longer *verb* 13
= to follow

longtemps *adverb*
= (for) a long time
il y a longtemps qu'il est parti = he left a
  long time ago
ça fait longtemps que tu attends? = have
  you been waiting long?

longue ▶ long

longuement *adverb*
= for a long time

longueur *noun, feminine*
la longueur = the length
à longueur de journée = all day long

lorsque (**lorsqu'** *before vowel or mute h*)
conjunction
= (at the time) when

loterie *noun, feminine*
une loterie = a lottery

lotissement *noun, masculine*
un lotissement = a housing estate, a
  housing development

loto *noun, masculine*
le loto = lotto
= bingo

louche
1 *adjective*
= shady
2 *noun, feminine*
une louche = a ladle

louer *verb* 1
- *(as the owner)* = to rent out
  'à louer' = 'to let', 'for rent'
- *(as the tenant)* = to rent
  (as the hirer) = to hire, to rent

loufoque* *adjective*
= crazy

loup *noun, masculine*
un loup = a wolf

loupe *noun, feminine*
une loupe = a magnifying glass

lourd/lourde *adjective*
- *(weighty)* = heavy
- *(describing the weather)* = muggy, sultry
  il fait lourd = it's muggy

loyer *noun, masculine*
le loyer = the rent

lu/lue ▶ lire¹ 41

lucarne *noun, feminine*
une lucarne = a skylight

lueur *noun, feminine*
une lueur = a (faint) light
= a glow
= a gleam, a flash

luge *noun, feminine*
- *(the equipment)*
  une luge = a toboggan, a sled
- *(the sport)*
  la luge = tobogganing

✻ in informal situations

lui
1 *pronoun, masculine*
* = him
  à cause de lui = because of him
  la voiture est à lui = the car belongs to
    him, the car is his
  c'est à lui de jouer = it's his turn to play
* = he
  elle est restée, mais lui est parti = she
    stayed, but he left
2 *pronoun, feminine*
  = her
  je lui ai prêté ma robe = I lent her my dress

lui-même *pronoun, masculine*
  = himself
  = itself

luire *verb* 62
  = to shine, to glow

luisant/luisante *adjective*
  = shining, glowing

lumière *noun, feminine*
  la lumière = light

lunch *noun, masculine*
  un lunch = a buffet lunch

lundi *noun, masculine*
  lundi = Monday

lune *noun, feminine*
  la lune = the moon

lunette
1 *noun, feminine*
  une lunette = a telescope
2 lunettes *noun, feminine plural*
  des lunettes = glasses, spectacles
  des lunettes de soleil = sunglasses

lustrer *verb* 1
  = to polish

lutin *noun, masculine*
  un lutin = an imp

lutte *noun, feminine*
* (*a fight*)
  une lutte = a struggle
* (*the sport*)
  la lutte = wrestling

lutter *verb* 1
  = to fight
  = to struggle

luxe *noun, masculine*
  le luxe = luxury

Luxembourg *noun, masculine*
  le Luxembourg = Luxembourg

lycée *noun, masculine*
  un lycée = a secondary school, ≈ a senior
    high school (*for students aged 15 to 18*)

lycéen/lycéenne *noun,*
masculine/feminine
  un lycéen/une lycéenne = a secondary
    school student, a high school student
    (*aged 15 to 18*)

m *noun, masculine* (**!** *never changes*)
(*abbreviation of* **mètre**)
  m = m

m' ▶ **me**

M. (*abbreviation of* **Monsieur**)
  M. = Mr

ma ▶ **mon**

macaron *noun, masculine*
  un macaron = a macaroon

macédoine *noun, feminine*
* **une macédoine de légumes** = mixed diced
  vegetables
* **une macédoine de fruits** = a fruit salad

machin✗ *noun, masculine*
  un machin✗ = a thing, a what's it

machine *noun, feminine*
  une machine = a machine
  une machine à coudre = a sewing
    machine
  une machine à écrire = a typewriter
  une machine à laver = a washing
    machine
  une machine à sous = a one-armed
    bandit

maçon *noun, masculine*
  un maçon = a bricklayer
    = a mason
    = a builder

madame *noun, feminine*
(*plural*) **mesdames**
  Madame Martin = Mrs Martin
  bonjour madame = good morning
  mesdames et messieurs = ladies and
    gentlemen

mademoiselle *noun, feminine*
(*plural*) **mesdemoiselles**
  Mademoiselle Martin = Miss Martin
  bonjour mademoiselle = good morning
  mesdames, mesdemoiselles et messieurs
    = ladies and gentlemen

magasin *noun, masculine*
  un magasin = a shop, a store
un grand magasin = a deparment store

magazine *noun, masculine*
  un magazine = a magazine

magique *adjective*
  = magic

magnétophone *noun, masculine*
  un magnétophone = a tape recorder

magnétoscope *noun, masculine*
  un magnétoscope = a video recorder

M

magnifique *adjective*
  = magnificent
  = wonderful

mai *noun, masculine*
  mai = May
  le 1er Mai = May Day

maigre *adjective*
• = thin
• = lean

maigrir *verb* ③
  = to lose weight

maillot *noun, masculine*
  un maillot (*for a dancer*) = a leotard
  (*in football*) = a shirt, a jersey
  (*for cyclists*) = a jersey
un maillot de corps = a vest, an
  undershirt
un maillot de bain = a swimsuit

main *noun, feminine*
  une main = a hand
  fait (à la) main = handmade
  se donner la main = to hold hands
  se serrer la main = to shake hands
  je vais te donner un coup de main = I'll
    give you a hand
  haut les mains! = hands up!

maintenant *adverb*
  = now
  = nowadays

maire *noun, masculine*
  le maire = the mayor

mairie *noun, feminine*
  la mairie = the town hall

mais *conjunction*
  = but

maïs *noun, masculine* (**!** *never changes*)
  le maïs = maize, corn
  = sweetcorn

maison
1 *adjective* (**!** *never changes*)
  = homemade
2 *noun, feminine*
  la maison = the house
  = home
  rester à la maison = to stay at home
  une maison de campagne = a house in
    the country
  une maison de la culture = a
    community arts centre
  **une maison des jeunes (et de la
    culture)** = a youth club
  une maison de retraite = a retirement
    home

maître/maîtresse *noun, masculine/
feminine*

• (*in a school*)
  le maître/la maîtresse = the teacher
• (*of a pet*)
  le maître/la maîtresse = the master/the
    mistress

majeur/majeure *adjective*
• = major, main
  en majeure partie = for the most part
• être majeur = to be over 18 years of age

mal
1 *adjective* (**!** *never changes*)
  = bad
  c'est mal de mentir = it's bad to lie
  les photos ne sont pas mal✶ = the photos
    aren't bad
2 *adverb*
  mal = badly
  = not well
  ils ont mal dormi = they slept badly
  elle va mal = she isn't well at all
  être mal élevé = to be bad mannered
3 faire mal = to hurt
  ça me fait mal = it hurts
  tu me fais mal = you're hurting me
  je me suis fait mal = I hurt myself
4 avoir mal
  avoir mal à la tête = to have a headache
  avoir mal aux dents = to have (a)
    toothache
  avoir mal à la gorge = to have a sore throat
  avoir mal au cœur = to feel sick
  il a mal au genou = his knee hurts
  avoir le mal de mer = to be seasick

malade
1 *adjective*
  = ill, sick
  tomber malade = to fall ill
2 *noun, masculine/feminine*
  un malade/une malade = a patient
  = a sick person

maladie *noun, feminine*
  une maladie = an illness, a disease

maladroit/maladroite *adjective*
  = clumsy

malaise *noun, masculine*
• (*faintness*)
  un malaise = a dizzy turn
  avoir un malaise = to feel faint
• (*nervousness*)
  un malaise = unease

malfaiteur *noun, masculine*
  un malfaiteur = a criminal

malgré *preposition*
  = despite, in spite of

malheur *noun, masculine*
  un malheur = a misfortune

malheureusement *adverb*
  = unfortunately

✶ in informal situations

malheureux/malheureuse *adjective*
= unhappy
= unfortunate

malhonnête *adjective*
= dishonest

malin/maligne *adjective*
= clever
= crafty

malsain/malsaine *adjective*
= unhealthy

maltraiter *verb* 1
= to ill-treat

maman *noun, feminine*
une maman = a mum, a mom

mamie✶ *noun, feminine*
ma mamie✶ = my gran, my granny

manche
1 *noun, feminine*
une manche = a sleeve
sans manches = sleeveless
2 *noun, masculine*
un manche = a handle
un manche à balai = a broomstick
= a joystick

Manche *noun, feminine*
la Manche = the (English) Channel

mandat *noun, masculine*
un mandat = a money order

manège *noun, masculine*
un manège = a fairground ride

manger *verb* 13
= to eat
inviter des amis à manger = to invite
   friends for a meal
manger au restaurant = to eat out

mangue *noun, feminine*
une mangue = a mango

manière *noun, feminine*
• (*a method*)
la manière = the way
c'est leur manière de remercier = it's their
   way of saying thank you
• (*conduct*)
des manières = manners

manif✶ *noun, feminine*
une manif✶ = a demo

manifestation *noun, feminine*
une manifestation = a demonstration
une manifestation sportive = a
sporting event

mannequin *noun, masculine*
un mannequin (*in a shop window*) = a
   dummy, a mannequin
(*a person*) = a (fashion) model

manquer *verb* 1
• (*to fail to catch, hit, reach, see, hear*) = to
   miss
manquer le train = to miss the train
• mes amis me manquent = I miss my
   friends
ça t'a manqué? = did you miss it?
• (*impersonal use*) = to be missing
il manque un bouton = there's a button
   missing
je ne peux pas l'acheter, il me manque dix
   francs = I can't buy it, I'm ten francs
   short
il te manque cinq francs pour payer la note
   = you need five francs more to pay the
   bill
• manquer de = to be short of
= to lack
• manquer à sa promesse = to break one's
   promise

mansarde *noun, feminine*
une mansarde = an attic room

manteau *noun, masculine*
(*plural*) **manteaux**
un manteau = a coat

maquereau *noun, masculine*
(*plural*) **maquereaux**
un maquereau = a mackerel

maquette *noun, feminine*
une maquette = a scale model

maquillage *noun, masculine*
le maquillage = make-up

maquiller: se maquiller *verb* 1
(**!** + *être*)
se maquiller = to put on make-up
= to wear make-up

marbre *noun, masculine*
le marbre = marble

marchand/marchande *noun,
masculine/feminine*
un marchand/une marchande = a
   shopkeeper
= a stallholder

marchandise *noun, feminine*
de la marchandise = goods

marche *noun, feminine*
• (*stair*)
une marche = a step
les marches = the stairs
• (*the sport*)
la marche = walking
• (*when talking about a machine, a
   mechanism*)
être en marche = to be running
mettre le moteur en marche = to start the
   engine up
• (*when talking about a vehicle*)
un train en marche = a moving train
faire marche arrière = to reverse
la marche à suivre = the procedure

M

marché *noun, masculine*
* (*a place*)
  un marché = a market
  faire son marché = to go shopping
* (*in business*)
  un marché = a deal
* **être bon marché** = to be cheap
le Marché Commun = the Common Market
un marché aux puces = a flea market

marcher *verb* [1]
* = to walk
* = to work
  comment marche la tondeuse? = how does the mower work?
* (*if it's an event, a fest*)**✗** = to go well
  les affaires marchent✗ bien = business is going well
  l'examen a marché✗? = how did the exam go?

mardi *noun, masculine*
  mardi = Tuesday
Mardi gras = Shrove Tuesday

mare *noun, feminine*
  une mare = a pond

marée *noun, feminine*
  la marée = the tide
  la marée monte = the tide is coming in
  la marée descend = the tide is going out
une marée noire = an oil slick

marelle *noun, feminine*
  la marelle = hopscotch

marge *noun, feminine*
  la marge = the margin

mari *noun, masculine*
  un mari = a husband

mariage *noun, masculine*
  un mariage = a wedding
  = a marriage

marié/mariée
1 *adjective*
  = married
2 *noun, masculine/feminine*
  le marié/la mariée = the bridegroom/the bride

marier *verb* [2]
1 (**!** + *avoir*)
  = to marry
  ils ont marié leur fille = they married their daughter
2 se marier (**!** + *être*)
  se marier = to get married, to marry
  elle s'est mariée avec son cousin = she got married to her cousin, she married her cousin

marin/marine¹
1 *adjective*

* **le sel marin** = sea salt
* **un pull marin** = a seaman's jersey
2 marin *noun, masculine*
  un marin = a sailor

marine² *noun, feminine*
  la marine = the navy

marionnette *noun, feminine*
  une marionnette = a puppet

Maroc *noun, masculine*
  le Maroc = Morocco

marocain/marocaine *adjective*
  = Moroccan

maroquinerie *noun, feminine*
  une maroquinerie = a leather shop, a leather store

marque *noun, feminine*
* (*in commerce*)
  une marque = a brand, a make
  de marque française = French
* (*a trace*)
  une marque = a mark

marquer *verb* [1]
* = to note (down), to write
* = to score
* = to mark, to make an impression

marraine *noun, feminine*
  une marraine = a godmother

marrant/marrante✗ *adjective*
  = funny

marre✗ *adverb*
  en avoir marre✗ = to be fed up

marrer: se marrer✗ *verb* [1] (**!** + *être*)
* **se marrer✗** = to laugh
* **se marrer✗** = to have a good laugh

marron
1 *adjective* (**!** *never changes*)
  = brown
2 *noun, masculine*
  un marron = a chestnut
  un marron (d'Inde) = a horse chestnut
des marrons chauds = roast chestnuts

mars *noun, masculine*
  mars = March

Marseillaise *noun, feminine*
  la Marseillaise = the Marseillaise (*the French national anthem*)

marteau *noun, masculine*
(*plural*) **marteaux**
  un marteau = a hammer
un marteau piqueur = a pneumatic drill, a jackhammer

mas *noun, masculine* (**!** *never changes*)
  un mas = a farmhouse (*in Provence*)

masque *noun, masculine*
  un masque = a mask

mât *noun, masculine*
un mât = a mast

match *noun, masculine*
un match de football = a football match, a football game

matelas *noun, masculine* (**!** *never changes*)
un matelas = a mattress
un matelas pneumatique = an air bed, an air mattress

matériel *noun, masculine*
le matériel = the equipment

mathématiques *noun, feminine plural*
les mathématiques = mathematics

maths✗ *noun, feminine plural*
les maths✗ = math(s)

matière *noun, feminine*
• (*something studied*)
une matière = a subject
• (*a substance*)
une matière = a material
les matières grasses = fats
les matières premières = raw materials

matin *noun, masculine*
un matin = a morning
demain matin = tomorrow morning
de bon matin = early in the morning

matinal/matinale *adjective*
(*plural*) **matinaux/matinales**
= early
être matinal = to be an early riser

matinée *noun, feminine*
la matinée = the morning
faire la grasse matinée = to have a lie-in, to sleep in

mauvais/mauvaise
1 *adjective*
• = bad
le mauvais temps = bad weather
être mauvais en algèbre = to be bad at algebra
• = wrong
la mauvaise adresse = the wrong address
2 mauvais *adverb*
• il fait mauvais = the weather is bad
• ça sent mauvais = it smells
une mauvaise herbe = a weed

maximum *noun, masculine*
un maximum = a maximum
100 francs au maximum = 100 francs at (the) most

mayonnaise *noun, feminine*
la mayonnaise = mayonnaise

me (**m'** *before vowel or mute h*) *pronoun*
• = me
il m'a vu = he saw me
elle ne me parle pas = she won't speak to me

• = myself
je me suis coupé = I cut myself

mec✗ *noun, masculine*
un mec✗ = a bloke, a guy

mécanicien/mécanicienne
un mécanicien/une mécanicienne (*in a garage*) = a mechanic
(*on a train*) = an engine driver, a locomotive engineer

mécanique
1 *adjective*
= mechanical
(*describing a toy*) = clockwork
2 *noun, feminine*
la mécanique = mechanics

méchant/méchante *adjective*
= nasty, mean

méchoui *noun, masculine*
un méchoui = a North African style barbecue

mécontent/mécontente *adjective*
= dissatisfied, displeased

médaille *noun, feminine*
une médaille = a medal

médecin *noun, masculine*
un médecin = a doctor

médical/médicale *adjective*
(*plural*) **médicaux/médicales**
= medical

médicament *noun, masculine*
un médicament = a medicine, a drug

médiéval/médiévale *adjective*
(*plural*) **médiévaux/médiévales**
= medieval

Méditerranée *noun, feminine*
la (mer) Méditerranée = the Mediterranean (Sea)

méfiant/méfiante *adjective*
= suspicious, mistrustful

méfier: **se méfier** *verb* 2 (**!** + *être*)
• se méfier = to distrust
je me méfie de ce garçon = I don't trust that boy
• se méfier = to be careful
méfie-toi! = be careful

meilleur/meilleure
1 *adjective*
• = better
le film est meilleur que le roman = the film is better than the novel
• = best
le meilleur vin de la région = the best wine in the area
2 *noun, masculine/feminine*
le meilleur/la meilleure = the best one

M

3 meilleur *adverb*
= better
il fait meilleur qu'hier = the weather is better than yesterday

mélanger *verb* [13]
• *(to combine)* = to mix
• *(to muddle up)* = to mix up

melon *noun, masculine*
un melon = a melon

membre *noun, masculine*
• *(a person)*
un membre = a member
• *(an arm, a leg)*
un membre = a limb

même
1 *adjective*
= same
les mêmes bottes que les miennes = the same boots as mine
2 *pronoun*
le même/la même = the same one
3 *adverb*
• *(used for emphasis)* = even
il n'a même pas répondu = he didn't even reply
j'irai, même s'il pleut = I'll go, even if it rains
• *(exactly)* = very
aujourd'hui même = this very day
ici même = in this very place, right here

mémé * *noun, feminine*
ma mémé* = my gran, my granny

mémoire *noun, feminine*
la mémoire = memory

mémoriser *verb* [1]
= to memorize

menacer *verb* [12]
= to threaten

ménage *noun, masculine*
• *(cleaning)*
le ménage = the housework
• *(the people)*
un ménage = a couple
= a household

ménager/ménagère¹ *adjective*
= domestic
= household

ménagère² *noun, feminine*
une ménagère = a housewife

mendiant/mendiante *noun, masculine/feminine*
un mendiant/une mendiante = a beggar

mener *verb* [16]
• = to lead
• = to take

mensonge *noun, masculine*
un mensonge = a lie

mensuel/mensuelle *adjective*
= monthly

menteur/menteuse *noun, masculine/feminine*
un menteur/une menteuse = a liar

menthe *noun, feminine*
la menthe = mint
une menthe à l'eau = a mint cordial

mentionner *verb* [1]
= to mention

mentir *verb* [30]
= to lie

menton *noun, masculine*
le menton = the chin

menu/menue
1 *adjective*
= small
2 menu *adverb*
hacher menu = to chop finely
3 menu *noun, masculine*
le menu = the menu
le menu à prix fixe = the set menu

mer *noun, feminine*
la mer = the sea

merci *noun, masculine* (also *exclamation*)
merci! = thank you!

mercredi *noun, masculine*
mercredi = Wednesday

merde ✦ *exclamation*
= shit!

mère *noun, feminine*
une mère = a mother

méridional/méridionale *adjective*
(plural) **méridionaux/méridionales**
= southern

mériter *verb* [1]
= to deserve

merveille *noun, feminine*
une merveille = a marvel, a wonder
faire des merveilles = to work wonders

merveilleux/merveilleuse *adjective*
= marvellous, wonderful

mes ▶ mon

mesdames ▶ madame

mesdemoiselles ▶ mademoiselle

messe *noun, feminine*
une messe = a mass

messieurs ▶ monsieur

mesure *noun, feminine*
• *(when determining size)*
une mesure = a measurement
sur mesure = made to measure

✱ in informal situations   **✦** may be considered offensive

- (*a decision, a step*)
  une mesure = a measure

mesurer *verb* 1
= to measure
combien mesures-tu? = how tall are you?
Paul mesure 1,80 m = Paul is six foot tall

météo *noun, feminine*
la météo = the weather forecast
la météo marine = the shipping forecast
la météo annonce de la pluie = the
  forecast is for rain

méthode *noun, feminine*
- (*a way of doing things*)
  une méthode = a method
- (*a book*)
  une méthode = a handbook
  = a textbook

métier *noun, masculine*
un métier = a job
= a trade

mètre *noun, masculine*
- (*a unit of measurement*)
  un mètre = a metre, a meter
- (*an instrument*)
  un mètre = a tape measure

métro *noun, masculine*
le métro = the underground, the subway

mets ▶ **mettre** 60

mettre *verb* 60
1 (**!** + *avoir*)
- = to put
  j'ai mis la lettre sur la table = I put the
    letter on the table
- = to put on
  il a mis son chapeau = he put on his hat
- (*other uses*)
  mettre le couvert = to set the table
  elle met une heure pour aller au bureau
    = it takes her one hour to get to the
    office
2 se mettre (**!** + *être*)
- (*to place oneself*)
  se mettre debout = to stand up
  il s'est mis à table = he sat down at the
    table
- (*to apply, to wear*)
  se mettre = to put on
  se mettre du rouge à lèvres = to put
    lipstick on
- (*to begin*)
  se mettre à [chanter | pleurer | écrire …] = to
    start [singing | crying | writing …]
  se mettre en colère = to lose one's temper,
    to get angry
  se mettre en route = to set off

meuble *noun, masculine*
un meuble = a piece of furniture
des meubles = furniture

meubler *verb* 1
= to furnish

meurtre *noun, masculine*
un meurtre = a murder

micro *noun, masculine*
un micro = a microphone

microbe *noun, masculine*
un microbe = a germ, a microbe

midi *noun, masculine*
- = twelve o'clock, midday, noon
  il est midi et demi = it's half past twelve, it's
    twelve thirty
- = lunchtime

Midi *noun, masculine*
le Midi = the South of France

miel *noun, masculine*
le miel = honey

mien/mienne *pronoun*
le mien/la mienne = mine
les miens/les miennes = mine

miette *noun, feminine*
une miette = a crumb

mieux *adverb, adjective* (**!** *never changes*)
= better

mignon/mignonne *adjective*
= sweet, cute

M

mijoter *verb* 1
- = to simmer
- = to prepare

milieu
(*plural*) **milieux**
1 *noun, masculine*
- (*the centre*)
  le milieu = the middle
- (*the world around*)
  le milieu (*nature*) = the environment
  (*family*) = the background
2 au milieu de = in the middle of
= among

militaire
1 *adjective*
= military
2 *noun, masculine*
un militaire = a soldier

mille
1 *number* (**!** *never changes*)
= a thousand, one thousand
2 *noun, masculine*
un mille (marin) = a (nautical) mile

milliard *noun, masculine*
un milliard = a billion

millier *noun, masculine*
un millier = a thousand
= about a thousand

million *noun, masculine*
un million = a million, one million

minable* *adjective*
= pathetic
= shabby

mince
1 *adjective*
= slim, thin, slender
2 *exclamation**
mince*! (*expressing annoyance*) = damn!
(*expressing amazement*) = wow!

minéral/minérale *adjective*
(*plural*) **minéraux/minérales**
= mineral

mineur/mineure
1 *adjective*
• (*under 18*) = underage
• (*not important*) = minor
2 *noun, masculine|feminine*
un mineur/une mineure = a minor
3 *mineur noun, masculine*
un mineur = a miner

Minitel® *noun, masculine*
le Minitel = Minitel (*a terminal linking phone users to interactive databases*)

minuit *noun, masculine*
minuit = twelve o'clock, midnight

minuscule *adjective*
= tiny, minute

minute *noun, feminine*
une minute = a minute, one minute

miroir *noun, masculine*
un miroir = a mirror

mis/mise ▶ mettre 60

misérable *adjective*
= poor
= wretched

misère *noun, feminine*
la misère = poverty

mistral *noun, masculine*
le mistral = the mistral (*a cold north wind*)

mite *noun, feminine*
une mite = a (clothes) moth

mixte *adjective*
= mixed
(*describing a school*) = coeducational

Mlle (*abbreviation of* **Mademoiselle**)
Mlle = Miss, Ms

Mme (*abbreviation of* **Madame**)
Mme = Mrs, Ms

mobilier *noun, masculine*
le mobilier = the furniture

mobylette® *noun, feminine*
une mobylette = a moped

---

moche* *adjective*
• = ugly
• = awful

mode
1 *noun, feminine*
une mode = a fashion
être à la mode (*if it's clothes*) = to be fashionable
(*if it's a singer, an actor*) = to be popular
2 *noun, masculine*
un mode de vie = a lifestyle

modèle *noun, masculine*
un modèle = a model
= a pattern

modéré/modérée *adjective*
= moderate

moi *pronoun*
= me
moi non plus = nor me, me neither
donne-la-moi = give it to me
ce sac est à moi = this bag belongs to me, this bag is mine
c'est à moi de jouer = it's my turn to play
viens chez moi = come to my house
moi, je reste ici = I'm staying here

moi-même *pronoun*
= myself

moineau *noun, masculine*
(*plural*) **moineaux**
un moineau = a sparrow

moins
1 *preposition*
• = minus
= less
il fait moins cinq (degrés) = it's minus five (degrees)
550 francs, moins la caution = 550 francs, minus the deposit
• (*when talking about time*) = to
il est une heure moins le quart = it's a quarter to one
2 *adverb*
• = less
moins intéressant = less interesting
moins cher que d'habitude = cheaper than usual
de moins en moins = less and less
deux fois moins cher = twice as cheap
• moins de = less
= fewer
= less than
= under
un peu moins de sucre = a little less sugar
il a moins d'amis maintenant = he has fewer friends now
moins de la moitié = less than half
• moins… moins… = the less… the less…
moins… plus… = the less… the more…
moins je travaille, moins j'ai envie de travailler = the less I work, the less I feel like working

---

* in informal situations

* **le moins/la moins** = the least
  = the less
  le coin le moins ensoleillé du jardin = the least sunny spot in the garden
  le moins cher des deux = the cheaper of the two
3 au moins = at least
4 du moins = at least
4 à moins que, à moins de = unless

mois *noun, masculine* (**!** *never changes*)
  un mois = a month
  au mois de mai = in May

moisson *noun, feminine*
  la moisson = the harvest

moitié *noun, feminine*
  une moitié = a half
  à moitié prix = half-price

molle ▶ mou

moment *noun, masculine*
  un moment = a moment, one moment
  en ce moment = at the moment
  par moments = at times
  juste au moment où il allait partir = just as he was about to leave

mon/ma *determiner*
(*plural*) **mes**
  = my

monde *noun, masculine*
* **le monde** = the world
  faire le tour du monde en bateau = to sail around the world
  le monde des affaires = the business world
* **il y a du monde, il y a beaucoup de monde** = there are a lot of people
  tout le monde = everybody

moniteur/monitrice
1 *noun, masculine|feminine*
  un moniteur/une monitrice (*for skiers, drivers*) = an instructor
  (*in a holiday camp*) = a group leader, a counselor
2 moniteur *noun, masculine*
  un moniteur (*a screen*) = a monitor

monnaie *noun, feminine*
* **la monnaie** = change
* **une monnaie** = a currency

monsieur *noun, masculine*
(*plural*) **messieurs**
  un monsieur = a gentleman
  bonjour messieurs = good morning (gentlemen)
  Monsieur Martin = Mr Martin

monstre
1 *adjective*
  monstre* = huge
2 *noun, masculine*
  un monstre = a monster

montagne *noun, feminine*
  une montagne = a mountain

montagneux/montagneuse
adjective
  = mountainous

montant/montante
1 *adjective*
* **un col montant** = a high collar
* **la marée montante** = the rising tide
2 montant *noun, masculine*
  le montant (*on a bill*) = the total

monter *verb* ⬚1
1 (**!** *+ être*)
* = to go up
  elle est montée au village = she's gone up to the village
  tu es monté à pied? = did you walk up?
  nous sommes montés en courant = we ran up
* = to go upstairs
  montez, le bureau est à l'étage au-dessus = go upstairs, the office is on the next floor
* = to come up
  = to come upstairs
  je suis dans le grenier, monte = I'm in the attic, come up
* = to get in(to)
  = to get on
  elle est montée dans la voiture = she got into the car
  monter dans un avion = to get on a plane
* = to climb
  ne monte pas sur la table = don't climb onto the table
* = to rise, to go up
  les prix montent = prices are rising, prices are going up
* (*other uses*)
  monter à bicyclette = to ride a bicycle
  monter à cheval = to ride
2 (**!** *+ avoir*)
* = to go up
  il a monté la colline en vélo = he cycled up the hill
* = to take up(stairs)
  je vais monter les bagages = I'm going to take the luggage up(stairs)
* = to bring up
  peux-tu me monter mes lunettes? = can you bring my glasses up to me?
* = to put up
  monter une tente = to put up a tent

montgolfière *noun, feminine*
  une montgolfière = a hot air balloon

montre *noun, feminine*
  une montre = a watch

montrer *verb* ⬚1
  = to show

monument *noun, masculine*
  un monument = a monument
  un monument historique = a historical building
  un monument aux morts = a war memorial

M

moquer: **se moquer de** verb $\boxed{1}$
(**!** + *être*)
• (*to mock*)
  se moquer de = to make fun of
• (*to dismiss*)
  se moquer de = not to care about
  je m'en moque = I don't care

moquette noun, feminine
  une moquette = a fitted carpet, wall-to-wall carpeting

moral noun, masculine
  le moral = morale
  avoir le moral, avoir bon moral = to be in good spirits
  avoir le moral à zéro* = to feel very down

morceau noun, masculine
(*plural*) **morceaux**
  un morceau = a piece
  un morceau de sucre = a lump of sugar

mordre verb $\boxed{6}$
  = to bite

morpion noun, masculine
  le morpion = noughts and crosses

mort¹ noun, feminine
  la mort = death

mort²/morte
1 ▶ **mourir** $\boxed{25}$
2 adjective
  = dead
  être mort de peur = to be scared stiff
3 noun, masculine/feminine
  un mort/une morte = a dead man/a dead woman

mosquée noun, feminine
  une mosquée = a mosque

mot noun, masculine
• **un mot** = a word
• (*a message*)
  un mot = a note
  des mots croisés = a crossword puzzle

motard noun, masculine
  un motard = a motorcyclist, a biker
  = a police motorcyclist

mot-clé noun, masculine
(*plural*) **mots-clés**
  un mot-clé = a key word

moteur noun, masculine
  un moteur = an engine
  = a motor

moto noun, feminine
  une moto = a motorbike, a motorcycle

mou/molle adjective
• (*describing things*) = soft
  = limp

• (*describing a person*) = spineless
  = lethargic

mouche noun, feminine
  une mouche = a fly

mouchoir noun, masculine
  un mouchoir = a handkerchief

mouette noun, feminine
  une mouette = a seagull

mouiller verb $\boxed{1}$
1 (**!** + *avoir*)
  = to wet
2 se mouiller (**!** + *être*)
  se mouiller = to get wet

moule
1 noun, feminine
  une moule = a mussel
2 noun, masculine
  un moule = a mould
  = a (baking) tin, a pan

mourir verb $\boxed{25}$ (**!** + *être*)
  = to die
  il est mort en avril = he died in April
  je meurs [**de faim** | **de soif** | **de froid** ...]**!** = I'm [starving | parched | freezing ...]!
  il meurt d'envie de te le dire = he's dying to tell you

mousse noun, feminine
• (*a plant*)
  la mousse = moss
• (*bubbles*)
  la mousse = foam
  = lather
  = froth
• (*in cooking*)
  une mousse au chocolat = a chocolate mousse
• (*a material*)
  la mousse = foam rubber

moustache noun, feminine
• (*on a man*)
  une moustache = a moustache
• (*on an animal*)
  des moustaches = whiskers

moustique noun, masculine
  un moustique = a mosquito

moutarde noun, feminine
  la moutarde = mustard

mouton noun, masculine
  un mouton = a sheep

moyen/moyenne¹
1 adjective
  = average
  = medium
2 moyen noun, masculine
  un moyen = a means
  = a way
  un moyen de transport = a means of transport
  c'est le seul moyen = it's the only way

---
* in informal situations

3 moyens *noun, masculine plural*
  des moyens (*money*) = means
  je n'ai pas les moyens de voyager = I can't
    afford to travel
le Moyen Âge = the Middle Ages

moyenne² *noun, feminine*
• (*in statistics*)
  la moyenne = the average
  en moyenne = on average
• (*in an exam*)
  la moyenne = half marks, 50%

moyennement *adverb*
  = moderately
  = fairly

Moyen-Orient *noun, masculine*
  le Moyen-Orient = the Middle East

muet/muette *adjective*
• = dumb
• = silent

muguet *noun, masculine*
  le muguet = lily of the valley

multiplier *verb* 2
  = to multiply

municipal/municipale *adjective*
(*plural*) **municipaux/municipales**
  = municipal

municipalité *noun, feminine*
  la municipalité = the (local) council

munir: se munir de *verb* 3 (**!** + *être*)
  se munir de = to equip oneself with

mur *noun, masculine*
  un mur = a wall
  le mur du son = the sound barrier

mûr/mûre¹ *adjective*
• (*describing fruit*) = ripe
• (*describing people*) = mature

muraille *noun, feminine*
  une muraille = a great wall

mûre² *noun, feminine*
  une mûre = a blackberry

murmurer *verb* 1
• = to murmur
• = to whisper

musclé/musclée *adjective*
  = muscular

musculation *noun, feminine*
  la musculation = body-building

musée *noun, masculine*
  un musée = a museum, a gallery

musicien/musicienne *noun,*
masculine/feminine
  un musicien/une musicienne = a musician

musique *noun, feminine*
  la musique = music

mutinerie *noun, feminine*
  une mutinerie = a mutiny

mystère *noun, masculine*
  un mystère = a mystery

mystérieux/mystérieuse *adjective*
  = mysterious

Nn

n' ▶ **ne**

nage *noun, feminine*
  la nage = swimming
  traverser le fleuve à la nage = to swim
    across the river

nager *verb* 13
  = to swim

nain/naine
1 *adjective*
  = dwarf
  = miniature
2 *noun, masculine/feminine*
  un nain/une naine = a dwarf

naissance *noun, feminine*
  la naissance = birth
  à ma naissance = when I was born

naître *verb* 64 (**!** + *être*)
  = to be born
  il est né le 10 janvier = he was born on 10
    January

nappe *noun, feminine*
  une nappe = a tablecloth
  une nappe de brouillard = a blanket of fog

narine *noun, feminine*
  une narine = a nostril

natal/natale *adjective*
(*plural*) **natals/natales**
  = native

natation *noun, feminine*
  la natation = swimming

national/nationale¹ *adjective*
(*plural*) **nationaux/nationales**
  = national

nationale² *noun, feminine*
  une nationale = a trunk road, a highway

nature
1 *adjective* (**!** *never changes*)
  = plain
  un yaourt nature = a plain yogurt
  un thé nature = a black tea

2 *noun, feminine*
la nature = nature
la protection de la nature = the protection of the environment
une nature morte = a still life

naturel/naturelle
1 *adjective*
= natural
2 naturel *noun, masculine*
• **être d'un naturel timide** = to be shy by nature
• **il manque de naturel** = he's not very natural
• **du thon au naturel** = tuna in brine

naufrage *noun, masculine*
un naufrage = a shipwreck
faire naufrage (*if it's a ship*) = to be wrecked
(*if it's a crew*) = to be shipwrecked

nausée *noun, feminine*
la nausée = nausea
avoir la nausée = to feel sick, to feel nauseous

nautique *adjective*
les sports nautiques = water sports

navet *noun, masculine*
un navet = a turnip

navette *noun, feminine*
une navette = a shuttle
= a shuttle service
faire la navette = to travel back and forth
= to commute

navire *noun, masculine*
un navire = a ship

navré/navrée *adjective*
je suis vraiment navré = I'm terribly sorry
avoir l'air navré = to look upset

ne (n' *before vowel or mute h*) *adverb*
> ! *In cases where* ne *is used with* aucun, guère, jamais, pas, personne, plus, rien *etc, one should consult the corresponding entry.* ne + verb + que *is treated in the entry below.*

je ne sais pas = I don't know
je n'ai que 10 francs = I've only got 10 francs
tu n'avais qu'à le dire = you only had to say so

né/née ▶ naître 64

néanmoins *adverb*
= nevertheless

nécessaire
1 *adjective*
= necessary

2 *noun, masculine*
• **faire le nécessaire pour les billets** = to see about the tickets
• **le strict nécessaire** = the bare essentials

néerlandais/néerlandaise
1 *adjective*
= Dutch
2 néerlandais *noun, masculine*
le néerlandais = Dutch

néfaste *adjective*
= harmful

négatif/négative *adjective*
= negative

négliger *verb* 13
= to neglect

neige *noun, feminine*
la neige = snow
des blancs d'œufs battus en neige
= stiffly beaten eggwhites

neiger *verb* 13
= to snow
il neige = it's snowing

nénuphar *noun, masculine*
un nénuphar = a waterlily

nerf *noun, masculine*
un nerf = a nerve
il me tape sur les nerfs✗ = he gets on my nerves

nerveux/nerveuse *adjective*
= nervous, tense

n'est-ce pas *adverb*
c'est grand, n'est-ce pas? = it's big, isn't it?
tu viendras, n'est-ce pas? = you will come, won't you?

net/nette
1 *adjective*
• (*describing prices or weights*) = net
• (*free from stains or clutter*) = clean
• (*easy to see or understand*) = clear
2 net *adverb*
s'arrêter net = to stop dead
refuser net = to refuse flatly

nettoyer *verb* 23
= to clean

neuf¹ *number*
= nine

neuf²/neuve *adjective*
= new
une voiture toute neuve = a brand new car

neuvième *number*
= ninth

neveu *noun, masculine*
(*plural*) **neveux**
un neveu = a nephew

nez *noun, masculine* (! *never changes*)
le nez = the nose

✗ in informal situations

ni *conjunction*
ni anglais ni espagnol = neither English nor Spanish
elle ne veut pas le voir ni lui parler = she doesn't wish to see him or talk to him
ni l'un ni l'autre = neither of them

niche *noun, feminine*
• (*for a dog*)
une niche = a kennel, a doghouse
• (*in a wall*)
une niche = a recess

nid *noun, masculine*
un nid = a nest

nièce *noun, feminine*
une nièce = a niece

nier *verb* $\boxed{2}$
= to deny

n'importe ▶ importer $\boxed{1}$

niveau *noun, masculine*
(*plural*) **niveaux**
un niveau = a level
= a standard
le niveau de vie = the standard of living

noce *noun, feminine*
une noce = a wedding
des noces d'argent = a silver wedding anniversary

nocturne *adjective*
= nocturnal
= night

Noël *noun, masculine*
Noël = Christmas

nœud *noun, masculine*
un nœud = a knot
un nœud papillon = a bow tie

noir/noire *adjective*
• = black
• = dark

noisette *noun, feminine*
une noisette = a hazelnut

noix *noun, feminine* (**!** *never changes*)
une noix = a walnut, an English walnut

nom
1 *noun, masculine*
• un nom = a name
• un nom = a noun
2 au nom de = in the name of
= on behalf of
un nom de famille = a surname, a last name
un nom de jeune fille = a maiden name

nombre *noun, masculine*
un nombre = a number
un certain nombre de personnes = some people

nombreux/nombreuse *adjective*
= large
= many
une foule nombreuse = a large crowd
de nombreuses personnes = many people
ils sont peu nombreux = there are few of them

nommer *verb* $\boxed{1}$
1 (**!** + *avoir*)
• = to name
= to call
nommer un enfant Olivier = to name a child Olivier
une plage nommée 'La Salie' = a beach called 'La Salie'
• = to appoint
être nommé à Paris = to be posted to Paris
2 se nommer (**!** + *être*)
se nommer = to be called

non
1 *adverb*
• = no
ah, ça non! = definitely not
je pense que non = I don't think so
• = non
non alcoolisé = nonalcoholic
2 non plus
je ne suis pas d'accord non plus = I don't agree either
il n'a pas aimé le film, moi non plus = he didn't like the film, neither did I

nonante *number*
= ninety

nord
1 *noun, masculine*
le nord = the north
2 *adjective* (**!** *never changes*)
= north
= northern

normal/normale *adjective*
(*plural*) **normaux/normales**
= normal
il est normal qu'il soit triste = it's natural that he should be sad

normalement *adverb*
= normally

normand/normande *adjective*
= Norman
= from Normandy
la côte normande = the Normandy coast

Normandie *noun, feminine*
la Normandie = Normandy

Norvège *noun, feminine*
la Norvège = Norway

norvégien/norvégienne
1 *adjective*
= Norwegian
2 norvégien *noun, masculine*
le norvégien = Norwegian

N

nos ▶ **notre**

note *noun, feminine*
* (*in a hotel*)
  la note = the bill, the check
* (*in music*)
  une note = a note
* (*at school*)
  une note = a mark, a grade
* (*words taken down*)
  des notes = notes

noter *verb* [1]
* = to write down
* = to notice
* = to mark, to grade

notre *determiner*
(*plural*) **nos**
  = our

nôtre *pronoun*
  le nôtre/la nôtre/les nôtres = ours

nouille *noun, feminine*
  les nouilles = noodles, pasta

nourrir *verb* [3]
1 (**!** + *avoir*)
  = to feed
  = to nourish
2 se nourrir (**!** + *être*)
  se nourrir = to feed
  = to eat

nourriture *noun, feminine*
  la nourriture = food

nous *pronoun*
* = we
  = us
  nous avons froid = we're cold
  donne-nous le livre = give us the book
  la voiture est à nous = the car is ours
  c'est à nous de jouer = it's our turn to play
  il nous l'a prêté = he lent it to us
* = ourselves
  nous nous soignons = we look after
    ourselves
  nous nous levons tôt = we get up early
* = each other
  nous nous aimons = we love each other

nouveau/nouvelle¹
(*plural*) **nouveaux/nouvelles**
1 *adjective*

> **!** nouvel *is used instead of* nouveau
> *before masculine nouns that begin with a*
> *vowel or a mute h. The plural of* nouvel *is*
> nouveaux.

  = new
  le Nouvel An = the New Year
  c'est tout nouveau = it's brand new
2 *noun, masculine|feminine*
  le nouveau/la nouvelle (*a pupil*) = the new
    boy/the new girl

3 de nouveau = (once) again

nouveau-né *noun, masculine*
(*plural*) **nouveau-nés**
  un nouveau-né = a newborn baby

nouvel ▶ **nouveau 1**

nouvelle² *noun, feminine*
  une nouvelle = a piece of news
  la nouvelle = the news
  les nouvelles = the news
  tu connais la nouvelle? = have you heard
    the news?

Nouvelle-Zélande *noun, feminine*
  la Nouvelle-Zélande = New Zealand

novembre *noun, masculine*
  novembre = November

noyau *noun, masculine*
(*plural*) **noyaux**
  un noyau = a stone, a pit

noyé/noyée *noun, masculine/feminine*
  un noyé/une noyée = a drowned person

noyer
1 *noun, masculine*
  un noyer = a walnut tree
2 *verb* [23] (**!** + *avoir*)
  = to drown
3 se noyer (**!** + *être*)
  se noyer = to drown

nu/nue *adjective*
  = naked, bare

nuage *noun, masculine*
  un nuage = a cloud

nuageux/nuageuse *adjective*
  = cloudy

nuance *noun, feminine*
* (*a colour*)
  une nuance = a shade
* (*between two things*)
  une nuance = a slight difference

nuée *noun, feminine*
  une nuée = a swarm

nuire *verb* [62]
  nuire à = to harm
  = to be harmful to

nuisible *adjective*
  = harmful

nuit *noun, feminine*
  une nuit = a night
  cette nuit = last night
  = tonight
  il fait nuit = it's dark
une nuit blanche = a sleepless night

nul/nulle
1 *adjective*
* (*describing a person*)✘ = hopeless
  (*describing a piece of work*)✘ = worthless
  (*describing a film, a book*)✘ = trashy

─────────
✘ in informal situations

- (*in sports*)
  un match nul = a draw, a tie
  faire match nul = to draw, to tie
2 *determiner*
  nul [**homme | pays | besoin** …] = no [man |
    country | need …]
  nul autre que vous = no-one else but you
3 *pronoun*
  = no-one
4 nulle part = nowhere

numéro *noun, masculine*
- (*for a house, a telephone, a ticket*)
  un numéro = a number
  un numéro de téléphone = a telephone
    number
- (*a magazine*)
  un numéro = a copy, an issue

nuque *noun, feminine*
  la nuque = the nape (of the neck)

obéir *verb* ③
  = to obey
  obéir à son maître = to obey one's master

obéissant/obéissante *adjective*
  = obedient

objet *noun, masculine*
  un objet = an object
  des objets de valeur = valuables
  objets trouvés = lost property, lost and
    found

obligatoire *adjective*
  = compulsory

obliger *verb* ⑬
  obliger un enfant à manger = to make a
    child eat, to force a child to eat
  je suis obligé de partir = I have to go

obscur/obscure *adjective*
- = dark
- = obscure

obscurité *noun, feminine*
  l'obscurité = darkness

obsèques *noun, feminine plural*
  les obsèques = the funeral

observateur/observatrice *noun,
masculine/feminine*
  un observateur/une observatrice = an
    observer

observer *verb* ①
- = to watch
- = to notice
- = to observe

obtenir *verb* ㊱
  = to get, to obtain

occasion *noun, feminine*
- (*a chance*)
  une occasion = an opportunity
- **une voiture d'occasion** = a second-hand
    car
- (*a circumstance*)
  une occasion = an occasion

occident *noun, masculine*
  l'occident = the west

occidental/occidentale *adjective*
(*plural*) **occidentaux/occidentales**
  = western

occupé/occupée *adjective*
- (*having a lot to do*) = busy
- (*not vacant*) = engaged

occuper *verb* ①
1 (**!** + *avoir*)
- = to occupy
- = to keep busy
  ça m'occupe = it keeps me busy
2 s'occuper (**!** + *être*)
- **s'occuper** = to keep oneself busy, to
    occupy oneself
- **s'occuper de** = to take care of, to look
    after

océan *noun, masculine*
  un océan = an ocean

octante *number*
  = eighty

octobre *noun, masculine*
  octobre = October

odeur *noun, feminine*
  une odeur = a smell

odieux/odieuse *adjective*
  = horrible, hateful

œil *noun, masculine*
(*plural*) **yeux**
  un œil = an eye

œillet *noun, masculine*
  un œillet = a carnation

œuf *noun, masculine*
  un œuf = an egg
  un œuf à la coque = a boiled egg
  un œuf dur = a hard-boiled egg
  un œuf sur le plat = a fried egg

œuvre *noun, feminine*
  une œuvre = a work

offense *noun, feminine*
  une offense = an insult

offenser *verb* ①
  = to offend

office *noun, masculine*
- (*in church*)
  un office = a service

O

- (*an organization*)
un office = an office
l'office du tourisme = the tourist office

offre *noun, feminine*
une offre = an offer
'offres d'emploi' = 'situations vacant'

offrir *verb* 4
1 (! + *avoir*)
- = to offer
- = to give
2 s'offrir (! + *être*)
s'offrir une croisière = to treat oneself to a cruise

oie *noun, feminine*
une oie = a goose

oignon *noun, masculine*
un oignon = an onion

oiseau *noun, masculine*
(*plural*) **oiseaux**
un oiseau = a bird

olivier *noun, masculine*
un olivier = an olive tree

ombre *noun, feminine*
- (*darkness*)
l'ombre = shade
- (*a shape*)
une ombre = a shadow

ombrelle *noun, feminine*
une ombrelle = a sunshade, a parasol

omnibus *noun, masculine* (! *never changes*)
un (train) omnibus = a slow train, a local train

omoplate *noun, feminine*
l'omoplate = the shoulder blade

on *pronoun*
- = someone
on t'appelle = someone's calling you
- = we
on a eu un accident = we had an accident
- = one
= you
= they
on est obligé de payer à l'avance = one has to pay in advance
= you have to pay in advance
on vend des fleurs au supermarché = they sell flowers at the supermarket
- = people
je me moque de ce qu'on dit = I don't care what people say
- (*other possible translations*)
on m'a demandé ma carte = I was asked for my card
on a réparé la route = the road has been repaired

oncle *noun, masculine*
un oncle = an uncle

ondulé/ondulée *adjective*
= wavy

ongle *noun, masculine*
un ongle = a nail

ont ▶ avoir 8

onze *number*
= eleven

onzième *number*
= eleventh

opération *noun, feminine*
- (*in mathematics*)
une opération = a calculation
- (*on a patient*)
une opération = an operation

opérer *verb* 14
= to operate
se faire opérer = to have an operation

opinion *noun, feminine*
une opinion = an opinion

opposé/opposée *adjective*
= opposite

optimiste *adjective*
= optimistic

or *noun, masculine*
l'or = gold
une montre en or = a gold watch

orage *noun, masculine*
un orage = a storm

orageux/orageuse *adjective*
= stormy

orchestre *noun, masculine*
un orchestre = an orchestra
= a band

ordinaire *adjective*
= ordinary

ordinateur *noun, masculine*
un ordinateur = a computer

ordonnance *noun, feminine*
une ordonnance = a prescription

ordre *noun, masculine*
- (*a command*)
un ordre = an order
- (*a way of arranging things*)
dans l'ordre = in order
- (*neatness*)
l'ordre = tidiness
mettre de l'ordre = to tidy up, to clean up

ordures *noun, feminine plural*
les ordures = rubbish, garbage, trash

oreille *noun, feminine*
une oreille = an ear

oreiller *noun, masculine*
un oreiller = a pillow

organisateur/organisatrice noun, masculine/feminine
un organisateur/une organisatrice = an organizer

organiser verb 1
1 (! + avoir)
= to organize
2 s'organiser (! + être)
s'organiser = to get organized

organisme noun, masculine
un organisme = an organization, a body

orge noun, feminine
l'orge = barley

orgueil noun, masculine
l'orgueil = pride

orgueilleux/orgueilleuse adjective
= proud

orient noun, masculine
l'orient = the east

oriental/orientale adjective
(plural) **orientaux/orientales**
= eastern

originaire adjective
être originaire d'un pays = to come from a country, to be a native of a country

original/originale adjective
(plural) **originaux/originales**
• = original
• = eccentric, unusual

origine noun, feminine
l'origine = the origin

orner verb 1
= to decorate

orphelin/orpheline noun,
masculine/feminine
un orphelin/une orpheline = an orphan

orteil noun, masculine
un orteil = a toe

orthographe noun, feminine
l'orthographe = spelling

ortie noun, feminine
une ortie = a (stinging) nettle

os noun, masculine (! never changes)
un os = a bone

oser verb 1
= to dare

osier noun, masculine
l'osier = wicker

otage noun, masculine
un otage = a hostage

ôter verb 1
= to take off, to remove

ou conjunction
• = or
ou bien = or else
• ou (bien)… ou (bien)… = either… or…

où
1 adverb
= where
d'où vient le bus? = where does the bus come from?
2 pronoun
• = where
restez où vous êtes = stay where you are
• = when
juste au moment où il partait = just as he was leaving

oublier verb 2
= to forget

ouest
1 noun, masculine
l'ouest = the west
2 adjective (! never changes)
= west, western

ouf exclamation
ouf! = phew!

oui adverb
= yes
je crois que oui = I think so

ouragan noun, masculine
un ouragan = a hurricane

ourlet noun, masculine
un ourlet = a hem

ours noun, masculine (! never changes)
un ours = a bear
un ours en peluche = a teddy bear

oursin noun, masculine
un oursin = a sea urchin

outil noun, masculine
un outil = a tool

outre-mer adverb
= overseas

ouvert/ouverte
1 ▶ ouvrir 32
2 adjective
= open

ouverture noun, feminine
une ouverture = an opening

ouvrable adjective
un jour ouvrable = a working day

ouvrage noun, masculine
un ouvrage = a (piece of) work, a project
= a book, a work

ouvre-boîtes noun, masculine (! never changes)
un ouvre-boîtes = a can-opener

ouvreur/ouvreuse noun,
masculine/feminine
un ouvreur/une ouvreuse = an usher/an usherette

o

ouvrier/ouvrière
1 *noun, masculine/feminine*
un ouvrier/une ouvrière = a worker
2 *adjective*
= working-class

ouvrir *verb* 32
1 (**!** + *avoir*)
= to open
2 s'ouvrir (**!** + *être*)
s'ouvrir = to open

---

pagaille*
1 *noun, feminine*
une pagaille* = a mess
mettre la pagaille* = to cause chaos
2 en pagaille*
il y a du vin en pagaille* = there's loads of
wine, there's lots of wine

page *noun, feminine*
une page = a page

paille *noun, feminine*
la paille = straw

pain *noun, masculine*
• le pain = bread
• un pain = a loaf
le pain grillé = toast
un petit pain = a bread roll

pair/paire¹
1 *adjective*
les nombres pairs = even numbers
2 au pair
une jeune fille au pair = an au pair

paire² *noun, feminine*
une paire = a pair

paisible *adjective*
= peaceful

paix *noun, feminine* (**!** *never changes*)
la paix = peace
= peace and quiet

palais *noun, masculine* (**!** *never changes*)
• un palais = a palace
• le palais = the palate

pâle *adjective*
= pale

palier *noun, masculine*
le palier = the landing

palmier *noun, masculine*
un palmier = a palm tree

pamplemousse *noun, masculine*
un pamplemousse = a grapefruit

panaché *noun, masculine*
un (demi-)panaché = a shandy, a beer with
lemonade

pancarte *noun, feminine*
une pancarte = a notice, a sign
= a placard

panier *noun, masculine*
un panier = a basket

paniquer* *verb* 1
= to panic

panne *noun, feminine*
une panne = a breakdown
tomber en panne = to break down
tomber en panne d'essence = to run out
of petrol, to run out of gas
une panne de courant = a power failure

panneau *noun, masculine*
(*plural*) **panneaux**
• un panneau = a panel
• un panneau = a sign
un panneau d'affichage = a noticeboard
un panneau de signalisation routière
= a road sign

pansement *noun, masculine*
un pansement = a dressing, a bandage
un pansement adhésif = a plaster, a
Band-Aid®

pantalon *noun, masculine*
un pantalon = (a pair of) trousers, (a pair
of) pants

pantoufle *noun, feminine*
une pantoufle = a slipper

paon *noun, masculine*
un paon = a peacock

papa *noun, masculine*
un papa = a dad

pape *noun, masculine*
le pape = the pope

papeterie *noun, feminine*
une papeterie = a stationer's

papier *noun, masculine*
le papier = paper
le papier alu(minium) = aluminium foil,
aluminum foil
le papier d'emballage = wrapping paper
le papier hygiénique = toilet paper
le papier peint = wallpaper
les papiers (d'identité) = (identity)
papers

papillon *noun, masculine*
un papillon = a butterfly

pâquerette *noun, feminine*
une pâquerette = a daisy

Pâques *noun, masculine*
Pâques = Easter

---

* in informal situations

paquet *noun, masculine*
* un paquet = a packet
* un paquet = a parcel, a package

par
1 *preposition*
* = by
  il a été piqué par une abeille = he was stung by a bee
  payer par carte de crédit = to pay by credit card
* = through
  le chemin passe par la forêt = the path goes through the forest
  par ici = this way, through here
* = per
  = a
  par personne = per person
  trois par [jour | mois | an ...] = three a [day | month | year ...]
* = in
  mettez-vous deux par deux = stand in twos
  sortir par mauvais temps = to go out in bad weather
* = on
  par une froide journée d'hiver = on a cold winter's day
* = out of
  regarder par la fenêtre = to look out (of) the window
  par bêtise = out of stupidity
2 par contre = on the other hand

parachute *noun, masculine*
* (*the equipment*)
  un parachute = a parachute
* (*the sport*)
  le parachute = parachuting

parages *noun, masculine plural*
  dans les parages = in the area

paraître *verb* 63
1 (*! + avoir*)
* (*to create an impression*) = to seem, to look
* (*to be seen*) = to appear
  paraître en public = to appear in public
2 (*! + être*)
  (*if it's a book, a record*) = to come out
3 il paraît que = apparently
  il paraît que non = apparently not

parapente *noun, masculine*
* (*the equipment*)
  un parapente = a paraglider
* (*the sport*)
  le parapente = paragliding

parapluie *noun, masculine*
  un parapluie = an umbrella

parasol *noun, masculine*
  un parasol = a sunshade, a beach umbrella

parc *noun, masculine*
  un parc = a park
un parc d'attractions = an amusement park

parce que (**parce qu'** *before vowel or mute h*) *conjunction*
  = because

par-ci *adverb*
  par-ci par-là = here and there

parcmètre *noun, masculine*
  un parcmètre = a parking meter

parcourir *verb* 26
* = to cover
  parcourir une distance = to cover a distance
* = to go all over
  parcourir toute la ville = to go all over the town
* = to glance through
  parcourir un article = to glance through an article

parcours *noun, masculine* (**!** *never changes*)
  un parcours = a journey
  = a route

parcouru/parcourue ▶ **parcourir** 26

pardessus *noun, masculine* (**!** *never changes*)
  un pardessus = an overcoat

pardon *noun, masculine*
* le pardon = forgiveness
  demander pardon = to apologize
  = to ask for forgiveness
* pardon! = sorry!
  pardon monsieur, je cherche la mairie = excuse me, I'm looking for the town hall

pardonner *verb* 1
  = to forgive

pare-brise *noun, masculine* (**!** *never changes*)
  un pare-brise = a windscreen, a windshield

pareil/pareille
1 *adjective*
* = the same
  = similar
  = identical
* = such
  je n'ai jamais vu un luxe pareil = I've never seen such luxury
2 pareil✗ *adverb*
  = the same
  faisons pareil✗ = let's do the same

parent/parente
1 *noun, masculine/feminine*
  un parent/une parente = a relative, a relation
2 parents *noun, masculine plural*
  les parents = parents

parenthèse *noun, feminine*
  entre parenthèses = between brackets

P

paresse *noun, feminine*
la paresse = laziness

paresseux/paresseuse *adjective*
= lazy

parfait/parfaite *adjective*
= perfect

parfois *adverb*
= sometimes

parfum *noun, masculine*
un parfum = a perfume
= a flavo(u)r

parfumé/parfumée *adjective*
= scented
= flavo(u)red

parier *verb* 2
= to bet

parisien/parisienne *adjective*
= Parisian

parking *noun, masculine*
un parking = a car park, a parking lot

parler *verb* 1
= to talk
= to speak

parmi *preposition*
= among

paroisse *noun, feminine*
une paroisse = a parish

parole *noun, feminine*
une parole = a word
prendre la parole = to speak
à vous la parole! = your turn to speak!

parrain *noun, masculine*
un parrain = a godfather

part
1 *noun, feminine*
• (*when dividing*)
une part (*of food*) = a portion
(*of a legacy*) = a share
• (*meaning direction, place*)
de toutes parts = from all sides, from
everywhere
nulle part = nowhere
quelque part = somewhere
d'une part... d'autre part = on the one
hand... on the other hand
faire part d'une naissance = to announce
a birth
2 de la part de = from
= on behalf of
elle m'a fait part de sa décision = she
informed me of her decision
3 à part = apart (from)

partager *verb* 13
= to share

partenaire *noun, masculine/feminine*
un partenaire/une partenaire = a partner

parterre *noun, masculine*
• (*in a garden*)
un parterre = a bed
• (*in a theatre*)
le parterre = the stalls, the orchestra

participer *verb* 1
• participer (à) = to take part (in)
• participer à = to share in

particulier/particulière *adjective*
= particular
= special

partie
1 *noun, feminine*
• (*not the whole*)
une partie = (a) part
• (*at cards, in sport*)
une partie = a game
2 en partie = partly, in part
3 faire partie de = to be part of
ça fait partie de mon travail = it's part of
my job
faire partie d'un club = to be a member of
a club

partir
1 *verb* 30 (**!** + *être*)
• = to leave
partir en courant = to run off
• = to go
partir à Paris = to go to Paris
• = to start
le sentier part du bois = the path starts in
the wood
2 à partir de = from
à partir de maintenant = from now on

partout *adverb*
= everywhere

paru ▶ paraître 63

parvenir *verb* 36 (**!** + *être*)
• parvenir à = to achieve
parvenir à son but = to achieve one's goal
parvenir à faire = to manage to do
• parvenir à = to reach
parvenir à New York = to reach New York

parvenu/parvenue ▶ parvenir 36

pas
1 *adverb*
= not
pas du tout = not at all
le film n'est pas mal✘ = the film isn't bad
2 *noun, masculine* (**!** *never changes*)
• (*a movement*)
un pas = a step
c'est à deux pas d'ici = it's very near here
• (*speed*)
le pas = the pace
d'un pas lent = slowly

passage *noun, masculine*
• (*a section of a text, a film*)
un passage = a passage

✘ in informal situations

- (*a means of access*)
  un passage = a way
  céder le passage = to give way, to yield
  'passage interdit' = 'no entry'
- **être de passage** = to be passing through
un passage à niveau = a level crossing, a grade crossing
un passage pour piétons = a pedestrian crossing, a crosswalk
un passage souterrain = a subway, a pedestrian underpass

passager/passagère *noun,*
masculine/feminine
  un passager/une passagère = a passenger
un passager clandestin = a stowaway

passant/passante *noun,*
masculine/feminine
  un passant/une passante = a passer-by

passé/passée
1 ▶ **passer** ⬚1
2 *adjective*
- **l'an passé** = last year
- **il est cinq heures passées** = it's past five o'clock
3 passé *noun, masculine*
  le passé = the past

passer *verb* ⬚1
1 (**!** + *avoir*)
- = to spend
  passer son temps à lire = to spend one's time reading
- = to take, to sit
  passer un examen = to take an examination

  > **!** *Note that* **réussir à un examen** *means to pass an exam.*

- = to show
  = to play
  passer un film = to show a film
  passer un disque = to play a record
- = to pass
  = to give
  peux-tu passer le sel? = can you pass the salt?
  il m'a passé son rhume = he gave me his cold
  je vous la passe (*on the telephone*) = I'll put her on
- (*to miss*)
  passer son tour = to pass
2 (**!** + *être*)
- (*to walk, to drive, to fly past*) = to go past, to go by
  un bus vient de passer = a bus has just gone past
  passer devant l'église = to go past the church, to pass the church
- (*to go a certain way*)
  passer par = to go through, to go by
  passer par la porte de derrière = to go through the back door

- (*to make one's way*) = to get past
  je ne peux pas passer = I can't get past
  laisser passer les enfants = to let the children past
- (*to call, to arrive*) = to come
  le facteur passe vers dix heures = the postman comes at about ten o'clock
- (*to pay a visit*) = to drop in
  passer voir un ami = to drop in on a friend
- (*to move to a different level*)
  passer dans la classe supérieure = to move up to the next class
- = to pass
  le temps passe trop vite = time passes too quickly
3 se passer (**!** + *être*)
- **se passer** = to happen
  qu'est-ce qui se passe? = what's happening?, what's going on?
- **se passer** = to go
  ça s'est bien passé = it went well
- **se passer de** = to do without

passerelle *noun, feminine*
  une passerelle = a footbridge
  = a gangway

passe-temps *noun, masculine* (**!** *never changes*)
  un passe-temps = a hobby

passion *noun, feminine*
  une passion = a passion

passionnant/passionnante
adjective
  = fascinating
  = exciting

passionné/passionnée
1 ▶ **passionner** ⬚1
2 *adjective*
  = passionate
3 *noun, masculine/feminine*
  un passionné/une passionnée de football = a football enthusiast, a football fan

passionner *verb* ⬚1
1 (**!** + *avoir*)
  = to fascinate
2 se passionner pour (**!** + *être*)
  se passionner pour = to have a passion for

passoire *noun, feminine*
  une passoire = a colander
  = a strainer

pastèque *noun, feminine*
  une pastèque = a watermelon

pasteur *noun, masculine*
  un pasteur = a parson, a minister

pastille *noun, feminine*
  une pastille = a lozenge, a cough drop

patate✶ *noun, feminine*
  une patate✶ = a spud, a potato

patauger *verb* ⬚13
  = to splash about

P

pâte
1 *noun, feminine*
- la pâte = pastry
  = dough
  = batter
- une pâte = a paste
2 **pâtes** *noun, feminine plural*
  des pâtes (alimentaires) = pasta

pâté *noun, masculine*
- le pâté = pâté
  un pâté (en croûte) = a pie
- un pâté de maisons = a block (of houses)

patience *noun, feminine*
- (*a virtue*)
  la patience = patience
- (*a game of cards*)
  faire une patience = to play patience, to
  play solitaire

patient/patiente
1 *adjective*
  = patient
2 *noun, masculine/feminine*
  un patient/une patiente = a patient

patienter *verb* 1
  = to wait

patin *noun, masculine*
  un patin = a skate
des patins de frein = brake blocks
des patins à glace = ice-skates
des patins à roulettes = roller-skates

patinage *noun, masculine*
  le patinage = skating

patinoire *noun, feminine*
  une patinoire = an ice rink

pâtisserie *noun, feminine*
- (*a place*)
  une pâtisserie = a cake shop
- (*a sweet*)
  une pâtisserie = a pastry, a cake

pâtissier/pâtissière *noun,*
masculine/feminine
  un pâtissier/une pâtissière = a
  confectioner

patron/patronne
1 *noun, masculine/feminine*
  le patron/la patronne = the boss
  = the manager
2 **patron** *noun, masculine*
  un patron = a pattern

patronne ▶ patron 1

patte *noun, feminine*
  une patte = a leg
  = a paw
  = a foot
  à quatre pattes = on all fours

---

paupière *noun, feminine*
  une paupière = an eyelid

pause *noun, feminine*
  une pause = a break
  faire une pause = to take a break

pauvre *adjective*
  = poor

pauvreté *noun, feminine*
  la pauvreté = poverty

pavé/pavée
1 *adjective*
  = cobbled
2 **pavé** *noun, masculine*
  un pavé = a cobblestone

payant/payante *adjective*
  (*describing a person*) = paying
  (*describing a show*) = not free

payer *verb* 21
1 (! + *avoir*)
  = to pay
2 **se payer*** (! + *être*)
  se payer* un repas = to treat oneself to a
  meal

pays *noun, masculine* (! never changes)
  un pays = a country

paysage *noun, masculine*
  un paysage = a landscape

Pays-Bas *noun, masculine plural*
  les Pays-Bas = the Netherlands, Holland

Pays de Galles *noun, masculine*
  le Pays de Galles = Wales

PCV *noun, masculine*
  appeler en PCV = to make a reverse-
  charge call, to call collect

péage *noun, masculine*
  le péage = the toll
  = the tollbooth

peau *noun, feminine*
(*plural*) **peaux**
  la peau = skin

pêche *noun, feminine*
- une pêche = a peach
- la pêche = fishing

péché *noun, masculine*
  un péché = a sin

pêcher
1 *verb* 1
- = to catch
- = to go fishing
2 *noun, masculine*
  un pêcher = a peach tree

pêcheur *noun, masculine*
  un pêcheur = a fisherman

pédale *noun, feminine*
  une pédale = a pedal

---

* in informal situations

pédaler verb 1
= to pedal

pédestre adjective
une randonnée pédestre = a ramble, a walk

peigne noun, masculine
un peigne = a comb

peignoir noun, masculine
un peignoir = a dressing gown, a robe

peindre verb 55
= to paint

peine
1 noun, feminine
• avoir de la peine à finir un travail = to have difficulty finishing a job
• ce n'est pas la peine d'essayer = it's not worth trying
ça vaut la peine d'y aller = it's worth going
• (sorrow)
la peine = grief
faire de la peine à ses amis = to upset one's friends
avoir de la peine = to be sad
• (punishment)
une peine de prison = a prison sentence
la peine de mort = capital punishment
2 **à peine** = hardly

peint/peinte ▶ **peindre** 55

peintre noun, masculine
un peintre = a painter

peinture noun, feminine
• la peinture (substance) = paint
(the activity) = painting
• une peinture = a painting

pêle-mêle adverb
= higgledy-piggledy, pell-mell

peler verb 17
= to peel

pèlerinage noun, masculine
un pèlerinage = a pilgrimage

pelle noun, feminine
une pelle = a shovel

pellicule
1 noun, feminine
une pellicule = a film
2 **pellicules** noun, feminine plural
des pellicules = dandruff

pelouse noun, feminine
la pelouse = the lawn

peluche noun, feminine
une peluche = a soft toy
un animal en peluche = a soft toy, a stuffed animal

pencher verb 1
1 (**!** + avoir)
= to tilt
pencher la tête = to bend one's head

2 se pencher (**!** + être)
se pencher = to lean
= to bend down

pendant
1 preposition
• = for
pendant des heures = for hours
pendant tout le voyage = for the whole journey, throughout the journey
• = during
pendant la nuit = during the night
pendant ce temps = meanwhile
2 **pendant que** = while

penderie noun, feminine
une penderie = a wardrobe, a closet

pendre verb 6
• = to hang
• = to dangle

pendu/pendue
1 ▶ **pendre** 6
2 **pendu** noun, masculine
jouer au pendu = to play hangman

pendule noun, feminine
une pendule = a clock

pénétrer verb 14
pénétrer dans un bâtiment = to enter a building, to get into a building

pénible adjective
= hard, difficult

péniblement adverb
= with difficulty

péniche noun, feminine
une péniche = a barge

pensée noun, feminine
• (an idea)
une pensée = a thought
• (a flower)
une pensée = a pansy

penser verb 1
• = to think
qu'en pensez-vous? = what do you think (about it)?
• penser à = to think of
= to remember
je pense à toi = I'm thinking of you
j'y ai pensé = I thought about it

pension noun, feminine
• (money)
une pension = a pension
• (a school)
une pension = a boarding school
• (a hotel)
une pension = a boarding house
la pension complète = full board
une pension de famille = a family hotel

pensionnaire noun, masculine/feminine
un pensionnaire/une pensionnaire (in a school) = a boarder
(in a hotel) = a resident

P

pensionnat *noun, masculine*
un pensionnat = a boarding school

pente *noun, feminine*
une pente = a slope
en pente = sloping

Pentecôte *noun, feminine*
la Pentecôte = Whitsun, Pentecost

pépé✶ *noun, masculine*
un pépé✶ = a grandad

pépin *noun, masculine*
• un pépin = a pip, a seed
• un pépin✶ = a slight problem

perche *noun, feminine*
une perche = a pole
la saut à la perche = pole vaulting

perdant/perdante
1 *adjective*
= losing
2 *noun, masculine/feminine*
un perdant/une perdante = a loser

perdre *verb* 6
1 (**!** + *avoir*)
= to lose
perdre son temps = to waste one's time
2 se perdre (**!** + *être*)
se perdre = to get lost

perdu/perdue
1 ▶ **perdre** 6
2 *adjective*
• = lost
= stray
• = wasted
c'est du temps perdu = it's a waste of time
• = remote, isolated

père *noun, masculine*
un père = a father
le père Noël = Father Christmas, Santa
Claus

perfectionner *verb* 1
1 (**!** + *avoir*)
= to perfect
= to improve
= to refine
2 se perfectionner (**!** + *être*)
se perfectionner = to improve

périmé/périmée *adjective*
= out-of-date

périphérique *noun, masculine*
le périphérique = the ring road, the
beltway

permanence
1 *noun, feminine*
une permanence = a permanently
manned office
(*in school*) = a (supervised) study room, a
study hall

2 en permanence = permanently

permettre *verb* 60
1 (**!** + *avoir*)
= to allow
permettre à un enfant de sortir = to allow a
child to go out
2 se permettre (**!** + *être*)
• (*to act without asking*)
se permettre de se servir = to take the
liberty of helping oneself
• (*to have money*)
pouvoir se permettre d'aller au restaurant
= to be able to afford to eat out

permis/permise
1 ▶ **permettre** 60
2 *adjective*
= permitted, allowed
3 permis *noun, masculine* (**!** *never
changes*)
un permis = a permit
= a licence, a license
un permis de conduire = a driving
licence, a driver's license

perroquet *noun, masculine*
un perroquet = a parrot

perruche *noun, feminine*
une perruche = a budgerigar, a budgie

perruque *noun, feminine*
une perruque = a wig

persienne *noun, feminine*
une persienne = a shutter

persil *noun, masculine*
le persil = parsley

personnage *noun, masculine*
un personnage = a character

personne
1 *pronoun*
= nobody
= anybody
2 *noun, feminine*
une personne = a person
quelques personnes = a few people

personnel/personnelle
1 *adjective*
= personal
2 personnel *noun, masculine*
le personnel = the staff

perte *noun, feminine*
une perte = a loss
une perte de temps = a waste of time

peser *verb* 16
= to weigh

pétanque *noun, feminine*
la pétanque = pétanque, *French bowls*

pétard *noun, masculine*
un pétard = a banger, a firecracker

pétillant/pétillante *adjective*
= sparkling

✶ in informal situations

petit/petite
1 *adjective*
   (*in size or importance*) = small, little
   (*in duration, length*) = short
2 *noun, masculine/feminine*
   un petit/une petite = a child
   (*in school*) = a junior
3 **petit** *noun, masculine*
   un petit = a little one
   les petits = the young
4 **petit à petit** = little by little, gradually
   les petits chevaux ≈ ludo, Parcheesi®

petite-fille *noun, feminine*
(*plural*) **petites-filles**
   une petite-fille = a granddaughter

petit-fils *noun, masculine*
(*plural*) **petits-fils**
   un petit-fils = a grandson

petits-enfants *noun, masculine plural*
   des petits-enfants = grandchildren

pétrole *noun, masculine*
   le pétrole = oil, petroleum

peu
1 *noun, masculine*
   un peu = a little
   un tout petit peu = just a little
2 *adverb*
* = not much
   il mange peu = he doesn't eat very much
* = not very
   peu intelligent = not very intelligent
   peu après = soon afterwards
3 **peu de** *determiner*
   = few, not many
   = little, not much
   peu de livres = few books
   peu de nourriture = little food
   c'est peu de chose = it's not much
4 **peu à peu** = gradually
5 **à peu près** = more or less
   = approximately

peuple *noun, masculine*
   un peuple = a people

peur *noun, feminine*
   la peur = fear
   avoir peur = to be afraid
   faire peur à quelqu'un = to frighten
      someone

peut-être *adverb*
   = perhaps, maybe

peux ▶ pouvoir 2 49

phare *noun, masculine*
   un phare (*on a car*) = a headlight
   (*on the coast*) = a lighthouse

pharmacie *noun, feminine*
   une pharmacie = a chemist's (shop), a
      drugstore

pharmacien/pharmacienne *noun,*
masculine/feminine
   un pharmacien/une pharmacienne = a
      chemist, a pharmacist

philatélie *noun, feminine*
   la philatélie = stamp collecting

phoque *noun, masculine*
   un phoque = a seal

photo *noun, feminine*
* (*a picture*)
   une photo = a photograph
* (*the activity*)
   la photo = photography

photocopie *noun, feminine*
   une photocopie = a photocopy

photocopieuse *noun, feminine*
   une photocopieuse = a photocopier

photographe *noun, masculine/feminine*
   un photographe/une photographe = a
      photographer

photographie *noun, feminine*
* (*a picture*)
   une photographie = a photograph
* (*the activity*)
   la photographie = photography

phrase *noun, feminine*
   une phrase = a sentence

physicien/physicienne *noun,*
masculine/feminine
   un physicien/une physicienne = a
      physicist

physique
1 *adjective*
   = physical
2 *noun, feminine*
   la physique = physics
3 *noun, masculine*
   le physique = physical appearance

picorer *verb* 1
   = to peck

pièce *noun, feminine*
* (*in a house, an apartment*)
   une pièce = a room
   un trois-pièces cuisine = a three-roomed
      apartment with kitchen
* (*money*)
   une pièce (de monnaie) = a coin
* (*at the theatre*)
   une pièce (de théâtre) = a play
* (*a component*)
   une pièce = a part
   une pièce de rechange = a spare part
* (*an item*)
   une pièce = a piece
   ils coûtent dix francs pièce = they cost ten
      francs each
   un (maillot) deux-pièces = a two-piece
      swimsuit
* (*in a file*)
   une pièce = a document

P

une pièce détachée = a spare part
une pièce d'identité = identification

pied noun, masculine
* (part of the body)
  un pied = a foot
  à pied = on foot
  il va à l'école à pied = he walks to school
  pieds nus = barefoot
  un coup de pied = a kick
* (the lower end)
  le pied = the foot, the bottom
  au pied de l'escalier = at the bottom of the stairs
* (an upright part)
  un pied (on a table) = a leg
  (on a lamp) = a base
  (on a glass) = a stem
* (a measurement)
  un pied = a foot

piège noun, masculine
  un piège = a trap

pierre noun, feminine
  une pierre = a stone

piéton/piétonne noun,
masculine/feminine
  un piéton/une piétonne = a pedestrian

pieuvre noun, feminine
  une pieuvre = an octopus

pigeon noun, masculine
  un pigeon = a pigeon
  pigeon vole = Simon says

pile
1 noun, feminine
* (in a flashlight, a toy)
  une pile = a battery
  à piles = battery-operated
* (on a coin)
  pile = tails
  jouer à pile ou face = to play heads or tails
* (things on top of one another)
  une pile = a pile, a stack
2 adverb✘
  à trois heures pile✘ = at three o'clock on the dot
  s'arrêter pile✘ = to stop dead
  tu tombes pile✘ = you've come at just the right moment

pilier noun, masculine
  un pilier = a pillar

pilote noun, masculine
  un pilote = a pilot
pilote automobile = racing driver
pilote de rallye = rally driver

pilule noun, feminine
  une pilule = a pill

pin noun, masculine
  un pin = a pine (tree)

pinceau noun, masculine
(plural) **pinceaux**
  un pinceau = a (paint)brush

pincée noun, feminine
  une pincée = a pinch

pincer verb [12]
  = to pinch

pinède noun, feminine
  une pinède = a pine forest

pingouin noun, masculine
  un pingouin = a penguin

ping-pong® noun, masculine
(plural) **ping-pongs**
  le ping-pong = table tennis, ping-pong

pin's noun, masculine (✘ never changes)
  un pin's = a (lapel) badge, a pin

pioche noun, feminine
  une pioche = a pickaxe

pipe noun, feminine
  une pipe = a pipe

pipi✘ noun, masculine
  faire pipi✘ = to have a pee, to take a pee

pique noun, masculine
  pique = spades

pique-nique noun, masculine
(plural) **pique-niques**
  un pique-nique = a picnic

piquer verb [1]
1 (✘ + avoir)
* (if it's a bee, a nettle, smoke) = to sting
  (if it's a snake, a mosquito) = to bite
  (if it's a thorn) = to prick
* (to take)✘ = to pinch, to steal
  = to borrow
2 se piquer (✘ + être)
  se piquer = to prick oneself

piqûre noun, feminine
  une piqûre (with a syringe) = an injection
  (from an insect) = a sting
  = a bite

pire
1 adjective
  = worse
  = worst
2 noun, masculine
  le pire = the worst (about it)

piscine noun, feminine
  une piscine = a swimming pool
  une piscine couverte = an indoor swimming pool

pistache noun, feminine
  une pistache = a pistachio nut

piste noun, feminine
* (a clearly marked path)
  une piste (in a forest) = a trail, a track
  (when skiing) = a piste, a run

✘ in informal situations

(*in racing events*)
= a (race)track
= a racecourse
• (*in a circus*)
la piste = the ring
• (*in a police investigation*)
une piste = a lead
une piste d'atterrissage = a runway
une piste cyclable = a cycle lane
une piste de danse = a dance floor

pistolet *noun, masculine*
un pistolet = a gun

pitre *noun, masculine*
un pitre = a clown, a buffoon

pittoresque *adjective*
= picturesque

placard *noun, masculine*
un placard = a cupboard

place *noun, feminine*
• (*in a town*)
une place = a square
• (*for a passenger, a spectator*)
une place = a seat
une place assise = a seat
une place debout = a standing ticket
• (*a position*)
une place = a place
remettre un livre à sa place = to put a book back in its place
obtenir la première place = to take first place
à la place de = instead of
• (*a vacant spot*)
une place (*at a table*) = a place
(*for a car*) = a parking space
• (*enough empty space*)
de la place = room, space

plafond *noun, masculine*
le plafond = the ceiling

plage *noun, feminine*
la plage = the beach

plaie *noun, feminine*
une plaie = a wound

plaindre *verb* 54
1 (**!** + *avoir*)
= to feel sorry for
2 se plaindre (**!** + *être*)
se plaindre = to complain

plaint/plainte[1] ▶ **plaindre** 54

plainte[2] *noun, feminine*
• (*expressing dissatisfaction*)
une plainte = a complaint
• (*a sound of pain*)
une plainte = a moan, a groan

plaire *verb* 59
• **s'il te plaît, s'il vous plaît** = please
• **Marc plaît aux filles** = girls find Marc attractive
le film leur a plu = they liked the film

plaisanterie *noun, feminine*
une plaisanterie = a joke

plaisir *noun, masculine*
le plaisir = pleasure
ma visite leur a fait plaisir = they were pleased to see me

plaît ▶ **plaire** 59

plan *noun, masculine*
• (*of an area*)
un plan = a map
• (*for an essay*)
un plan = an outline
• (*for a line of action*)
un plan = a plan
• (*in films, photography*)
au premier plan = in the foreground
un gros plan = a close-up

planche *noun, feminine*
une planche = a plank
= a board
une planche à repasser = an ironing board
une planche à roulettes = a skateboard
une planche à voile = a windsurfing board

plancher *noun, masculine*
le plancher = the floor

planète *noun, feminine*
une planète = a planet

planeur *noun, masculine*
• (*the equipment*)
un planeur = a glider
• (*the sport*)
le planeur = gliding

planifier *verb* 2
= to plan

plante *noun, feminine*
une plante = a plant
une plante grasse = a succulent
une plante verte = a houseplant

planter *verb* 1
• = to plant
• **planter une tente** = to pitch a tent

plaque *noun, feminine*
une plaque (*of metal, glass*) = a plate
une plaque d'immatriculation = a number plate, a license plate

plastique *noun, masculine*
le plastique = plastic

plat/plate
1 *adjective*
= flat
2 plat *noun, masculine*
un plat = a dish
= a course
le plat du jour = today's special

P

3 à plat
- (*the way something lies*)
  à plat = flat
  poser une carte à plat = to lay a map down flat
  à plat ventre = flat on one's stomach
- (*describing a tyre*)
  à plat = flat
- (*describing a person*)
  à plat✱ = run down

plateau *noun, masculine*
(*plural*) **plateaux**
  un plateau (*for serving*) = a tray
  un plateau de fromages = a cheeseboard

platine *noun, feminine*
  une platine = a turntable
  une platine CD = a CD player

plâtre *noun, masculine*
  le plâtre = plaster

plein/pleine
1 *adjective*
- = full
- en pleine forêt = (right) in the middle of the forest
  en plein jour = in broad daylight
  en plein air = in the open air
  en pleine forme = in great shape, really fit
2 plein *noun, masculine*
  faire le plein (d'essence) = to fill up (with petrol)

pleurer *verb* ⬚1
  = to cry, to weep

pleut ▶ **pleuvoir** ⬚33

pleuvoir *verb* ⬚33
  = to rain
  il pleut = it's raining

plier *verb* ⬚2
  = to fold
  = to bend

plombier *noun, masculine*
  un plombier = a plumber

plongée *noun, feminine*
  la plongée = diving
  la plongée sous-marine = deep-sea diving

plongeoir *noun, masculine*
  un plongeoir = a diving-board

plongeon *noun, masculine*
  un plongeon = a dive

plonger *verb* ⬚13
- = to dive
- = to plunge

plongeur/plongeuse *noun,*
masculine/feminine
  un plongeur/une plongeuse = a diver

plu
- ▶ **plaire** ⬚59
- ▶ **pleuvoir** ⬚33

pluie *noun, feminine*
  la pluie = rain

plume *noun, feminine*
- (*on a bird*)
  une plume = a feather
- (*on a pen*)
  une plume = a nib

plupart *noun, feminine*
  la plupart de = most of

pluriel *noun, masculine*
  le pluriel = the plural

plus
1 *conjunction*
  = plus
2 *adverb*
- = more
  c'est plus intéressant = it's more interesting
  arriver plus tôt que d'habitude = to arrive earlier than usual
  de plus en plus prudent = more and more careful
  deux fois plus cher = twice as expensive
- plus de = more
  = more than, over
  plus de la moitié = more than half
  elle a plus de seize ans = she's over sixteen
  il est plus de minuit = it's past midnight
- plus… plus = the more… the more
  plus… moins = the more… the less
  plus… mieux = the more… the better
  plus on lit, plus on apprend = the more you read, the more you learn
- le plus/la plus = the most
  = the more
  les plus belles fleurs du jardin = the most beautiful flowers in the garden
  le plus cher des deux = the more expensive of the two
- en plus = on top of (that)
  il fait froid et en plus il pleut = it's cold and on top of that it's raining
  en plus de mon travail = on top of my work
3 ne… plus = no more, not any more
  = no longer
  il n'y a plus de pain = there's no more bread, there's no bread left
  elle ne travaille plus = she doesn't work any more, she no longer works
  je n'ai plus que dix francs = I've only got ten francs left
  il ne te reste plus rien = you've nothing left
  plus jamais = never again
  il n'y va pas, et moi non plus = he's not going and neither am I

plusieurs *adjective*
  = several

---

plutôt *adverb*
= rather
= instead

pluvieux/pluvieuse *adjective*
= rainy

pneu *noun, masculine*
un pneu = a tyre, a tire

pneumatique *adjective*
= inflatable

poche *noun, feminine*
une poche = a pocket

poêle
1 *noun, feminine*
une poêle (à frire) = a frying pan
2 *noun, masculine*
un poêle = a stove

poésie *noun, feminine*
* la poésie = poetry
* une poésie = a poem

poids *noun, masculine* (**!** *never changes*)
le poids = the weight
prendre du poids = to put on weight
un poids lourd = a heavy goods vehicle

poignée *noun, feminine*
* (*on a door*)
une poignée = a handle
* (*an amount*)
une poignée = a handful
une poignée de main = a handshake

poignet *noun, masculine*
un poignet = a wrist
= a cuff

poil *noun, masculine*
un poil (*on the body, on an animal*) = a hair
(*on a brush*) = a bristle

poing *noun, masculine*
le poing = the fist
un coup de poing = a punch

point
1 *noun, masculine*
* (*a punctuation mark*)
un point = a full stop, a period
deux points = a colon
* (*when scoring*)
un point = a point
* (*in sewing, in knitting*)
un point = a stitch
* (*a small round mark*)
un point = a dot, a speck
* (*a particular place or position*)
un point de rencontre = a meeting point
2 à point
un bifteck (cuit) à point = a medium rare
steak
un point de départ = a starting point
un point d'exclamation = an
exclamation mark
un point d'interrogation = a question
mark

un point de repère = a landmark
des points de suspension = suspension
points

pointe *noun, feminine*
la pointe = the point, the tip
sur la pointe des pieds = on tiptoe

pointer: **se pointer✶** *verb* $\boxed{1}$ (**!** + *être*)
se pointer✶ = to show up

pointu/pointue *adjective*
= pointed
= with a sharp point

pointure *noun, feminine*
une pointure = a shoe size

point-virgule *noun, masculine*
(*plural*) **points-virgules**
un point-virgule = a semicolon

poire *noun, feminine*
une poire = a pear

poireau *noun, masculine*
(*plural*) **poireaux**
un poireau = a leek

pois *noun, masculine* (**!** *never changes*)
* (*on material*)
un pois = a dot
à pois = polka dot, dotted
* (*in a pod*)
un pois = a pea
des petits pois = garden peas, petits pois

poisson *noun, masculine*
un poisson = a fish
un poisson d'avril = an April fool's joke
un poisson rouge = a goldfish

poissonnerie *noun, feminine*
une poissonnerie = a fishmonger's, a fish
shop

poissonnier/poissonnière *noun,*
masculine/feminine
un poissonnier/une poissonnière = a
fishmonger, a fish dealer

Poissons *noun, masculine plural*
Poissons = Pisces

poitrine *noun, feminine*
la poitrine = the chest
= the bust

poivre *noun, masculine*
le poivre = pepper

poivron *noun, masculine*
un poivron = a sweet pepper, a capsicum

poli/polie *adjective*
* (*well-mannered*) = polite
* (*shiny*) = polished

police *noun, feminine*
la police = the police
police secours ≈ emergency services

policier *noun, masculine*
un policier = a policeman

P

polluer *verb* 1
= to pollute

Pologne *noun, feminine*
la Pologne = Poland

polonais/polonaise
1 *adjective*
= Polish
2 polonais *noun, masculine*
le polonais = Polish

pommade *noun, feminine*
une pommade = an ointment

pomme *noun, feminine*
une pomme = an apple
une pomme de pin = a pine cone
une pomme de terre = a potato

pommier *noun, masculine*
un pommier = an apple tree

pompe *noun, feminine*
une pompe = a pump

pompier *noun, masculine*
un pompier = a fireman, a firefighter
les pompiers = the fire brigade, the fire
   department

pompiste *noun, masculine|feminine*
un pompiste/une pompiste = a petrol
   pump attendant, a gas station
   attendant

pont *noun, masculine*
• (*over a river*)
un pont = a bridge
• (*on a ship*)
un pont = a deck
• (*extra time off*)
faire le pont *to have the day(s) off between
   a public holiday and a weekend*

populaire *adjective*
• (*describing an area*) = working-class
• (*meaning well-liked*) = popular

porc *noun, masculine*
• (*the animal*)
un porc = a pig
• (*the meat*)
le porc = pork

porc-épic *noun, masculine*
(*plural*) **porc-épics**
un porc-épic = a porcupine

porcherie *noun, feminine*
une porcherie = a pigsty

port *noun, masculine*
un port = a harbo(u)r, a port
un port de pêche = a fishing harbo(u)r
un port de plaisance = a marina

portail *noun, masculine*
un portail = a gate

porte *noun, feminine*
une porte = a door
= a gate
mettre à la porte = to throw out
une porte d'embarquement = a
   departure gate
la porte d'entrée = the front door

porte-clés, **porte-clefs** *noun,
masculine* (**!** *never changes*)
un porte-clés = a key ring

porte-fenêtre *noun, feminine*
(*plural*) **portes-fenêtres**
une porte-fenêtre = a French window

portefeuille *noun, masculine*
un portefeuille = a wallet

portemanteau *noun, masculine*
(*plural*) **portemanteaux**
un portemanteau = a coat rack
= a coat stand

porte-monnaie *noun, masculine*
(**!** *never changes*)
un porte-monnaie = a purse, a coin purse

porter *verb* 1
1 (**!** + *avoir*)
• = to carry
• = to wear
• porter bonheur = to bring good luck
porter malheur = to bring bad luck
2 se porter (**!** + *être*)
se porter bien = to be well

porteur *noun, masculine*
un porteur = a porter

portier *noun, masculine*
un portier = a doorman

portière *noun, feminine*
une portière = a door

portillon *noun, masculine*
un portillon = a gate, a barrier

portrait *noun, masculine*
• (*a likeness*)
un portrait = a portrait
• (*in words*)
un portrait = a description

portrait-robot *noun, masculine*
(*plural*) **portraits-robots**
un portrait-robot = a photofit®, an
   identikit®

portugais/portugaise
1 *adjective*
= Portuguese
2 portugais *noun, masculine*
le portugais = Portuguese

Portugal *noun, masculine*
le Portugal = Portugal

✷ in informal situations

poser *verb* 1
1 (**!** + *avoir*)
• = to put down
  poser un sac sur une table = to put a bag down on a table
• = to ask
  poser une question = to ask a question
2 se poser (**!** + *être*)
  se poser (*if it's a bird*) = to settle, to alight
  (*if it's a plane*) = to land, to touch down

posséder *verb* 14
  = to own
  = to possess

possible
1 *adjective*
  = possible
  le plus de temps possible = as much time as possible
  le plus tôt possible = as soon as possible
2 *noun, masculine*
  faire tout son possible = to do one's utmost

poste
1 *noun, feminine*
  la poste = the post office
2 *noun, masculine*
• (*employment*)
  un poste = a job, a position
• (*a receiver*)
  un poste de télévision = a television set
• (*a place*)
  le poste (de police) = the police station
• (*for telephoning*)
  un poste = an extension

poster *verb* 1
  = to post, to mail

pot *noun, masculine*
• **un pot** = a pot
  = a jar
• **un pot**✱ = a drink

potable *adjective*
  l'eau potable = drinking water

potage *noun, masculine*
  le potage = soup

potager *noun, masculine*
  un (jardin) potager = a vegetable garden

poteau *noun, masculine*
  (*plural*) **poteaux**
  un poteau = a post
  un poteau indicateur = a signpost

potier/potière *noun, masculine/feminine*
  un potier/une potière = a potter

poubelle *noun, feminine*
  une poubelle = a dustbin, a trash can

pouce *noun, masculine*
• **un pouce** = a thumb
• **un pouce** = an inch

poudre *noun, feminine*
  la poudre = powder

poule *noun, feminine*
  une poule = a hen

poulet *noun, masculine*
  un poulet = a chicken

poulpe *noun, masculine*
  un poulpe = an octopus

pouls *noun, masculine* (**!** *never changes*)
  le pouls = the pulse

poumon *noun, masculine*
  un poumon = a lung

poupée *noun, feminine*
  une poupée = a doll

pour
1 *preposition*
• = for
  c'est pour toi = it's for you
  un produit pour nettoyer les vitres = a product for cleaning windows
• = to, in order to, so as to
  j'ai écrit pour les remercier = I've written to thank them
  pour ne pas manquer le train = so as not to miss the train
• = per
  dix pour cent = ten per cent
2 *noun, masculine*
  le pour et le contre = the pros and the cons

pourboire *noun, masculine*
  un pourboire = a tip

pourpre *adjective*
  = crimson

pourquoi *adverb, conjunction*
  = why

pourrai ▶ **pouvoir 2** 49

pourri/pourrie *adjective*
  = rotten

pourtant *adverb*
  = yet

pousser *verb* 1
1 (**!** + *avoir*)
• = to push
• = to move
• = to let out
  pousser un cri = to let out a cry
• (*if it's a plant, hair*) = to grow
  faire pousser des fleurs = to grow flowers
2 se pousser (**!** + *être*)
  se pousser = to move over

poussette *noun, feminine*
  une poussette = a pushchair, a stroller

poussière *noun, feminine*
  la poussière = dust

poussin *noun, masculine*
  un poussin = a chick

pouvoir
1 *noun, masculine*
  le pouvoir = power

P

2 verb 49
- • = to be able to
  il ne pourra pas venir = he won't be able to come
  elle n'a pas pu partir = she wasn't able to leave, she couldn't leave
  je ne peux pas payer ce prix = I can't pay that sort of price
  pourriez-vous me dire où se trouve la gare? = could you tell me where the station is?
  je n'en peux plus! (after an effort) = I've had it!
  (after a meal) = I'm full!
- • = to be allowed to
  puis-je téléphoner? = may I use the phone?
  tu ne peux pas te garer là = you can't park there
- • (expressing a possibility)
  attention, tu pourrais glisser = careful, you might slip
  vous auriez pu m'avertir! = you might have warned me!
  il pouvait avoir dix ans = he would have been about ten
  il pouvait être dix heures = it was probably about ten o'clock
3 il se peut (! + être)
  il se peut que j'y aille = I might go
  il se pourrait bien que l'avion ait du retard = the plane might well be delayed
  ça se peut = it's possible

prairie noun, feminine
  une prairie = a meadow

pratique adjective
  = practical
  = handy, convenient

pratiquer verb 1
  pratiquer le tennis = to play tennis
  pratiquer le yoga = to do yoga

pré noun, masculine
  un pré = a meadow

précieux/précieuse adjective
  = precious

précipiter: se précipiter verb 1
(! + être)
  se précipiter = to rush
  se précipiter sur le journal = to pounce on the newspaper

précis/précise adjective
  = precise
  = accurate
  à trois heures précises = at exactly three o'clock, at three o'clock sharp

préféré/préférée
1 ▶ préférer 14
2 adjective
  = favo(u)rite

préférence noun, feminine
  une préférence = a preference
  de préférence = preferably

préférer verb 14
  = to prefer

premier/première¹
1 adjective
  = first
2 noun, masculine
  habiter au premier (in Britain) = to live on the first floor
  (in the US) = to live on the second floor
  le premier de l'an = New Year's Day

première² noun, feminine
- • (in school)
  la première the class for secondary school students aged 16 to 17
- • (when travelling)
  voyager en première = to travel first class

prendre verb 52
1 (! + avoir)
- • = to take
- • = to have
  allons prendre un verre = let's go and have a drink
  qu'est-ce que tu prends? = what'll you have?
- • = to go
  prenez à gauche = go left, turn left
- • = to catch
  prendre froid = to catch a chill
  prendre feu = to catch fire
- • **qu'est-ce qui te prend✘?** = what's up with you?
2 se prendre (! + être)
- • **pour qui se prend-il?** = who does he think he is?
- • **elle s'y prend mal** = she's going about it the wrong way

prénom noun, masculine
  un prénom = a first name

préparer verb 1
1 (! + avoir)
- • **préparer un repas** = to prepare a meal
- • **préparer un examen** = to prepare for an examination
- • **préparer ses affaires** = to get one's things ready
2 se préparer (! + être)
  se préparer = to get ready

près
1 adverb
  = close, near(by)
  tout près du magasin = near the shop
  près de trois mètres = nearly three metres
2 de près = closely
3 à peu près = about
  = practically

présenter verb 1
1 (! + avoir)
- • = to present
  = to show

- = to introduce
présenter son passeport = to show one's
  passport
il m'a présenté à ses amis = he introduced
  me to his friends
2 se présenter (**!** + *être*)
- (*to give one's name*)
se présenter = to introduce oneself
- (*to show up*)
se présenter = to present oneself
- (*if it's an opportunity*)
se présenter = to arise

président/présidente *noun,*
masculine/feminine
un président/une présidente = a president
  = a chairman/a chairwoman, a
  chairperson

presque *adverb*
= nearly, almost

pressé/pressée *adjective*
être pressé = to be in a hurry

pressing *noun, masculine*
un pressing = a dry-cleaner's

pression *noun, feminine*
la pression = pressure

prêt/prête
1 *adjective*
= ready
2 prêt *noun, masculine*
un prêt = a loan

prêt-à-porter *noun, masculine*
le prêt-à-porter = ready-to-wear (clothes)

prêter *verb* ①
= to lend

prêtre *noun, masculine*
un prêtre = a priest

preuve *noun, feminine*
- **une preuve** = a piece of evidence
des preuves = evidence
- **la preuve** = the proof
c'est la preuve qu'il est innocent = it's
  proof that he's innocent
- **faire preuve de** = to show

prévenir *verb* ㊱
- = to warn
- = to prevent

prévenu/prévenue ▶ **prévenir** ㊱

prévision *noun, feminine*
une prévision = a forecast
les prévisions météorologiques = the
  weather forecast

prévoir *verb* ㉟
- = to predict
  = to anticipate, to expect
- = to plan
comme prévu = as planned

prévu/prévue ▶ **prévoir** ㉟

prier *verb* ②
= to request, to ask
je vous en prie = don't mention it

primaire *adjective*
= primary

primeurs *noun, feminine plural*
les primeurs = early produce

principal/principale *adjective*
(*plural*) **principaux/principales**
= main

principauté *noun, feminine*
une principauté = a principality

printemps *noun, masculine* (**!** *never*
changes)
le printemps = spring

priorité *noun, feminine*
la priorité = priority
(*on the road*) = the right of way

pris/prise[1] ▶ **prendre** ㊾

prise[2] *noun, feminine*
- (*electrical*)
une prise = a plug
  = a socket
- (*when fishing*)
une prise = a catch

prisonnier/prisonnière *adjective*
être prisonnier = to be a prisoner

privé/privée *adjective*
= private

prix *noun, masculine* (**!** *never changes*)
- (*the cost*)
le prix = the price
à tout prix = at all costs
- (*a reward*)
un prix = a prize

problème *noun, masculine*
un problème = a problem
  = an issue

procès *noun, masculine* (**!** *never changes*)
un procès = a trial

prochain/prochaine *adjective*
= next
à l'année prochaine! = see you next year!

proche *adjective*
= nearby
le garage le plus proche = the nearest
  garage

producteur/productrice *noun,*
masculine/feminine
un producteur/une productrice = a
  producer

produire *verb* ㊷
1 (**!** + *avoir*)
- = to produce
- = to cause

P

2 se produire (! + *être*)
　se produire = to happen

produit/produite
1 ▶ produire [62]
2 produit *noun, masculine*
　un produit = a product
un produit de beauté = a beauty product
un produit chimique = a chemical

prof* *noun, masculine/feminine*
　un prof*/une prof* = a teacher, a lecturer

professeur *noun, masculine*
　un professeur = a teacher, a lecturer

profiter *verb* [1]
　profiter de = to take advantage of
　= to make the most of

profond/profonde *adjective*
　= deep
　peu profond = shallow

profondeur *noun, feminine*
　la profondeur = the depth
　avoir dix mètres de profondeur = to be ten
　　metres deep

programmateur *noun, masculine*
　un programmateur = a timer

programme *noun, masculine*
　un programme = a program(me)
　(*for an examination*) = a syllabus
　(*for a computer*) = a program

programmer *verb* [1]
　= to program

progrès *noun, masculine* (! *never changes*)
　le progrès = progress

projecteur *noun, masculine*
• (*a light*)
　un projecteur = a floodlight
　= a searchlight
• (*for slides*)
　un projecteur = a projector

projet *noun, masculine*
　un projet = a plan
　des projets de vacances = holiday plans,
　　vacation plans

projeter *verb* [20]
　= to plan

promenade *noun, feminine*
　une promenade (*on foot*) = a walk
　(*by car*) = a drive
　(*on a bike*) = a ride

promener *verb* [16]
1 (! + *avoir*)
　promener le chien = to take the dog for a
　　walk
2 se promener (! + *être*)
　se promener (*on foot*) = to go for a walk

　(*by car*) = to go for a drive
　(*on a bike*) = to go for a ride

promesse *noun, feminine*
　une promesse = a promise

promettre *verb* [60]
　= to promise

promis/promise ▶ promettre [60]

promotion *noun, feminine*
• (*in a shop*)
　une promotion = a special offer
• (*in one's career*)
　une promotion = promotion

pronom *noun, masculine*
　un pronom = a pronoun

prononcer *verb* [12]
• = to pronounce
• = to deliver

propos *noun, masculine plural*
　des propos = words
à propos = by the way
　à propos, je n'y vais pas = by the way, I'm
　　not going
à propos de = about

proposer *verb* [1]
• = to suggest
• = to offer
　elle m'a proposé sa voiture = she offered
　　me her car

proposition *noun, feminine*
　une proposition = a suggestion
　= a proposal

propre *adjective*
• = clean
　une serviette propre = a clean towel
• = own
　avec mon propre argent = with my own
　　money

propriétaire *noun, masculine/feminine*
　le propriétaire/la propriétaire = the owner
　(*with tenants*) = the landlord/the landlady

propriété *noun, feminine*
　la propriété = property
　'propriété privée' = 'private property'

prospère *adjective*
　= prosperous

protéger *verb* [15]
　= to protect

protester *verb* [1]
　= to protest

prouver *verb* [1]
　= to prove

provenance *noun, feminine*
　la provenance = the origin
　le train en provenance de Paris = the train
　　from Paris

provençal/provençale
(*plural*) **provençaux/provençales**
1 *adjective*
= of Provence
= from Provence
2 provençal *noun, masculine*
le provençal = Provençal

proviseur *noun, masculine*
le proviseur = the headteacher, the
principal

provision
1 *noun, feminine*
une provision de = a stock of, a supply of
faire une provision de papier = to stock up
on paper
2 provisions *noun, feminine plural*
faire des provisions = to go shopping for
food

provisoire *adjective*
= provisional, temporary

provoquer *verb* [1]
• = to cause
• = to provoke

proximité: **à proximité** *adverb*
= near(by)

prudence *noun, feminine*
la prudence = caution

prudent/prudente *adjective*
= careful, cautious

prune *noun, feminine*
une prune = a plum

pruneau *noun, masculine*
(*plural*) **pruneaux**
un pruneau = a prune

PTT *noun, feminine plural*
les PTT *formerly the French postal and
telecommunications service*

pu ▶ **pouvoir 2** [49]

pub* *noun, feminine* ▶ **publicité**

public/publique
1 *adjective*
= public
(*describing a school, education*) = state
(*in the US*) = public
2 public *noun, masculine*
le public (*all the people*) = the public
(*at a meeting, a show*) = the audience

publicitaire
1 *adjective*
= advertising
2 *noun, masculine|feminine*
un publicitaire/une publicitaire = an
advertising executive

publicité *noun, feminine*
• **la publicité** = advertising
• **une publicité** = an advertisement, a
commercial

publier *verb* [2]
= to publish

puer *verb* [1]
= to stink
ça pue le poisson! = it stinks of fish!

puis *adverb*
= then
= next

puisque (**puisqu'** *before vowel or mute
h*) *conjunction*
= as
= since

puissant/puissante *adjective*
= powerful

puisse ▶ **pouvoir 2** [49]

puits *noun, masculine* (**!** *never changes*)
un puits = a well

pull *noun, masculine*
un pull = a jumper, a sweater

punaise *noun, feminine*
• (*for pinning*)
une punaise = a drawing pin, a
thumbtack
• (*an insect*)
une punaise = a bug

punir *verb* [3]
= to punish

punition *noun, feminine*
une punition = a punishment

pur/pure *adjective*
= pure
(*describing wine or spirits*) = neat

purée *noun, feminine*
• **la purée (de pommes de terre)** = mashed
potatoes
• **la purée** = puree

PV* *noun, masculine*
un PV* = a fine
= a parking ticket

pyjama *noun, masculine*
un pyjama = pyjamas, pajamas

Qq

qu' ▶ **que**

quai *noun, masculine*
un quai (*in a station*) = a platform
(*in a port*) = a quay
(*along a river*) = a bank
le navire est à quai = the ship has docked

qualité noun, feminine
• **une qualité** = a quality
• **nom, prénom et qualité** = surname, first
  name and occupation
  en sa qualité de représentant = in his/her
  capacity as a representative

quand
1 conjunction
  = when
  quand il sera vieux = when he's old
  tu sortiras quand tu auras fini = you'll go
  out when you've finished
2 adverb
  = when
  quand est-ce que vous partez? = when are
  you leaving?
  depuis quand est-il malade? = how long
  has he been ill?
3 quand même = still, even so

quant à preposition
  = as for

quantité noun, feminine
  une quantité = a quantity, an amount
  des quantités de = lots of

quarante number
  = forty

quart noun, masculine
  un quart = a quarter
  un quart d'heure = a quarter of an hour
  une heure moins le quart = a quarter to
  one
  une heure et quart = a quarter past one

quartier noun, masculine
• (part of a town)
  un quartier = an area, a district
  les gens du quartier = the locals
• (a segment)
  un quartier = a quarter
  le premier quartier de la lune = the moon's
  first quarter
un quartier général = headquarters

quatorze number
  = fourteen

quatorzième number
  = fourteenth

quatre number
  = quatre

quatre-vingt(s) number
  = eighty

quatre-vingt-dix number
  = ninety

quatrième
1 number
  = fourth
2 noun, feminine
  la quatrième the class for secondary
  school students aged 13 to 14

que (**qu'** before vowel or mute h)
  ! The construction ne + verb + que is
  treated under ne.

1 conjunction
• = that
  elle a dit qu'elle le ferait = she said that she
  would do it
  je veux que tu m'accompagnes = I want
  you to come with me
• = than, as
  plus gros que moi = fatter than me
  aussi fort que mon père = as strong as my
  father
  c'est le même que le mien = it's the same
  as mine
• = whether
  que tu le veuilles ou non = whether you
  like it or not
2 pronoun
• = what
  que dire? = what can you say?
  je ne sais pas ce qu'il a dit = I don't know
  what he said
  qu'est-ce que c'est? = what's that?
• = that
  = who
  la voiture que tu as achetée = the car
  (that) you've bought
  l'ami que j'ai invité = the friend whom I
  invited
3 adverb
  que c'est joli! = it's so pretty!

québécois/québécoise adjective
  = of Quebec
  = from Quebec

quel/quelle
1 determiner
  = what
  = which
  quelle est la capitale du Togo? = what's
  the capital of Togo?
2 adjective
• = what
  = which
  quelle heure est-il? = what time is it?
  quels disques as-tu achetés? = which
  records did you buy?
• **quelle coïncidence!** = what a coincidence!
• **quel que soit le temps** = whatever the
  weather
  quelles que soient leurs habitudes
  = whatever their habits

quelque determiner
• (in the singular) = some
  depuis quelque temps = for some time
• (in the plural) = some, a few
  = any
  quelques élèves = some pupils, a few
  pupils

quelquefois adverb
  = sometimes

quelques-uns/quelques-unes
pronoun
= some, a few

quelqu'un *pronoun*
= someone, somebody
= anyone, anybody

quenelle *noun, feminine*
une quenelle *a dumpling made of flour and egg, flavo(u)red with meat or fish*

querelle *noun, feminine*
une querelle = a quarrel

question *noun, feminine*
* (*a sentence asking something*)
une question = a question
poser une question à un élève = to ask a pupil a question
* (*something to be examined*)
une question = a matter
= an issue
c'est une question de vie ou de mort = it's a matter of life and death
pas question! = no way!

questionnaire *noun, masculine*
un questionnaire = a questionnaire

questionner *verb* ⒈
= to question

quête *noun, feminine*
une quête = a collection
faire la quête = to pass the hat around
= to collect for charity
= to take the collection

queue *noun, feminine*
* (*on an animal*)
une queue = a tail
* (*people or cars waiting*)
une queue = a queue, a line
faire la queue = to stand in a queue, to stand in line

queue-de-cheval *noun, feminine*
(*plural*) **queues-de-cheval**
une queue-de-cheval = a ponytail

qui *pronoun*
* = who
= whom
qui est-ce? = who is it?
l'homme à qui tu as parlé = the man to whom you spoke
à qui sont ces chaussures? = whose shoes are these?
* = who
= that
= which
qui que vous soyez = whoever you are
je n'ai jamais frappé qui que ce soit = I've never hit anybody

quille *noun, feminine*
une quille = a skittle

quincaillerie *noun, feminine*
une quincaillerie = a hardware shop, a hardware store

quinzaine *noun, feminine*
* une quinzaine = about fifteen
* une quinzaine (de jours) = a fortnight, two weeks

quinze *number*
= fifteen
quinze jours = fifteen days
= a fortnight, two weeks

quinzième *number*
= fifteenth

quittance *noun, feminine*
une quittance = a receipt
= a bill

quitter *verb* ⒈
1 (**!** + *avoir*)
* = to leave
* ne quittez pas = hold the line please, hold on please
2 se quitter (**!** + *être*)
se quitter = to part

quoi *pronoun*
= what
quoi de neuf? = what's new?
je ne sais pas quoi faire = I don't know what to do
à quoi penses-tu? = what are you thinking about?
à quoi bon? = what's the point?
si je peux faire quoi que ce soit = if there's anything I can do
il n'y a pas de quoi = my pleasure, don't mention it
il n'y a pas de quoi s'inquiéter = there's nothing to worry about

quotidien/quotidienne
1 *adjective*
= daily, everyday
2 quotidien *noun, masculine*
un quotidien = a daily (paper)

R

Rr

rabais *noun, masculine* (**!** *never changes*)
un rabais = a reduction

raccompagner *verb* ⒈
raccompagner quelqu'un = to take someone home

raccourci *noun, masculine*
un raccourci = a short cut

raccourcir *verb* ⒊
= to shorten

raccrocher *verb* ⒈
(*when telephoning*) = to hang up

racine noun, feminine
une racine = a root

raconter verb [1]
= to tell

radiateur noun, masculine
un radiateur = a radiator

radin/radine✗ adjective
= mean

radio noun, feminine
• (for broadcasts)
la radio = (the) radio
à la radio = on the radio
• (a medical examination)
une radio = an X-ray

radis noun, masculine (! never changes)
un radis = a radish

radoucir: **se radoucir** verb [3] (! + être)
se radoucir = to turn milder

rafale noun, feminine
une rafale de vent = a gust of wind

raffiné/raffinée adjective
= refined

raffinerie noun, feminine
une raffinerie = a refinery

rafraîchir verb [3]
1 (! + avoir)
= to cool (down)
2 se rafraîchir (! + être)
• (if it's the weather)
se rafraîchir = to get cooler
• (if it's a person)
se rafraîchir = to freshen up, to wash up
= to have a drink

rafraîchissement noun, masculine
un rafraîchissement = a cold drink

ragoût noun, masculine
un ragoût = a stew

raide adjective
(describing a slope) = steep
(describing hair) = straight
(describing a collar, a person) = stiff

raie noun, feminine
• (in hair)
une raie = a parting, a part
• (a narrow band of colour)
une raie = a stripe

rail noun, masculine
un rail = a rail
les rails = the track(s)

raisin noun, masculine
le raisin = grapes
un grain de raisin = a grape
les raisins de Corinthe = currants
les raisins secs = raisins

raison noun, feminine
• une raison = a reason
• avoir raison = to be right

raisonnable adjective
= reasonable, moderate
= sensible

ralenti noun, masculine
le ralenti = slow motion
le moteur tourne au ralenti = the engine is (just) ticking over

ralentir verb [3]
= to slow down

ralentisseur noun, masculine
un ralentisseur = a speed ramp

râler✗ verb [1]
= to moan

ramasser verb [1]
= to pick (up)
= to collect

rame noun, feminine
• une rame = an oar
• une rame de métro = a (metro) train

ramer verb [1]
= to row

rampe noun, feminine
une rampe (on a staircase) = a banister
une rampe d'accès
(to a motorway) = a sliproad, an entrance ramp
(to a building) = a ramp

ramper verb [1]
= to crawl

rance adjective
= rancid

rançon noun, feminine
une rançon = a ransom

randonnée noun, feminine
• (a walk)
une randonnée = a ramble, a hike
• (an activity)
la randonnée = hiking
la randonnée à cheval = pony-trekking
la randonnée pédestre = rambling, hiking

rang noun, masculine
• (a line)
un rang = a row
se mettre en rangs = to get into line
• (a position)
un rang = a rank

rangée noun, feminine
une rangée = a row

ranger verb [13]
• = to put away
• = to tidy
= to sort out, to put in order

râper verb [1]
= to grate

---

rapide
1 *adjective*
 = fast, quick
 = prompt
2 *noun, masculine*
• (*a train*)
 un rapide = an express
• (*in a river*)
 un rapide = rapids

rapidement *adverb*
 = quickly, fast

rappel *noun, masculine*
 un rappel = a reminder

rappeler *verb* 19
1 (**!** + *avoir*)
• = to call back
• = to remind
2 se rappeler (**!** + *être*)
 se rappeler = to remember

rapport
1 *noun, masculine*
• (*an account*)
 un rapport = a report
• (*a link*)
 un rapport = a connection
2 par rapport à = compared with

rapporter *verb* 1
1 (**!** + *avoir*)
 = to take back, to bring back
2 se rapporter à (**!** + *être*)
 se rapporter à = to relate to

rapprocher *verb* 1
 = to move closer
 = to bring closer

raquette *noun, feminine*
 une raquette (*in tennis*) = a racket
 (*in table tennis*) = a bat, a paddle

rare *adjective*
 = rare
 = scarce

ras/rase *adjective*
• **des cheveux ras** = close-cropped hair,
  short hair
• **une cuillère à café rase** = a level
  teaspoonful
 plein à ras bord = full to the brim
• **en rase campagne** = in (the) open country

raser: **se raser** *verb* 1 (**!** + *être*)
 se raser = to shave

rasoir
1 *noun, masculine*
 un rasoir = a razor
2 *adjective*✶ (**!** *never changes*)
 = boring

rassembler *verb* 1
1 (**!** + *avoir*)
 = to gather
 = to bring together

2 se rassembler (**!** + *être*)
 se rassembler = to gather
 = to get together

rassurer *verb* 1
 = to reassure

rat *noun, masculine*
 un rat = a rat

râteau *noun, masculine*
(*plural*) **râteaux**
 un râteau = a rake

rater *verb* 1
• = to miss
• = to fail

rattraper *verb* 1
• = to catch up with
 rattraper un concurrent = to catch up with
  a competitor
• = to make up for
 rattraper le temps perdu = to make up for
  lost time
• = to recapture, to catch

ravin *noun, masculine*
 un ravin = a ravine

ravissant/ravissante *adjective*
 = beautiful, delightful

ravitailler *verb* 1
 ravitailler une ville = to provide a town
  with fresh supplies
 ravitailler un avion = to refuel a plane

rayé/rayée *adjective*
 = striped

rayer *verb* 21
• = to cross out
• = to scratch

rayon *noun, masculine*
• (*of light*)
 un rayon = a ray, a beam
• (*for books, goods*)
 un rayon = a shelf
• (*of a circle*)
 le rayon = the radius

rayure *noun, feminine*
• (*on material*)
 une rayure = a stripe
• (*on glass, on metal*)
 une rayure = a scratch

réaction *noun, feminine*
 une réaction = a reaction

réagir *verb* 3
 = to react

réaliser *verb* 1
1 (**!** + *avoir*)
• (*to make something happen*)
 réaliser son ambition = to achieve one's
  ambition
• (*to understand*) = to realize

R

2 se réaliser (**!** + *être*)
  se réaliser = to come true
  = to be fulfilled

réaliste *adjective*
  = realistic

réalité *noun, feminine*
  la réalité = reality

réanimation *noun, feminine*
  la réanimation = resuscitation

rebord *noun, masculine*
  le rebord de la fenêtre = the windowsill

récemment *adverb*
  = recently

récent/récente *adjective*
  = recent

récepteur *noun, masculine*
  un récepteur = a (telephone) receiver

recette *noun, feminine*
* (*a set of instructions*)
  une recette = a recipe
* (*money*)
  la recette = the takings

recevoir *verb* 5
* = to receive, to get
* = to receive, to welcome
* **être reçu à un examen** = to pass an exam

rechange *noun, masculine*
  une pièce de rechange = a spare part

recharge *noun, feminine*
  une recharge = a refill

réchaud *noun, masculine*
  un réchaud = a (portable) stove

réchauffer *verb* 1
* (*if it's food*) = to reheat, to heat up
* (*if it's a person, a part of the body*) = to
  warm up

recherche *noun, feminine*
* (*into a subject*)
  la recherche = research
* (*looking for something*)
  une recherche = a search

récipient *noun, masculine*
  un récipient = a container

récit *noun, masculine*
  un récit = a story

réciter *verb* 1
  = to recite

réclamation *noun, feminine*
  une réclamation = a complaint

réclame *noun, feminine*
* **la réclame** = publicity
* **une réclame** = an advertisement
* '**en réclame**' = 'on offer', 'on sale'

réclamer *verb* 1
* = to ask for
* = to complain

récolter *verb* 1
  = to harvest, to reap

recommandé/recommandée
adjective
  une lettre recommandée = a registered
  letter

recommander *verb* 1
* = to recommend
* = to advise

recommencer *verb* 12
  = to start again, to start over

récompense *noun, feminine*
  une récompense = a reward

récompenser *verb* 1
  = to reward

reconnaissance *noun, feminine*
  la reconnaissance = gratitude

reconnaissant/reconnaissante
adjective
  = grateful

reconnaître *verb* 63
* = to recognize
* = to admit
  = to acknowledge

recopier *verb* 2
  = to copy out
  = to write out

record *noun, masculine*
  le record du monde = the world record

recouvrir *verb* 32
  = to cover

récréation *noun, feminine*
  la récréation (*in school*) = break, recess

reçu/reçue
1 ▶ **recevoir** 5
2 **reçu** *noun, masculine*
  un reçu = a receipt

recueillir *verb* 27
  = to collect

reculer *verb* 1
* = to move back
  = to reverse
* = to postpone

reculons: **à reculons** *adverb*
  à reculons = backwards

récupérer *verb* 14
* (*after an illness*) = to recover
* (*having lost or lent something*) = to get
  back
  = to collect
* (*in order to reuse*) = to salvage

recyclage *noun, masculine*
  le recyclage (*of waste*) = recycling
  (*of staff*) = retraining

rédaction *noun, feminine*
  une rédaction = an essay, a theme

redescendre verb 6
1 (**!** + *être*)
= to go down again, to come down again
2 (**!** + *avoir*)
= to take down again, to bring down again

rediffusion noun, feminine
une rediffusion = a repeat (broadcast)

redoubler verb 1
redoubler (une classe) = to repeat a year

redresser verb 1
• = to put up again
• = to straighten (up)

réduction noun, feminine
une réduction = a reduction, a discount

réduire verb 62
= to reduce

réduit/réduite
1 ▶ réduire 62
2 réduit noun, masculine
un réduit = a cubbyhole

réel/réelle adjective
= real

réexpédier verb 2
• = to forward, to redirect
• = to send back

refaire verb 10
= to do again
= to redo
= to make again

réfectoire noun, masculine
un réfectoire = a refectory, a dining hall

refermer verb 1
= to close

réfléchir verb 3
• = to reflect
réfléchir la lumière = to reflect light
• réfléchir = to think

reflet noun, masculine
• (*an image*)
un reflet = a reflection
• (*a flash of light*)
un reflet = a glint
= a shimmer
cheveux châtain à reflets roux = brown hair with auburn highlights

refléter verb 14
= to reflect

réflexion noun, feminine
• la réflexion = reflection
• une réflexion = a remark

refrain noun, masculine
• le refrain = the chorus
• c'est toujours le même refrain = it's the same old refrain

refroidir verb 3
• = to cool down
• = to get cold

refus noun, masculine (**!** *never changes*)
un refus = a refusal

refuser verb 1
= to refuse
= to turn down

regagner verb 1
• = to get back to, to return to
• = to regain

régaler: se régaler verb 1 (**!** + *être*)
je me suis régalé = I really enjoyed that

regard noun, masculine
un regard = a look

regarder verb 1
• = to look at
• = to watch
• = to concern
ça ne te regarde pas = it's none of your business

régime noun, masculine
• (*what one eats*)
un régime = a diet
• (*in politics*)
un régime = a regime

région noun, feminine
une région = a region, an area

règle
1 noun, feminine
• (*for measuring*)
une règle = a ruler
• (*to be obeyed*)
une règle = a rule
2 règles noun, feminine plural
avoir ses règles = to have a period

règlement noun, masculine
le règlement = the regulations, the rules

régler verb 14
• = to pay
• = to settle
• = to adjust

réglisse noun, feminine
la réglisse = liquorice, licorice

règne noun, masculine
un règne = a reign

regretter verb 1
• = to be sorry
• = to regret
• = to miss

régulier/régulière adjective
• = regular
un vol régulier = a scheduled flight
• = steady
= even

rein
1 noun, masculine
un rein = a kidney

R

2 reins noun, masculine plural
 les reins = the small of the back
 avoir mal aux reins = to have (a) backache

reine noun, feminine
 une reine = a queen

rejoindre verb 56
• = to join
• = to meet up with
• = to catch up with

relais noun, masculine (! never changes)
• (a place)
 un relais = an inn
 un relais routier = a roadside café, a truck stop
• (in sport)
 un relais = a relay

relever verb 16
1 (! + avoir)
• (after something has fallen) = to pick up
 = to put back up
• (to become aware of) = to notice
2 se relever (! + être)
 se relever (after a fall) = to get up

relier verb 2
• = to connect
• = to bind

religieuse¹ noun, feminine
• ▶ religieux 2
• (a cake)
 une religieuse = a round éclair

religieux/religieuse²
1 adjective
 = religious
2 noun, masculine|feminine
 un religieux/une religieuse = a monk/a nun

relire verb 41
 = to read again
 = to read over

reliure noun, feminine
 une reliure = a binding

remarier: **se remarier** verb 2 (! + être)
 se remarier = to remarry

remarquer verb 1
 = to notice
 faire remarquer = to point out

rembourser verb 1
 = to reimburse, to pay back

remède noun, masculine
 un remède = a medicine
 = a cure

remerciement noun, masculine
 des remerciements = thanks

remercier verb 2
 = to thank

remettre verb 60
1 (! + avoir)
• = to put back
 remettre une lettre dans un tiroir = to put a letter back in a drawer
 remettre son manteau = to put one's coat back on
• = to hand over, to give
 je leur ai remis les clés = I handed the keys over to them
2 se remettre (! + être)
• **se remettre** = to recover
 se remettre d'une maladie = to recover from an illness, to get over an illness
• **se remettre à** [travailler | marcher | pleurer …] = to start [working | walking | crying …] again

remonter verb 1
1 (! + être)
• = to go back up(stairs), to come back up(stairs)
• **remonter au dix-septième siècle** = to go back to the seventeenth century
2 (! + avoir)
• **remonter les escaliers** = to go back up the stairs
• **remonter ses bagages** = to take one's luggage back up(stairs)

remorque noun, feminine
 une remorque = a trailer

remplacer verb 12
 = to replace

remplir verb 3
 = to fill

remuer verb 1
• = to move
 = to wriggle
• = to stir

renard noun, masculine
 un renard = a fox

rencontre noun, feminine
• **une rencontre** = an encounter
 = a meeting
 faire la rencontre d'un garçon = to meet a boy
• (in sport)
 une rencontre (sportive) = a match, a game

rencontrer verb 1
 = to meet
 = to come across

rendez-vous noun, masculine (! never changes)
 un rendez-vous = an appointment
 = a date

rendre verb 6
1 (! + avoir)
• = to give back, to return
• **rendre visite à un ami** = to visit a friend

2 se rendre (! + *être*)
* **se rendre** = to surrender
* **se rendre à Paris** = to go to Paris
* **se rendre compte**
  = to realize
* **se rendre malade** = to make oneself ill

renne *noun, masculine*
  un renne = a reindeer

renoncer *verb* [12]
  renoncer à = to give up

renouveler *verb* [19]
* = to renew
* = to replace

rénover *verb* [1]
  = to renovate

renseignement
1 *noun, masculine*
  un renseignement = (a piece of)
    information
  des renseignements = information
2 renseignements *noun, masculine plural*
  les renseignements (*on the telephone*)
    = directory enquiries, information
  (*an office*) = enquiries, information

renseigner *verb* [1]
1 (! + *avoir*)
  = to give information
  être bien renseigné = to be well-informed
2 se renseigner (! + *être*)
  se renseigner = to find out
  = to enquire, to make enquiries

rentrée *noun, feminine*
  la rentrée (**scolaire** *or* **des classes**) = the
    start of the school year

rentrer *verb* [1]
1 (! + *être*)
* = to go in, to come in
  rentrer dans une pièce = to go/come back
    into a room
* = to go home, to come home
* = to fit
  rentrer dans une boîte = to fit into a box
* **rentrer dans un mur** = to crash into a wall
2 (! + *avoir*)
  = to take in, to bring in

renverser *verb* [1]
* = to spill
* = to knock over

renvoyer *verb* [24]
* = to return
  = to throw back
  = to send back
* = to expel
  = to dismiss

réparation *noun, feminine*
  une réparation = a repair

réparer *verb* [1]
  = to mend, to repair

repas *noun, masculine* (! *never changes*)
  un repas = a meal

repassage *noun, masculine*
  le repassage = ironing

repasser *verb* [1]
1 (! + *avoir*)
* **repasser une jupe** = to iron a skirt
* **repasser un examen** = to resit an exam
2 (! + *être*)
* = to go past again
* = to call again

répéter *verb* [14]
* = to repeat
* = to rehearse

répétition *noun, feminine*
* (*in a text*)
  une répétition = a repetition
* (*for actors*)
  une répétition = a rehearsal

répondre *verb* [6]
  = to answer, to reply

réponse *noun, feminine*
  une réponse = an answer, a reply

reportage *noun, masculine*
  un reportage = a report, an article

repos *noun, masculine* (! *never changes*)
  le repos = rest
  = relaxation
  mon jour de repos = my day off

reposer: se reposer *verb* [1] (! + *être*)
  se reposer = to rest

reprendre *verb* [52]
* **reprendre du pain** = to have some more
    bread
* = to take back
* **reprendre le travail** = to go back to work
  reprendre ses études = to take up one's
    studies again
  reprendre la conversation = to continue
    the conversation
* = to start again
  l'école a repris = school has started again

représentant/représentante *noun,
masculine/feminine*
  un représentant/une représentante = a
    representative

représenter *verb* [1]
  = to represent

réprimander *verb* [1]
  = to tell off

repris/reprise ▶ reprendre [52]

république *noun, feminine*
  une république = a republic

requin *noun, masculine*
  un requin = a shark

R

RER *noun, masculine*
le RER *a rapid-transit rail system in the Paris area*

réseau *noun, masculine*
(*plural*) **réseaux**
un réseau = a network

réservation *noun, feminine*
une réservation = a reservation, a booking

réserver *verb* ⓵
• = to reserve, to book
• = to put aside, to set aside

résidence *noun, feminine*
une résidence = a residence
= a place of residence
une résidence secondaire = a second home

résolu/résolue
1 ▶ résoudre ⑥⑤
2 *adjective*
= resolute, determined

résoudre *verb* ⑥⑤
= to solve, to resolve

respecter *verb* ⓵
= to respect
= to treat with respect

respiration *noun, feminine*
la respiration = breathing

respirer *verb* ⓵
= to breathe

responsable
1 *adjective*
= responsible
2 *noun, masculine/feminine*
• un responsable/une responsable = a person in charge
• le responsable de l'accident = the person responsible for the accident

ressembler *verb* ⓵
1 (**!** + *avoir*)
ressembler à = to look like, to resemble
= to be like
2 se ressembler (**!** + *être*)
se ressembler = to look alike

ressort *noun, masculine*
un ressort = a spring

reste *noun, masculine*
• (*the remaining part*)
le reste = the rest
• (*the remains of a meal*)
les restes = the leftovers

rester *verb* ⓵ (**!** + *être*)
• = to stay
= to remain

× in informal situations

• **il me reste dix francs** = I've got ten francs left
il ne reste que quelques personnes = there are only a few people left

restituer *verb* ⓵
= to return, to hand back

résultat *noun, masculine*
le résultat = the result

résumé *noun, masculine*
un résumé = a summary

rétablir *verb* ③
1 (**!** + *avoir*)
= to restore
2 se rétablir (**!** + *être*)
se rétablir = to recover

retard *noun, masculine*
un retard = a delay
avoir du retard = to be late
être en retard = to be late

retarder *verb* ⓵
• = to be slow
• = to postpone, to put off
• = to delay, to hold up

retenir *verb* ㊱
1 (**!** + *avoir*)
• = to reserve
retenir des places = to reserve seats
• = to hold (back)
retenir son souffle = to hold one's breath
• = to remember
2 se retenir (**!** + *être*)
• se retenir à une branche = to hold on to a branch
• se retenir de pleurer = to stop oneself from crying

retenu/retenue¹ ▶ retenir ㊱

retenue² *noun, feminine*
une retenue (*in school*) = a detention

retirer *verb* ⓵
= to withdraw, to take out

retour *noun, masculine*
• le retour = the return
• le retour = the return journey
au retour = on the way back

retourner *verb* ⓵
1 (**!** + *avoir*)
• = to turn over
= to turn inside out
= to turn upside down
• = to send back
2 (**!** + *être*)
= to go back, to return
3 se retourner (**!** + *être*)
se retourner = to turn around, to turn over

retraite *noun, feminine*
la retraite = retirement

retraité/retraitée noun,
masculine/feminine
　un retraité/une retraitée = a retired person

rétrécir verb ③
　= to shrink

retrouver verb ①
1 (**!** + *avoir*)
* (*after losing something*) = to find
* (*after arranging to get together*) = to meet
* (*after losing touch*) = to see again
2 se retrouver (**!** + *être*)
* (*by arrangement*)
　se retrouver = to meet
* (*to end up*)
　se retrouver = to find oneself
　se retouver dans une situation difficile = to
　　find oneself in a difficult situation

rétroviseur noun, *masculine*
　un rétroviseur = a rearview mirror

réunion noun, *feminine*
　une réunion = a meeting

réunir verb ③
1 (**!** + *avoir*)
* = to gather together
* = to collect
2 se réunir (**!** + *être*)
　se réunir = to meet
　= to get together

réussir verb ③
* = to succeed
　= to be successful
* réussir à ouvrir la porte = to manage to
　open the door
　réussir à un examen = to pass an exam

réussite noun, *feminine*
* (*an achievement*)
　une réussite = success
* (*a game*)
　une réussite = patience, solitaire

rêve noun, *masculine*
　un rêve = a dream

réveil noun, *masculine*
　un réveil = an alarm clock

réveiller verb ①
1 (**!** + *avoir*)
　= to wake (up)
2 se réveiller (**!** + *être*)
　se réveiller = to wake up

réveillon noun, *masculine*
　le réveillon de Noël = Christmas Eve
　　celebrations
　le réveillon du Nouvel An = New Year's Eve
　　celebrations

révéler verb ⑭
　= to reveal
　= to show

revenir verb ㊱ (**!** + *être*)
　= to come back

revenu/revenue
1 ▶ revenir ㊱
2 revenu noun, *masculine*
　mon revenu = my income

rêver verb ①
　= to dream

réverbère noun, *masculine*
　un réverbère = a streetlamp

rêveur/rêveuse *adjective*
　= dreamy

réviser verb ①
* = to revise
* réviser un moteur = to overhaul an engine

revoir
1 verb ㊻
* = to see again
* = to go over
　revoir un exercice = to go over an exercise
2 au revoir = goodbye

revu/revue¹ ▶ revoir 1 ㊻

revue² noun, *feminine*
* une revue = a magazine
* une revue = a show

rez-de-chaussée noun, *masculine*
(**!** *never changes*)
　au rez-de-chaussée (*in Britain*) = on the
　　ground floor
　(*in the US*) = on the first floor

Rhin noun, *masculine*
　le Rhin = the Rhine

rhum noun, *masculine*
　le rhum = rum

rhume noun, *masculine*
　un rhume = a cold
　le rhume des foins = hay fever

riant ▶ rire 1 ㊸

riche *adjective*
　= rich, wealthy

ride noun, *feminine*
　une ride = a wrinkle

rideau noun, *masculine*
(*plural*) **rideaux**
　un rideau = a curtain
　des rideaux = curtains, drapes

ridicule *adjective*
　= ridiculous

rien *pronoun*
　= nothing
　je ne veux rien = I don't want anything
　ça ne fait rien = it doesn't matter
　de rien = don't mention it

rigoler* verb ①
* = to laugh
* = to have fun
* = to joke

R

rigolo/rigolote✻ *adjective*
= funny

rimer *verb* 1
= to rhyme

rinçage *noun, masculine*
le rinçage = rinsing

rincer *verb* 12
= to rinse

rire
1 *verb* 43
• = to laugh
• = to have fun
  il a dit ça pour rire = he said that as a joke
2 *noun, masculine*
un rire = a laugh, laughter

risque *noun, masculine*
un risque = a risk

risquer *verb* 1
• = to risk
  vos bagages ne risquent rien = your
    luggage is quite safe
• = to venture
• tu risques de tomber = you might fall
  il risque de faire froid = it might be cold
  ça ne risque pas de se produire = there's
    no chance of that happening

rivage *noun, masculine*
le rivage = the shore

rive *noun, feminine*
la rive (*of a river*) = the bank
(*of a lake*) = the shore

rivière *noun, feminine*
une rivière = a river

riz *noun, masculine* (✻ *never changes*)
le riz = rice

robe *noun, feminine*
une robe = a dress
une robe de chambre = a dressing gown,
a robe

robinet *noun, masculine*
un robinet = a tap, a faucet

robuste *adjective*
(*describing a person*) = robust, sturdy

rocher *noun, masculine*
un rocher = a rock

rognon *noun, masculine*
un rognon = a kidney

roi *noun, masculine*
un roi = a king

rôle *noun, masculine*
un rôle = a role
= a part

romain/romaine *adjective*
= Roman

roman *noun, masculine*
un roman = a novel
un roman policier = a detective novel, a
thriller

romarin *noun, masculine*
le romarin = rosemary

ronce *noun, feminine*
une ronce = a bramble

rond/ronde
1 *adjective*
• = round
• = chubby
2 rond *noun, masculine*
un rond = a circle
en rond = in a circle

rondelle *noun, feminine*
une rondelle = a slice

rond-point *noun, masculine*
(*plural*) **ronds-points**
un rond-point = a roundabout, a traffic
circle

ronfler *verb* 1
= to snore

ronger *verb* 13
1 (**!** + *avoir*)
= to gnaw
= to eat into
2 se ronger (**!** + *être*)
se ronger les ongles = to bite one's nails

ronronner *verb* 1
= to purr

rosbif *noun, masculine*
un rosbif = a joint of beef, a roast of beef
= roast beef

rose
1 *adjective*
= pink
2 *noun, feminine*
une rose = a rose

roseau *noun, masculine*
(*plural*) **roseaux**
un roseau = a reed

rosée *noun, feminine*
la rosée = dew

roseraie *noun, feminine*
une roseraie = a rose garden

rosier *noun, masculine*
un rosier = a rose bush

rossignol *noun, masculine*
un rossignol = a nightingale

rôti *noun, masculine*
un rôti = a joint
= a roast

✻ in informal situations

roue *noun, feminine*
une roue = a wheel
une roue de secours = a spare wheel, a spare tire

rouge
1 *adjective*
= red
2 *noun, masculine*
le rouge = red
le rouge à lèvres = lipstick

rouge-gorge *noun, masculine*
(*plural*) **rouges-gorges**
un rouge-gorge = a robin

rougeole *noun, feminine*
la rougeole = measles

rouille *noun, feminine*
la rouille = rust

rouleau *noun, masculine*
(*plural*) **rouleaux**
un rouleau = a roll

rouler *verb* ⬚1
• (*if it's a ball, a coin*) = to roll
• (*if it's a car*) = to go
  (*if it's a driver*) = to drive
• **rouler*** = to trick

roumain/roumaine
1 *adjective*
= Romanian
2 roumain *noun, masculine*
le roumain = Romanian

Roumanie *noun, feminine*
la Roumanie = Romania

rouspéter* *verb* ⬚14
= to grumble, to complain

rousse *adjective, feminine* ▶ **roux**

route *noun, feminine*
• une route = a road, a highway
• la route = the way
  en (cours de) route = on the way
  se mettre en route = to set off
  en route! = let's go!
  il y a deux heures de route = it's a two-hour drive
une route départementale = a secondary road
une route nationale = a trunk road, a national highway

routier/routière
1 *adjective*
= road
2 routier *noun, masculine*
un routier = a lorry driver, a truck driver

roux/rousse
1 *adjective*
= red
= red-haired
2 *noun, masculine|feminine*
un roux/une rousse = a redhead

Royaume-Uni *noun, masculine*
le Royaume-Uni = the United Kingdom

ruban *noun, masculine*
un ruban = a ribbon

ruche *noun, feminine*
une ruche = a beehive

rude *adjective*
(*describing a task*) = hard, tough
(*describing a climate, a voice*) = harsh

rue *noun, feminine*
une rue = a street

ruée *noun, feminine*
une ruée = a rush
= a stampede

ruelle *noun, feminine*
une ruelle = an alley

ruine *noun, feminine*
• (*financial*)
  la ruine = ruin
• (*remains*)
  des ruines = ruins

ruisseau *noun, masculine*
(*plural*) **ruisseaux**
un ruisseau = a stream, a brook

rumeur *noun, feminine*
une rumeur (*gossip*) = a rumo(u)r
(*a noise*) = a rumble

ruse *noun, feminine*
• une ruse = a trick
• la ruse = cunning

rusé/rusée *adjective*
= cunning, crafty

russe
1 *adjective*
= Russian
2 *noun, masculine*
le russe = Russian

Russie *noun, feminine*
la Russie = Russia

rustine® *noun, feminine*
une rustine = a patch

rythme *noun, masculine*
le rythme = (the) rhythm
= the rate, the pace

R

Ss

s'
1 *pronoun* ▶ **se**
2 *conjunction* ▶ **si 2**

sa ▶ **son²**

sable *noun, masculine*
le sable = sand

sac *noun, masculine*
un sac = a bag
un sac de couchage = a sleeping bag
un sac à dos = a rucksack, a backpack
un sac à main = a handbag, a purse
un sac à provisions = a shopping bag, a carry-all

saccade *noun, feminine*
une saccade = a jerk

saccager *verb* 13
= to wreck, to devastate
= to vandalize

sache ▶ **savoir** 47

sachet *noun, masculine*
un sachet = a packet
= a sachet
= a bag

sacoche *noun, feminine*
une sacoche = a bag
(*on a bicycle*) = a pannier, a saddlebag

sacré/sacrée *adjective*
= sacred, holy

sage *adjective*
• = good, well-behaved
• = wise

Sagittaire *noun, masculine*
le Sagittaire = Sagittarius

saignant/saignante *adjective*
(*describing steak*) = rare

saigner *verb* 1
= to bleed

sain/saine *adjective*
= healthy

sais ▶ **savoir** 47

saisir *verb* 3
• (*to catch hold of*) = to grab, to seize
saisir une balle au vol = to catch a ball
• (*to affect deeply*) = to grip
être saisi de panique = to be panic-stricken
• (*to get the meaning*) = to understand

---

saison *noun, feminine*
une saison = a season
en cette saison = at this time of year
en toute saison = all year round

saisonnier/saisonnière *adjective*
= seasonal

salade *noun, feminine*
une salade = a (head of) lettuce
= a salad

salaire *noun, masculine*
un salaire = a salary, wages

sale *adjective*
= dirty

salé/salée *adjective*
= salty, salted
= savoury

saler *verb* 1
= to salt

saleté *noun, feminine*
• la saleté = dirtiness
= dirt, filth
• **ramasser les saletés** = to pick up the rubbish, to pick up the trash

salir *verb* 3
1 (! + *avoir*)
= to dirty, to soil
2 se salir (! + *être*)
se salir = to get dirty

salle *noun, feminine*
une salle = a room
= a hall
une salle de bains = a bathroom
une salle de classe = a classroom
la salle d'embarquement = the departure lounge
une salle à manger = a dining room
une salle de séjour = a living room

salon *noun, masculine*
un salon = a lounge, a sitting room, a parlor

salopette *noun, feminine*
une salopette = dungarees

saluer *verb* 1
• = to greet
• = to salute

salut✕ *exclamation*
salut✕! = hi!
= goodbye!

salutations *noun, feminine plural*
des salutations = greetings
'sincères salutations' = 'yours sincerely'
= 'yours faithfully'

samedi *noun, masculine*
samedi = Saturday

sang *noun, masculine*
le sang = blood

✕ in informal situations

sang-froid noun, masculine (**!** never changes)
le sang-froid = calm, composure

sanglier noun, masculine
un sanglier = a wild boar

sangloter verb 1
= to sob

sans preposition
= without
sans doute = probably

santé noun, feminine
la santé = health
à votre santé! = cheers!

santon noun, masculine
un santon a Christmas crib figure

saoul/saoule adjective
= drunk

sapin noun, masculine
un sapin = a fir tree
un sapin de Noël = a Christmas tree

satisfaire verb 10
= to satisfy

satisfaisant/satisfaisante adjective
• = satisfactory
• = satisfying

satisfait/satisfaite adjective
= satisfied

sauce noun, feminine
une sauce = a sauce
= gravy

saucisse noun, feminine
une saucisse = a sausage

saucisson noun, masculine
le saucisson ≈ salami

sauf¹ preposition
= except
sauf si = unless

sauf²/sauve adjective
= safe
sain et sauf/saine et sauve = safe and sound

saumon noun, masculine
un saumon = a salmon

saurai ▶ savoir 47

saut noun, masculine
un saut = a jump
le saut en hauteur = the high jump

saute-mouton noun, masculine
jouer à saute-mouton = to play leapfrog

sauter verb 1
= to jump
= to skip
sauter à la corde = to skip, to jump rope

sauterelle noun, feminine
une sauterelle = a grasshopper

sauvage adjective
= wild

sauve ▶ sauf 2

sauvegarder verb 1
= to save

sauver verb 1
1 (**!** + avoir)
= to save
= to rescue
2 se sauver (**!** + être)
se sauver = to escape
= to run away

sauvetage noun, masculine
un sauvetage = a rescue

sauveteur noun, masculine
un sauveteur = a rescuer

savant/savante
1 adjective
• = learned
• les animaux savants = performing animals
2 noun, masculine|feminine
un savant/une savante = a scholar
= a scientist

saveur noun, feminine
la saveur = the flavo(u)r

savoir verb 47
• = to know
je n'en sais rien = I've no idea
• = to know how to

savon noun, masculine
le savon = soap

savonnette noun, feminine
une savonnette = a small bar of soap

savoureux/savoureuse adjective
= tasty

scène noun, feminine
• (in a theatre)
la scène = the stage
• (something seen)
une scène = a scene

schéma noun, masculine
un schéma = a diagram

scie noun, feminine
une scie = a saw

science noun, feminine
la science = science
les sciences (as a school subject)
= science

scier verb 2
= to saw

scintiller verb 1
= to twinkle, to sparkle, to glisten

scolaire adjective
= school

S

Scorpion noun, masculine
  le Scorpion = Scorpion

scotch noun, masculine
(plural) **scotches**
* le scotch® = Sellotape®, Scotch tape®
* le scotch = Scotch (whisky)

scout/scoute noun, masculine/feminine
  un scout/une scoute = a boy scout/a girl
  scout

se (**s'** before vowel or mute h) pronoun
* = oneself
  = himself/herself
  = itself
  = themselves
  se faire mal = to hurt oneself
  elles se sont fait mal = they hurt
  themselves
* = each other
  ils s'aimaient = they loved each other

séance noun, feminine
  une séance = a session
  (in a cinema) = a showing

seau noun, masculine
(plural) **seaux**
  un seau = a bucket

sec/sèche adjective
* (without moisture) = dry
  des fruits secs = dried fruit
* (abrupt) = sharp

sèche ▶ sec

sèche-cheveux noun, masculine
(! never changes)
  un sèche-cheveux = a hairdryer

sèche-linge noun, masculine (! never
changes)
  un sèche-linge = a tumble dryer

sécher verb 14
  = to dry (up)

sécheresse noun, feminine
  la sécheresse = drought

séchoir noun, masculine
* un séchoir = a hairdryer
* un séchoir = a clothes horse, a drying rack
  = a rotary clothes dryer

second/seconde¹ number
  = second

secondaire
1 adjective
  = secondary
2 noun, masculine
  le secondaire = secondary-school
  education, high-school education (for
  students aged 11 to 18)

seconde² noun, feminine
* (a unit of time)
  une seconde = a second
* (in school)
  la seconde the class for secondary school
  students aged 15 to 16
* (when travelling)
  voyager en seconde = to travel second
  class
  un billet de seconde = a second-class
  ticket

secouer verb 1
  = to shake

secourir verb 26
  = to rescue
  = to help

secours
1 noun, masculine (! never changes)
  un secours = help
  au secours! = help!
  une sortie de secours = an emergency exit
2 noun, masculine plural
  des secours = rescuers
  = (relief) supplies

secousse noun, feminine
  une secousse = a jolt

secret/secrète
1 adjective
  = secret
2 secret noun, masculine
  un secret = a secret

secrétaire noun, masculine/feminine
  un secrétaire/une secrétaire = a secretary

secrétariat noun, masculine
  le secrétariat = the secretary's office

secrète ▶ secret 1

sectionner verb 1
  = to cut

sécuriser verb 1
  = to reassure
  = to give a feeling of security

sécurité noun, feminine
  la sécurité = security
  = safety
  se sentir en sécurité = to feel safe
la sécurité sociale the French national
  health and pensions organization

séduisant/séduisante adjective
  = attractive

seigneur noun, masculine
  un seigneur = a lord

sein noun, masculine
  un sein = a breast

seize number
  = sixteen

seizième number
  = sixteenth

séjour noun, masculine
• (a room)
  un séjour = a living room, a parlor
• (time spent somewhere)
  un séjour = a stay
  faire un séjour à l'étranger = to spend
    some time abroad
un séjour linguistique = a language-
  study holiday, a language-study vacation

sel noun, masculine
  le sel = salt

sélectionner verb [1]
  = to select

selle noun, feminine
  une selle = a saddle

selon preposition
• = according to
  selon moi = in my opinion
• = depending on
  selon le temps = depending on the
    weather

semaine noun, feminine
  une semaine = a week

semblable adjective
  = similar

semblant noun, masculine
  faire semblant [de dormir | d'être malade |
    d'avoir mal ...] = to pretend [to be asleep | to
    be ill | to be in pain ...]

sembler verb [1]
  = to seem
  il me semble que = it seems to me that
  il me semble qu'il pleut = I think it's
    raining

semelle noun, feminine
  une semelle = a sole

semer verb [1]
• = to sow
• = to scatter

semoule noun, feminine
  la semoule = semolina

sens noun, masculine (**!** never changes)
• **un sens** = a meaning
• **le sens** = sense
  le bon sens = common sense
  ça n'a pas de sens = it doesn't make sense
• **le sens** = the way
  = the direction
  plie-le dans l'autre sens = fold it the other
    way
  dans le sens de la flèche = in the
    direction of the arrow
  dans le sens des aiguilles d'une montre
    = clockwise
  une rue à sens unique = a one-way street
  'sens obligatoire' = 'one way'

sensationnel/sensationnelle
adjective
• (causing a stir) = sensational
• (very good)✖ = fantastic

sensé/sensée adjective
  = sensible

sensible adjective
  = sensitive

senti ▶ **sentir** 30

sentier noun, masculine
  un sentier = a path
un sentier de grande randonnée = a
  long-distance footpath

sentiment noun, masculine
  un sentiment = a feeling

sentir verb 30
1 (**!** + avoir)
• = to feel
• = to sense
• = to smell
• = to smell of
  ça sent le brûlé = there's a smell of
    burning
2 se sentir (**!** + être)
  se sentir = to feel

séparer verb [1], **se séparer** (**!** + être)
  = to separate
  = to part
  = to divide

sept number
  = seven

septante number
  = seventy

septembre noun, masculine
  septembre = September

septième number
  = seventh

serai ▶ **être** [7]

série noun, feminine
• (a succession)
  une série = a series
• (a collection)
  une série = a set

sérieux/sérieuse adjective
• = serious
• = reliable

seringue noun, feminine
  une seringue = a syringe

serpent noun, masculine
  un serpent = a snake

serre noun, feminine
  une serre = a greenhouse

serré/serrée adjective
• (not big enough) = tight
• (too close together)
  être serrés = to be packed together

S

serrer verb 1
1 (! + *avoir*)
* = to grip
  = to squeeze
  serrer la main d'un ami = to shake hands with a friend
* = to tighten
  serrer une ceinture = to tighten a belt
* = to be too tight
  ma jupe me serre à la taille = my skirt is too tight around the waist
* (*on the road*)
  'serrez à droite' = 'keep to the right'
2 se serrer (! + *être*)
  se serrer = to squeeze up
  je me suis serré contre elle = I huddled up against her

serrure noun, feminine
  une serrure = a lock
  le trou de la serrure = the keyhole

serrurier noun, masculine
  un serrurier = a locksmith

serveur/serveuse noun, masculine/feminine
  un serveur/une serveuse = a waiter/a waitress

servi/servie ▶ **servir** 30

serviable adjective
  = obliging

service noun, masculine
* **le service** = service
  service compris = service included
* **un service** = a favo(u)r
  rendre service à un ami = to be helpful to a friend, to do a friend a favo(u)r

serviette noun, feminine
* (*household linen*)
  une serviette de toilette = a towel
  une serviette de table = a napkin
* (*a kind of bag*)
  une serviette = a briefcase

serviette-éponge noun, feminine
(*plural*) **serviettes-éponges**
  une serviette-éponge = a terry(-cloth) towel

servir verb 30
1 (! + *avoir*)
* = to serve
  qu'est-ce que je vous sers (à boire)? = what would you like to drink?
* = to be of use
  = to come in handy
  garde-le, ça peut servir = keep it, it might come in handy
* **servir à quelque chose** = to be used for something
  servir à quelqu'un = to be used by someone
  à quoi sert cet outil? = what's this tool used for?
  ça va me servir pour faire un coussin = I'm going to use it to make a cushion
  ça ne sert à rien de se mettre en colère = there's no point in losing one's temper
  j'ai écrit, mais ça n'a servi à rien = I wrote, but it didn't do any good

* **servir de** = to serve as
  = to be used as
  mon sac m'a servi d'oreiller = I used my bag as a pillow
2 se servir (! + *être*)
* **se servir** = to help oneself
* **se servir de** = to use
  il s'est servi d'un dictionnaire = he used a dictionary

ses ▶ **son²**

seuil noun, masculine
  le seuil = the threshold

seul/seule adjective
* = alone, by oneself, on one's own
  vivre seul = to live alone
* = lonely
  se sentir seul = to feel lonely
* = single
  pas un seul arbre = not a single tree
  une seule fois = once only

seulement adverb
  = only

sévère adjective
  = strict, harsh
  = severe

shampooing noun, masculine
  un shampooing = a shampoo

short noun, masculine
  un short = shorts

si
1 adverb
* = yes
  'tu n'y vas pas?'—'si!' = 'aren't you going?'—'yes I am!'
* = so
  elle est si jolie! = she's so pretty!
2 conjunction (**s'** before **il** or **ils**)
* (*introducing a supposition*) = if
  si j'étais riche = if I were rich
  si j'avais su = if only I had known, if I'd only known
  et s'il ne peut pas le réparer? = and what if he can't repair it?
  s'il vous plaît = please
* (*introducing a suggestion*)
  et si on allait en ville? = how about going into town?

sida noun, masculine
  le sida = Aids

siècle noun, masculine
  un siècle = a century
  au vingtième siècle = in the twentieth century

siège noun, masculine
* (*a piece of furniture*)
  un siège = a seat
* (*a place*)
  le siège (social) = the headquarters, the head office

sien/sienne *pronoun*
le sien/la sienne = his/hers
les siens/les siennes = his/hers

sieste *noun, feminine*
une sieste = a siesta, a snooze, a nap

siffler *verb* 1
• = to whistle
• = to blow one's whistle
• = to boo

sifflet *noun, masculine*
un sifflet = a whistle
un coup de sifflet = a whistle blast, a
whistle blow

sigle *noun, masculine*
un sigle = an acronym

signalement *noun, masculine*
un signalement = a description

signaler *verb* 1
• (*by informing*) = to report
rien à signaler = nothing to report
• (*by drawing attention*) = to point out
je vous signale qu'il est huit heures = may
I point out that it's eight o'clock
• (*by means of a notice, a sign*) = to indicate
= to signpost

signalisation *noun, feminine*
la signalisation = signs
la signalisation routière = road signs and
markings

signe *noun, masculine*
un signe = a sign

signer *verb* 1
= to sign

signifier *verb* 2
= to mean

silencieux/silencieuse *adjective*
= silent
= quiet

silhouette *noun, feminine*
• (*a shape*)
une silhouette = a silhouette
= an outline
• (*a person*)
une silhouette = a figure

sillon *noun, masculine*
un sillon = a furrow

simple *adjective*
• = simple
• = ordinary
c'est une simple formalité = it's just a
formality
• = single
un aller simple = a single (ticket)

singe *noun, masculine*
un singe = a monkey

sinistre
1 *adjective*
= sinister

2 *noun, masculine*
un sinistre = a (natural) disaster
= a fire

sinistré/sinistrée *adjective*
= stricken
une région sinistrée = a disaster area

sinon *conjunction*
= otherwise

sirène *noun, feminine*
une sirène = a siren

sirop *noun, masculine*
un sirop = a syrup
un sirop (de fruits) = a (fruit) cordial
un sirop (pour la toux) = a cough mixture

site *noun, masculine*
un site = a site
un site classé = a conservation area
un site pittoresque = a beauty spot, a
scenic area
un site touristique = a place of interest

situation *noun, feminine*
• (*a site*)
la situation d'une ville = the location of a
town
• (*the circumstances*)
la situation est grave = the situation is
serious
• (*a position*)
une bonne situation = a good job

situé/située *adjective*
= situated, located
la ville est bien située = the town is in a
good location

situer: se situer *verb* 1 (**!** + *être*)
• (*if it's a building, a town*)
se situer = to be situated
• (*if it's an event*)
se situer = to take place

six *number*
= six

sixième
1 *number*
= sixth
2 *noun, feminine*
la sixième *the class for secondary school
students aged 11 to 12*

ski *noun, masculine*
• (*the equipment*)
un ski = a ski
• (*the sport*)
le ski = skiing
le ski de fond = cross-country skiing
le ski nautique = water-skiing

skier *verb* 2
= to ski

slip *noun, masculine*
un slip (*for men*) = pants, shorts
(*for women*) = knickers, panties

slovaque
1 adjective
= Slovak
2 noun, masculine
le slovaque = Slovak

smoking noun, masculine
un smoking = a dinner jacket, a tuxedo

SNCF noun, feminine
la SNCF the French national railway
company

snob adjective
= snobbish

société noun, feminine
• **la société** = society
• **une société** = a company

soda noun, masculine
le soda = soda water

sœur noun, feminine
une sœur = a sister

soi pronoun
= oneself
= itself

soi-disant
1 adjective (**!** never changes)
= so-called
2 adverb
= supposedly

soie noun, feminine
la soie = silk

soif noun, feminine
la soif = thirst
avoir soif = to be thirsty

soigné/soignée adjective
= meticulous, neat

soigner verb [1]
1 (**!** + avoir)
• = to treat
• = to look after
= to take care of
= to take care over
2 se soigner (**!** + être)
se soigner = to look after oneself

soigneusement adverb
= carefully

soi-même pronoun
= oneself

soin
1 noun, masculine
le soin = care
avec soin = carefully
2 soins noun, masculine plural
les soins = treatment
= care
donner les premiers soins aux blessés
= to give first aid to the injured

soir noun, masculine
un soir = an evening
à ce soir = see you tonight

soirée noun, feminine
• **la soirée** = the evening
• **une soirée** = a party

soit
1 ▶ être [7]
2 conjunction
soit lundi soit mardi = either Monday or
Tuesday

soixante number
= sixty

soixante-dix number
= seventy

soja noun, masculine
le soja = soya

sol noun, masculine
le sol = the floor
= the ground
= the soil

solaire adjective
= sun
= suntan
= solar

soldat noun, masculine
un soldat = a soldier

solde
1 noun, masculine
articles en solde = reduced items, sales
bargains, sale items
acheter une veste en solde = to buy a
jacket in a sale, to buy a jacket on sale
2 soldes noun, masculine plural
les soldes (the event) = the sales
(the goods) = sales goods, sale items

soleil noun, masculine
le soleil = the sun
au soleil = in the sun
il fait (du) soleil = it's sunny
un coup de soleil = sunburn
attraper un coup de soleil = to get
sunburned

solennel/solennelle adjective
= solemn

solide adjective
= solid, strong
= sturdy

sombre adjective
= dark
il fait sombre = it's dark

sombrer verb [1]
= to sink

somme
1 noun, feminine
une somme = a sum
2 noun, masculine
un somme = a nap, a snooze

✺ in informal situations

sommeil noun, masculine
le sommeil = sleep
avoir sommeil = to be sleepy

sommes ▶ être 7

sommet noun, masculine
le sommet = the summit, the peak, the top

sommier noun, masculine
un sommier = a (bed) base

somnifère noun, masculine
un somnifère = a sleeping pill

son¹ noun, masculine
un son = a sound

son²/sa determiner
(plural) ses
= his/her
= its
son mari = her husband
sa femme = his wife
ses livres = his/her books
ses pattes = its paws

sondage noun, masculine
un sondage = a survey
= a(n opinion) poll

sonner verb 1
= to ring
(if it's a clock) to strike

sonnerie noun, feminine
• (a noise)
la sonnerie = the ringing
• (a mechanism)
la sonnerie (on an alarm clock) = the alarm
(on a door) = the bell

sonnette noun, feminine
une sonnette = a bell

sonore adjective
• (loud) = resounding
• effets sonores = sound effects

sont ▶ être 7

sorcier noun, masculine/feminine
un sorcier/une sorcière = a wizard/a witch

sordide adjective
= squalid
= sordid

sort noun, masculine
• le sort = fate
tirer au sort = to draw lots
• son sort = one's lot
être satisfait de son sort = to be satisfied
with one's lot
• un sort = a curse, a spell
jeter un sort à un ennemi = to put a curse
on an enemy

sorte noun, feminine
une sorte = a sort, a kind

sortie noun, feminine
• (a way out)
une sortie = an exit
• (the action of leaving a place)
il a été attaqué à sa sortie du bureau = he
was mugged as he left the office
se retrouver à la sortie de l'école = to meet
after school
• (a trip)
une sortie = an outing

sortir verb 30
1 (! + être)
• = to go out, to come out
• sortir de = to leave, to come out of
2 (! + avoir)
= to take out
= to get out
sortir une lettre de sa poche = to take a
letter out of one's pocket
sors ton frère du lit! = get your brother out
of bed!

sou noun, masculine
• un sou ≈ a penny, a cent
• avoir des sous✻ = to have money

souci noun, masculine
un souci = a worry
se faire du souci = to worry

soucoupe noun, feminine
une soucoupe = a saucer

soudain/soudaine
1 adjective
= sudden
2 soudain adverb
= suddenly

souffler verb 1
• = to blow
• = to prompt
on t'a soufflé la réponse = you were
prompted, you were told the answer
• = to breathe out
• = to get one's breath back

souffrant/souffrante adjective
= unwell

souffrir verb 4
= to suffer
= to be in pain

souhait noun, masculine
un souhait = a wish

souhaiter verb 1
= to wish
souhaite-moi bonne chance = wish me
luck
souhaiter la bienvenue à un visiteur = to
welcome a visitor
je souhaite qu'il ne fasse pas froid
= I hope that it won't be cold

soûl/soûle adjective
= drunk

S

soulager verb 13
= to relieve
le comprimé m'a soulagé = the pill made me feel better

soulever verb 16
= to lift
= to raise

soulier noun, masculine
un soulier = a shoe

souligner verb 1
• = to underline
• = to emphasize, to stress

soupçon noun, masculine
un soupçon = a suspicion

soupçonner verb 1
= to suspect

soupe noun, feminine
la soupe = soup

souper
1 noun, masculine
le souper = supper
2 verb 1
= to have supper

soupir noun, masculine
un soupir = a sigh

soupirer verb 1
= to sigh

souple adjective
• = supple
• = flexible

source noun, feminine
• (water)
une source = a spring
• (the origin or cause of something)
une source = a source

sourcil noun, masculine
un sourcil = an eyebrow

sourd/sourde adjective
• (unable to hear) = deaf
• (describing a noise, a pain) = dull

souriant/souriante adjective
= smiling

sourire
1 verb 43
= to smile
2 noun, masculine
un sourire = a smile

souris noun, feminine (**!** never changes)
une souris = a mouse

sous
1 preposition
= under, underneath
sous terre = underground
sous la pluie = in the rain
2 ▶ sou

sous-marin/sous-marine
(plural) **sous-marins/sous-marines**
1 adjective
= submarine, underwater
= deep-sea
2 sous-marin noun, masculine
un sous-marin = a submarine

sous-sol noun, masculine
(plural) **sous-sols**
le sous-sol = the basement

sous-titre noun, masculine
(plural) **sous-titres**
un sous-titre = a subtitle

sous-vêtement noun, masculine
(plural) **sous-vêtements**
des sous-vêtements = underwear

soutenir verb 36
= to support

soutenu/soutenue ▶ soutenir 36

souterrain/souterraine
1 adjective
= underground
2 souterrain noun, masculine
un souterrain = a subway, a pedestrian underpass

soutien-gorge noun, masculine
(plural) **soutiens-gorge**
un soutien-gorge = a bra

souvenir
1 noun, masculine
• (something remembered)
un souvenir = a memory
• (an object)
un souvenir = a souvenir
2 se souvenir verb 36 (**!** + être)
se souvenir de = to remember

souvent adverb
= often
le plus souvent = more often than not

soyons ▶ être 7

spacieux/spacieuse adjective
= spacious

sparadrap noun, masculine
le sparadrap = (sticking) plaster, surgical tape

spatial/spatiale adjective
(plural) **spatiaux/spatiales**
= space

spécial/spéciale adjective
(plural) **spéciaux/spéciales**
• (not ordinary) = special
• (strange) = odd

spécialement adverb
= specially
= especially

spectacle noun, masculine
• (in a theatre, a circus)
un spectacle = a show

- (*something seen*)
  un **spectacle** = a sight

spectateur/**spectatrice** *noun,
masculine*/*feminine*
  un **spectateur**/une **spectatrice** = a member
    of the audience
  = a spectator

spéléologie *noun, feminine*
  la **spéléologie** = potholing, spelunking
  = speleology

sponsoriser *verb* [1]
  = to sponsor

sport *noun, masculine*
  le **sport** = sport

sportif/**sportive**
1 *adjective*
- (*describing an event, a magazine*) = sports
- (*describing a person*)
  être sportif = to be the sporty type, to be
    athletic
2 *noun, masculine*/*feminine*
  un **sportif**/une **sportive** = a sportsman/a
    sportswoman

square *noun, masculine*
  un **square** = a small public garden

squelette *noun, masculine*
  le **squelette** = the skeleton

squelettique *adjective*
  = scrawny, thin as a rake

stade *noun, masculine*
  un **stade** = a stadium

stage *noun, masculine*
  un **stage** = a course
  = (a period of) work experience

station *noun, feminine*
- (*in a town*)
  une **station de métro** = a tube station, a
    subway station
  une **station de taxis** = a taxi rank, a taxi
    stand
- (*a town or a village*)
  une **station balnéaire** = a seaside resort
  une **station de ski** = a ski resort
  une **station thermale** = a spa

stationnement *noun, masculine*
  le **stationnement** = parking

station-service *noun, feminine*
(*plural*) **stations-service**
  une **station-service** = a service station, a
    gas station

steak *noun, masculine*
  un **steak** = a steak
  un **steak haché** = a beefburger

sténodactylo
1 *noun, masculine*/*feminine*
  un **sténodactylo**/une **sténodactylo** = a
    shorthand typist, a stenographer

2 *noun, feminine*
  la **sténodactylo** = shorthand typing,
    stenographing

stop *noun, masculine*
- un **stop** = a stop sign
- le **stop**✘ = hitch-hiking
  faire du stop✘ = to hitch-hike

store *noun, masculine*
  un **store** = a blind
  = an awning

studio *noun, masculine*
- (*accommodation*)
  un **studio** = a studio flat, a studio
    apartment
- (*a place of work*)
  un **studio** = a studio

stupéfait/**stupéfaite** *adjective*
  = astounded

stylo *noun, masculine*
  un **stylo** = a (fountain) pen
  un **stylo (à) bille** = a ball-point pen, a bic®
  un **stylo feutre** = a felt-tip pen

su/**sue** ▶ **savoir** [47]

subir *verb* [3]
  subir une opération = to undergo an
    operation
  subir des dégâts = to suffer damage

subitement *adverb*
  = suddenly

succès *noun, masculine* (❗ *never
changes*)
  le **succès** = success

sucer *verb* [12]
  = to suck

sucette *noun, feminine*
  une **sucette** = a lollipop, a lolly

sucre *noun, masculine*
  le **sucre** = sugar
  un **sucre** = a lump of sugar
  le **sucre d'orge** = barley sugar

sucré/**sucrée** *adjective*
  = sweet
  = sweetened

sucrer *verb* [1]
  = to put sugar in
  = to sweeten

sucreries *noun, feminine plural*
  les **sucreries** = sweets, candies

sud
1 *noun, masculine*
  le **sud** = the south
2 *adjective* (❗ *never changes*)
  = south
  = southern

Suède *noun, feminine*
  la **Suède** = Sweden

S

suédois/suédoise
1 *adjective*
= Swedish
2 suédois *noun, masculine*
le Suédois = Swedish

sueur *noun, feminine*
la sueur = sweat

suffire *verb* 39
• = to be enough
ça me suffit = that's enough for me
• il suffit de demander = all you have to do
is ask
il suffit d'une étincelle = one spark is
enough

suffisamment *adverb*
= enough

suffisant/suffisante *adjective*
= sufficient

suis
• ▶ être 7
• ▶ suivre 37

suisse *adjective*
= Swiss

Suisse *noun, feminine*
la Suisse = Switzerland

suite
1 *noun, feminine*
• la suite = the rest
(*if it's another film or novel*) = the sequel
'suite page 45' = 'continued on page 45'
• une suite de = a succession of, a series of
2 de suite = in a row
à la suite de = following
trois jours de suite = three days in a row
3 tout de suite = straight away, right
away
4 par la suite = subsequently

suivant/suivante
1 *adjective*
= next
= following
2 *noun, masculine/feminine*
le suivant/la suivante = the next (one)
au suivant! = next!
3 suivant = according to

suivi/suivie ▶ **suivre** 37

suivre *verb* 37
= to follow
'à suivre' = 'to be continued'
faire suivre le courrier = to forward the
mail

sujet *noun, masculine*
un sujet = a subject

super
1 *adjective*✱ (**!** *never changes*)
= great

✱ *in informal situations*

2 *noun, masculine*
le super ≈ 4-star (petrol), super

superficie *noun, feminine*
la superficie = the area

supérieur/supérieure *adjective*
• = upper, top
• = higher
• = superior

supermarché *noun, masculine*
un supermarché = a supermarket

supplémentaire *adjective*
= additional, extra

supportable *adjective*
= bearable

supporter *verb* 1
• = to support, to bear the weight of
• = to put up with, to bear

supprimer *verb* 1
= to remove
= to cancel
= to withdraw
= to do away with
= to cut

sur *preposition*
• = on
sur la table = on the table
• = over
un pont sur la rivière = a bridge over the
river
• = about
un livre sur la guerre = a book about war
• = out of
9 sur 20 = 9 out of 20
• = by
faire 10 mètres sur 15 = to measure 10
metres by 15

sûr/sûre
1 *adjective*
• = sure, certain
c'est sûr = it's certain
j'en suis sûr = I'm sure of it, I'm certain of
it
j'en étais sûr! = I knew it!
être sûr de soi = to be self-confident
• = safe
= reliable
un endroit sûr = a safe place
un homme sûr = a reliable man
2 bien sûr = of course

sûreté *noun, feminine*
la sûreté = safety
= security

surf *noun, masculine*
le surf = surfing

surface *noun, feminine*
la surface = the surface (area)

surgelé/surgelée *adjective*
= (deep-)frozen
les produits surgelés = frozen food

surligneur *noun, masculine*
un surligneur = a highlighter

surnaturel/surnaturelle *adjective*
= supernatural

surnom *noun, masculine*
un surnom = a nickname

surprenant/surprenante *adjective*
= surprising
= amazing

surprise *noun, feminine*
une surprise = a surprise

sursauter *verb* 1
= to jump, to start

surtout *adverb*
= above all
= especially

surveillant/surveillante *noun,*
masculine/feminine
un surveillant/une surveillante (*in a*
school) = a supervisor
(*in a store*) = a store detective
(*in a prison*) = a warder, a guard

surveiller *verb* 1
• = to watch, to keep an eye on
• = to supervise

survenir *verb* 36
= to occur, to happen

survêtement *noun, masculine*
un survêtement = a tracksuit

survivant/survivante *noun,*
masculine/feminine
un survivant/une survivante = a survivor

survoler *verb* 1
= to fly over

sus: **en sus** *adverb*
en sus = in addition, on top

svelte *adjective*
= slender

SVP (*abbreviation of* **s'il vous plaît**)
SVP = please

sympa* *adjective* (! *never changes*)
= nice

sympathie *noun, feminine*
avoir de la sympathie pour quelqu'un = to
like someone

sympathique *adjective*
= nice, pleasant

syndicat *noun, masculine*
un syndicat = a trade union
un syndicat d'initiative = a tourist
information office

synthétique *adjective*
= man-made

tabac *noun, masculine*
• (*a substance*)
le tabac = tobacco
• (*a shop*)
un tabac = a tobacconist's, a smoke shop

tabagisme *noun, masculine*
le tabagisme = tobacco addiction

table *noun, feminine*
une table = a table
mettre la table = to set the table
se mettre à table = to sit down at the table
à table! = dinner is served!
une table des matières = a table of
contents
une table de nuit = a bedside table, a
night stand

tableau *noun, masculine*
(*plural*) **tableaux**
• (*ornamental*)
un tableau = a painting
= a picture
• (*a surface*)
un tableau = a board
un tableau d'affichage = a noticeboard,
a bulletin board
le tableau de bord = the dashboard
le tableau (noir) = the blackboard

tablier *noun, masculine*
un tablier = an apron

tabouret *noun, masculine*
un tabouret = a stool

tache *noun, feminine*
une tache = a stain

tâche *noun, feminine*
une tâche = a task, a job
les tâches ménagères = household chores

tacher *verb* 1
= to stain

tâcher *verb* 1
tâcher de = to try to

taille *noun, feminine*
• (*the middle of the body*)
la taille = the waist, the waistline
• (*overall dimensions*)
la taille = the size
quelle taille faites-vous? = what size do
you take?
taille unique = one size
• (*tallness*)
la taille = the height

T

taille-crayon noun, masculine
(plural) **taille-crayons**
　un taille-crayon = a pencil sharpener

tailler verb 1
　= to cut
　= to prune
　= to carve
　= to sharpen

tailleur noun, masculine
• (a garment)
　un tailleur = a (woman's) suit
• (a person)
　un tailleur = a tailor

taire: se taire verb 59 (! + être)
　se taire = to stop talking
　= to be silent, to fall silent
　taisez-vous! = be quiet!

talent noun, masculine
　le talent = talent
　un acteur de talent = a talented actor

talkie-walkie noun, masculine
(plural) **talkies-walkies**
　un talkie-walkie = a walkie-talkie

talon noun, masculine
　un talon = a heel

talus noun, masculine (! never changes)
　un talus = an embankment

tambour noun, masculine
　un tambour = a drum

Tamise noun, feminine
　la Tamise = the Thames

tampon noun, masculine
　un tampon (for documents) = a stamp

tamponner verb 1
1 (! + avoir)
• (to put a mark on) = to stamp
• (to wipe) = to mop, to dab
2 se tamponner (! + être)
　se tamponner = to collide

tandis que (**tandis qu'** before vowel or
mute h) conjunction
　= while, whilst

tant adverb
• = so much
　il t'aime tant! = he loves you so much!
　tant mieux! = so much the better!
　tant mieux pour vous! = good for you!
　tant pis! = too bad!
• tant de = so much, so many
• tant que = as much as, as many as
　= as long as
　mange tant que tu veux = eat as much as
　　you like
　il restera tant qu'il voudra = he'll stay as
　　long as he likes

tante noun, feminine
　une tante = an aunt

tapage noun, masculine
　du tapage = a din, a racket

taper verb 1
• taper sur un clou = to hit a nail
　il m'a tapé sur l'épaule = he tapped me on
　　the shoulder
• taper des mains = to clap one's hands
　taper du pied = to tap one's foot
　taper à la porte = to knock at the door
• taper (à la machine) = to type

tapis noun, masculine (! never changes)
　un tapis = a rug
　= a carpet
un tapis roulant = a moving walkway

tapisser verb 1
• = to wallpaper
• = to line

tapisserie noun, feminine
• (woven or embroidered cloth)
　une tapisserie = a tapestry
• (paper)
　la tapisserie = the wallpaper

taquiner verb 1
　= to tease

tard adverb
　= late
　plus tard = later
　au plus tard = at the latest
　pas plus tard qu'hier = only yesterday

tarder verb 1
• tarder à arriver = to be a long time coming
　tes parents ne vont pas tarder = your
　　parents won't be long
• tarder à répondre à une lettre = to take a
　　long time replying to a letter
　= to put off replying to a letter
• il me tarde de les revoir = I'm longing to
　　see them again, I can't wait to see them
　　again

tarif noun, masculine
　le tarif = the price
　= the price list

tarte noun, feminine
　une tarte = a tart, a flan

tartelette noun, feminine
　une tartelette = a (small) tart

tartine noun, feminine
　une tartine = a slice of bread and butter

tas noun, masculine (! never changes)
• un tas = a pile, a heap
　en tas = in a pile, in a heap
• un (or des) tas✷ d'amis = loads of friends

tasse noun, feminine
　une tasse = a cup

tâter verb 1
　= to feel

✷ in informal situations

tâtonner *verb* [1]
= to grope about

tâtons: **à tâtons** *adverb*
avancer à tâtons = to grope one's way
  along

taudis *noun, masculine* (**!** *never changes*)
un taudis = a slum

taupe *noun, feminine*
une taupe = a mole

taureau *noun, masculine*
(*plural*) **taureaux**
un taureau = a bull

Taureau *noun, masculine*
le Taureau = Taurus

taux *noun, masculine* (**!** *never changes*)
le taux = the rate
  = the level
le taux de change = the exchange rate

tchèque
1 *adjective*
= Czech
2 *noun, masculine*
le tchèque = Czech

tchin(-tchin)ˣ *exclamation*
tchin(-tchin)ˣ! = cheers!

TD *noun, masculine plural* ▶ **travail**

te (**t'** *before vowel or mute h*) *pronoun*
• = you
je te vois = I can see you
elle te l'a donné = she gave it to you
• = yourself
tu t'es fait mal? = did you hurt yourself?

technicien/technicienne *noun,*
masculine/feminine
un technicien/une technicienne = a
  technician

teindre *verb* [55]
= to dye
= to stain

teint/teinte¹
1 ▶ **teindre** [55]
2 **teint** *noun, masculine*
un teint = a complexion

teinte² *noun, feminine*
une teinte = a shade
= a colo(u)r

teinture *noun, feminine*
une teinture = a dye

teinturerie *noun, feminine*
une teinturerie = a dry cleaner's

teinturier/teinturière *noun,*
masculine/feminine
un teinturier/une teinturière = a dry cleaner

tel/telle *adjective*
= such
de telle sorte qu'il l'a cassé = in such a
  way that he broke it
les pays tels que la France = countries
  like France

téléˣ *noun, feminine*
la télé ˣ = TV

télécommandé/télécommandée
adjective
= remote control

télécopieur *noun, masculine*
un télécopieur = a fax (machine)

téléfilm *noun, masculine*
un téléfilm = a TV film, a TV movie

téléphérique *noun, masculine*
un téléphérique = a cable car

téléphone *noun, masculine*
un téléphone = a (tele)phone

téléphoner *verb* [1]
= to (tele)phone

télésiège *noun, masculine*
un télésiège = a chair lift

téléski *noun, masculine*
un téléski = a ski tow

téléspectateur/téléspectatrice
noun, masculine/feminine
un téléspectateur/une téléspectatrice = a
  viewer

téléviseur *noun, masculine*
un téléviseur = a television (set)

télévision *noun, feminine*
la télévision = television, TV

tellement *adverb*
• = so (much)
il est tellement riche! = he's so rich!
c'est tellement mieux maintenant! = it's so
  much better now!
• tellement de = so much, so many
elle a tellement de temps libre = she has so
  much free time
il y avait tellement de monde que je suis
  parti = there were so many people that I
  left

témoignage *noun, masculine*
un témoignage = a personal account
(*in court*) = evidence

témoin *noun, masculine*
un témoin = a witness
être témoin d'un incident = to witness an
  incident

tempérament *noun, masculine*
un tempérament = a disposition, a
  temperament

température *noun, feminine*
la température = the temperature

T

tempête *noun, feminine*
  une tempête = a storm
  = a gale

temporaire *adjective*
  = temporary

temps *noun, masculine* (**!** *never changes*)
• (*outside conditions*)
  le temps = the weather
  quel temps fait-il? = what's the weather
    like?
  il fait beau temps = the weather is fine
  il a fait mauvais temps = the weather has
    been bad
  quel temps de chien! = what awful
    weather!, it's terrible weather!
• (*as measured in hours*)
  le temps = time
  je n'ai pas le temps de me reposer = I
    haven't got time to rest
  il est grand temps de partir = it's high time
    we left
  ils ont fini à temps = they finished in time
  de temps en temps = from time to time
  pendant ce temps = meanwhile
• (*in grammar*)
  un temps = a tense

tenace *adjective*
  = stubborn, persistent

tenir *verb* 36
1 (**!** + *avoir*)
• = to hold
• **tiens!, tenez!** (*when giving something*)
  = here!
  (*expressing surprise*) = hey!
2 tenir à (**!** + *avoir*)
  tenir à sa famille = to be fond of one's
    family
3 se tenir (**!** + *être*)
• **se tenir** = to hold on
  se tenir à la rampe = to hold on to the
    banister
• **se tenir** = to stand
  se tenir droit (*if standing*) = to stand up
    straight
  se tenir tranquille = to keep still
• **se tenir** = to behave
  tenez-vous bien! = behave yourselves!
• **ils se tenaient par la main** = they were
  holding hands
4 si cela ne tenait qu'à moi = if I had my way

tennis *noun, masculine* (**!** *never changes*)
• (*the sport*)
  le tennis = tennis
• (*footwear*)
  un tennis = a tennis shoe

tentation *noun, feminine*
  la tentation = temptation

tentative *noun, feminine*
  une tentative = an attempt

✖ in informal situations

tente *noun, feminine*
  une tente = a tent

tenter *verb* 1
• = to attempt
  = to try
  tenter sa chance = to try one's luck
• = to tempt
  ça ne me tente guère = it doesn't appeal to
    me very much

tenu/tenue[1] ▶ **tenir** 36

tenue[2] *noun, feminine*
  une tenue = an outfit, clothes
  en tenue de soirée = in evening dress

terminale *noun, feminine*
  la terminale *the class for secondary school*
    students aged 17 to 18

terminer *verb* 1
1 (**!** + *avoir*)
  = to finish, to end
2 se terminer (**!** + *être*)
  se terminer = end
  se terminer par une bagarre = to end in a
    fight

terminus *noun, masculine* (**!** *never changes*)
  le terminus (*for a train*) = the end of the
    line
  (*for a bus*) = the terminus

terne *adjective*
  = dull

terrain *noun, masculine*
• (*a site*)
  un terrain = a piece of land
  (*used for sport*) = a pitch, a ground
• (*the surface underfoot*)
  le terrain = the ground
  un terrain d'atterrissage = a landing
    strip
  un terrain à bâtir = a building plot
  un terrain de camping = a campsite
  un terrain de jeux = a playground
  un terrain de sports = a sports ground, a
    sports field
  un terrain vague = a piece of wasteland

terrasse *noun, feminine*
  une terrasse = a terrace
  = a flat roof
  s'asseoir à la terrasse d'un café = to sit at
    a table outside a café

terre *noun, feminine*
• (*the surface underfoot*)
  la terre = the ground
  sous terre = underground
  par terre = on the ground, on the floor
• (*the substance*)
  la terre = the earth, the soil
  (*as opposed to the sea*) = land
  aller à terre = to go ashore
• (*a type of clay*)
  un pot en terre = an earthenware pot

- (*an area in private ownership*)
  une terre = a piece of land
  des terres = land

Terre *noun, feminine*
  la Terre = Earth

terrestre *adjective*
  (*describing plants or animals*) = land
  (*relating to the Earth*) = of the Earth

terrible *adjective*
- = terrible
- (*excellent*)✗ = terrific
  le livre n'est pas terrible✗ = it's not a great
    book

tes ▶ ton²

testament *noun, masculine*
  un testament = a will

tester *verb* ①
  = to test

tête *noun, feminine*
- (*part of the body*)
  la tête = the head
  se laver la tête = to wash one's hair
- (*the front part of the head*)
  la tête = the face
  tu fais une drôle de tête = you look funny
  faire la tête = to sulk
  n'en faire qu'à sa tête = to get one's way
- (*as opposed to the end*)
  la tête = the front
  = the head
  être en tête = to be at the front
une tête en l'air = a scatterbrain

têtu/têtue *adjective*
  = stubborn, obstinate

TGV *noun, masculine*
  un TGV = a high speed train

thé *noun, masculine*
- **le thé** = tea
- **un thé** = a cup of tea

théâtre *noun, masculine*
  un théâtre = a theatre, a theater
  faire du théâtre = to be an actor/an actress,
    to act

théière *noun, feminine*
  une théière = a teapot

thème *noun, masculine*
- (*of a speech*)
  le thème = the theme
- (*a translation*)
  un thème = a prose

thermal/thermale *adjective*
  (*plural*) **thermaux/thermales**
  une source thermale = a thermal spring
  une station thermale = a spa

thermos® *noun, masculine* (**!** *never
changes*)
  un thermos® = a (vacuum) flask

thon *noun, masculine*
  le thon = tuna

thym *noun, masculine*
  le thym = thyme

tibia *noun, masculine*
  le tibia = the shin

ticket *noun, masculine*
  un ticket = a ticket

tiède *adjective*
  = warm
  = lukewarm, tepid

tien/tienne: *pronoun*
  le tien/la tienne = yours
  les tiens/les tiennes = yours

tiens ▶ tenir ③⑥

tiers *noun, masculine* (**!** *never changes*)
  un tiers = one third

tiers-monde *noun, masculine*
  le tiers-monde = the Third World

tige *noun, feminine*
  une tige = a stem

tigre *noun, masculine*
  un tigre = a tiger

tilleul *noun, masculine*
- (*a tree*)
  un tilleul = a lime tree
- (*a drink*)
  le tilleul = lime tea

timbre *noun, masculine*
  un timbre = a (postage) stamp

timbrer *verb* ①
  = to put a stamp on

timide *adjective*
  = shy

timidité *noun, feminine*
  la timidité = shyness

tir *noun, masculine*
- **le tir** (*in an attack*) = firing
  (*as a sport*) = shooting
- **le tir à l'arc** = archery

tirage *noun, masculine*
- (*in a lottery*)
  le tirage (au sort) = the draw
- (*for a newspaper*)
  le tirage = the circulation
  un quotidien à grand tirage = a mass
    circulation daily

tire-bouchon *noun, masculine*
  (*plural*) **tire-bouchons**
  un tire-bouchon = a corkscrew

tirelire *noun, feminine*
  une tirelire = a piggy bank

tirer *verb* ①
- = to pull
- = to draw

T

• = to fire
= to shoot
• **tirer au sort** = to draw lots

tiroir *noun, masculine*
un tiroir = a drawer

tiroir-caisse *noun, masculine*
(*plural*) **tiroirs-caisses**
un tiroir-caisse = a cash register

tisane *noun, feminine*
la tisane = herbal tea

tisser *verb* 1
= to weave

tissu *noun, masculine*
le tissu = material, fabric

titre *noun, masculine*
un titre = a title

toc *exclamation*
toc toc! = knock! knock!

toi *pronoun*
= you
plus jeune que toi = younger than you
toi, tu as de la chance = you're lucky, you
    are
ce livre est à toi = this book belongs to
    you, this book is yours
à toi (de jouer)! = it's your turn (to play)!
allons chez toi = let's go to your house
lève-toi! = get up!

toile *noun, feminine*
• (*material*)
la toile = cloth
= canvas
• (*in art*)
une toile = a canvas
une toile d'araignée = a cobweb, a
    spider's web
une toile cirée = an oilcloth

toilette
1 *noun, feminine*
faire sa toilette = to have a wash
2 toilettes *noun, feminine plural*
les toilettes (*in a house*) = the toilet, the
    bathroom
(*in a public place*) = the toilets

toi-même *pronoun*
= yourself

toise *noun, feminine*
une toise = a height gauge

toit *noun, masculine*
un toit = a roof
un toit ouvrant = a sunroof

tôle *noun, feminine*
la tôle = sheet metal
la tôle ondulée = corrugated iron

tomate *noun, feminine*
une tomate = a tomato

tombe *noun, feminine*
une tombe = a grave

tomber *verb* 1 (**!** + *être*)
• = to fall
= to fall over
c'est tombé de ma poche = it fell out of
    my pocket
il est tombé de l'arbre = he fell off the tree
tomber en panne = to break down
• laisser tomber = to drop
• (*to see or meet by chance*)
tomber sur = to come across
= to run into
• (*to happen*)
ça tombe bien, moi aussi je suis libre
    = that's good, I'm free too

ton[1] *noun, masculine*
• (*a way of speaking*)
un ton = a tone
d'un ton sec = drily
• (*a colour*)
un ton = a shade

ton[2]/**ta** *determiner*
(*plural*) **tes**
= your

tonalité *noun, feminine*
la tonalité = the dialling tone, the dial
    tone

tondeuse *noun, feminine*
une tondeuse (à gazon) = a lawnmower

tondre *verb* 6
tondre le gazon = to mow the grass
tondre un mouton = to shear a sheep
tondre quelqu'un = to shave someone's
    head

tondu/tondue ▶ tondre 6

tonneau *noun, masculine*
(*plural*) **tonneaux**
un tonneau = a barrel

tonnerre
1 *noun, masculine*
le tonnerre = thunder
un coup de tonnerre = a clap of thunder
2 du tonnerre✘ = fabulous

torchon *noun, masculine*
un torchon = a tea towel, a dish towel

tordre *verb* 6
1 (**!** + *avoir*)
= to twist
= to wring
= to bend
2 se tordre (**!** + *être*)
se tordre la cheville = to twist one's ankle

tordu/tordue *adjective*
1 ▶ tordre 6
2 *adjective*
= crooked
= twisted

✘ in informal situations

tornade *noun, feminine*
une tornade = a tornado

torrent *noun, masculine*
un torrent = a torrent
pleuvoir à torrents = to rain very heavily

torse *noun, masculine*
le torse = the chest

tort *noun, masculine*
avoir tort = to be wrong

tortue *noun, feminine*
une tortue = a tortoise, a turtle

tôt *adverb*
= early
tôt le matin = early in the morning
le plus tôt possible = as soon as possible

toucher *verb* ⌐1⌐
• = to touch
• = to get
toucher un salaire = to get a wage
• = to cash

touffe *noun, feminine*
une touffe (*of hair, grass*) = a tuft

toujours *adverb*
• (*all the time*) = always
il est toujours en retard = he's always late
• (*showing that something is continuing*)
= still
tu habites toujours Paris? = are you still
living in Paris?
il n'est toujours pas levé = he's still not up
elle est toujours aussi jolie = she's as pretty
as ever

tour
1 *noun, feminine*
• (*a building*)
une tour = a tower
= a tower block, a high rise
• (*in chess*)
une tour = a rook, a castle
2 *noun, masculine*
• (*a turning movement*)
un tour = a turn
faire un tour de manège = to have a go on
a fairground ride
faire le tour du lac (*on foot*) = to walk
round the lake
faire le tour du monde en bateau = to sail
round the world
• (*in a game, a rota*)
un tour = a turn
à tour de rôle = in turn
• (*an outing*)
(aller) faire un tour = to go for a stroll
aller faire un tour à Rome = to go to Rome
• (*a piece of mischief*)
un tour = a trick
jouer un tour à un ami = to play a trick on
a friend
• (*a size*)
un tour = a measurement
mon tour de taille = my waist
measurement

tourbillon *noun, masculine*
un tourbillon = a whirlpool
un tourbillon (de vent) = a whirlwind
un tourbillon de poussière = a whirl of
dust

tourisme *noun, masculine*
le tourisme = tourism

touristique *adjective*
= tourist
un endroit touristique = a popular tourist
spot

tournée *noun, feminine*
• une tournée (*for a postman*) = a round
(*for a singer, a theatre company*) = a tour
• (*in a café*)
une tournée = a round (of drinks)

tourner *verb* ⌐1⌐
1 (**!** + *avoir*)
• = to turn
• tourner un film = to shoot a film
2 se tourner (**!** + *être*)
se tourner = to turn around

tournoi *noun, masculine*
un tournoi = a tournament

tous ▶ **tout** 1, 2

Toussaint *noun, feminine*
la Toussaint = All Saints' Day

tousser *verb* ⌐1⌐
= to cough

tout/toute
(*plural*) **tous/toutes**
1 *adjective*
• = all
= every
il a plu toute la journée = it rained all day
(long)
c'est tout ce que tu veux? = is that all you
want?
tout le reste = everything else
tout le monde = everyone
tous les jours = every day
tous les deux ans = every other year
ils sont venus tous les deux = they both
came
• tout un/tout une = a whole
manger tout un pain = to eat a whole loaf
• = any
à toute heure = at any time
de toute façon = in any case
2 *pronoun*
= everything
= anything
= all
il a tout oublié = he's forgotten everything
tout peut arriver = anything can happen
100 francs en tout = 100 francs in all
tous ensemble = all together

T

3 *adverb*
- = quite
  = very
  c'est tout naturel = it's quite natural
  c'est tout près d'ici = it's very near
  être tout seul = to be all by oneself
  continuer tout droit = to carry straight on
  tout neuf/toute neuve = brand-new
  des rideaux tout faits = ready-made
  curtains
- **tout en** [marchant | travaillant | écoutant la
  radio …] = while [walking | working | listening
  to the radio …]
- (*in some phrases*)
  tout à coup = suddenly
  tout à fait = quite
  tout à l'heure = in a moment
  à tout à l'heure! = see you later!
  tout de même = all the same, even so
  tout de suite = at once
4 tout *noun, masculine*
- **le tout** = the lot
- **pas du tout** = not at all

toux *noun, feminine* (**!** *never changes*)
  une toux = a cough

TP *noun, masculine plural* ▶ **travail**

tracasser *verb* 1
  = to bother

trace *noun, feminine*
- **une trace** = a trail, a track
- **une trace** = a mark, a trace
  des traces de pas = footprints
  des traces de doigts = fingermarks

tracer *verb* 12
  = to draw
  = to write

traduire *verb* 62
  = to translate

trafic *noun, masculine*
  le trafic = traffic

trafiquant/trafiquante *noun,*
masculine/feminine
  un trafiquant/une trafiquante = a
  trafficker, a dealer

train
1 *noun, masculine*
  un train = a train
2 en train de = in the process of
  être en train de [travailler | dormir | se
  doucher …] = to be [working | sleeping |
  having a shower …]

traîneau *noun, masculine*
(*plural*) **traîneaux**
  un traîneau = a sledge

traîner *verb* 1
- = to drag (along)

✗ in informal situations

- **traîner dans les rues** = to hang around
  (on) the streets
- (*to be scattered*) = to be lying around
  laisser traîner ses affaires = to leave one's
  things lying around

trait
1 *noun, masculine*
  un trait = a line
2 traits *noun, masculine plural*
  des traits (*of a face*) = features

traitement *noun, masculine*
  un traitement = a treatment

traiter *verb* 1
  = to treat

trajet *noun, masculine*
  un trajet = a journey

tranche *noun, feminine*
  une tranche (*of cheese, bread*) = a slice

tranquille *adjective*
  = quiet
  = calm, peaceful

tranquillité *noun, feminine*
  la tranquillité = peace and quiet

transmettre *verb* 60
- = to broadcast
- = to pass on, to convey
- = to transmit

transpirer *verb* 1
  = to sweat, to perspire

transport *noun, masculine*
- **le transport** = transport, transportation
- **les transports en commun** = public
  transport

transporter *verb* 1
  = to carry

travail
(*plural*) **travaux**
1 *noun, masculine*
- **le travail** = work
- **un travail** = a job
2 travaux *noun, masculine plural*
  des travaux = work
  = roadwork(s)
  les travaux ménagers = housework
les travaux dirigés, TD = practicals
les travaux manuels = handicrafts
les travaux pratiques, TP = practical
  work
les travaux publics = civil engineering

travailler *verb* 1
  = to work
  = to practise

travailleur/travailleuse
1 *adjective*
  = hardworking
2 *noun, masculine/feminine*
  un travailleur/une travailleuse = a worker

travaux ▶ travail

travers *noun, masculine*
1 à travers = through
= across
2 de travers
ta cravate est de travers = your tie is crooked
boutonné de travers = buttoned up wrongly
j'ai avalé de travers = it went down the wrong way
3 en travers de
= across

traversée *noun, feminine*
une traversée = a crossing

traverser *verb* 1
• = to cross
• = to go through

traversin *noun, masculine*
un traversin = a bolster

trèfle *noun, masculine*
• (*a plant*)
le trèfle = clover
• (*at cards*)
trèfle = clubs

treille *noun, feminine*
une treille = a climbing vine

treize *number*
= thirteen

treizième *number*
= thirteenth

tremblement *noun, masculine*
un tremblement = a tremor
un tremblement de terre = an earthquake

trembler *verb* 1
= to shake
= to tremble, to quiver

trempé/trempée *adjective*
= soaked, sodden, soaking wet
trempé jusqu'aux os = soaked to the skin

tremper *verb* 1
• = to soak
• = to dip

trente *number*
= thirty

très *adverb*
= very
avoir très faim = to be very hungry
très volontiers = gladly

trésor *noun, masculine*
un trésor = a treasure

tresse *noun, feminine*
une tresse = a plait, a braid

tribu *noun, feminine*
une tribu = a tribe

tribune *noun, feminine*
la tribune (*in a stadium*) = the grandstand

tricher *verb* 1
= to cheat

tricolore *adjective*
le drapeau tricolore = the French flag

tricot *noun, masculine*
• (*a craft*)
le tricot = knitting
• (*a knitted garment*)
un tricot = a jumper, a sweater

tricoter *verb* 1
= to knit

trier *verb* 2
• = to sort (out)
• = to select

trimestre *noun, masculine*
un trimestre = a term

triste *adjective*
= sad

tristesse *noun, feminine*
la tristesse = sadness

trois *number*
= three

troisième
1 *number*
= third
2 *noun, feminine*
la troisième *the class for secondary school students aged 14 to 15*

trombone *noun, masculine*
• (*an instrument*)
un trombone = a trombone
• (*for fastening papers*)
un trombone = a paper clip

trompe *noun, feminine*
une trompe d'éléphant = an elephant trunk

tromper *verb* 1
1 (**!** + *avoir*)
= to deceive
2 se tromper (**!** + *être*)
• se tromper = to make a mistake
se tromper de bus = to take the wrong bus
se tromper de date = to get the date wrong
• se tromper = to be mistaken

trompette *noun, feminine*
une trompette = a trumpet

tronc *noun, masculine*
un tronc = a trunk

trop
1 *adverb* = too
= too much
c'est trop petit = it's too small
tu parles trop = you talk too much
2 trop de = too much, too many

T

trottoir noun, masculine
un trottoir = a pavement, a sidewalk
le bord du trottoir = the kerb, the curb

trou noun, masculine
• **un trou** = a hole
  (in a hedge) = a gap
• (a small town)✱
  un trou✱ (perdu) = a dump

troupeau noun, masculine
(plural) **troupeaux**
un troupeau = a herd
= a flock

trousse noun, feminine
une trousse = a (small) case
= a kit
une trousse d'écolier = a pencil case
une trousse de secours = a first-aid kit
une trousse de toilette = a toilet bag

trouver verb 1
1 (! + avoir)
• = to find
• = to think
  je trouve qu'il a raison = I think he's right
  comment trouves-tu mon copain? = what
    do you think of my friend?
2 se trouver (! + être)
• **se trouver** = to be
  se trouver à Nice = to be in Nice
• **se trouver** = to find
  se trouver une excuse = to find an excuse
• **je me trouve bien ici** = I like it here
  se trouver mal = to pass out, to faint

truc noun, masculine
• (when referring vaguely to something)
  un truc = a thing
• (a clever way)✱
  un truc✱ = a trick
  = a knack

truffe noun, feminine
une truffe = a truffle

truite noun, feminine
une truite = a trout

TTC (abbreviation of **toutes taxes
comprises**)
TTC = inclusive of tax

tu pronoun
= you

tube noun, masculine
• **un tube** = a tube, a pipe
• (a song)✱
  un tube✱ = a hit

tuer verb 1
= to kill

tue-tête: **à tue-tête** adverb
chanter à tue-tête = to sing at the top of
one's voice

---

tuile noun, feminine
une tuile = a tile

Tunisie noun, feminine
la Tunisie = Tunisia

tunisien/tunisienne adjective
= Tunisian

tunnel noun, masculine
un tunnel = a tunnel
le tunnel sous la Manche = the Channel
Tunnel

turc/turque
1 adjective
= Turkish
2 turc noun, masculine
le turc = Turkish

Turquie noun, feminine
la Turquie = Turkey

tutoyer verb 23
tutoyer quelqu'un = to address someone
using the 'tu' form

tuyau noun, masculine
(plural) **tuyaux**
un tuyau = a pipe
un tuyau d'arrosage = a hosepipe
le tuyau d'échappement = the exhaust

TVA noun, feminine
la TVA = VAT

type noun, masculine
• (a sort)
  un type = a type, a kind
• (a man)✱
  un type✱ = a bloke, a guy

typique adjective
= typical

Uu

ULM noun, masculine (! never changes)
• (the equipment)
  un ULM = a microlight
• (the sport)
  l'ULM = microlighting

un/une
1 number
= one
trente et un jours = thirty-one days
une fois = once
un jour sur deux = every other day
2 determiner
(plural) **des**
= a(n)
un chat = a cat
des enfants = children

3 *pronoun*
(*plural*) **uns/unes**
   (l')un/(l')une = one
   les uns/les unes = some
   l'un d'entre vous = one of you
   pourquoi les uns et pas les autres? = why
      some and not others?

uni/unie *adjective*
• (*not at odds*) = united
   = close-knit
• (*not patterned*) = plain

unique *adjective*
• = only
   être fils/fille unique = to be an only child
• = unique
   une occasion unique = a unique
      opportunity

uniquement *adverb*
   = only

unir *verb* 3
   = to unite

unité *noun, feminine*
• une unité = a unit
• l'unité = unity

univers *noun, masculine* (**!** *never
changes*)
   l'univers = the universe

universitaire *adjective*
   = university

université *noun, feminine*
   l'université = university, college

uns/unes ▶ un 3

urbain/urbaine *adjective*
   = urban
   la vie urbaine = city life

urbanisme *noun, masculine*
   l'urbanisme = town planning, city
      planning

urgence *noun, feminine*
• l'urgence = the urgency
   téléphonez d'urgence = phone
      immediately
   des mesures d'urgence = emergency
      measures
   on l'a transporté d'urgence à l'hôpital = he
      was rushed to the hospital
• (*in a hospital*)
   une urgence = an emergency
   le service des urgences = the casualty
      department, the accident and
      emergency department

urticaire *noun, feminine*
   l'urticaire = nettle rash

usage *noun, masculine*
   l'usage = the use
   'à usage externe' = 'for external use only'

usager *noun, masculine*
   un usager (*of a service*) = a user
   les usagers de la route = road-users

usé/usée *adjective*
   = worn

user *verb* 1
1 (**!** + *avoir*)
   = to wear out
   = to wear down
2 s'user (**!** + *être*)
   s'user = to wear out

usine *noun, feminine*
   une usine = a factory

ustensile *noun, masculine*
   un ustensile = a utensil

utile *adjective*
   = useful

utiliser *verb* 1
   = to use

va ▶ aller 1 9

vacances *noun, feminine plural*
   des vacances = holidays, a vacation
   être en vacances = to be on holiday, to be
      on vacation

vacancier/vacancière *noun,
masculine/feminine*
   un vacancier/une vacancière = a
      holidaymaker, a vacationer

vache *noun, feminine*
   une vache = a cow

vagabonder *verb* 1
   = to wander

vague
1 *adjective*
   = vague
2 *noun, masculine*
   il regardait dans le vague = he was staring
      into space
3 *noun, feminine*
• une vague = a wave
• une vague de froid = a cold spell

vaincre *verb* 57
   = to defeat
   = to overcome

vaincu/vaincue
1 ▶ vaincre 57
2 *noun, masculine/feminine*
   les vaincus = the losers

V

vainqueur noun, masculine
  un vainqueur = a winner
  = a victor

vais ▶ aller 1 ⑨

vaisselle noun, feminine
  la vaisselle = crockery, dishes
  faire la vaisselle = to do the dishes

valable adjective
  = valid

valet noun, masculine
• (a person)
  un valet = a manservant
• (at cards)
  un valet = a jack

valeur noun, feminine
  la valeur (in terms of money) = value
  (in terms of merit) = worth
  les objets de valeur = valuables
  sans valeur = worthless

valise noun, feminine
  une valise = a suitcase
  faire ses valises = to pack

vallée noun, feminine
  une vallée = a valley

valoir verb ㊺
• = to be worth
  = to cost
  ça en vaut la peine = it's worth it
• il vaut mieux partir tôt = it's better to leave
  early
  il vaut mieux que tu y ailles = you'd better
  go

valu ▶ valoir ㊺

vanille noun, feminine
  la vanille = vanilla

vapeur
1 noun, feminine
  la vapeur = steam
  un bateau à vapeur = a steamboat
  faire cuire des légumes à la vapeur = to
  steam vegetables
2 vapeurs noun, feminine plural
  des vapeurs = fumes

vaporisateur noun, masculine
  un vaporisateur = a spray

vaporiser verb ①
  = to spray
  = to vaporize

varappe noun, feminine
  la varappe = rock-climbing

variable adjective
• = variable
• = changeable, unpredictable

variante noun, feminine
  une variante = a variation

× in informal situations

varié/variée adjective
  = varied
  = various
  'sandwichs variés' = 'a selection of
  sandwiches'

variété
1 noun, feminine
• la variété = variety
• une variété = a variety
2 variétés noun, feminine plural
  un spectacle de variétés = a variety show

vas ▶ aller 1 ⑨

vase
1 noun, masculine
  un vase = a vase
2 noun, feminine
  la vase = mud

vaste adjective
  = vast, huge
  = large

vaudrait ▶ valoir ㊺

vaut ▶ valoir ㊺

vautour noun, masculine
  un vautour = a vulture

veau noun, masculine
(plural) **veaux**
• (the animal)
  un veau = a calf
• (the meat)
  le veau = veal

vécu/vécue
1 ▶ vivre ㊳
2 adjective
  = real-life

vedette noun, feminine
• (a person)
  une vedette = a star
• (a boat)
  une vedette = a motor launch

véhicule noun, masculine
  un véhicule = a vehicle

veille noun, feminine
  la veille = the day before
  la veille au soir = the night before

veiller verb ①
• (to remain awake) = to stay up
• (to be alert) = to be watchful

veilleur noun, masculine
  un veilleur de nuit = a night watchman

veilleuse noun, feminine
  une veilleuse = a night light
  = a pilot light

veine noun, feminine
• une veine = a vein
• la veine× = luck
  avoir de la veine× = to be lucky

vélo noun, masculine
  un vélo = a bike
  un vélo tout terrain = a mountain bike
  faire du vélo = to cycle

vélomoteur noun, masculine
  un vélomoteur = a moped

velours noun, masculine (**!** never changes)
  le velours = velvet
  = corduroy

venais ▶ venir 36

vendanges noun, feminine plural
  les vendanges = the grape harvest

vendeur/vendeuse noun, masculine/feminine
  un vendeur/une vendeuse = a seller, a vendor
  = a shop assistant
  = a salesman/a saleswoman

vendre verb 6
1 (**!** + avoir)
  = to sell
  'à vendre' = 'for sale'
2 se vendre (**!** + être)
  se vendre = to be sold
  ça se vend bien = it sells well

vendredi noun, masculine
  vendredi = Friday
  le vendredi = on Fridays

vendu/vendue ▶ vendre 6

vénéneux/vénéneuse adjective
  = poisonous

vengeance noun, feminine
  la vengeance = revenge

venger verb 13
1 (**!** + avoir)
  = to avenge
2 se venger (**!** + être)
  se venger = to get one's revenge

venir verb 36 (**!** + être)
• = to come
  viens déjeuner = come for lunch
  faire venir un plombier = to call a plumber
  ça ne m'est jamais venu à l'idée = it never crossed my mind
• venir de faire = to have just done

vent noun, masculine
  le vent = the wind
  il y a du vent, il fait du vent = it's windy

vente noun, feminine
  une vente = a sale
  des médicaments en vente libre = drugs available over the counter
la vente par correspondance = mail-order selling
une vente aux enchères = an auction

ventre noun, masculine
  le ventre (a person's) = the stomach
  (an animal's) = the (under)belly

venu/venue ▶ venir 36

ver noun, masculine
  un ver = a worm
  = a maggot
un ver de terre = an earthworm

verbe noun, masculine
  un verbe = a verb

verdure noun, feminine
  la verdure = greenery

verger noun, masculine
  un verger = an orchard

verglacé/verglacée adjective
  = icy

verglas noun, masculine (**!** never changes)
  le verglas = black ice

vérifier verb 2
  = to check

véritable adjective
  = real, true, genuine

vérité noun, feminine
  la vérité = the truth

vernis noun, masculine (**!** never changes)
  le vernis = varnish
  = glaze
  du vernis à ongles = nail polish

verrai ▶ voir 46

verre noun, masculine
• (a substance)
  le verre = glass
• (a container)
  un verre = a glass
  un verre à vin = a wine glass
  un verre de vin = a glass of wine
  aller prendre un verre = to go for a drink
• (on spectacles)
  un verre = a lens
des verres de contact = contact lenses

vers
1 noun, masculine (**!** never changes)
  un vers = a line (of verse)
  des vers = poetry
2 preposition
• = toward(s)
  rouler vers Paris = to go toward(s) Paris
  vers le soir = toward(s) evening
• = about
  vers six heures = at about six o'clock

Verseau noun, masculine
  le Verseau = Aquarius

verser verb 1
• = to pour
• = to pay

V

version noun, feminine
• (an exercise)
  une version = a translation (into one's own language)
• (an account, an adaptation)
  une version = a version
  un film en version originale = a film in the original language

vert/verte adjective
  = green

vertèbre noun, feminine
  une vertèbre = a vertebra
  se déplacer une vertèbre = to slip a disc

vertical/verticale adjective
(plural) **verticaux/verticales**
  = vertical
  = upright

verticalement adverb
• = vertically
• (in a crossword) = down

vertige noun, masculine
  le vertige = dizziness
  = vertigo
  avoir le vertige = to feel dizzy

veste noun, feminine
  une veste = a jacket

vestiaire noun, masculine
  un vestiaire (in a gym) = a changing room
  (in a theatre, a museum) = a cloakroom

vestibule noun, masculine
  un vestibule = a hall
  = a foyer, a lobby

veston noun, masculine
  un veston = a (man's) jacket

vêtement noun, masculine
  un vêtement = a garment
  des vêtements = clothes, clothing
  'vêtements pour hommes' = 'menswear'

vétérinaire noun, masculine|feminine
  un vétérinaire/une vétérinaire = a veterinary surgeon, a veterinarian

vêtu/vêtue adjective
  = dressed
  elle était vêtue d'une robe noire = she was wearing a black dress

veuf/veuve
1 adjective
  = widowed
2 noun, masculine|feminine
  un veuf/une veuve = a widower/a widow

veuille ▶ vouloir 48

veulent ▶ vouloir 48

veuve ▶ veuf

veux ▶ vouloir 48

vexer verb 1
1 (! + avoir)
  = to offend, to upset

2 se vexer (! + être)
  se vexer = to take offence, to get upset

viande noun, feminine
  la viande = meat
  de la viande de bœuf = beef

victime noun, feminine
  une victime = a victim
  = a casualty

victoire noun, feminine
  une victoire = a victory

vide
1 adjective
  = empty, vacant
  = blank
2 noun, masculine
• (a space)
  un vide = a gap
• (absence of air)
  le vide = a vacuum
  emballé sous vide = vacuum-packed
• sauter dans le vide = to jump

vidéothèque noun, feminine
  une vidéothèque = a video library
  = a video collection

vider verb 1
1 (! + avoir)
  = to empty
2 se vider (! + être)
  se vider = to empty

vie noun, feminine
  la vie = life
  être en vie = to be alive
  la vie active = working life
  la vie est chère = the cost of living is high

vieil ▶ vieux 1

vieillard/vieillarde noun,
masculine|feminine
  un vieillard/une vieillarde = an old man/an old woman
  les vieillards = old people

vieille ▶ vieux

vieillir verb 3
  = to get old(er)
  = to age

viendrai ▶ venir 36

viens ▶ venir 36

vierge adjective
  = virgin
  = blank
  = new

Vierge noun, feminine
• la Vierge = Virgo
• la (Sainte) Vierge = the (Blessed) Virgin

vietnamien/vietnamienne
1 adjective
  = Vietnamese

2 vietnamien noun, masculine
le vietnamien = Vietnamese

vieux/vieille
(plural) **vieux/vieilles**
1 adjective
= old

> ! vieil is used instead of vieux before masculine nouns that begin with a vowel or a mute h. The plural of vieil is vieux.

un vieil homme = an old man
de vieilles photos = old photographs
2 noun, masculine|feminine
un vieux/une vieille = an old man/an old woman
les vieux = old people

vif/vive¹ adjective
• (describing a person) = lively
• (describing a pace, a movement) = brisk
rouler à vive allure = to drive at high speed
• (describing a light, a colour) = bright
• (describing the cold, the wind) = biting
• (describing a pain) = sharp

vigne noun, feminine
la vigne = vine
une vigne = a vineyard
la vigne vierge = Virginia creeper

vigneron/vigneronne noun,
masculine|feminine
un vigneron/une vigneronne = a winegrower

vignette noun, feminine
une vignette = a label
(on a car) = a tax disc

vignoble noun, masculine
un vignoble = a vineyard

vilain/vilaine adjective
• = naughty, nasty
• = ugly

villa noun, feminine
une villa = a detached house
= a villa

village noun, masculine
un village = a village

ville noun, feminine
une ville = a town, a city
aller en ville = to go into town

vin noun, masculine
le vin = wine

vinaigre noun, masculine
le vinaigre = vinegar

vinaigrette noun, feminine
la vinaigrette = vinaigrette, oil and vinegar dressing

vingt number
= twenty

vingtaine noun, feminine
une vingtaine = about twenty
= twenty

vingt et un/vingt et une number
= twenty-one

vingt et unième number
= twenty-first

vingtième number
= twentieth

violent/violente adjective
= violent

violet/violette¹ adjective
= purple

violette² noun, feminine
une violette = a violet

violon noun, masculine
un violon = a violin

violoncelle noun, masculine
un violoncelle = a cello

vipère noun, feminine
une vipère = an adder, a viper

virage noun, masculine
un virage = a bend

virgule noun, feminine
une virgule = a comma
= a decimal point

vis
1 ▶ vivre 38
2 noun, feminine (! never changes)
une vis = a screw

visage noun, masculine
le visage = the face

viser verb 1
• = to aim at
• = to be aimed at

visite noun, feminine
une visite = a visit
= a call
rendre visite à un ami = to pay a visit to a friend
avoir de la visite = to have visitors
une visite médicale = a medical examination

visiter verb 1
visiter une ville = to visit a town
visiter un appartement = to view a flat, to look at an apartment

visser verb 1
= to screw on

vite adverb
= quickly, fast
vite! = quick!
j'ai parlé trop vite = I spoke too hastily

vitesse noun, feminine
• la vitesse = speed
en vitesse = quickly
à toute vitesse = at top speed
• une vitesse = a gear

V

vitre noun, feminine
   une vitre = a windowpane
   = a pane of glass
   les vitres d'une voiture = the windows of a
    car

vitrine noun, feminine
• (in a shop)
   une vitrine = a (shop) window
   faire les vitrines = to go window shopping
• (in a museum)
   une vitrine = a display cabinet, a curio
    cabinet

vivant/vivante adjective
• = alive, living
   être vivant = to be alive
   les êtres vivants = living creatures
• = lively

vive²
1 adjective, feminine ▶ **vif**
2 verb ▶ **vivre** 38

vivre verb 38
   = to live
   se laisser vivre = to take things easy

vocabulaire noun, masculine
   le vocabulaire = vocabulary

vœu noun, masculine
(plural) **vœux**
   un vœu = a wish
   meilleurs vœux = best wishes
   les vœux du Nouvel An = New Year's
    greetings

voici preposition
   = here is, this is
   = here are, these are
   me voici = here I am
   voici un mois = a month ago

voie noun, feminine
• (for traffic)
   une voie = a road
   = a street
   la voie publique = the public highway
   une voie sans issue = a dead end
• (part of a road)
   une voie = a lane
• (for a train)
   une voie = a track
• **en voie de** = in the process of
   un pays en voie de développement = a
    developing country
   une espèce en voie de disparition = an
    endangered species
   la voie ferrée = the railway track, the
    railroad track

voilà preposition
   = here is, this is
   = here are, these are
   te voilà enfin! = here you are at last!
   voilà tout = that's all
   voilà un mois = a month ago

voile
1 noun, feminine
• **une voile** = a sail
• **la voile** = sailing
2 noun, masculine
   un voile = a veil

voir verb 46
1 (**!** + avoir)
• = to see
   on verra = we'll see
   un film à voir = a film worth seeing
   faire voir quelque chose à quelqu'un = to
    show someone something
• = to be able to see
   je ne vois rien, je n'y vois rien = I can't see
    a thing
• (to be connected)
   ça n'a rien à voir = that's got nothing to do
    with it
• (when encouraging someone)
   voyons, soyez sages! = come on, be good!
2 se voir (**!** + être)
• (to be visible)
   se voir = to show
   ça se voit de loin = it can be seen from a
    distance
• (to meet)
   se voir = to see each other

voisin/voisine
1 adjective
   = neighbo(u)ring
   = nearby
2 noun, masculine|feminine
   un voisin/une voisine = a neighbo(u)r

voiture noun, feminine
   une voiture = a car, an automobile
   = a carriage, a car
   en voiture! = all aboard!

voix noun, feminine (**!** never changes)
• (the way one speaks)
   une voix = a voice
   à voix basse = in a low voice
   à haute voix = out loud
• (in an election)
   une voix = a vote

vol noun, masculine
• (through the air)
   un vol = a flight
   à vol d'oiseau = as the crow flies
• (an offence)
   un vol = a theft, a robbery
   un vol à main armée = an armed robbery
   le vol à voile = gliding

volaille noun, feminine
   la volaille = poultry

volant/volante
1 adjective
   = flying
2 volant noun, masculine
• (in a car)
   un volant = a steering wheel
   donner un coup de volant = to turn the
    wheel sharply

- (*in badminton*)
  un volant = a shuttlecock
- (*on a skirt*)
  un volant = a flounce

volcan *noun, masculine*
  un volcan = a volcano

voler *verb* 1
- = to steal
  il s'est fait voler sa voiture = he had his car stolen
- **voler un passant** = to rob a passer-by
- = to fly

volet *noun, masculine*
  un volet (*on a window*) = a shutter

voleur/voleuse *noun,*
masculine|feminine
  un voleur/une voleuse = a thief

volontaire
1 *adjective*
  = deliberate
2 *noun, masculine|feminine*
  un volontaire/une volontaire = a volunteer

volonté *noun, feminine*
  la volonté = will
  = will-power

volontiers *adverb*
  = gladly, willingly
  = with pleasure

vomir *verb* 3
- = to vomit, to bring up
- = to be sick, to throw up

vont ▶ **aller 1** 9

vos ▶ **votre**

voter *verb* 1
  = to vote

votre *determiner*
(*plural*) **vos**
  = your

vôtre *pronoun*
  le vôtre/la vôtre/les vôtres = yours
  à la vôtre! = cheers!

voudrais ▶ **vouloir** 48

vouloir *verb* 48
- (*expressing determination*) = to want
  je veux partir = I want to leave
  il ne voulait pas que tu viennes = he didn't want you to come
- (*expressing a wish, a polite request*)
  que veux-tu boire?, que voulez-vous boire? = what would you like to drink?
  je voudrais des poires = I'd like pears
  comme tu veux = as you wish
  veuillez vous asseoir = please sit down
- **vouloir dire** = to mean
  qu'est-ce que ça veut dire? = what does it mean?

voulu/voulue
1 ▶ **vouloir** 48

2 *adjective*
- = required
- = deliberate, planned

vous *pronoun*
- = you
  vous avez gagné = you've won
  à cause de vous = because of you
  la voiture est à vous = the car is yours
- = yourself
  = yourselves
  soignez-vous = look after yourself
  = look after yourselves
  allez vous laver les mains = go and wash your hands
- = each other
  vous vous aimez? = do you love each other?

vous-même *pronoun*
(*plural*) **vous-mêmes**
  = yourself
  = yourselves

vouvoyer *verb* 23
  vouvoyer quelqu'un = to address someone using the "vous" form

voyage *noun, masculine*
  un voyage = a trip, a journey
  aimer les voyages = to love travel(l)ing
un voyage de noces = a honeymoon
un voyage organisé = a package tour

voyager *verb* 13
  = to travel

voyageur/voyageuse *noun,*
masculine|feminine
  un voyageur/une voyageuse = a passenger
  = a travel(l)er

voyant/voyante
1 *adjective*
  = loud
2 *noun, masculine|feminine*
  un voyant/une voyante = a clairvoyant
3 voyant *noun, masculine*
  un voyant lumineux = a warning light

voyelle *noun, feminine*
  une voyelle = a vowel

voyons ▶ **voir** 46

voyou *noun, masculine*
  un voyou = a lout
  = a rascal

vrai/vraie
1 *adjective*
  = true
  = real, genuine
2 vrai *noun, masculine*
  le vrai = the truth
  à vrai dire = to tell the truth
  pour de vrai = for real

vraiment *adverb*
  = really

vrombir verb ③
= to roar

VTT noun, masculine
un VTT = a mountain bike

vu/vue¹
1 ▶ **voir** ④⑥
2 adjective
• **être bien vu** = to be well thought of
  ce serait plutôt mal vu = it wouldn't go
  down well
• **bien vu!** = good point!
• **c'est tout vu** = my mind is made up
3 vu = in view of

vue² noun, feminine
• **la vue** = sight
  avoir une bonne vue = to have good
  eyesight
  je la connais de vue = I know her to see
  perdre un ami de vue = to lose touch with
  a friend
  à vue d'œil = visibly
• **une vue** = a view
  avoir vue sur le lac = to look out onto the
  lake

wagon noun, masculine
  un wagon = a wagon, a car
  = a carriage, a car

wagon-lit noun, masculine
(plural) **wagons-lits**
  un wagon-lit = a sleeper, a sleeping car

wagon-restaurant noun, masculine
(plural) **wagons-restaurants**
  un wagon-restaurant = a restaurant car, a
  dining car

WC noun, masculine plural
  les WC = the toilet, the bathroom

y pronoun
• = it
  j'y pense souvent = I often think about it
  il s'y attendait = he was expecting it
  tu n'y peux rien = you can't do anything
  about it
  elle n'y arrivera jamais = she'll never
  manage it
  je n'y comprends rien = I don't understand
  a thing

• = there
  j'y mange parfois = I sometimes eat there
  j'y vais = I'm going
• **il y a** = there is
  = there are
  il n'y en a plus = there's none left
  = there aren't any left

yaourt noun, masculine
  un yaourt = a yogurt

yeux ▶ **œil**

yoga noun, masculine
  le yoga = yoga

Z z

zapper* verb ①
= to flick through the TV channels

zèbre noun, masculine
  un zèbre = a zebra

zéro
1 number
  = zero
2 noun, masculine
  zéro (in school) = nought, zero
  (in a match) = nil, nothing
  il est zéro heure quinze = it's a quarter
  past midnight
  trois (buts) à zéro = three nil, three
  nothing
  avoir le moral à zéro* = to feel very down
  repartir à zéro = to start all over again

zeste noun, masculine
  un zeste de citron = the zest of a lemon

zigzag noun, masculine
  un zigzag = a zigzag
  une route en zigzag = a winding
  road

zodiaque noun, masculine
  le zodiaque = the zodiac

zone noun, feminine
  une zone = a zone, an area
  une zone industrielle = an industrial
  estate, an industrial park

zoo noun, masculine
  un zoo = a zoo

zoologique adjective
= zoological

zut* exclamation
= blast!
= oh dear!

---

* in informal situations

Dictionary know-how

This section contains a number of short exercises which will help you to use your dictionary more effectively. You will find answers to all of the exercises at the end of the section p. 182.

1 Identifying French nouns and adjectives

Here is an extract from a French advertisement for a gas oven. See if you can find fourteen different nouns and underline them, and six different adjectives and circle them (or make two lists). If you are not sure of some words, look them up in the French–English half of the dictionary and see if the term 'noun' or 'adjective' is used to describe them.

> ### GAZ DE FRANCE, LE CHOIX DE LA QUALITÉ
>
> Pourquoi les Français préfèrent-ils le gaz naturel?
>
> Si vous venez dîner chez moi, vous verrez un magnifique objet, écran plat, coins carrés, dont la beauté luisante saute aux yeux.
>
> Un poste de télévision? Non, non, ce n'est pas mon téléviseur, c'est mon nouveau four au gaz naturel.

The publishers would like to thank Gaz de France for permission to reproduce copyright material.

2 Checking the gender of French nouns

Here are some English nouns which appear in the English–French half of the dictionary. Find out what their French equivalents are and make two separate lists, masculine nouns and feminine nouns.

bag	hippopotamus	magic	saddle
cake shop	island	oyster	thunderstorm
doorbell	jumper	peach	waitress
felt-tip pen	library	raincoat	worm

3 Identifying French and English pronouns

Each of the following phrases appears in the French–English half of this dictionary in entries where a pronoun is the headword. In each one, underline the pronoun(s) and give the English equivalent(s).

ça ne fait rien

c'est un cadeau

ce sont des détails sans importance

il l'a invitée

elle ne me parle pas

donne-la-moi

je lui ai prêté ma robe

elles se sont fait mal

il vous l'a prêté

donne-nous l'adresse

4 Recognizing French verbs

Underline the verb in each sentence.

Pierre descend la rue sur son vélo.

Sophie ne connaît pas le nom du magasin.

Les sapeurs pompiers arriveront dans cinq minutes.

Chaque année nous passons nos vacances d'été en France.

Ma sœur a un bassin avec des poissons dans son jardin.

5 Identifying French adverbs

Here is a list of twelve French words. Eight of them are adverbs and four are not. Underline the ones which are not, or make a list, and say what they are. If you are not sure of some of them, look them up in the French–English half of the dictionary.

absolument	enseignement	seulement
certainement	facilement	stationnement
directement	heureusement	vêtement
énormément	médicament	vraiment

6 **Identifying subjects and objects**

We have left out the subjects and objects from this French newspaper report. Choose suitable words from the list below in order to complete it. When you have finished, list the subjects and objects separately.

L'OURS FÉLIX ATTAQUE

.... a dévoré ....

depuis son arrivée dans les Pyrénées. Hier, ... ,

transplanté des forêts de Slovénie, a entièrement dévoré

.... qui se trouvait près de Portet-d'Aspet en

Haute-Garonne. .... a aussitôt

compensé .... de la perte de sa bête.

.... est de 600F pour l'attaque, qui ne sont versés

qu'une seule fois, puis de 800F par mouton. Pourtant, ...

devraient se rassurer: .... sont toujours plus

prédateurs que les vieux. Avec le temps, ... perdra

.... pour la chasse.

---

l'animal	Le département	Félix
le berger	les jeunes ours	sa passion
les bergers	neuf moutons	Le 'tarif'
une brebis	L'ours Félix	

The publishers would like to thank *Libération* for permission to use copyright material.

---

7 **Word search**

Here is a grid in which are hidden eleven French words: 3 masculine nouns, 3 feminine nouns, 2 adjectives, 2 verbs and 1 pronoun. They may appear horizontally or vertically, and in either direction. When you have found them, circle them. If you are not sure of any of them, look them up in the French–English section of the dictionary.

B	G	R	A	N	D	K	Y	S	T		**abandonner**
H	O	E	P	M	Q	C	E	L	A		**baguette**
S	T	N	D	N	O	R	U	I	V		**cela**
Z	E	N	X	A	K	E	B	F	C		**dent**
D	F	O	G	H	J	S	K	L	P		**excuser**
M	R	D	E	N	T	U	A	P	Q		**fils**
M	O	N	D	E	P	C	O	A	D		**grand**
P	G	A	W	C	U	X	V	R	N		**monde**
C	U	B	A	G	U	E	T	T	E		**nez**
R	H	A	N	F	Q	E	M	T	K		**part**
											rond

8 Accents are important!

Here is part of a letter typed by somebody who does not know how to find the accents on a word processor. Use your dictionary as necessary to help you put them in:

> Ma chere Louise,
>
> Merci pour ta lettre que j'ai reçue hier. Ce matin, comme
> d'habitude, je suis allee faire mes courses au marche ou j'ai
> rencontre Madame Bonnard, que tu connais tres bien, je crois. Elle
> m'a dit que sa fille ainee, Sandrine, a fini ses etudes et qu'elle part
> en Grece faire un stage de six mois dans un hotel. Ça devrait etre
> amusant, non? Qu'est-ce que tu comptes faire toi-meme cet ete? Est-
> ce que tu restes en France ou esperes-tu toujours visiter la Norvege?
> Moi, je vais passer deux semaines dans la maison de campagne de
> mon frere a Gaillac...

9 Using page headings

In order to help you find what you are looking for quickly, every page of the main section of the dictionary has a word at the top which identifies the first entry on that page. In this exercise the left-hand column contains a list of entries and the right-hand column a selection of page headings. Choose the page where you would expect to find the entry you are looking for.

Entry	Page headings
encourager	énerver | enseigne en | énervé
historique	hâte | histoire historique | hôtesse
liquide	librairie | loge logé | luge
mener	mélanger | mesure mesurer | million
renseigner	reine | rendre renne | requin
sérieux	séjour | serré serrer | siège
vieil	version | vietnamien vieux | vitesse

10 Masculine or feminine?

Some French nouns can be both masculine and feminine, and change their
meaning accordingly. Use your dictionary to find the following nouns and list them
with their different meanings in two columns, masculine and feminine, e.g.

un livre = ...   *une* livre = ...

livre
manche
mode
moule
poêle
tour
vase
voile

11 Which preposition, à or de?

Many verbs in French take a preposition, either *à* or *de*, before an infinitive e.g. *il m'a
demandé de venir demain*; *elle a réussi à ouvrir la porte*. In the following extract, all of
the prepositions have been left out. Use your dictionary to check what they should
be.

> Jean-Pierre a longtemps refusé . . . accepter la proposition de son ami,
> Michel, mais finalement il a décidé . . . dire oui. Michel avait envie . . . faire
> une randonnée de plusieurs semaines à vélo à travers l'Europe et avait tout
> fait pour convaincre son ami . . . venir avec lui. A vrai dire, Jean-Pierre
> préférait passer son temps . . . se faire bronzer sur la plage, mais il essayait
> toujours . . . faire plaisir à son copain et c'est pour cette raison que Michel
> est parvenu . . . le persuader. Bien entendu, c'est Michel qui s'est chargé
> . . . faire tous les préparatifs du voyage, alors que Jean-Pierre a commencé
> . . . tracer l'itinéraire sur la carte.

12 **Find the verb**

Some words in English can be both nouns and verbs e.g. race. In this exercise, you have to find the following English words in the English–French half of the dictionary and then give the French for the verb only.

aim	**iron**	**question**
block	**joke**	**sail**
camp	**kiss**	**train**
dance	**milk**	**welcome**
finish	**paint**	**yell**

13 **Choosing the right word**

Very often you cannot use a word exactly as it is given in the dictionary. In the case of adjectives with an irregular feminine form, for example, you have to make sure that you select the form which is appropriate to the noun you are using. Use your dictionary to find the correct form of the adjective to match the nouns in the following sentences.

Elle a de .... yeux et de .... dents. (*beautiful*)

Notre .... maison était très .... (*former*) (*old*)

C'est une très .... idée. (*good*)

La .... chose à faire est de trouver l'entrée ....
(*first*) (*secret*)

Elles sont si .... (*happy*)

La neige est .... (*white*)

Il a une .... voiture. (*new*)

Mon père est ...., mais ma mère est ....
(*Italian*) (*Norwegian*)

14 **Which part of speech?**

Use your dictionary to help you arrange these words in separate lists according to their parts of speech (masculine noun, feminine noun, adjective etc). Some words may belong to more than one category and will therefore appear in more than one list.

chasse	inscrire	pâle
dessous	juste	que
en	mouche	relire
facilement	notre	toi-même
gendre	ouest	vers

15 **Translating phrasal verbs**

Use your dictionary to find the correct translation for the following English sentences containing phrasal verbs.

The button's **come off**.

The dustmen have **taken** the rubbish **away**.

She is **bringing up** her children on her own.

They've **given up** smoking.

I'm going to **take** my shoes **off**.

16 **Find the plural**

Use your dictionary as necessary to find the plural of the following nouns (be careful, some of them are exceptions to the general guidelines):

un bijou, des ....

un cas, des ....

un cheval, deux ....

un cheveu, mes ....

une croix, deux ....

un manteau, deux ....

un pneu, quatre ....

du travail, des ....

un trou, deux ....

un vieux, des ....

17 **Faux amis**

Some French words look the same as, or similar to English words, but in fact have a different meaning. These are known as *faux amis* or false friends. Use your dictionary to find the meanings of the following French words:

actuellement	éventuellement
un bonnet	gentil
un car	le matériel
une cave	le pétrole
une course	un pin
décevoir	sale
délivrer	sensible
un engin	

18 **False friends**

Now use your dictionary to find a French meaning for each of these English 'lookalikes'.

actually	eventually
a bonnet	gentle
a car	material
a cave	petrol
a course	a pin
to deceive	a sale
to deliver	sensible
an engine	

19 Male or female?

Some French masculine nouns also have a feminine form. This is particularly true of words denoting an occupation—*un commerçant, une commerçante*. Some simply add -e to the masculine form but many do not. Use your dictionary to find the feminine form of the following nouns:

un astronaute	un piéton
un conseiller	un religieux
un enquêteur	un scout
un jongleur	un skieur
un musicien	un téléspectateur

20 Which meaning?

Some words have more than one meaning and it's important to check that you have chosen the right one. In this dictionary different meanings of a word are marked by a bullet point (•). We have given you one meaning of the French words below. Use your dictionary to find another one.

une baie	• a bay	• ....
blanc	• white	• ....
un centimètre	• a centimetre	• ....
enlever	• to remove	• ....
un gorille	• a gorilla	• ....
le jour	• the day	• ....
mauvais	• bad	• ....
noir	• black	• ....
un pépin	• a pip	• ....
une radio	• a radio	• ....
un tailleur	• a tailor	• ....
voler	• to steal	• ....

21 **Mots croisés**

Across

1 avoid (*verb*) (6)
4 washing (*noun*) (7)
6 stadium (*noun*) (5)
7 him (*pronoun*) (2)
8 studies (*plural noun*) (6)

Down

1 church (*noun*) (6)
2 moment (*noun*) (7)
3 thorn (*noun*) (5)
5 they (*pronoun*) (5)
7 the (*determiner*) (2)

22 **Odd one out**

Hidden in this list of nouns is a verb. See if you can find it, then use your dictionary to check whether you are right.

abattoir	givre
bagarre	injure
colorier	lecture
enfer	ordre
foudre	sentier

23 **Filling in the gaps**

Here is a dialogue between a market stall holder and someone shopping for fruit and vegetables. Use your dictionary to help you fill in the names of the things she buys.

CLIENTE: Bonjour, monsieur.

MARCHAND: Bonjour, madame. Que voulez-vous aujourd'hui?

CLIENTE: Eh bien, nous avons des invités ce soir et j'ai besoin de plusieurs choses. Pour commencer je voudrais un kilo de belles (*tomatoes*), s'il vous plaît, et deux bottes de (*radishes*). C'est tellement bon, les (*radishes*) au beurre.

MARCHAND: Très bien, et avec ça?

CLIENTE: J'ai besoin d'une (*lettuce*), une grosse.

MARCHAND: Voilà. Il y a autre chose?

CLIENTE: Oui, oui. Je voudrais, deux kilos de (*potatoes*), une livre d'(*onions*), une livre de (*carrots*), un (*cauliflower*) et un (*cucumber*).

MARCHAND: Et avec ça?

CLIENTE: Les (*peaches*) sont bonnes aujourd'hui?

MARCHAND: Oui, elles sont très bonnes.

CLIENTE: Donnez-m'en un kilo et puis avec ça une livre de (*plums*) et une barquette de (*raspberries*).

MARCHAND: Bien, madame. Ce sera tout?

CLIENTE: Oui, merci, c'est tout pour aujourd'hui.

---

24 **French reflexive verbs**

Use your dictionary to find the French equivalents of the following English sentences:

(a) I'm going to get changed.

(b) We argue about money.

(c) He easily gets bored.

(d) She always parks near the office.

(e) Sometimes I get impatient.

(f) What's happening?

(g) I always wake up at 7 o'clock.

(h) The war's coming to an end.

(i) Stamps are sold in the cafés.

(j) She's great fun.

Answers

1

Nouns: gaz, France, choix, qualité, Français, objet, écran, coins, beauté, yeux, poste, télévision, téléviseur, four.

Adjectives: naturel, magnifique, plat, carrés, luisante, nouveau.

2

Masculine nouns: sac, feutre, hippopotame, pull, imperméable, orage, ver.

Feminine nouns: pâtisserie, sonnette, île, bibliothèque, magie, huître, pêche, selle, serveuse.

3

ça ne fait rien (*it doesn't matter*)

c'est un cadeau (*it's a present*)

ce sont des détails sans importance (*these are unimportant details*)

il l'a invitée (*he invited her*)

elle ne me parle pas (*she won't speak to me*)

donne-la-moi (*give it to me*)

je lui ai prêté ma robe (*I lent her my dress*)

elles se sont fait mal (*they hurt themselves*)

il vous l'a prêté (*he lent it to you*)

donne-nous l'adresse (*give us the address*)

4

Pierre **descend** la rue sur son vélo.

Sophie ne **connaît** pas le nom du magasin.

Les sapeurs pompiers **arriveront** dans cinq minutes.

Chaque année nous **passons** nos vacances d'été en France.

Ma sœur **a** un bassin avec des poissons dans son jardin.

5

enseignement, médicament, stationnement, vêtement (*all masculine nouns*).

6

L'ours Félix a dévoré **neuf moutons** depuis son arrivée dans les Pyrénées. Hier, **l'animal** (*or* **Félix**), transplanté des forêts de Slovénie, a entièrement dévoré une brebis qui se trouvait près de Portet-d'Aspet en Haute-Garonne. **Le département** a aussitôt compensé **le berger** de la perte de sa bête. **Le 'tarif'** est de 600F pour l'attaque, qui ne sont versés qu'une seule fois, puis de 800F par mouton. Pourtant, **les bergers** devraient se rassurer: **les jeunes ours** sont toujours plus prédateurs que les vieux. Avec le temps, **Félix** (*or* **l'animal**) perdra **sa passion** pour la chasse.

Subjects: l'ours Félix, l'animal, le département, le 'tarif', les bergers, les jeunes ours, Félix.

Objects: neuf moutons, une brebis, le berger, sa passion.

7

B	G	R	A	N	D	K	Y	S	T
H	O	E	P	M	Q	C	E	L	A
S	T	N	D	N	O	R	U	I	V
Z	E	N	X	A	K	E	B	F	C
D	F	O	G	H	J	S	K	L	P
M	R	D	E	N	T	U	A	P	Q
M	O	N	D	E	P	C	O	A	D
P	G	A	W	C	U	X	V	R	N
C	U	B	A	G	U	E	T	T	E
R	H	A	N	F	Q	E	M	T	K

8

Ma chère Louise,

Merci pour ta lettre que j'ai reçue hier. Ce matin, comme d'habitude, je suis allée faire mes courses au marché où j'ai rencontré Madame Bonnard, que tu connais très bien, je crois. Elle m'a dit que sa fille aînée, Sandrine, a fini ses études et qu'elle part en Grèce faire un stage de six mois dans un hôtel. Ça devrait être amusant, non? Qu'est-ce que tu comptes faire toi-même cet été? Est-ce que tu restes en France ou espères-tu toujours visiter la Norvège? Moi, je vais passer deux semaines dans la maison de campagne de mon frère à Gaillac . . .

9

encourager   **en** | énerver

horreur   **historique** | hôtesse

liquide   **librairie** | loge

mener   **mélanger** | mesure

renseigner   **renne** | requin

sérieux   **séjour** | serré

vieil   **version** | vietnamien

10

un livre = *a book*
une livre = *a pound*

un manche = *a handle*
une manche = *a sleeve*

un mode (de vie) = *a (life)style*
une mode = *a fashion*

un moule = *a mould*
une moule = *a mussel*

un poêle = *a stove*
une poêle = *a frying pan*

un tour = *a trick, a turn*
une tour = *a tower*

un vase = *a vase*
la vase = *mud*

un voile = *a veil*
une voile = *a sail*

11

Jean-Pierre a longtemps refusé d'accepter la proposition de son ami, Michel, mais finalement il a décidé de dire oui. Michel avait envie de faire une randonnée de plusieurs semaines à vélo à travers l'Europe et avait tout fait pour convaincre son ami de venir avec lui. A vrai dire, Jean-Pierre préférait passer son temps à se bronzer sur la plage, mais il essayait toujours de faire plaisir à son copain et c'est pour cette raison que Michel est parvenu à le persuader. Bien entendu, c'est Michel qui s'est chargé de faire tous les préparatifs du voyage, alors que Jean-Pierre a commencé à tracer l'itinéraire sur la carte.

12

to aim *viser*; to block *bloquer*; to camp *camper*; to dance *danser*; to finish *finir*; to iron *repasser*; to joke *plaisanter*; to kiss *embrasser*; to milk *traire*; to paint *peindre*; to question *interroger*; to sail *voyager en bateau*; to train *former, entraîner*; to welcome *accueillir*; to yell *crier*.

13

Elle a de **beaux** yeux et de **belles** dents.

Notre **ancienne** maison était très **vieille**.

C'est une très **bonne** idée.

La **première** chose à faire est de trouver l'entrée **secrète**.

Elles sont si **heureuses**.

La neige est **blanche**.

Il a une **nouvelle** voiture.

Mon père est **italien**, mais ma mère est **norvégienne**.

14

Masculine noun: dessous, gendre, ouest, vers.

Feminine noun: chasse, mouche.

Pronoun: en, que, toi-même.

Adjective: juste, ouest, pâle.

Preposition: en, vers.

Verb: inscrire, relire.

Adverb: dessous, facilement, juste, que.

Determiner: notre.

Conjunction: que.

15

Le bouton s'est détaché.
Les éboueurs ont enlevé les déchets.
Elle élève ses enfants toute seule.
Ils ont cessé de fumer.
Je vais enlever mes chaussures.

16

bijoux, cas, chevaux, cheveux, croix, manteaux, pneus, travaux, trous, vieux

17

actuellement currently, at the moment
un bonnet a cap, a hat
un car a coach, bus
une cave a cellar
une course a race, an errand
décevoir to disappoint
délivrer to free, to issue
un engin a device, a vehicle
éventuellement possibly, if necessary
gentil kind, nice
le matériel the equipment
le pétrole oil, petroleum
un pin a pine
sale dirty
sensible sensitive

18

actually *en fait, vraiment, exactement*
a bonnet *un capot*
a cap *une casquette, un capuchon, une capsule*
a car *une voiture*
a cave *une grotte*
a course *un cours, un plat*
to deceive *tromper*
to deliver *livrer*
an engine *un moteur, une locomotive*
eventually *finalement*
gentle *doux*
material *la documentation* (a material *une matière, une substance, un tissu, une étoffe*)
petrol *l'essence*
a pin *une épingle*
a sale *une solde*
sensible *raisonnable, judicieux, pratique*

19

une astronaute
une conseillère
une enquêtrice
une jongleuse
une musicienne
une piétonne
une religieuse
une scoute
une skieuse
une téléspectatrice

20

une baie	• a bay	• a berry
blanc	• white	• blank
un centimètre	• a centimetre	• a tape measure
enlever	• to remove	• to kidnap
un gorille	• a gorilla	• a bodyguard
le jour	• the day	• daylight
mauvais	• bad	• wrong
noir	• black	• dark
un pépin	• a pip	• a slight problem
une radio	• a radio	• an X-ray
un tailleur	• a tailor	• a (woman's) suit
voler	• to steal	• to fly

21

22
The verb is *colorier*.

23
tomates, radis, salade (*or* laitue), pommes de terre, oignons, carottes, chou-fleur, concombre, pêches, prunes, framboises

24
(a) Je vais **me changer**.
(b) Nous **nous disputons** pour des questions d'argent.
(c) Il **s'ennuie** facilement.
(d) Elle **se gare** toujours près du bureau.
(e) Parfois je **m'impatiente**.
(f) Qu'est-ce qui **se passe**?
(g) Je **me réveille** toujours à sept heures.
(h) La guerre **se termine**.
(i) Les timbres **se vendent** dans les cafés.
(j) On **s'amuse** bien avec elle.

a, **an** *determiner*
  a, an = un/une
  a dog = un chien
  an exhibition = une exposition
  my mother's a doctor = ma mère est
    médecin

able *adjective*
* (*having the possibility*)
  to be able to [walk | travel | sleep ...]
    = pouvoir [marcher | voyager | dormir ...]
* (*having the skill or knowledge*)
  to be able to [drive | read | type ...] = savoir
    [conduire | lire | taper à la machine ...]

aboard *adverb*
  to go aboard = monter à bord

about
> ! Often *about occurs in combinations with
> verbs, for example:* bring about, run about
> *etc. To find the correct translations for this
> type of verb, look up the separate
> dictionary entries at* bring, run *etc.*

1 *preposition*
  it's a book about France = c'est un livre
    sur la France
  I need some information about the town
    = j'ai besoin de renseignements sur la
    ville
2 *adverb*
  = environ
  I have about 200 francs left = il me reste
    environ 200 francs
  Oxford is about 40 km from here = Oxford
    est à environ 40 km d'ici
  we arrived at about midnight = nous
    sommes arrivés vers minuit
3 to be about to = être sur le point de
  to be about to [leave | cry | fall asleep ...]
    = être sur le point de [partir | pleurer |
    s'endormir ...]

above
1 *preposition*
  = au-dessus de
  their apartment is above the shop = leur
    appartement se trouve au-dessus de la
    boutique
  there is a shelf above it = il y a une
    étagère au-dessus
2 above all = surtout

abroad *adverb*
  = à l'étranger
  to go abroad = aller à l'étranger

absent *adjective*
  = absent/absente

accent *noun*
  an accent = un accent

accept *verb*
  = accepter

accident *noun*
* (*causing injury or damage*)
  an accident = un accident
  a car accident = un accident de voiture
* I heard about it by accident = je l'ai appris
  par hasard

accommodation *noun*
  to look for accommodation = chercher un
    logement

accompany *verb*
  = accompagner

account *noun*
* (*in a bank or post office*)
  an account = un compte
  there's money in my account = il y a de
    l'argent sur mon compte
* to take travelling expenses into account
  = tenir compte des frais de voyage

accountant *noun* ▶ 315 |
  an accountant = un comptable/une
    comptable

accuse *verb*
  to accuse someone of cheating = accuser
    quelqu'un de tricher

across *preposition*
* to go across the street = traverser la rue
  to run across the street = traverser la rue
    en courant
  to swim across the Channel = traverser la
    Manche à la nage
  a journey across the desert = un voyage à
    travers le désert
* (*on the other side of*) = de l'autre côté de
  he lives across the street = il habite de
    l'autre côté de la rue

act *verb*
* (*to do something*) = agir
* (*to play a role*) = jouer

activity *noun*
  an activity = une activité
  sports activities = les activités sportives

actor *noun* ▶ 315 |
  an actor = un acteur

actress *noun* ▶ 315 |
  an actress = une actrice

actually *adverb*
> ! Note that *actually is not translated by*
> actuellement.

  actually, she's a very good athlete = en
    fait, c'est une très bonne athlète
  what actually happened? = qu'est-ce qui
    s'est passé exactement?

adapt verb
= s'adapter (**!** + être)

add verb
* (to put in) = ajouter
* (in arithmetic) = additionner

address noun
an address = une adresse

admire verb
= admirer

admit verb
* (to recognize as being true) = reconnaître
* (to own up) = avouer
  did she admit that she'd stolen the
  money? = est-ce qu'elle a avoué avoir
  volé l'argent?
* to be admitted to (the) hospital = être
  hospitalisé/hospitalisée

adolescent noun
an adolescent = un adolescent/une
adolescente

adopt verb
= adopter

adult noun
an adult = un adulte/une adulte

advantage noun
* (a positive point)
  an advantage = un avantage
* to take advantage of a situation = profiter
  d'une situation

adventure noun
an adventure = une aventure

advertisement noun
* (on TV, in the cinema)
  an advertisement = une publicité
* (in a newspaper)
  an advertisement = une (petite) annonce
  to answer job advertisements = répondre
  aux offres d'emploi

advertising noun
advertising = la publicité

advice noun
a piece of advice = un conseil
advice = des conseils

advise verb
to advise someone to rest = conseiller à
quelqu'un de se reposer
I've been advised not to go there = on m'a
déconseillé d'y aller

aerial noun
an aerial = une antenne

aerobics noun ▶ 248 |
aerobics = l'aérobic (masculine)

affect verb
the farmers have been affected by the
drought = les fermiers ont été touchés
par la sécheresse
the war is bound to affect tourism = la
guerre va sûrement avoir des
conséquences pour le tourisme

afford verb
to be able to afford a car = avoir les
moyens d'acheter une voiture

afraid adjective
to be afraid = avoir peur
to be afraid of spiders = avoir peur des
araignées
to be afraid to go out = avoir peur de
sortir

Africa noun ▶ 218 |
Africa = l'Afrique (feminine)

African ▶ 275 |
1 adjective
= africain/africaine
2 noun
the Africans = les Africains (masculine)

after
1 preposition
= après
we'll leave after breakfast = nous
partirons après le petit déjeuner
the day after tomorrow = après-demain
2 conjunction
after we had eaten, we went for a walk
= après avoir mangé, nous sommes allés
nous promener
they went in after the film had started = ils
sont entrés après le début du film
3 after all = après tout

afternoon noun ▶ 211 |, ▶ 356 |
an afternoon = un après-midi, une après-
midi

afterwards, afterward (US English)
adverb
* (after) = après
* (later) = plus tard

again adverb
= encore
are you going camping again this year?
= est-ce que vous allez encore camper
cette année?

! Note that there will very often be a
specific French verb to translate the idea
of doing something again—to start again
= recommencer, to do the work again
= refaire le travail, to see someone again
= revoir quelqu'un.

against preposition
= contre

age noun ▶ 187 |
age = l'âge (masculine)
he's my age, he's the same age as me = il
a mon âge

aged adjective
= âgé de/âgée de
a boy aged 13 = un garçon âgé de 13 ans

ago adverb
two weeks ago = il y a deux semaines
long ago = il y a longtemps

Age

Note that, where English says **to be X years old**, French says **avoir X ans** (*to have X years*).

How old?

*how old **are you**?*	= quel âge **as-tu**?
*what age **is she**?*	= quel âge **a-t-elle**?

The word **ans** (*years*) is never dropped:

he is forty-one (years old)	= il a quarante et un **ans**
the house is a hundred years old	= la maison a cent **ans**
a man of fifty	= un homme de cinquante **ans**

Note the use of **de** after **âgé**:

a woman aged thirty	= une femme âgée **de** trente ans

Comparing ages

*I'm older **than** you*	= je suis plus âgé **que** toi
*she's younger **than** him*	= elle est plus jeune **que** lui
*Anne's two years **younger***	= Anne a deux ans **de moins**
*Tom's five years **older than** Jo*	= Tom a cinq ans **de plus que** Jo

Approximate ages

*he is **about** fifty*	= il a **environ** cinquante ans
*she's **just over** sixty*	= elle **vient** d'avoir soixante ans
*games for **the under** twelves*	= jeux pour **les moins de** douze ans
*only for **the over** eighteens*	= seulement pour **les plus de** dix-huit ans

---

agree *verb*
- (*to have the same opinion*) = être d'accord
  I don't agree with you = je ne suis pas
  d'accord avec toi
- (*to be ready*)
  to agree to come a week later = accepter
  de venir une semaine plus tard
- (*to reach a decision*) = se mettre d'accord
  (**!** + *être*)

agriculture *noun*
  agriculture = l'agriculture (*feminine*)

ahead *adverb*
  to go on ahead = partir en avant

Aids *noun* ▶ **266** |
  Aids = le sida

aim
1 *noun*
  an aim = un but
2 *verb*
- (*to be directed at*)
  to be aimed at young people = viser les
  jeunes
- (*when using a weapon*)
  to aim a rifle at someone = braquer un
  fusil sur quelqu'un

air *noun*
  air = l'air (*masculine*)
  to throw a ball up into the air = lancer un
  ballon en l'air
  to let the air out of a tyre = dégonfler un
  pneu

air force *noun*
  the air force = l'armée de l'air
  ! *Note that* armée *is feminine.*

air hostess *noun* ▶ **315** | (*British English*)
  an air hostess = une hôtesse de l'air

airmail *noun*
  to send a letter by airmail = envoyer une
  lettre par avion

airport *noun*
  an airport = un aéroport

alarm clock *noun*
  an alarm clock = un réveil

alcohol *noun*
  alcohol = l'alcool (*masculine*)

alive *adjective*
  = vivant/vivante

all
1 *determiner*
  = tout/toute (+ *singular*)
  = tous/toutes (+ *plural*)
  I spent all week working = j'ai passé toute
  la semaine à travailler
  all the men have left = tous les hommes
  sont partis
2 *pronoun*
  = tout
  that's all = c'est tout
  after all we've done = après tout ce que
  nous avons fait

3 *adverb*
to be all alone = être tout seul/toute seule
all along the street = tout le long de la rue

allow *verb*
to allow someone to [work | play | leave ...]
= permettre à quelqu'un de [travailler | jouer | partir ...]
they don't allow me to smoke at home
= on ne me permet pas de fumer à la maison
smoking is not allowed = il est interdit de fumer

all right *adjective*
• (*when giving your opinion*) = pas mal✴
the film was all right = le film n'était pas mal✴
• (*when talking about health*)
are you all right? = ça va?
• (*when asking someone's opinion*)
is it all right if I come later? = est-ce que ça va si je viens plus tard?
come at about nine, all right? = viens vers neuf heures, d'accord?
• (*when agreeing*) = d'accord

almond *noun*
an almond = une amande

almost *adverb*
= presque
we're almost there = nous sommes presque arrivés
I almost forgot = j'ai failli oublier

alone
1 *adjective*
= seul/seule
to be all alone = être tout seul/toute seule
leave me alone! = laisse-moi tranquille!
2 *adverb*
[to work | to live | to travel ...] **alone**
= [travailler | vivre | voyager ...] seul/seule

along *preposition*
= le long de
there are seats all along the canal = il y a des bancs tout le long du canal

aloud *adverb*
to read aloud = lire à haute voix

already *adverb*
= déjà
it's ten o'clock already = il est déjà dix heures
have you finished already? = tu as déjà fini?

also *adverb*
= aussi

although *conjunction*
= bien que
although she's strict, she's fair = bien qu'elle soit sévère, elle est juste

✴ in informal situations

! *Note that the subjunctive is used after* bien que.

always *adverb*
= toujours
I always go to France in (the) summer = je vais toujours en France en été

amazed *adjective*
= stupéfait/stupéfaite

amazing *adjective*
= extraordinaire

ambition *noun*
an ambition = une ambition

ambitious *adjective*
= ambitieux/ambitieuse

ambulance *noun*
an ambulance = une ambulance

America *noun* ▶ 218 |
America = l'Amérique (*feminine*)

American ▶ 275 |
1 *adjective*
= américain/américaine
2 *noun*
the Americans = les Américains (*masculine*)

among, amongst *preposition*
• (*in the middle of*) = parmi
the ruins are hidden among the trees = les ruines sont cachées parmi les arbres
• (*in a particular group*) = chez
unemployment among young people = le chômage chez les jeunes

amount *noun*
an amount = une quantité

amusement arcade *noun*
an amusement arcade = une salle de jeux électroniques

amusement park *noun*
an amusement park = un parc d'attractions

an ▶ a

ancestor *noun*
an ancestor = un ancêtre/une ancêtre

and *conjunction*
• and = et
a red and white sweater = un pull rouge et blanc
she stood up and went out = elle s'est levée et elle est sortie
to go faster and faster = aller de plus en plus vite
• (*in numbers, and is not translated*)
three hundred and sixty-five = trois cent soixante-cinq

anger *noun*
anger = la colère

angry *adjective*
to be angry = être en colère
to be angry with someone = être en colère
  contre quelqu'un

animal *noun*
an animal = un animal
farm animals = les animaux de la ferme

ankle *noun* ▶ 201 |
the ankle = la cheville

announcement *noun*
an announcement = une annonce

annoy *verb*
= agacer

annoyed *adjective*
to be annoyed with someone = être
  fâché/fâchée contre quelqu'un

another
1 *determiner*
• another = un autre/une autre, encore
  un/une
  another cup of coffee? = encore un café?
  I'll buy another ticket for Alison = je vais
  acheter un autre billet pour Alison
• (*different*) = un autre/une autre
  there's another way of doing it = il y a une
  autre façon de le faire
  she's got another boyfriend now = elle a
  un nouveau copain maintenant
2 *pronoun*
  there's some pears left—would you like
  another? = il reste des poires—est-ce que
  tu en veux encore une?

  ! *Note that it is necessary to use* en,
  which might be translated as 'of it' *or* 'of
  them', *with pronouns like* another. *See
  also* any, a few, a lot *etc for this use of* en.

answer
1 *noun*
an answer = une réponse
did you get an answer? = est-ce que tu as
  eu une réponse?
there's no answer (*at the door*) = il n'y a
  personne
(*on the phone*) = ça ne répond pas
2 *verb*
= répondre
to answer a question = répondre à une
  question
to answer the phone = répondre au
  téléphone
answer back = répondre

answering machine *noun*
an answering machine = un répondeur
  (téléphonique)

ant *noun*
an ant = une fourmi

antique *noun*
an antique = un objet ancien

antique shop *noun*
an antique shop = un magasin
  d'antiquités

anxious *adjective*
= inquiet/inquiète, anxieux/anxieuse
then I started to get anxious = j'ai
  commencé à m'inquiéter à ce moment-
  là

any
1 *determiner*
• (*in questions*) = du/de la (**!** de l' + *vowel or
  mute h*)
  = des (+ *plural*)
  is there any tea? = est-ce qu'il y a du thé?
  is there any tart left? = est-ce qu'il reste de
  la tarte?
  have you got any money? = est-ce que
  vous avez de l'argent?
• (*with the negative*) = de (**!** d' + *vowel or
  mute h*)
  we don't have any bread = nous n'avons
  pas de pain
  I didn't have any friends = je n'avais pas
  d'amis
• (*whatever*)
  take any cup you like = prenez n'importe
  quelle tasse
2 *pronoun*
= en
do you have any? = est-ce que vous en
  avez?
he doesn't have any = il n'en a pas

  ! *Note that it is necessary to use* en,
  which might be translated as 'of it' *or* 'of
  them', *with pronouns like* any. *See also*
  another, a few, a lot *etc for this use of* en.

anyone *pronoun* (*also* **anybody**)
• (*in questions*) = quelqu'un
  do you know anyone who could help us?
  = est-ce que tu connais quelqu'un qui
  pourrait nous aider?
• (*with the negative*) = personne
  there isn't anyone in the house = il n'y a
  personne dans la maison
• (*everyone*)
  anyone could do it = n'importe qui
  pourrait le faire

anything *pronoun*
• (*in questions*) = quelque chose
  can I do anything to help? = est-ce que je
  peux faire quelque chose pour vous
  aider?
• (*with the negative*) = rien
  she didn't say anything = elle n'a rien dit
  there isn't anything to do here = il n'y a
  rien à faire ici
• (*everything*) = tout
  I like anything to do with sports = j'aime
  tout ce qui a rapport au sport

anyway *adverb*
= de toute façon
I didn't want to go there anyway = de
  toute façon je ne voulais pas y aller

anywhere *adverb*
- (*in questions*) = quelque part
  can you see a phone booth anywhere?
  = est-ce que tu vois une cabine
  téléphonique quelque part?
- (*with the negative*) = nulle part
  you can't go anywhere = on ne peut aller
  nulle part
- (*any place*)
  we can meet anywhere you like = nous
  pouvons nous retrouver où tu veux

apart
1 *adjective*
  they don't like being apart = ils n'aiment
  pas être séparés
2 apart from = à part

apartment *noun*
  an apartment = un appartement

apartment block *noun*
  an apartment block = un immeuble

apologize *verb*
  = s'excuser (**!** + *être*)

apology *noun*
  an apology = des excuses (*feminine plural*)

appear *verb*
- (*to seem*)
  to appear happy = avoir l'air
  heureux/heureuse
- (*to come into view*) = apparaître (**!** + *être*)

appetite *noun*
  the appetite = l'appétit (*masculine*)
  to have a good appetite = avoir bon
  appétit

apple *noun*
  an apple = une pomme

apple juice *noun*
  apple juice = le jus de pomme

appliance *noun*
  an appliance = un appareil

application *noun*
  an application = une candidature

apply *verb*
  to apply for a job = poser sa candidature
  pour un emploi
  to apply for a passport = faire une
  demande de passeport

appointment *noun*
  an appointment = un rendez-vous
  to make an appointment = prendre
  rendez-vous

appreciate *verb*
  ! *Note that* **apprécier** *usually means to
  like.*

  I'd appreciate it if you could let me know
  = je vous serais reconnaissant de
  m'informer

approach *verb*
  = s'approcher de (**!** + *être*)

approve *verb*
  to approve of someone = apprécier
  quelqu'un

apricot *noun*
  an apricot = un abricot

April *noun* ▶ **222** |
  April = avril (*masculine*)

Aquarius *noun*
  Aquarius = Verseau (*masculine*)

architect *noun* ▶ **315** |
  an architect = un architecte/une
  architecte

area *noun*
  an area (*of a country*) = une région
  (*of a city*) = un quartier
  in the poorer areas of Paris = dans les
  quartiers plus défavorisés de Paris

area code *noun* (*US English*)
  an area code = un indicatif

argue *verb*
- (*to quarrel*) = se disputer (**!** + *être*)
  to argue about money = se disputer pour
  des questions d'argent
- (*to discuss a subject*) = discuter
  to argue about politics = discuter de
  politique

argument *noun*
  an argument = une dispute
  to have an argument with someone = se
  disputer avec quelqu'un

Aries *noun*
  Aries = Bélier (*masculine*)

arm *noun* ▶ **201** |
  the arm = le bras
  she's hurt her arm = elle s'est fait mal au
  bras

armchair *noun*
  an armchair = un fauteuil

armed *adjective*
  = armé/armée

arms *noun*
  arms = les armes (*feminine*)

army *noun*
  an army = une armée
  to join the army = s'engager (**!** + *être*)

around

  ! *Often* **around** *occurs in combinations
  with verbs, for example:* **run around, turn
  around** *etc. To find the correct
  translations for this type of verb, look up
  the separate dictionary entries at* **run, turn**
  etc.

1 *preposition*
= autour de
there are trees all around the garden = il y
a des arbres tout autour du jardin
**the people around me were speaking
French** = les gens autour de moi
parlaient français
to go around the world = faire le tour du
monde
2 *adverb*
= environ
it costs around £200 = ça coûte environ
200 livres sterling
we'll be there at around four o'clock
= nous serons là vers quatre heures

arrange *verb*
to arrange a break in Italy = organiser des
vacances en Italie
to arrange to have lunch together
= s'arranger pour déjeuner ensemble

arrest *verb*
= arrêter

arrive *verb*
= arriver (**!** + *être*)
we arrived at the station at noon = nous
sommes arrivés à la gare à midi

arrow *noun*
an arrow = une flèche

art *noun*
• art = l'art (*masculine*)
• (*as a school subject*)
art = le dessin

art gallery *noun*
an art gallery = un musée d'art

artificial *adjective*
= artificiel/artificielle

artist *noun* ▶ 315
an artist = un artiste/une artiste

arts and crafts *noun*
arts and crafts = les travaux manuels
! *Note that* **travaux** *is masculine plural.*

as
1 *conjunction*
• as = comme
as you know, we're leaving = comme vous
le savez, nous partons
• (*at the time when*)
**the phone rang as I was getting out of the
bath** = le téléphone a sonné au moment
où je sortais du bain
I used to live there as a child = j'habitais
là quand j'étais enfant
• (*British English*) (*because, since*) = comme
as you were out, I left a message
= comme tu étais sorti j'ai laissé un
message
• (*when used with* **the same**)
my coat is the same as yours = j'ai le
même manteau que toi

2 *preposition*
she's got a job as a teacher = elle a trouvé
un poste d'enseignante
he was dressed as a sailor = il était
habillé en marin
3 *adverb*
as [intelligent | rich | strong …] **as** = aussi
[intelligent | riche | fort …] que
go there as fast as you can = vas-y aussi
vite que possible
I have as much work as you = j'ai autant
de travail que toi
he plays the piano as well as his sister
= il joue du piano aussi bien que sa sœur
4 as usual = comme d'habitude

ashamed *adjective*
to be ashamed = avoir honte

ashes *noun*
ashes = les cendres (*feminine*)

ashtray *noun*
an ashtray = un cendrier

Asia *noun* ▶ 218
Asia = l'Asie (*feminine*)

Asian *adjective* ▶ 275
(*from China, Japan*) = asiatique

ask *verb*
• **to ask** = demander
he asked me my name = il m'a demandé
mon nom
to ask someone to [phone | take a message |
do the shopping …] = demander à
quelqu'un de [téléphoner | prendre un
message | faire les courses …]
I'll ask them if they want to come = je vais
leur demander s'ils veulent venir
to ask for money = demander de l'argent
to ask to speak to someone = demander à
parler à quelqu'un
to ask a question = poser une question
• (*to invite*) = inviter
to ask some friends to dinner = inviter des
amis à dîner
he asked her out = il l'a invitée à sortir
avec lui
• (*to look for information*) = se renseigner
(**!** + *être*)
did you ask about the tickets? = est-ce que
tu t'es renseigné pour les billets?

asleep *adjective*
to be asleep = dormir
to fall asleep = s'endormir (**!** + *être*)

assemble *verb*
= se rassembler (**!** + *être*)

assignment *noun*
a school assignment = un devoir

assistant *noun*
an assistant = un assistant/une assistante

at *preposition*

! There are many verbs which involve the use of *at*, *like* look at, laugh at, point at *etc. For translations, look up the entries at* look, laugh, point *etc.*

* (*when talking about a position or place*) = à
  we met at a concert = nous nous sommes rencontrés à un concert
  she's at an exhibition = elle est allée à une exposition
  he's not at his desk = il n'est pas à son bureau
  at the = au/à la (! à l' + *vowel or mute h*)
  = aux (+ *plural*)
  they're at the clinic = ils sont à la clinique
  I saw her at the races = je l'ai vue aux courses
  to be [at home | at school | at work …] = être [à la maison | à l'école | au travail …]
* (*at the house, shop, practice of*) = chez
  we'll be at Nathalie's = nous serons chez Nathalie
  he's got an appointment at the dentist's = il a rendez-vous chez le dentiste
* (*when talking about time*) = à
  the film starts at nine o'clock = le film commence à neuf heures
  I was here at dawn = j'étais ici à l'aube
* (*when talking about age*) = à
  she was able to read at four years of age = elle savait lire à l'âge de quatre ans

athlete *noun* ▶ 315 |
  an athlete = un athlète/une athlète

athletics *noun* ▶ 248 |
  athletics (*in Britain*) = l'athlétisme (*masculine singular*)
  (*in the US*) = les sports (*masculine*)

Atlantic *noun*
  the Atlantic = l'Atlantique (*masculine*)

atmosphere *noun*
* (*the air*)
  the atmosphere = l'atmosphère (*feminine*)
* (*a mood, a feeling*)
  an atmosphere = une ambiance

attach *verb*
  = attacher
  to be attached to the wall = être fixé/fixée au mur

attack *verb*
  to attack a town = attaquer une ville
  to attack someone in the street = agresser quelqu'un dans la rue

attempt
1 *verb*
  to attempt to break the record = tenter de battre le record
2 *noun*
  an attempt = une tentative

attend *verb*
  to attend the village school = fréquenter l'école du village
  to attend evening classes = suivre des cours du soir

attention *noun*
  attention = l'attention (*feminine*)
  to get someone's attention = attirer l'attention de quelqu'un
  to pay attention to the teacher = écouter le professeur

attic *noun*
  an attic = un grenier

attitude *noun*
  an attitude = une attitude
  he has a strange attitude toward(s) people = il a une attitude bizarre envers les gens

attract *verb*
  = attirer

attractive *adjective*
  to be attractive = être séduisant/séduisante

auburn *adjective* ▶ 213 |
  = auburn (! *never changes*)

audience *noun*
  an audience = un public

August *noun* ▶ 222 |
  August = août (*masculine*)

aunt *noun*
  an aunt = une tante

au pair *noun*
  an au pair = une jeune fille au pair

Australia *noun* ▶ 218 |
  Australia = l'Australie (*feminine*)

Australian ▶ 275 |
1 *adjective*
  = australien/australienne
2 *noun*
  the Australians = les Australiens (*masculine*)

Austria *noun* ▶ 218 |
  Austria = l'Autriche (*feminine*)

Austrian ▶ 275 |
1 *adjective*
  = autrichien/autrichienne
2 *noun*
  the Austrians = les Autrichiens (*masculine*)

author *noun* ▶ 315 |
  an author = un écrivain

automatic *adjective*
  = automatique

autumn *noun*
  autumn = l'automne (*masculine*)
  in (the) autumn = en automne

available *adjective*
* (*on sale*)
  tickets for the concert are still available = il reste encore des billets pour le concert

- (*free*) = disponible
  are you available? = est-ce que vous êtes
    disponible?

average *adjective*
= moyen/moyenne
the average teenager = l'adolescent
  moyen

avoid *verb*
- (*to prevent*) = éviter
  to avoid spending money = éviter de
    dépenser de l'argent
- (*to stay away from*) = éviter

awake *adjective*
  to be awake (*having slept*) = être
    réveillé/réveillée
  to stay awake = rester éveillé/éveillée
  to keep someone awake = empêcher
    quelqu'un de dormir

award *noun*
  an award = un prix
  she got the award for best actress = elle a
    reçu le prix de la meilleure actrice

aware *adjective*
  to be aware of the [problem | danger | risk ...]
    = être conscient/consciente du [problème |
    danger | risque ...]

away *adverb*
- (*absent*)
  to be away = être absent/absente
  she's away on business = elle est en
    voyage d'affaires
- (*when talking about distances*)
  to be far away = être loin
  London is 40 km away = Londres est à 40
    km d'ici

awful *adjective*
- (*no good*) = épouvantable
  I thought the film was awful = j'ai trouvé le
    film épouvantable
- (*causing shock*) = terrible
- **I feel awful** = je ne me sens pas bien du
    tout

awkward *adjective*
  (*describing a situation, a problem*)
    = délicat/délicate
  I feel awkward about telling him = ça me
    gêne de le lui dire

axe, **ax** (*US English*) *noun*
  an axe = une hache

Bb   B

baby[hg]*noun*
  a baby = un bébé

babysit *verb*
= faire du babysitting

back

> ! *Often* back *occurs in combinations with
> verbs, for example:* come back, get back,
> give back *etc. To find the correct
> translations for this type of verb, look up
> the separate dictionary entries at* come,
> get, give *etc.*

1 *noun*
- (*part of the body*) ▶ **201**
  the back = le dos
  I've hurt my back = je me suis fait mal au
    dos
- (*the rear*)
  at the back of the supermarket = derrière
    le supermarché
  to sit in the back of the car = s'asseoir à
    l'arrière de la voiture
2 *adverb*
- **to be back** = être de retour
  I'll be back in five minutes = je serai de
    retour dans cinq minutes
- (*before in time*)
  back in January = en janvier

back door *noun*
  the back door = la porte de derrière

background *noun*
- (*of a person*)
  a background = un milieu
- (*of a picture*)
  the background = l'arrière-plan
    (*masculine*)
  in the background = à l'arrière-plan

backpack *noun*
  a backpack = un sac à dos

back seat *noun*
  the back seat = le siège arrière

back to front *adverb*
= sens devant derrière
  to put a sweater on back to front = mettre
    un pull sens devant derrière

backwards, **backward** (*US English*)
adverb
= en arrière

bacon *noun*
  bacon = le bacon

bad *adjective*
- bad = mauvais/mauvaise (**!** *before the noun*)

  a bad film = un mauvais film

  a bad idea = une mauvaise idée

  I have some bad news = j'ai une mauvaise nouvelle

  to be bad [at maths | at tennis | at chess ...] = être mauvais/mauvaise [en maths | au tennis | aux échecs ...]

  it's a bad time to go on holiday = ce n'est pas le bon moment pour partir en vacances

  'was the film good?'—'not bad' = 'est-ce que le film était bien?'—'pas mal✲'

  smoking is bad for you = fumer est mauvais pour ta santé
- (*serious*) = grave

  a bad accident = un accident grave
- (*when talking about food*) = mauvais/mauvaise (**!** *before the noun*)
- (*not kind, not honest*) = méchant/méchante

  to feel bad = culpabiliser
- (*severe*)

  to have a bad cold = avoir un gros rhume

badger *noun*

  a badger = un blaireau

badly *adverb*
- (*not well*) = mal

  she slept badly = elle a mal dormi
- (*seriously*) = gravement

  he was badly injured = il a été gravement blessé

badminton *noun* ▶ 248 |

  badminton = le badminton

bad-tempered *adjective*

  to be bad-tempered = avoir mauvais caractère

bag *noun*

  a bag = un sac

baggage *noun*

  baggage = les bagages (*masculine plural*)

bake *verb*
- (*to prepare bread or cakes*) (*bread*) = faire du pain

  (*cakes*) = faire des gâteaux
- (*to be cooked in the oven*) = cuire (au four)

baker *noun* ▶ 315 |

  a baker = un boulanger/une boulangère

bakery *noun* ▶ 315 |

  a bakery = une boulangerie

balance *noun*

  balance = l'équilibre (*masculine*)

  to lose one's balance = perdre l'équilibre

balcony *noun*

  a balcony = un balcon

bald *adjective*

  = chauve

ball *noun*

  a ball (*in football, rugby or basketball*) = un ballon

  (*in tennis, golf or cricket*) = une balle

  (*in billiards*) = une bille

  to play ball = jouer au ballon

ballet *noun*

  ballet = le ballet

balloon *noun*

  a balloon = un ballon en baudruche

ban *verb*

  = interdire

banana *noun*

  a banana = une banane

band *noun*

  a band = un groupe

  a rock band = un groupe de rock

bandage *noun*

  a bandage = un bandage

bang

1 *noun*
- (*a loud noise*)

  a bang = une détonation
- (*US English*) (*a fringe*)

  bangs = une frange

2 *verb*
- (*to close with a bang*) = claquer
- (*to hurt*)

  to bang one's head on the wall = se cogner la tête contre le mur
- (*to hit*)

  to bang one's fist on the table = taper du poing sur la table

bank *noun*

  a bank = une banque

bank account *noun*

  a bank account = un compte bancaire

bank holiday *noun* (*British English*)

  a bank holiday = un jour férié

bank manager *noun* ▶ 315 |

  a bank manager = un directeur de banque

bar *noun*
- (*a place*)

  a bar = un bar

  to go to a bar = aller dans un bar
- (*a piece of metal*)

  a bar = une barre
- (*on a cage or window*)

  a bar = un barreau
- (*other uses*)

  a bar of soap = une savonnette

  a bar of chocolate = une tablette de chocolat

barbecue *noun*

  a barbecue = un barbecue

✲ in informal situations

barely *adverb*
= à peine
he was barely able to walk = il pouvait à peine marcher

bargain *noun*
a bargain = une affaire

bark *verb*
= aboyer

barn *noun*
a barn = une grange

barrel *noun*
a barrel = un tonneau

base *verb*
to be based in London = être basé/basée à Londres
to be based on a true story = être basé/basée sur une histoire vécue

baseball *noun* ▶ 248 |
baseball = le base-ball

basement *noun*
a basement = un sous-sol

basically *adverb*
= au fond

basin *noun*
a basin = une cuvette

basket *noun*
a basket = un panier

basketball *noun* ▶ 248 |
basketball = le basket

bat *noun*
* (*in cricket or baseball*)
  a bat = une batte
* (*an animal*)
  a bat = une chauve-souris

bath *noun*
* **to have a bath** = prendre un bain
  he's in the bath = il est dans son bain
* (*a bathtub*)
  a bath = une baignoire

bathroom *noun*
* **a bathroom** = une salle de bains
* (*US English*) (*the toilet*)
  to go to the bathroom = aller aux toilettes

battery *noun*
a battery (*for a torch*) = une pile
(*for a car*) = une batterie

battle *noun*
a battle = une bataille

bay *noun*
a bay = une baie

be *verb*
▶ 196 | *See the boxed note on* **be** *for more information and examples.*

* **to be** = être
  to be intelligent = être intelligent/intelligente
  he is tall = il est grand
  we are rich = nous sommes riches
  be polite! = sois poli!
  it's a girl = c'est une fille
  it's Monday = c'est lundi
  it's past midnight = il est minuit passé
  it's late = il est tard
  the house has been sold = la maison a été vendue
  he'll be famous = il sera célèbre
* (*when talking about jobs*) ▶ 315 |
  she is a lawyer = elle est avocat
  he is a good doctor = c'est un bon médecin
* (*when describing a physical or mental state*)
  to be [cold | hungry | afraid ...] = avoir [froid | faim | peur ...]
  my feet are cold = j'ai froid aux pieds
  I am 18 = j'ai 18 ans
* (*when describing the weather*)
  the weather is [fine | awful | cold ...] = il fait [beau | mauvais | froid ...]
  it's not too hot = il ne fait pas trop chaud
  it's raining = il pleut
* (*when talking about travelling*)
  I've never been to Spain = je ne suis jamais allé en Espagne
  have you ever been to Africa? = est-ce que tu es déjà allé en Afrique?
* (*when talking about health*)
  how are you? = comment allez-vous?, comment vas-tu?
  I'm very well = je vais très bien
  how is your mother? = comment va ta mère?
* (*in continuous tenses*)
  I'm coming = j'arrive
  it was snowing = il neigeait
  he is reading = il lit, il est en train de lire
* (*in questions and short answers*)
  it's a lovely house, isn't it? = c'est une belle maison, n'est-ce-pas?
  'he's not here'—'yes he is' = 'il n'est pas là'—'si'

beach *noun*
a beach = une plage

beak *noun*
a beak = un bec

beam *noun*
a beam = une poutre

bean *noun*
a bean = un haricot

bear
1 *noun*
a bear = un ours
2 *verb*
= supporter

beard *noun*
a beard = une barbe

be

As an ordinary verb

When **be** is used as a simple verb in *subject + verb* sentences, it is generally translated by **être**:

*I **am** tired*	= je **suis** fatigué
*Paul **is** a doctor*	= Paul **est** médecin

As an auxiliary verb in progressive tenses

In English, **be** can be used in combination with another verb to form a progressive tense which allows us to express *an idea of duration, of something happening over a period of time.*

The present
French uses the present tense to translate both forms of the English present tense, the simple and the progressive:

I work in London	= je travaille à Londres
I am working in London	= je travaille à Londres

To emphasize the idea of duration, **être en train de** + *infinitive* can be useful:

I'm working	= je suis **en train de** travailler
he's reading the paper	= il est **en train de** lire le journal

The future
By using the progressive form of the present tense, you can also refer to the future:

we're going to Paris next week	= nous allons à Paris la semaine prochaine

The past
To express the difference between *she watched TV* and *she was watching TV*, French uses the perfect and the imperfect tenses:

*she **watched** TV*	= elle a **regardé** la télévision
*she **was watching** TV*	= elle **regardait** la télévision

Again, to emphasize the idea of an activity happening over a period of time, the phrase **être en train de** + *infinitive* is useful:

*she **was watching** TV when I phoned her*	= elle **était en train de regarder** la télévision quand je lui ai téléphoné

As part of the passive

In French, as in English, the passive is formed in exactly the same way using **être**:

*the rabbit **was killed by** a fox*	= le lapin **a été tué** par un renard
*the window **has been fixed***	= la fenêtre **a été réparée**

However, in spoken French, the impersonal pronoun **on** is often used to translate the passive if there is a person clearly involved:

the window has been fixed	= **on** a réparé la fenêtre

In short questions

With questions like *aren't you?, wasn't she?*, the general French phrase **n'est-ce pas?** can be useful in specific cases:

*you're a doctor, **aren't you?***	= vous êtes médecin, **n'est-ce pas?**

With negative questions, **par hasard** can be useful:

*he's not there, **is he?***	= il n'est pas là **par hasard?**

In short answers

There is no French equivalent for the verb in short answers such as *no, he's not, yes, we were* etc.

'is he around?' — 'no, he's not'	= 'est-ce qu'il est là?' — 'non'
'are you coming?'— 'yes, I am'	= 'est-ce que tu viens?' — 'oui'

If answering 'yes' to contradict a negative statement, the most useful translation is **si**:

*'you're **not** coming, are you?' — '**yes, I am**'*	= 'tu **ne** viens pas?' — '**si**'

beat *verb*
- (*to hit hard*) = battre
- (*in cooking*) = battre
- (*to win against*) = battre
  Scotland beat England two nil = l'Écosse a
    battu l'Angleterre deux à zéro
beat up = battre

beautiful *adjective*
= beau/belle (**!** *before the noun*)

> **!** *Note that* bel *is used instead of* beau
> *before masculine nouns beginning with a*
> *vowel* (endroit) *or a mute h* (hôtel). *The*
> *plural of* beau *and* bel *is* beaux.

a beautiful garden = un beau jardin
a beautiful girl = une belle fille
a beautiful place = un bel endroit
they are beautiful cities = ce sont de belles
  villes

beauty *noun*
beauty = la beauté

because
1 *conjunction*
= parce que
he did it because it was necessary = il l'a
  fait parce que c'était nécessaire
2 because of = à cause de
we didn't go out because of the rain
  = nous ne sommes pas sortis à cause de
  la pluie

become *verb*
= devenir
to become an adult = devenir adulte

bed *noun*
a bed = un lit
to go to bed = se coucher (**!** + *être*)

bedroom *noun*
a bedroom = une chambre

bee *noun*
a bee = une abeille

beef *noun*
beef = le bœuf
roast beef = le rosbif

beer *noun*
- (*the product*)
  beer = la bière
- (*a glass of beer*)
  a beer = une bière

beet, **beetroot** (*British English*) *noun*
a beet(root) = une betterave

before
1 *preposition*
= avant
before the holidays = avant les vacances
the day before yesterday = avant-hier
the day before the exam = la veille de
  l'examen

2 *adjective*
= précédent/précédente, d'avant
the week before = la semaine précédente,
  la semaine d'avant
the day before = la veille
3 *adverb*
= avant
two months before = deux mois avant
have you been to Paris before? = est-ce
  que tu es déjà allé à Paris?
4 *conjunction*
I'd like to see him before I go = j'aimerais
  le voir avant de partir
I'd like to see him before he goes
  = j'aimerais le voir avant son départ

beg *verb*
= mendier

beggar *noun*
a beggar = un mendiant/une mendiante

begin *verb*
= commencer
to begin [working | laughing | raining ...]
  = commencer à [travailler | rire | pleuvoir ...]

beginner *noun*
a beginner = un débutant/une débutante

beginning *noun*
the beginning = le début
in the beginning = au début
at the beginning of May = début mai

behave *verb*
= se conduire (**!** + *être*)
he behaved badly = il s'est mal conduit
to be well behaved = être sage
behave yourself! = tiens-toi bien!

behaviour (*British English*), **behavior**
(*US English*) *noun*
behaviour = la conduite

behind *preposition*
= derrière
I looked behind me = j'ai regardé derrière
  moi

Belgian ▶ 275 |
1 *adjective*
= belge
2 *noun*
the Belgians = les Belges (*masculine*)

Belgium *noun* ▶ 218 |
Belgium = la Belgique

believe *verb*
= croire

bell *noun*
- (*in a church*)
  a bell = une cloche
- (*on a door or bicycle*)
  a bell = une sonnette

B

belong verb
• (to be the property of)
  to belong to someone = appartenir à
    quelqu'un
  that book belongs to me = ce livre
    m'appartient
• (to be a member of)
  to belong to a club = faire partie d'un club

belongings noun
  belongings = les affaires (feminine)

below preposition
  = au-dessous de
  the kitchen is below my bedroom = la
    cuisine se trouve au-dessous de ma
    chambre
  there's a cupboard below it = il y a un
    placard au-dessous

belt noun
  a belt = une ceinture

bench noun
  a bench = un banc

bend
1 verb
• (to lean, to move) = se pencher (**!** + être)
  to bend one's head = pencher la tête
  to bend one's knees = plier les genoux
• (to make crooked) = tordre
2 noun
  a bend = un tournant, un virage
bend down = se pencher (**!** + être)

beneath preposition
  = sous

beside preposition
  = à côté de
  he is sitting beside me = il est assis à côté
    de moi
  to live beside the sea = habiter au bord de
    la mer

best
1 noun
  the best = le meilleur/la meilleure
  to be the best at French = être le
    meilleur/la meilleure en français
  who is the best at drawing? = qui dessine
    le mieux?
  to do one's best = faire de son mieux
2 adjective
  = meilleur/meilleure
  the best hotel in town = le meilleur hôtel
    de la ville
  she speaks the best French = c'est elle
    qui parle le mieux français
  my best friend = mon meilleur ami/ma
    meilleure amie
  the best book I've ever read = le meilleur
    livre que j'aie jamais lu

  ! Note that the subjunctive is used after
  the superlative le meilleur... que.

  **the best thing to do would be to phone
    him** = le mieux serait de lui téléphoner

3 adverb
  = le mieux
  the best dressed man = l'homme le
    mieux habillé
  I like tennis best = le tennis est mon sport
    préféré

bet verb
  = parier

better
1 adjective
  = meilleur/meilleure
  her new film is better than the others
    = son nouveau film est meilleur que les
    précédents
  he is better at sports than me = il est
    meilleur en sport que moi
  the weather is going to get better = le
    temps va s'améliorer
  he was ill but now he's better = il était
    malade mais maintenant il va mieux
2 adverb
  = mieux
  he speaks French better than I do = il
    parle mieux le français que moi
  we'd better go = nous ferions mieux de
    partir
  it's better to [phone | write | check ...] = il
    vaut mieux [téléphoner | écrire | vérifier ...]

between
1 preposition
  = entre
  there is a wall between the two gardens
    = il y a un mur entre les deux jardins
  between now and next year = d'ici l'année
    prochaine
2 in between = au milieu

beyond preposition
  = au-delà de
  beyond the village = au-delà du village

bicycle noun
  a bicycle = un vélo

big adjective
• (large) = grand/grande (**!** before the noun)
  a big garden = un grand jardin
  a big party = une grande fête
  they have big houses = ils ont de grandes
    maisons
  a big car = une grosse voiture
• (heavy, thick) = gros/grosse (**!** before the
  noun)
  a big parcel = un gros paquet
  a big book = un gros livre
• (important, serious) = gros/grosse (**!** before
  the noun)
  a big salary = un gros salaire
  to make a big mistake = faire une grave
    erreur

bike noun
  a bike = un vélo

bill noun
• (for gas, electricity, telephone)
  a bill = une facture

- (*in a restaurant*)
  a bill = une addition
  could we have the bill please?
     = l'addition, s'il vous plaît
- (*in a hotel*)
  a bill = une note
- (*US English*) (*money*)
  a bill = un billet de banque

billiards *noun* ▶ **248**
   billiards = le billard

bin *noun* (*British English*)
   a bin = une poubelle

biology *noun*
   biology = la biologie

bird *noun*
   a bird = un oiseau

biro® *noun* (*British English*)
   a biro = un stylo-bille

birth *noun*
   a birth = une naissance
   a place of birth = un lieu de naissance

birthday *noun*
   a birthday = un anniversaire
   Happy birthday! = Bon anniversaire!

biscuit *noun* (*British English*)
   a biscuit = un gâteau sec, un biscuit

bit
1 *noun*
   (*of cheese, bread, wood*) = un morceau
   (*of string, paper*) = un bout
2 a bit (*British English*)
   a bit [early | nasty | odd …] = un peu [tôt |
    méchant | bizarre …]

bite *verb*
   = mordre
   to bite one's nails = se ronger les ongles

bitter *adjective*
   = amer/amère

black *adjective* ▶ **213**
   = noir/noire

blackberry *noun*
   a blackberry = une mûre

blackboard *noun*
   a blackboard = un tableau noir

blackcurrants *noun*
   blackcurrants = le cassis (*singular*)

blade *noun*
- (*of a knife, a sword*)
  a blade = une lame
- **a blade of grass** = un brin d'herbe

blame
1 *verb*
   to blame someone = en vouloir à
    quelqu'un
2 *noun*
   to take the blame = prendre la
    responsabilité

blank *adjective*
   (*describing a page*) = blanc/blanche
   (*describing a cassette*) = vierge

blanket *noun*
   a blanket = une couverture

blaze *verb*
   = être en flammes

bleed *verb*
   = saigner
   my nose is bleeding = je saigne du nez

blind
1 *adjective*
   = aveugle
2 *verb*
- (*destroy someone's sight*) = aveugler
- (*to dazzle*) = éblouir
3 *noun*
   a blind = un store

blink *verb*
   = cligner des yeux

blister *noun*
   a blister = une ampoule

block
1 *noun*
- (*a building*)
  a block of apartments = un immeuble
- (*a group of houses*)
  a block of houses = une pâté de maisons
- (*a large piece*)
  a block = un bloc
  a block of ice = un bloc de glace
2 *verb*
   = bloquer
   to block a road = bloquer une route

blond, blonde *adjective* ▶ **213**
   = blond/blonde
   he has blond hair = il a les cheveux blonds
   my sister's blonde = ma sœur est blonde

blood *noun*
   blood = le sang

blouse *noun*
   a blouse = un chemisier

blow
1 *verb*
- (*if it's the wind*) = souffler
  the wind blew the door shut = un coup de
     vent a fermé la porte
- (*if it's a person*) = souffler
  to blow a whistle = donner un coup de
     sifflet
  to blow one's nose = se moucher
     (**!** + *être*)
  to blow bubbles = faire des bulles
- (*if it's a light bulb*) = sauter
2 *noun*
   a blow = un coup
blow away
   to be blown away = être
    emporté/emportée par le vent

B

blow down
  to be blown down = être abattu/abattue (par le vent)
blow out = souffler
  to blow out a candle = souffler une bougie
blow up
- (to destroy) = faire sauter
  to blow up a car = faire sauter une voiture
- (to be destroyed) = sauter
- (to put air into) = gonfler

blue adjective ▶ 213 |
  = bleu/bleue

blush verb
  = rougir

board
1 noun
- (a piece of wood)
  a board = une planche
- (for games)
  a board (in chess) = un échiquier
  (in draughts, checkers) = un damier
- (a blackboard)
  a board = un tableau noir
2 verb
  to board a ship = monter à bord d'un navire
3 on board = à bord

boarding school noun
  a boarding school = une pension

boast verb
  = se vanter (**!** + être)

boat noun
  a boat = un bateau

body noun
  the body = le corps
  a dead body = un cadavre

boil verb
- (if it's a person)
  to boil water = faire bouillir de l'eau
  to boil an egg = faire cuire un œuf
- (if it's water, milk) = bouillir

boiled egg noun
  a boiled egg = un œuf à la coque

boiler noun
  a boiler = une chaudière

boiling adjective
  = bouillant/bouillante

bomb
1 noun
  a bomb = une bombe
2 verb
  = bombarder

bone noun ▶ 201 |
  a bone (in the body, in meat) = un os
  (in fish) = une arête

bonnet noun (British English)
  the bonnet (in a car) = le capot

book
1 noun
  a book = un livre
2 verb
  = réserver
  to book a room = réserver une chambre
  the flight is fully booked = le vol est complet

booking noun
  a booking = une réservation

bookshop, **bookstore** noun ▶ 315 |
  a bookshop, a bookstore = une librairie

boot noun
- (worn on the feet)
  a boot = une botte
- (British English) (of a car)
  the boot = le coffre

border noun
  a border = une frontière
  to cross the border = passer la frontière

bore verb
  = ennuyer

bored adjective
  to be bored, to get bored = s'ennuyer (**!** + être)

boring adjective
  = ennuyeux/ennuyeuse

born adjective
  to be born = naître (**!** + être)
  he was born in February = il est né au mois de février
  she was born in Italy = elle est née en Italie

borrow verb
  = emprunter
  to borrow some money from someone = emprunter de l'argent à quelqu'un

boss noun
  the boss = le patron/la patronne

both
1 determiner
  both girls are blonde = les deux filles sont blondes
  both my sons = mes deux fils
  both Anne and Brian came = Anne et Brian sont venus tous les deux
2 pronoun
  = tous les deux/toutes les deux
  you are both wrong, both of you are wrong = vous avez tort tous les deux/toutes les deux

bother verb
- (to take the trouble)
  don't bother calling back = ce n'est pas la peine de rappeler
- (to worry, to upset) = tracasser

The human body

Note the use of **le**, **la**, **l'** or **les** in French where English uses a possessive adjective:

he raised his hand	= il a levé **la** main
she closed her eyes	= elle a fermé **les** yeux
my eye hurts	= j'ai mal à **l'**œil

For expressions such as *he hurt his foot* or *she brushed her teeth*, where the action involves more than the simple movement of a body part, use a reflexive verb in French:

she has broken her leg	= elle s'est **cassé** la jambe
he was washing his hands	= il **se lavait** les mains

Note also the following:

she broke his nose	= elle lui a cassé le nez (literally *she broke to him the nose*)

Describing people

Here are some ways of describing people in French:

his hair is long	= il a les cheveux longs
he has long hair	= il a les cheveux longs
a boy with long hair	= un garçon aux cheveux longs
her eyes are blue	= elle a les yeux bleus
she has blue eyes	= elle a les yeux bleus
the girl with blue eyes	= la fille aux yeux bleus
his nose is red	= il a le nez rouge
he has a red nose	= il a le nez rouge
a man with a red nose	= un homme au nez rouge

▶ For other expressions with terms relating to parts of the body, **▶ 266 |**.

---

* (*in polite apologies*) = déranger
  I'm sorry to bother you = je suis désolé de vous déranger

bottle *noun*
  a bottle = une bouteille

bottle-opener *noun*
  a bottle-opener = un décapsuleur

bottom
1 *noun*
* (*the lowest part*)
  the bottom of the hill = le pied de la colline
  at the bottom of [the page | the stairs | the street ...] = en bas [de la page | de l'escalier | de la rue ...]
  at the bottom [of the lake | of the sea | of the garden ...] = au fond [du lac | de la mer | du jardin ...]
* (*at the lowest level*)
  to be bottom of the class = être dernier/dernière de la classe
* (*part of the body*) **▶ 201 |**
  the bottom = le derrière**✗**
2 *adjective*
  the bottom [shelf | drawer | cupboard ...] = [l'étagère | le tiroir | le placard ...] du bas

bound: **to be bound to** *verb*
  it's bound to create problems = ça va sûrement créer des problèmes
  she's bound to complain = elle va sûrement se plaindre
  it was bound to happen = cela devait arriver

bow¹ *noun*
* (*a knot*)
  a bow = un nœud
* (*a weapon*)
  a bow = un arc

bow² *verb*
  = saluer
  to bow one's head = baisser la tête

bowl *noun*
  a bowl = un bol
  (*shallow*) = une assiette

bowling *noun* **▶ 248 |**
  bowling = le bowling

box *noun*
  a box = une boîte
  (*when moving*) = un carton

boxing *noun* **▶ 248 |**
  boxing = la boxe

boy *noun*
  a boy = un garçon

boyfriend *noun*
  a boyfriend = un copain

bra *noun*
  a bra = un soutien-gorge

bracelet *noun*
  a bracelet = un bracelet

braid *noun* (*US English*)
  a braid = une natte, une tresse

brain *noun* ▶ 201
the brain = le cerveau

brake *noun*
a brake = un frein

branch *noun*
a branch = une branche

brand-new *adjective*
= tout neuf/toute neuve

brandy *noun*
brandy = le cognac

brave *adjective*
= courageux/courageuse

Brazil *noun* ▶ 218
Brazil = le Brésil

bread *noun*
bread = le pain

break
1 *verb*
• (*to be damaged*) = se casser (**!** + *être*)
the chair broke = la chaise s'est cassée
• (*to crack, to smash or damage*) = casser
to break an egg = casser un œuf
• (*to injure*)
to break one's leg = se casser la jambe
she broke her arm = elle s'est cassé le bras
• (*not to keep*)
to break a promise = manquer à une promesse
to break the rules = enfreindre le règlement
2 *noun*
• a break (*a short rest*) = une pause
(*at school*) = une récréation
to take a break = faire une pause
• (*a holiday*)
a break = des vacances (*feminine plural*)
break down
• (*if it's a TV, a car*) = tomber en panne (**!** + *être*)
• (*to get upset*) = s'effondrer (**!** + *être*)
break into = cambrioler
to be broken into = être cambriolé/cambriolée
break out
(*if it's a fire*) = se déclarer (**!** + *être*)
(*if it's violence*) = éclater
break up
• (*if it's a crowd*) = se disperser (**!** + *être*)
• (*if it's a couple*) = se séparer (**!** + *être*)
to break up with someone = rompre avec quelqu'un
• (*to put an end to*) = mettre fin à
the police broke up the demonstration = la police a mis fin à la manifestation

breakfast *noun*
breakfast = le petit déjeuner
to have breakfast = prendre le petit déjeuner

breast *noun* ▶ 201
a breast = un sein

breath *noun*
breath = le souffle
to be out of breath = être hors d'haleine
to hold one's breath = retenir sa respiration

breathe *verb*
= respirer
breathe in = inspirer
breathe out = expirer, souffler

breeze *noun*
a breeze = une brise

brick *noun*
a brick = une brique

bride *noun*
a bride = une mariée

bridegroom *noun*
a bridegroom = un marié

bridge *noun*
a bridge = un pont

brief *adjective*
= bref/brève (**!** *before the noun*)

bright *adjective*
• (*describing colours, light*) = vif/vive
a bright yellow dress = une robe jaune vif
• (*having plenty of light, sun*) = clair/claire
this room is not very bright = cette pièce n'est pas très claire
a bright spell = une belle éclaircie
to get brighter = s'éclaircir (**!** + *être*)
• (*intelligent*) = intelligent/intelligente

brilliant *adjective*
• (*very intelligent*) = brillant/brillante
• (*British English*) (*used for emphasis*) = génial/géniale✗

bring *verb*
• to bring = apporter
to bring someone a present = apporter un cadeau à quelqu'un
it will bring us good luck = ça va nous porter chance
• (*to be accompanied by*) = amener
he brought his sister to the party = il a amené sa sœur à la soirée
bring about
to bring about a change = provoquer un changement
bring back = rapporter
he brought me back some perfume = il m'a rapporté du parfum
bring up = élever
to bring up a child = élever un enfant

Britain *noun* ▶ 218
Britain = la Grande-Bretagne

British ▶ 275
1 *adjective*
= britannique

✗ in informal situations

2 noun
the British = les Britanniques (*masculine plural*)

broad adjective
= large

broadcast verb
= diffuser
to be broadcast live = être diffusé/diffusée en direct

brochure noun
a brochure = une brochure

broke adjective
= fauché/fauchée✱

broken adjective
= cassé/cassée

bronze noun
bronze = le bronze

brother noun
a brother = un frère

brother-in-law noun
a brother-in-law = un beau-frère

brown adjective ▶ 213 |
• (*in colour*) = marron (! *never changes*)
to have brown eyes = avoir les yeux marron
• (*describing hair*) = châtain (! *never changes*)
• to go brown = bronzer

bruise noun ▶ 266 |
a bruise = un bleu

brush
1 noun
• (*for hair, teeth, clothes or shoes*)
a brush = une brosse
• (*for sweeping up*)
a brush = un balai
• (*for painting*)
a brush = un pinceau
2 verb
to brush one's hair = se brosser les cheveux
to brush one's teeth = se brosser les dents

Brussels noun ▶ 218 |
Brussels = Bruxelles

bubble noun
a bubble = une bulle

bucket noun
a bucket = un seau

budgerigar, **budgie** noun
a budgerigar = une perruche

build verb
= construire
to build a house = construire une maison

building noun
a building = un bâtiment

Bulgaria noun ▶ 218 |
Bulgaria = la Bulgarie

bull noun
a bull = un taureau

bullet noun
a bullet = une balle

bulletin noun
a bulletin = un bulletin
a news bulletin = un bulletin d'informations

bully verb
= tyranniser

bump verb
to bump one's head = se cogner la tête
bump into
• (*to hit*) = rentrer dans (! + *être*)
• (*to meet*) = tomber sur (! + *être*)

bunch noun
a bunch of flowers = un bouquet de fleurs
a bunch of grapes = une grappe de raisins
a bunch of keys = un trousseau de clés

burger noun
a burger = un hamburger

burglar noun
a burglar = un cambrioleur/une cambrioleuse

burglar alarm noun
a burglar alarm = une sirène d'alarme

burglary noun
a burglary = un cambriolage

burn
1 verb
• (*to destroy, to get rid of*) = brûler
to burn rubbish = brûler des ordures
• (*to injure*)
to burn oneself = se brûler (! + *être*)
to burn one's finger = se brûler le doigt
• (*to be on fire*) = brûler
• (*when cooking*) = laisser brûler
• (*in the sun*)
to burn easily = attraper facilement des coups de soleil
2 noun
a burn = une brûlure
burn down = brûler

burst verb
• (*if it's a balloon*) = éclater
• (*if it's a pipe*) = éclater
• (*if it's a river*)
to burst its banks = déborder
burst into
to burst into tears = fondre en larmes
burst out
to burst out laughing = éclater de rire

bury verb
= enterrer

bus noun
a bus = un bus

bus conductor *noun* ▶ 315 |
   a bus conductor = un receveur/une
   receveuse d'autobus

bus driver *noun* ▶ 315 |
   a bus driver = un conducteur/une
   conductrice d'autobus

bush *noun*
   a bush = un buisson

business *noun*
 • (*commercial activities*)
   business = les affaires (*feminine plural*)
   to go to London on business = aller à
      Londres pour affaires
 • (*a company*)
   a business = une entreprise
 • (*when protecting one's privacy*)
   that's my business = ça me regarde
   it's none of your business = ça ne te
      regarde pas

businessman *noun* ▶ 315 |
   a businessman = un homme d'affaires

businesswoman *noun* ▶ 315 |
   a businesswoman = une femme d'affaires

bus station *noun*
   a bus station = une gare routière

bus stop *noun*
   a bus stop = un arrêt d'autobus

busy *adjective*
   = occupé/occupée
   to be busy packing = être occupé à faire
      ses valises
   to have a busy day = avoir une journée
      chargée
   to lead a busy life = mener une vie
      active

but *conjunction*
   = mais
   he understands French but he doesn't
      speak it = il comprend le français mais
      il ne le parle pas

butcher *noun* ▶ 315 |
   a butcher = un boucher

butter *noun*
   butter = le beurre

butterfly *noun*
   a butterfly = un papillon

button *noun*
   a button = un bouton

buy *verb*
   = acheter
   to buy a present for someone = acheter
      un cadeau à quelqu'un
   she bought herself a new coat = elle s'est
      acheté un nouveau manteau

buzz *verb*
   = bourdonner

by *preposition*

 • by = par
   by accident = accidentellement
   by chance = par hasard
   by mistake = par erreur
   one by one = un par un/une par une
   he was bitten by a dog = il a été mordu
      par un chien
 • (*on one's own*)
   by oneself = tout seul/toute seule
 • (*using*)
   to travel by bus = voyager en bus
   we went there by bicycle = nous y
      sommes allés à bicyclette
   to pay by cheque = payer par chèque
   to book by phone = réserver par
      téléphone
   to come in by the back door = entrer par
      la porte de derrière
 • (*as a result of*)
   he succeeded by working hard = il a
      réussi en travaillant beaucoup
 • (*beside*)
   by the sea = au bord de la mer
   by the side of the road = au bord de la
      route
 • (*indicating the author or painter*) = de
   a book by Charles Dickens = un livre de
      Charles Dickens
   a painting by Chagall = un tableau de
      Chagall
 • (*when talking about time*)
   by next Thursday = d'ici jeudi prochain
   he should be here by now = il devrait
      déjà être là
 • (*when talking about figures, rates*)
   to increase by 20% = augmenter de 20%
   to be paid by the hour = être payé/payée à
      l'heure
   8 metres by 4 metres = 8 mètres sur 4

Cc

cab *noun*
   a cab = un taxi

cabbage *noun*
   cabbage = le chou

cable car *noun*
   a cable car = un téléphérique

café *noun*
   a café = un café

cake *noun*
   a cake = un gâteau

cake shop *noun* ▶ 315 |
   a cake shop = une pâtisserie

calculator *noun*
   a calculator = une calculatrice, une
      calculette

calendar *noun*
  a calendar = un calendrier

calf *noun*
• (*the animal*)
  a calf = un veau
• (*part of the leg*) ▶ **201** |
  the calf = le mollet

call *verb*
• (*to name*) = appeler
  he's called Michael = il s'appelle Michael
  it's called 'un robinet' in French = en
    français ça s'appelle 'un robinet'
• (*to describe as*)
  to call someone a coward = traiter
    quelqu'un de lâche
• (*to call out (to)*) = appeler
  the teacher is calling us = le professeur
    nous appelle
  to call the register (*British English*) = faire
    l'appel
• (*to phone*) = appeler
  who's calling? = qui est à l'appareil?
• (*to get to come*) = appeler
  to call the doctor = faire venir le médecin
• (*to wake*) = réveiller
• (*to pay a visit*) = passer (**!** + *être*)
  they called yesterday = ils sont passés
    hier
call back
• (*to come back*) = repasser (**!** + *être*)
• (*to phone back*) = rappeler
call off = annuler
call out
  to call out the numbers for the lottery
    = annoncer les numéros gagnants du
    loto
call up = appeler

calm
1 *adjective*
  = calme
2 *verb*
  = calmer
calm down = se calmer (**!** + *être*)

camcorder *noun*
  a camcorder = un caméscope®

camel *noun*
  a camel = un chameau

camera *noun*
  a camera (*for taking photos*) = un appareil
    photo
  (*in a studio, for videos*) = une caméra

camp
1 *noun*
  a summer camp = un camp de vacances
2 *verb*
  = camper
  to go camping = faire du camping

camping *noun*
  camping = le camping

campsite *noun*
  a campsite = un camping

can¹ *verb*
• (*to have the possibility*)
  can you come? = est-ce que tu peux
    venir?
  where can I buy stamps? = où est-ce que
    je peux acheter des timbres?
  he can't sleep when it's hot = il ne peut
    pas dormir quand il fait chaud
• (*when talking about* seeing, hearing,
  understanding, *you don't usually translate*
  can)
  I can hear you better now = je t'entends
    mieux maintenant
  can they see us? = est-ce qu'ils nous
    voient?
  he can't understand Japanese = il ne
    comprend pas le japonais
• (*to be allowed to*)
  can I smoke? = est-ce que je peux fumer?
  we can't turn right here = nous ne
    pouvons pas tourner à droite ici
• (*to know how to*)
  she can swim = elle sait nager
  he can't drive yet = il ne sait pas encore
    conduire
  can you speak French? = est-ce que tu
    parles français?
• (*when asking, offering or suggesting*)
  can we borrow your car? = est-ce que
    nous pouvons emprunter ta voiture?
  can I help you? = est-ce que je peux vous
    aider?
  you can phone back later if you like
    = vous pouvez rappeler plus tard si vous
    voulez

can² *noun*
  a can = une boîte

Canada *noun* ▶ **218** |
  Canada = le Canada

Canadian ▶ **275** |
1 *adjective*
  = canadien/canadienne
2 *noun*
  the Canadians = les Canadiens
    (*masculine*)

canal *noun*
  a canal = un canal

cancel *verb*
  = annuler

cancer *noun* ▶ **266** |
  cancer = le cancer

candle *noun*
  a candle (*in a room, on a cake*) = une
    bougie
  (*in a church*) = un cierge

candy *noun* (*US English*)
• candy = la confiserie
• (*a sweet*)
  a candy = un bonbon

canoe *noun*
  a canoe = un canoë, un canoë-kayak

canoeing noun ▶ 248|
canoeing = le canoë-kayak

can-opener noun
a can-opener = un ouvre-boîtes

canteen noun
a canteen = une cantine

cap noun
a cap = une casquette
a baseball cap = une casquette de base-ball

capable adjective
• to be capable of looking after oneself
= être capable de se débrouiller tout seul
• (having ability, skill)
= compétent/compétente

capital
1 noun
the capital = la capitale
Paris is the capital of France = Paris est la capitale de la France
2 adjective
= majuscule
capital P = P majuscule

captain noun
a captain = un capitaine

car noun
a car = une voiture

caravan noun (British English)
a caravan = une caravane

card noun
• (for sending to someone)
a card = une carte
• (for playing games)
a card = une carte (à jouer)
to play cards = jouer aux cartes

cardphone noun
a cardphone = un téléphone à carte

care
1 noun
• (to take care) = faire attention
to take care crossing the street = faire attention en traversant la rue
• to take care of someone = s'occuper de quelqu'un
2 verb
I don't care = ça m'est égal
to care about the environment
= s'intéresser à l'environnement

career noun
a career = une carrière

careful adjective
to be careful = faire attention
to be careful crossing the street = faire attention en traversant la rue
to be careful not to make mistakes = faire attention de ne pas faire d'erreurs

careless adjective
to be careless = être négligent/négligente

car ferry noun
a car ferry = un ferry, un transbordeur

carnival noun
• (British English) (a festival)
a carnival = un carnaval
• (US English) (a fair)
a carnival = une fête foraine

car park noun (British English)
a car park = un parking, un parc de stationnement

carpet noun
carpet = la moquette

car phone noun
a car phone = un téléphone de voiture

carrot noun
a carrot = une carotte

carry verb
• (to hold) = porter
I can't carry the shopping = je ne peux pas porter les courses
• (to move)
to carry the baggage upstairs = monter les bagages
to carry the boxes downstairs = descendre les cartons
carry on = continuer

cartoon noun
a cartoon (a comic strip) = une bande dessinée, une BD
(a film) = un dessin animé

case¹: in case conjunction
= au cas où
keep the bike in case you need it = garde le vélo au cas où tu en aurais besoin
! Note that the conditional is used after au cas où.

case² noun
a case = une valise

cash
1 noun
cash = l'argent liquide
! Note that argent is masculine.
I don't have any cash = je n'ai pas d'argent liquide
to pay in cash = payer en espèces
2 verb
= encaisser

cash dispenser noun
a cash dispenser = un distributeur automatique de billets

cassette noun
a cassette = une cassette

cassette player noun
a cassette player = un lecteur de cassettes

castle noun
a castle = un château

cat *noun*
a cat = un chat/une chatte

catch *verb*
* (*to capture*) = attraper
  to catch a fish = attraper un poisson
* (*to take hold of*) = attraper
* (*to pinch, to stick*)
  he caught his finger in the door = il s'est
    pris le doigt dans la porte
  my shirt got caught in the thorns = ma
    chemise s'est prise dans les ronces
* (*to get*)
  he was running to catch his train = il
    courait pour attraper son train
* (*to take by surprise*)
  to catch someone stealing = surprendre
    quelqu'un en train de voler
  to get caught = se faire prendre (**!** + *être*)
* (*to become ill with*)
  to catch flu = attraper la grippe
  to catch a cold = s'enrhumer (**!** + *être*),
    attraper un rhume
* to catch fire = prendre feu
catch up
  to catch up with someone = rattraper
    quelqu'un

caterpillar *noun*
a caterpillar = une chenille

cathedral *noun*
a cathedral = une cathédrale

cauliflower *noun*
cauliflower = le chou-fleur

cause *verb*
  the storm will cause damage = l'orage va
    causer des dégâts
  it has caused us a lot of problems = ça
    nous a causé beaucoup de problèmes
  it's going to cause delays = ça va
    provoquer des retards

cautious *adjective*
= prudent/prudente

cave *noun*
a cave = une grotte

CD *noun*
a CD = un disque compact, un CD

CD player *noun*
a CD player = une platine laser

ceiling *noun*
the ceiling = le plafond

celebrate *verb*
= faire la fête
  to celebrate someone's birthday = fêter
    l'anniversaire de quelqu'un

celery *noun*
celery = le céleri

cell *noun*
a cell = une cellule

cellar *noun*
a cellar = une cave

cello *noun* ▶ **290**
a cello = un violoncelle

cement *noun*
cement = le ciment

cemetery *noun*
a cemetery = un cimetière

centimetre (*British English*),
centimeter (*US English*) *noun* ▶ **285**
a centimetre = un centimètre

central heating *noun*
central heating = le chauffage central

centre (*British English*), **center** (*US
English*) *noun*
* (*a place for activities, meetings*)
  a centre = un centre
  a leisure centre = un centre de loisirs
* (*the middle*)
  the centre = le centre
  near the centre of London = près du
    centre de Londres

century *noun* ▶ **356**
a century = un siècle

certain *adjective*
= certain/certaine

certainly *adverb*
= certainement

chain *noun*
a chain = une chaîne

chair *noun*
a chair = une chaise

chalk *noun*
chalk = la craie

champagne *noun*
champagne = le champagne

champion *noun*
a champion = un champion/une
  championne
a tennis champion = un champion/une
  championne de tennis

chance *noun*
* (*when talking about a possibility*)
  there is a chance that she'll have a job in
    Paris = il est possible qu'elle ait un
    travail à Paris

  ! *Note that the subjunctive is used after* il
  est possible que.

* (*an opportunity*)
  a chance = une occasion
  to have a chance to meet people = avoir
    l'occasion de rencontrer des gens
* by chance = par hasard

change
1 *noun*
* a change = un changement
  a change of temperature = un
    changement de température

* (*a different experience*)
  it makes a change from homework = ça
    change des devoirs
  let's go to the beach for a change = allons
    à la plage pour changer
* (*cash*)
  change = la monnaie
  have you got change for 50 francs?
    = pouvez-vous me faire la monnaie de
    50 francs?
2 *verb*
* (*to become different, to make different*)
    = changer
  the town has changed a lot = la ville a
    beaucoup changé
  I've changed my mind = j'ai changé d'avis
* (*to replace*) = changer
  to change a wheel = changer une roue
* (*to exchange in a shop*) = échanger
  change a shirt for a smaller size
    = échanger une chemise pour une taille
    plus petite
* (*to switch*) = changer de
  to change places with someone
    = changer de place avec quelqu'un
  she keeps changing channels = elle
    n'arrête pas de changer de chaîne
* (*when talking about one's clothes*) = se
  changer (**!** + *être*)
  to get changed = se changer (**!** + *être*)
* (*when using transport*) = changer
* **to change dollars into French francs**
    = changer des dollars en francs français

changing room *noun*
  a changing room = un vestiaire

channel *noun*
  a TV channel = une chaîne de télévision

Channel *noun*
  the (English) Channel = la Manche

chapter *noun*
  a chapter = un chapitre

charge
1 *verb*
  to charge someone for the damage = faire
    payer les dégâts à quelqu'un
  they'll charge you for the electricity = ils
    te feront payer l'électricité
2 *noun*
* (*a price, a fee*)
  a charge = des frais (*masculine plural*)
  there's no charge = c'est gratuit
3 in charge = responsable
  to be in charge of the money = être
    responsable de l'argent

charming *adjective*
    = charmant/charmante

chase *verb*
  (*on foot*) = courir après
  (*in a car*) = poursuivre

× in informal situations

chase away = chasser

chat
1 *verb*
    = bavarder, discuter
2 *noun*
  a chat = une conversation
chat up (*British English*) = draguer**×**

cheap *adjective*
* (*not expensive*) = bon marché (**!** *never
  changes*)
  it's cheap = c'est bon marché, ça ne coûte
    pas cher
  it's cheaper to take the bus = ça coûte
    moins cher de prendre le bus
* (*of poor quality*) = de mauvaise qualité

cheat *verb*
    = tricher

check
1 *verb*
* (*to make sure*) = vérifier
  you should check whether it's true = tu
    devrais vérifier si c'est vrai
* (*to inspect*) = contrôler
  they didn't even check our passports = ils
    n'ont même pas contrôlé nos passeports
2 *noun*
* (*US English*) (*a bill*)
  a check = une addition
* (*US English*) (*a cheque*)
  a check = un chèque
check in = se présenter à l'enregistrement
check out = partir (**!** + *être*)

checkbook *noun* (*US English*)
  a checkbook = un carnet de chèques, un
    chéquier

checkers *noun* ▶ **248** | (*US English*)
  checkers = les dames (*feminine*)

check-in *noun*
  the check-in = l'enregistrement
    (*masculine*)

checkout *noun*
  a checkout = une caisse

cheek *noun* ▶ **201** |
  the cheek = la joue

cheeky *adjective*
    = effronté/effrontée, insolent/insolente

cheerful *adjective*
    = gai/gaie

cheese *noun*
  cheese = le fromage

chef *noun* ▶ **315** |
  a chef = un chef cuisinier

chemist *noun* ▶ **315** |
* (*in a shop*)
  a chemist = un pharmacien/une
    pharmacienne
* (*in a laboratory*)
  a chemist = un chimiste/une chimiste

chemistry *noun*
chemistry = la chimie

cheque *noun* (*British English*)
a cheque = un chèque
to write a cheque for £50 = faire un
chèque de 50 livres

cheque book *noun* (*British English*)
a cheque book = un carnet de chèques,
un chéquier

cherry *noun*
a cherry = une cerise

chess *noun* ▶ 248
chess = les échecs (*masculine plural*)

chest *noun* ▶ 201
the chest = la poitrine

chestnut
1 *noun*
a chestnut = un marron, une châtaigne
2 *adjective*
= châtain (**!** *never changes*)
to have chestnut hair = avoir les cheveux
châtain

chew *verb*
(*if it's a person*) = mâcher
(*if it's an animal*) = ronger

chewing gum *noun*
chewing gum = le chewing-gum

chicken *noun*
• (*the bird*)
a chicken = une poule
• (*the meat*)
chicken = le poulet

child *noun*
a child = un enfant/une enfant

chilly *adjective*
it's chilly = il fait froid

chimney *noun*
a chimney = une cheminée

chin *noun* ▶ 201 , ▶ 237
the chin = le menton

China *noun* ▶ 218
China = la Chine

Chinese ▶ 275
1 *adjective*
= chinois/chinoise
2 *noun*
• (*the people*)
the Chinese = les Chinois (*masculine
plural*)
• (*the language*)
Chinese = le chinois

chips *noun*
• (*British English*) (*French fries*)
chips = les frites (*feminine*)
• (*US English*) (*crisps*)
(potato) chips = les chips (*feminine*)

chocolate *noun*
chocolate = le chocolat
a box of chocolates = une boîte de
chocolats

choice *noun*
a choice = un choix
we had no choice = nous n'avions pas le
choix

choir *noun*
a choir = une chorale

choke *verb*
= s'étouffer (**!** + *être*)

choose *verb*
= choisir

chore *noun*
a chore = une tâche
to do the chores = faire le ménage

Christian *adjective*
= chrétien/chrétienne

Christian name *noun*
a Christian name = un nom de baptême

Christmas *noun*
Christmas (Day) = (le jour de) Noël
Merry Christmas!, Happy Christmas!
= Joyeux Noël!

Christmas carol *noun*
a Christmas carol = un chant de Noël

Christmas cracker *noun* (*British
English*)
a Christmas cracker = un diablotin

Christmas Eve *noun*
Christmas Eve = la veille de Noël

Christmas tree *noun*
a Christmas tree = un sapin de Noël

church *noun*
a church (*Catholic or Anglican*) = une
église
(*Protestant*) = un temple

cider *noun*
cider = le cidre

cigar *noun*
a cigar = un cigare

cigarette *noun*
a cigarette = une cigarette

cigarette lighter *noun*
a cigarette lighter = un briquet

cinema *noun* (*British English*)
a cinema = un cinéma

circle *noun*
a circle = un cercle
we were sitting in a circle = nous étions
assis en cercle

circus *noun*
a circus = un cirque

C

citizen noun
* (of a country)
  a citizen = un citoyen/une citoyenne
* (of a city or town)
  a citizen = un habitant/une habitante

city noun
  a city = une (grande) ville

city centre (British English), **city center** (US English) noun
  the city centre = le centre-ville

civilized adjective
  = civilisé/civilisée

civil servant noun ▶ 315 |
  a civil servant = un fonctionnaire/une fonctionnaire

clap verb
  = applaudir

clarinet noun ▶ 290 |
  a clarinet = une clarinette

class noun
* (a group of students)
  a class = une classe
* (a lesson)
  a class = un cours
  a history class = un cours d'histoire
* (a social group)
  a (social) class = une classe (sociale)

classical music noun
  classical music = la musique classique

classmate noun
  a classmate = un camarade/une camarade de classe

classroom noun
  a classroom = une salle de classe

clean
1 adjective
* (not dirty) = propre
  my hands are clean = j'ai les mains propres
  to keep the house clean = tenir la maison propre
* (not polluted) = pur/pure
2 verb
  = nettoyer
  to have a jacket cleaned = faire nettoyer une veste

clear
1 adjective
* (easy to understand, making sense) = clair/claire
  is that clear? = est-ce que c'est clair?
* (obvious)
  it is clear that no-one is happy = il est clair que personne n'est content
* (easy to see or hear, distinct)
  a clear voice = une voix claire
  your writing must be clear = votre écriture doit être lisible
* (with no rain or cloud) = clair/claire
  on a clear day = par temps clair

2 verb
* (to empty, to remove from)
  to clear the table = débarrasser la table
  to clear the building = évacuer le bâtiment
  to clear the snow off the road = dégager la neige de la route
* (if it's fog, mist) = se dissiper (**!** + être)

clever adjective
* (intelligent) = intelligent/intelligente
  to be clever at mathematics = être doué/douée pour les mathématiques
* (smart) = astucieux/astucieuse

cliff noun
  a cliff = une falaise

climate noun
  a climate = un climat

climb verb
* **to climb (up) a tree** = grimper à un arbre
  to climb a mountain = faire l'ascension d'une montagne
  to climb over a wall = passer par-dessus un mur
* (to rise higher) = monter (**!** + être)

climbing noun ▶ 248 |
  climbing = l'escalade (feminine)

clinic noun
  a clinic = un centre médical

cloakroom noun
  a cloakroom = un vestiaire

clock noun
  a clock (on a building, in a classroom) = une horloge
  (smaller, as an ornament) = une pendule
  (in sporting events) = un chronomètre

close¹
1 adjective
* (near) = proche
  the station is quite close = la gare est assez proche
  is the house close to the school? = est-ce que la maison est près de l'école?
* (as a friend or relation) = proche
2 adverb
  to live close (by) = habiter tout près
  to come closer = s'approcher (**!** + être)

close² verb
  = fermer
  close your eyes = ferme les yeux
  the shop closes at noon = le magasin ferme à midi
  the door closed suddenly = tout d'un coup, la porte s'est fermée
close down = fermer définitivement

closed adjective
  = fermé/fermée

cloth noun
* (material)
  cloth = le tissu

The clock

What time is it?

what time is it?	= quelle heure est-il?
could you tell me the time?	= pouvez-vous me donner l'heure?
it's exactly four o'clock	= il est exactement quatre heures

It is ...	**Il est ...**	**say**
4 o'clock	4 heures	
	4 h	quatre heures
*4 o'clock in the morning	4 am*	4 h 00	quatre heures du matin
*4 o'clock in the afternoon	4 pm*	16 h 00	quatre heures de l'après-midi
		seize heures*
*4.10	ten past four*	4 h 10	quatre heures dix
4.15	4 h 15	quatre heures quinze
a quarter past four	4 h 15	quatre heures et quart
4.20	4 h 20	quatre heures vingt
4.25	4 h 25	quatre heures vingt-cinq
4.30	4 h 30	quatre heures trente
half past four	4 h 30	quatre heures et demie†
4.35	4 h 35	quatre heures trente-cinq
twenty-five to five	4 h 35	cinq heures moins vingt-cinq
4.40	4 h 40	quatre heures quarante
twenty to five	4 h 40	cinq heures moins vingt
*4.45	a quarter to five*	4 h 45	cinq heures moins le quart
4.50	4 h 50	quatre heures cinquante
ten to five	4 h 50	cinq heures moins dix
4.55	4 h 55	quatre heures cinquante-cinq
five to five	4 h 55	cinq heures moins cinq
5 o'clock	5 h 00	cinq heures
16.15	16 h 15	seize heures quinze
8 o'clock in the evening	8 h du soir	huit heures du soir
8 pm	20 h 00	vingt heures
12.00	12 h 00	douze heures
*noon	12 noon*	12 h 00	midi
*midnight	12 midnight*	24 h 00	minuit

* In timetables etc, the twenty-four hour clock is used, so that **4 pm** is **seize heures**. In ordinary usage, one says **quatre heures (de l'après-midi)**.

† Note that **demi** agrees with the noun it follows:

une heure et demie
un jour et demi
minuit et demi
midi et demi

Note also that, when it comes before the noun, **demi** is hyphenated and does not change:

une **demi**-journée
les **demi**-heures.

When?

French never drops the word **heures**: **at five** is **à cinq heures** and so on:

French always uses **à**, whether or not English includes the word **at**. The only exception is when there is another preposition present, as in **vers cinq heures** (*about five o'clock*), **avant cinq heures** (*before five o'clock*) etc:

what *time did it happen?*	= **à quelle** heure cela s'est-il passé?
what *time will he come at?*	= **à quelle** heure va-t-il venir?
*it happened **at** two o'clock*	= c'est arrivé **à** deux heures
*he'll come **at** four*	= il viendra **à** quatre heures
*at **about** five*	= **vers** cinq heures / **à** cinq heures **environ**
*it must be ready **by** ten*	= il faut que ce soit prêt **avant** dix heures
*closed **from** 1 **to** 2 pm*	= fermé **de** treize **à** quatorze heures
*every hour **on** the hour*	= toutes les heures **à** l'heure juste

- **a cloth** (*for dusting*) = un chiffon
  (*for the floor*) = une serpillière
  (*for dishes*) = un torchon

clothes *noun*
  clothes = les vêtements (*masculine*)
  to put on one's clothes = s'habiller
    (**!** + *être*)
  to take off one's clothes = se déshabiller
    (**!** + *être*)
  to have no clothes on = être tout nu/toute
    nue

cloud *noun*
  a cloud = un nuage

clown *noun*
  a clown = un clown

club *noun*
- **a club** = un club
  a tennis club = un club de tennis
  to be in a club = faire partie d'un club
- (*a nightclub*)
  a club = une boîte de nuit

clue *noun*
- (*in an investigation*)
  a clue = un indice
- (*in a crossword*)
  a clue = une définition

clumsy *adjective*
  = maladroit/maladroite

coach
1 *noun* (*British English*)
- (*a bus*)
  a coach = un car
- (*of a train*)
  a coach = un wagon
2 *verb*
  = entraîner

coach station *noun*
  a coach station = une gare routière

coal *noun*
  coal = le charbon

coast *noun*
  the coast = la côte

coat *noun*
- **a coat** = un manteau
- (*of an animal*)
  the coat (*of a dog*) = le poil
  (*of a cat*) = la fourrure

coat hanger *noun*
  a coat hanger = un cintre

cobweb *noun*
  a cobweb = une toile d'araignée

cock *noun*
  a cock = un coq

× in informal situations

cocoa *noun*
- (*the drink*)
  cocoa = le chocolat
- (*the product*)
  cocoa = le cacao

coconut *noun*
  a coconut = une noix de coco

cod *noun*
  cod = le cabillaud

coffee *noun*
- (*the product*)
  coffee = le café
- (*a cup of coffee*)
  a coffee = un café

coffee machine *noun*
  a coffee machine (*an appliance*) = une
    cafetière électrique
  (*a machine*) = une machine à café

coin *noun*
  a coin = une pièce
  a ten-franc coin = une pièce de dix francs

coincidence *noun*
  a coincidence = une coïncidence

cold
1 *adjective*
  = froid/froide
  to be cold, to feel cold = avoir froid
  I'm very cold = j'ai très froid
  it's cold in the classroom = il fait froid
    dans la salle de classe
  you'll get cold = tu vas prendre froid
  to go cold = refroidir
  a cold meal = un repas froid
2 *noun*
- (*the lack of heat*)
  the cold = le froid
- (*a common illness*)
  a cold = un rhume

collapse *verb*
  (*if it's a building, a chair*) = s'effondrer
    (**!** + *être*)
  (*if it's a wall*) = s'écrouler (**!** + *être*)

collar *noun*
- (*on a shirt or jacket*)
  a collar = un col
- (*for a pet*)
  a collar = un collier

colleague *noun*
  a colleague = un collègue/une collègue

collect *verb*
- (*to gather*) = ramasser
  to collect the exercise books = ramasser
    les cahiers
- (*to make a collection of*) = collectionner
  he collects stamps = il collectionne les
    timbres
- (*to take away*)
  to collect the post = faire la levée du
    courrier
  to collect the rubbish = ramasser les
    ordures

Colours

Most colour adjectives agree with the noun they are describing:

a blue coat	= un manteau bleu
a blue dress	= une robe bleue

There are exceptions, labelled (**!** *never changes*) in the dictionary. Even with a plural noun, this type of adjective remains the same:

brown shoes	= des chaussures marron
orange curtains	= des rideaux orange

This rule also applies to shades of colour:

a dark blue dress	= une robe bleu foncé
pale blue curtains	= des rideaux bleu pâle

Describing the colour of something

what colour is your car?	= ta voiture est de quelle couleur?
	(*more formally*) de quelle couleur est ta voiture?
it's green	= elle est verte
to paint something green	= peindre quelque chose en vert

Describing people

Note the use of **les**:

to have brown eyes	= avoir **les** yeux marron

Note the use of **à**:

the girl with the blond hair = la fille **aux** cheveux blonds

---

collection *noun*
- (*a set*)
  a collection = une collection
  she has a great collection of posters
     = elle a une super* collection d'affiches
- (*money collected*)
  a collection = une collecte

college *noun*
  a college = un établissement
     d'enseignement supérieur
  to go to college, to be at college = faire
     des études supérieures

colour (*British English*), **color** (*US English*)
1 *noun*
  a colour = une couleur
  what colour is the car? = de quelle
     couleur est la voiture?
2 *verb*
  to colour the drawings (in) = colorier les
     dessins

colourful (*British English*), **colorful** (*US English*) *adjective*
  a colourful shirt = une chemise aux
     couleurs vives

colour television (*British English*),
color television (*US English*) *noun*
  a colour television = une télévision (en)
     couleur

comb
1 *noun*
  a comb = un peigne
2 *verb*
  to comb one's hair = se peigner (**!** + *être*)

come *verb*
- **to come** = venir (**!** + *être*)
  she's coming today = elle vient
     aujourd'hui
  come to Paris with us = viens avec nous à
     Paris
  we came by bike = nous sommes venus à
     bicyclette
  come and see! = venez voir!
  I'm coming! = j'arrive!
  is the bus coming? = est-ce que le bus
     arrive?
  **be careful when you come down the
     stairs** = faites attention en descendant
     l'escalier
  he won't come into the house = il ne veut
     pas entrer dans la maison
  to come through the city centre = passer
     par le centre-ville
- (*to call around*) = passer (**!** + *être*)
- (*to reach*)
  **turn left when you come to the traffic
     lights** = tournez à gauche quand vous
     arriverez aux feux
- (*to attend*) = venir (**!** + *être*)
  will you be able to come to the meeting?
     = est-ce que tu pourras venir à la
     réunion?

- (*to be a native or a product of*)
  she comes from Italy = elle est italienne
  the strawberries all come from Spain
    = toutes les fraises viennent d'Espagne
- (*in a contest*)
  to come first = arriver premier/première
come around ▶ come round
come back = revenir (**!** + *être*)
  to come back home = rentrer (**!** + *être*)
come in
- (*to enter*) = entrer (**!** + *être*)
- (*if it's a plane, a train*) = arriver (**!** + *être*)
- **the tide's coming in** = la marée monte
come off
  (*if it's a cover, a lid*) = s'enlever (**!** + *être*)
  (*if it's a button, a label*) = se détacher
    (**!** + *être*)
come on
- (*to start to work*) (*if it's heating*) = se mettre
  en marche
  (*if it's a light*) = s'allumer (**!** + *être*)
- (*when encouraging someone*)
  come on, hurry up! = allez, dépêchez-
  vous!
  come on, you can do better than that!
    = allez, tu peux faire mieux!
come on to (*US English*)
  to come on to someone = draguer
  quelqu'un*
come out
- (*to leave a place*) = sortir (**!** + *être*)
  I saw him as I was coming out of the shop
    = je l'ai vu en sortant du magasin
- (*to become available*)
  (*if it's a film*) = sortir (**!** + *être*)
  (*if it's a book*) = paraître (**!** + *être*)
- (*to wash out*) = s'en aller (**!** + *être*)
- (*if it's a photo*)
  the photo didn't come out = la photo est
  ratée
- (*if it's smoke, fire*)
  **there are flames coming out of the
  windows** = il y a des flammes qui
  sortent par les fenêtres
come round
- (*to visit*) = venir (**!** + *être*)
- (*after a faint*) = reprendre connaissance
come to
  the meal came to 75 francs = le repas a
  coûté 75 francs
  how much does it come to? = ça fait
  combien?
come up
- (*to be discussed*)
  to come up in conversation = être
  abordé/abordée dans la conversation
- (*if it's the sun*) = se lever (**!** + *être*)

comfortable *adjective*
- (*if it's a chair, a bed*) = confortable
  are you comfortable? = êtes-vous bien
  installés?
- (*relaxed*) = à l'aise
- (*having enough money*) = aisé/aisée

comforter *noun* (*US English*)
  a comforter = une couette

comic strip *noun*
  a comic strip = une bande dessinée, une
  BD

commercial
1 *adjective*
  = commercial/commerciale
2 *noun*
  a commercial = une publicité

commit *verb*
  to commit a crime = commettre un crime

common *adjective*
  = courant/courante

communicate *verb*
  = communiquer

community *noun*
  a community = une communauté

company *noun*
- (*a business*)
  a company = une société
- (*a group of actors*)
  a theatre company = une troupe de
  théâtre
- (*other people*)
  company = la compagnie
  to keep someone company = tenir
  compagnie à quelqu'un
  to keep bad company = avoir de
  mauvaises fréquentations

company secretary *noun* ▶ 315
  a company secretary = un secrétaire
  général

compare *verb*
  = comparer
  to compare France with Italy = comparer
  la France à l'Italie
  she compares herself to her older sister
    = elle se compare à sa sœur aînée

compass *noun*
  a compass = une boussole

competition *noun*
- **competition** = la concurrence
  **there's a lot of competition between the
  schools** = il y a beaucoup de
  concurrence entre les écoles
- (*a contest*)
  a competition = un concours
  a drawing competition = un concours de
  dessin

competitive *adjective*
  to be competitive = avoir l'esprit de la
  compétition

complain *verb*
  = se plaindre (**!** + *être*)
  to complain about the food = se plaindre
  de la nourriture

complete
1 *adjective*
it was a complete disaster = c'était un désastre total
this is a complete waste of time = c'est vraiment du temps perdu
2 *verb*
= terminer
to complete a training course = terminer un stage de formation

completely *adverb*
= complètement

complicate *verb*
= compliquer

complicated *adjective*
= compliqué/compliquée

compliment
1 *noun*
a compliment = un compliment
2 *verb*
to compliment someone = faire des compliments à quelqu'un

comprehensive *noun* (*British English*)
a comprehensive = une école (publique) secondaire

compulsory *adjective*
= obligatoire

computer *noun*
a computer = un ordinateur

computer game *noun*
a computer game (*the game*) = un jeu électronique
(*the software*) = un logiciel de jeu

computer programmer *noun* ▶ 315 |
a computer programmer = un programmeur/une programmeuse

computer scientist *noun* ▶ 315 |
a computer scientist = un informaticien/une informaticienne

computer studies *noun*
computer studies = l'informatique (*feminine*)

concentrate *verb*
= se concentrer (**!** + *être*)

concert *noun*
a concert = un concert
in concert at Wembley = en concert à Wembley

concert hall *noun*
a concert hall = une salle de concert

concrete *noun*
concrete = le béton

condemn *verb*
to condemn someone to death
= condamner quelqu'un à mort

condition
1 *noun*
a condition = un état
in a terrible condition = dans un état lamentable
the car is in good condition = la voiture est en bon état
2 on condition that = à condition que
you can go on condition that her parents drive you home = tu peux y aller à condition que ses parents te ramènent
! *Note that the subjunctive is used after* à condition que.

condom *noun*
a condom = un préservatif

conductor *noun* ▶ 315 |
a conductor = un chef d'orchestre

cone *noun*
a cone = un cornet

conference *noun*
a conference = une conférence

confidence *noun*
• confidence = l'assurance (*feminine*)
• (*trust*)
to have confidence in someone = avoir confiance en quelqu'un

confident *adjective*
= sûr de soi
she's a confident girl = c'est une fille sûre d'elle

confidential *adjective*
= confidentiel/confidentielle

confiscate *verb*
= confisquer

conflict *noun*
a conflict = un conflit

confused *adjective*
to get confused = s'embrouiller (**!** + *être*)

congratulate *verb*
= féliciter

congratulations *noun* (also exclamation)
congratulations! = félicitations!

connection *noun*
a connection = un rapport
it has no connection with the strike = cela n'a aucun rapport avec la grève

conscientious *adjective*
= consciencieux/consciencieuse

conscious *adjective*
• (*aware*) = conscient/consciente
• (*after an operation*) = réveillé/réveillée

construct *verb*
= construire

consult *verb*
= consulter

contact
1 *noun*
  to be in contact with someone = être en contact avec quelqu'un
  to lose contact = perdre contact
2 *verb*
  = contacter

contact lens *noun*
  a contact lens = une lentille de contact

contain *verb*
  = contenir

content *adjective*
  = content/contente

contest *noun*
  a contest = un concours
  the Eurovision song contest = le concours Eurovision de la chanson

continent *noun*
• (*a large mass of land*)
  a continent = un continent
• (*British English*) (*Europe*)
  the Continent = l'Europe continentale

continental quilt *noun* (*British English*)
  a continental quilt = une couette

continue *verb*
  = continuer
  to continue to talk, to continue talking = continuer à parler
  to continue down the street = continuer à descendre la rue

continuous *adjective*
  = incessant/incessante
  the continuous noise of the traffic = le bruit incessant de la circulation

contraception *noun*
  contraception = la contraception

contract *noun*
  a contract = un contrat
  to have a two-year contract = avoir un contrat de deux ans

contradict *verb*
  = contredire

contradiction *noun*
  a contradiction = une contradiction

contrast *noun*
  a contrast = un contraste

contribute *verb*
• (*to give money*) = donner (de l'argent)
• **to contribute to a discussion** = participer à une discussion

control
1 *noun*
  to take control of a situation = prendre une situation en main
  to lose control of a car = perdre le contrôle d'une voiture

2 *verb*
  to control a region = contrôler une région
  to control traffic = diriger la circulation

convenient *adjective*
• (*useful, practical*) = pratique
  it's more convenient to take the bus = il est plus pratique de prendre le bus
• (*suitable*) = pratique
  it's a convenient place to meet = c'est un endroit pratique pour se retrouver
  it's not convenient for me = ça ne me convient pas

conversation *noun*
  a conversation = une conversation
  to make conversation = faire la conversation

convince *verb*
  = convaincre

cook
1 *verb*
• (*to prepare food*) = faire la cuisine, cuisiner
  to cook a meal = préparer un repas
  to cook vegetables = faire cuire des légumes
• (*to be cooked in the oven*) = cuire
2 *noun* ▶ **315** |
  a cook = un cuisinier/une cuisinière

cooker *noun* (*British English*)
  a cooker = une cuisinière

cookie *noun* (*US English*)
  a cookie = un gâteau sec, un biscuit

cooking *noun*
  cooking = la cuisine
  to do the cooking = faire la cuisine

cool *adjective*
• (*fresh, not hot*) = frais/fraîche
  a cool drink = une boisson fraîche
  it's much cooler today = il fait beaucoup plus frais aujourd'hui
• (*calm*) = calme
• (*fashionable*) = branché/branchée✱
• (*relaxed*) = décontracté/décontractée

cool down
• (*to get colder*) = refroidir
• (*to calm down*) = se calmer (**!** + *être*)

cooperate *verb*
  = coopérer

cope *verb*
• (*to manage*) = se débrouiller (**!** + *être*)
• **to cope with pain** = supporter la douleur

copper *noun*
  copper = le cuivre

copy
1 *noun*
  a copy = une copie
2 *verb*
  = copier
  to copy in an exam = copier à un examen

✱ in informal situations

copy down, copy out = recopier

cork *noun*
- a cork = un bouchon
- cork = le liège

corkscrew *noun*
a corkscrew = un tire-bouchon

corner *noun*
- (*of a street, a building*)
the corner = l'angle (*masculine*)
= le coin
the shop on the corner = le magasin qui fait l'angle
to go around the corner = tourner au coin de la rue
- (*in football, hockey*)
a corner = un corner

correct
1 *adjective*
= bon/bonne (**!** *before the noun*), correct/correcte
the correct answer = la bonne réponse, la réponse correcte
that is correct = c'est exact
2 *verb*
= corriger

correction *noun*
a correction = une correction

corridor *noun*
a corridor = un couloir

cost *verb*
= coûter
how much does it cost? = ça coûte combien?
it costs a lot of money = ça coûte très cher

costume *noun*
a costume = un costume

cosy *adjective* (*British English*)
a cosy room = une pièce confortable

cot *noun* (*British English*)
a cot = un lit de bébé

cottage *noun*
a cottage = une petite maison

cotton *noun*
- (*the material*)
cotton = le coton
- (*the thread*)
cotton = le fil de coton

cotton wool *noun* (*British English*)
cotton wool = le coton hydrophile

couch *noun*
a couch = un canapé

cough *verb*
= tousser

could *verb*
- (*had the possibility*)
I couldn't move = je ne pouvais pas bouger
he couldn't sleep for weeks = il n'a pas pu dormir pendant des semaines

- (*knew how to*)
she could read at the age of three = elle savait lire à l'âge de trois ans
he couldn't type = il ne savait pas taper à la machine
I couldn't speak any German = je ne parlais pas allemand
- (*when talking about seeing, hearing, understanding, you don't translate* could)
I couldn't see a thing = je n'y voyais rien
he could hear them = il les entendait
they couldn't understand me = ils ne me comprenaient pas
- (*when implying that something did not happen*)
she could have become a doctor = elle aurait pu devenir médecin
you could have apologized! = tu aurais pu t'excuser!
- (*when indicating a possibility*)
they could be wrong = ils se trompent peut-être
a bike could be useful = un vélo pourrait être utile
- (*when asking, offering or suggesting*)
could I speak to Annie? = est-ce que je pourrais parler à Annie?
could you take a message? = est-ce que vous pourriez prendre un message?
we could ask Gary = nous pourrions demander à Gary

count *verb*
= compter
count on
to count on someone = compter sur quelqu'un

counter *noun*
a counter (*in a shop*) = un comptoir
(*in a bank, a post office*) = un guichet
(*in a bar*) = un bar, un comptoir

country *noun*
- (*a state*)
a country = un pays
- (*the countryside*)
the country = la campagne
to live in the country = vivre à la campagne

countryside *noun*
the countryside = la campagne

couple *noun*
- a couple of days (*two days*) = deux jours
(*a few days*) = deux ou trois jours
- (*two people*)
a couple = un couple

courage *noun*
courage = le courage

courageous *adjective*
= courageux/courageuse

course
1 *noun*
- (*a series of lessons or lectures*)
a course = un cours

Countries, cities, and continents

Countries and continents

Most countries and all continents are used with the definite article in French:

*I like France	Canada*	= j'aime **la** France / **le** Canada
to visit the United States	= visiter **les** États-Unis

All the continent names are feminine in French. Generally, the names of countries ending in **e** are feminine and the rest are mostly masculine. Some names of countries are plural, eg **les États-Unis**.

In, to, and from somewhere

With continent names and feminine singular names of countries, for **in** and **to** use **en**, and for **from** use **de** (or **d'** before a vowel or mute 'h'):

*to go **to** Europe / **to** France*	= aller **en** Europe / **en** France
*to come **from** France / **from** Germany*	= venir **d'**Europe / **d'**Allemagne

With masculine names of countries beginning with a consonant, use **au** for **in** and **to**, and **du** for **from** and with masculine names of countries beginning with a vowel use **en** for **in** and **to**, and **d'** for from

*to live **in** Canada / **in** Iraq*	= vivre **au** Canada / **en** Irak
*to come **from** Japan / **from** Iraq*	= venir **du** Japon / **d'**Irak

With plurals, use **aux** for **in** and **to**, and **des** for **from**

*to live **in the** United States*	= vivre **aux** États-Unis
*to come **from the** United States*	= venir **des** États-Unis

Towns and cities

For **in** and **to** with the name of a town, use **à** in French; if the French name includes the definite article, **à** will become **au**, **à la**, **à l'** or **aux**.

*to live **in** Toulouse / **in le** Havre /*	= vivre **à** Toulouse / **au** Havre /
***in la** Rochelle / **in les** Arcs*	**à la** Rochelle / **aux** Arcs

Similarly, **from** is **de**, becoming **du**, **de la**, **de l'** or **des** when it combines with the definite article in town names:

*to come **from** Toulouse / **from le** Havre /*	= venir **de** Toulouse / **du** Havre /
***from la** Rochelle / **from les** Arc*	**de la** Rochelle / **des** Arcs

---

a language course = un cours de langue
- (*part of a meal*)
  a course = un plat
  what's the main course? = qu'est-ce qu'il y a comme plat principal?

2 of course = bien sûr
  of course not! = bien sûr que non!

court *noun*
- (*of law*)
  a court = une cour, un tribunal
  to go to court = aller devant les tribunaux
- (*for playing sports*)
  a tennis court = un court de tennis
  a basketball court = un terrain de basket

court case *noun*
  a court case = un procès

cousin *noun*
  a cousin = un cousin/une cousine

cover
1 *verb*
- **to cover** = couvrir
  to be covered in spots = être couvert/couverte de boutons
- (*to decorate*)
  to cover a cake with chocolate = recouvrir un gâteau de chocolat
2 *noun*
- (*a lid*)
  a cover = un couvercle
- (*for a cushion, a quilt*)
  a cover = une housse
- (*a blanket*)
  a cover = une couverture
- (*on a book, a magazine, an exercise book*)
  the cover = la couverture

cow *noun*
  a cow = une vache

coward *noun*
  a coward = un lâche/une lâche

cowboy noun
a cowboy = un cowboy

cozy adjective (US English)
a cozy room = une pièce confortable

crab noun
a crab = un crabe

crack verb
• (to damage) = fêler
• (to get damaged) = se fêler (**!** + être)
• (to get broken) = se casser (**!** + être)

cradle noun
a cradle = un berceau

cramp noun
a cramp = une crampe

crash
1 noun
a crash = un accident
a car crash = un accident de voiture
2 verb
to crash into a tree = rentrer dans un arbre
the plane crashed = l'avion s'est écrasé

crayon noun
a crayon = une craie grasse

crazy adjective
= fou/folle

cream noun
cream = la crème

create verb
= créer
to create employment = créer des emplois

credit noun
credit = le crédit
they don't give credit = ils ne font pas crédit

credit card noun
a credit card = une carte de crédit

cricket noun ▶ 248 |
cricket = le cricket

crime noun
• (a criminal act)
a crime (serious) = un crime
(minor) = un délit
• (in general)
crime = la criminalité

criminal
1 noun
a criminal = un criminel/une criminelle
2 adjective
= criminel/criminelle

crisis noun
a crisis = une crise

crisps noun (British English)
crisps = les chips (feminine)

critical adjective
= critique

criticize verb
= critiquer

crocodile noun
a crocodile = un crocodile

crooked adjective
a crooked line = une ligne brisée
the picture is crooked = le tableau est de travers

cross
1 verb
• (to go across)
to cross the road = traverser la rue
to cross the Channel = traverser la Manche
to cross the border = passer la frontière
to cross into Italy = passer en Italie
• (other uses)
to cross one's legs = croiser les jambes
our letters crossed = nos lettres se sont croisées
2 noun
a cross = une croix
3 adjective
= fâché/fâchée
to get cross = se fâcher (**!** + être)
cross out = rayer

crossroads noun
a crossroads = un carrefour

crossword puzzle noun
a crossword puzzle = des mots croisés
! Note that mots is masculine plural.

crow noun
a crow = un corbeau

crowd noun
• (a large number of people)
a crowd = une foule
crowds of people = une foule de gens
• (watching a game)
the crowd = les spectateurs (masculine plural)

crown noun
a crown = une couronne

cruel adjective
= cruel/cruelle

cruelty noun
cruelty = la cruauté

cruise noun
a cruise = une croisière

crush verb
= écraser

crutch noun
a crutch = une béquille

cry
1 verb
= pleurer
2 noun
a cry = un cri

C

cub *noun*
a cub = un petit

cuckoo *noun*
a cuckoo = un coucou

cucumber *noun*
a cucumber = un concombre

cuddle *noun*
a cuddle = un câlin
to give someone a cuddle = faire un câlin à quelqu'un

culprit *noun*
a culprit = un coupable/une coupable

cultural *adjective*
= culturel/culturelle

culture *noun*
culture = la culture

cunning *adjective*
(*describing a person*) = rusé/rusée
(*describing a plan*) = habile

cup *noun*
• a cup = une tasse
a cup of coffee = une tasse de café
• (*in sport*)
a cup = une coupe

cupboard *noun*
a cupboard = un placard

curb *noun* (*US English*)
the curb = le bord du trottoir

cure
1 *verb*
= guérir
2 *noun*
a cure = un traitement

curious *adjective*
= curieux/curieuse

curly *adjective*
= frisé/frisée
to have curly hair = avoir les cheveux frisés

currency *noun*
a currency = une monnaie
foreign currency = les devises étrangères
  ! *Note that* **devises** *is feminine plural.*

curry *noun*
a curry = un curry

curtain *noun*
a curtain = un rideau
to draw the curtains = tirer les rideaux

cushion *noun*
a cushion = un coussin

custard *noun* (*British English*)
custard ≈ la crème anglaise

custom *noun*
a custom = une coutume

customer *noun*
a customer = un client/une cliente

customs *noun*
customs = la douane
to go through customs = passer à la douane

customs officer *noun* ▶ 315|
a customs officer = un douanier/une douanière

cut
1 *verb*
= couper
to cut an apple in half = couper une pomme en deux
to cut [one's fingers | one's knee | one's foot …] = se couper [les doigts | le genou | le pied …]
she cut herself = elle s'est coupée
to have one's hair cut = se faire couper les cheveux
I got my hair cut = je me suis fait couper les cheveux
2 *noun*
a cut = une coupure
cut down = abattre
cut out
to cut a photo out of a magazine = découper une photo dans un magazine
cut up = couper

cute *adjective*
= mignon/mignonne

CV *noun*
a CV = un CV, un curriculum vitae

cycle *verb*
to cycle to school = aller à l'école à vélo
to go cycling = faire du vélo

cycle lane, cycle path *noun*
a cycle lane = une piste cyclable

cycling *noun* ▶ 248|
cycling = le cyclisme

cyclist *noun*
a cyclist = un cycliste/une cycliste

cynical *adjective*
= cynique

Czech Republic *noun* ▶ 218|
the Czech Republic = la République tchèque

Dd

dad, Dad noun
  a dad = un papa

daffodil noun
  a daffodil = une jonquille

daisy noun
  a daisy = une pâquerette

damage
1 verb
• to damage = abîmer
  the building was damaged by the fire = le bâtiment a été endommagé par l'incendie
• (to harm) = nuire à
  it can damage your health = cela nuit à la santé
2 noun
  damage = les dégâts (masculine plural)
  to cause damage = faire des dégâts

damp adjective
  = humide

dance
1 verb
  = danser
2 noun
  a dance = une danse

dancer noun ▶ 315 |
  a dancer = un danseur/une danseuse

dancing noun
  dancing = la danse

danger noun
  danger = le danger
  to be in danger = être en danger

dangerous adjective
  = dangereux/dangereuse

Danish ▶ 275 |
1 adjective
  = danois/danoise
2 noun
  Danish = le danois

dare verb
• (to have the courage) = oser
• (when testing someone)
  to dare someone to play a trick = défier quelqu'un de jouer un tour
• (when expressing anger)
  don't dare speak to me like that! = je t'interdis de me parler sur ce ton!

dark
1 adjective
• (lacking light) = sombre
  it's getting dark = il commence à faire nuit

• (describing a colour, clothes) ▶ 213 |
  = sombre
  he always wears dark clothes = il porte toujours des vêtements sombres
  a dark blue dress = une robe bleu foncé
• (describing a person) = brun/brune
2 noun
  the dark = le noir, l'obscurité (feminine)

darts noun ▶ 248 |
  darts = les fléchettes (feminine)

date noun ▶ 222 |
• (in a calendar)
  a date = une date
  what date is today? = quelle est la date aujourd'hui?
• (with a friend)
  a date = un rendez-vous
  to go out on a date with someone = sortir avec quelqu'un

daughter noun
  a daughter = une fille

daughter-in-law noun
  a daughter-in-law = une belle-fille

dawn noun
  dawn = l'aube (feminine)
  at dawn = à l'aube

day noun ▶ 356 |

  ! Note that day is usually translated by jour in French. However it is sometimes translated by journée, when there is an emphasis on the idea of duration.

  a day = un jour
  what day is it today? = quel jour sommes-nous aujourd'hui?
  during the day = pendant la journée
  we had a very nice day = nous avons passé une journée très agréable
  the next day, the day after = le lendemain
  the day before = la veille

daylight noun
  daylight = le jour, la lumière du jour

dazzle verb
  = éblouir

dead adjective
  = mort/morte
  he is dead = il est mort

deaf adjective
  = sourd/sourde

deal
1 noun
• a deal (in business) = une affaire
  (with a friend) = un marché
• a great deal [of money | of time | of energy …]
  = beaucoup [d'argent | de temps | d'énergie …]
2 verb
  to deal the cards = distribuer les cartes
deal with = s'occuper de (! + être)
  to deal with a problem = s'occuper d'un problème

Dates, days, and months

The days of the week

Note that French uses lower-case letters for the names of days.

Write the names of days in full; do not abbreviate as in English (*Tues, Sat* and so on).

Monday	= lundi
Tuesday	= mardi
Wednesday	= mercredi
Thursday	= jeudi
Friday	= vendredi
Saturday	= samedi
Sunday	= dimanche

lundi in the notes below stands for any day; they all work the same way. Note the use of **le** for regular occurrences, and no article for single ones. (*Remember: do not translate* **on**.)

on Monday	= lundi
on Mondays	= le lundi
Monday afternoon	= lundi après-midi
*last	next Monday*	= lundi dernier	prochain
last Monday night	= la nuit de lundi dernier
	(*if evening*) lundi dernier dans la soirée
early on Monday	= lundi matin de bonne heure
late on Monday	= lundi soir tard
a month from Monday	= dans un mois lundi
from Monday on	= à partir de lundi

The months of the year

As with the days of the week, do not use capitals to spell the names of the months in French, and do not abbreviate as in English (*Jan, Feb* and so on).

January	= janvier	*July*	= juillet
February	= février	*August*	= août
March	= mars	*September*	= septembre
April	= avril	*October*	= octobre
May	= mai	*November*	= novembre
June	= juin	*December*	= décembre

May in the notes below stands for any month; they all work the same way.

in May	= en mai	au mois de mai
next May	= en mai prochain
last May	= l'année dernière en mai
*in early	late May*	= début	fin mai

Dates

French has only one generally accepted way of writing dates: **le 10 mai** (say **le dix mai**).

If the days of the week is included, put it after the **le**:

Monday, May 1st 1901	= le lundi 1er mai 1901
what's the date?	= quel jour sommes-nous?
it's the tenth of May	= nous sommes le 10 mai	on est le 10 mai
in 1968	= en 1968
in the year 2000	= en l'an 2000
in the seventeenth century	= au dix-septième siècle

	Write	**Say**
May 1	le 1er mai	le premier mai
May 2	le 2 mai	le deux mai
from 4th to 16th May	du 4 au 16 mai	du quatre au seize mai
May 6 1968	le 6 mai 1968	le six mai mille neuf cent soixante-huit
in the 1980s	dans les années 80	dans les années quatre-vingt
the 16th century	le XVIe siècle	le seizième siècle

dear
1 *adjective*
• (*in letters*) = cher/chère
  Dear Anne = Chère Anne
  Dear Anne and Paul = Chers Anne et Paul
  Dear Sir/Madam = Monsieur, Madame
• (*expensive*) = cher/chère
2 *exclamation* ▶ **237** |
  oh dear! = oh mon Dieu!

death *noun*
  death = la mort

death penalty *noun*
  the death penalty = la peine de mort

debate *noun*
  a debate = un débat

debt *noun*
  a debt = une dette
  to be in debt = avoir des dettes

decade *noun*
  a decade = une décennie

decaffeinated *adjective*
  = décaféiné/décaféinée

deceive *verb*
  = tromper

December *noun* ▶ **222** |
  December = décembre (*masculine*)

decide *verb*
  = décider
  he decided [to accept | to stay | to get
  married …] = il a décidé [d'accepter | de
  rester | de se marier …]

decision *noun*
  a decision = une décision
  to make a decision = prendre une
  décision

deck *noun*
  a deck = un pont
  on deck = sur le pont

deckchair *noun*
  a deckchair = une chaise longue

decorate *verb*
• (*with ornaments*) = décorer
• (*with wallpaper*) = tapisser
  (*to paint*) = peindre

decoration *noun*
  a decoration = une décoration

deep *adjective* ▶ **285** |
  = profond/profonde
  how deep is the lake? = quelle est la
  profondeur du lac?
  the hole is three metres deep = le trou fait
  trois mètres de profondeur

deer *noun*
  a deer (*male*) = un cerf
  (*female*) = une biche

defeat
1 *verb*
  to defeat an enemy = vaincre un ennemi
  the team was defeated = l'équipe a été
  battue
2 *noun*
  a defeat = une défaite

defence (*British English*), **defense** (*US
English*) *noun*
  defence = la défense

defend *verb*
  = défendre

definite *adjective*
• (*describing a decision*) = ferme
  (*describing a plan*) = précis/précise
  nothing is definite = rien n'est sûr
• (*obvious, visible*) = net/nette
  a definite improvement = une nette
  amélioration

definitely *adverb*
  = sans aucun doute
  they're definitely lying = ils mentent sans
  aucun doute
  I'm definitely coming = c'est décidé, je
  viens
  'definitely!' = 'absolument!'

defy *verb*
  = défier

degree *noun*
• (*from a university*)
  a degree = un diplôme universitaire
• (*in measurements*)
  a degree = un degré

delay
1 *verb*
  = retarder
2 *noun*
  a delay = un retard

deliberate *adjective*
  = délibéré/délibérée

deliberately *adverb*
  = exprès
  he did it deliberately = il l'a fait exprès

delicious *adjective*
  = délicieux/délicieuse

delighted *adjective*
  = ravi/ravie
  to be delighted with a present = être
  ravi/ravie d'un cadeau

deliver *verb*
  = livrer
  to deliver goods = livrer des marchandises
  to deliver mail = distribuer le courrier

demand *verb*
  = exiger

demolish *verb*
  = démolir

D

demonstration *noun*
a demonstration = une manifestation

denim jacket *adjective*
a denim jacket = un blouson en jean

Denmark *noun* ▶ 218 |
Denmark = le Danemark

dentist *noun* ▶ 315 |
a dentist = un dentiste/une dentiste

deny *verb*
= nier

department *noun*
a department (*in a firm*) = un service
(*in a large store*) = un rayon
(*in a school*) = une section
(*in a university*) = un département

department store *noun*
a department store = un grand magasin

depend *verb*
= dépendre
to depend on someone = dépendre de
    quelqu'un
it depends on you = cela dépend de toi
it depends = ça dépend

depressed *adjective*
= déprimé/déprimée

depressing *adjective*
= déprimant/déprimante

deprive *verb*
= priver

depth *noun* ▶ 285 |
depth = la profondeur

describe *verb*
= décrire

description *noun*
a description = une description

desert *noun*
a desert = un désert

deserve *verb*
= mériter
he deserves to be punished = il mérite
    d'être puni

design
1 *verb*
• (*to plan*) = concevoir
the house was designed for a hot climate
    = la maison a été conçue pour un climat
    chaud
• (*in fashion*)
to design clothes = créer des vêtements
2 *noun*
• (*a subject of study*)
(fashion) design = le stylisme
• (*a pattern*)
a design = un motif

desk *noun*
a desk = un bureau

desperate *adjective*
= désespéré/désespérée

dessert *noun*
a dessert = un dessert

destroy *verb*
= détruire

detail *noun*
a detail = un détail
to go into details = entrer dans les détails

detective *noun* ▶ 315 |
a detective = un inspecteur de police
a private detective = un détective

detective story *noun*
a detective story = un roman policier

determined *adjective*
= déterminé/déterminée
to be determined to go = être
    décidé/décidée à y aller

develop *verb*
= développer

development *noun*
a development = un développement

diagram *noun*
a diagram = un schéma

dial *verb*
to dial a number = composer un numéro

dialling code *noun* (*British English*)
a dialling code = un indicatif

dialling tone (*British English*), **dial
tone** (*US English*) *noun*
a dialling tone = une tonalité

diamond *noun*
a diamond = un diamant

diary *noun*
• (*for personal thoughts*)
a diary = un journal
• (*for appointments*)
a diary = un agenda

dice *noun*
a dice = un dé

dictionary *noun*
a dictionary = un dictionnaire

die *verb*
• to die = mourir (**!** + *être*)
he died in the war = il est mort à la guerre
to be dying of cancer = être
    atteint/atteinte d'un cancer incurable
• (*used for emphasis*)
I'm dying to go on holiday = je meurs
    d'envie de partir en vacances

diet *noun*
a diet = un régime
to go on a diet = se mettre au régime

difference noun
a difference = une différence
I can't tell the difference = je ne vois pas la différence
it won't make any difference = ça ne changera rien
what difference does it make? = qu'est-ce que ça change?

different adjective
= différent/différente

difficult adjective
= difficile
Spanish is not difficult to learn = l'espagnol n'est pas difficile à apprendre
to be difficult to get along with = être difficile à vivre

difficulty noun
a difficulty = une difficulté, un problème
to have difficulty concentrating = avoir du mal à se concentrer

dig verb
= creuser
dig up
• (when gardening) = bêcher
• (to find what was buried) = déterrer

dim adjective
• (describing a light) = faible
• (describing a room) = sombre

diner noun (US English)
a diner = un café-restaurant

dinghy noun
a dinghy = un dériveur

dining room noun
a dining room = une salle à manger

dinner noun
a dinner = un dîner
dinner's ready! = à table!

dip verb
= tremper

direct
1 adjective
= direct/directe
2 verb
• (when talking about directions)
could you direct me to the station? = pourriez-vous m'indiquer le chemin pour aller à la gare?
• (in cinema or theatre)
to direct a film = réaliser un film
to direct a play = mettre en scène une pièce

direction noun
a direction = une direction, un sens
is this the right direction? = est-ce que c'est la bonne direction?
they were going in the other direction = ils allaient dans l'autre sens

directions noun
directions = les indications (feminine)
to give someone directions = donner des indications à quelqu'un
to ask someone for directions = demander le chemin à quelqu'un

director noun ▶ 315 |
• (of a film or play)
a director = un metteur en scène
• (of a company)
a director = un directeur/une directrice

dirt noun
dirt = la saleté

dirty
1 adjective
= sale
to get dirty = se salir (**!** + être)
2 verb
= salir

disabled adjective
= handicapé/handicapée

disadvantage noun
a disadvantage = un désavantage

disagree verb
= ne pas être d'accord
I disagree with you = je ne suis pas d'accord avec toi

disappear verb
= disparaître

disappoint verb
= décevoir

disappointed adjective
= déçu/déçue

disappointing adjective
= décevant/décevante

disappointment noun
disappointment = la déception

disapprove verb
to disapprove of someone = ne pas apprécier quelqu'un

disaster noun
a disaster = une catastrophe, un désastre

discipline noun
discipline = la discipline

disco noun
a disco = une discothèque

disconnect verb
• (to pull out a plug) = débrancher
• (to cut off) = couper

discourage verb
= décourager

discover verb
= découvrir

discovery noun
a discovery = une découverte

D

discreet adjective
= discret/discrète

discrimination noun
discrimination = la discrimination

discuss verb
= discuter de
to discuss politics = discuter de politique

discussion noun
a discussion = une discussion

disease noun ▶ 266|
a disease = une maladie

disguise
1 noun
a disguise = un déguisement
to wear a disguise = être déguisé/déguisée
2 verb
to disguise oneself as a woman = se
déguiser en femme

disgusting adjective
= dégoûtant/dégoûtante

dish noun
• (food)
a dish = un plat
• the dishes = la vaisselle (singular)
to wash the dishes = faire la vaisselle

dishonest adjective
= malhonnête

dishwasher noun
a dishwasher = un lave-vaisselle

dislike verb
= ne pas aimer
I dislike him = je ne l'aime pas

dismiss verb
= renvoyer

disobedient adjective
= désobéissant/désobéissante

disobey verb
to disobey someone = désobéir à
quelqu'un

display noun
a display = un étalage
a window display = une vitrine

dispute noun
a dispute (between individuals) = une
dispute
(between groups) = un conflit

disqualify verb
= disqualifier

disrupt verb
= perturber

dissatisfied adjective
= mécontent/mécontente

distance noun
a distance = une distance
in the distance = au loin
to keep one's distance = garder ses
distances

distinct adjective
• (easy to see, to hear) = distinct/distincte
• (definite) = net/nette (! before the noun)

distinguish verb
= distinguer
to distinguish between truth and lies
= faire la distinction entre la vérité et les
mensonges

distract verb
= distraire
to distract someone from working
= empêcher quelqu'un de travailler

distressed adjective
= bouleversé/bouleversée

distribute verb
= distribuer

disturb verb
= déranger

disturbing adjective
= troublant/troublante

dive verb ▶ 248|
= plonger
to go diving = faire de la plongée

divide verb
• (in arithmetic) = diviser
• (to share) = partager

diving board noun
a diving board = un plongeoir

divorce
1 noun
a divorce = un divorce
2 verb
= divorcer

DIY noun (British English)
DIY = le bricolage

dizzy adjective
to feel dizzy = avoir la tête qui tourne

do verb ▶ 237|
▶ 227| See the boxed note on **do** for more
information and examples.
• to do = faire
to do the cooking = faire la cuisine
to do one's homework = faire ses devoirs
what has he done with the newspaper?
= qu'est-ce qu'il a fait du journal?
what has she done to her hair? = qu'est-ce
qu'elle a fait à ses cheveux?
do as you're told = fais ce qu'on te dit
• (in questions, negatives)
do you like cats? = est-ce que tu aimes les
chats?
I don't like cats = je n'aime pas les chats
I didn't do anything = je n'ai rien fait
don't shout! = ne crie pas!

do

As an ordinary verb

Usually, the French equivalent of the verb **to do** is **faire**:

    *she is **doing** her homework*   = elle **fait** ses devoirs
    *what **has** he **done** with the newspaper?*   = qu'est-ce qu'il **a fait** du journal?

As an auxiliary verb

In questions

In French there is no auxiliary verb in questions equivalent to **do** in English.

When the subject is a pronoun, use either of these structures: *verb + hyphen + subject* or, less formally, **est-ce que** + *subject* + *verb*:

    ***do** you like Mozart?*   = aimes-tu Mozart?
     = **est-ce que** tu aimes Mozart?

When the subject is a noun, there are again two possibilities:

    ***did** your sister ring?*   = **est-ce que** ta sœur a téléphoné?
     = ta sœur a-t-elle téléphoné?

In negatives

Equally, auxiliaries are not used in negatives in French:

    *I **don't** like Mozart*   = je n'aime pas Mozart.

In emphatic uses

There is no verbal equivalent for the use of **do** in such expressions as *I do like your dress*. In emphatic uses, French may use an adverb like *beaucoup, vraiment*:

    *I **do** like your dress*   = j'aime **beaucoup** ta robe
    *I **do** think you should go*   = je pense **vraiment** que tu devrais y aller

When referring back to another verb

In this case the verb **to do** is not translated at all:

    *I live in Oxford and so **does** Lily*   = j'habite à Oxford et Lily aussi
    *she gets paid more than I **do***   = elle est payée plus que moi
    *'I don't like carrots' — 'neither **do** I'*   = 'je n'aime pas les carottes' — 'moi non plus'

In polite requests

In polite requests the phrase *je vous en prie* or *je t'en prie* is useful:

    ***do** sit down*   = asseyez-vous, **je vous en prie**

In imperatives

In French there is no use of an auxiliary verb in imperatives:

    ***don't** shut the door*   = ne ferme pas la porte
    ***do** be quiet*   = tais-toi!

In short questions

With questions like **doesn't he?** or **didn't he?**, there is a general French phrase question **n'est-ce pas?** which will work in many cases:

    *you like fish, **don't you?***   = tu aimes les poisson, **n'est-ce pas?**

With positive tag questions, **par hasard** can often be used as a translation:

    Lola didn't phone, did she?   = Lola n'a pas téléphoné **par hasard?**

In short answers

There is no direct French equivalent for the verb such as *no, he doesn't, yes, we did* etc.

    *'does he play tennis?' — '**no, he doesn't**'* = 'est-ce qu'il joue au tennis?' — '**non**'
    *'do you like strawberries?' —'**yes I do**'* = 'aimez-vous les fraises?' — '**oui**'

If answering 'yes' to contradict a negative statement, the most useful translation is **si**:

    *'Marion didn't say that' —'**yes she did**'* = 'Marion n'a pas dit ça' — '**si**'

▶ For more examples, see the entry **do**.

• (*in short answers and tag questions*)
  'do you like strawberries?'—'yes, I do'
  = 'est-ce que tu aimes les fraises?'—'oui'
  'I never said I liked him'—'yes, you did'
  = 'je n'ai jamais dit que je l'aimais'—'si,
  tu l'as dit'
  'I love chocolate'—'so do I!' = 'j'adore le
  chocolat'—'moi aussi!'
  'who wrote it?'—'I did' = 'qui l'a écrit?'
  —'moi'
  he lives in London, doesn't he? = il habite
  à Londres, n'est-ce-pas?
  Martine didn't phone, did she? = Martine
  n'a pas téléphoné, par hasard?
  'may I sit down?'—'yes, please do'
  = 'puis-je m'asseoir?'—'je t'en prie'
• (*to be enough*) = suffire
  ten pounds will do = dix livres suffiront
  that box will do = cette boîte fera l'affaire
• (*to perform*)
  he did well = il s'est bien débrouillé
  he did badly = il s'est mal débrouillé
do up (*British English*)
  to do up one's buttons = se boutonner
  (**!** + *être*)
  to do up a house = refaire une maison
do with
  it's got something to do with computers
  = ça a quelque chose à voir avec
  l'informatique
  it has nothing to do with him = ça n'a rien
  à voir avec lui
do without = se passer de (**!** + *être*)
  I can do without a television = je peux me
  passer de télévision

dock *noun*
  a dock = un dock

doctor *noun* ▶ 315 |
  a doctor = un médecin

document *noun*
  a document = un document

documentary *noun*
  a documentary = un documentaire

dog *noun*
  a dog = un chien

doll *noun*
  a doll = une poupée

dollar *noun*
  a dollar = un dollar

dolphin *noun*
  a dolphin = un dauphin

dominoes *noun* ▶ 248 |
  dominoes = les dominos (*masculine*)

donkey *noun*
  a donkey = un âne

door *noun*
  a door = une porte

doorbell *noun*
  a doorbell = une sonnette

dormitory *noun*
  a dormitory = un dortoir

dose *noun*
  a dose = une dose

double
1 *adjective*
• (*of an amount*) = double
  a double helping of strawberries = une
  double portion de fraises
• (*when spelling or giving a number*)
  Annie is spelled with a double 'n' = Annie
  s'écrit avec deux 'n'
  three double five (*British English*) = trois
  cent cinquante cinq
2 *verb*
  = doubler

double bass *noun* ▶ 290 |
  a double bass = une contrebasse

double bed *noun*
  a double bed = un grand lit

double-decker *noun*
  a double-decker = un autobus à impériale

double room *noun*
  a double room = une chambre pour deux
  personnes

doubt
1 *noun*
  a doubt = un doute
  there's no doubt that he is innocent = son
  innocence ne fait aucun doute
  I've no doubt that it's true = je suis certain
  que c'est vrai
2 *verb*
  = douter
  I doubt if she'll come = je doute qu'elle
  vienne

  ! *Note that the subjunctive is used after*
  douter que.

dough *noun*
  dough = la pâte

doughnut, donut (*US English*) *noun*
  a doughnut = un beignet

down

  ! *Often* down *occurs in combinations with
  verbs, for example:* calm down, let down,
  slow down *etc. To find the correct
  translations for this type of verb, look up
  the separate dictionary entries at* calm,
  let, slow *etc.*

1 *preposition*
  to go down the street = descendre la rue
  he walked down the corridor = il a
  descendu le couloir
  he ran down the hill = il a descendu la
  colline en courant
  the kitchen is down those stairs = la
  cuisine est en bas de cet escalier

2 *adverb*
  she's down in the cellar = elle est dans la cave
  down in Brighton = à Brighton
  to go down to the country = aller à la campagne
  to go down = descendre (**!** + *être*)
  to fall down = tomber (**!** + *être*)
  down there = là-bas

downstairs *adverb*
  = en bas
  to go downstairs = descendre (l'escalier)
  to bring the boxes downstairs
    = descendre les cartons

dozen *noun* ▶ 317 |
  a dozen = une douzaine
  a dozen eggs = une douzaine d'œufs

draft *noun* (*US English*)
  a draft = un courant d'air

drag *verb*
  = traîner

drain *verb*
- (*when cooking*) = égoutter
- (*if it's water*)
  to drain (away) = s'écouler (**!** + *être*)

drama *noun*
- (*a play, an event*)
  a drama = un drame
- (*theatre*)
  drama = le théâtre

dramatic *adjective*
  = spectaculaire

drapes *noun* (*US English*)
  drapes = les rideaux (*masculine*)

draught *noun* (*British English*)
  a draught = un courant d'air

draughts *noun* ▶ 248 | (*British English*)
  draughts = les dames (*feminine*)

draw
1 *verb*
- (*with a pen or pencil*) = dessiner
  to draw a rabbit = dessiner un lapin
  to draw a picture = faire un dessin
  to draw a line = tracer une ligne
  she drew his portrait = elle a fait son portrait
- (*to pull*) = tirer
  to draw the curtains = tirer les rideaux
- (*to take out*) = sortir
  to draw a knife = sortir un couteau
- (*in a lottery*)
  to draw a ticket = tirer un ticket au sort
- (*to attract*) = attirer
  the circus drew a large crowd = le cirque a attiré beaucoup de monde
- (*British English*) (*in sport*) = faire match nul
- **Christmas is drawing near** = Noël approche

2 *noun*
- (*in sport*)
  a draw = un match nul
- (*in a lottery*)
  a draw = un tirage au sort

draw aside
  to draw someone aside = prendre quelqu'un à part

draw back
  to draw back the curtains = ouvrir les rideaux

draw up
  to draw up a list = dresser une liste

drawer *noun*
  a drawer = un tiroir

drawing *noun*
  drawing = le dessin

dread *verb*
  = appréhender

dreadful *adjective*
  = épouvantable

dream
1 *noun* ▶ 237 |
  a dream = un rêve
  to have a dream = faire un rêve
2 *verb*
  = rêver
  to dream of going to Japan = rêver d'aller au Japon

dress
1 *noun*
  a dress = une robe
2 *verb*
- (*to put one's own clothes on*) = s'habiller (**!** + *être*)
- (*to put clothes on someone*) = habiller

dress up
- (*in good clothes*) = s'habiller (**!** + *être*)
- (*in a disguise*) = se déguiser (**!** + *être*)
  she dressed up as a clown = elle s'est déguisée en clown

dressing gown *noun*
  a dressing gown = une robe de chambre

drill
1 *noun*
  a drill = une perceuse
2 *verb*
  to drill a hole = percer un trou
  to drill through the wall = percer un trou dans le mur

drink
1 *verb*
  = boire
2 *noun*
  a drink = une boisson
  a drink of water = un verre d'eau

D

drive

1 *verb*
- (*in a car*) = conduire
  to learn to drive = apprendre à conduire
  he drives to work = il va au travail en voiture
  to drive someone home = ramener quelqu'un en voiture
- (*to make*)
  to drive someone mad = rendre quelqu'un fou/folle

2 *noun*
  a drive = un tour (en voiture)
  to go for a drive = aller faire un tour (en voiture)

drive away
- (*in a car*) = démarrer
- (*to chase away*) = chasser

drive back = rentrer (en voiture) (**!** + *être*)

driver *noun*
  a driver = un conducteur/une conductrice

driver's license (*US English*), **driving licence** (*British English*) *noun*
  a driver's license = un permis de conduire

drizzle *verb*
= bruiner

drop

1 *verb*
- (*to come down*) = baisser
  the temperature has dropped = la température a baissé
- (*to let fall*) = laisser tomber
  she dropped her suitcase = elle a laissé tomber sa valise
- (*to fall*) = tomber (**!** + *être*)

2 *noun*
- (*a fall*)
  a drop = une baisse
  a drop in temperature = une baisse de température
- (*of liquid*)
  a drop = une goutte

drop in = passer (**!** + *être*)
  he dropped in to see me = il est passé me voir

drop off = déposer
  could you drop me off at the station? = est-ce que tu pourrais me déposer à la gare?

drop out
  to drop out of school = abandonner ses études
  to drop out of a race = se retirer d'une course

drought *noun*
  a drought = une sécheresse

drown *verb*
= se noyer (**!** + *être*)

drug

1 *noun*
- (*for illegal use*)
  a drug = une drogue
  to be on drugs = se droguer (**!** + *être*)
- (*for medical use*)
  a drug = un médicament

2 *verb*
  to drug someone = droguer quelqu'un

drug addict *noun*
  a drug addict = un toxicomane/une toxicomane

drum *noun* ▶ **290**
  a drum = un tambour
  to play drums = jouer de la batterie

drunk *adjective*
= ivre

dry

1 *adjective*
= sec/sèche
  a dry day = une journée sans pluie

2 *verb*
  to dry clothes = faire sécher des vêtements
  to dry oneself = se sécher (**!** + *être*)
  he dried his hands = il s'est séché les mains
  to dry the dishes = essuyer la vaisselle

duck

1 *noun*
  a duck = un canard

2 *verb*
= baisser la tête

due

1 due to = à cause de
  the game was cancelled due to bad weather = le match a été annulé à cause du mauvais temps

2 *adjective*
- (*expected*)
  the train is due (in) at two o'clock = le train doit arriver à deux heures
- (*owed*) = dû/due
  the amount due = la somme due

dull *adjective*
- (*describing a person or book*) = terne
- (*describing a colour*) = terne
- (*describing the weather or a landscape*) = morne

dumb *adjective*
- (*unable to speak*) = muet/muette
- (*stupid*) = bête

dump

1 *verb*
= jeter

2 *noun*
  a dump = une décharge

during *preposition*
= pendant
  during the summer = pendant l'été

dust

1 *noun*
  dust = la poussière

2 *verb*
= épousseter

dustbin *noun* (*British English*)
a dustbin = une poubelle

dustman *noun* (*British English*)
a dustman = un éboueur

dustpan *noun*
a dustpan = une pelle (à poussière)

Dutch ▶ 275 |
1 *adjective*
= hollandais/hollandaise
2 *noun*
the Dutch = les Hollandais (*masculine plural*)

duty *noun*
• (*a task, part of one's job*)
a duty = une fonction
to take up one's duties = prendre ses fonctions
• (*of a soldier, a nurse*)
to be on duty = être de service
• (*what one must do*)
duty = le devoir
it's my duty to go = il est de mon devoir d'y aller
• (*a tax*)
customs duties = les droits de douane
! Note that **droits** is masculine.

dye *verb*
= teindre
to dye one's hair = se teindre les cheveux

Ee

each
1 *determiner*
= chaque
each time I see him = chaque fois que je le vois
2 *pronoun*
= chacun/chacune
each of the boys = chacun des garçons
each of them has a car, they each have a car = ils ont chacun/elles ont chacune une voiture

each other *pronoun*
! Note that **each other** is very often translated by using a reflexive pronoun like **se**, **s'**, **nous** or **vous**.

they know each other already = ils se connaissent déjà
we write to each other every year = nous nous écrivons tous les ans

eager *adjective*
= enthousiaste

eagle *noun*
an eagle = un aigle

ear *noun* ▶ 201 |
an ear = une oreille

early *adverb*
• **early** = tôt
to get up early = se lever tôt
early in the afternoon = en début d'après-midi
• (*ahead of time*) = en avance
to arrive early = arriver en avance

earn *verb*
to earn lots of money = gagner beaucoup d'argent

earring *noun*
an earring = une boucle d'oreille

earth *noun*
• (*the planet*)
the earth = la terre
• (*soil*)
earth = la terre

easily *adverb*
= facilement

east
1 *noun*
the east = l'est (*masculine*)
in the east of France = dans l'est de la France
2 *adverb*
to go east = aller vers l'est
to live east of Paris = vivre à l'est de Paris
3 *adjective*
= est (! *never changes*)
to work in east London = travailler dans l'est de Londres

Easter *noun*
Easter = Pâques (*feminine plural*)
Happy Easter! = Joyeuses Pâques!

Easter egg *noun*
an Easter egg = un œuf de Pâques

easy *adjective*
= facile
it's easy to fix = c'est facile à réparer
it's not easy to find work there = il n'est pas facile d'y trouver du travail

eat *verb*
= manger
eat out = manger au restaurant

EC *noun*
the EC = la Communauté Européenne

echo *noun*
an echo = un écho

economic *adjective*
= économique

economics noun
economics = les sciences économiques
! Note that **sciences** is feminine plural.

economy noun
the economy = l'économie (feminine)

edge noun
* (of a road, table, an object)
the edge = le bord
the edge of the lake = le bord du lac
at the edge of the town = aux abords de la ville
* (of a forest, a wood or field)
the edge = la lisière
* (of a blade or knife)
the edge = le tranchant

educate verb
= instruire
he was educated in Paris = il a fait ses études à Paris

education noun
education = l'instruction (feminine)
to get a good education = recevoir une bonne instruction

effect noun
an effect = un effet

effective adjective
= efficace

efficient adjective
= efficace

effort noun
an effort = un effort
to make an effort = faire un effort

egg noun
an egg = un œuf

eggcup noun
an eggcup = un coquetier

eight number ▶ 187 |, ▶ 211 |
eight = huit
eight apples = huit pommes
I've got eight (of them) = j'en ai huit

eighteen number ▶ 187 |, ▶ 211 |
eighteen = dix-huit

eighteenth number
* (in a series) = dix-huitième
* (in dates) ▶ 222 |
the eighteenth of August = le dix-huit août

eighth number
* (in a series) = huitième
* (in dates) ▶ 222 |
the eighth of August = le huit août

eighty number ▶ 187 |
eighty = quatre-vingts

either
1 conjunction
they're coming on either Tuesday or Wednesday = ils viendront soit mardi, soit mercredi
he didn't contact either Helen or Paul = il n'a contacté ni Helen ni Paul
2 pronoun
take either (of them) = prends l'un ou l'autre/l'une ou l'autre
I don't know either (of them) = je ne connais ni l'un ni l'autre/l'une ni l'autre
3 determiner
take either road = prenez l'une ou l'autre route
I don't want to live in either country = je ne veux habiter dans aucun des deux pays
4 adverb
= non plus
she can't do it either = elle ne peut pas le faire non plus

elbow noun ▶ 201 |
the elbow = le coude

elder adjective
= aîné/aînée

elderly adjective
= âgé/âgée

eldest adjective
= aîné/aînée
the eldest daughter = l'aînée

elect verb
= élire

election noun
an election = une élection
to win an election = remporter les élections

electric adjective
= électrique

electrician noun ▶ 315 |
an electrician = un électricien/une électricienne

electricity noun
electricity = l'électricité (feminine)

elegant adjective
= élégant/élégante

elephant noun
an elephant = un éléphant

elevator noun (US English)
an elevator = un ascenseur

eleven number ▶ 187 |, ▶ 211 |
eleven = onze
eleven apples = onze pommes
I've got eleven (of them) = j'en ai onze

eleventh number
* (in a series) = onzième
* (in dates) ▶ 222 |
the eleventh of May = le onze mai

else
1 *adverb*
= d'autre
someone else = quelqu'un d'autre
nothing else = rien d'autre
what else did he say? = qu'est-ce qu'il a dit d'autre?
something else = autre chose
everything else = tout le reste
2 or else = sinon
be quiet or else I'll get angry = taisez-vous sinon je vais me fâcher

elsewhere *adverb*
= ailleurs

embarrassed *adjective*
= gêné/gênée

embarrassing *adjective*
= gênant/gênante

embassy *noun*
an embassy = une ambassade

emergency *noun*
an emergency = une urgence
in an emergency = en cas d'urgence

emergency exit *noun*
an emergency exit = une sortie de secours

emigrate *verb*
= émigrer

emotion *noun*
an emotion = une émotion

emotional *adjective*
• (*describing a scene or moment*)
= émouvant/émouvante
• (*describing a person*) = émotif/émotive

emperor *noun*
an emperor = un empereur

employ *verb*
= employer

employed *adjective*
to be employed = avoir un emploi

employee *noun*
an employee = un employé/une employée

employer *noun*
an employer = un employeur

employment *noun*
employment = le travail, l'emploi (*masculine*)

empty
1 *adjective*
= vide
2 *verb*
= vider

encourage *verb*
= encourager

end
1 *noun*
• (*the final part*)
the end = la fin

at the end of the film = à la fin du film
at the end of May = fin mai
in the end = finalement
• (*the furthest part*)
the end = le bout
at the end of the street = au bout de la rue
2 *verb*
• (*to come to an end*) = se terminer (**!** + *être*)
• (*to put an end to*) = mettre fin à
to end the war = mettre fin à la guerre
• (*to finish*) = terminer
to end a concert = terminer un concert
end up
to end up in London = se retrouver à Londres
to end up going abroad = finir par aller à l'étranger

ending *noun*
the ending = la fin

enemy *noun*
an enemy = un ennemi/une ennemie

energetic *adjective*
= énergique

energy *noun*
energy = l'énergie (*feminine*)

engaged *adjective*
• **to get engaged** = se fiancer (**!** + *être*)
to be engaged = être fiancé/fiancée
• (*British English*) (*describing a phone, toilet*) = occupé/occupée

engine *noun*
• (*of a car*)
an engine = un moteur
• (*for a train*)
an engine = une locomotive

engineer *noun* ▶ 315 |
an engineer = un ingénieur

England *noun* ▶ 218 |
England = l'Angleterre (*feminine*)

English ▶ 275 |
1 *adjective*
= anglais/anglaise
2 *noun*
• (*the people*)
the English = les Anglais (*masculine plural*)
• (*the language*)
English = l'anglais (*masculine*)

enjoy *verb*
• (*to like*) = aimer
he enjoys fishing = il aime la pêche
did you enjoy your holiday? = est-ce que tu as passé de bonnes vacances?
• (*to have a good time*) ▶ 237 |
to enjoy oneself = s'amuser (**!** + *être*)

enjoyable *adjective*
= agréable

enormous *adjective*
= énorme

enough
1 *determiner*
= assez de
I don't have enough [money | time | friends …] = je n'ai pas assez [d'argent | de temps | d'amis …]
there's enough room for everyone = il y a assez de place pour tout le monde
2 *adverb*
= assez
is it big enough? = est-ce que c'est assez grand?
you're not old enough = tu n'es pas assez grand
3 *pronoun*
= assez
we have enough to eat = nous avons assez à manger
I've had enough = j'en ai assez
that's enough = ça suffit

enquire *verb*
= se renseigner (**!** + *être*)
I'll enquire about the price = je vais me renseigner sur le prix

enter *verb*
• (*to go into*) = entrer dans (**!** + *être*)
• (*to take part in*) = participer à
to enter a competition = participer à un concours

entertain *verb*
= divertir

entertaining *adjective*
= divertissant/divertissante

entertainment *noun*
entertainment = le divertissement, les distractions (*feminine plural*)

enthusiasm *noun*
enthusiasm = l'enthousiasme (*masculine*)

enthusiastic *adjective*
= enthousiaste

entrance *noun*
an entrance = une entrée
the entrance to the castle = l'entrée du château

envelope *noun*
an envelope = une enveloppe

environment *noun*
the environment = l'environnement (*masculine*)

envy
1 *noun*
envy = l'envie (*feminine*)
2 *verb*
= envier

episode *noun*
an episode = un épisode

equal
1 *adjective*
= égal/égale
to fight for equal rights = lutter pour l'égalité des droits
2 *verb*
= égaler
six and four equals ten = six et quatre égalent dix

equality *noun*
equality = l'égalité (*feminine*)

equator *noun*
the equator = l'équateur (*masculine*)

equipment *noun*
equipment (*in an office, a laboratory, a factory*) = le matériel
(*for an activity*) = l'équipement (*masculine*)

eraser *noun*
an eraser = une gomme

escalator *noun*
an escalator = un escalier mécanique

escape *verb*
• (*to get away*) = s'échapper (**!** + *être*)
he escaped from prison = il s'est échappé de prison
• (*to avoid*) = échapper à
to escape death = échapper à la mort

especially *adverb*
= surtout

essay *noun*
an essay (*by a pupil*) = une rédaction
(*by a student*) = une dissertation

essential *adjective*
= essentiel/essentielle

ethnic *adjective*
= ethnique

eurocheque *noun*
a eurocheque = un Eurochèque

Europe *noun* ▶ **218**
Europe = l'Europe (*feminine*)

European *adjective* ▶ **275**
= européen/européenne

European Union *noun*
the European Union = l'Union européenne
! *Note that* **Union** *is feminine.*

evacuate *verb*
= évacuer

even¹
1 *adverb*
• (*when expressing surprise*) = même
he didn't even try = il n'a même pas essayé
she even works on weekends = elle travaille même le week-end
• (*in comparisons*) = encore
it's even colder today = il fait encore plus froid aujourd'hui

2 even though = bien que
he's bored even though he's with other
people = bien qu'il soit avec d'autres
personnes, il s'ennuie

! *Note that the subjunctive is used after*
bien que.

even² *adjective*
• (*flat, smooth*) = régulier/régulière
• (*when talking about numbers*)
an even number = un nombre pair

evening *noun* ▶ 211 , ▶ 356

! *Note that* evening *is usually translated
by* soir *in French. However it is sometimes
translated by* soirée, *when there is an
emphasis on the idea of duration.*

an evening = un soir
at eight o'clock in the evening = à huit
heures du soir
to spend the evening at home = passer la
soirée à la maison

event *noun*
an event = un événement

eventually *adverb*

! *Note that* eventually *is never translated
by* éventuellement.

= finalement

ever *adverb*
• (*at any time*)
nothing ever happens here = il ne se
passe jamais rien ici
no-one will ever know = personne ne le
saura jamais
have you ever been to Greece? = est-ce
que tu es déjà allé en Grèce?
I hardly ever go there = je n'y vais presque
jamais
• (*always*)
he's as lazy as ever = il est toujours aussi
paresseux

every *determiner* ▶ 356
= tous les/toutes les
every time I meet her = toutes les fois que
je la rencontre
every day = tous les jours
every second day, every other day = tous
les deux jours
two out of every three people = deux
personnes sur trois

everyone *pronoun* (*also* **everybody**)
= tout le monde
everyone else = tous les autres

everything *pronoun*
= tout

everywhere *adverb*
= partout
everywhere else = partout ailleurs

evidence *noun*
a piece of evidence = une preuve
to give evidence = témoigner

evil *noun*
evil = le mal

exact *adjective*
= exact/exacte

exactly *adverb*
= exactement

exaggerate *verb*
= exagérer

exam *noun*
an exam = un examen
to pass an exam = réussir à un examen
to take an exam = passer un examen

examine *verb*
= examiner

example *noun*
an example = un exemple
for example = par exemple

excellent *adjective*
= excellent/excellente

except *preposition*
= sauf

exchange *verb*
= échanger
to exchange a hat for a scarf = échanger
un chapeau contre une écharpe

exchange rate *noun*
the exchange rate = le taux de change

excited *adjective*
= excité/excitée

exciting *adjective*
= passionnant/passionnante

exclude *verb*
= exclure

excuse
1 *noun*
an excuse = une excuse
to make excuses = trouver des excuses
2 *verb*
= excuser
excuse me! = excusez-moi!

exercise *noun*
• (*to keep fit*)
an exercise = un exercice
to take exercise, to do exercise = faire de
l'exercice
• (*a piece of work*)
an exercise = un exercice

exercise book *noun*
an exercise book = un cahier

exhausted *adjective*
= épuisé/épuisée

exhibition *noun*
an exhibition = une exposition

exit *noun*
an exit = une sortie

expect verb
- (to be prepared for) = s'attendre à (! + être)
  to expect bad news = s'attendre à de
    mauvaises nouvelles
  they expect to win = ils s'attendent à
    gagner
- (to wait for) = attendre
- (to want) = vouloir
  they expect us to do the work = ils
    veulent que nous fassions le travail
  ! Note that the subjunctive is used after
  vouloir que.

expenses noun
  expenses = les frais (masculine)

expensive adjective
  = cher/chère

experience noun
  an experience = une expérience

experienced adjective
  = expérimenté/expérimentée

experiment
1 noun
  an experiment = une expérience
2 verb
  = expérimenter

expert noun
  an expert = un spécialiste/une spécialiste
  a computer expert = un spécialiste/une
    spécialiste en informatique

explain verb
  = expliquer
  to explain a rule to someone = expliquer
    une règle à quelqu'un

explanation noun
  an explanation = une explication

explode verb
  = exploser

exploit verb
  = exploiter

explosion noun
  an explosion = une explosion

export verb
  = exporter

express
1 verb
  to express oneself = s'exprimer (! + être)
2 adverb
  to send a letter express = envoyer une
    lettre en exprès

expression noun
  an expression = une expression

express train noun
  an express train = un rapide

extinct adjective
  (describing an animal) = disparu/disparue
  (describing a volcano) = éteint/éteinte

extra
1 adjective
  = supplémentaire
  an extra bed = un lit supplémentaire
  to pay an extra ten pounds = payer dix
    livres de plus
2 adverb
  to pay extra = payer un supplément

extraordinary adjective
  = extraordinaire

extreme adjective
  = extrême

extremely adverb
  = extrêmement

eye noun ▶ 201 |
  an eye = un œil
  to have green eyes = avoir les yeux verts

eyebrow noun ▶ 201 |
  an eyebrow = un sourcil

eyelash noun ▶ 201 |
  an eyelash = un cil

eyelid noun ▶ 201 |
  an eyelid = une paupière

eye shadow noun
  eye shadow = le fard à paupières

eyesight noun
  eyesight = la vue
  to have good eyesight = avoir une bonne
    vue

Ff

face
1 noun
  the face = le visage, la figure
  to make a face = faire une grimace
2 verb
- (to be opposite) = être face à
  she was facing me = elle était face à moi
- (to have to deal with) = confronter
  I can't face seeing them again = je n'ai pas
    le courage de les revoir
- (to look toward(s))
  my room faces the sea = ma chambre
    donne sur la mer
  face up to = faire face à

fact
1 noun
  a fact = un fait
2 **in fact** = en fait

factory noun
  a factory = une usine

Useful everyday expressions in spoken French

When things are going well

well done!	= bravo!	congratulations!	= félicitations!
	= chapeau✘!	good luck!	= bonne chance!
	(*I take my hat*	way to go! *(US English)*	= bravo!
	off to him / you etc)	wow!	= super✘!, génial✘!

When things are not so good

hard luck!	= pas de chance!	good luck! (*you'll need it*)	= bon courage!
too bad !	= tant pis!	ouch!	= aïe!, ouïlle!
cheer up!, chin up!	= courage!	shit!	= merde❢ !
oh dear!	= oh là là✘!	yuck!, ugh!	= beurk✘!
	= ça alors!	phew! (*that was close*)	= ouf!
damn!	= ah, mince✘!	get well soon!	= bon rétablissement!,
blast!	= zut✘!		remets-toi vite!

Coming

welcome!	= bienvenue!
nice to meet you, pleased to meet you	= enchanté/enchantée de faire votre connaissance
hello!	= bonjour! (*face to face*)
	= allô, bonjour! (*on the phone*)
hi!	= salut✘!
hi again!	= rebonjour✘!

Going

goodbye!	= au revoir!
bye!	= salut✘! tchao✘!
cheers! (*British English*)	= salut✘!
see you soon / later / next week!	= à bientôt! / plus tard! / la semaine prochaine!
see you around!	= à un de ces jours!
(have a) safe journey!	= bon voyage!
all the best!	= bonne continuation!

Wishing someone well

have a nice day!	= bonne journée!
have a good weekend!	= bon week-end!
have a great holiday or vacation!	= bonnes vacances!
have a good time!, enjoy yourself!	= amuse-toi bien!, amusez-vous bien!
have a good trip!	= bon voyage!

Special greetings

Happy birthday!	= Bon anniversaire!	Happy New Year!	= Bonne année!
Happy Christmas!	= Joyeux Noël!	April fool!	= poisson d'avril!

In reply to: 'Would you like ... ?'

yes, please	= volontiers
	= oui, je veux bien!
	= pourquoi pas?

In reply to: 'Thank you'

you're very welcome	= je t'en prie, je vous en prie
don't mention it	= (il n'y a) pas de quoi
no problem, not at all	= de rien

Eating and drinking

enjoy your meal!	= bon appétit!
cheers!	= santé!, à la tienne!, à la vôtre!, tchin! tchin!

Sleeping

good night!	= bonne nuit!	sweet dreams!	= fais de beaux rêves!
sleep well!	= dors bien!		

✘ in informal situations   ❢ may be considered offensive

F

fade *verb*
(*if it's a material*) = se décolorer (**!** + *être*)
(*if it's a colour*) = passer (**!** + *être*)

fail *verb*
= échouer
to fail an exam = échouer à un examen

failure *noun*
a failure (*an event, an attempt*) = un échec
(*a person*) = un raté/une ratée

faint *verb*
= s'évanouir (**!** + *être*)

fair
1 *adjective*
• (*just*) = juste
it's not fair = ce n'est pas juste
• (*in colour*)
to have fair hair = avoir les cheveux
  blonds
to have fair skin = avoir le teint clair
2 *noun*
• (*British English*) (*a funfair*)
a fair = une fête foraine
• (*a display of goods*)
a (trade) fair = une foire

fairly *adverb*
= assez

faith *noun*
to have faith in someone = avoir
  confiance en quelqu'un

faithful *adjective*
= fidèle

fall
1 *verb*
• (*if it's a person*) = tomber (**!** + *être*)
she fell to the ground = elle est tombée
  par terre
• (*to come down, to be reduced*) = baisser
• (*other uses*)
to fall asleep = s'endormir (**!** + *être*)
to fall ill = tomber malade (**!** + *être*)
to fall in love with someone = tomber
  amoureux/amoureuse de quelqu'un
2 *noun*
• (*in prices, temperature*)
a fall = une baisse
a fall in prices = une baisse des prix
• (*US English*) (*autumn*)
fall = l'automne (*masculine*)
fall down
• (*if it's a person*) = tomber (**!** + *être*)
• (*if it's a building*) = s'effondrer (**!** + *être*)
fall off = tomber (**!** + *être*)
to fall off a chair = tomber d'une chaise
fall out
• (*from somewhere*) = tomber (**!** + *être*)
the letter fell out of his pocket = la lettre
  est tombée de sa poche
• (*to quarrel*) = se brouiller (**!** + *être*)

fall over = tomber (par terre) (**!** + *être*)
fall through = tomber à l'eau

false *adjective*
= faux/fausse

false teeth *noun*
false teeth = un dentier (*singular*)

familiar *adjective*
= familier/familière

family *noun*
a family = une famille

famous *adjective*
= célèbre

fan *noun*
• (*of a pop star, an actor, a sport*)
a fan = un fan/une fan
• (*for cooling*)
a fan (*electric*) = un ventilateur
(*hand-held*) = un éventail

fancy dress party *noun* (*British English*)
a fancy dress party = une soirée costumée

fantastic *adjective*
= formidable, super✶

far
1 *adverb*
• ▶ 285 |
far (away) = loin
how far is it to London? = Londres est à
  combien de kilomètres?
how far is Oxford from London? = Oxford
  est à quelle distance de Londres?
we went as far as the coast = nous
  sommes allés jusqu'à la côte
• (*in time*)
as far back as 1950 = déjà en 1950
• (*very much*) = beaucoup
you're eating far too much bread = tu
  manges beaucoup trop de pain
we know far fewer people here = on
  connaît beaucoup moins de monde ici
2 *adjective*
= autre (**!** *before the noun*)
at the far side of the room = de l'autre côté
  de la pièce
3 **so far** = jusqu'ici

fare *noun*
the fare (*on a bus or the underground*) = le
  prix du ticket
(*on a train or plane*) = le prix du billet

farm *noun*
a farm = une ferme

farmer *noun* ▶ 315 |
a farmer = un fermier

fascinating *adjective*
= fascinant/fascinante

fashion *noun*
fashion = la mode
to be in fashion = être à la mode
to go out of fashion = se démoder
  (**!** + *être*)

✶ in informal situations

fashionable *adjective*
= à la mode

fast
1 *adjective*
• (*describing movement*) = rapide
• **to be fast** = avancer
  my watch is ten minutes fast = ma montre avance de dix minutes
2 *adverb*
= vite, rapidement

fasten *verb*
  to fasten a seatbelt = attacher une ceinture de sécurité

fast-forward *verb*
  to fast-forward a cassette = faire avancer rapidement une cassette

fat *adjective*
= gros/grosse (**!** *before the noun*)
  to get fat = grossir

fatal *adjective*
= mortel/mortelle

father *noun*
  a father = un père

Father Christmas *noun* (*British English*)
  Father Christmas = le père Noël

father-in-law *noun*
  a father-in-law = un beau-père

faucet *noun* (*US English*)
  a faucet = un robinet

fault *noun*
  to be someone's fault = être (de) la faute de quelqu'un
  it's not my fault = ce n'est pas (de) ma faute
  whose fault was it? = à qui la faute?

favour (*British English*), **favor** (*US English*)
1 *noun*
  a favour = un service
  to do someone a favour = rendre (un) service à quelqu'un
  to ask someone a favour = demander un service à quelqu'un
2 in favour of
  to be in favour of a change in the law = être pour un changement de la loi

favourite (*British English*), **favorite** (*US English*) *adjective*
= préféré/préférée
  it's my favourite film = c'est mon film préféré

fax *noun*
  a fax = un fax

fear *noun*
  fear = la peur

feather *noun*
  a feather = une plume

February *noun* ▶ **222** |
  February = février (*masculine*)

fed up *adjective*
  to be fed up = en avoir marre✘

fee *noun*
  a fee (*to attend an event, a show*) = un droit d'entrée
  (*to join a club, a union*) = une cotisation

feeble *adjective*
= faible

feed *verb*
= nourrir
  I must feed the children = je dois donner à manger aux enfants

feel *verb*
• (*referring to an emotion, an impression*)
  to feel happy = être heureux/heureuse
  he's feeling uncomfortable = il se sent mal à l'aise
  to feel afraid = avoir peur
  I feel as if I'm being followed = j'ai l'impression qu'on me suit
  it feels like winter = on se croirait en hiver
  it feels good to be back home = ça fait du bien d'être chez soi
• (*referring to a physical feeling*)
  to feel [hot | cold | sleepy ...] = avoir [chaud | froid | sommeil ...]
  to feel ill = se sentir malade
  to feel a draught = sentir un courant d'air
  I don't feel a thing = je ne sens rien
• (*describing how something seems*)
  the box felt very heavy = la boîte était lourde
  the room feels very cold = la pièce est très froide
• (*to touch*) = tâter, toucher
• **to feel like** [going out | eating | dancing ...] = avoir envie de [sortir | manger | danser ...]
  I don't feel like it = je n'en ai pas envie

feeling *noun*
• (*emotional*)
  a feeling = un sentiment
  to hurt someone's feelings = blesser quelqu'un
• (*physical*)
  a feeling = une sensation
• **I have a feeling he's right** = j'ai l'impression qu'il a raison

felt-tip pen *noun*
  a felt-tip pen = un crayon feutre

female *adjective*
• (*in biology*) = femelle
• (*relating to women*) = féminin/féminine

feminine *adjective*
= féminin/féminine

fence *noun*
  a fence = une clôture

fencing *noun* ▶ **248** |
  fencing = l'escrime (*feminine*)

F

festival *noun*
a festival = une fête

fetch *verb*
= aller chercher
go and fetch some water = va chercher de l'eau

fever *noun*
to have a fever = avoir de la fièvre

few ▶ 317 |
1 a few
a few [people | houses | books …] = quelques [personnes | maisons | livres …]
a few of the houses were burned down = quelques-unes des maisons ont été brûlées
a few of them speak Greek = quelques-uns d'entre eux parlent grec
I would like a few more = j'en voudrais quelques-uns/quelques-unes de plus

! *Note that it is necessary to use* en, *which may be translated as* 'of them', *with phrases like* a few. *See also* another, a lot, none *etc for this use of* en.

2 *determiner*
• (*not many*) = peu de
few [visitors | letters | meals …] = peu de [visiteurs | lettres | repas …]
• (*several*)
the first few weeks = les premières semaines
3 *pronoun*
= peu
few of us succeeded = peu d'entre nous ont réussi
there are so few of them (*of people*) = ils sont si peu nombreux
(*of things*) = il y en a tellement peu

fewer ▶ 317 |
1 *determiner*
= moins de
fewer shops = moins de magasins
2 *pronoun*
= moins
fewer than ten people = moins de dix personnes

fewest
1 *determiner*
the fewest = le moins de
they have the fewest advantages = ce sont eux qui ont le moins d'avantages
2 *pronoun*
the fewest = le moins

field *noun*
a field = un champ

fifteen *number* **▶ 187 |, ▶ 211 |**
fifteen = quinze

fifteenth *number*
• (*in a series*) = quinzième
• (*in dates*) **▶ 222 |**
the fifteenth of May = le quinze mai

fifth *number*
• (*in a series*) = cinquième
• (*in dates*) **▶ 222 |**
the fifth of June = le cinq juin

fifty *number* **▶ 187 |, ▶ 211 |**
fifty = cinquante

fight
1 *verb*
• to fight (against) prejudice = lutter contre les préjugés
to fight for justice = lutter pour la justice
• (*in war*) = se battre (**!** + *être*)
to fight the enemy = combattre l'ennemi
• (*physically*) = se battre (**!** + *être*)
• (*to quarrel*) = se disputer (**!** + *être*)
2 *noun*
• (*a campaign*)
a fight = une lutte
• (*physical*)
a fight = une bagarre
fight back = se défendre (**!** + *être*)

figure *noun*
• (*a number*)
a figure = un chiffre
• to have a good figure = être bien fait/bien faite

file *noun*
• a file (*for documents*) = un dossier
(*in a computer*) = un fichier
• in single file = en file indienne

fill *verb*
• (*to make full*) = remplir
• (*to become full*) = se remplir (**!** + *être*)
fill in = remplir

film
1 *noun*
• (*in cinema or on TV*)
a film = un film
• (*for a camera*)
a film = une pellicule
2 *verb*
= filmer

filthy *adjective*
= sale

final
1 *adjective*
= dernier/dernière (**!** *before the noun*)
2 *noun*
a final = une finale

finally *adverb*
= finalement

find *verb*
= trouver
find out
to find out the truth = découvrir la vérité
if he ever finds out he'll be furious = si jamais il l'apprend il sera furieux

fine
1 *adjective*
• (*very good, excellent*) = beau/belle
(**!** *before the noun*)
the weather is fine = il fait beau

- (*in good health*)
  I feel fine = je me sens très bien
- (*expressing agreement*)
  (that's) fine = d'accord
2 *noun*
  a fine = une amende

finger *noun* ▶ 201 |
  a finger = un doigt

finish
1 *verb*
- (*to end*) = finir
  to finish writing a letter = finir d'écrire
  une lettre
- (*to come to an end*) = finir
2 *noun*
  the finish (*in a race*) = l'arrivée (*feminine*)

Finland *noun* ▶ 218 |
  Finland = la Finlande

fire
1 *noun*
  fire = le feu
  a fire (*for heat*) = un feu
  (*causing damage*) = un incendie
  to catch fire = prendre feu
  to be on fire = être en feu
2 *verb*
- (*to shoot*) = tirer
- (*to dismiss*) = renvoyer

fire alarm *noun*
  a fire alarm = une sonnerie d'alarme
  incendie

fire brigade (*British English*), fire department (*US English*) *noun*
  the fire brigade = les pompiers (*masculine plural*)

fire engine *noun*
  a fire engine = une voiture de pompiers

fireman *noun* ▶ 315 |
  a fireman = un pompier

fire station *noun*
  a fire station = une caserne de pompiers

fireworks display *noun*
  a fireworks display = un feu d'artifice

firm
1 *noun*
  a firm = une entreprise
2 *adjective*
  = ferme

first
1 *adjective*
  = premier/première (**!** *before the noun*)
  the first time = la première fois
  the first three weeks = les trois premières
  semaines
2 *adverb*
- (*to begin with*) = d'abord
  first of all = tout d'abord
- (*for the first time*) = pour la première fois

- **to arrive first** = arriver le premier/la
  première
3 *noun*
- (*in a series or group*)
  the first = le premier/la première
  he was the first to congratulate us = il a
  été le premier à nous féliciter
- (*in dates*) ▶ 222 |
  the first of June = le premier juin
4 at first = au début

first aid *noun*
  first aid = les premiers soins
  | **!** *Note that* soins *is masculine plural.*

first class *adverb*
  to travel first class = voyager en première
  classe

first floor *noun*
  the first floor (*in Britain*) = le premier étage
  (*in the US*) = le rez-de-chaussée

first name *noun*
  a first name = un prénom

fish
1 *noun*
  a fish = un poisson
2 *verb*
  to go fishing = aller à la pêche

fisherman *noun* ▶ 315 |
  a fisherman = un pêcheur

fishing *noun* ▶ 248 |
  fishing = la pêche

fishing rod *noun*
  a fishing rod = une canne à pêche

fist *noun* ▶ 201 |
  the fist = le poing

fit
1 *verb*
  the shoes don't fit me = les chaussures ne
  me vont pas
  the photo won't fit into the envelope = la
  photo ne rentre pas dans l'enveloppe
  will the table fit here? = est-ce qu'il y a de
  la place pour la table ici?
2 *adjective*
- (*suitable, capable*)
  the house isn't fit to live in = la maison
  n'est pas habitable
  to be fit to drive = être en état de conduire
  he's not fit to be a minister = il n'est pas
  capable d'être ministre
- (*healthy*)
  to be fit = être en forme
fit in
- (*in a room or car*)
  can you all fit in? = est-ce qu'il y a de la
  place pour vous tous?
- (*in a group or team*) = s'intégrer (**!** + *être*)

fitness *noun*
  (physical) fitness = la forme (physique)

five number ▶ **187**, ▶ **211**
five = cinq
five apples = cinq pommes
I've got five (of them) = j'en ai cinq

fix verb
• (to decide on, to set) = fixer
• (to repair) = réparer
to get a watch fixed = faire réparer une
montre
• (to prepare) = préparer

flag noun
a flag = un drapeau

flame noun
a flame = une flamme
to go up in flames = s'enflammer
(! + être)

flash
1 noun
a flash (for a camera) = un flash
2 verb
to flash (on and off) = clignoter

flashlight noun
a flashlight = une lampe de poche

flask noun
a flask = un thermos®

flat
1 noun (British English)
a flat = un appartement
2 adjective
= plat/plate
to have a flat tyre = avoir un pneu à plat

flavour (British English), **flavor** (US
English) noun
a flavour (of food) = une saveur, un goût
(of ice cream, yogurt) = un parfum

flea noun
a flea = une puce

flight noun
a flight = un vol

flight attendant noun ▶ **315**
a flight attendant = un steward/une
hôtesse de l'air

float verb
= flotter
to float up into the air = s'envoler (! + être)

flock noun
• (of sheep, goats, geese)
a flock = un troupeau
• (of birds)
a flock = une volée

flood noun
a flood = une inondation

floor noun
• (a surface)
a floor = un plancher
to sit on the floor = s'asseoir par terre
• (a storey)
a floor = un étage

florist noun ▶ **315**
a florist = un fleuriste/une fleuriste

flour noun
flour = la farine

flow verb
• (if it's a liquid) = couler
• (if it's traffic) = circuler

flower
1 noun
a flower = une fleur
2 verb
= fleurir

flu noun ▶ **266**
flu = la grippe

fluently adverb
= couramment

flush verb
to flush the toilet = tirer la chasse d'eau

flute noun ▶ **290**
a flute = une flûte

fly
1 noun
a fly = une mouche
2 verb
• (if it's a bird, a kite, a plane, an insect)
= voler
• (if it's a passenger) = prendre l'avion
to fly from London to Paris = aller de
Londres à Paris en avion
• to fly a plane = piloter un avion
• (if it's a flag) = flotter
fly away = s'envoler (! + être)

fog noun
fog = le brouillard

fold verb
• to fold a shirt = plier une chemise
• to fold one's arms = croiser les bras

folder noun
a folder (for work) = une chemise
(in computing) = un dossier

follow verb
• (to go or come after) = suivre
• (to use, to look at) = suivre
I followed the signposts = j'ai suivi les
panneaux indicateurs

following adjective
= suivant/suivante

fond adjective
I'm very fond of you = je t'aime beaucoup

food noun
food = la nourriture

fool verb
= tromper, duper

foot noun
• (part of the leg) ▶ **201**
the foot = le pied
on foot = à pied

* (of a rabbit, a cat, a dog, a cow)
  the foot = la patte
* (in measurements) ▶ 285 |
  a foot = un pied
  ! Note that a **foot** = 30.48 cm.

football noun ▶ 248 |
* **football** (soccer) = le football
  (American football) = le football américain
* (a ball)
  a football = un football

footballer (British English), **football player** (US English) noun ▶ 315 |
  a footballer = un joueur/une joueuse de football

footprint noun
  a footprint = une trace de pas

footstep noun
  a footstep = un pas

for preposition
▶ 244 | See the boxed note on for for more information and examples.
* **for** = pour
  the letter is for you = la lettre est pour toi
  to work for a company = travailler pour une entreprise
  he cooked dinner for us = il nous a préparé à manger
* (when talking about time)
  we've been living here for two years = on habite ici depuis deux ans, ça fait deux ans qu'on habite ici
  he's going to Paris for a year = il va à Paris pour un an
  she read for two hours = elle a lu pendant deux heures
  I've been waiting for three hours = ça fait trois heures que j'attends
  he won't arrive for another two weeks = il ne va pas arriver avant deux semaines
* (when talking about distance) = pendant
  we drove for 80 kilometres = nous avons roulé pendant 80 kilomètres
* (when talking about money)
  he bought it for £50 = il l'a acheté pour 50 livres
  a cheque for £20 = un chèque de 20 livres
* (in favour (of)) = pour
* **say hello to her for me** = donne-lui le bonjour de ma part
* (other uses)
  T for Tom = T comme Tom
  the Minister for Education = le ministre de l'éducation
  what is the French for 'badger'? = comment dit-on 'badger' en français?
  we went [for a swim | for a run | for a walk …] = nous sommes allés [nager | courir | nous promener …]

forbid verb
  = interdire
  to forbid someone to go out = interdire à quelqu'un de sortir
  smoking is forbidden = il est interdit de fumer

force
1 verb
  = forcer
  to force someone to leave = forcer quelqu'un à partir
2 noun
  force = la force
  by force = de force

forecast noun
  the forecast = les prévisions (feminine plural)
  the forecast is for rain = la météo prévoit de la pluie

forehead noun ▶ 201 |
  the forehead = le front

foreign adjective
  = étranger/étrangère

foreigner noun
  a foreigner = un étranger/une étrangère

forest noun
  a forest = une forêt

forever, for ever adverb
  = pour toujours

forget verb
  = oublier
  to forget about someone = oublier quelqu'un
  to forget [to do the shopping | to eat | to call …] = oublier [de faire les courses | de manger | de téléphoner …]

forgive verb
  to forgive someone = pardonner à quelqu'un

fork noun
  a fork = une fourchette

form
1 noun ▶ 245 |
* (a shape)
  a form = une forme
* (a document)
  a form = un formulaire
* (referring to mood or fitness)
  to be in good form = être en bonne forme
* (British English) (a class)
  a form = une classe
  to be in the sixth form = être en terminale
2 verb
* (to create, to make) = former
  to form a circle = former un cercle
* (to start, to set up) = créer

formal adjective
* (describing language) = soutenu/soutenue
* **to wear formal clothes** (for the evening) = être en tenue de soirée
* (official) = officiel/officielle

former adjective
  = ancien/ancienne (**!** before the noun)

fortnight noun ▶ 356 | (British English)
  a fortnight = quinze jours (masculine plural)

for

Some general uses

for is generally translated by **pour**:

for my sister	= **pour** ma sœur
for me	= **pour** moi

When **for** followed by a verb is used to explain the purpose of something, it is translated by **pour** + *infinitive*:

a product *for* losing weight	= un produit **pour** maigrir

When talking about time

for in time expressions may be translated by **depuis**, **pendant** or **pour**. The following examples are designed to show you which translation to choose. Note that tense is very important in distinguishing between them.

● When **for** is used to express the time period of something that started in the past and is still going on, French uses either *present tense* + **depuis** or **ça fait✗** ... **que** + *present tense*:

I have been waiting for three hours	= j'attends **depuis** trois heures
(and I am still waiting)	= **ça fait✗** trois heures **que** j'attends
we've been together for two years	= nous sommes ensemble **depuis** deux ans
(and we're still together)	= **ça fait✗** deux ans **que** nous sommes ensemble

When **for** is used after a verb in the past perfect tense placing an event even further back in time, French uses either *imperfect* + **depuis** or **ça faisait✗** ... **que** + *imperfect*:

I had been waiting for two hours	= j'attendais **depuis** deux heures
(and was still waiting)	= **ça faisait✗** deux heures **que** j'attendais

● When **for** is used in negative sentences with the present perfect tense to express the time that has elapsed since something has happened, French uses the same tense as English, either *perfect* + **depuis** or **ça fait✗** ... **que** + *perfect*:

I haven't seen him for ten years	= je ne l'ai pas vu **depuis** dix ans
(and I still haven't seen him)	= **ça fait✗** dix ans que je ne l'ai pas vu

When **for** is used in negative sentences after a verb in the past perfect tense, again placing events further back in time, French uses either *past perfect* + **depuis** or **ça faisait✗** ... **que** + *past perfect*:

I hadn't seen him for ten years	= je ne l'avais pas vu **depuis** dix ans
	= **ça faisait✗** dix ans que je ne l'avais pas vu

● When **for** is used to express the time period of something that happened in the past and is no longer going on, French uses *present perfect* + **pendant**:

last Sunday I read for two hours	= dimanche dernier j'ai lu **pendant** deux heures

● When **for** is used to express a time period in the future, French uses *present* or *future* + **pour**:

I'm going to Montreal for six weeks	= je vais à Montréal **pour** six semaines
I will go to Montreal for six weeks	= j'irai à Montréal **pour** six semaines

● When the verb **to be** is used in the future with **for** to emphasize the period of time, French uses *future* + **pendant**:

I will be in Brussels for six weeks	= je serai à Bruxelles **pendant** six semaines

✗ in informal situations

---

fortunately *adverb*
= heureusement

fortune *noun*
• **a fortune** = une fortune
  to make a fortune = faire fortune
• **to tell someone's fortune** = dire la bonne
  aventure à quelqu'un

forty *number* ▶ **187** |, ▶ **211** |
  forty = quarante

forward
1 *adverb*
  = en avant
  to step forward = faire un pas en
  avant

Forms of address (Miss, Mr, Mrs)

When speaking to someone

Where English puts the surname after the title, French normally uses the title alone:

*Good morning, **Miss Jones***	= bonjour, **Mademoiselle**	
*Good evening, **Mr Halpin***	= bonsoir, **Monsieur**	
*Good morning, **Mrs Davies***	= bonjour, **Madame**	

When speaking about someone

In this case, French and English behave the same:

Miss Jones | Mr Halpin | Mrs Davies = Mademoiselle Jones / Monsieur Halpin /
is here   Madame Davies est là

When writing to someone

When starting a letter, translations will differ according to the degree of formality involved:

	formal	less formal
Dear Miss Jones	= Mademoiselle	= Chère Mademoiselle
Dear Mr Halpin	= Monsieur	= Cher Monsieur
Dear Mrs Davies	= Madame	= Chère Madame

▶ There is no French equivalent of **Ms** but one can use **Madame** in similar circumstances.

---

2 *verb*
 to forward a letter to someone = faire
 suivre une lettre à quelqu'un

found *verb*
 = fonder

fountain *noun*
 a fountain = une fontaine

four *number* ▶ **187 |**, ▶ **211 |**
 four = quatre
 four apples = quatre pommes
 I've got four (of them) = j'en ai quatre

fourteen *number* ▶ **187 |**, ▶ **211 |**
 fourteen = quatorze

fourteenth *number*
• (*in a series*) = quatorzième
• (*in dates*) ▶ **222 |**
 the fourteenth of July = le quatorze juillet

fourth *number*
• (*in a series*) = quatrième
• (*in dates*) ▶ **222 |**
 the fourth of July = le quatre juillet

fox *noun*
 a fox = un renard

fragile *adjective*
 = fragile

frame *noun*
 a frame = un cadre

France *noun* ▶ **218 |**
 France = la France

frank *adjective*
 = franc/franche

freckle *noun*
 a freckle = une tache de rousseur

free
1 *adjective*
• (*costing nothing*) = gratuit/gratuite
• (*independent, able to come and go*) = libre
 he is free to do what he likes = il est libre
 de faire ce qu'il veut
• (*not occupied, available*) = libre
 are you free on Monday? = est-ce que tu
 es libre lundi?
2 *verb*
 = libérer
3 *adverb*
 = gratuitement

freedom *noun*
 freedom = la liberté

freeway *noun* (*US English*)
 a freeway = une autoroute

freeze *verb*
• (*in cold weather*) = geler
 the river froze = la rivière a gelé
 the ground was frozen = le sol était gelé
• (*in a freezer*) = congeler
• **to freeze to death** = mourir de froid

freezer *noun*
 a freezer = un congélateur

freezing *adjective*
  it's freezing = il fait un temps glacial
  this room is freezing = cette pièce est
    glaciale
  to be freezing (*if it's a person*) = être
    gelé/gelée

French ▶ 275
1 *adjective*
  = français/française
2 *noun*
• (*the people*)
  the French = les Français (*masculine
    plural*)
• (*the language*)
  French = le français

French fries *noun*
  French fries = les frites (*feminine*)

fresh *adjective*
  = frais/fraîche

Friday *noun* ▶ 222
  Friday = vendredi (*masculine*)

fridge *noun*
  a fridge = un frigo✶

fried *adjective*
  = frit/frite

fried egg *noun*
  a fried egg = un œuf sur le plat

friend *noun*
  a friend = un ami/une amie
  to make friends = se faire des amis
  to make friends with someone = devenir
    ami/amie avec quelqu'un

friendly *adjective*
  = gentil/gentille

fright *noun*
  to get a fright = avoir peur
  to give someone a fright = faire peur à
    quelqu'un

frightened *adjective*
  to be frightened = avoir peur

fringe *noun* (*British English*)
  a fringe = une frange

frog *noun*
  a frog = une grenouille

from *preposition*

  ! *There are many verbs which involve the
  use of* from, *like* borrow from, escape from
  etc. For translations, look up the entries at
  borrow, escape *etc.*

✶ in informal situations

• from = de (**!** d' + *vowel or mute h*)
  the boy from London = le garçon (qui
    vient) de Londres
  where is she from? = d'où vient-elle?
  to come back from the office = rentrer du
    bureau
  to return from a holiday = rentrer de
    vacances
  there's a message from Paul = il y a un
    message de Paul
  the train from Oxford is late = le train en
    provenance d'Oxford est en retard
  we live ten minutes from the city centre
    = nous habitons à dix minutes du
    centre-ville
• (*when talking about time*) = de, à partir de
  the shop is open from eight to six = le
    magasin est ouvert de huit heures à
    dix-huit heures
  from Monday to Saturday = du lundi au
    samedi
  from April on = à partir du mois d'avril
  from then on = à partir de ce moment-là
  fifty years from now = d'ici cinquante ans
• (*British English*) (*in arithmetic*)
  5 from 8 leaves 3 = 5 ôté de 8, il reste 3

front
1 *noun*
• (*of a building*)
  the front of a house = la façade d'une
    maison
  the front of a shop = la devanture d'un
    magasin
  my room is at the front of the house = ma
    chambre est sur le devant de la maison
• (*of a car, a train or queue*)
  at the front of the bus = à l'avant du bus
  at the front of the queue = au début de la
    queue
2 in front of = devant

front door *noun*
  the front door = la porte d'entrée

front page *noun*
  the front page = la première page

front seat *noun*
  the front seat = le siège avant

frost *noun*
  frost = le givre, la gelée

frozen *adjective*
  = congelé/congelée

fruit *noun*
  a piece of fruit = un fruit
  he likes fruit = il aime les fruits

frustrated *adjective*
  = frustré/frustrée

fry *verb*
  to fry potatoes = faire frire des pommes de
    terre

frying pan *noun* (*British English*)
  a frying pan = une poêle

full *adjective*
- (*not empty*) = plein/pleine
  the streets were full of people = les rues étaient pleines de monde
- (*describing a flight, a hotel*) = complet/complète
- (*maximum*)
  to travel at full speed = rouler à toute vitesse
  to get full marks = obtenir la note maximale
- (*complete*)
  to pay the full fare = payer plein tarif
  his full name = ses nom et prénom

full-time *adverb*
= à plein temps
to work full-time = travailler à plein temps

fumes *noun*
fumes = les fumées (*feminine*)

fun *noun*
it's fun = c'est amusant
skiing is fun = c'est amusant de faire du ski
to have fun = s'amuser (**!** + *être*)
she's fun = on s'amuse bien avec elle

function *verb*
= fonctionner

funeral *noun*
a funeral = un enterrement

funfair *noun* (*British English*)
a funfair = une fête foraine

funny *adjective*
- (*amusing*) = drôle, amusant/amusante
- (*odd*) = drôle, bizarre

fur *noun*
fur (*an animal's coat*) = les poils (*masculine plural*)
(*on a garment*) = la fourrure

furious *adjective*
= furieux/furieuse

furniture *noun*
a piece of furniture = un meuble
furniture = les meubles

further *adverb*
= plus loin
he lives further away from the school = il habite plus loin de l'école
how much further is it? = c'est encore loin?

fuss *noun*
a fuss = des histoires (*feminine plural*)

future
1 *noun*
the future = l'avenir (*masculine*)
in the future = dans l'avenir
in future, let us know = à l'avenir, préviens-nous
2 *adjective*
= futur/future

Gg

gallery *noun*
a gallery = un musée

game *noun*
a game = un jeu
a game of football = un match de football
a game of tennis = une partie de tennis

games *noun* (*British English*)
games = le sport

game show *noun*
a game show = un jeu télévisé

gang *noun*
a gang (*a group of friends, young people*) = une bande
(*of criminals*) = un gang

gap *noun*
- **a gap** (*in a fence or hedge*) = un trou
  (*between buildings, cars*) = un espace
- (*a period of time*)
  a gap = un intervalle

garage *noun*
a garage = un garage

garbage *noun* (*US English*)
garbage = les ordures (*feminine plural*)

garden
1 *noun*
a garden = un jardin
2 *verb*
= faire du jardinage

gardener *noun* ▶ 315|
a gardener = un jardinier/une jardinière

gardening *noun*
gardening = le jardinage

garlic *noun*
garlic = l'ail (*masculine*)

gas *noun*
- (*for cooking, heating*)
  gas = le gaz
- (*US English*) (*gasoline*)
  gas = l'essence (*feminine*)

gas station *noun* (*US English*)
a gas station = une station-service

gate *noun*
a gate (*to a garden, a town, a prison*) = une porte
(*to a field*) = une barrière

gather *verb*
- (*to come together*) = se rassembler
  (**!** + *être*)

Games and sports

With or without the definite article?

French normally uses **le, la, l'** or **les** with names of games and sports:

football	= le football
chess	= les échecs (*masculine plural*)
to play football	= jouer au football
to play tennis	= jouer au tennis
to play chess	= jouer aux échecs
to go climbing	= faire de l'escalade
to beat somebody at tennis	= battre quelqu'un au tennis
to win at chess	= gagner aux échecs
to lose at marbles	= perdre aux billes

Players and events

a tennis player	= un joueur de tennis

but

I'm not a tennis player	= je ne joue pas au tennis
he's a good tennis player	= il joue bien au tennis
a game of tennis	= une partie de tennis
a tennis champion	= un champion de tennis
the French tennis champion	= le champion de France de tennis
a tennis championship	= un championnat de tennis
the rules of tennis	= les règles du tennis

- (*to collect*)
  to gather wood = ramasser du bois
  to gather fruit = cueillir des fruits

gay *adjective*
= homosexuel/homosexuelle

gear *noun*
- (*in a car or bus, on a bike*)
  a gear = une vitesse
- (*equipment*)
  gear = le matériel
  fishing gear = le matériel de pêche
- (*clothes*)
  my football gear = ma tenue de football
  your swimming gear = tes affaires pour la piscine

Gemini *noun*
Gemini = Gémeaux (*masculine*)

general
1 *noun*
  a general = un général
2 *adjective*
  = général/générale
3 **in general** = en général

generation *noun*
  a generation = une génération

generous *adjective*
  = généreux/généreuse

Geneva *noun* ▶ 218 |
  Geneva = Genève

genius *noun*
  a genius = un génie

gentle *adjective*
= doux/douce

gentleman *noun*
  a gentleman = un monsieur

geography *noun*
  geography = la géographie

germ *noun*
  a germ = un microbe

German ▶ 275 |
1 *adjective*
  = allemand/allemande
2 *noun*
- (*the people*)
  the Germans = les Allemands (*masculine*)
- (*the language*)
  German = l'allemand (*masculine*)

Germany *noun* ▶ 218 |
  Germany = l'Allemagne (*feminine*)

get *verb*
▶ See the boxed note on **get** for more
information and examples.
get away
- (*to escape*) = s'échapper (**!** + *être*)
- **he won't get away with it** = il ne va pas s'en
  tirer comme ça
get back
- (*to return*) = revenir (**!** + *être*)
- (*to have back*) = récupérer
  I got my bike back = j'ai récupéré mon
    vélo
  he'll get his money back = il va être
    remboursé

get

A multi-purpose verb

The word **get** is extremely common in English and does not have a multi-purpose French equivalent.

However, it is helpful to try to find a synonym (a word which has the same sense) and from there, a suitable translation:

*he's gone to **get** (or **fetch**) help* = il est parti **chercher** de l'aide
*I'll call when **we get** (or **arrive**) there* = j'appellerai quand **nous arriverons**

Main senses

When changing from one state (of mind) to another

French very often has a specific verb for the various combinations of **to get** + *adjective*:

to get old | angry | worried = vieillir / se fâcher / s'inquiéter

devenir + *adjective* is also useful:

to get jealous = **devenir** jaloux / jalouse

When asking, telling or persuading

The translations **dire (à quelqu'un)** and **demander (à quelqu'un)** are helpful:

get him to call me = **dis-lui** de m'appeler
I'll get her to help me = je **lui demanderai** de m'aider

When getting things done by someone else

The construction **faire** + *infinitive verb* is useful here:

to get the car cleaned = **faire nettoyer** la voiture
to get a TV repaired = **faire réparer** une télévision
to get one's hair cut = **se faire couper** les cheveux

When to get means to obtain

to get (or buy)someone a present = **acheter** un cadeau à quelqu'un
I got (or found) a job in Paris = j'**ai trouvé** un travail à Paris

When to get means to receive

The best translation is **recevoir**:

we got a letter from Mark = nous **avons reçu** une lettre de Mark
but
to get good grades = **avoir** de bonnes notes

When cooking

A translation which will work well is **préparer**:

to get dinner = **préparer** le déjeuner

With illnesses:

In this context **attraper** is useful:

to get measles = **attraper** la rougeole
to get a cold = **s'enrhumer** (+ *être*)

When using transport

The most reliable translation is **prendre**:

we can get the bus = on peut **prendre** le bus
to get a taxi to the station = **prendre** un taxi pour aller à la gare

▶ To find translations for other expressions using get—**to get sick, to get a surprise, to get better**, etc. —look up the entries at **sick, surprise, better**, etc.

▶ You will also find translations for *phrasal verbs* using get (**get down, get away, get on get up**) listed separately in the dictionary.

get down
- (*to come or go down*) = descendre
  (**!** + *être*)
  can he get down from the tree? = est-ce
  qu'il peut descendre de l'arbre?
- (*to take down*) = descendre (**!** + *avoir*)
  I got the box down from the shelf = j'ai
  descendu la boîte de l'étagère
- (*to depress*) = déprimer
  it gets him down = ça le déprime
get in = entrer (**!** + *être*)
get off
- (*to leave a bus or train*) = descendre
  (**!** + *être*)
  I'm getting off at the next stop = je
  descends au prochain arrêt
  he fell as he was getting off the train = il
  est tombé en descendant du train
- (*to remove*) = enlever
  to get a stain off = enlever une tache
get on
- (*to climb on board a bus or train*) = monter
  (**!** + *être*)
  to get on the bus = monter dans le bus
- **to get on well** = bien s'entendre (**!** + *être*)
  I get on well with her = je m'entends bien
  avec elle
- (*in polite enquiries*)
  how did you get on? = comment est-ce
  que ça s'est passé?
  how is she getting on at school? = et ses
  études, ça marche**✱**?
get out
- (*to leave*) = sortir (**!** + *être*)
  she got out of the building = elle est sortie
  du bâtiment
- (*to take out*) = sortir (**!** + *avoir*)
  to get the furniture out of the house
  = sortir les meubles de la maison
get over
  to get over a shock = se remettre d'un
  choc
get through to
  to get through to someone = avoir
  quelqu'un au téléphone
get together = se réunir (**!** + *être*)
get up = se lever (**!** + *être*)

ghost *noun*
  a ghost = un fantôme

gift *noun*
- (*a present*)
  a gift = un cadeau
- (*an ability*)
  a gift = un don
  to have a gift for languages = avoir le don
  des langues

ginger *adjective* ▶ **213**|
  = roux/rousse
  to have ginger hair (*British English*) = avoir
  les cheveux roux

girl *noun*
  a girl = une fille

girlfriend *noun*
  a girlfriend (*in a couple*) = une (petite)
  amie
  (*a female friend*) = une amie

give *verb*
  ! *For translations of expressions like* to
  give someone a lift, to give someone an
  injection, to give someone a fright *etc*,
  look up the entries lift, injection, fright.

- **to give** = donner
  to give someone a book = donner un livre
  à quelqu'un
  I gave him the photos = je lui ai donné les
  photos
  give me the newspapers = donne-moi les
  journaux
  give them to me = donne-les-moi
  to give someone a drink = donner à boire
  à quelqu'un
  to give one's seat to someone = laisser sa
  place à quelqu'un
- (*to offer*) = offrir
  he gave us one of his pictures = il nous a
  offert un de ses tableaux
  to give someone a present = faire un
  cadeau à quelqu'un
- **to give someone a message** = transmettre
  un message à quelqu'un
give away
- (*to make a present of*) = donner
- **to give away a secret** = révéler un secret
give back = rendre
give in = céder
give off
  to give off fumes = dégager des vapeurs
give out
  to give out the exercise books
  = distribuer les cahiers
give up
- (*to stop*)
  to give up smoking = cesser de fumer
  to give up the idea of working abroad
  = renoncer à l'idée de travailler à
  l'étranger
- **to give oneself up to the police** = se livrer à
  la police

glad *adjective*
  = content/contente

glass *noun*
  a glass = un verre

glasses *noun*
  glasses = les lunettes (*feminine*)

glove *noun*
  a glove = un gant

glow *verb*
  = luire

glue
1 *noun*
  glue = la colle

✱ in informal situations

2 *verb*
= coller

go *verb*
▶ **253 |** *See the boxed note on* go *for more information and examples.*
go across = traverser
go after = poursuivre
go ahead
* (*if it's an event*) = avoir lieu
  the concert's going ahead after all = le concert aura finalement lieu
* (*if it's a person*)
  go ahead, there's no-one there = vas-y, il n'y a personne
go around ▶ **go round**
go around with ▶ **go round with**
go away = partir (**!** + *être*)
  go away! = allez-vous-en!, va-t'en!
go back = retourner (**!** + *être*)
  Gary went back to Paris = Gary est retourné à Paris
  to go back to school = reprendre les cours
  to go back to work = reprendre le travail
  to go back to sleep = se rendormir (**!** + *être*)
go by = passer (**!** + *être*)
go down
* (*if it's quality, a price, a salary*) = baisser
* (*if it's a person*) = descendre
  she went down into the basement = elle est descendue au sous-sol
  we went down the hill = nous avons descendu la pente
* (*if it's the sun*) = se coucher (**!** + *être*)
* (*if it's a computer*) = tomber en panne (**!** + *être*)
go in
* (*to enter*) = entrer (**!** + *être*)
* (*to return inside*) = rentrer (**!** + *être*)
go off
* (*to explode*) = exploser
* (*to ring*) (*if it's an alarm clock*) = sonner (*if it's an alarm*) = se déclencher (**!** + *être*)
* (*to leave*) = partir (**!** + *être*)
* **the milk will go off** = le lait va tourner
* (*to be switched off*) = s'éteindre (**!** + *être*)
go on
* (*to continue*) = continuer
  to go on talking = continuer à parler
* (*to happen*)
  what's going on? = qu'est-ce qui se passe?
* (*to keep talking*)
  he goes on (and on) about his work = il n'arrête pas de parler de son travail
* (*to be switched on*) (*if it's a light*) = s'allumer (**!** + *être*)
  (*if it's heating, a machine*) = se mettre en marche (**!** + *être*)
go out
* (*to leave the house*) = sortir (**!** + *être*)
  are you going out this evening? = est-ce que tu sors ce soir?
* (*as a boyfriend, a girlfriend*)
  to go out with someone = sortir avec quelqu'un

* (*to be switched off, to stop burning*) = s'éteindre (**!** + *être*)
* **the tide's going out** = la marée descend
go over
* (*to check*)
  to go over some grammar = vérifier quelques points de grammaire
* (*to revise*) = revoir
go round
* (*British English*) (*to call on*) = passer (**!** + *être*)
  to go round to see someone = passer voir quelqu'un
* (*to walk around, to visit*) = visiter
  to go round the museums = visiter les musées
  to go round the shops = faire les magasins
* (*to be enough*)
  is there enough bread to go round? = est-ce qu'il y a assez de pain pour tout le monde?
go round with
* (*British English*) (*to spend time with*) = fréquenter
go through
* (*to have, to live through*)
  to go through a difficult time = traverser une période difficile
  I don't want to go through that again = je ne voudrais pas revivre ça
* (*to search*) = fouiller
* (*to check*) = examiner
go together = aller ensemble
  the skirt and blouse go well together = la jupe et la chemise vont bien ensemble
go up
* (*if it's a person*) = monter
  he went up to bed = il est monté se coucher
  he went up the stairs = il a monté l'escalier
  to go up to the top of the hill = monter jusqu'en haut de la colline
  to go up to the top floor = monter jusqu'au dernier étage
* (*if it's a price, a salary*) = augmenter
go with = aller avec (**!** + *être*)
  the trousers don't really go with your jacket = le pantalon ne va pas très bien avec ta veste

goal *noun*
  a goal = un but

goalkeeper *noun*
  a goalkeeper = un gardien de but

goat *noun*
  a goat = une chèvre

god *noun*
  a god = un dieu
  God = Dieu

goddaughter *noun*
  a goddaughter = une filleule

godfather *noun*
  a godfather = un parrain

G

godmother noun
a godmother = une marraine

godson noun
a godson = un filleul

going: to be going to
= aller
I'm going to [leave | go to Ireland | learn to
drive …] = je vais [partir | aller en Irlande |
apprendre à conduire …]
we were going to phone you = on allait te
téléphoner

gold
1 noun
gold = l'or (masculine)
2 adjective
= en or
a gold ring = une bague en or

goldfish noun
a goldfish = un poisson rouge

golf noun ▶ 248 |
golf = le golf

golf course noun
a golf course = un terrain de golf

good
1 adjective
• good = bon/bonne (❗ before the noun)
a good book = un bon livre
a good party = une bonne soirée
we've got some good news = nous avons
de bonnes nouvelles
to have good eyesight = avoir une bonne
vue
to be good [at chemistry | at drawing | at
chess …] = être bon/bonne [en chimie | en
dessin | aux échecs …]
it's a good time to visit Paris = c'est le bon
moment pour visiter Paris
exercise is good for you = ça fait du bien
de faire de l'exercice
to look good (healthy) = avoir bonne mine
I don't feel too good = je ne me sens pas
très bien
I had a good time = je me suis bien amusé
• (talking about food) = bon/bonne (❗ before
the noun)
• (obedient) = sage
• (kind) = gentil/gentille
it's very good of you to let me know = c'est
très gentil de votre part de me prévenir
2 noun
it's no good shouting = ça ne sert à rien
de crier
to be no good at Latin = être nul/nulle❌ en
latin
the change will do you good = le
changement te fera du bien
3 exclamation
• (when pleased)
good = c'est bien

❌ in informal situations

• (when relieved)
'he's much better'—'good' = 'il va
beaucoup mieux'—'tant mieux'
• (when praising)
good! = très bien!
4 for good = pour toujours

good afternoon noun (also
exclamation)
good afternoon (when meeting) = bonjour
(when leaving) = au revoir

goodbye noun (also exclamation)
goodbye = au revoir

good evening noun (also exclamation)
good evening = bonsoir

good-looking adjective
= beau/belle (❗ before the noun)

good morning noun (also exclamation)
good morning (when meeting) = bonjour
(when leaving) = au revoir

goodnight noun (also exclamation)
goodnight = bonne nuit

goods noun
goods = la marchandise (singular)

goose noun
a goose = une oie

gooseberry noun
a gooseberry = une groseille à maquereau

gorilla noun
a gorilla = un gorille

gossip verb
• (to chat) = bavarder
• (to talk in a harmful way) = faire des
commérages

got: to have got verb
▶ See the boxed note on got for more
information and examples.
• (to have) = avoir
I've got work to do = j'ai du travail
have you got a cold? = est-ce que tu as un
rhume?
• (to be obliged to)
to have got to = devoir
I've got to [go | work | get dressed …] = je
dois [partir | travailler | m'habiller …], il faut
que [je parte | je travaille | je m'habille …]
❗ Note that the subjunctive is used after il
faut que.

government noun
a government = un gouvernement

GP noun ▶ 315 | (British English)
a GP = un médecin, un généraliste

grab verb
to grab someone by the arm = saisir
quelqu'un par le bras
he tried to grab my handbag = il a essayé
d'arracher mon sac à main

go

▶ You will find translations for phrasal verbs like **go away**, **go back**, **go round**, etc listed separately in the dictionary.

▶ For translations of expressions like **I'm going to leave** / **go to London** / **learn to drive**, see the entry **going**.

Getting from A to B

Generally **go** is translated by **aller** (**!** + *être*):

we went to the cinema	= nous sommes allés au cinéma
to go to town | *to school* | *to the market*	= aller en ville | à l'école | au marché
to go to Brussels | *to Germany* | *to Japan*	= aller à Bruxelles | en Allemagne | au Japon
to go to the dentist's | *the doctor's* | *the chemist's*	= aller chez le dentiste | le médecin | le pharmacien
to go for a swim | *for a coffee* | *for a walk*	= aller nager | prendre un café | se promener

G

Translating verbs of movement in French

Moving in, out, back, away etc is usually translated using a single verb in French which takes **être**:

to go into a room	= entrer dans une pièce
to go away on vacation	= partir en vacances
to go back to work in France	= retourner travailler en France
to go home	= rentrer
to go outside	= sortir
to go upstairs	= monter

See also the phrasal verbs listed separately for further translations.

go meaning *to become*

There is often a single French verb to translate the structure **to go** + *adjective*:

to go pale	= pâlir
to go red	= rougir

but

the light went red	= le feu est passé au rouge

devenir + *adjective* is a useful alternative:

to go crazy	= devenir fou / folle
to go blind	= devenir aveugle

In polite inquiries

how's it going?	= comment ça va?
everything's going very well	= tout va très bien
how did the exam go?	= comment s'est passé l'examen?

Talking about time, money, food ...

the time goes so quickly	= le temps passe si vite
200 francs won't go far here	= on n'ira pas loin avec 200 francs ici
the money's | *bread's* | *petrol's gone*	= il n'y a plus d'argent / de pain / d'essence

Describing how (and if) something works

is the car going?	= est-ce que la voiture marche?
it's still not going	= ça ne marche toujours pas
to get the heating going	= mettre le chauffage en marche

grade noun
* (a mark)
  a grade = une note
* (US English) (a class)
  a grade = une classe
  he's in the eighth grade = il est en
    quatrième

grade school noun (US English)
  grade school = l'école primaire
  ! Note that école is feminine.

gradually adverb
= peu à peu

gram(me) noun ▶ 285 |
  a gram = un gramme

grammar noun
  grammar = la grammaire

grandchild noun
  a grandchild = un petit-fils/une petite-
    fille
  the grandchildren = les petits-enfants

granddaughter noun
  a granddaughter = une petite-fille

grandfather noun
  a grandfather = un grand-père

grandmother noun
  a grandmother = une grand-mère

grandparents noun
  grandparents = les grands-parents
    (masculine)

grandson noun
  a grandson = un petit-fils

grapefruit noun
  a grapefruit = un pamplemousse

grapes noun
  grapes = le raisin (singular)
  a bunch of grapes = une grappe de raisin

grass noun
  grass = l'herbe (feminine)
  (in gardens) = la pelouse
  to cut the grass = tondre la pelouse

grasshopper noun
  a grasshopper = une sauterelle

grateful adjective
= reconnaissant/reconnaissante
  **I would be grateful if you could let me
    know** = je vous serais reconnaissant de
    me prévenir

grave noun
  a grave = une tombe

gray (US English) ▶ **grey**

grease noun
  grease = la graisse

greasy adjective
= gras/grasse

great adjective
* (stressing size, amount, importance)
  = grand/grande (**!** before the noun)
  a great improvement = une grande
    amélioration
  to have great difficulty reading = avoir
    beaucoup de mal à lire
  the guide book was a great help = le
    guide a été très utile
* (showing enthusiasm)
  that's great! = c'est formidable!, c'est
    génial✶!
  I had a great time = je me suis bien amusé

Great Britain noun ▶ 218 |
  Great Britain = la Grande-Bretagne

great grandfather noun
  a great grandfather = un arrière-grand-
    père

great grandmother noun
  a great grandmother = une arrière-grand-
    mère

Greece noun ▶ 218 |
  Greece = la Grèce

greedy adjective
= gourmand/gourmande

Greek ▶ 275 |
1 adjective
= grec/grecque
2 noun
* (the people)
  the Greeks = les Grecs (masculine)
* (the language)
  Greek = le grec

green adjective ▶ 213 |
= vert/verte

greenhouse noun
  a greenhouse = une serre

grey (British English), **gray** (US English)
adjective ▶ 213 |
= gris/grise
  to have grey hair = avoir les cheveux gris

grill verb
= faire griller

grin verb
= sourire

grocer noun ▶ 315 |
  a grocer = un épicier/une épicière

grocery noun ▶ 315 |
  a grocery = une épicerie

ground noun
* **the ground** = le sol
  the ground is hard in winter = le sol est
    dur en hiver
  to throw papers on the ground = jeter des
    papiers par terre
  to get up off the ground = se lever
    (**!** + être)

- (*land used for sports*)
  a **sports ground** = un terrain de sport

ground floor *noun* (*British English*)
  the **ground floor** = le rez-de-chaussée

group *noun*
- (*a number of people*)
  a **group** = un groupe
- (*a band*)
  a (**rock**) **group** = un groupe (de rock)

grow *verb*
- (*to get big, strong*) (*if it's a person, an animal*) = grandir
  (*if it's a plant*) = pousser
- (*as a gardener, a farmer*) = cultiver
  to **grow vegetables** = cultiver des légumes
- (*to get long*) = pousser
  she's decided to let her hair grow = elle a décidé de se laisser pousser les cheveux
- (*to let grow*)
  to **grow a beard** = se laisser pousser la barbe
- (*to become*) = devenir (**!** + *être*)
  she's grown more cynical = elle est devenue plus cynique
  to **grow old** = vieillir
- (*to increase in size*)
  the **population will grow** = la population va augmenter
grow up = grandir
  when I grow up, I want to be a doctor = je veux être médecin quand je serai grand

grumble *verb*
  = ronchonner

guard *noun*
- (*in a prison, at a bank*)
  a **guard** = un gardien/une gardienne
- (*in the army*)
  a **guard** = un garde
  to **be on guard** = être de garde

guard dog *noun*
  a **guard dog** = un chien de garde

guess *verb*
  = deviner

guest *noun*
- (*a person invited to stay*)
  a **guest** = un invité/une invitée
- (*at a hotel*)
  a **guest** = un client/une cliente

guesthouse *noun*
  a **guesthouse** = une pension de famille

guide
1 *noun*
- (*a person*)
  a (**tour**) **guide** = un guide
- (*British English*) (*a Girl Guide*)
  a **guide** = une guide
2 *verb*
  = guider

guide book *noun*
  a **guide book** = un guide

guided tour *noun*
  a **guided tour** = une visite guidée

guilty *adjective*
  = coupable
  to **feel guilty** = culpabiliser

guinea pig *noun*
  a **guinea pig** = un cochon d'Inde

guitar *noun* ▶ **290**
  a **guitar** = une guitare

gum *noun*
  the **gum** = la gencive

gun *noun*
  a **gun** (*a weapon*) = une arme à feu
  (*a rifle*) = un fusil
  (*a revolver*) = un revolver

gym *noun*
  a **gym** = une salle de gym**✶**

gymnasium *noun*
  a **gymnasium** = un gymnase

gymnastics *noun* ▶ **248**
  gymnastics = la gymnastique

gypsy *noun*
  a **gypsy** = un gitan/une gitane

Hh

habit *noun*
  a **habit** = une habitude

hail *noun*
  hail = la grêle

hair *noun*
  hair (*on the head*) = les cheveux (*masculine plural*)
  (*on the body*) = les poils (*masculine plural*)

hairbrush *noun*
  a **hairbrush** = une brosse à cheveux

hairdresser *noun* ▶ **315**
  a **hairdresser** = un coiffeur/une coiffeuse

hairdryer *noun*
  a **hairdryer** = un sèche-cheveux

hairstyle *noun*
  a **hairstyle** = une coiffure

half ▶ **317**
1 *noun*
- a **half** = une moitié
  to **cut a melon in half** = couper un melon en deux
- (*in a game*)
  the **first half** = la première mi-temps

2 *adjective*
a half-litre of milk, half a litre of milk = un demi-litre de lait
3 *pronoun*
• (*when talking about quantities, numbers*)
to spend half of one's pocket money = dépenser la moitié de son argent de poche
half the pupils speak French = la moitié des élèves parlent français
• (*when talking about time, age*) ▶ 211 ▮, ▶ 187 ▮
an hour and a half = une heure et demie
he's three and a half = il a trois ans et demi
it's half (past) three (*British English*) = il est trois heures et demie
4 *adverb*
Sam's half French half Irish = Sam est moitié français moitié irlandais

half hour *noun* ▶ 356 ▮
a half hour = une demi-heure

half term *noun* (*British English*)
half term = les vacances de la mi-trimestre
! *Note that* **vacances** *is feminine plural.*

hall *noun*
• (*in a house, an apartment*)
a hall = une entrée
• (*for public events*)
a hall = une grande salle

ham *noun*
ham = le jambon

hamburger *noun*
a hamburger = un hamburger

hammer *noun*
a hammer = un marteau

hamster *noun*
a hamster = un hamster

hand *noun*
• (*the part of the body*) ▶ 201 ▮
the hand = la main
he had a pencil in his hand = il avait un crayon à la main
to hold someone's hand = tenir quelqu'un par la main
• (*help*)
a hand = un coup de main
• (*on a clock or watch*)
a hand = une aiguille
• (*when judging a situation or subject*)
on the one hand..., on the other... = d'un côté..., d'un autre côté...

handbag *noun*
a handbag = un sac à main

handball *noun* ▶ 248 ▮
handball = le handball

handicapped *adjective*
= handicapé/handicapée

handkerchief *noun*
a handkerchief = un mouchoir

handle *noun*
a handle = une poignée

handsome *adjective*
= beau/belle (! *before the noun*)
a handsome man = un bel homme

handwriting *noun*
handwriting = l'écriture (*feminine*)

handy *adjective*
• (*practical*) = pratique
• (*helpful*) = utile

hang *verb*
• (*on a hook, a coat hanger, a line*)
to hang a picture (up) on the wall = accrocher un tableau au mur
to hang clothes (up) in a wardrobe = suspendre des vêtements dans une armoire
to hang clothes on a line = étendre du linge
• (*to be attached*)
the portrait hangs over the piano = le portrait est accroché au-dessus du piano
to be hanging from the ceiling = être suspendu/suspendue au plafond
• (*to kill*) = pendre
hang around
• (*to wait*) = attendre
• (*to waste time, to do nothing*) = traîner
hang on to = s'agripper à (! + *être*)
she was hanging on to the rope = elle s'agrippait à la corde
hang up
• (*on a hook, a coat hanger, a line*)
to hang up one's coat = accrocher son manteau
to hang clothes up to dry = mettre des vêtements à sécher
• **your coat's hanging up in the hall** = ton manteau est suspendu dans l'entrée
• (*when phoning*) = raccrocher

hang-gliding *noun* ▶ 248 ▮
hang-gliding = le deltaplane

happen *verb*
• (*to occur*) = se passer (! + *être*), arriver (! + *être*)
what happened? = qu'est-ce qui s'est passé?, qu'est-ce qui est arrivé?
the accident happened last week = l'accident est arrivé la semaine dernière
to happen again = se reproduire (! + *être*)
• (*to affect someone*)
what happened to you? = qu'est-ce qui t'est arrivé?
something odd happened to me = il m'est arrivé quelque chose de bizarre

happy *adjective*
- (*content*) = heureux/heureuse
  to make someone happy = rendre quelqu'un heureux
  they were happy to hear from you = ils ont été heureux d'avoir de tes nouvelles
  he's happy with the language course = le cours de langue lui plaît
- (*in greetings*)
  Happy birthday! = Bon anniversaire!
  Happy New Year! = Bonne année!

hard
1 *adjective*
- (*firm, stiff*) = dur/dure
  the ground is hard = le sol est dur
- (*difficult*) = difficile
  a hard question = une question difficile
  it's not hard to change a light bulb = ce n'est pas difficile de changer une ampoule
  it's hard to understand = c'est difficile à comprendre
  I find it hard to concentrate = j'ai du mal à me concentrer
- (*harsh, tough*)
  a hard winter = un hiver rude
  to be having a hard time = traverser une période difficile
- (*severe*) = dur/dure, sévère
2 *adverb*
  to work hard = travailler dur
  they hit him hard = ils l'ont frappé fort
  to try hard to concentrate = faire beaucoup d'efforts pour se concentrer

hardly *adverb*
= à peine
  I hardly know them = je les connais à peine

hardware *noun*
  hardware (*for computers*) = le matériel (informatique)

hard-working *adjective*
= travailleur/travailleuse

hare *noun*
  a hare = un lièvre

harm *verb*
  to harm someone = faire du mal à quelqu'un
  to harm the environment = nuire à l'environnement

harmful *adjective*
= nocif/nocive

harmless *adjective*
= inoffensif/inoffensive

harp *noun* ▶ **290**
  a harp = une harpe

harvest *noun*
  the harvest (*of wheat*) = la moisson
  (*of fruit*) = la récolte
  (*of grapes*) = la vendange

hat *noun*
  a hat = un chapeau

hate *verb*
- (*to feel a strong dislike for*)
  to hate someone = détester quelqu'un
- (*to feel hatred for*) = haïr

hatred *noun*
  hatred = la haine

have
1 *verb*
▶ **258** *See the boxed note on* have *for more information and examples.*
- (*to eat, to drink*)
  to have a sandwich = manger un sandwich
  to have a glass of wine = boire un verre de vin
  to have dinner = dîner
- (*to get*)
  I had a letter from Bob yesterday = j'ai reçu une lettre de Bob hier
  I'll let you have the money soon = je te donnerai l'argent bientôt
- (*to hold or organize*)
  to have a party = faire une fête
  to have a competition = organiser un concours
- (*to spend*) ▶ **237**
  we had a nice day at the beach = nous avons passé une journée agréable à la plage
  I'll have a good time in Paris = je m'amuserai bien à Paris
- (*to suffer*)
  to have [flu | a headache | a toothache ...] = avoir [la grippe | mal à la tête | mal aux dents ...]
- (*to get something done*)
  to have the house painted = faire peindre la maison
  she had her hair cut = elle s'est fait couper les cheveux
- **to have a baby** = avoir un enfant
2 *auxiliary verb*

  ! *For a detailed note on the use of* have *as an auxiliary verb, see the boxed note on* have. *All verbs which don't take* avoir *as an auxiliary verb are marked (***!** *+ être) in this dictionary.*

  you've seen her, haven't you? = tu l'as vue, n'est-ce pas?
  he hasn't called, has he? = il n'a pas téléphoné, par hasard?
  'I've no money'—'yes you have!' = 'je n'ai pas d'argent'—'mais si tu en as!'
3 to have to = devoir
  I have to [study | pay | go home ...] = je dois [étudier | payer | rentrer ...]
  you don't have to go back to France = tu n'es pas obligé de retourner en France

hay *noun*
  hay = le foin

H

have

As an ordinary verb

● When **have** or **have got** is used as a verb meaning *possess*, it can generally be translated by **avoir**:

> *I **have** (got) a car* = j'**ai** une voiture
> *she **has** (got) a good memory* = elle **a** une bonne mémoire
> *they **have** (got) problems* = ils **ont** des problèmes

For examples and particular usages see the entry **have**; see also the entry **got**.

● **have** is also used with certain noun objects where the whole expression is equivalent to a verb: *to have dinner* = to dine; *to have a walk* = to walk; *to have a swim* = to swim. In such cases, the phrase is very often translated by the equivalent verb in French (*dîner, se promener, se baigner*).

As an auxiliary verb

● When used as an auxiliary in present perfect and past perfect tenses, **have** is normally translated by **avoir**:

> *I **have** seen* = j'**ai** vu
> *I **had** seen* = j'**avais** vu

● However, some verbs in French, especially verbs of movement and change of state (*aller, venir, descendre, mourir*), always take **être** in these tenses:

> *he **has** left* = il **est** parti
> *she's fallen* = elle **est** tombée

In this case, remember the past participle agrees with the subject of the verb:

> *she **has** gone* = elle **est** allée
> *they **had** come back* = ils **étaient** revenus
> *we **had** stayed at home* = nous **étions** restés chez nous

If you are in doubt as to whether a verb conjugates with **être** or **avoir**, consult the French entry, where verbs taking **être** will be indicated like this: (**!** + *être*).

● Reflexive verbs (*se lever, se coucher*) always conjugate with **être**:

> *she **has** fainted* = elle **s'est** évanouie
> *have you **had** a rest?* = est-ce que tu **t'es** reposé?
> *he **had** fallen asleep* = il **s'était** endormi
> *I **had** changed my clothes* = je **m'étais** changé

In this case, the past participle agrees with the reflexive pronoun only when the pronoun is a direct object. Otherwise there is no agreement:

> *she **has** hurt herself* = elle **s'est** fait mal
> *I've washed my hair* = je **me suis** lavé les cheveux
> *he's broken his leg* = il **s'est** cassé la jambe

to have (got) to

● **to have (got) to** meaning *must* is translated by either **devoir** or the impersonal construction **il faut que** + *subjunctive*:

> *I **have** to leave now* = je **dois** partir maintenant
> = **il faut que** je parte maintenant
> *you've **got** to understand* = tu **dois** comprendre
> = **il faut que** tu comprennes

● In negative sentences, **not to have to** is usually translated by **ne pas être obligé / obligée de**:

> *you **don't have** to go* = tu **n'es pas obligé d'**y aller
> *we **don't have** to accept* = nous **ne sommes pas obligés d'**accepter

▶ For have used with illnesses, see usage note **Illnesses, aches, and pains ▶ 266 |**.

hazel *adjective* ▶ **213** |
= noisette (**!** *never changes*)

hazelnut *noun*
a hazelnut = une noisette

he *pronoun*
he = il
he's coming next week = il vient la
  semaine prochaine
there he is = le voilà!
HE didn't write the letter = ce n'est pas lui
  qui a écrit la lettre
I work in London but he doesn't = je
  travaille à Londres mais lui non
he's a strange man = c'est un homme
  bizarre

head
1 *noun*
• (*the part of the body*) ▶ **201** |
  the head = la tête
• (*the mind*)
  he's got it into his head that he's ugly = il
    s'est mis dans la tête qu'il était laid
• a head of cabbage = un chou
  a head of lettuce = une laitue
• (*the person in charge*)
  the head = le responsable/la responsable,
    le directeur/la directrice
  a head of State = un chef d'État
2 *verb*
• (*to be in charge of*)
  to head a team = être à la tête d'une
    équipe
• (*in soccer*)
  to head the ball = faire une tête
head for = se diriger vers (**!** + *être*)

headache *noun* ▶ **266** |
  to have a headache = avoir mal à la tête
  my headache's gone = mon mal de tête
    est passé

headlamp, **headlight** *noun*
  a headlamp = un phare

headline *noun*
  a headline = un gros titre
  to hit the headlines = faire la une des
    journaux
  the news headlines = les grands titres de
    l'actualité

headquarters *noun*
  the headquarters (*of a company, a
    business*) = le siège social
  (*of an army*) = le quartier général

headteacher *noun* ▶ **315** |
  a headteacher = un directeur/une
    directrice

health *noun*
  health = la santé

healthy *adjective*
• (*in good health*) = en bonne santé
• (*good for the health*) = sain/saine

hear *verb*
• to hear = entendre
  he can't hear anything = il n'entend rien
  I heard someone coming in = j'ai entendu
    quelqu'un entrer
  you can hear him practising the piano
    = on l'entend qui travaille le piano
• (*to learn, to discover*)
  to hear the news = apprendre la nouvelle
  I've heard about that school = j'ai
    entendu parler de cette école
  we've heard a lot about you = nous avons
    beaucoup entendu parler de vous
• (*to listen to*) = écouter
hear from = avoir des nouvelles de
  have you heard from Cathy? = est-ce que
    tu as eu des nouvelles de Cathy?
hear of = entendre parler de
  I've never heard of the place = je n'ai
    jamais entendu parler de cet endroit

heart *noun*
• (*part of the body*) ▶ **201** |
  the heart = le cœur
• (*the centre*)
  right in the heart of London = en plein
    cœur de Londres
• by heart = par cœur

heart attack *noun* ▶ **266** |
  a heart attack = une crise cardiaque

heat
1 *verb*
  = chauffer
2 *noun*
• the heat = la chaleur
  I can't stand the heat = je ne supporte pas
    la chaleur
• (*on a cooker*)
  to cook at a low heat = faire cuire à feu
    doux
• (*in a sporting contest*)
  a heat = une épreuve éliminatoire
heat up
• (*to cook*) = faire chauffer
• (*to warm up again*) = réchauffer

heater *noun*
  a heater = un appareil de chauffage

heating *noun*
  heating = le chauffage

heatwave *noun*
  a heatwave = une vague de chaleur

heaven *noun*
  heaven = le paradis

heavy *adjective*
• (*in weight*) ▶ **285** | = lourd/lourde
• (*in quantity, intensity*)
  the traffic is very heavy = il y a beaucoup
    de circulation
  to be a heavy smoker = beaucoup fumer
  to have a heavy cold = avoir un gros
    rhume
• (*describing food*) = lourd/lourde

H

- it's very heavy today = il fait très lourd aujourd'hui

hedge noun
a hedge = une haie

hedgehog noun
a hedgehog = un hérisson

heel noun ▶ 201 |
the heel = le talon

height noun ▶ 285 |
height (of a person) = la taille
(of a building, a tree) = la hauteur
to be afraid of heights = avoir le vertige

helicopter noun
a helicopter = un hélicoptère

hell noun
hell = l'enfer

hello noun (also exclamation) ▶ 237 |
hello! (when greeting someone) = bonjour!
(on the phone) = allô!

helmet noun
a helmet = un casque

help
1 verb
- to help = aider
  to help someone to [walk | do the housework | escape …] = aider quelqu'un à [marcher | faire le ménage | s'échapper …]
  the medicine helps to cure the illness = le médicament aide à guérir la maladie
  to help each other = s'aider, s'entraider (! + être)
- (at a meal)
  to help oneself = se servir (! + être)
  help yourselves! = servez-vous!
- I can't help thinking about it = je ne peux pas m'empêcher d'y penser
2 exclamation
help! = au secours!
3 noun
help (a helping hand) = l'aide (feminine)
(urgent assistance) = le secours
to ask someone for help = demander de l'aide à quelqu'un
to shout for help = crier au secours
help out = donner un coup de main

helpful adjective
- (ready to help) = serviable, aimable
- (useful) = utile

helping noun
a helping = une portion

helpless adjective
- (having no power) = impuissant/impuissante
- (because of weakness, ill health) = impotent/impotente

✶ in informal situations

hen noun
a hen = une poule

her
1 pronoun

! Note that there is a boxed usage note at them. The entries me, him, her and us are modelled on this note where you will find detailed grammatical information and fuller explanations.

- her = la (! l' + vowel or mute h)
  I know her! = je la connais
  I don't know her = je ne la connais pas
  do I know her? = est-ce que je la connais?
- he's seen her = il l'a vue
  he hasn't seen her = il ne l'a pas vue
  has he seen her? = est-ce qu'il l'a vue?
- catch her! = attrape-la!
  help her! = aide-la!
  don't help her! = ne l'aide pas!
  don't hit her! = ne la frappe pas!
- I gave the book to her = je lui ai donné le livre
  I didn't give the book to her = je ne lui ai pas donné le livre
  did I give the book to her? = est-ce que je lui ai donné le livre?
- her = lui
  write to her! = écris-lui!
  say it to her! = dis-le-lui!
  don't show it to her! = ne le lui montre pas!
- her = elle
  he did it for her = il l'a fait pour elle
  it's her = c'est elle
  stand in front of her = mets-toi devant elle
2 determiner
her = son/sa (+ singular)
= ses (+ plural)

! Note that sa becomes son before a vowel or mute h.

I hate her dog = je déteste son chien
what do you think of her house? = qu'est-ce que tu penses de sa maison?
she licked her plate = elle a léché son assiette
did you see all her CDs? = est-ce que tu as vu tous ses disques compacts?
she broke her leg = elle s'est cassé la jambe

! Note that, when talking about parts of the body, son, sa, ses are not used. See the usage note on The human body ▶ 201 | for further examples.

herd noun
a herd = un troupeau

here adverb
- (when talking about location) = ici
  is it far from here? = est-ce que c'est loin d'ici?
  I'm up here = je suis là

• (*when drawing attention*)
here's the post office = voici la poste
here they are = les voici
here's my telephone number = voici mon numéro de téléphone
here comes the train = voilà le train
here—take my pencil = tiens—prends mon crayon

• (*in general statements*) = là
tell him I'm not here = dis-lui que je ne suis pas là
we're here to help you = nous sommes là pour vous aider

hers *pronoun*
the green pen is hers = le stylo vert est à elle
which bag is hers? = lequel de ces sacs est le sien?
my jacket is red but hers is green = ma veste est rouge mais la sienne est verte
my parents are younger than hers = mes parents sont plus jeunes que les siens

! Note that, when comparing objects, people, etc, one of the following translations—le sien, la sienne, les siens or les siennes—will be used. To know which one to use, find out whether the object, person, etc being described is masculine or feminine, singular or plural.

herself *pronoun*
• (*when used as a reflexive pronoun*)
she wants to enjoy herself = elle veut s'amuser
she's cut herself with a knife = elle s'est coupée avec un couteau
• (*when used for emphasis*)
she said it herself = elle l'a dit elle-même
she did it all by herself = elle l'a fait toute seule

hesitate *verb*
= hésiter

hi *exclamation*
hi! = salut✶!

hiccups *noun*
to have hiccups = avoir le hoquet

hidden *adjective*
= caché/cachée

hide *verb*
• (*to avoid showing*) = cacher
to hide documents from the police = cacher des documents à la police
• (*to avoid being seen*) = se cacher (! + *être*)

hi-fi *noun*
a hi-fi = une chaîne hi-fi

high
1 *adjective* ▶ 285 |
• (*having a great height*) = haut/haute
the mountains are high = les montagnes sont hautes
• (*describing a level, a price, a speed*) = élevé/élevée
prices are high = les prix sont élevés
the train travels at high speed = le train roule très vite

• (*describing a standard, grades*)
the standard is high = le niveau est élevé
to get high grades = avoir de très bonnes notes
• (*describing a voice*) = aigu/aiguë
2 *adverb*
don't go any higher = ne montez pas plus haut

high rise block *noun*
a high rise block = une tour d'habitation

high school *noun*
a high school (*in the US*) = un établissement secondaire
(*in Britain*) = un lycée

hijack *verb*
= détourner

hike *verb*
to go hiking = faire de la randonnée

hiking *noun* ▶ 248 |
hiking = la randonnée

hill *noun*
a hill = une colline
(*a rise in the road*) = une pente

him *pronoun*

! Note that there is a boxed usage note at them. The entries me, him, her and us are modelled on this note where you will find detailed grammatical information and fuller explanations.

• **him** = le (! l' + *vowel or mute h*)
I know him = je le connais
I don't know him = je ne le connais pas
do I know him? = est-ce que je le connais?
• **she's seen him** = elle l'a vu
she hasn't seen him = elle ne l'a pas vu
has she seen him? = est-ce qu'elle l'a vu?
• **catch him!** = attrape-le!
help him! = aide-le!
don't help him! = ne l'aide pas!
don't hit him! = ne le frappe pas!
• **I gave the book to him** = je lui ai donné le livre
I didn't give the book to him = je ne lui ai pas donné le livre
did I give the book to him? = est-ce que je lui ai donné le livre?
• **him** = lui
write to him! = écris-lui!
say it to him! = dis-le-lui!
don't show it to him! = ne le lui montre pas!
• **him** = lui
he did it for him = il l'a fait pour lui
it's him = c'est lui
stand in front of him = mets-toi devant lui

himself *pronoun*
• (*when used as a reflexive pronoun*)
he wants to enjoy himself = il veut s'amuser
he's cut himself with a knife = il s'est coupé avec un couteau

H

* (when used for emphasis)
  he said it himself = il l'a dit lui-même
  he did it all by himself = il l'a fait tout seul

hip noun ▶ 201|
  the hip = la hanche

hippopotamus, **hippo** noun
  a hippopotamus = un hippopotame

hire verb
* (to employ) = embaucher
* (British English) (to rent) = louer
  to hire a car = louer une voiture
* (to lend for a fee) = louer
  they hire (out) the skates = ils louent les patins

his
1 determiner
  his = son/sa (+ singular)
  = ses (+ plural)

  ! Note that **sa** becomes **son** before a vowel or mute h.

  I hate his dog = je déteste son chien
  what do you think of his house? = qu'est-ce que tu penses de sa maison?
  he licked his plate = il a léché son assiette
  did you see all his CDs? = est-ce que tu as vu tous ses disques compacts?
  he broke his arm = il s'est cassé le bras

  ! Note that, when talking about parts of the body, **son**, **sa**, **ses** are not used. See the usage note on **The human body** ▶ 201| for further examples.

2 pronoun
  the blue pen is his = le stylo bleu est à lui
  which house is his? = laquelle de ces maisons est la sienne?
  my shirt is white but his is yellow = ma chemise est blanche mais la sienne est jaune
  my brother is taller than his = mon frère est plus grand que le sien

  ! Note that, when comparing objects, people, etc, one of the following translations—**le sien**, **la sienne**, **les siens** or **les siennes**—will be used. To know which one to use, find out whether the object, person, etc which is being described is masculine or feminine, singular or plural.

history noun
  history = l'histoire (feminine)

hit
1 verb
* (to strike) = frapper
  to hit someone on the head = frapper quelqu'un à la tête
  to hit one's head on a chair = se cogner la tête contre une chaise

* (to crash into)
  to hit a wall = heurter un mur
  to hit a pedestrian = renverser un piéton
2 noun
  a hit (a song) = un tube✱
  (a film, a play) = un succès
hit back = riposter
  to hit someone back = rendre un coup à quelqu'un

hitchhike verb
  = faire de l'auto-stop, faire du stop✱

hitchhiker noun
  a hitchhiker = un auto-stoppeur/une auto-stoppeuse

hoarse adjective
  to be hoarse = être enroué/enrouée

hobby noun
  a hobby = un passe-temps

hockey noun ▶ 248|
  hockey = le hockey

hold
1 verb
* **to hold** = tenir
  he held some coins in his hand = il avait quelques pièces dans la main
* (to arrange)
  to hold a competition = organiser un concours
  the party will be held in the school = la fête aura lieu dans l'école
* (to keep or hide) = détenir
  to hold someone hostage = garder quelqu'un en otage
* (to keep back) = garder
  to hold a seat for someone = garder une place pour quelqu'un
* (other uses)
  to hold the world record = détenir le record mondial
  to hold someone responsible = tenir quelqu'un pour responsable
  to hold, to hold the line = patienter
2 noun
* **to get hold of the ball** = attraper le ballon
* **to get hold of someone** (to find) = trouver quelqu'un
  (by phone) = joindre quelqu'un
hold on
* (to wait) = attendre
* **hold on tight!** = tiens-toi bien!
hold on to = s'agripper à (! + être)
hold up
* (to raise) = lever
  to hold up one's hand ≈ lever le doigt
* (to delay)
  to hold someone up = retarder quelqu'un
  to hold up the traffic = ralentir la circulation
* (to rob) = attaquer

hole noun
  a hole = un trou

✱ in informal situations

holiday *noun*
- (*British English*) (*a vacation*)
  a holiday = des vacances (*feminine plural*)
  to go on holiday = partir en vacances
- (*a national or religious festival*)
  a (public) holiday = un jour férié
- (*British English*) (*time taken off work*)
  a day's holiday = un jour de congé
  to take two weeks' holiday = prendre
    quinze jours de congé

Holland *noun* ▶ **218**|
  Holland = la Hollande

holly *noun*
  holly = le houx

home
1 *noun*
- **a home** (*a place to live*) = un logement
  (*a house*) = une maison
  to leave home = quitter la maison
  to work from home = travailler à domicile
- (*for elderly, ill or disabled people*)
  a home for handicapped children = un
    établissement pour enfants handicapés
  an old people's home = une maison de
    retraite
2 *adverb*

  ! *Note that chez soi changes to chez moi,
  chez lui, chez eux, etc depending on the
  person whose home is being talked
  about.*

  to go home (*to one's house*) = retourner à
    la maison, rentrer (chez soi)
  (*to one's home country*) = rentrer (dans son
    pays)
  on my way home = en rentrant chez moi
  to be home (*from school, work*) = être
    rentré/rentrée
  I can take you home = je peux te
    raccompagner chez toi
3 at home
- (*in one's house*) = à la maison, chez soi
  she's working at home = elle travaille à la
    maison, elle travaille chez elle
  he lives at home = il habite chez ses
    parents
- **to feel at home** = se sentir à l'aise
  make yourselves at home = faites comme
    chez vous
- (*when talking about a sports team*) = à
    domicile

homeless *adjective*
  to be homeless = être sans abri, être sans
    logement

homesick *adjective*
  to be homesick (*when abroad*) = avoir le
    mal du pays

homework *noun*
  homework = les devoirs (*masculine plural*)

homosexual *noun*
  a homosexual = un homosexuel/une
    homosexuelle

honest *adjective*
- **honest** = honnête
- (*frank, sincere*) = franc/franche
  to be honest, I'd rather stay here = à vrai
    dire, je préfère rester ici

honestly *adverb*
  = franchement, honnêtement

honey *noun*
  honey = le miel

honeymoon *noun*
  a honeymoon = un voyage de noces

hood *noun*
- (*to cover the head*)
  a hood = un capuchon
- (*US English*) (*of a car*)
  the hood = le capot

hoof *noun*
  a hoof = un sabot

hook *noun*
- (*for hanging clothes, pictures*)
  a hook = un crochet
- (*for fishing*)
  a hook = un hameçon

hooligan *noun*
  a hooligan = un voyou, un vandale
  a football hooligan = un hooligan

hoover *verb* (*British English*)
  to hoover the house = passer l'aspirateur
    dans la maison

hop *verb*
  = sauter à cloche-pied

hope
1 *verb*
  = espérer
  I hope you don't mind = j'espère que cela
    ne vous dérange pas
  I hope she remembers to come = j'espère
    qu'elle pensera à venir

  ! *Note that, when talking about the future,
  espérer que is followed by the future
  tense.*

  we hope to meet lots of people = nous
    espérons rencontrer beaucoup de
    monde
  I hope so = j'espère que oui
2 *noun*
  hope = l'espoir (*masculine*)
  to give up hope = abandonner tout espoir

hopeless *adjective*
- (*without hope of success*)
  = désespéré/désespérée
- (*without any ability*) = nul/nulle
  to be hopeless at cooking = être
    incapable de faire la cuisine

horn *noun*
- (*on a car, a bus*)
  a horn = un klaxon®
  to blow a horn = klaxonner

H

- *(of an animal)*
  a horn = une corne
- *(an instrument)* ▶ **290** |
  a horn = un cor

horoscope *noun*
  the horoscope = l'horoscope *(masculine)*

horrible *adjective*
  = affreux/affreuse

horror film *noun*
  a horror film = un film d'épouvante

horse *noun*
  a horse = un cheval
  he likes horses = il aime les chevaux

horseracing *noun* ▶ **248** |
  horseracing = les courses *(feminine plural)*

horseriding *noun* ▶ **248** |
  horseriding = l'équitation *(feminine)*

hospital *noun*
  a hospital = un hôpital
  he's still in (the) hospital = il est toujours
    à l'hôpital
  to be taken to (the) hospital = être
    hospitalisé/hospitalisée

host *noun*
  a host = un hôte

hostage *noun*
  a hostage = un otage

hostel *noun*
  a hostel = un foyer

hostess *noun*
  a hostess = une hôtesse

hot *adjective*
- *(very warm)* = chaud/chaude
  to be hot, to feel hot = avoir chaud
  I'm very hot = j'ai très chaud
  it's too hot in the office = il fait trop chaud
    au bureau
  a hot meal = un repas chaud
- *(strong, with a lot of spices)*
  a hot mustard = une moutarde forte
  a very hot dish = un plat très épicé

hot air balloon *noun*
  a hot air balloon = une montgolfière

hot dog *noun*
  a hot dog = un hot dog

hotel *noun*
  a hotel = un hôtel

hour *noun* ▶ **211** |, ▶ **356** |
  an hour = une heure
  I earn two pounds an hour = je gagne
    deux livres (de) l'heure

house *noun*
  a house = une maison
  to go to someone's house = aller chez
    quelqu'un
  the bike is at my house = le vélo est chez
    moi

housewife *noun* ▶ **315** |
  a housewife = une femme au foyer

housework *noun*
  to do the housework = faire le ménage

housing estate *(British English)*,
housing development *(US English)*
noun
  a housing estate = une cité (ouvrière)

hovercraft *noun*
  a hovercraft = un aéroglisseur

how *adverb*
- *(in what way)* = comment
  how did you find us? = comment est-ce
    que tu nous as trouvés?
  I know how [to swim | to ride a horse | to cook
    a curry …] = je sais [nager | monter à cheval |
    préparer un curry …]
- *(in polite questions)*
  how are you? = comment allez-vous?,
    comment vas-tu?
  how is your sister? = comment va ta sœur?
  how was your holiday? = est-ce que tes
    vacances se sont bien passées?
- *(in questions requiring specific information)*
  how long will it take? = combien de temps
    faudra-t-il?
  how tall are you? = combien mesures-tu?
  how old is he? = quel âge a-t-il?
- *(when making a suggestion)*
  how would you like to eat out? = est-ce
    que ça te dirait d'aller au restaurant?
  how about going to the cinema tonight?
    = et si on allait au cinéma ce soir?

however *adverb*
- *(nevertheless)* = toutefois, cependant
- however hard I try, I can't understand
  grammar = j'ai beau essayer, je ne
  comprends pas la grammaire

how many ▶ **317** |
1 *pronoun*
  = combien
  how many do you want? = combien en
    voulez-vous?
  how many of you are there? = combien
    êtes-vous?
2 *determiner*
  = combien de
  how many children are going on the trip?
    = combien d'enfants vont participer à
    l'excursion?

how much ▶ **317** |
1 *pronoun*
  = combien
  how much does it come to? = ça fait
    combien?
  how much is the jacket? = combien coûte
    la veste?
2 *determiner*
  = combien de
  how much money do you have left?
    = combien d'argent est-ce qu'il te reste?

huge *adjective*
= énorme

human being *noun*
a human being = un être humain

humour (*British English*), **humor** (*US English*) *noun*
humour = l'humour (*masculine*)
to have a sense of humour = avoir le sens de l'humour

hundred *number* ▶ **187**
one hundred, a hundred = cent
three hundred = trois cents
five hundred and fifty francs = cinq cent cinquante francs
about a hundred people = une centaine de personnes

Hungary *noun* ▶ **218**
Hungary = la Hongrie

hungry *adjective*
to be hungry = avoir faim
I'm very hungry = j'ai très faim

hunt *verb* ▶ **248**
= chasser
to go hunting = aller à la chasse

hurdles *noun* ▶ **248**
the hurdles = la course de haies

hurrah, **hurray** *noun* (*also exclamation*)
hurrah! = hourra!

hurry
1 *verb*
• = se dépêcher (**!** + *être*)
hurry home! = dépêche-toi de rentrer!
• to hurry someone = bousculer quelqu'un
2 *noun*
to be in a hurry = être pressé/pressée
there's no hurry = ça ne presse pas
hurry up = se dépêcher (**!** + *être*)

hurt *verb*
• (*to injure*)
to hurt oneself = se faire mal (**!** + *être*)
to hurt one's leg = se faire mal à la jambe
• (*to be painful*)
my throat hurts = j'ai mal à la gorge
that hurts = ça fait mal
• (*to upset*) = blesser
to hurt someone's feelings = blesser quelqu'un

husband *noun*
a husband = un mari

I i

I *pronoun*
I = je (**!** *j'* + *vowel or mute h*)
I've got to go = je dois m'en aller
here I am = me voilà
I didn't do it = ce n'est pas moi qui l'ai fait
I'm the one who does all the work = c'est moi qui fais tout le travail
she drives but I don't = elle conduit mais moi non

ice *noun*
• (*frozen water*)
ice = la glace
• (*on roads*)
ice = le verglas
• (*in a drink*)
ice = des glaçons (*masculine plural*)

ice cream *noun*
ice cream = la glace
an ice cream = une glace

ice hockey *noun* ▶ **248**
ice hockey = le hockey sur glace

ice rink *noun*
an ice rink = une patinoire

ice-skate *noun*
an ice-skate = un patin à glace

ice-skating *noun* ▶ **248**
ice-skating = le patin à glace

icing *noun*
icing = le glaçage

idea *noun*
an idea = une idée
what a good idea! = quelle bonne idée!
I've no idea how much it costs = je ne sais pas du tout combien ça coûte

identity card *noun*
an identity card = une carte d'identité

idiot *noun*
an idiot = un idiot/une idiote

if *conjunction*
= si
if you like = si tu veux
if it rains, we won't go = s'il pleut, nous n'irons pas
if I were rich, I would travel = si j'étais riche, je voyagerais
I wonder if they'll come = je me demande s'ils vont venir
if I were you, I'd refuse = à ta place, je refuserais

Illnesses, aches, and pains

Where does it hurt?

where does it hurt? = où est-ce que ça vous fait mal?
his leg hurts = il a mal à la jambe

(Do not confuse, **faire mal à quelqu'un** with **faire du mal à quelqu'un**, which means *to harm somebody*.)

Note that with **avoir mal à** French uses the definite article (**le, la, les,** or **l'**) with the part of the body, where English has a possessive, hence:

*he **has a pain in his** leg* = il **a mal à la** jambe
his head was hurting = il **avait mal à la** tête

Accidents

*she broke **her** leg* = elle s'est cassé **la** jambe
*I twisted **my** ankle* = je me suis foulé **la** cheville

Being ill

French mostly uses the definite article with the name of an illness:

to have flu | measles = avoir **la** grippe | **la** rougeole
but
to have cancer = avoir **un** cancer

Falling ill

French has no general equivalent of **to get**. However, where English can use **catch**, French can use **attraper**:

*to **catch** measles* = **attraper** la rougeole
*to **catch** a cold* = **attraper** un rhume

Treatment

to be treated for rabies = **se faire soigner contre** la rage
to take tablets for indigestion = **prendre des comprimés contre** l'indigestion
to be operated on for cancer = **être opéré d'**un cancer

---

ignore *verb*
 to ignore a person = faire semblant de ne pas voir quelqu'un
 to ignore a problem = ne prêter aucune attention à un problème

ill *adjective*
 = malade

illegal *adjective*
 = illégal/illégale

illness *noun*
 an illness = une maladie

imagination *noun*
 imagination = l'imagination (*feminine*)
 to have imagination = avoir de l'imagination

imagine *verb*
 = imaginer

imitate *verb*
 = imiter

immediately *adverb*
 = immédiatement

impatient *adjective*
 = impatient/impatiente
 to get impatient = s'impatienter (**!** + *être*)

import *verb*
 = importer

important *adjective*
 = important/importante
 it is important to eat well = il est important de bien manger

impossible *adjective*
 = impossible
 it's impossible to argue with him = c'est impossible de discuter avec lui

impress *verb*
 = impressionner

impression *noun*
 an impression = une impression
 to make a good impression = faire bonne impression

improve *verb*
* (*to make better*) = améliorer
  to improve living conditions = améliorer les conditions de vie
  to improve one's French = se perfectionner en français
* (*to get better*) = s'améliorer (**!** + *être*)

improvement *noun*
  an improvement = une amélioration

in

> **!** Often **in** *occurs in combinations with verbs, for example:* **drop in, fit in, move in** *etc. To find the correct translations for this type of verb, look up the separate dictionary entries at* **drop, fit, move** *etc.*

1 *preposition*
* (*inside*) = dans
  in the house = dans la maison
  I read it in the newspaper = je l'ai lu dans le journal
  there's a letter in the envelope = il y a une lettre dans l'enveloppe
  there's a letter in it = il y a une lettre dedans
  the woman in the photograph = la femme sur la photo
* (*at*) = à
  I learned German in school = j'ai fait de l'allemand à l'école
  in the countryside = à la campagne
* (*when talking about countries or cities*)
  to live [**in Ireland** | **in Japan** | **in Paris** ...] = vivre [**en Irlande** | **au Japon** | **à Paris** ...]
* (*dressed in*) = en
  in a skirt = en jupe
  to be dressed in black = être habillé/habillée en noir
* (*showing the way in which something is done*) = en
  written in French = écrit en français
  we paid in cash = nous avons payé en espèces
  they were sitting in a circle = ils étaient assis en cercle
  in ink = à l'encre
* (*during*)
  in October = en octobre
  in the night = pendant la nuit
  in the morning = le matin
* (*within*)
  I'll be ready in ten minutes = je serai prêt en dix minutes
  she'll be back in half an hour = elle sera de retour dans une demi-heure
* (*other uses*)
  to stay in the rain = rester sous la pluie
  she's in her twenties = elle a entre vingt et trente ans
  one in ten = un sur dix
  to cut an apple in two = couper une pomme en deux

2 *adverb*
* (*at home, available*) = là
  tell her I'm not in = dis-lui que je ne suis pas là
* (*arrived*)
  the train is in = le train est en gare
  the tide is in = c'est la marée haute

inch *noun* ▶ **285 |**
  an inch = un pouce
  ! *Note that an* **inch** = *2.54 cm.*

include *verb*
  = comprendre
  service is included in the bill = le service est compris dans la note

including *preposition*
  = y compris
  they were all invited, including the children = ils étaient tous invités, y compris les enfants

income *noun*
  an income = un revenu

income tax *noun*
  income tax = l'impôt sur le revenu
  ! *Note that* **impôt** *is masculine.*

inconvenient *adjective*
  it's an inconvenient place to meet = c'est un endroit peu pratique pour se retrouver
  an inconvenient time = un moment inopportun
  I hope that's not inconvenient for you = j'espère que cela ne vous dérange pas

increase
1 *verb*
  = augmenter
  to increase in value = augmenter de valeur
  to increase by 10% = augmenter de 10%
2 *noun*
  an increase = une augmentation

incredible *adjective*
  = incroyable

independent *adjective*
  = indépendant/indépendante

India *noun* ▶ **218 |**
  = l'Inde (*feminine*)

Indian ▶ **275 |**
1 *adjective*
  = indien/indienne
2 *noun*
* (*from India*)
  the Indians = les Indiens (*masculine*)
* (*from North America*)
  the Indians = les Indiens d'Amérique

indicate *verb*
  = indiquer

indifferent *adjective*
  = indifférent/indifférente

indigestion noun ▶ 266 |
  to have indigestion = avoir mal à
    l'estomac

individual
1 adjective
  = individuel/individuelle
2 noun
  an individual = un individu

indoor adjective
  = couvert/couverte
  an indoor swimming pool = une piscine
    couverte

indoors adverb
  = à l'intérieur

industrial adjective
  = industriel/industrielle

industry noun
  industry = l'industrie (feminine)

inevitable adjective
  = inévitable

infant school noun (British English)
  an infant school = une école maternelle

infection noun
  an infection = une infection

influence
1 noun
  an influence = une influence
  to have influence = avoir de l'influence
2 verb
• (to persuade) = influencer
• (to make a strong impression on)
  to influence someone = avoir une
    influence sur quelqu'un
  to be too influenced by someone = se
    laisser trop influencer par quelqu'un

inform verb
  to inform the police of an accident
    = signaler un accident à la police
  to keep someone informed = tenir
    quelqu'un au courant

informal adjective
• (describing a person, a person's manner)
  = simple
• (describing a word, a language)
  = familier/familière
• (describing a discussion or an interview)
  = informel/informelle

information noun
  a piece of information = un
    renseignement
  information = des renseignements

information desk noun
  the information desk = l'accueil
    (masculine)

information technology noun
  information technology = l'informatique
    (feminine)

ingredient noun
  an ingredient = un ingrédient

inhabitant noun
  an inhabitant = un habitant/une habitante

injection noun
  an injection = une piqûre
  to give someone an injection = faire une
    piqûre à quelqu'un

injured adjective
  = blessé/blessée

injury noun
  an injury = une blessure

ink noun
  ink = l'encre (feminine)

innocent adjective
  = innocent/innocente

inquiry noun
  an inquiry = une enquête

insect noun
  an insect = un insecte

inside
1 preposition
  = à l'intérieur de
  inside the house = à l'intérieur de la
    maison
2 adverb
  = à l'intérieur
  he's inside = il est à l'intérieur
  I looked inside = j'ai regardé à l'intérieur
  let's bring the chairs inside = rentrons les
    chaises
3 noun
  the inside = l'intérieur (masculine)
  the inside of the palace = l'intérieur du
    palais
4 adjective
  = intérieur/intérieure
5 inside out = à l'envers
  to put one's shirt on inside out = mettre sa
    chemise à l'envers

inspect verb
• (if it's an official) = inspecter
• (if it's a conductor) = contrôler

inspector noun
• (of a school)
  an inspector = un inspecteur/une
    inspectrice
• (on a bus, a train)
  an inspector = un contrôleur/une
    contrôleuse
• (in the police)
  a police inspector = un inspecteur de
    police

instantly adverb
  = immédiatement

instead
1 instead of
- *(rather than)* = au lieu de
  he hired a van instead of a car = il a loué une camionnette au lieu d'une voiture
  instead of working he watched TV = au lieu de travailler il a regardé la télévision
- *(in place of)* = à la place de
  use oil instead of butter = utilisez de l'huile à la place du beurre
  his wife came instead of him = sa femme est venue à sa place
2 *adverb*
  I don't feel like going to the cinema—let's stay at home instead = je n'ai pas envie d'aller au cinéma—restons plutôt à la maison

instruction *noun*
  an instruction = une instruction
  to give someone instructions to check the baggage = donner l'ordre à quelqu'un de vérifier les bagages
  the instructions for use = le mode d'emploi

instrument *noun* ▶ 290|
  an instrument = un instrument
  to play an instrument = jouer d'un instrument

insult *verb*
  = insulter

insurance *noun*
  insurance = l'assurance *(feminine)*

insure *verb*
  = assurer
  to insure a car against theft = assurer une voiture contre le vol

intelligent *adjective*
  = intelligent/intelligente

intend *verb*
  he intends [to leave | to learn Spanish | to travel abroad …] = il a l'intention [de partir | d'apprendre l'espagnol | d'aller à l'étranger …]

intense *adjective*
  = intense

intensive care *noun*
  to be in intensive care = être en soins intensifs

interest
1 *noun*
- *(enthusiasm)*
  interest = l'intérêt *(masculine)*
  to have an interest in music = s'intéresser à la musique
- *(financial)*
  interest = l'intérêt *(masculine)*
2 *verb*
  = intéresser

interested *adjective*
  = intéressé/intéressée
  to be interested [in politics | in sport | in painting …] = s'intéresser [à la politique | au sport | à la peinture …]
  are you interested? = ça t'intéresse?

interesting *adjective*
  = intéressant/intéressante

interfere *verb*
- *(to get involved in)*
  to interfere in someone's business = se mêler des affaires de quelqu'un
- *(to have a bad effect on)*
  it's going to interfere with his work = ça va l'empêcher de travailler

intermission *noun*
  an intermission = un entracte

international *adjective*
  = international/internationale

interpreter *noun* ▶ 315|
  an interpreter = un interprète/une interprète

interrupt *verb*
  = interrompre

interval *noun*
- *(in time or at a location)*
  an interval = un intervalle
  at regular intervals = à intervalles réguliers
- *(British English) (during a play, a show)*
  an interval = un entracte

interview
1 *noun*
  an interview *(for a job)* = un entretien *(with a journalist)* = une interview
2 *verb*
  to interview someone *(if it's an employer)* = faire passer un entretien à quelqu'un *(if it's a journalist)* = interviewer quelqu'un *(if it's the police)* = interroger quelqu'un

intimidate *verb*
  = intimider

into *preposition*
- *(when talking about a location)* = dans
  to go into the garden = aller dans le jardin
  to get into a car = monter dans une voiture
  to get into bed = se mettre au lit
- *(indicating a change)* = en
  to translate a letter into French = traduire une lettre en français
  to turn someone into a frog = transformer quelqu'un en grenouille

introduce *verb*
- *(to bring in)* = introduire
  to introduce a law = introduire une loi
- *(when people meet)* = présenter
  he introduced me to Peter = il m'a présenté à Peter

it

- When **it** is used as a subject pronoun to stand for a specific object (or animal), **il** or **elle** is used in French depending on whether the object referred to is masculine or feminine:

  'where is the book | chair?' — 'it's   = 'où est le livre | la chaise?' — 'il | elle est
  in the kitchen'   dans la cuisine'

- When **it** is used as an object pronoun, it is translated by **le** or **la** (**l'** before a vowel or mute h) depending on whether the object referred to is masculine or feminine:

  it's my book | my chair and I want it = c'est mon livre | ma chaise et je **le | la** veux

  Note that the object pronoun normally comes before the verb in French and that in tenses like the perfect and the past perfect, the past participle agrees with it:

  I liked his shirt, did you notice it? = sa chemise m'a plu, est-ce que tu **l'**as remarquée?
     sa chemise m'a plu, **l'**as-tu remarquée?

  In imperatives the pronoun comes after the verb:

  it's my book, give it to me = c'est mon livre, donne-**le**-moi*
  * Note the hyphens.

  However, in negative commands, the pronoun comes before the verb:

  it's my book, don't give it to him! = c'est mon livre, ne **le** lui donne pas!

- When **it** is used after a preposition in English, the two words (*preposition* + **it**) are often translated by one word in French. If the preposition would normally be translated by **de** in French (**of**, **about**, **from** etc), the preposition + **it** = **en**:

  we talked a lot about it = on **en** a beaucoup parlé
  have you heard of it? = est-ce que tu **en** as entendu parler?

  If the preposition would normally be translated by **à** in French (**to**, **in**, **at** etc), the preposition + **it** = **y**:

  they went to it = ils **y** sont allés

  For translations of **it** following prepositions not normally translated by **de** or **à** (*above*, *under*, *over*, *etc*) consult the entry for the preposition.

- When **it** is used in expressions like *it's raining, it will snow* etc, the translation will always be **il**: **il** pleut, **il** va neiger. See the entry for the verb in question.

  ▶ For translations of *it's Friday, it's five o'clock* etc, consult the usage notes on **Dates, days, and months** and **The clock**.

- *(on radio or television)* = présenter
  to introduce a programme = présenter
  une émission

invade *verb*
= envahir

invent *verb*
= inventer

invention *noun*
an invention = une invention

investigate *verb*
to investigate a crime = enquêter sur un
crime

investigation *noun*
an investigation = une enquête

invisible *adjective*
= invisible

invitation *noun*
an invitation = une invitation

invite *verb*
= inviter
to invite someone to a party = inviter
quelqu'un à une fête

involved *adjective*
to be involved in an accident = avoir un
accident
to get involved in someone's problems
= se mêler des problèmes de quelqu'un

Ireland *noun* ▶ 218 |
Ireland = l'Irlande (*feminine*)

Irish ▶ 275 |
1 *adjective*
= irlandais/irlandaise
2 *noun*
- *(the people)*
  the Irish = les Irlandais (*masculine
  plural*)
- *(the language)*
  Irish = l'irlandais (*masculine*)

iron
1 *noun*
- iron = le fer
- an iron = un fer à repasser

2 *verb*
= repasser

island *noun*
an island = une île

it *pronoun*
▶ **270** *See the boxed note on* it *for more information and examples.*

where is it? (*if it's an object*) = où est-il/elle?
(*if it's a place*) = où est-ce?
who is it? = qui est-ce?
it's me = c'est moi
it's a nice house = c'est une jolie maison
it is [difficult | easy | complicated ...] = c'est [difficile | facile | compliqué ...]
it doesn't matter = ça ne fait rien
it's easy to make a mistake = il est facile de se tromper
it's [cold | warm | mild ...] = il fait [froid | chaud | doux ...]
I've heard about it = j'en ai entendu parler
did you go to it? = est-ce que tu y es allé?

Italian ▶ **275**
1 *adjective*
= italien/italienne
2 *noun*
- (*the people*)
  the Italians = les Italiens (*masculine*)
- (*the language*)
  Italian = l'italien (*masculine*)

Italy *noun* ▶ **218**
Italy = l'Italie (*feminine*)

itchy *adjective*
my leg is itchy = j'ai la jambe qui me démange

its *determiner*
its = son/sa (+ *singular*)
= ses (+ *plural*)

! *Note that* sa *becomes* son *before a vowel or mute h.*

its nose = son nez
its tail = sa queue
its ear = son oreille
its eyes = ses yeux

itself *pronoun*
- (*when used as a reflexive pronoun*)
  the cat's going to hurt itself = le chat va se faire mal
- (*when used for emphasis*)
  the car itself was not damaged = la voiture elle-même n'a pas été endommagée
  the heating comes on by itself = le chauffage se met en marche tout seul

Jj

jacket *noun*
a jacket = une veste
(*gathered at the waist*) = un blouson

jail *noun*
a jail = une prison

jam *noun* (*British English*)
jam = la confiture

Jamaica *noun* ▶ **218**
Jamaica = la Jamaïque

January *noun* ▶ **222**
January = janvier (*masculine*)

Japan *noun* ▶ **218**
Japan = le Japon

Japanese ▶ **275**
1 *adjective*
= japonais/japonaise
2 *noun*
- (*the people*)
  the Japanese = les Japonais (*masculine plural*)
- (*the language*)
  japanese = le japonais

jaw *noun* ▶ **201**
the jaw = la mâchoire

jazz *noun*
jazz = le jazz

jealous *adjective*
= jaloux/jalouse
he is jealous of her = il est jaloux d'elle

jeans *noun*
jeans = un jean (*singular*)

jeer *verb*
to jeer someone = se moquer de quelqu'un

jelly *noun*
- (*US English*) (*jam*)
  jelly = la confiture
- (*British English*) (*a dessert*)
  jelly = la gelée de fruits

Jesus *noun*
Jesus = Jésus

jet *noun*
a jet = un jet, un avion à réaction

jewellery (*British English*), jewelry (*US English*) *noun*
a piece of jewellery = un bijou
jewellery = les bijoux (*plural*)

Jewish *adjective*
= juif/juive

jigsaw puzzle *noun*
  a jigsaw puzzle = un puzzle

job *noun*
* (*work*)
  a job = un emploi
  to look for a job = chercher un emploi
* (*a task*)
  a job = un travail, une tâche

jogging *noun* ▶ 248|
  jogging = le jogging

join *verb*
* (*meet up with*) = rejoindre
  I'll join you in half an hour = je vous
    rejoins dans une demi-heure
* (*become a member of*)
  to join a club = s'inscrire dans un club
  to join a company = entrer dans une
    entreprise
join in
  to join in a game = participer à un jeu

joke
1 *noun*
  a joke = une plaisanterie, une blague✱
2 *verb*
  = plaisanter

journalist *noun* ▶ 315|
  a journalist = un journaliste/une
    journaliste

journey *noun*
  a journey = un voyage
  to go on a journey = partir en voyage

joy *noun*
  joy = la joie

judge
1 *noun* ▶ 315|
  a judge = un juge
2 *verb*
  = juger

judo *noun* ▶ 248|
  judo = le judo

jug *noun*
  a jug = un pichet

juice *noun*
  juice = le jus
  fruit juice = le jus de fruits

July *noun* ▶ 222|
  July = juillet (*masculine*)

jump *verb*
* = sauter
  the children were jumping on the bed
    = les enfants sautaient sur le lit
  to jump across the stream = franchir le
    ruisseau d'un bond
  to jump rope = sauter à la corde
  to jump out of the window = sauter par la
    fenêtre

* to jump the queue (*British English*) = passer
  devant tout le monde

jumper *noun* (*British English*)
  a jumper = un pull

June *noun* ▶ 222|
  June = juin (*masculine*)

junior high school *noun* (*US English*)
  a junior high school ≈ un collège

junior school *noun* (*British English*)
  a junior school = une école primaire

jury *noun*
  the jury = le jury

just[1] *adverb*
* (*very recently*)
  I have just [arrived | seen her | received the
    letter …] = je viens [d'arriver | de la voir | de
    recevoir la lettre …]
  I had just turned on the TV = je venais
    d'allumer la télévision
* (*at this or that very moment*) = juste
  I was just about to phone you = j'étais
    juste sur le point de t'appeler, j'allais
    t'appeler
  you've just missed him = il vient juste de
    partir
  I arrived just as he was leaving = je suis
    arrivé juste au moment où il partait
* (*only*) = juste
  just two days ago = il y a juste deux jours
  he's just a child = ce n'est qu'un enfant
* (*barely*) = tout juste
  I got there just in time = je suis arrivé juste
    à temps
  she's just 18 = elle a tout juste 18 ans
* (*when comparing*)
  she is just as intelligent as he is = elle est
    tout aussi intelligente que lui
* (*immediately*) = juste
  just before the weekend = juste avant le
    week-end

just[2] *adjective*
  = juste

justice *noun*
  justice = la justice

Kk

kangaroo *noun*
  a kangaroo = un kangourou

karate *noun* ▶ 248|
  karate = le karaté

✱ in informal situations

keen *adjective*
  a keen student = un étudiant/une
    étudiante enthousiaste
  to be keen on swimming = aimer la
    natation

keep *verb*
• = garder
  to keep someone in (the) hospital
    = garder quelqu'un à l'hôpital
  we keep the wine in the cellar = nous
    gardons le vin dans la cave
  this sweater will keep you warm = ce pull
    te tiendra chaud
  to keep someone waiting = faire attendre
    quelqu'un
• (*to delay*) = retenir
  what kept you? = qu'est-ce qui t'a retenu?
  I won't keep you long = je n'en ai pas pour
    longtemps
• (*to put*) = ranger
  where do you keep the cups? = où est-ce
    que tu ranges les tasses?
• (*not to break, not to reveal*)
  to keep a promise = tenir une promesse
  to keep a secret = garder un secret
• (*to continue*)
  to keep [walking | talking | running ...]
    = continuer à [marcher | parler | courir ...]
  to keep going = continuer
  to keep calm = rester calme
• (*if it's food*) = se conserver (**!** + *être*)
keep away = ne pas s'approcher (**!** + *être*)
  keep away from the fire! = ne t'approche
    pas du feu!
keep back = retenir
  he kept the children back after school = il
    a retenu les enfants après l'école
keep on
  to keep on [talking | walking | singing ...]
    = continuer à [parler | marcher | chanter ...]
keep out
  to keep out of the sun = ne pas se mettre
    au soleil
  to keep the rain out = empêcher la pluie
    d'entrer
keep up = suivre
  to keep up with the other pupils = suivre
    en classe

kerb *noun* (*British English*)
  the kerb = le bord du trottoir

kettle *noun*
  a kettle = une bouilloire

key *noun*
  a key = une clé

keyhole *noun*
  a keyhole = un trou de serrure

kick *verb*
  to kick someone = donner un coup de
    pied à quelqu'un
  he kicked the ball = il a donné un coup de
    pied dans le ballon
kick off = donner le coup d'envoi

kick out
  to kick someone out = mettre quelqu'un à
    la porte

kid *noun*
• (*a child*)
  a kid = un enfant/une enfant, un
    gamin/une gamine**✶**
• (*a young goat*)
  a kid = un chevreau

kidnap *noun*
  = enlever

kill *verb*
  = tuer
  to kill oneself = se suicider (**!** + *être*)

kilo *noun* ▶ **285**
  a kilo = un kilo

kilogram(me) *noun* ▶ **285**
  a kilogram = un kilogramme

kilometre (*British English*), **kilometer**
(*US English*) *noun* ▶ **285**
  a kilometre = un kilomètre

kind
1 *noun*
  it's a kind of [fish | novel | hotel ...] = c'est
    une sorte [de poisson | de roman | d'hôtel ...]
  what kind of film is it? = c'est quel genre
    de film?
  what kind of car is it? = qu'est-ce que c'est
    comme voiture?
2 *adjective*
  = gentil/gentille

king *noun*
  a king = un roi

kingdom *noun*
  a kingdom = un royaume

kiss
1 *verb*
  to kiss someone = embrasser quelqu'un
  to kiss (each other) = s'embrasser
    (**!** + *être*)
2 *noun*
  a kiss = un baiser

kitchen *noun*
  a kitchen = une cuisine

kite *noun*
  a kite = un cerf-volant

kitten *noun*
  a kitten = un chaton

knee *noun* ▶ **201**
  the knee = le genou

kneel down *verb*
  = se mettre à genoux (**!** + *être*)

knife *noun*
  a knife = un couteau

knit *verb*
  = tricoter

K

knock
1 *verb*
  to knock on the door = frapper à la porte
2 *noun*
  a knock = un coup
  to get a knock on the head = recevoir un
    coup sur la tête

knock down
• (*in an accident*) = renverser
• (*to demolish*) = démolir

knock out
• (*to make unconscious*) = assommer
• (*in a contest*) = éliminer

knock over = renverser

knot *noun*
  a knot = un nœud

know *verb*
• (*when talking about facts, information*)
  = savoir
  he thinks he knows everything = il croit
    tout savoir
  I know why he phoned = je sais pourquoi
    il a téléphoné
  she knows how to swim = elle sait nager
  I don't know the French word for it = je ne
    sais pas comment ça se dit en français
  let me know = tenez-moi au courant
  does he know about the party? = est-ce
    qu'il est au courant pour la soirée?
  to know all about art = s'y connaître en art
• (*when talking about people, places*)
  = connaître
  do you know Paris? = est-ce que tu
    connais Paris?
  to get to know someone = faire la
    connaissance de quelqu'un

knowledge *noun*
  knowledge = les connaissances (*feminine
    plural*)

laboratory *noun*
  a laboratory = un laboratoire

lace *noun*
• (*the material*)
  lace = la dentelle
• (*for shoes*)
  a lace = un lacet
  to tie one's laces = lacer ses chaussures

lack
1 *noun*
  a lack [of food | of money | of interest …] = un
    manque [de nourriture | d'argent | d'intérêt …]

2 *verb*
  = manquer de
  he lacks confidence = il manque
    d'assurance

ladder *noun*
  a ladder = une échelle

lady *noun*
  a lady = une dame

lake *noun*
  a lake = un lac

lamb *noun*
  a lamb = un agneau

lamp *noun*
  a lamp = une lampe

lampshade *noun*
  a lampshade = un abat-jour

land
1 *noun*
• (*for farming, as opposed to the sea*)
  land = la terre
• (*property*)
  a piece of land = un terrain
  to own land = posséder des terres
• (*the countryside*)
  the land = la campagne
2 *verb*
• (*to fall*) = tomber (**!** + *être*)
• (*if it's a plane*) = atterrir
• (*if it's a passenger*) = débarquer

landscape *noun*
  a landscape = un paysage

language *noun*
• a language = une langue
  foreign languages = les langues
    étrangères
• bad language = le langage grossier

language laboratory *noun*
  a language laboratory = un laboratoire de
    langues

large *adjective*
• (*big*) = grand/grande (**!** *before the noun*)
  a large garden = un grand jardin
  a large house = une grande maison
• (*when talking about numbers*) = gros/grosse
  (**!** *before the noun*)
  a large sum of money = une grosse
    somme
  a large population = une forte population
• (*bulky*) = gros/grosse (**!** *before the noun*)
  a large parcel = un gros paquet

last
1 *adjective*
  = dernier/dernière
  last week = la semaine dernière
  that's the last time I saw her = c'est la
    dernière fois que je l'ai vue
2 *adverb*
• (*most recently*)
  when I was last here = la dernière fois que
    je suis venu ici

Languages and nationalities

Languages

The names of languages in French are always written with a small letter, not a capital as in English. French almost always uses the definite article **le** or **l'** with languages:

to learn French	= apprendre **le** français

except after **en**:

*to translate a word **into** French*	= traduire un mot **en** français

and it may be omitted with **parler**:

to speak French	= parler français / parler le français

but

*to speak **in** French*	= parler **en** français

When **French** means **in French** or **of the French**, it is translated by **français**:

*the **French** language*	= la langue **française**

If you want to make it clear you mean **in French** and not **from France**, use **en français**:

*a **French** book*	= un livre **en français**

When **French** means **relating to French** or **about French**, it is translated by **de français**:

*a **French** class*	= une classe **de français**

Nationalities

Adjectives indicating nationality **never** have capitals in French:

*a **French** student*	= un étudiant **français** / une étudiante **française**

Nouns have capitals in French when they mean *a person of a specific nationality*:

*a **Frenchman** / a **Frenchwoman***	= un **Français** / une **Française**
French** people or the **French	= les **Français** (*masculine plural*)

English sometimes has a special word for a person *of a specific nationality*; in French, the same word is almost always either an adjective (no capitals) or a noun (with capitals):

Spanish	= espagnol
*a **Spaniard***	= un **Espagnol** / une **Espagnole**
*the **Spaniards***	= les **Espagnols** (*masculine plural*)

You can use either the adjective or the noun to refer to nationality:

*he / she is **French***	= il est **français** / elle est **française**
	= c'est **un Français** / c'est **une Française**

- (*at the end*) = en dernier
  I'll do the dishes last (of all) = je ferai la vaisselle en dernier
- (*in final position*)
  he came last in the race = il est arrivé dernier dans la course

3 *pronoun*
  the last = le dernier/la dernière
  they were the last to arrive = ils ont été les derniers à arriver
  the night before last = avant-hier soir

4 *verb*
  = durer
  the film lasts two hours = le film dure deux heures

late
1 *adverb*
- (*far into the day or night*) = tard
  late in the afternoon = tard dans l'après-midi
  it's getting late = il se fait tard

- (*not on time*) = en retard
  to arrive half an hour late = arriver avec une demi-heure de retard

2 *adjective*
  = en retard
  to be late for work = arriver en retard au travail
  the train was two hours late = le train a eu deux heures de retard
  to make someone late = retarder quelqu'un

later *adverb*
  = plus tard
  I'll call back later = je rappellerai plus tard
  see you later! = à plus tard!

latest
1 *adjective*
  = dernier/dernière (**!** *before the noun*)
  the latest news = les dernières nouvelles
2 at the latest = au plus tard

Latin noun
　　Latin = le latin

laugh
1 verb
　　= rire
　　to laugh at a joke = rire d'une plaisanterie
　　to make someone laugh = faire rire
　　　quelqu'un
　　to laugh at someone = se moquer de
　　　quelqu'un
2 noun
　　a laugh = un rire

laundry noun
　　the laundry = le linge (sale)
　　to do the laundry = faire la lessive

law noun
• (a set of rules in a country)
　　the law = la loi
　　to obey the law = respecter la loi
　　it's against the law = c'est interdit par la
　　　loi
• (a rule)
　　a law = une loi
• (as a subject)
　　law = le droit

lawn noun
　　a lawn = une pelouse

lawnmower noun
　　a lawnmower = une tondeuse à gazon

lawyer noun ▶ 315 |
　　a lawyer = un avocat/une avocate

lay verb
• (to put) = poser, mettre
　　lay some newspapers on the floor = mets
　　　des journaux par terre
• **to lay the table** = mettre le couvert
• (of a chicken)
　　to lay an egg = pondre un œuf
lay down = poser, mettre
　　he laid the tray down on the table = il a
　　　posé le plateau sur la table
lay off = licencier

lazy adjective
　　= paresseux/paresseuse

lead¹ verb
• (to guide) = mener, conduire
　　this road will lead you to the village
　　　= cette route vous mènera au village
• (in a match) = mener
　　(in a race) = être en tête
• **to lead a busy life** = mener une vie active
• (to have as a result)
　　to lead to an accident = entraîner un
　　　accident

lead² noun
　　lead = le plomb

leader noun
　　a leader (of a political party) = un leader,
　　　un dirigeant
　　(of a state) = un chef d'État

leaf noun
　　a leaf = une feuille

leak verb
• (if it's a container) = fuir
　　the pipe leaks = il y a une fuite dans le
　　　tuyau
• (if it's a boat, shoes) = prendre l'eau

lean
1 verb
• (to support oneself)
　　to lean against the wall = s'appuyer contre
　　　le mur
• (to put)
　　to lean a bicycle against the wall
　　　= appuyer un vélo contre le mur
• **to lean out of the window** = se pencher par
　　　la fenêtre
2 adjective
　　= maigre
lean back = se pencher en arrière
　　(! + être)
lean forward = se pencher en avant
　　(! + être)
lean on = s'appuyer sur (! + être)

learn verb
　　= apprendre
　　to learn how to drive = apprendre à
　　　conduire

leash noun
　　a leash = une laisse

least
1 determiner
　　the least
　　= le moins de
　　they have the least money = ce sont eux
　　　qui ont le moins d'argent
2 pronoun
　　it was the least I could do! = c'était la
　　　moindre des choses!
3 adverb
　　the least = le moins/la moins (+ singular)
　　= les moins (+ plural)
　　the least expensive shop = le magasin le
　　　moins cher
　　the least difficult question = la question la
　　　moins difficile
4 at least
• (at the minimum) = au moins
　　he's at least thirty = il a au moins trente
　　　ans
• (when expressing some doubt) = du moins
　　he's gone out—at least, I think so = il est
　　　sorti—du moins, il me semble

leather noun
　　leather = le cuir

leave verb
• (to go away from) = quitter
　　to leave school = quitter l'école
　　she left her husband = elle a quitté son
　　　mari

- (*to go away*) = partir (**!** + *être*)
he left the next day = il est parti le
lendemain
- (*to go out of*) = sortir de (**!** + *être*)
she left the room = elle est sortie de la
pièce
- (*to allow to remain*) = laisser
leave your coat here = laisse ton manteau
ici
she left the window open = elle a laissé la
fenêtre ouverte
- (*to put, to give*) = laisser
he didn't leave a message = il n'a pas
laissé de message
she left him some money = elle lui a laissé
de l'argent
- (*to put off*) = laisser
leave it until tomorrow = laisse ça pour
demain
- (*to remain*)
there's nothing left = il ne reste rien
we've got ten minutes left = il nous reste
dix minutes
- (*other uses*)
I left them to clean the windows = je les ai
laissés nettoyer les fenêtres
leave behind = laisser
he left his belongings behind = il a laissé
ses affaires
leave out
- (*not to show or talk about*) (*by accident*)
= oublier
(*deliberately*) = omettre
- (*to exclude*) = exclure
to feel left out = se sentir exclu/exclue
leave over
there was not much left over = il ne restait
plus grand-chose
there is some food left over = il reste un
peu de nourriture

lecture *noun*
a lecture (*to students*) = un cours
magistral
(*to the public*) = une conférence

left
1 *noun*
the left = la gauche
the first street on the left = la première rue
à gauche
2 *adjective*
= gauche
his left hand = sa main gauche
3 *adverb*
= à gauche
to turn left = tourner à gauche

leg *noun*
- (*of a person*) ▶ **201**
the leg = la jambe
- (*of animals*)
the leg = la patte
- (*of meat*)
a leg of lamb = un gigot d'agneau

legal *adjective*
= légal/légale

leisure *noun*
leisure = les loisirs (*masculine plural*)

leisure centre (*British English*),
leisure center (*US English*) *noun*
a leisure centre = un centre de loisirs

lemon *noun*
a lemon = un citron

lemonade *noun*
lemonade = la limonade

lend *verb*
= prêter
to lend someone money = prêter de
l'argent à quelqu'un

length *noun* ▶ **285**
- (*in measurements*)
length = la longueur
- **length** (*of a book, a film, a list*) = la
longueur
(*of an event*) = la durée

leopard *noun*
a leopard = un léopard

less ▶ **317**
1 *determiner*
= moins de
less [money | food | time …] = moins
[d'argent | de nourriture | de temps …]
I have less work than he does = j'ai moins
de travail que lui
2 *pronoun*
= moins
to cost less = coûter moins cher
he reads less than she does = il lit moins
qu'elle
they have less than you = ils en ont
moins que toi

> **!** *Note that it is necessary to use* en,
> *which might be translated as* 'of it', *with
> pronouns like* less. *See also* another, a
> few, a lot *etc for this use of* en.

3 *adverb*
= moins
we travel less in winter = nous voyageons
moins l'hiver
4 *preposition*
(*minus*) = moins
5 **less and less** = de moins en moins
less and less often = de moins en moins
souvent
6 **less than** = moins de
in less than half an hour = en moins d'une
demi-heure

lesson *noun*
a lesson = un cours
a riding lesson = une leçon d'équitation

let[1] *verb*
- (*when making suggestions*)
let's go home = rentrons
let's go! = allons-y!

- *(to allow)* = laisser
  to let someone in = laisser entrer
  quelqu'un
  he let me help him = il m'a laissé l'aider
  she lets him do what he likes = elle le
  laisse faire ce qu'il veut
  he's letting his hair grow = il se laisse
  pousser les cheveux
let down = décevoir
let go
- *(to stop holding)* = lâcher prise
  he let go of me = il m'a lâché
- *(to release)* = relâcher
  he let the prisoners go = il a relâché les
  prisonniers
let in
- *(to a room or house)* = faire entrer
  he let me in = il m'a fait entrer
- **to let in the rain** = laisser entrer la pluie
let out
- *(to allow to go out)* = laisser sortir
  let me out! = laisse-moi sortir!
- **to let out a scream** = laisser échapper un
  cri
let through
  to let someone through = laisser passer
  quelqu'un

let² *verb (British English)*
= louer

letter *noun*
  a letter = une lettre

letter box *noun (British English)*
  a letter box = une boîte aux lettres

lettuce *noun*
  a lettuce = une laitue

level
1 *noun*
  a level = un niveau
2 *adjective*
  = plat/plate

library *noun*
  a library = une bibliothèque

licence *(British English)*, **license** *(US English) noun*
  a licence = un permis

license plate *noun (US English)*
  a license plate = une plaque
  minéralogique

lick *verb*
  = lécher

lid *noun*
  a lid = un couvercle

lie
1 *verb*
- *(on the ground, on a bed)* = s'allonger
  (**!** + *être*)
  he lay down on the sofa = il s'est allongé
  sur le canapé
  he was lying on the sofa = il était allongé
  sur le canapé

- *(to be situated)* = se trouver (**!** + *être*)
- *(not to tell the truth)* = mentir
2 *noun*
  a lie = un mensonge
  to tell a lie = mentir
lie around = traîner
  he always leaves his keys lying around
  = il laisse toujours traîner ses clés
lie down = s'allonger (**!** + *être*)

life *noun*
  life = la vie
  a way of life = un mode de vie

lifestyle *noun*
  a lifestyle = un style de vie

lift
1 *verb*
  to lift one's arm = lever le bras
  to lift a lid = soulever un couvercle
2 *noun*
- *(British English) (an elevator)*
  a lift = un ascenseur
- *(in a car)*
  to give someone a lift to the station
  = conduire quelqu'un à la gare
lift up = soulever

light
1 *noun*
- *(from the sun, moon)*
  light = la lumière
- *(in a room, on a machine)*
  a light = une lumière
  to switch on a light = allumer
- *(for traffic)*
  the lights are green = le feu est au vert
- *(in a street)*
  a light = un réverbère
- **have you got a light?** = est-ce que vous
  avez du feu?
2 *adjective*
- *(not dark)* ▶ **213** = clair/claire
  it's still light outside = il fait encore jour
  dehors
  a light blue dress = une robe bleu clair
- *(not heavy)* = léger/légère
3 *verb*
  = allumer
  he lit a cigarette = il a allumé une
  cigarette
  to light a fire = faire un feu

light bulb *noun*
  a light bulb = une ampoule

lighthouse *noun*
  a lighthouse = un phare

lightning *noun*
  a flash of lightning = un éclair

like¹ *preposition*
  = comme
  people like you and me = des gens comme
  toi et moi
  what's it like? = c'est comment?

like² *verb*
- (*when expressing an interest*) = aimer
  I like [**swimming** | **reading** | **dancing** …]
    = j'aime (bien) [nager | lire | danser …]
  I like it! = ça me plaît!
  how do you like America? = est-ce que
    l'Amérique te plaît?
- (*when expressing a wish*) = vouloir, aimer
  I'd like coffee please = je voudrais un café
    s'il vous plaît
  I'd like to live here = j'aimerais vivre ici

limit *noun*
  a limit = une limite

line
1 *noun*
- a line = une ligne
  a straight line = une ligne droite
- (*US English*) (*a queue*)
  a line = une queue
  to stand in line = faire la queue
- (*a row*)
  a line = une rangée
- the line is bad = la ligne est mauvaise
2 *verb*
  to be lined with trees = être bordé/bordée
    d'arbres

link *verb*
- (*by train*) = relier
  to link Paris to Brussels = relier Paris à
    Bruxelles
- (*to make a connection between*) = lier
  the two murders are linked = les deux
    meurtres sont liés

lion *noun*
  a lion = un lion

lip *noun*
  a lip = une lèvre

lipstick *noun*
  lipstick = le rouge à lèvres

list *noun*
  a list = une liste

listen *verb*
  = écouter
  to listen to someone = écouter quelqu'un

litre (*British English*), **liter** (*US English*)
noun
  a litre = un litre

little¹
1 *determiner*
  = peu de
  little [**food** | **wine** | **money** …] = peu [de
    nourriture | de vin | d'argent …]
  there is very little time = il y a très peu de
    temps
2 *pronoun*
  a little = un peu
  I only ate a little = je n'en ai mangé qu'un
    peu

! *Note that it is necessary to use* **en**,
which might be translated as 'of it',*with
pronouns like* **a little.** *See also* **a lot, more,
none,** *etc for this use of* **en.**

3 *adverb*
  = peu
4 a little (bit) = un peu
5 little by little = peu à peu

little² *adjective*
  = petit/petite (! *before the noun*)

live¹ *verb*
- (*to have one's home*) = vivre, habiter
  he lives in London = il habite à Londres, il
    vit à Londres
- (*to be alive*) = vivre
  that's not enough to live on = ça ne suffit
    pas pour vivre

live² *adjective*
- (*alive*) = vivant/vivante
- (*of a match, a show*) = en direct

lively *adjective*
  = vivant/vivante

living room *noun*
  a living room = une salle de séjour

load *noun*
- (*on a truck, being carried*)
  a load = un chargement
- loads of money = beaucoup d'argent

loaf *noun*
  a loaf (*of bread*) = un pain

loan *noun*
  a loan (*money lent*) = un prêt
  (*money borrowed*) = un emprunt

lobster *noun*
  a lobster = un homard

local *adjective*
  a local newspaper = un journal local
  the local people = les gens du coin

lock
1 *verb*
  = fermer à clé
  she locked the door = elle a fermé la porte
    à clé
2 *noun*
  a lock = une serrure
  a bicycle lock = un antivol
lock in
  to lock someone in = enfermer quelqu'un
  to lock oneself in = s'enfermer (! + *être*)

locker *noun*
  a locker = un casier

logical *adjective*
  = logique

London *noun* ▶ 218 |
  = Londres

lonely *adjective*
  = seul/seule

L

long
1 *adjective* ▶ **285**
= long/longue
a long letter = une longue lettre
to have long hair = avoir les cheveux longs
the film is two hours long = le film dure deux heures
I haven't seen him for a long time = ça fait longtemps que je ne l'ai pas vu
2 *adverb*
= longtemps
long ago = il y a longtemps
you can stay as long as you like = tu peux rester aussi longtemps que tu veux
I won't be long = je n'en ai pas pour longtemps
3 as long as = à condition que
as long as the weather is nice = à condition qu'il fasse beau

! *Note that the subjunctive is used after* à condition que.

look
1 *verb*
• = regarder
to look at a picture = regarder un tableau
to look out of the window = regarder par la fenêtre
• (*to appear*)
to look tired = avoir l'air fatigué/fatiguée
to look well = avoir bonne mine
he looks young = il fait jeune
she looks like her mother = elle ressemble à sa mère
what does he look like? = il est comment?
2 *noun*
a look = un regard
look after = s'occuper de (**!** + *être*)
to look after a child = s'occuper d'un enfant
look down
• (*to lower one's eyes*) = baisser les yeux
• **to look down on someone** = regarder quelqu'un de haut
look for = chercher
he is looking for a job = il cherche un emploi
look forward to
I am looking forward to meeting her = j'attends avec impatience le plaisir de faire sa connaissance
look onto = donner sur
my bedroom looks onto the garden = ma chambre donne sur le jardin
look out = faire attention
look through
to look through a book = feuilleter un livre
look up
• **to look up a word in a dictionary** = chercher un mot dans un dictionnaire
• (*to raise one's eyes*) = lever les yeux

loose *adjective*
• (*describing clothes*) = ample
• (*describing a screw*) = desserré/desserrée

lorry *noun* (*British English*)
a lorry = un camion

lose *verb*
= perdre

lost *adjective*
= perdu/perdue
to get lost = se perdre (**!** + *être*)

lot *pronoun* ▶ **317**
a lot = beaucoup
he eats a lot = il mange beaucoup
a lot [of money | of time | of books ...] = beaucoup [d'argent | de temps | de livres ...]
there's not a lot left = il n'en reste pas beaucoup

! *Note that it is necessary to use* en, *which may be translated as* 'of it' *or* 'of them', *with pronouns like* a lot. *See also* another, a few, any *etc for this use of* en.

lottery *noun*
a lottery = une loterie

loud *adjective*
= fort/forte
to talk in a loud voice = parler fort

loudspeaker *noun*
a loudspeaker = un haut-parleur

lounge *noun*
a lounge = un salon

love
1 *verb*
• (*when talking about people*) = aimer
to love each other = s'aimer (**!** + *être*)
• (*when talking about things, activities*) = adorer
2 *noun*
love = l'amour (*masculine*)
to be in love = être amoureux/amoureuse
to make love = faire l'amour

lovely *adjective*
• (*beautiful*) = beau/belle (**!** *before the noun*)
a lovely apartment = un bel appartement
you've got lovely eyes = tu as de beaux yeux
• (*very nice, kind*) = charmant/charmante

low
1 *adjective*
= bas/basse
to speak in a low voice = parler à voix basse
2 *adverb*
= bas
to turn the lights down low = baisser les lumières

lower *verb*
= baisser

loyal *adjective*
= loyal/loyale

✕ in informal situations

luck *noun* ▶ 237 |
　luck = la chance
　good luck! = bonne chance!
　to bring someone (good) luck = porter
　　bonheur à quelqu'un

lucky *adjective*
　to be lucky = avoir de la chance

lunch *noun*
　lunch = le déjeuner

lung *noun*
　the lung = le poumon

Luxembourg *noun* ▶ 218 |
　Luxembourg = le Luxembourg

luxury
1 *noun*
　luxury = le luxe
2 *adjective*
　a luxury hotel = un hôtel de luxe

Mm

machine *noun*
　a machine = une machine

mad *adjective*
• (*crazy*) = fou/folle
　to go mad = devenir fou/folle
• (*very angry*) = furieux/furieuse
• to be mad about someone = être fou/folle✗
　de quelqu'un

magazine *noun*
　a magazine = un magazine

magic *adjective*
　= magique

maiden name *noun*
　a maiden name = un nom de jeune fille

mail
1 *noun*
• (*the postal system*)
　the mail = la poste
• (*letters*)
　mail = le courrier
2 *verb* (*US English*)
　to mail a letter to someone = envoyer une
　　lettre à quelqu'un

mailbox *noun* (*US English*)
　a mailbox = une boîte aux lettres

mailman *noun* ▶ 315 | (*US English*)
　a mailman = un facteur

main *adjective*
　= principal/principale

main course *noun*
　a main course = un plat principal

major
1 *adjective*
　= majeur/majeure
　a major event = un événement majeur
2 *noun*
　a major = un commandant

majority *noun*
　a majority = une majorité

make *verb*

> ! Note that the word **make** *can often be
> translated by* faire. *This entry covers the
> most frequent uses of* make *but to find
> translations for other expressions like* to
> make a mess, to make a mistake, to make
> sure *etc., look up the entries at* mess,
> mistake, sure *etc.*

• to make = faire
　to make [the bed | a film | some coffee …]
　　= faire [le lit | un film | du café …]
　to make room = faire de la place
　to make a phone call = passer un coup de
　　fil
　to make friends = se faire des amis
　　(! + *être*)
　to make breakfast = préparer le petit
　　déjeuner
　to be made of [gold | metal | wood …] = être
　　en [or | métal | bois …]
　to be made in France = être
　　fabriqué/fabriquée en France
• (*to cause a particular reaction*)
　to make someone [happy | ill | jealous …]
　　= rendre quelqu'un [heureux | malade |
　　jaloux …]
　to make someone [annoyed | tired |
　　sleepy …] = [agacer | fatiguer | endormir …]
　　quelqu'un
　to make someone [cry | laugh | eat …]
　　= faire [pleurer | rire | manger …] quelqu'un
• to make someone wait = faire attendre
　　quelqu'un
• (*to earn*)
　to make a lot of money = gagner
　　beaucoup d'argent
　to make a living = gagner sa vie
　to make a profit = faire un bénéfice
make do = faire avec
make out = faire
　to make out a list = faire une liste
　to make a cheque out to someone = faire
　　un chèque à quelqu'un
make up
• (*to be friends again*) = se réconcilier
　　(! + *être*)
• to make up an excuse = inventer un
　　prétexte
• to make up a parcel = faire un paquet

make-up *noun*
　make-up = le maquillage
　to wear make-up = se maquiller (! + *être*)

male *adjective*
• (*in biology*) = mâle
• (*relating to men*) = masculin/masculine

man noun
- **a man** = un homme
  a single man = un célibataire
- **man** = l'homme

manage verb
- (to run) = gérer
- **to manage to finish one's homework** = réussir à finir ses devoirs

manager noun ▶ 315 |
  a manager (of a company, a bank, a project) = un directeur/une directrice
  (of a shop) = un gérant/une gérante
  (of a football team) = un manager

manner noun
  a manner = une attitude

manners noun
  manners = les manières (feminine)
  it's bad manners not to say hello = c'est impoli de ne pas dire bonjour

manufacture verb
  = fabriquer

many ▶ 317 |
1 determiner
- (a lot of) = beaucoup de
  were there many tourists? = est-ce qu'il y avait beaucoup de touristes?
  there weren't many people there = il n'y avait pas beaucoup de monde
- (when used with how, too, so, as)
  how many cases have you got? = combien de valises avez-vous?
  you eat too many chips = tu manges trop de frites
  there are so many things to do here = il y a tant de choses à faire ici
  I got as many presents as you did = j'ai reçu autant de cadeaux que toi
2 pronoun
  are there many left? = est-ce qu'il en reste beaucoup?
  I've got too many = j'en ai trop
  take as many as you like = prends-en autant que tu veux

  ! Note that it is necessary to use en, which might be translated as 'of them', with pronouns like many. See also another, a few, a lot etc for this use of en.

  many (of them) speak English = beaucoup (d'entre eux) parlent anglais

map noun
  a map (of a country or region) = une carte
  (of a town or a transport system) = un plan

marble noun
  marble = le marbre

marbles noun ▶ 248 |
  marbles = les billes (feminine)

march verb
- (in the army) = marcher au pas
- (in a demonstration) = manifester

March noun ▶ 222 |
  March = mars (masculine)

margarine noun
  margarine = la margarine

mark
1 noun
- **a mark** (on a surface) = une tache
  (on a person's body) = une marque
  to leave marks on the table = laisser des taches sur la table
- (British English) (a grade)
  a mark = une note
  to get good marks = avoir de bonnes notes
2 verb
- (to stain) = tacher
- **to mark the homework** = corriger les devoirs
- (to indicate) = indiquer

marker noun
  a marker (a pen) = un marqueur
  (a felt-tip pen) = un feutre

market noun
- (the place)
  a market = un marché
  a flea market = un marché aux puces
- (the system)
  the market = le marché
  the job market = le marché du travail

marmalade noun
  marmalade = la confiture d'oranges

marriage noun
  marriage = le mariage

married adjective
  = marié/mariée
  to be married to someone = être marié/mariée à quelqu'un

marry verb
  to marry someone = se marier avec quelqu'un (**!** + être)

marsh noun
  a marsh = un marécage

masculine adjective
  = masculin/masculine

mashed potatoes noun
  mashed potatoes = la purée de pommes de terre

mask noun
  a mask = un masque

mat noun
  a mat = un (petit) tapis

match
1 *noun*
- (*British English*) (*a game*)
  a match = un match
  a football match = un match de football
- (*a matchstick*)
  a match = une allumette

2 *verb*
  the shoes match the belt = les chaussures sont assorties à la ceinture

mate *noun* (*British English*)
  a mate = un copain/une copine

material *noun*
  a material = un tissu, une étoffe

math (*US English*), maths (*British English*) *noun*
  math(s) = les maths (*feminine plural*)

mathematics *noun*
  mathematics = les mathématiques (*feminine plural*)

matter
1 *noun*
  what's the matter? = qu'est-ce qu'il y a?
  what's the matter with her? = qu'est-ce qu'elle a?

2 *verb*
  does it really matter? = est-ce que c'est vraiment important?
  it doesn't matter = ça ne fait rien, ça n'a pas d'importance

maximum
1 *adjective*
  the maximum price = le prix maximum
  a maximum temperature of 80 degrees = une température maximale de 80 degrés

2 *noun*
  the maximum = le maximum

may *verb*
- (*when talking about a possibility*)
  they may be able to come = ils pourront peut-être venir
  she may not have seen him = elle ne l'a peut-être pas vu
  it may rain = il risque de pleuvoir
- (*when asking for or giving permission*)
  may I come in? = est-ce que je peux entrer?, puis-je entrer?
  you may sit down = vous pouvez vous asseoir

May *noun* ▶ 222 |
  May = mai (*masculine*)

maybe *adverb*
  = peut-être

mayor *noun* ▶ 315 |
  a mayor = un maire

me *pronoun*

> **!** *Note that there is a boxed usage note at* **them**. *The entries* **me**, **him**, **her** *and* **us** *are modelled on this note where you will find detailed grammatical information and fuller explanations.*

- **me** = me (**!** m' + *vowel or mute h*)
  they know me = ils me connaissent
  they don't know me = ils ne me connaissent pas
  do they know me? = est-ce qu'ils me connaissent?
- **he's seen me** = il m'a vu
  he hasn't seen me = il ne m'a pas vu
  has he seen me? = est-ce qu'il m'a vu?
- **help me!** = aide-moi!
  hold me! = tiens-moi!
  don't bother me! = ne m'embête pas!
  don't hit me! = ne me frappe pas!
- **she gave the book to me** = elle m'a donné le livre
  she didn't give the book to me = elle ne m'a pas donné le livre
  did she give the book to me? = est-ce qu'elle m'a donné le livre?
- **write to me!** = écris-moi!
  say it to me! = dis-le-moi!
  don't show it to me! = ne me le montre pas!
- **me** = moi
  he did it for me = il l'a fait pour moi
  it's me = c'est moi
  stand in front of me = mets-toi devant moi

meal *noun*
  a meal = un repas

mean
1 *verb*
- **to mean** = vouloir dire
  what does that mean? = qu'est-ce que ça veut dire?
  what does the word 'bête' mean? = que veut dire le mot 'bête'?
- (*to have as a result*)
  it means giving up my job = ça veut dire que je dois abandonner mon travail
- (*to intend*)
  I meant to order a pizza = je voulais commander une pizza
  she didn't mean to upset you = elle ne voulait pas te faire de la peine
  he meant it as a joke = il voulait plaisanter
- (*to intend to say*) = vouloir dire
  what do you mean? = qu'est-ce que tu veux dire?
- **her work means a lot to her** = son travail compte beaucoup pour elle
  money doesn't mean much to him = l'argent n'a pas beaucoup d'importance pour lui

2 *adjective*
- (*British English*) (*not generous*) = avare, radin/radine✱

M

• **to be mean to someone** = être
  méchant/méchante avec quelqu'un

meaning *noun*
  a meaning = un sens

means *noun*
  a means = un moyen
  a means of transport = un moyen de
    transport
  a means of earning money = un moyen de
    gagner de l'argent

meant: **to be meant to** *verb*
  to be meant to = être censé/censée
  I'm meant to be at my parents' house = je
    suis censé être chez mes parents

meanwhile *adverb*
  = pendant ce temps

measles *noun* ▶ 266 |
  measles = la rougeole

measure *verb*
  = mesurer

meat *noun*
  meat = la viande

mechanic *noun* ▶ 315 |
  a mechanic = un mécanicien/une
    mécanicienne

medal *noun*
  a medal = une médaille
  the gold medal = la médaille d'or

media *noun*
  the media = les médias (*masculine*)

medical *adjective*
  = médical/médicale
  to have medical treatment = suivre un
    traitement médical

medicine *noun*
  a medicine = un médicament

Mediterranean *noun*
  the Mediterranean = la (mer)
    Méditerranée

medium *adjective*
  = moyen/moyenne

meet *verb*
• (*by accident or appointment*) = rencontrer
  she met him at the butcher's = elle l'a
    rencontré à la boucherie
  can we meet (up) next week? = est-ce
    qu'on peut se voir la semaine
    prochaine?
  to meet again = se revoir (**!** + *être*)
• (*to be introduced to*) ▶ 237 | = faire la
    connaissance de
  she met him at a wedding = elle a fait sa
    connaissance à un mariage
  have you met Tom? = est-ce que vous
    connaissez Tom?

• (*to fetch*)
  I can meet you at the station = je peux
    aller te chercher à la gare
  can you meet me at the station? = peux-tu
    venir me chercher à la gare?
• (*to have a meeting*) = se réunir (**!** + *être*)

meeting *noun*
  a meeting = une réunion

melon *noun*
  a melon = un melon

melt *verb*
• **the snow is starting to melt** = la neige
    commence à fondre
• **the salt will melt the ice** = le sel fera fondre
    le verglas

member *noun* ▶ 315 |
  a member = un membre
  a member of staff (*in a school*) = un
    enseignant/une enseignante
  (*in a bank, a firm*) = un membre du
    personnel

memory *noun*
• **memory** = la mémoire
  to have a good memory = avoir bonne
    mémoire
  he's got a bad memory = il n'a pas de
    mémoire
• (*of a person, a place or time*)
  a memory = un souvenir

mend *verb*
• (*to fix*) = réparer
• (*by sewing*) = raccommoder

mental *adjective*
  = mental/mentale

menu *noun*
  a menu = un menu

mess *noun*
  a mess = le désordre
  your room is in a mess = ta chambre est
    en désordre
  to make a mess in the kitchen = mettre du
    désordre dans la cuisine

message *noun*
  a message = un message

metal *noun*
  a metal = un métal

method *noun*
  a method = une méthode

metre (*British English*), **meter** (*US
  English*) *noun* ▶ 285 |
  a metre = un mètre

Mexico *noun* ▶ 218 |
  Mexico = le Mexique

microphone *noun*
  a microphone = un microphone

microwave *noun*
  a microwave = un four à micro-ondes

Length and weight measurements

Length measurements

Note that French has a *comma* where English has a *decimal point*:

1 inch	= 2,54 cm	*1 yard*	= 91,44 cm
1 foot	= 30,48 cm	*1 mile*	= 1,61 km (kilomètres)

Length

how long is the rope?	= quelle est la longueur de la corde?
it's ten metres long	= elle fait dix mètres
the rope is three metres too short	= la corde est trop courte de trois mètres

Height

People	*how tall is he?*	= combien mesure-t-il?
	he's six feet tall	= il mesure un mètre quatre-vingts
	*Tom is taller	smaller than Jane*	= Tom est plus grand / plus petit que Jane
Things	*how high is the tower?*	= quelle est la hauteur de la tour?
	it's 100 metres high	= elle fait cent mètres de† haut / de† hauteur
	*A is higher	lower than B*	= A est plus haut / moins haut que B

Distance

how far is it from Paris to Nice?	= quelle distance y a-t-il entre Paris et Nice?
it's about 800 kilometres	= il y a environ 800 kilomètres

M

Width / breadth

how wide is the river?	= quelle est la largeur de la rivière?
it's seven metres wide	= elle fait sept mètres de† large / de† largeur

Depth

how deep is the lake	= quelle est la profondeur du lac?
it's four metres deep	= il fait quatre mètres de† profondeur

Note the French construction with **de**, coming after the noun it describes:

a street two kilometres long	= une rue **de** deux kilomètres de† long
a 100-metre-high tower	= une tour **de** cent mètres de† haut
a ten-kilometre walk	= une promenade **de** dix kilomètres
a river 50 metres wide	= une rivière **de** 50 mètres de† largeur

Weight measurements

Again, note that French has a *comma* where English has a *decimal point*:

1 ounce	= 28,35 g (grammes)	*1 stone*	= 6,35 kg (kilos)
1 pound *	= 453,60 g	*1 ton*	= 1 014,60 kg

* **a pound** (£1) is translated by **une livre** in French, but the French **livre** = 500 grammes (half a kilo).

People	*how much does he weigh?*	= combien pèse-t-il?
	*he weighs 10st	140 lbs*	= il pèse 63 kg 500 (soixante-trois kilos cinq cents)
Things	*what does the parcel weigh?*	= combien pèse le colis?
	how heavy is it?	= quel est son poids?
	it weighs 10 kilos	= il pèse 10 kilos
	A weighs more than B	= A pèse plus lourd que B
	sold by the kilo	= vendu au kilo

† The use of **de** is obligatory in these constructions.

midday noun ▶ 211 |, ▶ 356 |
  midday = midi (*masculine*)
  at midday = à midi

middle noun
  the middle = le milieu
  in the middle of the road = au milieu de la route
  to be in the middle of cooking a meal
    = être en train de préparer un repas

middle-aged adjective
  = d'âge mûr (**!** *never changes*)

midnight noun ▶ 211 |, ▶ 356 |
  midnight = minuit (*masculine*)
  at midnight = à minuit

might verb
• (*when talking about a possibility*)
  she might be right = elle a peut-être raison
  they might have got lost = ils se sont peut-être perdus
  'will you come?'—'I might' = 'est-ce tu viendras?'—'peut-être'
  we might miss the plane = nous risquons de rater l'avion
  he said he might not come = il a dit qu'il ne viendrait peut-être pas
• (*when implying something didn't happen*)
  you might have been killed! = tu aurais pu te faire tuer!
  she might have warned us = elle aurait pu nous prévenir
• (*when making suggestions*)
  you might try leaving a message = vous pourriez laisser un message
  it might be better to wait = ce serait peut-être mieux d'attendre

mild adjective
  = doux/douce
  the weather's mild, it's mild = il fait doux

mile noun ▶ 285 |
  a mile = un mile
  ! *Note that a mile = 1609 m.*

military adjective
  = militaire

milk
1 noun
  milk = le lait
2 verb
  = traire

milkman noun ▶ 315 |
  a milkman = un laitier

million number
  one million, a million = un million
  three million dollars = trois millions de dollars
  a million inhabitants = un million d'habitants

mind
1 noun
• the mind = l'esprit (*masculine*)
  to have a logical mind = avoir l'esprit logique
  I have a lot on my mind = j'ai beaucoup de soucis
• to make up one's mind to change jobs = se décider à changer de travail
  to change one's mind = changer d'avis
2 verb
• (*when expressing an opinion*)
  'where shall we go?'—'I don't mind' = 'où irons-nous?'—'ça m'est égal'
  she doesn't mind the heat = la chaleur ne la dérange pas
  I wouldn't mind some cake = je prendrais volontiers du gâteau
• (*in polite questions or requests*)
  do you mind if I smoke? = est-ce que cela vous dérange si je fume?
  would you mind coming? = est-ce que ça vous ennuierait de venir?
• (*to be careful*)
  mind the steps! = fais attention aux marches!
  mind you don't break the plates = fais attention de ne pas casser les assiettes
• (*to take care of*) = s'occuper de (**!** + *être*)
• never mind, she'll get the next train = ne t'en fais pas, elle prendra le train suivant

mine¹ pronoun
  the green pen is mine = le stylo vert est à moi
  guess which house is mine = devine laquelle de ces maisons est la mienne
  her coat is brown but mine is dark green = son manteau est marron mais le mien est vert foncé
  his sister's the same age as mine = sa sœur a le même âge que la mienne

  ! *Note that, when comparing objects, people, etc, one of the following translations—le mien, la mienne, les miens or les miennes—will be used. To know which one to use, find out whether the object, person, etc which is being described is masculine or feminine, singular or plural.*

mine² noun
  a mine = une mine

miner noun ▶ 315 |
  a miner = un mineur

mineral water noun
  a mineral water = une eau minérale

minimum
1 adjective
  the minimum price = le prix minimum
  a minimum temperature of 15 degrees = une température minimale de 15 degrés
2 noun
  the minimum = le minimum

minister noun ▶ 315 |
• (*in government*)
  a minister = un ministre
  the minister for Education = le ministre de
    l'Éducation
• (*in religion*)
  a minister = un ministre du culte

minor adjective
  = mineur/mineure
  a minor injury = une blessure légère

minority noun
  a minority = une minorité

minus preposition
  = moins
  it's minus four outside = il fait moins
    quatre dehors

minute noun ▶ 211 |, ▶ 356 |
  a minute = une minute
  they'll be here any minute now = ils vont
    arriver d'une minute à l'autre

mirror noun
  a mirror (*on a wall*) = un miroir, une glace
  (*on a car*) = un rétroviseur

miserable adjective
  = malheureux/malheureuse
  to feel miserable = avoir le cafard

miss verb
• (*to fail to hit*)
  to miss the target = manquer la cible
  the stone just missed his head = la pierre
    lui a frôlé la tête
• (*to fail to see*) = rater
  you can't miss it = tu ne peux pas le rater
• (*to fail to take*)
  to miss an opportunity = laisser passer
    une occasion
• (*to feel sad not to see*)
  I miss you = tu me manques
  we'll miss Oxford = Oxford va nous
    manquer
• (*other uses*)
  don't miss this film = ne rate pas ce film
  she missed her plane = elle a raté son
    avion
  to miss school (*due to illness*) = manquer
    l'école
  (*by skipping classes*) = sauter les cours

Miss noun
▶ See the boxed note on Forms of address.
  Miss = mademoiselle (*feminine*)

missing adjective
  to be missing = manquer
  there's a book missing = il manque un
    livre

mist noun
  mist = la brume

mistake noun
  a mistake = une erreur
  a spelling mistake = une faute
    d'orthographe
  to make a mistake = se tromper (**!** + *être*)

mistletoe noun
  mistletoe = le gui

mix verb
• (*to put together*) = mélanger
• (*to go together*) = se mélanger (**!** + *être*)
• to mix with the other students = fréquenter
  les autres étudiants
mix up = confondre
  to get the two languages mixed up
    = confondre les deux langues
  I'm always mixing him up with his brother
    = je le confonds toujours avec son frère

mixture noun
  a mixture = un mélange

model noun
• (*of a train, a car, a building*)
  a model = un modèle réduit, une
    maquette
• ▶ 315 |
  a (fashion) model = un mannequin

modern adjective
  = moderne

Mohammed noun
  Mohammed = Mahomet

mole noun
  a mole = une taupe

mom, Mom noun (*US English*)
  a mom = une maman

moment noun
  a moment = un instant
  there's no-one there at the moment = il
    n'y a personne en ce moment

Monday noun ▶ 222 |
  Monday = lundi (*masculine*)

money noun
  money = l'argent (*masculine*)

monkey noun
  a monkey = un singe

month noun ▶ 356 |
  a month = un mois
  he'll be back in two months' time = il sera
    de retour dans deux mois

Montreal noun ▶ 218 |
  Montreal = Montréal

monument noun
  a monument = un monument

mood noun
  to be in a good mood = être de bonne
    humeur
  I'm in a very bad mood = je suis de très
    mauvaise humeur

M

moon *noun*
　the moon = la lune

moped *noun*
　a moped = un vélomoteur

moral *adjective*
　= moral/morale

more ▶ 317 |
1 *determiner*
　= plus de
　more [friends | books | CDs …] = plus [d'amis |
　　de livres | de disques compacts …]
　more [money | food | time …] = plus [d'argent |
　　de nourriture | de temps …]
　I have more work than him = j'ai plus de
　　travail que lui
　there's no more bread = il n'y a plus de
　　pain
　there's more tea = il y a encore du thé
　would you like more coffee? = voulez-
　　vous encore du café?
　he bought two more tickets = il a acheté
　　deux billets de plus
2 *pronoun*
　= plus
　to cost more = coûter plus cher
　I did more than you = j'en ai fait plus que
　　toi
　I can't tell you any more = je ne peux pas
　　t'en dire plus
　we need more (of them) = il nous en faut
　　plus
　we need more (of it) = il nous en faut
　　davantage

　! *Note that it is necessary to use* en,
　which might be translated as 'of it' *or* 'of
　them', *with pronouns like* more. *See also*
　another, a few, a lot *etc for this use of* en.

3 *adverb*
　• (*when comparing*) = plus
　　it's more complicated than that = c'est
　　　plus compliqué que ça
　• (*when talking about time*)
　　he doesn't live there any more = il
　　　n'habite plus là
4 more and more = de plus en plus
　more and more expensive = de plus en
　　plus cher
5 more or less = plus ou moins
6 more than = plus de
　there were more than 20 people there = il
　　y avait plus de 20 personnes

morning *noun* ▶ 211 |, ▶ 356 |

　! *Note that* morning *is usually translated
　by* matin *in French. However it is some-
　times translated by* matinée, *when there
　is an emphasis on the idea of duration.*

　a morning = un matin
　at three o'clock in the morning = à trois
　　heures du matin
　to spend the morning reading the paper
　　= passer la matinée à lire le journal

mosquito *noun*
　a mosquito = un moustique

most
1 *determiner*
　• (*the majority of*) = la plupart de
　　most schools will be closed = la plupart
　　　des écoles seront fermées
　• (*in superlatives*)
　　the most = le plus de
　　who has the most money? = qui a le plus
　　　d'argent?
2 *pronoun*
　= la plupart de
　most of the time they phone each other
　　= la plupart du temps ils se téléphonent
　most (of them) speak Greek = la plupart
　　(d'entre eux) parlent grec
3 *adverb*
　the most
　= le plus/la plus (+ *singular*)
　= les plus (+ *plural*)
　the most expensive shop in London = le
　　magasin le plus cher de Londres
　the most beautiful town in France = la
　　plus belle ville de France
4 at (the) most = au maximum, au plus
5 most of all = par-dessus tout

mostly *adverb*
　= pour la plupart

mother *noun*
　a mother = une mère

mother-in-law *noun*
　a mother-in-law = une belle-mère

motor *noun*
　a motor = un moteur

motorbike *noun*
　a motorbike = une moto

motorcyclist *noun*
　a motorcyclist = un motocycliste/une
　　motocycliste

motorist *noun*
　a motorist = un automobiliste/une
　　automobiliste

motor racing *noun* ▶ 248 |
　motor racing = la course automobile

motorway *noun* (*British English*)
　a motorway = une autoroute

mountain *noun*
　a mountain = une montagne
　to go camping in the mountains = faire du
　　camping en montagne

mountain bike *noun*
　a mountain bike = un vélo tout terrain, un
　　VTT

mountain climbing *noun* ▶ 248 |
　mountain climbing = l'alpinisme
　　(*masculine*)

mouse *noun*
　a mouse = une souris

moustache, mustache (*US English*)
noun
  a moustache = une moustache

mouth *noun* ▶ **201**
• (*of a person*)
  the mouth = la bouche
  to have a big mouth = avoir une grande
    gueule✗
• (*of an animal*)
  the mouth = la gueule
• (*of a river*)
  the mouth = l'embouchure (*feminine*)

move *verb*
• (*to make a movement*) = bouger
  don't move! = ne bouge pas!
  the train's starting to move = le train
    démarre
• (*to put elsewhere*) = déplacer
  to move the car = déplacer la voiture
  to move a chair (out of the way)
    = déplacer une chaise
• (*to make a movement with*) = bouger
  I couldn't move my leg = je n'arrivais pas à
    bouger la jambe
  don't move the camera = ne bouge pas
    l'appareil photo
• (*to act*) = agir
• (*to move (house)*) = déménager
  to move to Paris = déménager à Paris
move away
• (*to live elsewhere*) = déménager
• (*to make a movement away*) = s'éloigner
  (**!** + *être*)
  to move away from the window
    = s'éloigner de la fenêtre
move back = reculer
move forward = s'avancer (**!** + *être*)
move in = emménager
  to move in with friends = s'installer avec
    des amis
move out = déménager
move over = se pousser (**!** + *être*)
  move over please = pousse-toi s'il te plaît

movement *noun*
  a movement = un mouvement

movie *noun* (*US English*)
  a movie = un film

movies *noun* (*US English*)
  the movies = le cinéma

movie theater *noun* (*US English*)
  a movie theater = un cinéma

moving *adjective*
  = émouvant/émouvante

mow *verb*
  to mow the lawn = tondre le gazon

MP *noun* ▶ **315** (*British English*)
  an MP = un député

Mr *noun*
▶ See the boxed note on **Forms of address**.
  Mr = monsieur (*masculine*)

Mrs *noun*
▶ See the boxed note on **Forms of address**.
  Mrs = madame (*feminine*)

much ▶ **317**
1 *adverb*
• (*a lot*) = beaucoup
  her work is much more tiring = son travail
    est beaucoup plus fatigant
  he doesn't read much = il ne lit pas
    beaucoup
• (*often*) = beaucoup
  they don't go out much = ils ne sortent
    pas beaucoup
• (*when used with* very, too *or* so)
  he misses her very much = elle lui
    manque beaucoup
  you talk too much = tu parles trop
  she loves him so much = elle l'aime
    tellement
2 *pronoun*
  (*in questions*) = beaucoup
  (*in negative statements*) = grand-chose
  is there much to be done? = est-ce qu'il y a
    beaucoup à faire?
  he didn't eat much = il n'a pas mangé
    grand-chose
3 *determiner*
• (*a lot of*) = beaucoup de
  I haven't got much time = je n'ai pas
    beaucoup de temps
  do you have much work? = est-ce que
    vous avez beaucoup de travail?
• (*when used with* how, very, too, so *or* as)
  how much money have you got?
    = combien d'argent as-tu?
  she doesn't eat very much meat = elle ne
    mange pas beaucoup de viande
  I spent too much money = j'ai dépensé
    trop d'argent
  don't use so much salt = ne mets pas tant
    de sel
  she has as much work as me = elle a
    autant de travail que moi

mud *noun*
  mud = la boue

mug
1 *noun*
  a mug = une grande tasse
2 *verb*
  to be mugged = se faire agresser (**!** + *être*)

multiply *verb*
  = multiplier

mum, Mum *noun* (*British English*)
  a mum = une maman

mumps *noun* ▶ **266**
  mumps = les oreillons (*masculine plural*)

murder
1 *noun*
  a murder = un meurtre

M

Musical instruments

Playing an instrument

Note the use of **de** with **jouer**:

to play the piano	= **jouer du** piano
to play the flute	= **jouer de la** flûte

but

to learn the piano	= **apprendre le** piano
to learn the guitar	= **apprendre la** guitare

Players

English **-ist** is very often French **-iste**. The gender will reflect the sex of the player:

a pianist	= **un** pian**iste** / **une** pian**iste**
a violonist	= **un** violon**iste** / **une** violon**iste**

But note the French when these words are used with **good** and **bad** like this:

he's a good pianist	= **il joue bien du** piano
he's a bad pianist	= **il joue mal du** piano

Use with another noun

de is usually correct:

to take piano lessons	= prendre des leçons **de** piano
a guitar solo	= un solo **de** guitare
a piano teacher	= un professeur **de** piano

---

2 *verb*
= assassiner

murderer *noun*
a murderer = un meurtrier

muscle *noun*
a muscle = un muscle

museum *noun*
a museum = un musée

mushroom *noun*
a mushroom = un champignon

music *noun*
music = la musique

musical *noun*
a musical = une comédie musicale

musical instrument *noun*
a musical instrument = un instrument de
musique

musician *noun* ▶ 315
a musician = un musicien/une
musicienne

Muslim *adjective*
= musulman/musulmane

mussel *noun*
a mussel = une moule

must *verb*

! *The verbs* **devoir** *and* **falloir** *are used to
translate* must. *Note that the subjunctive
is used after* il **faut que**.

- (*when stressing the importance of
something*)
you must go to the doctor = il faut que tu
ailles chez le médecin
we mustn't tell anyone = il ne faut en
parler à personne
- (*when talking about a rule*)
she must take the exam in June = elle
doit passer l'examen au mois de
juin
visitors must go to (the) reception = les
visiteurs doivent se présenter au bureau
d'accueil
- (*when assuming that something is
true*)
it must be nice to live there = ça doit être
agréable de vivre là-bas
you must be David's sister = tu dois être
la sœur de David
they must have been bored = ils ont dû
s'ennuyer

mustard *noun*
mustard = la moutarde

mutton *noun*
mutton = le mouton

Using the subjunctive

There are a number of examples in this dictionary which use the subjunctive. They are highlighted in the text with a note. The type of examples generating the subjunctive fall into three main categories. They are examples which contain:

- certain verbs, mainly:

  falloir
  vouloir

- certain conjunctions:

  bien que . . .
  jusqu'à ce que . . .
  à condition que . . .
  pour que . . .
  à moins que . . .

- certain phrases, often expressing a personal opinion:

  il est bizarre que . . .
  c'est dommage que . . .
  je suis content que . . .
  je doute que . . .

Verbs

- *falloir* is by far the most common verb requiring the subjunctive in this dictionary. The impersonal form **il faut que** is most often used to translate **must**.

I **must** go	= il **faut que** je m'en aille
you **must** come	= il **faut que** tu viennes

- *vouloir*, meaning **to want**, requires the subjunctive in specific cases. Compare:

I want **to come**	= je veux **venir**
I want you **to come**	= je veux que **tu viennes**

The second example uses the subjunctive because there are two 'subjects' involved, *I* and *you*. In the first example, there is only one subject, which means that no subjunctive is required.

Conjunctions

The most common conjunctions requiring the subjunctive in French in this dictionary are:

- **bien que** (= *although, even though, though*)

although she's quite old, she has lots of energy	= **bien qu**'elle soit assez âgée, elle a beaucoup d'énergie

- **jusqu'à ce que** (= *until*)

*let's watch television **until** they arrive*	= regardons la télévision **jusqu'à ce qu**'ils arrivent

- **à condition que** (= *provided, on condition that, as long as*)

*you can go out with them **provided** they bring you home*	= tu peux sortir avec eux **à condition qu**'ils te ramènent

- **pour que** (= *so that*)

*be quiet **so that** I can sleep*	= tais-toi **pour que** je puisse dormir!

- **à moins que** (= *unless*)

*I am not going **unless** you come with me*	= je n'y vais pas **à moins que** tu viennes avec moi

Phrases

When stating an opinion, the subjunctive is always used with the following phrases:

it's strange that she's never there	= il est bizarre qu'elle ne soit jamais là
it's a pity we can't go there	= c'est dommage qu'on ne puisse pas y aller
I'm glad he has lots of friends	= je suis content qu'il ait beaucoup d'amis
I doubt if he'll come	= je doute qu'il vienne

Superlatives

it's the best book (that) I have ever read	= c'est le meilleur livre **que j'aie jamais lu**
it's the most expensive watch (that) he's seen	= c'est la montre la plus chère **qu'il ait vue**

In French, the subjunctive is always used in clauses with **que** following a superlative adjective like *le meilleur* / *la meilleure*, *le plus mauvais* / *la plus mauvaise* etc.

▶ For more information on the subjunctive forms of French verbs, see the **verb tables ▶ 381** |.

▶ For information on grammar terms used in this note, see the **glossary page x**.

my *determiner*
  my = mon/ma (+ *singular*)
  = mes (+ *plural*)

  ! *Note that* ma *becomes* mon *before a vowel or mute h.*

  they hate my dog = ils détestent mon chien
  what do you think of my house? = qu'est-ce que tu penses de ma maison?
  he's my age = il a mon âge
  I sold all my CDs = j'ai vendu tous mes disques compacts
  I broke my leg = je me suis cassé la jambe

  ! *Note that, when talking about parts of the body,* mon, ma *and* mes *are not used. See the usage note on* **The human body ▶ 201** *for further examples.*

myself *pronoun*
• (*when used as a reflexive pronoun*)
  I want to enjoy myself = je veux m'amuser
  I didn't hurt myself = je ne me suis pas fait mal
• (*when used for emphasis*)
  I told them myself = je le leur ai dit moi-même
  I did it all by myself = je l'ai fait tout seul

mystery *noun*
  a mystery = un mystère

Nn

nail *noun* **▶ 201**
• (*for use in attaching, repairing*)
  a nail = un clou
• (*on the fingers or toes*)
  a nail = un ongle

nail polish *noun*
  nail polish = le vernis à ongles

naked *adjective*
  = nu/nue

name *noun*
• (*of a person*)
  a name = un nom
  what's your name? = comment t'appelles-tu?, comment vous appelez-vous?
  my name is Louis = je m'appelle Louis
• (*of a book, a play or film*)
  a name = un titre

narrow *adjective*
  = étroit/étroite

nasty *adjective*
• (*mean, unkind*) = méchant/méchante
• (*unpleasant*) = désagréable

national *adjective*
  = national/nationale

native *adjective*
  a native language = une langue maternelle
  a native French speaker = une personne de langue maternelle française

natural *adjective*
  = naturel/naturelle
  it's natural to be disappointed = c'est normal d'être déçu

naturally *adverb*
  = naturellement

nature *noun*
  nature = la nature

naughty *adjective*
  = vilain/vilaine

navy *noun*
  the navy = la marine

navy blue *adjective* **▶ 213**
  = bleu marine (**!** *never changes*)

near
1 *preposition*
  = près de
  he was sitting near us = il était assis près de nous
2 *adverb*
  they live quite near = ils habitent tout près

3 *adjective*
= proche
  the school is quite near = l'école est assez
    proche
  the nearest shops are several miles away
    = les magasins les plus proches sont à
    plusieurs kilomètres d'ici

nearby *adverb*
  = à proximité

nearly *adverb*
  = presque
  we're nearly there = nous sommes
    presque arrivés
  I nearly [forgot | gave up | fell asleep …] = j'ai
    failli [oublier | abandonner | m'endormir …]

neat *adjective*
  (*in one's habits*) = ordonné/ordonnée
  (*in how one looks*) = net/nette
  (*describing work, handwriting*)
    = soigné/soignée

necessary *adjective*
  = nécessaire

neck *noun* ▶ **201**
  the neck = le cou

necklace *noun*
  a necklace = un collier

need *verb*
• (*(to) have to*)
  you don't need to ask permission = tu
    n'es pas obligé de demander la
    permission
  they'll need to come early = il va falloir
    qu'ils viennent de bonne heure

  ! *Note that the subjunctive is used after*
  falloir que.

• (*to want*) = avoir besoin de
  they need [money | help | friends …] = ils ont
    besoin [d'argent | d'aide | d'amis …]
  we need to see the doctor = nous avons
    besoin de voir le médecin
  everything you need = tout ce qu'il vous
    faut

needle *noun*
  a needle = une aiguille

negative
1 *adjective*
• (*pessimistic*) = négatif/négative
• (*harmful*) = néfaste
2 *noun*
  a negative = un négatif

neighbour (*British English*), **neighbor**
(*US English*) *noun*
  a neighbour = un voisin/une voisine

neither
1 *conjunction*
• (*in* **neither… nor** *sentences*) = ni… ni

she speaks neither French nor English
    = elle ne parle ni français ni anglais
  I have neither the time nor the energy to
    argue = je n'ai ni le temps ni la force de
    discuter
• (*nor*)
  'I can't sleep'—'neither can I' = 'je
    n'arrive pas à dormir'—'moi non plus'
2 *determiner*
  = aucun des deux/aucune des deux
  neither girl answered = aucune des deux
    filles n'a répondu
3 *pronoun*
  = ni l'un/l'une ni l'autre
  neither of them is coming = ni l'un ni
    l'autre ne vient

  ! *Note that, in sentences with a verb, the*
  negative **ne** *or* **n'** *(before a vowel or mute*
  h) is used together with **ni… ni**,
  aucun/aucune des deux *and* **ni l'un/l'une**
  ni l'autre *to translate* **neither**. *Remember*
  that **ne** *comes before the verb or the*
  auxiliary verb.

nephew *noun*
  a nephew = un neveu

nerves *noun*
  nerves = les nerfs (*masculine*)
  to get on someone's nerves = énerver
    quelqu'un

nervous *adjective*
• (*frightened*)
  to be nervous = avoir peur
• (*anxious*) = angoissé/angoissée
  to feel nervous = être angoissé/angoissée

nest *noun*
  a nest = un nid

net *noun*
• (*for fishing*)
  a net = un filet
• (*in sport*)
  the net (*in football*) = les filets (*masculine*
    plural)
  (*in tennis*) = le filet

Netherlands *noun* ▶ **218**
  the Netherlands = les Pays-Bas (*masculine*
    plural)

network *noun*
  a network = un réseau

neutral *adjective*
  = neutre

never *adverb*

  ! *Note that, in sentences with a verb, the*
  negative **ne** *or* **n'** *(before a vowel or mute*
  h) is used together with **jamais** *to*
  translate **never**. *Remember that* **ne** *comes*
  before the verb or the auxiliary verb.

• (not ever) = jamais
  they never come to see us = ils ne
  viennent jamais nous voir
  she has never been to the opera = elle
  n'est jamais allée à l'opéra
  I'll never go back there again = je n'y
  retournerai plus jamais
• (when used for emphasis)
  she never even apologized = elle ne s'est
  même pas excusée

nevertheless adverb
= pourtant, néanmoins

new adjective
= nouveau/nouvelle (! before the noun)

> ! Note that **nouvel** is used instead of
> nouveau before masculine nouns
> beginning with a vowel (endroit, ordina-
> teur) or a mute h (hôtel). The plural of
> nouveau and nouvel is nouveaux.

  a new bike = un nouveau vélo
  a new car = une nouvelle voiture
  a new computer = un nouvel ordinateur
  new dresses = de nouvelles robes

newborn baby noun
  a newborn baby = un nouveau-né

news noun
• **a piece of news** = une nouvelle
  have you heard the news? = est-ce que tu
  connais la nouvelle?
  that's good news = c'est une bonne
  nouvelle
  have you any news of John? = est-ce que
  tu as des nouvelles de John?
• (on radio, TV)
  the news = le journal (singular)= , les
  informations (feminine)

newsagent's noun ▶ 315 | (British
English)
  a newsagent's = un magasin de journaux

newspaper noun
  a newspaper = un journal

New Year noun
  the New Year = le nouvel an
  Happy New Year! = Bonne année!

New Year's Day, **New Year's** (US
English) noun
  New Year's (Day) = le jour de l'an

New Year's Eve noun
  New Year's Eve = la Saint-Sylvestre

New Zealand noun ▶ 218 |
  New Zealand = la Nouvelle-Zélande

next
1 adjective
• (when talking about what is still to come)
  = prochain/prochaine

  I'll take the next train to London = je
  prendrai le prochain train pour Londres
  he'll be here next week = il sera là la
  semaine prochaine
• (when talking about what followed)
  = suivant/suivante
  I took the next train = j'ai pris le train
  suivant
  they arrived the next day = ils sont arrivés
  le lendemain
• (in a queue)
  'who's next?' = 'à qui le tour?'
  'I'm next' = 'c'est mon tour'
2 adverb
• (in the past) = ensuite
  what happened next? = qu'est-ce qui s'est
  passé ensuite?
• (now) = maintenant
  what'll we do next? = qu'est-ce qu'on fait
  maintenant?
• (in the future)
  **when you next go to Paris, give Gary a
  call** = la prochaine fois que tu iras à
  Paris, passe un coup de fil à Gary
3 next to = à côté de

next door adverb
= à côté

nice adjective
• (enjoyable) = agréable
  it's nice to be able to relax = c'est agréable
  de pouvoir se détendre
• (kind, friendly) = sympathique, sympa✕
  to be nice to someone = être
  gentil/gentille avec quelqu'un
• (attractive) = beau/belle (! before the noun)

nickname noun
  a nickname = un surnom

niece noun
  a niece = une nièce

night noun ▶ 356 |
• (as opposed to day)
  a night = une nuit
  I didn't sleep last night = je n'ai pas dormi
  cette nuit
  he stayed out all night = il n'est pas rentré
  de la nuit
• (evening)
  a night = un soir
  last night = hier soir
  a night at the cinema = une soirée au
  cinéma

> ! See the note at **evening** for information
> on soir and soirée.

nightclub noun
  a nightclub = une boîte de nuit

nightdress noun
  a nightdress = une chemise de nuit

nightmare *noun*
  a nightmare = un cauchemar
  to have a nightmare = faire un cauchemar

nil *noun*
  nil = zéro

nine *number* ▶ **187** |, ▶ **211** |
  nine = neuf
  nine books = neuf livres
  I have nine (of them) = j'en ai neuf

nineteen *number* ▶ **187** |, ▶ **211** |
  nineteen = dix-neuf

nineteenth *number*
• (*in a series*) = dix-neuvième
• (*in dates*) ▶ **222** |
  the nineteenth of July = le dix-neuf juillet

ninety *number* ▶ **187** |
  ninety = quatre-vingt-dix

ninth *number*
• (*in a series*) = neuvième
• (*in dates*) ▶ **222** |
  the ninth of December = le neuf décembre

no
1 *adverb*
• no = non
  no thanks = non merci
• he no longer works here = il ne travaille
  plus ici
2 *determiner*
• (*not any*)
  we have no money = nous n'avons pas
  d'argent
  there are no trains = il n'y a pas de trains
• (*when refusing permission*)
  no smoking = défense de fumer
  no talking! = silence!
• (*when used for emphasis*)
  this is no time to argue = ce n'est pas le
  moment de discuter
  it's no problem = ce n'est pas du tout un
  problème

nobody ▶ **no-one**

noise *noun*
  noise = le bruit
  to make noise = faire du bruit

noisy *adjective*
  = bruyant/bruyante

none *pronoun*
  ! *Note that, when there is a verb in the
  sentence, the negative ne or n' (before a
  vowel or mute h) is used together with
  aucun/aucune to translate none.
  Remember that ne comes before the verb
  or the auxiliary verb.*

  none = aucun/aucune
  none of the girls went to the class
    = aucune des filles n'est allée au cours
  none of [us | you | them ...] can speak
    German = aucun [de nous | de vous | d'entre
    eux ...] ne parle allemand
  there's none left = il n'y en a plus
  I've got none, I have none = je n'en ai pas

! *Note that it is necessary to use en which
might be translated as 'of it' or 'of them',
with pronouns like none. See also another,
a few, a lot etc for this use of en.*

nonsense *noun*
  that's nonsense! = c'est absurde!

noon *noun* ▶ **211** |, ▶ **356** |
  noon = midi (*masculine*)
  at noon = à midi

no-one *pronoun* (*also* **nobody**)
  ! *Note that, when there is a verb in the
  sentence, the negative ne or n' (before a
  vowel or mute h) is used together with
  personne to translate no-one. Remember
  that ne comes before the verb or the
  auxiliary verb.*

  no-one = personne
  no-one tells me anything = personne ne
    me dit rien
  no-one saw him = personne ne l'a vu
  there's no-one else in the office = il n'y a
    personne d'autre au bureau

nor *conjunction*
  ! *For translations of nor when used in
  combination with neither, look at the entry
  for neither in this dictionary.*

  'I don't like him'—'nor do I' = 'je ne l'aime
  pas'—'moi non plus'

normal *adjective*
  = normal/normale

normally *adverb*
  = normalement

north
1 *noun*
  the north = le nord
  in the north of France = dans le nord de la
  France
2 *adverb*
  to go north = aller vers le nord
  to live north of Paris = vivre au nord de
  Paris
3 *adjective*
  = nord (**!** *never changes*)
  to work in north London = travailler dans
  le nord de Londres

North America *noun* ▶ **218** |
  North America = l'Amérique du Nord
  ! *Note that Amérique is feminine.*

northeast *noun*
  the northeast = le nord-est

Northern Ireland *noun* ▶ **218** |
  Northern Ireland = l'Irlande du Nord
  ! *Note that Irlande is feminine.*

northwest *noun*
  the northwest = le nord-ouest

Norway *noun* ▶ **218** |
  Norway = la Norvège

N

not

Used without a verb

When **not** is used without a verb before an adjective, a noun, an adverb, a verb or a pronoun it is translated by **pas**:

not at all	= **pas** du tout
not bad	= **pas** mal
*it's a cat **not** a dog*	= c'est un chat **pas** un chien
*you should walk, **not** run*	= il faut marcher, **pas** courir
*she should apologise, **not** me*	= c'est elle qui devrait s'excuser, **pas** moi

Used with a verb

When **not** is used with the verbs *be, do, have, will* and *would*, the translation is **ne ... pas** (**n'** before a vowel or mute h): **ne** comes before the verb or the auxiliary, and **pas** comes after the verb or auxiliary:

*it's **not** a cat*	= ce n'est **pas** un chat
he doesn't like oranges	= il n'aime **pas** les oranges
I haven't seen him	= je ne l'ai **pas** vu
she hasn't arrived yet	= elle n'est **pas** encore arrivée
she won't come by car	= elle ne viendra **pas** en voiture
it wouldn't matter	= ce ne serait **pas** grave

When used with a verb in the infinitive, **ne** and **pas** are placed together before the verb:

*he decided **not** to go*	= il a décidé de **ne pas** y aller
*you were wrong **not** to tell her*	= tu as eu tort de **ne pas** le lui dire

Used in short questions

When **not** is used in short questions, the whole question can usually be translated by the French **n'est-ce pas**:

*she bought it, **didn't she**?*	= elle l'a acheté, **n'est-ce pas**?
*you were there too, **weren't you**?*	= tu y étais aussi, **n'est-ce pas**?
*they're living in Germany, **aren't they**?*	= ils habitent en Allemagne, **n'est-ce pas**?
*he's got a lot of money, **hasn't he**?*	= il a beaucoup d'argent, **n'est-ce pas**?
*you'll come too, **won't you**?*	= vous viendrez vous aussi, **n'est-ce pas**?
*he likes fish, **doesn't he**?*	= il aime le poisson, **n'est-ce pas**?

▶ For more examples, see the entry **not**.

Norwegian ▶ 275 |
1 *adjective*
= norvégien/norvégienne
2 *noun*
the Norwegians = les Norvégiens

nose *noun* ▶ 201 |
the nose = le nez

not
▶ *See the boxed note on* **not** *for more information and examples*
1 *adverb*
= ne... pas (**!** n' + *vowel or mute h...* pas)

! *Remember that ne or n' (before a vowel or mute h) comes before the verb or auxiliary verb and* pas *after.*

she's not at home = elle n'est pas chez elle
hasn't he phoned you? = il ne t'a pas téléphoné?
I hope not = j'espère que non

we're going to go out whether it rains or not = qu'il pleuve ou non, nous allons sortir
not everyone likes football = le football ne plaît pas à tout le monde
2 not at all
• (*in no way*) = pas du tout
he's not at all worried = il n'est pas du tout inquiet
• 'thanks a lot'—'not at all' = 'merci beaucoup'—'de rien'

note
1 *noun*
• (*to remind oneself*)
a note = une note
• (*a message*)
a note = un mot
I left you a note = je t'ai laissé un mot
• (*British English*) (*money*)
a note = un billet
a 50-franc note = un billet de 50 francs

- (*in music*)
  a note = une note
2 *verb*
  to note (down) = noter

notebook *noun*
a notebook = un carnet

nothing *pronoun*
nothing = rien

> **!** Note that, when there is a verb in the
> sentence, the negative ne or n' (before a
> vowel or mute h) is used together with
> rien to translate nothing. Remember that
> ne or n' comes before the verb or the
> auxiliary verb.

nothing has changed = rien n'a changé
there's nothing left = il ne reste rien
she said nothing = elle n'a rien dit
I knew nothing about it = je n'en savais
  rien
there's nothing we can do about it = nous
  n'y pouvons rien
I had nothing to do with it! = je n'y étais
  pour rien!
it's nothing to do with us = ça ne nous
  regarde pas

notice
1 *verb*
= remarquer
2 *noun*
- (*a written sign*)
  a notice = une pancarte
- (*warning people*)
  notice = le préavis
  a month's notice = un mois de préavis
  to be cancelled at short notice = être
    annulé/annulée à la dernière minute
- don't take any notice, take no notice = ne
  fais pas attention

novel *noun*
a novel = un roman

November *noun* ▶ 222 |
November = novembre (*masculine*)

now
1 *adverb*
= maintenant
we have to do it now = il faut le faire
  maintenant
I'm phoning her now = je suis en train de
  lui téléphoner
do it right now = fais-le tout de suite
now is the time to contact them = c'est le
  moment de les contacter
I should have told you before now
  = j'aurais dû te le dire avant
it hasn't been a problem until now = ça n'a
  pas posé de problème jusqu'à présent
between now and next Monday = d'ici
  lundi prochain
from now on = à partir de maintenant
2 now and again, now and then = de
  temps en temps

nowhere *adverb*
= nulle part
I go nowhere without my dog = je ne vais
  nulle part sans mon chien
there's nowhere to sit = il n'y a pas
  d'endroit pour s'asseoir

nuclear *adjective*
= nucléaire

nuisance *noun*
to be a nuisance = être pénible
it's a nuisance having to pay in cash
  = c'est agaçant de devoir payer en
  espèces

numb *adjective*
- to go numb = s'engourdir (**!** + *être*)
  my hands are numb = j'ai les mains
  engourdies
- (*before an operation*) = insensible

number
1 *noun*
- a number (*a figure*) = un chiffre
  (*of a house, a bus, a telephone, a passport*)
  = un numéro
  to dial the wrong number = faire un faux
  numéro
- (*when talking about quantities*) ▶ 317 |
  a number of [demonstrations | people |
  times …] = un certain nombre de
  [manifestations | personnes | fois …]
  a small number of tourists = quelques
  touristes
2 *verb*
= numéroter

numberplate *noun* (*British English*)
a numberplate = une plaque
  minéralogique

nun *noun* ▶ 315 |
a nun = une religieuse

nurse *noun* ▶ 315 |
a nurse = un infirmier/une infirmière

nursery *noun*
a nursery = une crèche

nursery school *noun*
a nursery school = une école maternelle

nut *noun*
a nut (*a walnut*) = une noix

nylon *noun*
nylon = le nylon®

N

oak *noun*
  an oak = un chêne

oar *noun*
  an oar = une rame

obedient *adjective*
  = obéissant/obéissante

obey *verb*
  = obéir
  to obey someone = obéir à quelqu'un
  to obey the law = se conformer à la loi

object
1 *noun*
  an object = un objet
2 *verb*
  = soulever des objections

oblige *verb*
• to be obliged to leave = être obligé/obligée
  de partir
• to oblige someone = rendre service à
  quelqu'un

obtain *verb*
  = obtenir

obvious *adjective*
  = évident/évidente

obviously *adverb*
  = manifestement

occasion *noun*
  an occasion = une occasion
  on special occasions = dans les grandes
  occasions

occasionally *adverb*
  = de temps à autre

occupy *verb*
• (*to take over*) = occuper
• (*to keep busy*)
  to keep oneself occupied = s'occuper
  (**!** + *être*)
  to keep the children occupied = occuper
  les enfants

occur *verb*
  = se produire (**!** + *être*)

ocean *noun*
  the ocean = l'océan (*masculine*)

o'clock *adverb* ▶ **211** |
  it's five o'clock = il est cinq heures
  at one o'clock = à une heure

October *noun* ▶ **222** |
  October = octobre (*masculine*)

octopus *noun*
  an octopus = une pieuvre

odd *adjective*
• (*strange*) = bizarre
• (*not matching*) = dépareillé/dépareillée
• (*when talking about numbers*)
  an odd number = un nombre impair

odour (*British English*), **odor** (*US English*)
noun
  an odour = une odeur

of *preposition*
• of = de (**!** d' + *vowel or mute h*)
  the sound of an engine = le bruit d'un
  moteur
  it's in the centre of Paris = c'est au centre
  de Paris
  a photo of the dog = une photo du chien
  half of the salad = la moitié de la salade
  at the top of the stairs = en haut de
  l'escalier
  the names of the pupils = le nom des
  élèves
• (*when talking about quantities*) ▶ **317** |
  of = de (**!** d' + *vowel or mute h*)
  a kilo of potatoes = un kilo de pommes
  de terre
  a bottle of mineral water = une bouteille
  d'eau minérale
  two cans of beer = deux cannettes de
  bière
  the flowers are lovely so we bought some
  of them = les fleurs sont belles alors
  nous en avons acheté
  have you heard of it? = est-ce que tu en as
  entendu parler?
  there are six of them in the family = ils
  sont six dans la famille
  there were too many of them = ils étaient
  trop nombreux
  ! *Note that* en *is used to translate* 'of it' *or*
  'of them' *when talking about things, but*
  not usually when referring to people.

off
  ! *Often* off *occurs in combinations with*
  verbs, for example: get off, go off, take off
  etc. To find the correct translations for this
  type of verb, look up the separate
  dictionary entries at get, go, take *etc.*

1 *adverb*
• (*leaving*)
  I'm off (*British English*) = je m'en vais
  they're off to Italy tomorrow = ils partent
  pour l'Italie demain
• (*away*)
  the coast is a long way off = la côte est
  loin d'ici
  we could see them from a long way off
  = on les voyait de loin
• (*free*)
  to take a day off = prendre un jour de
  congé
  today's her day off = elle ne travaille pas
  aujourd'hui

- (*not working, switched off*)
  the lights are all off = toutes les lumières sont éteintes
2 *adjective*
  the milk is off = le lait a tourné

offence (*British English*), **offense** (*US English*) *noun*
- (*a crime*)
  an offence = un délit
- **to take offence** = s'offenser (**!** + *être*)

offend *verb*
  = vexer

offer *verb*
  to offer someone a job = offrir un emploi à quelqu'un
  to offer to water the plants = se proposer pour arroser les plantes

office *noun*
  an office = un bureau

office block *noun* (*British English*)
  an office block = un immeuble de bureaux

officer *noun*
  an officer (*in the army or navy*) = un officier
  (*in the police*) = un policier

office worker *noun* ▶ 315 |
  an office worker = un employé/une employée de bureau

official *adjective*
  = officiel/officielle

often *adverb*
  = souvent

oil *noun*
- (*for heating, energy*)
  oil = le pétrole
- (*for a car*)
  oil = l'huile (*feminine*)
- (*for cooking, for health*)
  oil = l'huile (*feminine*)

okay, OK
1 *adjective*
- (*when asking or giving opinions*)
  is it okay if I come later? = est-ce que je peux venir plus tard?
  it's okay to invite them = on peut les inviter
- (*when talking about health*)
  to feel okay = aller bien
  are you okay? = ça va?
2 *adverb*
  okay = d'accord

old *adjective*
- (*not new, not young*) = vieux/vieille (**!** *before the noun*)

! *Note that* **vieil** *is used instead of* **vieux** *before masculine nouns beginning with a vowel (*ordinateur*) or a mute h (*hôtel*). The plural of* **vieux** *and* **vieil** *is* **vieux**.

  an old oak = un vieux chêne
  an old woman = une vieille femme
  an old man = un vieil homme
  old houses = de vieilles maisons
  old people = les personnes âgées
- (*when talking about a person's age*) ▶ 187 |
  how old are you? = quel âge as-tu?
  a three-year old girl = une fillette de trois ans
  I'm as old as he is = j'ai le même âge que lui
  she's eight years older than her brother = elle a huit ans de plus que son frère
  to be the oldest = être l'aîné/l'aînée
  to be old enough to go out at night = être en âge de sortir le soir
- (*previous*) = ancien/ancienne (**!** *before the noun*)
  that's my old address = c'est mon ancienne adresse
  in the old days = autrefois

old-fashioned *adjective*
  (*describing attitudes, ideas*)
  = démodé/démodée
  (*describing people*) = vieux jeu (**!** *never changes*)

olive
1 *noun*
  an olive = une olive
2 *adjective* ▶ 213 |
  = vert olive (**!** *never changes*)

olive oil *noun*
  olive oil = l'huile d'olive
  ! *Note that* **huile** *is feminine.*

Olympics *noun*
  the Olympics = les jeux Olympiques
  ! *Note that* **jeux** *is masculine plural.*

omelette *noun*
  an omelette = une omelette

on
  ! *Often* **on** *occurs in combinations with verbs, for example:* **count on, get on, keep on** *etc. To find the correct translations for this type of verb, look up the separate dictionary entries for* **count, get, keep** *etc.*

1 *preposition*
- **on** = sur
  it's on the table = c'est sur la table
  it's on top of the wardrobe = c'est sur l'armoire
  you've got a spot on your nose = tu as un bouton sur le nez
  there's a stain on it = il y a une tache dessus
  to fall on the floor = tomber par terre
  I like the picture on the wall = j'aime le tableau qui est au mur
  to live on Park Avenue = habiter Park Avenue

O

- (*when talking about transport*)
  to travel on the bus = voyager en bus
  I'm on my bike today = je suis à vélo
  aujourd'hui
- (*about*) = sur
  it's a book on Africa = c'est un livre sur
  l'Afrique
  a programme on primary schools = une
  émission sur les écoles primaires
- (*when talking about time*)
  she was born on the sixth of December
  = elle est née le six décembre
  I'll be there on Saturday = j'y serai samedi
  we went there on my birthday = nous y
  sommes allés le jour de mon
  anniversaire
- (*when talking about the media*)
  on television = à la télévision
  I saw it on the news = je l'ai vu aux
  informations
  is the film out on video? = est-ce que le
  film est sorti en vidéo?
- (*using*)
  to be on drugs = se droguer (**!** + *être*)
2 *adverb*
- (*when talking about what one wears*)
  to have a sweater on = porter un pull
  to have make-up on = être
  maquillé/maquillée
- (*working, switched on*)
  why are all the lights on? = pourquoi est-
  ce que toutes les lumières sont
  allumées?
  the radio was on all evening = la radio a
  marché toute la soirée
- (*showing*)
  what's on? (*on TV*) = qu'est-ce qu'il y a à la
  télévision?
  (*in the cinema*) = qu'est-ce qu'on joue (au
  cinéma)?
- (*when talking about time*)
  from Tuesday on, I'll be here = à partir de
  mardi, je serai là
  a little later on = un peu plus tard

once
1 *adverb*
- (*one time*) = une fois
  once a day = une fois par jour
- (*in the old days*) = autrefois
2 *conjunction*
= une fois que
  it'll be easier once we've found a house
  = ce sera plus facile une fois que nous
  aurons trouvé une maison
3 at once = tout de suite

one
1 *number* ▶ **187** |, ▶ **211** |
  one = un/une
  one child = un enfant/une enfant
  one of my colleagues = un/une de mes
  collègues
  one hundred = cent

2 *determiner*
- (*the only*)
  she's the one person who can help him
  = c'est la seule personne capable de
  l'aider
  it's the one thing that annoys me = c'est la
  seule chose qui m'agace
- (*the same*)
  to take three exams in the one day
  = passer trois examens dans la même
  journée
3 *pronoun*
- (*when referring to something generally*)
  I need an umbrella—have you got one?
  = j'ai besoin d'un parapluie—est-ce que
  tu en as un?

  ! *Note that it is necessary to use* en,
  which might be translated as 'of them',
  with pronouns like one. *See also* any, a
  few, many *etc for this use of* en.

- (*when referring to a specific person or
  thing*)
  **I like the new house but she prefers the
  old one** = j'aime la nouvelle maison
  mais elle préfère l'ancienne
  he's the one who told me to be quiet
  = c'est lui qui m'a dit de me taire
  which one? = lequel/laquelle?
  this one = celui-ci/celle-ci
- (*when used to mean 'you' or 'people'*)
  one never knows = on ne sait jamais
4 one by one = un par un/une par une

one another *pronoun*

  ! *Note that* one another *is very often
  translated by using a reflexive pronoun
  like* se, s', nous *or* vous.

  to love one another = s'aimer (**!** + *être*)
  **we don't like being apart from one
  another** = nous n'aimons pas être
  séparés (l'un de l'autre)

oneself *pronoun*
= se (**!** *s'* + vowel or mute h)
  to enjoy oneself = s'amuser (**!** + *être*)
  to hurt oneself = se blesser (**!** + *être*)

onion *noun*
  an onion = un oignon

only
1 *adverb*

  ! *Note that in sentences with a verb, the
  negative* ne *is often used together with*
  que *to translate* only. *Remember that* ne
  *comes before the verb or the auxiliary
  verb.*

  only = ne... que
  it's only a game = ce n'est qu'un jeu
  you only have to ask = vous n'avez qu'à
  demander
  they've only met once = ils ne se sont
  rencontrés qu'une fois
  he only hit his elbow = il s'est juste cogné
  le coude

2 *adjective*
= seul/seule (**!** *before the noun*)
**she was the only one who didn't speak
French** = elle était la seule à ne pas
parler français
the only problem is that I can't drive = le
seul problème c'est que je ne conduis
pas
an only daughter = une fille unique
3 only just
I've only just [arrived | heard the news | moved
house …] = je viens juste [d'arriver |
d'apprendre la nouvelle | de déménager …]
she had only just bought a car = elle
venait d'acheter une voiture

onto *preposition*
= sur

open
1 *verb*
• **to open** = ouvrir
to open a letter = ouvrir une lettre
what time do you open? = à quelle heure
est-ce que vous ouvrez?
the shop opens at eight = le magasin
ouvre à huit heures
the door opens very easily = la porte
s'ouvre facilement
• (*to start*) (*when talking about a film*) = sortir
(**!** + *être*)
(*when talking about a play*) = commencer
2 *adjective*
• (*not closed*) = ouvert/ouverte
leave the door open = laisse la porte
ouverte
the pool isn't open = la piscine n'est pas
ouverte
• (*frank*) = franc/franche
3 *noun*
out in the open = dehors, en plein air

opener *noun*
an opener (*for bottles*) = un décapsuleur
(*for cans*) = un ouvre-boîtes

open-minded *adjective*
to be open-minded = avoir l'esprit ouvert

opera *noun*
an opera = un opéra

operate *verb*
• (*to make something work*) = faire marcher
• (*to carry out an operation*) = opérer
to operate on someone = opérer
quelqu'un
to operate on someone's leg = opérer
quelqu'un à la jambe

operation *noun*
an operation = une opération
to have an operation = se faire opérer
(**!** + *être*)

operator *noun* ▶ 315 |
an operator = un standardiste/une
standardiste

opinion *noun*
an opinion (*a point of view*) = un avis
(*when judging a person, a situation*) = une
opinion
in my opinion, they're lying = à mon avis,
ils mentent

opponent *noun*
an opponent = un adversaire/une
adversaire

opportunity *noun*
an opportunity = une occasion
to take the opportunity to visit Paris
= profiter de l'occasion pour visiter Paris

oppose *verb*
to oppose a plan = s'opposer à un projet
to be opposed to nuclear weapons = être
contre les armes nucléaires

opposite
1 *preposition*
= en face de
she was sitting opposite me = elle était
assise en face de moi
2 *adjective*
the opposite sex = le sexe opposé
he was walking in the opposite direction
= il allait dans l'autre sens
3 *adverb*
= en face
4 *noun*
the opposite = le contraire
it's the exact opposite = c'est tout le
contraire

optician *noun* ▶ 315 |
an optician = un opticien/une opticienne

optimist *noun*
an optimist = un optimiste/une optimiste

optimistic *adjective*
= optimiste

or *conjunction*
• **or** = ou
once or twice a week = une ou deux fois
par semaine
we'll stay either here or at Martine's
= nous resterons soit ici soit chez
Martine
do you have any brothers or sisters?
= est-ce que tu as des frères et sœurs?
• (*in negative sentences*)
I can't come today or tomorrow = je ne
peux venir ni aujourd'hui ni demain
don't tell Mum or Dad = ne le dis ni à
maman ni à papa
• (*otherwise*) = sinon
be careful or you'll break the cups = fais
attention sinon tu vas casser les tasses

oral *adjective*
= oral/orale

orange
1 *noun*
an orange = une orange

O

2 *adjective* ▶ 213 |
= orange (**!** *never changes*)

orange juice *noun*
orange juice = le jus d'orange

orchard *noun*
an orchard = un verger

orchestra *noun*
an orchestra = un orchestre

order
1 *verb*
• (*to tell*)
to order someone to leave = ordonner à
quelqu'un de partir
• (*to ask for*) = commander
to order goods from a magazine
= commander des articles dans un
magazine
2 *noun*
• (*an instruction*)
an order = un ordre
to give orders = donner des ordres
• the right order = le bon ordre
the list is in alphabetical order = la liste
est dans l'ordre alphabétique
3 in order to = pour
I phoned them in order to change the date
= je leur ai téléphoné pour changer la
date

ordinary *adjective*
• (*not unusual*) = ordinaire
an ordinary family = une famille ordinaire
• (*average*) = moyen/moyenne

organ *noun*
• (*the musical instrument*) ▶ 290 |
an organ = un orgue
• (*a part of the body*)
an organ = un organe

organization *noun*
an organization = une organisation

organize *verb*
= organiser
to get organized = s'organiser (**!** + *être*)

original *adjective*
• (*first*) = original/originale
• (*true, real*) = originel/originelle
• (*new, fresh*) = original/originale

ornament *noun*
an ornament = un bibelot

orphan *noun*
an orphan = un orphelin/une orpheline

ostrich *noun*
an ostrich = une autruche

other
1 *adjective*
= autre (+ *singular*)
= autres (+ *plural*)
not that dress, the other one = pas cette
robe-là, l'autre
they sold the other car = ils ont vendu
l'autre voiture
to annoy the other pupils = embêter les
autres élèves

some people like driving, other people
hate it = certains aiment conduire,
d'autres détestent ça
every other Saturday = un samedi sur
deux
2 *pronoun*
he makes the others laugh = il fait rire les
autres
some students learn French easily,
others have problems = certains élèves
apprennent le français facilement,
d'autres ont des problèmes
they came in one after the other = ils sont
entrés l'un après l'autre

otherwise *conjunction*
= sinon
it's not dangerous, otherwise I wouldn't
go = ce n'est pas dangereux, sinon je
n'irais pas

otter *noun*
an otter = une loutre

ought *verb*
• (*when talking about what should be done*)
you ought not to say things like that = tu
ne devrais pas dire des choses pareilles
• (*when making a polite suggestion*)
you ought to be in bed = tu devrais être au
lit
• (*when saying something may happen*)
they ought to arrive tomorrow = ils
devraient arriver demain
• (*when saying something didn't happen*)
someone ought to have gone with them
= quelqu'un aurait dû les accompagner

our *determiner*
our = notre (+ *singular*)
= nos (+ *plural*)
he ran over our dog = il a écrasé notre
chien
what do you think of our house? = qu'est-
ce que tu penses de notre maison?
all our CDs have been stolen = on a volé
tous nos disques compacts

ours *pronoun*
the grey car is ours = la voiture grise est à
nous
which case is ours? = laquelle de ces
valises est la nôtre?
their garden is bigger than ours = leur
jardin est plus grand que le nôtre
their children are younger than ours
= leurs enfants sont plus jeunes que les
nôtres

! *Note that, when comparing objects,
people, etc, one of the following
translations—le nôtre, la nôtre or les
nôtres—will be used. To know which one
to use, find out whether the object,
person etc which is being described is
masculine singular, feminine singular or
just plural.*

ourselves *pronoun*
- (*when used as a reflexive pronoun*)
  we want to enjoy ourselves = nous
  voulons nous amuser, on veut s'amuser
  we didn't hurt ourselves = nous ne nous
  sommes pas fait mal, on ne s'est pas fait
  mal

  ! *Note that* **on** *is more usual in spoken
  French.*

- (*when used for emphasis*)
  we organized everything ourselves
  = nous avons tout organisé nous-mêmes
  we like to be by ourselves = nous aimons
  être seuls

out

  ! *Often* **out** *occurs in combinations with
  verbs, for example:* **blow out, come out,
  find out, give out** *etc. To find the correct
  translations for this type of verb, look up
  the separate dictionary entries at* **blow,
  come, find, give** *etc.*

1 *adverb*
- (*outside*) = dehors
  they're out there = ils sont dehors
  to stay out in the rain = rester dehors sous
  la pluie
  she's out in the garden = elle est dans le
  jardin
  I'm looking for the way out = je cherche la
  sortie
- (*absent*)
  to be out = être sorti/sortie
  someone called while you were out
  = quelqu'un a téléphoné pendant que tu
  étais sorti
- (*not lighting, not on*)
  to be out = être éteint/éteinte
  all the lights were out = toutes les
  lumières étaient éteintes
2 out of
  to walk out of the building = sortir du
  bâtiment
  to get out of the city = sortir de la ville
  to take a pencil out of the drawer
  = prendre un crayon dans le tiroir

outdoor *adjective*
  = en plein air
  an outdoor swimming pool = une piscine
  en plein air

outdoors *adverb*
  = dehors

outer space *noun*
  outer space = l'espace (*masculine*)

outside
1 *preposition*
- (*in front of*) = devant
  to wait outside the school = attendre
  devant l'école
- (*beyond*)
  outside the city = en dehors de la ville

2 *adverb*
  = dehors
  let's go outside = allons dehors
  let's bring the chairs outside = sortons les
  chaises
3 *noun*
  the outside = l'extérieur (*masculine*)
  the outside of the building = l'extérieur du
  bâtiment
4 *adjective*
  = extérieur/extérieure

oven *noun*
  an oven = un four

over

  ! *Often* **over** *occurs in combinations with
  verbs, for example:* **get over, move over**
  *etc. To find the correct translations for this
  type of verb, look up the separate
  dictionary entries at* **get, move** *etc.*

1 *preposition*
- **over** = par-dessus
  to climb over a wall = passer par-dessus un
  mur
  we climbed over it = nous sommes passés
  par-dessus
- (*across*)
  it's somewhere over there = c'est quelque
  part par là
  come over here = viens par ici
- (*above*) = au-dessus de
  the picture over the piano = le tableau au-
  dessus du piano
  young people over 18 = les jeunes de plus
  de 18 ans
- (*during*)
  we saw them over the weekend = nous les
  avons vus pendant le week-end
- (*everywhere*)
  I've looked all over the house for my keys
  = j'ai cherché mes clés partout dans la
  maison
2 *adverb*
- (*finished*)
  the term is over = le trimestre est terminé
  is the film over? = est-ce que le film est
  fini?
- (*to one's home*)
  to ask someone over = inviter quelqu'un
- **to start over again** = recommencer à zéro

overdose *noun*
  an overdose = une surdose

overtake *verb*
  = dépasser

overweight *adjective*
  = trop gros/trop grosse

owe *verb*
  = devoir
  to owe money to someone = devoir de
  l'argent à quelqu'un

owl *noun*
  an owl = un hibou, une chouette

O

own

1 *adjective*
= propre (**!** *before the noun*)
you should clean your own room = tu devrais ranger ta propre chambre
he'd like his own car = il voudrait une voiture à lui, il voudrait sa propre voiture

2 *pronoun*

! *Note that, when comparing objects, people etc, the translations given for the pronouns* mine, yours, his, hers, ours *or* theirs *work for* my own, your own *etc.*

I didn't use his pencil—I've got my own = je n'ai pas utilisé son crayon—j'ai le mien
they have a house of their own = ils ont une maison à eux, ils ont leur propre maison

3 *verb*
= avoir
he owns a shop in town = il a un magasin en ville
who owns that dog? = à qui est ce chien?

4 on one's own = tout seul/toute seule
own up = avouer

owner *noun*
an owner = un propriétaire/une propriétaire

ox *noun*
an ox = un bœuf

oxygen *noun*
oxygen = l'oxygène (*masculine*)

oyster *noun*
an oyster = une huître

Pacific *noun*
the Pacific = le Pacifique

pack

1 *verb*
= faire ses bagages
I've got to pack my suitcase = je dois faire ma valise

2 *noun*
a pack = un paquet
a pack of cigarettes = un paquet de cigarettes
a pack of cards = un jeu de cartes
pack up = faire ses bagages
to pack up one's belongings = emballer ses affaires

package *noun*
a package = un paquet, un colis

packed *adjective*
(*describing a room*) = plein/pleine à craquer
(*describing a train, a bus*) = bondé/bondée

packet *noun*
a packet = un paquet

page *noun*
a page = une page
on page six = (à la) page six

pain *noun*
pain = la douleur
I've got a pain in my back = j'ai mal au dos
to be in pain = souffrir

painful *adjective*
= douloureux/douloureuse

paint

1 *noun*
paint = la peinture

2 *verb*
= peindre

paintbrush *noun*
a paintbrush = un pinceau

painter *noun* ▶ **315**
a painter = un peintre

painting *noun*
• (*a picture*)
a painting = un tableau
• (*the activity*)
painting = la peinture

pair *noun*
a pair = une paire
a pair of shoes = une paire de chaussures

pajamas *noun* (*US English*)
pajamas = un pyjama (*singular*)

Pakistan *noun* ▶ **218**
Pakistan = le Pakistan

palace *noun*
a palace = un palais

pale *adjective*
= pâle
to go pale, to turn pale = pâlir

pancake *noun*
a pancake = une crêpe

panic *verb*
= s'affoler (**!** + *être*)

pants *noun*
• (*British English*) (*underwear*)
pants = un slip (*singular*)
• (*US English*) (*trousers*)
pants = un pantalon (*singular*)

pantyhose *noun* (*US English*)
pantyhose = un collant

paper *noun*
• (*for writing or drawing on*)
paper = le papier
a piece of paper = un bout de papier

- (*a newspaper*)
  a paper = un journal

parachuting *noun* ▶ 248 |
  parachuting = le parachutisme

parade *noun*
  a parade = un défilé

paragliding *noun* ▶ 248 |
  paragliding = le parapente

paralysed (*British English*), **paralyzed**
(*US English*) *adjective*
  = paralysé/paralysée

parcel *noun*
  a parcel = un paquet, un colis

parents *noun*
  parents = les parents (*masculine*)

Paris *noun* ▶ 218 |
  Paris = Paris

park
1 *noun*
  a park = un jardin public, un parc
2 *verb*
  to park a car = garer une voiture
  to park near the office = se garer près du
    bureau

parking lot *noun* (*US English*)
  a parking lot = un parking, un parc de
    stationnement

parking meter *noun*
  a parking meter = un parcmètre

parliament *noun*
  a parliament = un parlement

parrot *noun*
  a parrot = un perroquet

part
- **a part** = une partie
  part of the [book | film | time ...] = une partie
    du [livre | film | temps ...]
  it's part of the job = ça fait partie du
    travail
  in this part of the country = dans cette
    région
- (*a piece for a machine, a car*)
  a part = une pièce
- (*a section*)
  a part (*in a programme*) = une partie
  (*in a series*) = un épisode
- (*a role*)
  a part = un rôle
  to play the part of Tommy = jouer le rôle
    de Tommy

participate *verb*
  = participer

particular
1 *adjective*
  = particulier/particulière
2 in particular = en particulier

partner *noun*
- (*in a relationship*)
  a partner = un compagnon/une compagne
- (*in dancing, sport*)
  a partner = un partenaire/une partenaire

part-time *adverb*
  = à temps partiel
  to work part-time = travailler à temps
    partiel

party *noun*
- (*a social event*)
  a party = une fête
  (*held in the evening*) = une soirée
  a birthday party = une fête d'anniversaire,
    un anniversaire
  a children's party = un goûter d'enfants
- **a political party** = un parti politique

pass *verb*
- (*to go past*) = passer (**!** + *être*)
  to let someone pass = laisser passer
    quelqu'un
  to pass the school = passer devant l'école
  to pass a car = dépasser une voiture
  to pass someone in the street = croiser
    quelqu'un dans la rue
- (*to give*) = passer
  pass me the salt, please = passe-moi le
    sel, s'il te plaît
  to pass the ball to someone = passer le
    ballon à quelqu'un
- (*to spend*) = passer
  to pass the time [reading | painting | listening
    to the radio ...] = passer le temps [en lisant |
    en faisant de la peinture | en écoutant la
    radio ...]
- (*to succeed in an exam*) = réussir
  to pass an exam = réussir un examen
pass around
  to pass around the biscuits = faire passer
    les biscuits
pass on = transmettre
  to pass on a message to someone
    = transmettre un message à quelqu'un

passage *noun*
  a passage (*indoors*) = un couloir
  (*outdoors*) = un passage

passenger *noun*
  a passenger = un passager/une passagère

passport *noun*
  a passport = un passeport

past
1 *noun*
  the past = le passé
  in the past = dans le passé
2 *adjective*
  = dernier/dernière (**!** *before the noun*)
  the past few days have been difficult = ces
    derniers jours ont été difficiles
3 *preposition*
- (*when talking about time*) ▶ 211 |
  it's twenty past four = il est quatre heures
    vingt
  it's past midnight = il est minuit passé

P

- (by)
  to go past someone = passer devant
  quelqu'un
  she ran past me = elle est passée devant
  moi en courant
- (beyond) = après
  it's just past the traffic lights = c'est juste
  après les feux
4 adverb
  to go past, to walk past = passer (**!** + être)

pasta noun
  pasta = les pâtes (feminine)

pastry noun
- (for baking)
  pastry = la pâte
  to make pastry = faire de la pâte
- (a cake)
  a pastry = une pâtisserie, un gâteau

patch noun
- (on a garment)
  a patch = une pièce
- (on a tyre)
  a patch = une rustine®

path noun
  a path = un chemin
  (narrower) = un sentier
  (in a garden) = une allée

patience noun
  patience = la patience
  to lose patience with someone = perdre
  patience avec quelqu'un

patient
1 noun
  a patient = un patient/une patiente
2 adjective
  = patient/patiente

patrol car noun
  a patrol car = une voiture de police

pattern noun
- (a design)
  a pattern = un dessin, un motif
- (when making garments)
  a pattern (for knitting) = un modèle
  (for sewing) = un patron

pavement noun (British English)
  a pavement = un trottoir

paw noun
  a paw = une patte

pay
1 verb
- **to pay** = payer
  to pay the bills = payer les factures
  to pay for the shopping = payer les
  courses
  he paid for my meal = il a payé mon repas
- (when talking about wages)
  the work doesn't pay very well = le travail
  est mal payé
  I'm paid eight pounds an hour = je suis
  payé huit livres de l'heure

- (to give)
  to pay attention to the teacher = écouter
  le professeur
  to pay someone a visit = rendre visite à
  quelqu'un
  to pay someone a compliment = faire des
  compliments à quelqu'un
2 noun
  pay = le salaire
  the pay is very good = c'est très bien payé
pay back = rembourser

PE noun
  PE = l'éducation physique
  ! Note that éducation is feminine.

pea noun
  a pea = un petit pois

peace noun
  peace = la paix

peach noun
  a peach = une pêche

peacock noun
  a peacock = un paon

peanut noun
  a peanut = une cacahuète

pear noun
  a pear = une poire

pearl noun
  a pearl = une perle

pebble noun
  a pebble (on a beach) = un galet

pedestrian noun
  a pedestrian = un piéton

pedestrian crossing noun
  a pedestrian crossing = un passage pour
  piétons

peel verb
  = éplucher

pen noun
  a pen = un stylo

penalty noun
  a penalty (in soccer) = un tir de
  réparation, un penalty
  (in rugby) = une pénalité

pencil noun
  a pencil = un crayon

pencil case noun
  a pencil case = une trousse à crayons

pencil sharpener noun
  a pencil sharpener = un taille-crayon

penfriend (British English), **penpal**
noun
  a penfriend = un correspondant/une
  correspondante

penguin noun
  a penguin = un pingouin

penknife *noun*
a penknife = un canif

pensioner *noun*
a pensioner = un retraité/une retraitée

people *noun*
people (*in general*) = les gens (*masculine plural*)
(*if counting*) = les personnes (*feminine plural*)
we met very nice people = nous avons fait la connaissance de gens très sympathiques
most people don't know what's going on = la plupart des gens ne savent pas ce qui se passe
there were three people at the meeting = il y avait trois personnes à la réunion
there are too many people here = il y a trop de monde ici
to help other people = aider les autres

pepper *noun*
* (*the spice*)
pepper = le poivre
* (*the vegetable*)
a pepper = un poivron

per *preposition*
per person = par personne

per cent, **percent** (*US English*) *noun*
per cent = pour cent, %

perfect *adjective*
= parfait/parfaite
to speak perfect French = parler un français parfait
it's the perfect place for a picnic = c'est l'endroit idéal pour un pique-nique

perform *verb*
* (*to do*)
to perform a task = exécuter une tâche
* (*to act, to play*) = jouer

perfume *noun*
perfume = le parfum
to wear perfume = mettre du parfum

perhaps *adverb*
= peut-être

period *noun*
* (*in time*)
a period = une période
a trial period = une période d'essai
* (*in history*)
a period = une époque
* (*for women*)
a period = des règles (*feminine plural*)
to have one's period = avoir ses règles
* (*a school lesson*)
a period = un cours

permanent *adjective*
= permanent/permanente

permission *noun*
permission = la permission
to get permission to leave the country = obtenir la permission de quitter le pays

person *noun*
a person = une personne
an old person = une personne âgée
to be a kind person = être gentil/gentille
he's not a very patient person = il n'est pas très patient

personal *adjective*
= personnel/personnelle

personality *noun*
a personality = une personnalité

perspire *verb*
= transpirer

persuade *verb*
= persuader
to persuade someone to buy a car = persuader quelqu'un d'acheter une voiture

pessimist *noun*
a pessimist = un pessimiste/une pessimiste

pessimistic *adjective*
= pessimiste

pet *noun*
a pet = un animal de compagnie
do you have any pets? = est-ce que tu as des animaux?

petrol *noun* (*British English*)
petrol = l'essence (*feminine*)
to run out of petrol = tomber en panne d'essence

petrol station *noun* (*British English*)
a petrol station = une station d'essence

pet shop *noun* ▶ 315|
a pet shop = une animalerie

phone
1 *noun*
a phone = un téléphone
the phone's ringing = le téléphone sonne
to answer the phone = répondre au téléphone
he's on the phone = il est au téléphone
2 *verb*
= téléphoner
to phone someone = téléphoner à quelqu'un, passer un coup de fil à quelqu'un

phone book *noun*
a phone book = un annuaire téléphonique

phone booth *noun*
a phone booth = une cabine téléphonique

P

phone call *noun*
a phone call = un coup de fil, un appel
  téléphonique
to receive a phone call = recevoir un
  appel téléphonique, recevoir un coup
  de fil
to make a phone call = téléphoner, passer
  un coup de fil

phone card *noun*
a phone card = une télécarte®

phone number *noun*
a phone number = un numéro de
  téléphone

photo *noun*
a photo = une photo

photocopier *noun*
a photocopier = une photocopieuse

photocopy *noun*
a photocopy = une photocopie

photograph *noun*
a photograph = une photo
to take a photograph of someone
  = prendre quelqu'un en photo

photographer *noun* ▶ 315|
a photographer = un photographe/une
  photographe

physical *adjective*
= physique

physics *noun*
physics = la physique

piano *noun* ▶ 290|
a piano = un piano

pick *verb*
• (*to choose*) = choisir
  to pick a number = choisir un chiffre
• (*to collect*) = cueillir
  to pick blackberries = cueillir des mûres
• (*to take*)
  to pick a book off the shelf = prendre un
    livre sur l'étagère
pick on = s'en prendre à (! + *être*)
  he's always picking on me = il s'en prend
    toujours à moi
pick out = choisir
pick up
• (*to lift*) = ramasser
  to pick the clothes up off the floor
    = ramasser les vêtements par terre
  to pick a baby up = prendre un bébé dans
    ses bras
  to pick up the phone = décrocher le
    téléphone
• (*to collect*)
  to pick up passengers = prendre des
    passagers
  he's coming to pick me up = il vient me
    chercher

• (*to buy*) = prendre
  I stopped to pick up some milk = je me
    suis arrêté pour prendre du lait
• (*to learn*)
  to pick up a little German = apprendre un
    peu d'allemand

picnic *noun*
a picnic = un pique-nique
to go on a picnic = aller faire un pique-
  nique

picture *noun*
• a picture (*painted*) = une peinture, un
    tableau
  (*drawn*) = un dessin
  to paint someone's picture = faire le
    portrait de quelqu'un
• (*a photograph*)
  a picture = une photo
• the pictures = le cinéma (*singular*)

piece *noun*
• (*a bit*)
  a piece = un morceau
  a piece of cheese = un morceau de
    fromage
  a piece of string = un bout de ficelle
• (*a part of a machine*)
  a piece = une pièce
• (*a broken part*)
  a piece = un morceau
  to fall to pieces = tomber en morceaux
• (*a coin*)
  a 50-pence piece = une pièce de 50 pence
• (*other uses*)
  a piece of furniture = un meuble
  a piece of information = un
    renseignement
  a piece of advice = un conseil

pierce *verb*
= percer

pig *noun*
a pig = un porc, un cochon

pigeon *noun*
a pigeon = un pigeon

pile
• a pile = une pile
  (*untidy*) = un tas
  a pile of old shoes = un tas de vieilles
    chaussures
• (*lots*)
  piles of [toys | records | books ...] = des tas✱
    de [jouets | disques | livres ...]

pill *noun*
• (*a tablet*)
  a pill = un comprimé
• (*a method of contraception*)
  the pill = la pilule

pillow *noun*
a pillow = un oreiller

pilot *noun* ▶ 315|
a pilot = un pilote

✱ in informal situations

pin
1 *noun*
a pin = une épingle
2 *verb*
= accrocher

pinball *noun* ▶ 248 |
pinball = le flipper

pinch *verb*
- to pinch = pincer
  he pinched my arm, he pinched me on the arm = il m'a pincé le bras
- (*to hurt by being too tight*) = serrer
  my shoes are pinching = mes chaussures me serrent

pineapple *noun*
a pineapple = un ananas

pine tree *noun*
a pine tree = un pin

pink *adjective* ▶ 213 |
= rose

pint *noun*
- (*the quantity*)
  a pint ≈ un demi-litre

  ! *Note that a pint = 0.57 l in Britain and 0.47 l in the US.*

  a pint of milk ≈ un demi-litre de lait
- (*British English*) (*a drink*)
  to go for a pint = aller boire une bière

pipe *noun*
- (*for gas, water*)
  a pipe = un tuyau
- (*for smoking*)
  a pipe = une pipe

pirate *noun*
a pirate = un pirate

Pisces *noun*
Pisces = Poissons (*masculine plural*)

pitch *noun* (*British English*)
a pitch = un terrain
a football pitch = un terrain de football

pity
1 *noun*
- pity = la pitié
- (*when expressing regret*)
  what a pity! = quel dommage!
  it's a pity you can't come = c'est dommage que tu ne puisses pas venir

  ! *Note that the subjunctive is used after* c'est dommage que.

2 *verb*
= plaindre

pizza *noun*
a pizza = une pizza

place *noun*
- a place = un endroit
  it's the best place to buy salmon = c'est le meilleur endroit pour acheter du saumon
  Oxford is a nice place = Oxford est une belle ville
  they come from all over the place = ils viennent de partout
  this place is dirty = c'est sale ici
- (*a home*)
  at Alison's place = chez Alison
  I'd like a place of my own = j'aimerais avoir un chez-moi
- (*in a queue, on a bus, in a car park, at table*)
  a place = une place
  is this place free? = est-ce que cette place est libre?
  to take someone's place = prendre la place de quelqu'un
  to find a place to park = trouver une place pour se garer
- (*on a team, a course, in a firm*)
  a place = une place
  to get a place on a course = obtenir une place dans un cours
- (*in a contest*)
  a place = une place
  to win first place = gagner la première place

plain
1 *adjective*
- (*simple*) = simple
  a plain dress = une robe simple
- (*not good-looking*) = quelconque
2 *noun*
a plain = une plaine

plait *noun* (*British English*)
a plait = une natte, une tresse

plan
1 *noun*
- (*what one intends to do*)
  a plan = un plan
  we need a plan = il nous faut un plan
- (*what one has arranged to do*)
  a plan = un projet
  do you have any plans for the future? = est-ce que tu as des projets pour l'avenir?
  I don't have any plans for tonight = je n'ai rien de prévu pour ce soir
2 *verb*
- (*to prepare, to organize*)
  to plan [a trip | a school timetable | a meeting …] = organiser [un voyage | un emploi du temps | une réunion …]
- (*to intend*) = avoir l'intention de
  I'm planning to visit Scotland = j'ai l'intention de visiter l'Écosse

plane *noun*
a plane = un avion

P

planet noun
a planet = une planète

plant
1 noun
a plant = une plante
2 verb
= planter

plaster noun (British English)
a plaster = un pansement adhésif

plastic
1 noun
plastic = le plastique
2 adjective
= en plastique

plate noun
a plate = une assiette

platform noun
a platform = un quai
on platform 4 = au quai numéro 4

play
1 verb
* (to have fun) = jouer
  to play with friends = jouer avec des amis
  to play a trick on someone = jouer un
    tour à quelqu'un
  to play cards = jouer aux cartes
* (when talking about sports) ▶ 248 = jouer
  to play [football | cricket | tennis …] = jouer
    [au football | au cricket | au tennis …]
  France is playing (against) Ireland = la
    France joue contre l'Irlande
* (when talking about music) ▶ 290 = jouer
  to play [the piano | the flute | drums …] = jouer
    [du piano | de la flûte | de la batterie …]
* (to put on) = mettre
  to play [a video | a CD | a record …] = mettre
    [une cassette vidéo | un disque compact | un
    disque …]
* (when talking about theatre, cinema)
  to play the role of Richard II = jouer le rôle
    de Richard II
  the film will be playing at the Phoenix = le
    film va passer au Phoenix
2 noun
a play = une pièce
play around = faire l'imbécile
play back
to play back a tape = repasser une cassette

player noun ▶ 248
a player = un joueur/une joueuse
a tennis player = un joueur/une joueuse
  de tennis

playground noun
a playground = une aire de jeu
the school playground = la cour de
  récréation

please adverb
(formal, to several people) = s'il vous plaît
(informal) = s'il te plaît
please come in = entrez, je vous en prie
'more cake?'—'yes please' = 'encore du
  gâteau?'—'oui, je veux bien'

pleased adjective
= content/contente
I was very pleased with myself = j'étais
  très content de moi
pleased to meet you = enchanté

plenty pronoun
to have plenty [of time | of money | of
  friends …] = avoir beaucoup [de temps |
  d'argent | d'amis …]

plot noun
* (a plan)
  a plot = un complot
* (the story in a film, a novel, a play)
  a plot = une intrigue

plug noun
* (on an appliance)
  a plug = une prise
  to pull out the plug = débrancher la prise
* (in a sink or bath)
  a plug = une bonde
plug in = brancher

plum noun
a plum = une prune

plumber noun ▶ 315
a plumber = un plombier

plus preposition
= plus
three plus three are six = trois plus trois
  font six

pocket noun
a pocket = une poche

pocketbook noun (US English)
a pocketbook = un sac à main

pocket money noun
pocket money = l'argent de poche
! Note that argent is masculine.

poem noun
a poem = un poème

point
1 noun
* (a statement in a discussion)
  a point = une remarque
  to make a point = faire une remarque
* (the most important idea)
  the point = le point essentiel
  that's not the point = là n'est pas la
    question
* (use)
  there's no point in shouting = ça ne sert à
    rien de crier
* (when talking about time)
  to be on the point of [moving | leaving |
    selling the house …] = être sur le point de
    [déménager | partir | vendre la maison …]
* (the sharp end)
  the point = la pointe
  the point of a pencil = la pointe d'un
    crayon
* (in a contest, a game)
  a point = un point

2 *verb*
* (*to indicate*)
  to point (one's finger) at someone
  = montrer quelqu'un du doigt
  to point at a house = indiquer une maison
  to point the way to the station = indiquer
  la direction de la gare
* (*to aim*)
  to point a gun at someone = braquer un
  pistolet sur quelqu'un
point out = montrer
  can you point them out to me? = est-ce
  que tu peux me les montrer?

poison
1 *noun*
  poison = le poison
2 *verb*
  = empoisonner

Poland *noun* ▶ **218**
  Poland = la Pologne

pole *noun*
  a pole = une perche

police *noun*
  the police = la police

policeman *noun* ▶ **315**
  a policeman = un policier

police station *noun*
  a police station = un poste de police

policewoman *noun* ▶ **315**
  a policewoman = une femme policier

polish *verb*
  to polish shoes = cirer des chaussures
  to polish the car = lustrer la voiture

polite *adjective*
  = poli/polie

political *adjective*
  = politique

politician *noun* ▶ **315**
  a politician = un homme/une femme
  politique

politics *noun*
  politics = la politique

pollute *verb*
  = polluer

pollution *noun*
  pollution = la pollution

pond *noun*
  a pond (*large*) = un étang
  (*smaller*) = une mare
  (*in a garden*) = un bassin

pony *noun*
  a pony = un poney

ponytail *noun*
  a ponytail = une queue de cheval

pool *noun*
* (*a swimming pool*)
  a pool = une piscine

* (*on the ground, the floor*)
  a pool of water = une flaque d'eau
* (*the game*) ▶ **248**
  pool = le billard américain

poor *adjective*
* (*not wealthy*) = pauvre
* (*not satisfactory*) = mauvais/mauvaise
  (**!** *before the noun*)
  to be poor at languages = être faible en
  langues
* (*expressing sympathy*) = pauvre (**!** *before
  the noun*)
  the poor boy is exhausted = le pauvre
  garçon est épuisé

popular *adjective*

> **!** *Note that* **popular** *is not usually
> translated by* **populaire**.

  a popular hobby = un passe-temps
  répandu
  she's very popular = elle a beaucoup
  d'amis
  to be popular with the girls = avoir du
  succès auprès des filles

population *noun*
  a population = une population

pork *noun*
  pork = le porc

port *noun*
  a port = un port

portrait *noun*
  a portrait = un portrait

Portugal *noun* ▶ **218**
  Portugal = le Portugal

Portuguese ▶ **275**
1 *adjective*
  = portugais/portugaise
2 *noun*
* (*the people*)
  the Portuguese = les Portugais (*masculine
  plural*)
* (*the language*)
  Portuguese = le portugais

positive *adjective*
  = positif/positive

possibility *noun*
  a possibility = une possibilité

possible *adjective*
  = possible
  they came as quickly as possible = ils
  sont venus le plus vite possible
  I did as much as possible = j'ai fait tout ce
  que j'ai pu

post (*British English*)
1 *noun*
  the post (*the system*) = la poste
  (*the letters*) = le courrier
  has the post come yet? = est-ce que le
  courrier est arrivé?

P

2 *verb*
  to post a letter = poster une lettre

postbox *noun* (*British English*)
  a postbox = une boîte aux lettres

postcard *noun*
  a postcard = une carte postale

postcode *noun* (*British English*)
  a postcode = un code postal

poster *noun*
  a poster (*giving information*) = une affiche
  (*used as a picture*) = un poster

postman *noun* ▶ **315** (*British English*)
  a postman = un facteur

post office *noun*
  a post office = un bureau de poste

postpone *verb*
  to postpone a concert = reporter un
    concert
  let's postpone the party until next week
    = reportons la fête à la semaine
    prochaine

pot *noun*
• (*a container*)
  a pot = un pot
  to make a pot of tea = faire du thé
• (*a saucepan*)
  a pot = une casserole

potato *noun*
  a potato = une pomme de terre

pottery *noun*
  pottery = la poterie

pound *noun*
• (*the currency*)
  a pound = une livre
• (*the measurement*)
  a pound ≈ une livre
  | **!** Note that a **pound** = *453.6 g.*

  two pounds of apples ≈ un kilo de
    pommes

pour *verb*
• (*from a container*) = verser
  to pour milk into a bowl = verser du lait
    dans un bol
• (*to serve*) = servir
  to pour someone a vodka = servir une
    vodka à quelqu'un
• (*to flow*) = couler (à flots)
  the water was pouring into the kitchen
    = l'eau coulait dans la cuisine
• (*to escape*)
  there is smoke pouring out of the window
    = il y a de la fumée qui sort par la
    fenêtre
• (*to rain*)
  it's pouring (with rain) = il pleut à verse

• (*to enter or leave in large numbers*)
  to pour into the city = affluer dans la ville
  to pour out of the stadium = sortir en
    grand nombre du stade

powder *noun*
  a powder = une poudre

power *noun*
• (*control*)
  power = le pouvoir
  to be in power = être au pouvoir
• (*influence*)
  to have great power = avoir une grande
    influence
• (*electricity*)
  power = le courant

practical *adjective*
  = pratique

practise (*British English*), **practice** (*US
English*) *verb*
  (*at the piano, guitar*) = s'exercer (**!** + *être*)
  (*at a sport*) = s'entraîner (**!** + *être*)
  (*for a play, a concert*) = répéter
  to practise [the violin | one's French | a
    song ...] = travailler [le violon | son français |
    une chanson ...]

praise *verb*
  to praise someone (*when talking to
    someone else*) = faire l'éloge de
    quelqu'un
  (*when talking directly to someone*)
    = féliciter quelqu'un

prawn *noun* (*British English*)
  a prawn = une crevette rose

prayer *noun*
  a prayer = une prière

precaution *noun*
  a precaution = une précaution

precious *adjective*
  = précieux/précieuse

precise *adjective*
  = précis/précise

prefer *verb*
  = préférer, aimer mieux
  to prefer chocolate to vanilla = mieux
    aimer le chocolat que la vanille
  I'd prefer to phone = j'aimerais mieux
    téléphoner

pregnant *adjective*
  = enceinte

prejudice *noun*
  a prejudice = un préjugé

prepare *verb*
• (*to get something or someone ready*)
  = préparer
  to prepare pupils for an exam = préparer
    des élèves à un examen

✕ in informal situations

• (*to get ready*)
  to prepare for [an exam | a trip | a party ...]
  = se préparer pour [un examen | un voyage | une fête ...]

prepared *adjective*
• (*willing*)
  to be prepared to wait = être prêt/prête à attendre
• (*ready*)
  to be prepared for an exam = être prêt/prête pour un examen

prescription *noun*
  a prescription = une ordonnance

present
1 *noun*
• (*a gift*)
  a present = un cadeau
  to give someone a present = offrir un cadeau à quelqu'un
• (*now*)
  the present = le présent
  I'm staying here for the present = je reste ici pour l'instant
2 *verb*
• (*to give*)
  to present a prize to someone = remettre un prix à quelqu'un
• (*on radio or TV*)
  to present a programme = présenter une émission

president *noun* ▶ 315 |
  a president = un président/une présidente

press
1 *verb*
  = appuyer sur
  to press the bell = appuyer sur la sonnette
  to press (oneself) against the wall = se plaquer contre le mur
2 *noun*
  the press = la presse

pressure *noun*
  pressure = la pression
  to put pressure on someone = faire pression sur quelqu'un

pretend *verb*
  = faire semblant
  he's pretending to be annoyed = il fait semblant d'être vexé

pretty
1 *adjective*
  = joli/jolie
2 *adverb*
  = assez
  that's pretty good = ce n'est pas mal du tout*

prevent *verb*
  to prevent a war = éviter une guerre
  to prevent someone from [working | having fun | sleeping ...] = empêcher quelqu'un de [travailler | s'amuser | dormir ...]

previous *adjective*
  = précédent/précédente

price *noun*
  a price = un prix

pride *noun*
• **pride** = la fierté
• (*self-respect*)
  pride = l'amour-propre (*masculine*)

priest *noun* ▶ 315 |
  a priest = un prêtre

primary school *noun*
  a primary school = une école primaire

primary school teacher *noun* ▶ 315 |
  a primary school teacher = un instituteur/une institutrice, un professeur des écoles

prime minister *noun* ▶ 315 |
  the prime minister = le premier ministre

prince *noun*
  a prince = un prince

princess *noun*
  a princess = une princesse

principal *noun*
  a principal (*in a senior school*) = un proviseur
  (*in a junior school*) = un directeur/une directrice

print
1 *verb*
  = imprimer
  to print a book = imprimer un livre
2 *noun*
• (*of a photo*)
  a print = une épreuve
• (*of a finger, a foot*)
  a print = une empreinte

priority *noun*
  a priority = une priorité

prison *noun*
  a prison = une prison
  to put someone in prison = mettre quelqu'un en prison

prisoner *noun*
  a prisoner = un prisonnier/une prisonnière
  to be taken prisoner = être fait prisonnier/faite prisonnière

private
1 *adjective*
• (*personal*) = privé/privée
  my private life = ma vie privée
• (*not run by the state*) = privé/privée
  a private school = une école privée
2 in private = en privé

prize *noun*
  a prize = un prix

probably *adverb*
  = probablement

P

problem noun
a problem = un problème
to cause a problem = poser un problème

process noun
a process = un processus
to be in the process of writing a letter
= être en train d'écrire une lettre

produce
1 verb
• (to make) = produire
• (to create)
to produce a film = produire un film
to produce a play = mettre en scène une
pièce
2 noun
produce = les produits (masculine plural)

product noun
a product = un produit

production noun
production (of food) = la production
(of machinery, cars) = la fabrication

profession noun
a profession = une profession

professional adjective
= professionnel/professionnelle

professor noun ▶ 315 |
a professor = un professeur d'université

profit noun
a profit = un bénéfice

program
1 noun
• (for a computer)
a program = un programme
• (US English) ▶ **programme**
2 verb
= programmer

programme (British English), **program**
(US English)
1 noun
• (on radio, TV)
a programme = une émission
a programme about China = une émission
sur la Chine
• (for a play, a concert)
a programme = un programme
2 verb
= programmer

progress noun
progress = le progrès
to make progress = faire des progrès

project noun
a project (at school) = un dossier

promise
1 verb
= promettre
to promise [to write | to repay a loan | to say
nothing …] = promettre [d'écrire | de
rembourser un prêt | de ne rien dire …]

2 noun
a promise = une promesse

pronounce verb
= prononcer

proof noun
proof = une preuve

properly adverb
= correctement

property noun
property = la propriété

protect verb
= protéger
to protect oneself = se protéger (! + être)

protest verb
• (to complain) = protester
• (to demonstrate) = manifester

protester noun
a protester = un manifestant/une
manifestante

proud adjective
= fier/fière
she's proud of her work = elle est fière de
son travail

prove verb
= prouver

provide verb
to provide meals = fournir des repas
to provide work for people = fournir du
travail aux gens
to provide a transport service = assurer
un service de transport

provided conjunction
I'll lend you my car provided you pay me
= je te prête ma voiture à condition que
tu me paies
! Note that the subjunctive is used after à
condition que.

psychiatrist noun ▶ 315 |
a psychiatrist = un psychiatre/une
psychiatre

psychologist noun ▶ 315 |
a psychologist = un psychologue/une
psychologue

pub noun (British English)
a pub = un pub

public
1 noun
the public = le public
2 adjective
a public park = un jardin public
a public library = une bibliothèque
municipale
3 in public = en public

public holiday noun
a public holiday = un jour férié

Shops, trades, and professions

Work and Jobs

what does she do?	= qu'est-ce qu'elle fait comme métier?
what do you do for a living?	= qu'est-ce que vous faites dans la vie?

- There are various ways of saying what someone works at in French. In this area, the major difference between the two languages is the *absence of article* in French, whereas in the singular English always has **a**.

Note the following examples:

*he's got a job as **a** mechanic*	= il travaille comme mécanicien
*to work as **a** translator*	= travailler comme traducteur / traductrice
*Paul is **a** dentist*	= Paul est dentiste
*I want to be **a** policeman*	= je voudrais devenir agent de police

- The only case where you would use the article **un / une** or **des** in the plural would be in combination with **c'est** or **ce sont**, so:

she is a teacher	= elle est professeur
but	= **c'est** un professeur*
she's a judge	= elle est juge
but	= **c'est** un juge*
they are all doctors	= ils sont tous médecins
but	= **ce sont** tous **des** médecins*

- When using an adjective to describe what kind of doctor / teacher / worker a person is, you must use **c'est un / une** …

***she's a good** journalist*	= **c'est une bonne** journaliste
***he's a bad** teacher*	= **c'est un mauvais** professeur
***he's an** excellent chef*	= **c'est un** chef **excellent**

* Note that some professions do not have a feminine form and the article will always be masculine as in the examples using **professeur**, **juge**, **médecin**, **ministre**, …

Shops

In English you can say *at the baker's* or *at the baker's shop*. French also has this possibility but the translation for **at** will also differ depending on what follows:

***at** the baker's*	= **chez** le boulanger
***at** the baker's shop*	= **à** la boulangerie

chez means *at the house or premises of* and is used with the French word for the particular *tradesman* or *professional*:

*I'm going **to** the chemist's*	= je vais **chez** le pharmacien
*she's gone **to** the hairdresser's*	= elle est allée **chez** le coiffeur
I've got an appointment	
***at** the dentist's*	= j'ai rendezvous **chez** le dentiste
*is he **at** the doctor's?*	= est-ce qu'il est **chez** le médecin?

However you can also use **à la / au** (or **à l'** + *vowel* or *mute h*) with the French word for a shop:

*I'm going **to the chemist's***	= je vais **à la pharmacie**
*he's **at the grocer's***	= il est **à l'épicerie**
*they've gone **to the baker's***	= ils sont allés **à la boulangerie**

So in French you could have translations using either **à la** or **chez** in the following example:

*go **to** the butcher's*	= va **à la** boucherie
	= va **chez** le boucher

---

public transport *noun*
  public transport = les transports en
    commun

  ! *Note that* transports *is masculine
  plural.*

pudding *noun* (*British English*)
  a pudding = un dessert

puddle *noun*
  a puddle = une flaque

pull *verb*
* to pull = tirer
  to pull someone's hair = tirer les cheveux de quelqu'un
  to pull (on) a rope = tirer sur une corde
* (*to move*)
  to pull the piano into the hall = traîner le piano dans l'entrée
  to pull someone away from the door = éloigner quelqu'un de la porte
* (*to take out*)
  to pull a handkerchief out of one's pocket = tirer un mouchoir de sa poche
  to pull someone out of the river = sortir quelqu'un de la rivière
* to pull a face (*British English*) = faire une grimace

pull down
* (*to knock down*) = démolir
* (*to lower*) = baisser

pull out
  to pull a tooth out = arracher une dent

pull up
* (*to stop*) = s'arrêter (**!** + *être*)
* (*to remove*)
  to pull up the flowers = arracher les fleurs
* to pull up one's socks = remonter ses chaussettes

pullover *noun*
  a pullover = un pull

pump *noun*
  a pump = une pompe
  a bicycle pump = une pompe à bicyclette
pump up = gonfler

pumpkin *noun*
  a pumpkin = une citrouille

punch *verb*
  = donner des coups de poing
  she punched him in the face = elle lui a donné un coup de poing dans la figure

puncture *noun*
  a puncture = une crevaison

punish *verb*
  = punir

pupil *noun*
  a pupil = un élève/une élève

puppet *noun*
  a puppet = une marionnette

puppy *noun*
  a puppy = un chiot

pure *adjective*
  = pur/pure

purple *adjective* ▶ 213 |
  = violet/violette

purpose
1 *noun*
  a purpose = un but
2 on purpose = exprès
  you did it on purpose! = tu l'as fait exprès!

purse *noun*
* (*for money*)
  a purse = un porte-monnaie
* (*US English*) (*a handbag*)
  a purse = un sac à main

push *verb*
* to push = pousser
  to push a car = pousser une voiture
  to push someone down the stairs = pousser quelqu'un dans l'escalier
  to push someone out of the way = écarter quelqu'un
  to push past someone = bousculer quelqu'un
* (*to sell*) = vendre
  to push drugs = vendre de la drogue

pushchair *noun* (*British English*)
  a pushchair = une poussette

pusher *noun*
  a pusher = un revendeur/une revendeuse de drogue

put *verb*
  = mettre
  to put the cards on the table = mettre les cartes sur la table
  don't put sugar in my coffee = ne mets pas de sucre dans mon café
  to put someone in prison = mettre quelqu'un en prison
  to put someone in a bad mood = mettre quelqu'un de mauvaise humeur

put away = ranger

put back
* (*to return to its place*) = remettre
  to put a book back on a shelf = remettre un livre sur une étagère
* (*to change the time*)
  to put the clocks back = retarder les pendules

put down
* (*on a surface*) = poser
  put your cases down here, Laurence = pose tes valises ici, Laurence
* (*when phoning*)
  to put the phone down = raccrocher
* (*British English*) (*to give an injection to*) = piquer
  our dog had to be put down = on a dû faire piquer notre chien

put forward = avancer
  to put the clocks forward = avancer les pendules

put off
* (*to delay*)
  we'll have to put the party off till next week = il va falloir reporter la fête à la semaine prochaine
* (*to switch off*) = éteindre

put on
* (*when dressing*) = mettre
  to put jeans on = mettre un jean

Quantities

Note the use of **en** (*of it* or *of them*) in the following examples. This word must be included when the thing you are talking about is not expressed. However, **en** is not needed when the commodity is specified (*there is a lot of butter* = il y a beaucoup de beurre):

How much?

how much is there?	= combien y **en** a-t-il?
there's a lot	= il y **en** a beaucoup
there's not much	= il n'y **en** a pas beaucoup
there's two kilos	= il y **en** a deux kilos
how much sugar have you?	= combien de sucre as-tu?
I've got a lot	= j'**en** ai beaucoup
I haven't got (very) much	= je n'**en** ai pas beaucoup
I've got two kilos	= j'**en** ai deux kilos

How many?

how many are there?	= combien y **en** a-t-il?*
there are a lot	= il y **en** a beaucoup*
there aren't many	= il n'y **en** a pas beaucoup*
there are twenty	= il y **en** a vingt
how many apples have you?	= combien de pommes as-tu?*
	tu as combien de pommes?
I've got a lot	= j'**en** ai beaucoup
I haven't got many	= je n'**en** ai pas beaucoup

Comparisons

I've got twenty	= j'**en** ai vingt
Tim has got more than Tom	= Tim **en** a plus que Tom
Tim has got more money than Tom	= Tim a plus d'argent que Tom
much more than	= beaucoup plus que
a little more than	= un peu plus que
Tim has got more apples than Tom	= Tim a plus de pommes que Tom
many more apples than Tom	= beaucoup plus de pommes que Tom
a few more apples than Tom	= quelques pommes de plus que Tom
a few more people than yesterday	= quelques personnes de plus qu'hier
Tom has got less than Tim	= Tom **en** a moins que Tim
Tom has got less money than Tim	= Tom a moins d'argent que Tim
much less than	= beaucoup moins que
a little less than	= un peu moins que
Tom has got fewer than Tim	= Tom **en** a moins que Tim
Tom has got fewer apples than Tim	= Tom a moins de pommes que Tim
many fewer than	= beaucoup moins que

Relative quantities

how many are there to the kilo?	= combien y **en** a-t-il au kilo?*
there are ten to the kilo	= il y **en** a dix au kilo*
how many do you get for ten francs?	= combien peut-on **en** avoir pour dix francs?
you get five for ten francs	= il y **en** a cinq pour dix francs
how much does it cost a litre?	= combien coûte le litre?
it costs £5 a litre	= ça coûte cinq livres le litre
how much do apples cost a kilo?	= combien coûte le kilo de pommes?
how many glasses do you get to the bottle?	= combien y a-t-il de verres par bouteille?
you get six glasses to the bottle	= il y a six verres par bouteille

* Note the use of a singular verb in French in these examples.

- (*to switch on*)
  to put the heating on = allumer le chauffage
  to put the kettle on = mettre la bouilloire à chauffer
  to put a CD on = mettre un disque compact
- **to put on weight** = prendre du poids
- (*to organize, to produce*) = monter
  to put on a play = monter une pièce

put out
- **to put out a cigarette** = éteindre une cigarette
- (*to take out*) = sortir
  to put the bins out = sortir les poubelles

put up
- (*to lift*)
  to put one's hair up = remonter ses cheveux
  to put up one's hand (*in class*) ≈ lever le doigt
- (*to attach*)
  to put a sign up = mettre une pancarte
- (*when camping*)
  to put up a tent = planter une tente
- (*British English*) (*to raise*) = augmenter
  to put the rent up = augmenter le loyer
- (*to give someone a place to stay*) = héberger

put up with = supporter

puzzle *noun*
  a puzzle = un casse-tête

pyjamas *noun* (*British English*)
  pyjamas = un pyjama (*singular*)

---

qualified *adjective*
- (*having studied*) = diplômé/diplômée
- (*having experience, skills*) = qualifié/qualifiée

quality *noun*
  quality = la qualité

quantity *noun* ▶ 317 |
  a quantity = une quantité

quarrel
1 *noun*
  a quarrel = une dispute
2 *verb*
  = se disputer (**!** + *être*)

---

quarter
1 *noun*
  a quarter = un quart
  a quarter of an hour = un quart d'heure
  to cut the tomatoes in quarters = couper les tomates en quatre
2 *pronoun*
- (*when talking about quantities, numbers*) ▶ 317 |
  a quarter of the population can't read = un quart de la population ne sait pas lire
- (*when talking about time*) ▶ 211 |
  an hour and a quarter = une heure et quart
  it's (a) quarter past five = il est cinq heures et quart

quay *noun*
  a quay = un quai

queen *noun*
  a queen = une reine

question
1 *noun*
- (*a request for information*)
  a question = une question
  to ask someone a question = poser une question à quelqu'un
- (*a problem, a matter*)
  a question = un problème
2 *verb*
  = interroger

queue (*British English*)
1 *noun*
  a queue (*of people*) = une queue, une file d'attente
  (*of cars, trucks*) = une file
  to join the queue = se mettre à la queue
2 *verb*
  = faire la queue

quick *adjective*
  = rapide
  a quick answer = une réponse rapide
  it's quicker to go by train = c'est plus rapide d'y aller en train
  it's the quickest way [to get to London | to save money | to make friends ...] = c'est le moyen le plus rapide [d'aller à Londres | de gagner de l'argent | de se faire des amis ...]

quickly *adverb*
  = vite, rapidement

quiet
1 *adjective*
- (*silent*) = silencieux/silencieuse
  to keep quiet = garder le silence
  to go quiet = se taire (**!** + *être*)
  be quiet! = taisez-vous!
- (*not talkative*) = réservé/réservée
- (*calm*) = tranquille
  it's a quiet little village = c'est un petit village tranquille

2 *noun*
quiet = le silence
quiet please! = silence, s'il vous plaît!

quietly *adverb*
to speak quietly = parler doucement
to [play | sit | read …] **quietly** = [jouer | s'asseoir | lire …] en silence

quit *verb*
* (*to resign*) = démissionner
* (*US English*) (*to give up*)
to quit [smoking | drinking | working …] = arrêter de [fumer | boire | travailler …]

quite *adverb*
* (*rather*) = assez
they go back to France quite often = ils rentrent assez souvent en France
I quite like Chinese food = j'aime assez la cuisine chinoise
she earns quite a lot of money = elle gagne pas mal✽ d'argent
* (*completely*)
I'm not quite ready yet = je ne suis pas encore tout à fait prêt
you're quite right = vous avez entièrement raison
are you quite sure? = en êtes-vous certain?
* (*exactly*)
'is it true?'—'not quite' = 'est-ce que c'est vrai?'—'pas exactement'
I don't quite know what he does = je ne sais pas exactement ce qu'il fait

quiz *noun*
a quiz = un jeu de questions-réponses

Rr

rabbit *noun*
a rabbit = un lapin

rabies *noun* ▶ 266
rabies = la rage

race
1 *noun*
* (*a contest*)
a race = une course
to have a race = faire une course
* (*for horse-racing*)
the races = les courses (*feminine*)
2 *verb*
* (*to compete with*)
to race (against) someone = faire la course avec quelqu'un
I'll race you to the car = on fait la course jusqu'à la voiture
* (*to take part in a contest*) = courir

racehorse *noun*
a racehorse = un cheval de course

racetrack *noun*
a racetrack (*for horses*) = un champ de courses
(*for cars*) = un circuit

racism *noun*
racism = le racisme

racket, **racquet** *noun*
a racket = une raquette

radiator *noun*
a radiator = un radiateur

radio *noun*
a radio = une radio
on the radio = à la radio

radio station *noun*
a radio station = une station de radio

rage *noun*
rage = la rage, la colère
to fly into a rage = se mettre en colère

raid *verb*
to raid a bank = attaquer une banque
the police raided the building = la police a fait une descente dans le bâtiment

rail *noun*
* (*for holding on to*)
a rail = une rampe, une main courante
* (*for trains*)
rails = les rails (*masculine*)

railway (*British English*), **railroad** (*US English*) *noun*
* (*a track*)
a railway = une voie ferrée
* (*the rail system*)
the railway = le chemin de fer

railway line *noun* (*British English*)
a railway line = une ligne de chemin de fer

railway station *noun* (*British English*)
a railway station = une gare

rain
1 *noun*
rain = la pluie
to stand in the rain = rester sous la pluie
2 *verb*
= pleuvoir
it's raining = il pleut

rainbow *noun*
a rainbow = un arc-en-ciel

raincoat *noun*
a raincoat = un imperméable

raise *verb*
* (*to lift*) = lever
* (*to increase*) = augmenter
to raise prices = augmenter les prix
* (*in anger*)
to raise one's voice = hausser le ton

R

- (*to talk about*)
to raise a subject = soulever une question
- (*to bring up*)
to raise children = élever des enfants

range *noun*
- (*a selection*)
a range (*of goods, prices*) = une gamme
(*of activities, school subjects*) = un grand
choix
- (*of mountains*)
a range = une chaîne
- (*US English*) (*for cooking*)
a range = une cuisinière

rare *adjective*
- (*not common*) = rare
- (*very slightly cooked*) = saignant/saignante

rarely *adverb*
= rarement

rasher *noun* (*British English*)
a rasher (of bacon) = une tranche (de
bacon)

raspberry *noun*
a raspberry = une framboise

rat *noun*
a rat = un rat

rather *adverb*
- (*when saying what one would prefer*)
I'd rather [leave | stay here | read the paper ...]
= j'aimerais mieux [partir | rester ici | lire le
journal ...]
I'd rather you came with me = j'aimerais
mieux que tu viennes avec moi

! *Note that the subjunctive is used after*
j'aimerais mieux que.

- (*quite*) = plutôt
I think he's rather nice = je le trouve
plutôt sympathique

raw *adjective*
= cru/crue

razor *noun*
a razor = un rasoir

razor blade *noun*
a razor blade = une lame de rasoir

reach *verb*
- (*to arrive at*) = atteindre
they reached the town at midnight = ils
ont atteint la ville à minuit
- (*to be delivered to*) = parvenir à (**!** + *être*)
the letter never reached him = la lettre ne
lui est pas parvenue
- (*by stretching*)
to reach up = lever le bras
I can't reach the shelf = je n'arrive pas à
atteindre l'étagère
- (*to come to*) = arriver à (**!** + *être*)
to reach a decision = arriver à une
décision
- (*to contact by phone*) = joindre
I can be reached at this number = on peut
me joindre à ce numéro

reach out = tendre le bras

react *verb*
= réagir

read *verb*
= lire
the writing is difficult to read = l'écriture
est difficile à lire
to read to someone = faire la lecture à
quelqu'un
read out
to read out the names = lire les noms à
haute voix
read through (*once*) = lire
(*a second time*) = relire

reading *noun*
reading = la lecture

ready *adjective*
- (*prepared*) = prêt/prête
are you ready to leave? = est-ce que vous
êtes prêts à partir?
to get ready = se préparer (**!** + *être*)
to get a meal ready = préparer le repas
- (*happy*) = prêt/prête
I'm ready to help them = je suis prêt à les
aider

real *adjective*
- (*not imagined*) = réel/réelle
- (*not artificial*) = vrai/vraie (**!** *before the*
noun)
are they real diamonds? = est-ce que ce
sont de vrais diamants?
- **it's a real shame** = c'est vraiment
dommage

reality *noun*
reality = la réalité

realize *verb*
= se rendre compte (**!** + *être*)
I didn't realize (that) he was your boss
= je ne me suis pas rendu compte que
c'était ton patron

really *adverb*
= vraiment
it's really easy to make = c'est vraiment
facile à faire
what really happened? = qu'est-ce qui
s'est réellement passé?
really? = c'est vrai?

rear
1 *noun*
the rear = l'arrière (*masculine*)
2 *verb*
= élever

reason *noun*
a reason = une raison
that's a good reason to learn French
= c'est une bonne raison d'apprendre le
français
is there any reason why you shouldn't
drive? = pourquoi est-ce que vous ne
devriez pas conduire?
tell me the reason why = dis-moi pourquoi

reassure verb
= rassurer

receipt noun
a receipt = un reçu
a till receipt = un ticket de caisse

receive verb
• (to get) = recevoir
we received a letter from the teacher
= nous avons reçu une lettre du
professeur
• (to meet) = accueillir, recevoir
to be well received = être bien reçu/reçue

recent adjective
= récent/récente

recently adverb
= récemment

reception noun
• (in a hotel, a hospital, a company)
the reception = la réception
ask at (the) reception = adressez-vous à la
réception
• (a formal event)
a reception = une réception

receptionist noun ▶ 315 |
a receptionist = un réceptionniste/une
réceptionniste

recipe noun
a recipe = une recette

recognize verb
= reconnaître

recommend verb
= recommander

record
1 noun
• (information)
the records (historical, public) = les
archives (feminine)
(personal, medical) = le dossier (singular)
• (for playing music)
a record = un disque
• (in sport)
a record = un record
to break the world record = battre le
record du monde
2 verb
= enregistrer

recorder noun ▶ 290 |
a recorder = une flûte à bec

record player noun
a record player = un électrophone

recover verb
= se remettre (! + être)
to recover from an illness = se remettre
d'une maladie

recycle verb
= recycler

red adjective ▶ 213 |
= rouge
to go red, to turn red = rougir
to have red hair = avoir les cheveux roux

red-haired adjective
= roux/rousse

reduce verb
to reduce prices = baisser les prix
to reduce the number of employees
= réduire le nombre d'employés
to reduce speed = ralentir

reduction noun
a reduction = une réduction

redundant adjective (British English)
to be made redundant = être
licencié/licenciée pour raisons
économiques

referee noun ▶ 315 |
a referee = un arbitre

reflection noun
a reflection = un reflet

refreshing adjective
= rafraîchissant/rafraîchissante

refrigerator noun
a refrigerator = un réfrigérateur, un
frigidaire®

refugee noun
a refugee = un réfugié/une réfugiée

refuse¹ verb
= refuser
to refuse [to listen | to stop | to pay …]
= refuser [d'écouter | de s'arrêter | de payer …]

refuse² noun (British English)
refuse = les ordures (feminine plural)

regards noun
give her my regards = transmettez-lui
mes amitiés

region noun
a region = une région

regional adjective
= régional/régionale

register noun
the register = le cahier d'appel
to take the register = faire l'appel

regret verb
= regretter
I regret changing my mind = je regrette
d'avoir changé d'avis
he regrets that he can't come = il regrette
de ne pas pouvoir venir
I regret that he can't come = je regrette
qu'il ne puisse pas venir
! Note that the subjunctive is used after
regretter que.

regular adjective
regular = régulier/régulière

regularly adverb
= régulièrement

rehearsal noun
a rehearsal = une répétition

rehearse verb
= répéter

reject verb
to reject someone's advice = rejeter les
conseils de quelqu'un
to reject a candidate = refuser un
candidat

relationship noun
a relationship = une relation, des relations
(plural)
to have a good relationship = bien
s'entendre (**!** + être)
she has a good relationship with her
parents = elle s'entend bien avec ses
parents

relative noun
a relative = un parent/une parente
my relatives = ma famille

relax verb
= se détendre (**!** + être)

relaxed adjective
= détendu/détendue,
décontracté/décontractée

relay race verb
a relay race = une course de relais

release verb
= libérer

reliable adjective
a reliable person = une personne digne de
confiance
a reliable car = une voiture fiable

relieved adjective
= soulagé/soulagée

religion noun
religion = la religion

religious education, **RE** (British
English) noun
religious education = l'instruction
religieuse
! Note that instruction is feminine.

rely verb
• (to depend on) = dépendre de
• (to count on) = compter sur
can we rely on you? = est-ce qu'on peut
compter sur toi?

remain verb
= rester

remark noun
a remark = une remarque, une réflexion

remarkable adjective
= remarquable

remember verb
= se souvenir (**!** + être)
do you remember her? = est-ce que tu te
souviens d'elle?
I remember writing down the address = je
me souviens d'avoir noté l'adresse
to remember to [write the letter | water the
plants | turn off the lights …] = penser à
[écrire la lettre | arroser les plantes | éteindre les
lumières …]

remind verb
= rappeler
to remind someone to buy milk = rappeler
à quelqu'un d'acheter du lait
she reminds me of my sister = elle me
rappelle ma sœur

remote control noun
a remote control = une télécommande

remove verb
= enlever
to remove the stains from a carpet
= enlever les taches d'une moquette

rent
1 verb
= louer
to rent an apartment = louer un
appartement
2 noun
a rent = un loyer
rent out = louer

repair verb
= réparer
to have a bicycle repaired = faire réparer
un vélo

repeat verb
• (to say again) = répéter
• to repeat a year = redoubler une classe

replace verb
= remplacer
they replaced the fence with a wall = ils
ont remplacé la clôture par un mur

reply
1 verb
= répondre
to reply to a letter = répondre à une lettre
2 noun
a reply = une réponse

report
1 verb
• (to tell about) = signaler
to report an accident = signaler un
accident
• (in the news)
to report on an event = faire un reportage
sur un événement
• (to complain about)
to report the noise = se plaindre du bruit
2 noun
• (in the news)
a report = un communiqué
(longer) = un reportage

- (*an official document*)
  a **report** = un rapport
- (*British English*) (*from school*)
  a (**school**) **report** = un bulletin scolaire

report card noun (*US English*)
  a **report card** = un bulletin scolaire

reporter noun ▶ 315|
  a **reporter** = un journaliste/une journaliste, un reporter

represent verb
  = représenter

republic noun
  a **republic** = une république

request noun
  a **request** = une demande

rescue verb
  (*from danger*) = sauver

resemble verb
  = ressembler à
  to resemble each other = se ressembler (**!** + être)

resent verb
  to resent someone = en vouloir à quelqu'un
  he resents her for winning = il lui en veut d'avoir gagné

reservation noun
  a **reservation** = une réservation

reserve verb
  = réserver

resign verb
  = démissionner

resist verb
  = résister

respect
1 verb
  = respecter
2 noun
  respect = le respect
  out of respect = par respect

responsibility noun
  responsibility = la responsabilité

responsible adjective
- (*the cause of*) = responsable
  to be responsible for the damage = être responsable des dégâts
- (*in charge*) = responsable
  to be responsible for organizing a trip = être chargé/chargée d'organiser une sortie

rest
1 noun
- (*what is left*)
  the rest = le reste
  we spent the rest of the day in the garden = on a passé le reste de la journée dans le jardin

- (*time to recover*)
  rest = le repos
  to need rest = avoir besoin de repos
- (*a break*)
  a **rest** = une pause
  to have a rest = se reposer (**!** + être)
2 verb
  = se reposer (**!** + être)

restaurant noun
  a **restaurant** = un restaurant

result noun
  a **result** = un résultat
  the exam results = les résultats des examens
  as a result of an accident = à la suite d'un accident

résumé noun (*US English*)
  a **résumé** = un CV, un curriculum vitae

retire verb
  = prendre sa retraite

return verb
- (*to go back*) = retourner (**!** + être)
- (*to come back*) = revenir (**!** + être)
  (*from abroad, to one's home*) = rentrer (**!** + être)
- (*to give back*) = rendre
  can you return my book? = est-ce que tu peux me rendre mon livre?
- (*to send back*) = renvoyer
  to return goods = renvoyer des articles
- (*to start again*)
  to return to work = reprendre le travail
  to return to school = reprendre l'école

return ticket noun
  a **return ticket** = un billet aller-retour

reveal verb
  to reveal a secret = révéler un secret

revenge noun
  revenge = la vengeance
  to get one's revenge = se venger (**!** + être)

revolution noun
  a **revolution** = une révolution

reward
1 noun
  a **reward** = une récompense
2 verb
  = récompenser

rewind verb
  = rembobiner

rhinoceros, **rhino** noun
  a **rhinoceros** = un rhinocéros

rhythm noun
  rhythm = le rythme

rib noun ▶ 201|
  a **rib** = une côte

rice noun
  rice = le riz

R

rich *adjective*
= riche
to get rich = s'enrichir (**!** + *être*)

rid: **to get rid of** *verb*
= se débarrasser de (**!** + *être*)

ride
1 *verb* ▶ 248 |
to ride, to go riding = faire du cheval
to ride a horse = monter à cheval
to be riding a bike = rouler à vélo
2 *noun*
to go for a ride (*in a car, on a bike*) = aller faire un tour
(*on a horse*) = aller faire une promenade à cheval

ridiculous *adjective*
= ridicule

rifle *noun*
a rifle = un fusil

right
1 *adjective*
• (*not left*) = droit/droite
his right hand = sa main droite
• (*honest, good*) = bien
it's not right to steal = ce n'est pas bien de voler
to do the right thing = faire ce qu'il faut
• (*correct*) = bon/bonne (**!** *before the noun*)
the right answer = la bonne réponse
is this the right direction? = est-ce que c'est la bonne direction?
what's the right time? = quelle est l'heure exacte?
you're right = tu as raison
that's right = c'est ça
2 *noun*
• (*the direction*)
the right = la droite
the first street on the right = la première rue à droite
• (*what one is entitled to*)
a right = un droit
to have a right to education = avoir droit à l'instruction
human rights = les droits de l'homme
3 *adverb*
= à droite
to turn right = tourner à droite

ring
1 *verb*
• (*British English*) (*to phone*) = appeler
to ring for a taxi = appeler un taxi
• (*to make a sound*) = sonner
to ring the bell = sonner
the doorbell rang = on a sonné à la porte
2 *noun*
• (*a piece of jewellery*)
a ring = une bague
a wedding ring = une alliance
• (*a circle*)
a ring = un cercle
• (*in a circus*)
the ring = la piste

ring up (*British English*) = téléphoner

rinse *verb*
= rincer

ripe *adjective*
= mûr/mûre

rise *verb*
• (*if it's smoke, water*) = monter (**!** + *être*)
• (*if it's a price*) = augmenter
• (*if it's a plane*) = s'élever (**!** + *être*)
• (*if it's the sun or moon*) = se lever (**!** + *être*)

risk
1 *noun*
a risk = un risque
2 *verb*
= risquer
to risk losing one's job = risquer de perdre son travail

river *noun*
a river = une rivière
(*flowing into the sea*) = un fleuve

riverbank *noun*
a riverbank = une berge

road *noun*
a road = une route
the road to London = la route de Londres

road sign *noun*
a road sign = un panneau de signalisation

roadworks *noun*
roadworks = les travaux (*masculine*)

roar *verb*
(*if it's a lion*) = rugir
(*if it's a person*) = hurler
(*if it's an engine*) = vrombir

roast
1 *verb*
= rôtir
2 *adjective*
= rôti/rôtie
to eat roast beef = manger du rôti de bœuf
3 *noun*
a roast = un rôti

rob *verb*
to rob someone = voler quelqu'un
to rob a bank = dévaliser une banque

robbery *noun*
a robbery = un vol

robin *noun*
a robin = un rouge-gorge

robot *noun*
a robot = un robot

rock *noun*
• (*the material*)
rock = la roche
• (*a large stone*)
a rock = un rocher
• (*music*)
rock = le rock

rock climbing *noun* ▶ 248
  rock climbing = la varappe

rocket *noun*
  a rocket = une fusée

role *noun*
  a role = un rôle

roll
1 *verb*
  = rouler
  the ball rolled under a car = le ballon a roulé sous une voiture
  to roll the pastry into a ball = faire une boule de la pâte
2 *noun*
• (*of paper, cloth, plastic*)
  a roll = un rouleau
  a roll of film = une pellicule
• (*bread*)
  a roll = un petit pain
• (*US English*) (*at school*)
  to call the roll = faire l'appel
roll about, roll around (*if it's an object*) = rouler
roll over = se retourner (**!** + *être*)
roll up = enrouler
  to roll up a newspaper = rouler un journal

roller coaster *noun*
  a roller coaster = des montagnes russes
  ! *Note that* montagnes *is feminine plural.*

roller-skate *noun*
  a roller-skate = un patin à roulettes

roller-skating *noun* ▶ 248
  roller-skating = le patin à roulettes

Romania *noun* ▶ 218
  Romania = la Roumanie

romantic *adjective*
  = romantique

roof *noun*
  a roof = un toit

room *noun*
• a room = une pièce
  (*for sleeping*) = une chambre
  (*for working*) = un bureau
  (*for teaching, holding meetings*) = une salle
• (*space*)
  room = la place
  to make room = faire de la place
  is there room? = est-ce qu'il y a de la place?

root *noun*
  a root = une racine

rope *noun*
  a rope = une corde

rose *noun*
  a rose = une rose

rosy *adjective*
  = rose
  to have rosy cheeks = avoir les joues roses

rotten *adjective*
  = pourri/pourrie

rough *adjective*
• (*not smooth*) = rugueux/rugueuse
  to have rough skin = avoir la peau rugueuse
• (*not gentle*) = brutal/brutale
• (*tough*) = dur/dure
  to live in a rough area = habiter un quartier dur
• (*not exact, precise*)
  a rough figure = un chiffre approximatif
• (*difficult*) = dur/dure, difficile
  to have a rough time = traverser une période difficile
• (*caused by bad weather*)
  a rough sea = une mer agitée

round

  ! *Often* round *occurs in combinations with verbs. For more information, see the note at* around.

1 *preposition*
  = autour de
  to be sitting round a table = être assis/assises autour d'une table
  to sail round the world = faire le tour du monde en bateau
  to go round Oxford = visiter Oxford
2 *adverb*
  to go round and round = tourner en rond
  to go round to John's = passer chez John
  to invite someone round = inviter quelqu'un chez soi
3 *noun*
  a round (*in a quiz*) = une manche
  (*in showjumping*) = un parcours
  (*in boxing*) = un round
  (*in an election*) = un tour
4 *adjective*
  = rond/ronde

roundabout *noun*
• (*British English*) (*in a fair*)
  a roundabout = un manège
• (*for traffic*)
  a roundabout = un rond-point

route *noun*
  a route = un itinéraire
  a bus route = une ligne d'autobus

routine *noun*
  a routine = une routine

row¹
1 *noun*
• a row (*of people, trees*) = un rang
  (*of houses, seats*) = une rangée
  (*of cars*) = une file
  the pupils were sitting in rows = les élèves étaient assis en rangs
• (*when talking about frequency*)
  to be absent five days in a row = être absent/absente cinq jours de suite

R

2 *verb*
(*as an activity*) = ramer
(*as a sport*) ▶ **248**| = faire de l'aviron
to row across a lake = traverser un lac à la rame

row² *noun* (*British English*)
a row = une dispute
to have a row with someone = se disputer avec quelqu'un

rowing *noun* ▶ **248**|
rowing = l'aviron (*masculine*)

rowing boat (*British English*),
rowboat (*US English*) *noun*
a rowing boat = un bateau à rames

royal *adjective*
= royal/royale

rub *verb*
to rub a stain = frotter une tache
to rub one's eyes = se frotter les yeux
rub out (*British English*) = s'effacer
(**!** + *être*)
to rub out a mistake = effacer une erreur

rubber *noun*
• (*the material*)
  rubber = le caoutchouc
• (*British English*) (*an eraser*)
  a rubber = une gomme

rubbish *noun* (*British English*)
• (*refuse*)
  rubbish (*household*) = les ordures
  (*feminine plural*)
  (*in the street, in a dump*) = les déchets
  (*masculine plural*)
• (*poor quality goods*)
  rubbish = la camelote✱

rubbish bin *noun* (*British English*)
a rubbish bin = une poubelle

rucksack *noun*
a rucksack = un sac à dos

rude *adjective*
• (*not polite*) = impoli/impolie
  to be rude to someone = être
  impoli/impolie envers quelqu'un
• (*vulgar*) = grossier/grossière
  a rude word = un gros mot

rug *noun*
a rug = un tapis

rugby *noun* ▶ **248**|
rugby = le rugby

ruin
1 *verb*
• (*to spoil*) = gâcher
  to ruin a meal = gâcher un repas
• (*to damage*) = abîmer
  you'll ruin your shoes = tu vas abîmer tes chaussures

2 *noun*
a ruin = une ruine

rule
1 *noun*
a rule (*of a game, a language*) = une règle
(*in a school, an organization*) = un règlement
it's against the rules = c'est contraire au règlement
2 *verb*
(*if it's a leader*) = gouverner
(*if it's a king, queen*) = régner sur
(*if it's a party*) = diriger

ruler *noun*
a ruler = une règle

rumour (*British English*), **rumor** (*US English*) *noun*
a rumour = une rumeur

run
1 *verb*
• **to run** = courir
  to run after someone = courir après quelqu'un
  to run across the street = traverser la rue en courant
  to run a race = faire une course
• (*from danger*) = fuir, s'enfuir (**!** + *être*)
• (*to manage*) = diriger
• (*to work, to operate*) = marcher
  the car runs on unleaded petrol = la voiture marche à l'essence sans plomb
  the system is running well = le système marche bien
• (*to organize*) = organiser
  to run a competition = organiser un concours
• (*when talking about transport*) = circuler
  the buses don't run after midnight = les bus ne circulent pas après minuit
• (*to flow*) = couler
• (*to fill with water*)
  to run a bath = faire couler un bain
• (*to come off*) (*when talking about dyes*) = déteindre
  (*when talking about make-up*) = couler
• (*in an election*)
  to run for president = être candidat/candidate à la présidence
• (*other uses*)
  to be running late = être en retard
  to be running a temperature = avoir de la fièvre
2 *noun*
a run = une course
to go for a run = aller courir
run about, run around = courir
run away = s'enfuir (**!** + *être*)
run off = partir en courant (**!** + *être*)

runner *noun*
a runner = un coureur/une coureuse (à pied)

✱ in informal situations

rush
1 *verb*
- (*to hurry*) = se dépêcher (**!** + *être*)
  to rush to finish one's homework = se dépêcher de finir ses devoirs
  to rush into a shop = se précipiter dans un magasin
  to rush out of the house = se précipiter hors de la maison
  to be rushed to the hospital = être emmené/emmenée d'urgence à l'hôpital
- (*to put pressure on*) = bousculer
2 *noun*
  to be in a rush = être pressé/pressée
  to do one's homework in a rush = faire ses devoirs à la va-vite

rush hour *noun*
  the rush hour = les heures de pointe
  ! *Note that* **heures** *is feminine plural.*

Russia *noun* ▶ 218 |
  Russia = la Russie

Russian ▶ 275 |
1 *adjective*
  = russe
2 *noun*
- (*the people*)
  the Russians = les Russes (*masculine*)
- (*the language*)
  Russian = le russe

rusty *adjective*
  = rouillé/rouillée

Ss

sad *adjective*
  = triste

saddle *noun*
  a saddle = une selle

safe ▶ 237 |
1 *adjective*
- (*without risk*) = sûr/sûre
  a safe place = un endroit sûr
  it's not safe for children = c'est dangereux pour les enfants
  is it safe to go there? = est-ce qu'on peut y aller sans danger?
- (*free from danger*)
  to feel safe = se sentir en sécurité
  your car is safe here = ici, votre voiture ne risque rien
- (*out of danger*) = sain et sauf/saine et sauve
2 *noun*
  a safe = un coffre-fort

safety *noun*
  safety = la sécurité

Sagittarius *noun*
  Sagittarius = Sagittaire (*masculine*)

sail
1 *noun*
  a sail = une voile
  to set sail = prendre la mer
2 *verb*
  to sail around the world = faire le tour du monde en bateau
  to go sailing = faire de la voile

sailing *noun* ▶ 248 |
  sailing = la voile

sailing boat (*British English*), **sailboat** (*US English*) *noun*
  a sailing boat = un bateau à voiles

sailor *noun* ▶ 315 |
  a sailor = un marin

saint *noun*
  a saint = un saint/une sainte

salad *noun*
  a salad = une salade

salary *noun*
  a salary = un salaire

sale *noun*
- **to be on sale** (*British English*) = être en vente
  for sale = à vendre
- **the sales** = les soldes (*masculine*)

sales assistant *noun* ▶ 315 | (*British English*)
  a sales assistant = un vendeur/une vendeuse

salmon *noun*
  a salmon = un saumon

salt *noun*
  salt = le sel

same
1 *adjective*
  = même
  she's got the same coat as me = elle a le même manteau que moi
  they go to the same school = ils vont à la même école
  it's the same as the car I had before = c'est la même voiture que celle que j'avais avant
  it's all the same to me = ça m'est complètement égal
  the houses all look the same = les maisons sont toutes pareilles
  people are the same everywhere = les gens sont partout pareils
  things aren't the same without them = ce n'est pas la même chose sans eux
  it's the same as ever = c'est toujours la même chose

S

2 *pronoun*
  the same = la même chose
  I'll have the same = je prendrai la même chose
  to do the same as the others = faire comme les autres
  'Happy New Year!'—'the same to you!' = 'Bonne année!'—'à toi de même!'

sand *noun*
  sand = le sable

sandal *noun*
  a sandal = un nu-pied

sandwich *noun*
  a sandwich = un sandwich
  a ham sandwich = un sandwich au jambon

Santa (Claus) *noun*
  Santa (Claus) = le Père Noël

sardine *noun*
  a sardine = une sardine

satellite TV *noun*
  satellite TV = la télévision par satellite

satisfactory *adjective*
  = satisfaisant/satisfaisante

satisfied *adjective*
  = satisfait/satisfaite

Saturday *noun* ▶ **222**
  Saturday = samedi (*masculine*)

sauce *noun*
  a sauce = une sauce

saucepan *noun*
  a saucepan = une casserole

saucer *noun*
  a saucer = une soucoupe

sausage *noun*
  a sausage = une saucisse

save *verb*
• (*to rescue*) = sauver
  they saved his life = ils lui ont sauvé la vie
• (*to avoid spending*)
  to save (up) = faire des économies
  to save money = mettre de l'argent de côté
• (*to avoid wasting*)
  to save [time | energy | money …] = économiser [du temps | de l'énergie | de l'argent …]
• (*to keep*) = garder
  to save a piece of cake for someone = garder un morceau de gâteau pour quelqu'un
  to save a file = sauvegarder un fichier
• (*to spare*)
  to save someone a lot of work = éviter beaucoup de travail à quelqu'un
  it will save us from having to drive all night = ça nous évitera de conduire toute la nuit

savings *noun*
  savings = les économies (*feminine*)

saw *noun*
  a saw = une scie

saxophone *noun* ▶ **290**
  a saxophone = un saxophone

say *verb*
  = dire
  to say goodbye = dire au revoir
  she says (that) she can't go out tonight = elle dit qu'elle ne peut pas sortir ce soir
  he said to wait here = il a dit d'attendre ici
  they say she's very rich = on dit qu'elle est très riche
  I can't say who did it = je ne peux pas dire qui a fait ça
  she wouldn't say = elle n'a pas voulu le dire
  I said to myself that you'd like that = je me suis dit que ça te ferait plaisir
  what does the message say? = que dit le message?
  it says here that smoking is not allowed = il est dit ici qu'on n'a pas le droit de fumer
  I'd say she was forty = je lui donne quarante ans
  let's say there are twenty people at the party = supposons qu'il y ait vingt personnes à la fête
  ! *Note that the subjunctive is used after* supposer que.

scandal *noun*
  a scandal = un scandale

scare *verb*
  = faire peur à
  you scared me! = tu m'as fait peur!
  scare away = faire fuir

scared *adjective*
  to be scared = avoir peur

scarf *noun*
  a scarf (*long*) = une écharpe
  (*square*) = un foulard

scenery *noun*
  scenery = le paysage

school
1 *noun*
  a school = une école
  to be at school = être à l'école
2 *adjective*
  = scolaire
  a school bus = un car de ramassage scolaire

schoolbag *noun*
  a schoolbag = un cartable

schoolboy *noun*
  a schoolboy = un élève

schoolgirl *noun*
a schoolgirl = une élève

schoolwork *noun*
schoolwork = le travail de classe

science *noun*
science = la science
to study science = étudier les sciences

scientist *noun* ▶ 315 |
a scientist = un scientifique/une
scientifique

scissors *noun*
scissors = les ciseaux (*masculine*)
a pair of scissors = une paire de ciseaux

score *verb*
to score a goal = marquer un but

Scorpio *noun*
Scorpio = Scorpion (*masculine*)

Scotland *noun* ▶ 218 |
Scotland = l'Écosse

Scottish *adjective* ▶ 275 |
= écossais/écossaise

scratch *verb*
• (*when itchy*) = se gratter (**!** + *être*)
to scratch one's arm = se gratter le bras
• (*if it's a person or an animal*) = griffer
(*if it's a bush, thorns*) = égratigner
• (*to mark, to damage*) = érafler

scream *verb*
= hurler

screen *noun*
a screen = un écran

screw *noun*
a screw = une vis

sea *noun*
a sea = une mer
beside the sea, by the sea = au bord de la
mer

seagull *noun*
a seagull = une mouette

seal *verb*
a seal = un phoque

search *verb*
• to search = chercher
to search for someone = chercher
quelqu'un
• (*to examine a place, a person*) = fouiller
they searched me at the airport = on m'a
fouillé à l'aéroport

seashell *noun*
a seashell = un coquillage

seasick *adjective*
to be seasick, to get seasick = avoir le
mal de mer

seaside *noun*
at the seaside = au bord de la mer
to go to the seaside = aller à la mer

season *noun*
a season = une saison
strawberries are in season = c'est la
saison des fraises

seat *noun*
• (*a chair, a bench*)
a seat = un siège
have a seat = asseyez-vous
• (*on transport, in a theatre*)
a seat = une place

seatbelt *noun*
a seatbelt = une ceinture de sécurité

second
1 *adjective*
= deuxième, second/seconde
it's the second time I've called her = c'est
la deuxième fois que je l'appelle
every second Monday = un lundi sur
deux
2 *noun*
• (*in a series*)
the second = le deuxième/la deuxième, le
second/la seconde
• (*in time*)
a second = une seconde
(*a very short time*) = un instant
• (*in dates*) ▶ 222 |
the second of May = le deux mai
3 *adverb*
= deuxième
to come second = arriver deuxième

secondary school *noun*
a secondary school = une école
secondaire

second-hand *adjective*
a second-hand [car | coat | book ...] = [une
voiture | un manteau | un livre ...] d'occasion

secret
1 *adjective*
= secret/secrète
2 *noun*
a secret = un secret
to tell someone a secret = confier un
secret à quelqu'un
3 in secret = en secret

secretary *noun* ▶ 315 |
a secretary = un secrétaire/une secrétaire

see *verb* ▶ 237 |
• to see = voir
what can you see? = qu'est-ce que tu vois?
I can't see them = je ne les vois pas
he saw the people running = il a vu les
gens qui couraient
do they see each other often? = est-ce
qu'ils se voient souvent?
see you tomorrow! = à demain!
I'll go and see = je vais voir
• (*to accompany*)
I'll see you home = je vais te
raccompagner chez toi

S

seem *verb*
* (*to appear*)
  she seems [happy | annoyed | tired …] = elle a l'air [contente | vexée | fatiguée …]
  they seem to be looking for someone = on dirait qu'ils cherchent quelqu'un
* (*when talking about one's impressions*) = sembler
  it seems (that) there are a lot of problems = il semble qu'il y ait beaucoup de problèmes
  it seems strange (to me) = ça (me) paraît bizarre

seldom *adverb*
= rarement

self-confident ▶ **confident**

selfish *adjective*
= égoïste

sell *verb*
= vendre
  to sell books to the students = vendre des livres aux étudiants
  he sold me his car = il m'a vendu sa voiture
  water is sold in bottles = l'eau se vend en bouteilles

send *verb*
= envoyer
  to send help = envoyer des secours
  to send a package to someone = envoyer un paquet à quelqu'un
  he sent her a letter = il lui a envoyé une lettre
  to send someone to post a letter = envoyer quelqu'un mettre une lettre à la poste
  to send a pupil home from school = renvoyer un élève chez lui/une élève chez elle
send away = faire partir
send back = renvoyer
send for = faire venir
  to send for the doctor = faire venir le médecin
send off
  to send a player off = expulser un joueur
send on
  to send on baggage = expédier des bagages à l'avance
  to send on post = faire suivre du courrier

senior high school (*US English*), **senior school** (*British English*) *noun*
  a senior (high) school ≈ un lycée

sense *noun*
* (**common**) **sense** = le bon sens
  to have the sense to go home = avoir le bon sens de rentrer chez soi
* (*allowing one to see, hear, smell etc*)
  a sense = un sens
  the sense of taste = le goût
* (*a meaning*)
  a sense = un sens
  it doesn't make sense = ça n'a pas de sens
  it makes sense to check first = c'est une bonne idée de vérifier d'abord

sensible *adjective*

  ! Note that **sensible** in English is never translated by **sensible** in French.

  (*describing a person*) = raisonnable
  (*describing a decision*) = judicieux/judicieuse
  (*describing clothes*) = pratique

sensitive *adjective*
  (*describing a person*) = sensible
  (*describing a situation*) = délicat/délicate

sentence
1 *noun*
* (*in grammar*)
  a sentence = une phrase
* (*for a crime*)
  a (prison) sentence = une peine (de prison)
2 *verb*
  to sentence someone to one year in prison = condamner quelqu'un à un an de prison

separate
1 *adjective*
  a separate room = une pièce à part
  the children have separate rooms = les enfants ont chacun leur chambre
  there are two separate problems = il y a deux problèmes différents
2 *verb*
* **to separate** = séparer
* (*if it's a couple*) = se séparer (**!** + *être*)

separated *adjective*
= séparé/séparée

separately *adverb*
= séparément

September *noun* ▶ **222**
  September = septembre (*masculine*)

serial *noun*
  a serial = un feuilleton
  a TV serial = un feuilleton télévisé

series *noun*
  a series = une série

serious *adjective*
* (*causing worry*) = grave
  a serious accident = un accident grave
* (*describing a personality*) = sérieux/sérieuse
* **to be serious about football** = prendre le football au sérieux
  to be serious about going to college = avoir vraiment l'intention d'aller à l'université

serve *verb*
- (*in a shop*) = servir
  are you being served? = est-ce qu'on s'occupe de vous?
- (*at table*) = faire le service
  to serve the soup = servir la soupe
- (*in sport*) = servir

service *noun*
- (*which people need or find useful*)
  a service = un service
- (*in a shop, a restaurant*)
  service = le service
- (*in a church*)
  a service = un office

service station *noun*
  a service station = une station-service

set
1 *noun*
- (*a collection*)
  a set of keys = un jeu de clés
  a set of stamps = une série de timbres
- (*in tennis*)
  a set = un set
2 *verb*
- (*to decide on*) = fixer
  to set [a date | a price | a goal …] = fixer [une date | un prix | un but …]
- (*for a particular time*)
  to set an alarm clock = mettre un réveil
  to set a video (*British English*) = programmer un magnétoscope
- (*in school*)
  to set homework = donner des devoirs
  to set an exam = préparer les sujets d'un examen
- (*to be responsible for*)
  to set a record = établir un record
  to set a good example to someone = montrer le bon exemple à quelqu'un
- (*when talking about a story, a film*)
  the film is set in Paris = le film se passe à Paris
- (*when talking about the sun*) = se coucher (**!** + *être*)
- (*other uses*)
  to set the table = mettre la table
  to set fire to a house = mettre le feu à une maison
  to set someone free = libérer quelqu'un
set off
- (*to leave*) = partir (**!** + *être*)
- (*to cause to go off*)
  to set off fireworks = faire partir un feu d'artifice
  to set off a bomb = faire exploser une bombe
  to set off a burglar alarm = déclencher une sirène d'alarme
set up = monter (**!** + *avoir*)
  to set up a company = monter une entreprise

settle *verb*
- (*to end*)
  to settle an argument = mettre fin à une dispute
- (*to decide on*) = fixer
  nothing is settled yet = rien n'est encore fixé
- (*to make one's home*) = s'installer (**!** + *être*)
settle down
- (*to get comfortable*) = s'installer (**!** + *être*)
- (*to marry*) = se ranger (**!** + *être*)
settle in = s'adapter (**!** + *être*)

seven *number* ▶ **187** |, ▶ **211** |
  seven = sept
  seven exams = sept examens
  I've got seven (of them) = j'en ai sept

seventeen *number* ▶ **187** |, ▶ **211** |
  seventeen = dix-sept

seventeenth *number*
- (*in a series*) = dix-septième
- (*in dates*) ▶ **222** |
  the seventeenth of May = le dix-sept mai

seventh *number*
- (*in a series*) = septième
- (*in dates*) ▶ **222** |
  the seventh of July = le sept juillet

seventy *number* ▶ **187** |
  seventy = soixante-dix

several *determiner*
  = plusieurs

severe *adjective*
- (*serious*) = grave
- (*harsh*) = sévère

sew *verb*
  = coudre

sewing *noun*
  sewing = la couture

sewing machine *noun*
  a sewing machine = une machine à coudre

sex *noun*
  sex = le sexe
  to have sex = avoir des rapports sexuels

shade *noun*
- (*out of the sun*)
  shade = l'ombre (*feminine*)
  to sit in the shade = s'asseoir à l'ombre
- (*a colour*)
  a shade = un ton
- (*for a lamp*)
  a shade = un abat-jour

shadow *noun*
  a shadow = une ombre

shake *verb*
- **to shake** = secouer
  the earthquake shook the building = le tremblement de terre a ébranlé le bâtiment
  to shake a bottle = agiter une bouteille
  to shake hands with someone = serrer la main de quelqu'un

S

- (when saying no)
  to shake one's head = faire non de la tête
- (with cold, fear, shock) = trembler
  he was shaking with fear = il tremblait de
  peur
- (during an explosion, an earthquake)
  = trembler

shall verb

> ! Note that, when referring to the future,
> French uses the future tense of the verb to
> translate shall + verb: I shall leave = je
> partirai.

- (when talking about the future)
  I shall see you next Tuesday = je te verrai
  mardi prochain
- (when making suggestions)
  shall I set the table? = est-ce que je mets
  la table?
  shall we go to the cinema? = et si nous
  allions au cinéma?

shame noun
- **shame** = la honte
  shame on you! = tu devrais avoir honte!
- (when expressing regret)
  that's a shame = c'est dommage

shampoo noun
  shampoo = le shampooing

shape noun
- (a form)
  a shape = une forme
  a square shape = une forme carrée
  in the shape of a square = en forme de
  carré
- (when talking about health)
  to be in good shape = être en forme
  to get in shape = se mettre en forme

share
1 verb
  = partager
  to share a house = partager une maison
2 noun
  a share = une part
  to pay one's fair share = payer sa part
share out (British English) (amongst others)
  = répartir
  (within a group) = partager

shark noun
  a shark = un requin

sharp adjective
- (used for cutting) = tranchant/tranchante
- (with a point) = pointu/pointue
- (sudden) = brusque
  a sharp bend = un virage serré
- (intelligent) = vif/vive
- (aggressive) = acerbe
- (in taste) = acide

shave verb
  = se raser (! + être)

she pronoun
  she = elle
  she'll be there too = elle sera là aussi
  there she is! = la voilà!
  SHE **didn't say it** = ce n'est pas elle qui l'a
  dit
  he works in London but she doesn't = il
  travaille à Londres mais elle non
  she's an intelligent girl = c'est une fille
  intelligente

sheep noun
  a sheep = un mouton
  (female) = une brebis

sheet noun
- (for a bed)
  a sheet = un drap
- (a piece)
  a sheet (of paper) = une feuille
  (of glass) = une plaque

shelf noun
  a shelf (for books, ornaments) = une
  étagère
  (in a shop) = un rayon
  a set of shelves = une étagère

shell noun
  a shell (of an egg, a nut, a snail) = une
  coquille
  (of a crab, a tortoise) = une carapace

shelter
1 noun
- (from rain, danger)
  a shelter = un abri
- (for homeless people)
  a shelter = un refuge
2 verb
- (to take shelter) = se mettre à l'abri
- (to help) = donner refuge à

shin noun ▶ **201**
  the shin = le tibia

shine verb
- (to give out light) = briller
  the light is shining in my eyes = j'ai la
  lumière dans les yeux
- (to point)
  to shine a torch at someone = braquer
  une lampe sur quelqu'un
- (to reflect light) = reluire

ship noun
  a ship (large) = un navire
  (smaller) = un bateau
  a passenger ship = un paquebot

shirt noun
  a shirt = une chemise

shiver verb
  (with cold) = grelotter
  (with fear) = trembler

shock
1 *noun*
* (*an upsetting experience*)
  a shock = un choc
  to get a shock = avoir un choc
  to give someone a shock = faire un choc à
    quelqu'un
* (*the medical state*)
  to be in shock = être en état de choc
* (*from electricity*)
  a shock = une décharge
  to get a shock = recevoir une décharge
2 *verb*
* (*to upset*) = consterner
* (*to cause a scandal*) = choquer

shoe *noun*
  a shoe (*for a person*) = une chaussure
  (*for a horse*) = un fer

shoot *verb*
* (*using a weapon*) = tirer
  to shoot someone = tirer sur quelqu'un
  they shot him in the leg = ils lui ont tiré
    dans la jambe
  to shoot someone dead = abattre
    quelqu'un
* (*to move very fast*)
  to shoot past = passer en trombe
* (*to make*)
  to shoot a film = tourner un film

shop
1 *noun*
  a shop = un magasin
  (*small, fashionable*) = une boutique
2 *verb*
  to go shopping = aller faire des courses

shop assistant *noun* ▶ 315 ▮ (*British English*)
  a shop assistant = un vendeur/une
    vendeuse

shopkeeper *noun* ▶ 315 ▮
  a shopkeeper = un commerçant/une
    commerçante

shopping *noun*
  shopping = les courses (*feminine plural*)
  to do the shopping = faire les courses

shopping cart *noun* (*US English*)
  a shopping cart = un caddie®

shopping centre (*British English*),
shopping mall (*US English*) *noun*
  a shopping centre, a shopping mall = un
    centre commercial

shopping trolley *noun* (*British English*)
  a shopping trolley = un caddie®

shop window *noun*
  a shop window = une vitrine

shore *noun*
* (*the edge of the sea*)
  the shore = la côte, le rivage
* (*dry land*)
  the shore = la terre

short
1 *adjective*
* (*not lasting long*) = court/courte (**!** *before
  the noun*)
  to go for a short walk = faire une petite
    promenade
  a short speech = un bref discours
  the days are getting shorter = les jours
    diminuent
* (*not long*) = court/courte
  a short skirt = une jupe courte
  to have short hair = avoir les cheveux
    courts
* (*not tall*) = petit/petite (**!** + *être*)
* **to be short of** [money | food | ideas ...] = être à
    court [d'argent | de nourriture | d'idées ...]
2 in short = bref

short cut *noun*
  a short cut = un raccourci

shortly *adverb*
* (*soon*) = bientôt
* (*not long*) = peu de temps
  shortly before we left = peu de temps
    avant notre départ

shorts *noun*
  shorts = un short (*singular*)

shot *noun*
* (*from a gun*)
  a shot = un coup (de feu)
  to fire a shot at someone = tirer sur
    quelqu'un
* (*in sports*) ▶ 248 ▮
  a shot (*in football*) = un tir
  (*in tennis, golf, cricket*) = un coup

should *verb*

> **!** *Note that, in general,* should *is
> translated by* devoir *in the conditional,
> either present (*you shouldn't smoke = tu
> ne devrais pas fumer*) or past (*he
> shouldn't have left = il n'aurait pas dû
> partir*).*

* (*when talking about what is right, what one
  ought to do*)
  she should learn to drive = elle devrait
    apprendre à conduire
  shouldn't he be at school? = est-ce qu'il
    ne devrait pas être à l'école?
  you shouldn't have said that! = tu n'aurais
    pas dû dire ça!
* (*when saying something may happen*)
  we should be there by midday = nous
    devrions être là vers midi
  it shouldn't be too difficult = cela ne
    devrait pas être trop difficile
* (*when implying that something, though
  likely, didn't happen*)
  the letter should have arrived yesterday
    = la lettre aurait dû arriver hier
* (*when asking for advice or permission*)
  should I call the doctor? = est-ce que je
    devrais appeler le médecin?

S

shoulder noun ▶ 201 |
the shoulder = l'épaule
to wear a sweater over one's shoulders
= porter un pull sur les épaules
to have round shoulders = avoir le dos
rond

shout
1 verb
= crier
to shout at someone = crier après
quelqu'un
2 noun
a shout = un cri
shout out = pousser un cri

shovel noun
a shovel = une pelle

show
1 verb
• (to let someone see) = montrer
to show someone a photo = montrer une
photo à quelqu'un
I'll show you how it works = je vais te
montrer comment ça marche
• (to go with)
I'll show you to your room = je vais vous
accompagner à votre chambre
• (to point to, to indicate) = indiquer
to show someone where to go = indiquer
à quelqu'un où aller
there's a sign showing the way to the
pool = il y a un panneau qui indique la
direction de la piscine
• (to be on TV, at the cinema) = passer
(! + être)
the film is showing at the Phoenix = le
film passe au Phoenix
to be shown on TV = passer à la télévision
2 noun
• a show (on a stage) = un spectacle
(on TV, radio) = une émission
• (an exhibition)
a show = une exposition
show off = faire le fier/la fière
show round
to show someone around the town = faire
visiter la ville à quelqu'un
show up = se pointer✖ (! + être)

shower noun
• (for washing)
a shower = une douche
to have a shower = prendre une douche
• (rain)
a shower = une averse

showjumping noun ▶ 248 |
showjumping = le saut d'obstacles

shrimp noun
a shrimp = une crevette grise

shrink verb
= rétrécir

✖ in informal situations

shut
1 adjective
= fermé/fermée
my eyes were shut = j'avais les yeux
fermés
2 verb
= fermer
to shut the windows = fermer les fenêtres
the door doesn't shut properly = la porte
ne ferme pas bien
shut down = fermer
the factory shut down in May = l'usine a
fermé au mois de mai
shut out
to shut someone out = laisser quelqu'un
dehors
shut up
• (to be quiet) = se taire (! + être)
shut up! = tais-toi!
• (to lock inside) = enfermer

shy adjective
= timide

sick adjective
• (ill) = malade
to get sick = tomber malade (! + être)
to feel sick = avoir mal au cœur
to be sick (British English) (to vomit)
= vomir
• (fed up)
he's sick of the neighbours = il en a
marre✖ des voisins

sickness noun
a sickness = une maladie

side noun
• a side = un côté
it's an apartment block with shops on
either side = c'est un immeuble avec des
magasins de chaque côté
to be driving on the wrong side of the
road = rouler du mauvais côté de la
route
by the side of the river = au bord de la
rivière
the north side of the city = le nord de la
ville
he works on the other side of London = il
travaille à l'autre bout de Londres
• (of a person's body)
the side = le côté
to be lying on one's side = être
allongé/allongée sur le côté
on my right side = à ma droite
• (in a conflict, a contest)
a side = un camp
• (a team)
a side = une équipe
side with = se mettre du côté de

sidewalk noun (US English)
a sidewalk = un trottoir

sigh verb
= soupirer

sight *noun*
  sight = la vue
  to have good sight = avoir une bonne vue
  to catch sight of someone = apercevoir
    quelqu'un
  to be out of sight = être caché/cachée

sightseeing *noun*
  sightseeing = le tourisme

sign
1 *noun*
• (*a mark*)
  a sign = un signe
  the dollar sign = le symbole du dollar
• (*for traffic, for advertising*)
  a sign = un panneau
• (*a notice*)
  a sign = une pancarte
2 *verb*
  = signer
sign on (*British English*) = pointer au
chômage

signal
1 *noun*
  a signal = un signal
2 *verb*
• (*to make signs*) = faire des signes
  to signal to someone to come = faire
    signe à quelqu'un de venir
• (*when driving*) = mettre son clignotant

signature *noun*
  a signature = une signature

signpost *noun*
  a signpost = un panneau indicateur

silence *noun*
  silence = le silence

silent *adjective*
• (*quiet*) = silencieux/silencieuse
• (*without sound or words*) = muet/muette

silk *noun*
  silk = la soie

silly *adjective*
  = idiot/idiote

silver
1 *noun*
  silver = l'argent (*masculine*)
2 *adjective*
  = en argent
  a silver ring = une bague en argent

simple *adjective*
  = simple

since
1 *preposition*

> **!** Note that, when *since* is used to
> describe an event or an action that is still
> going on, rather than an event or an
> action that belongs to the past and has
> finished, the present tense + **depuis** is
> used in French. In the same way, if the
> event or action has its starting point
> further back in the past, in French the
> imperfect tense + **depuis** is used.

  = depuis
  I haven't seen him since yesterday = je ne
    l'ai pas vu depuis hier
  I haven't been feeling well since Monday
    = je ne me sens pas bien depuis lundi
  she had been living in France since 1988
    = elle vivait en France depuis 1988
2 *conjunction*
• (*from the time when*) = depuis que
  since she left = depuis qu'elle est partie,
    depuis son départ
  I've lived here since I was ten = j'habite
    ici depuis l'âge de dix ans
  it's ten years since she died = cela fait dix
    ans qu'elle est morte
• (*because*) = comme
  since she was ill, she couldn't go
    = comme elle était malade, elle ne
    pouvait pas y aller
3 *adverb*
  = depuis

sincere *adjective*
  = sincère

sincerely *adverb*
  = sincèrement
  Yours sincerely (*British English*),
  Sincerely yours (*US English*) = Veuillez
    agréer, Monsieur/Madame, l'expression
    de mes sentiments les meilleurs
  (*less formal*) = Meilleures salutations

sing *verb*
  = chanter

singer *noun* **▶ 315 |**
  a singer = un chanteur/une chanteuse

singing *noun*
  singing = le chant

single *adjective*
• (*one*) = seul/seule (**!** *before the noun*)
  we visited three towns in a single day
    = nous avons visité trois villes en une
    seule journée
• (*when used for emphasis*)
  every single day = tous les jours sans
    exception
  I didn't see a single person = je n'ai vu
    absolument personne
• (*without a partner*) = célibataire

single bed *noun*
  a single bed = un lit pour une personne

single room *noun*
  a single room = une chambre à une
    personne

single ticket *noun* (*British English*)
  a single ticket = un aller simple

sink
1 *noun*
  a sink = un évier
2 *verb*
  = couler

S

sister noun
  a sister = une sœur

sister-in-law noun
  a sister-in-law = une belle-sœur

sit verb
* (to take a seat) = s'asseoir (! + être)
  to be sitting on the floor = être assis/assise
    par terre
* (British English) (to take)
  to sit an exam = passer un examen
  sit down = s'asseoir (! + être)
    to be sitting down = être assis/assise
  sit up = se redresser (! + être)
    sit up straight! = tiens-toi droit!

sitting room noun
  a sitting room = un salon

situated adjective
  = situé/située
  situated near the town centre
    = situé/située près du centre-ville

situation noun
  a situation = une situation

six number ▶ 187 |, ▶ 211 |
  six = six
  six weeks = six semaines
  I've got six (of them) = j'en ai six

sixteen number ▶ 187 |, ▶ 211 |
  sixteen = seize

sixteenth number
* (in a series) = seizième
* (in dates) ▶ 222 |
  the sixteenth of July = le seize juillet

sixth number
* (in a series) = sixième
* (in dates) ▶ 222 |
  the sixth of February = le six février

sixty number ▶ 187 |
  sixty = soixante

size noun
* (when talking about a person)
  a size = une taille
  she's about your size = elle est à peu près
    de ta taille
* (when talking about clothes)
  a size (of garment) = une taille
  (of shoe) = une pointure
  I'd like this in a smaller size = je voudrais
    ce modèle en plus petit
  what size do you take? (in clothes)
    = quelle taille faites-vous?
  (in shoes) = vous chaussez du combien?
* (when talking about how big something is)
  the size (of a building, a region) = la
    grandeur
  (of an apple, a parcel) = la grosseur

skateboard noun ▶ 248 |
  a skateboard = un skateboard, une
    planche à roulettes

skating noun ▶ 248 |
  skating = le patin

skating rink noun
  a skating rink (for ice-skating) = une
    patinoire
  (for roller-skating) = une piste de patin à
    roulettes

sketch noun
* (a drawing)
  a sketch = un croquis
* (a funny scene)
  a sketch = un sketch

ski
1 noun
  a ski = un ski
2 verb
  to go skiing = faire du ski

skiing noun ▶ 248 |
  skiing = le ski

skilful (British English), **skillful** (US
English) adjective
  = habile, adroit/adroite

skill noun
* (the quality)
  skill (mental) = l'habileté (feminine)
  (physical) = la dextérité
* (a particular ability)
  a skill (learned) = une compétence
  (natural) = une aptitude

skin noun
  the skin = la peau

skinny adjective
  = maigre

skip verb
* (to give little jumps) = sautiller
* (with a rope) = sauter à la corde
* **to skip classes** = sauter les cours

ski resort noun
  a ski resort = une station de ski

skirt noun
  a skirt = une jupe

sky noun
  the sky = le ciel
  a clear sky = un ciel dégagé

skydiving noun ▶ 248 |
  skydiving = le parachutisme (en chute
    libre)

slap verb
  to slap someone = donner une tape à
    quelqu'un
  (across the face) = gifler quelqu'un

sled, **sledge** (British English)
1 noun
  a sled (for fun) = une luge
  (for transport) = un traîneau
2 verb
  to go sledging (British English) = faire de
    la luge

sleep
1 *noun*
  sleep = le sommeil
  to go to sleep = s'endormir (**!** + *être*)
  to go back to sleep = se rendormir
    (**!** + *être*)
  to put someone to sleep = endormir
    quelqu'un
2 *verb*
• (*to be asleep*) = dormir
• **to sleep with someone** = coucher avec
    quelqu'un
sleep in = faire la grasse matinée

sleeping bag *noun*
  a sleeping bag = un sac de couchage

sleepy *adjective*
  to be sleepy, to feel sleepy = avoir
    sommeil, avoir envie de dormir

sleet *noun*
  sleet = la neige fondue

sleeve *noun*
  a sleeve = une manche
  to roll up one's sleeves = retrousser ses
    manches

slice
1 *noun*
  a slice (*of bread, meat*) = une tranche
    (*of lemon, cucumber*) = une rondelle
2 *verb*
  to slice bread = couper du pain en
    tranches

slide
1 *verb*
  = glisser
  the plates slid off the table = les assiettes
    ont glissé de la table
2 *noun*
• (*an image*)
  a slide = une diapositive
• (*in a playground*)
  a slide = un toboggan

slim
1 *adjective*
  = mince
2 *verb* (*British English*)
  = maigrir

slip *verb*
• (*to slide*) = glisser
• **the glass slipped out of my hands** = le
    verre m'a échappé des mains

slipper *noun*
  a slipper = une pantoufle

slippery *adjective*
  = glissant/glissante

slot machine *noun*
  a slot machine = une machine à sous

Slovakia *noun* ▶ 218 |
  Slovakia = la Slovaquie

slow *adjective*
• (*not fast*) = lent/lente
  to make slow progress = avancer
    lentement
• (*not bright*) = lent/lente (d'esprit)
• (*describing a watch, a clock*)
  to be slow = retarder
  the clock is 20 minutes slow = la pendule
    retarde de 20 minutes
slow down = ralentir

slowly *adverb*
  = lentement

sly *adjective*
  = rusé/rusée

small *adjective*
  = petit/petite (**!** *before the noun*)
  a small car = une petite voiture
  a small quantity = une faible quantité

small ad *noun* (*British English*)
  a small ad = une petite annonce

smart *adjective*
• (*British English*) (*elegant*)
  = élégant/élégante
• (*intelligent*) = intelligent/intelligente
• (*expensive*) = chic (**!** *never changes*)

smash *verb*
• (*to break*) = briser, fracasser
• (*to get broken*) = se briser, se fracasser
    (**!** + *être*)
smash up = démolir

smell
1 *noun*
• (*an odour*)
  a smell = une odeur
• (*the sense*)
  the sense of smell = l'odorat (*masculine*)
2 *verb*
  = sentir
  that smells nice = ça sent bon
  I can smell burning = ça sent le brûlé

smile
1 *verb*
  = sourire
  to smile at someone = sourire à quelqu'un
2 *noun*
  a smile = un sourire

smoke
1 *noun*
  smoke = la fumée
2 *verb*
  = fumer

smooth *adjective*
  (*not rough*) = lisse
  a smooth road = une route plane
  a smooth crossing = une traversée sans
    heurts

smother *verb*
  = étouffer

snack *noun*
  a snack = un casse-croûte

S

snail *noun*
  a snail = un escargot

snake *noun*
  a snake = un serpent

snapshot *noun*
  a snapshot = une photo

sneaker *noun*
  a sneaker (*high*) = une basket
  (*low*) = un tennis

sneeze *verb*
  = éternuer

snobbish *adjective*
  = snob

snooker *noun* ▶ 248 |
  snooker = le billard anglais

snore *verb*
  = ronfler

snow
1 *noun*
  snow = la neige
2 *verb*
  = neiger
  it's snowing = il neige

snowball *noun*
  a snowball = une boule de neige

snowman *noun*
  a snowman = un bonhomme de neige

so
1 *adverb*
• so = si, tellement
  he's so [happy | stupid | smart …] = il est si
    [content | bête | malin …]
  they speak so fast = ils parlent si vite, ils
    parlent tellement vite
  it's so much easier = c'est tellement plus
    facile
  she has so many clothes = elle a tant de
    vêtements
  I've so much work to do = j'ai tant de
    travail à faire
• (*also*)
  I'm fifteen and so is he = j'ai quinze ans et
    lui aussi
  if you go, so will I = si tu y vas, j'y vais
    aussi
• (*other uses*)
  I think so = je pense que oui
  I'm afraid so = j'ai bien peur que oui
  I told you so = je te l'avais bien dit
  who says so? = qui dit ça?
  so what? = et alors?
  and so on = et ainsi de suite
2 **so (that)** = pour que
  be quiet so I can work = tais-toi pour que
    je puisse travailler

! *Note that the subjunctive is used after*
  pour que.

3 **so as** = pour
  we left early so as not to miss the train
    = nous sommes partis tôt pour ne pas
    rater le train

soap *noun*
• (*for washing*)
  soap = le savon
• (*on TV*)
  a soap = un feuilleton

soccer *noun* ▶ 248 |
  soccer = le football
  = sociable

social *adjective*
  = social/sociale

social studies *noun*
  social studies = l'instruction civique

! *Note that* instruction *is feminine.*

social worker *noun* ▶ 315 |
  a social worker = un travailleur social/une
    travailleuse sociale

sock *noun*
  a sock = une chaussette

sofa *noun*
  a sofa = un canapé

soft *adjective*
• (*not hard or tough*) = doux/douce
  to have soft skin = avoir la peau douce
  the ground is soft here = la terre est
    meuble ici
  a soft toffee = un caramel mou
• (*not harsh or severe*) = doux/douce
• (*not strict*) = indulgent/indulgente

software *noun*
  a software = un logiciel

soldier *noun* ▶ 315 |
  a soldier = un soldat

sole *noun*
• the sole (*of the foot*) = la plante du pied
• (*of a shoe*)
  a sole = une semelle

solicitor *noun* ▶ 315 | (*British English*)
  a solicitor (*for documents*) ≈ un notaire
  (*for court work*) ≈ un avocat/une avocate

solution *noun*
  a solution = une solution

solve *verb*
  = résoudre
  to solve a problem = résoudre un
    problème

some

1 *determiner*
* (*an amount or a number of*) = du/de la (**!** de l' + *vowel or mute h*)
  = des (+ *plural*)
  I have to buy some bread = je dois acheter du pain
  have some water = prenez de l'eau
  we bought some beer = nous avons acheté de la bière
  she ate some strawberries = elle a mangé des fraises
  we visited some beautiful towns = nous avons visité des villes superbes
* (*certain*) = certains/certaines
  some people don't like travelling by plane = certaines personnes n'aiment pas voyager en avion

2 *pronoun*
* (*an amount or a number of*) = en
  I know where you can find some = je sais où tu peux en trouver
  have some more! = reprenez-en!

  ! *Note that it is necessary to use* en, *which might be translated as* 'of it' *or* 'of them', *with pronouns like* some. *See also* any, a few, a lot *etc for this use of* en.

* (*certain people or things*)
  some are quite expensive = certains sont assez chers/certaines sont assez chères
  some (of them) are French = certains d'entre eux sont français/certaines d'entre elles sont françaises

someone *pronoun* (*also* **somebody**)
= quelqu'un
someone famous = quelqu'un de célèbre

something *pronoun*
= quelque chose
I saw something interesting = j'ai vu quelque chose d'intéressant
there's something odd about him = il a quelque chose de bizarre

sometimes *adverb*
= quelquefois, parfois

somewhere *adverb*
= quelque part
they live somewhere in Ireland = ils habitent quelque part en Irlande
let's go somewhere else = allons ailleurs

son *noun*
a son = un fils

song *noun*
a song = une chanson

son-in-law *noun*
a son-in-law = un gendre

soon *adverb*
* (*in a short time*) = bientôt
  see you soon! = à bientôt!
* (*early*)
  the sooner the better = le plus tôt sera le mieux
  as soon as possible = dès que possible
  come as soon as you can = viens dès que tu pourras

  ! *Note that, if talking about future time, the future tense is used after* dès que.

sore *adjective*
to have a sore [throat | leg | back …] = avoir mal [à la gorge | à la jambe | au dos …]
it's very sore = ça fait très mal

sorry

1 *exclamation*
* (*when apologizing*)
  sorry! = pardon!, désolé/désolée!
* (*when asking someone to repeat*)
  sorry? = pardon?

2 *adjective*
* (*when apologizing*) = désolé/désolée
  I'm sorry I'm late = je suis désolé d'être en retard
  to say sorry = s'excuser (**!** + *être*)
* (*when expressing regret*)
  I'm sorry you can't come = je suis désolé que tu ne puisses pas venir

  ! *Note that the subjunctive is used after* être désolé que.

* (*to feel pity for*)
  to feel sorry for someone = plaindre quelqu'un
  to feel sorry for oneself = s'apitoyer sur son sort

sort

1 *noun*
it's a sort of [bird | computer | loan …] = c'est une sorte [d'oiseau | d'ordinateur | de prêt …]
I don't like that sort of thing = je n'aime pas ce genre de choses
he's not that sort of person = ce n'est pas son genre

2 *verb*
to sort files = classer des dossiers
to sort the books into piles = ranger les livres en piles

sort out
* (*to solve*) = régler
  to sort out a problem = régler un problème
* (*to deal with*) = s'occuper de (**!** + *être*)
  I'll sort it out = je m'en occuperai
* (*to organize*) = classer
  to sort out the documents = classer les documents
* (*to pick out, to choose*)
  to sort out the photos = trier les photos
  to sort out the old clothes from the new = séparer les vieux vêtements des neufs

sound

1 *noun*
* **a sound** (*a noise*) = un bruit
  (*of an instrument, a bell*) = un son

S

I heard the sound of voices = j'ai entendu un bruit de voix
• (*of a radio, a television*)
the sound = le son
to turn the sound up = monter le son
2 *verb*
it sounds [dangerous | odd | interesting …] = ça a l'air [dangereux | bizarre | intéressant …]
it sounds like a piano = on dirait un piano

soup *noun*
a soup = une soupe, un potage

sour *adjective*
= aigre
to go sour = tourner

south
1 *noun*
the south = le sud
in the south of France = dans le sud de la France
2 *adverb*
to go south = aller vers le sud
to live south of Paris = vivre au sud de Paris
3 *adjective*
= sud (**!** *never changes*)
to work in south London = travailler dans le sud de Londres

South Africa *noun* ▶ 218 |
South Africa = l'Afrique du Sud
! *Note that* Afrique *is feminine.*

South America *noun* ▶ 218 |
South America = l'Amérique du Sud
! *Note that* Amérique *is feminine.*

southeast *noun*
the southeast = le sud-est

southwest *noun*
the southwest = le sud-ouest

souvenir *noun*
a souvenir = un souvenir

space *noun*
• (*room*)
space = la place
to take up space = prendre de la place
• (*an area of land*)
an open space = un espace libre
• (*outer space*)
space = l'espace (*masculine*)
• (*a gap*)
a space = un espace

Spain *noun* ▶ 218 |
Spain = l'Espagne (*feminine*)

Spanish ▶ 275 |
1 *adjective*
= espagnol/espagnole
2 *noun*
Spanish = l'espagnol (*masculine*)

spare *adjective*
• (*extra*) = en plus
I've got a spare ticket = j'ai un billet en plus
• (*available*) = disponible
are there any spare seats? = est-ce qu'il y a des places disponibles?

spare part *noun*
a spare part = une pièce de rechange

spare room *noun*
a spare room = une chambre d'amis

spare time *noun*
spare time = les loisirs (*masculine plural*)

speak *verb*
= parler
to speak German = parler (l')allemand
they're not speaking (to each other) = ils ne se parlent pas
who's speaking, please? = qui est à l'appareil?
generally speaking = en règle générale
speak up = parler plus fort

special *adjective*
= spécial/spéciale
! *Note that* spécial *can also mean* odd *or* strange *in French:* il est assez spécial = he's rather strange.

a special offer = une offre spéciale
she's a special friend = c'est une amie très chère

speciality (*British English*), **specialty** (*US English*) *noun*
a speciality = une spécialité

specially *adverb*
= spécialement

spectator *noun*
a spectator = un spectateur/une spectatrice

speech *noun*
a speech = un discours

speed
1 *noun*
speed = la vitesse
2 *verb*
• to speed away = s'éloigner à toute allure
• (*to drive too fast*) = conduire trop vite
speed up = accélérer

speed limit *noun*
a speed limit = une limitation de vitesse

spell *verb*
(*when speaking*) = épeler
(*when writing*) = écrire
how do you spell it? = comment ça s'écrit?

spelling *noun*
spelling = l'orthographe (*feminine*)

spend *verb*
• (*to pay money*) = dépenser

- (*to pass*)
  to spend (some) time [reading | painting | writing letters ...] = passer du temps [à lire | à faire de la peinture | à écrire des lettres ...]

spider *noun*
  a spider = une araignée

spill *verb*
- (*if it's a person*) = renverser
  don't spill the milk = ne renverse pas le lait
- (*if it's a liquid*) = se répandre (**!** + *être*)

spinach *noun*
  spinach = les épinards (*masculine plural*)

spit *verb*
  = cracher

spite: **in spite of** *preposition*
  = malgré
  we went out in spite of the weather = nous sommes sortis malgré le temps

spiteful *adjective*
  = méchant/méchante

spoil *verb*
- (*to take away from*) = gâcher
  to spoil the evening = gâcher la soirée
- (*to ruin, to damage*) = abîmer
- (*as a parent*) = gâter
  to spoil a child = gâter un enfant

sponge *noun*
  a sponge = une éponge

spoon *noun*
  a spoon = une cuillère

sport *noun* ▶ 248 |
  a sport = un sport
  to be good at sports = être bon/bonne en sport

sports centre (*British English*), **sports center** (*US English*) *noun*
  a sports centre = un centre sportif

sports club *noun*
  a sports club = un club sportif

spot
1 *noun*
- (*on an animal*)
  a spot = une tache
- (*British English*) (*on the face or body*)
  a spot = un bouton
- (*a place*)
  a spot = un endroit
  on the spot (*there and then*) = sur-le-champ
2 *verb*
- (*to see*) = apercevoir
- (*to recognize*) = repérer

sprain *verb*
  to sprain one's wrist = se fouler le poignet

spring *noun*
  spring = le printemps
  in spring = au printemps

spy *noun*
  a spy = un espion/une espionne

square
1 *noun*
- (*the shape*)
  a square = un carré
- (*in a town*)
  a square = une place
2 *adjective*
  = carré/carrée

squash
1 *noun* ▶ 248 |
  squash = le squash
2 *verb*
  = écraser

squeak *verb*
  (*if it's a door, a wheel*) = grincer
  (*if it's a shoe, a chair*) = craquer

squeeze *verb*
  to squeeze a lemon = presser un citron
  to squeeze someone's hand = serrer la main de quelqu'un

squirrel *noun*
  a squirrel = un écureuil

stable *noun*
  a stable = une écurie

stadium *noun*
  a stadium = un stade

staff *noun*
  the staff (*of a company*) = le personnel
  (*of a school, a college*) = le personnel enseignant

stage *noun*
  a stage = une scène

stain
1 *noun*
  a stain = une tache
2 *verb*
  = tacher

stairs *noun*
  the stairs = l'escalier (*masculine singular*)
  to fall down the stairs = tomber dans l'escalier

stamp *noun*
- (*for an envelope*)
  a stamp = un timbre
  a three-franc stamp = un timbre à trois francs
- (*on a document, a passport*)
  a stamp = un cachet

stamp-collecting *noun*
  stamp-collecting = la philatélie

stand *verb*
- **to be standing** = être debout
  to stay standing, to remain standing = rester debout (**!** + *être*)
  to be able to stand = tenir debout
  you're standing in my way = tu me bloques le passage

S

- (*to put*)
  to stand a vase on a table = mettre un vase sur une table
- (*to step*)
  to stand on a nail = marcher sur un clou
- (*to bear*)
  I can't stand French = je déteste le français
  he can't stand playing football = il déteste jouer au football
- (*other uses*)
  to stand for election (*British English*) = se présenter aux élections
  to stand trial = passer en jugement
stand back = reculer
stand for
- (*to represent*) = représenter
- (*to mean*) = vouloir dire
stand out
  (*if it's a person*) = sortir de l'ordinaire
stand up
- **to stand up** = se lever (**!** + *être*)
- **to stand someone up** = poser un lapin✖ à quelqu'un
stand up for = défendre
  to stand up for oneself = se défendre (**!** + *être*)
stand up to = tenir tête à
  to stand up to someone = tenir tête à quelqu'un

star *noun*
- (*in space*)
  a star = une étoile
- (*a famous person*)
  a star = une vedette, une star

stare *verb*
  to stare at someone = dévisager quelqu'un

start
1 *verb*
- (*to begin*) = commencer
  to start [working | writing | running ...] = commencer à [travailler | écrire | courir ...]
  you should start by phoning them = tu devrais commencer par leur téléphoner
- (*to begin one's working life*)
  to start (out) as a teacher = débuter comme professeur
- (*to set up*) = lancer
  to start a fashion = lancer une mode
- (*to cause*) = déclencher
  to start a war = déclencher une guerre
- (*to begin working*) = démarrer
  the car won't start = la voiture ne veut pas démarrer
- (*to put into action*)
  to start a car = faire démarrer une voiture
  to start a machine = mettre une machine en marche

2 *noun*
  a start = un début
  at the start of the week = au début de la semaine
start off = commencer
start over (*US English*) = recommencer

starter *noun* (*British English*)
  a starter = un hors-d'œuvre

state *noun*
- (*a country, part of a country*)
  a state = un état
- (*a government*)
  the State = l'État
- (*a condition*)
  a state = un état
  to be in a bad state (of repair) = être en mauvais état
  she's in no state to work = elle n'est pas en état de travailler

statement *noun*
  a statement = une déclaration
  (*official*) = un communiqué

station *noun*
- (*for trains*)
  a station = une gare
- (*on TV*)
  a station = une chaîne

statue *noun*
  a statue = une statue

stay
1 *verb*
- (*to remain*) = rester (**!** + *être*)
  we stayed there for a week = nous sommes restés là une semaine
- (*to have accommodation*) = loger
  to stay with friends = loger chez des amis
2 *noun*
  a stay = un séjour
stay away from = éviter
  to stay away from school = ne pas aller à l'école
stay in = rester à la maison
stay out
  to stay out late = rentrer tard
stay up (*to wait*) = veiller
  (*to keep late hours*) = se coucher tard

steady *adjective*
- (*continuous*)
  to make steady progress = faire des progrès réguliers
- (*not likely to move*) = stable

steak *noun*
  a steak = un steak

steal *verb*
  = voler
  to steal from someone = voler quelqu'un
  to steal money from someone = voler de l'argent à quelqu'un

steam *noun*
  steam = la vapeur

✖ in informal situations

steel *noun*
  steel = l'acier (*masculine*)

steep *adjective*
  = raide

steering wheel *noun*
  a steering wheel = un volant

step
1 *noun*
• (*when walking*)
  a step = un pas
  to take a step = faire un pas
• (*in stairs, at a door*)
  a step = une marche
• (*a series of actions*)
  to take steps = prendre des mesures
2 *verb*
  to step in a puddle = marcher dans une
    flaque
step aside = s'écarter (**!** + *être*)

stepbrother *noun*
  a stepbrother = un demi-frère

stepfather *noun*
  a stepfather = un beau-père

stepmother *noun*
  a stepmother = une belle-mère

stepsister *noun*
  a stepsister = une demi-sœur

stereo *noun*
  a stereo = une chaîne stéréo

stewardess *noun* ▶ 315 |
  a stewardess = une hôtesse de l'air

stick
1 *verb*
• (*using glue or tape*) = coller
• (*to become attached*) = coller
• (*to get blocked*) = se coincer (**!** + *être*)
  the door is stuck = la porte est coincée
2 *noun*
• (*a piece of wood*)
  a stick = un bâton
• (*for walking*)
  a stick = une canne
stick at
  to stick at a task = persévérer dans une
    tâche
stick out = dépasser
  there's a nail sticking out = il y a un clou
    qui dépasse
  his ears stick out = il a les oreilles
    décollées

sticky tape *noun* (*British English*)
  sticky tape = le scotch®, le ruban adhésif

stiff *adjective*
• (*not soft, not supple*) = raide
  to have stiff legs (*after sport, walking*)
    = avoir des courbatures dans les jambes
• (*not easy to use*)
  to be stiff (*if it's a door, a drawer*) = être
    dur/dure à ouvrir

(*if it's a handle*) = être dur/dure à tourner

still¹ *adverb*
• (*when there has been no change*)
  = toujours
  does she still play the piano? = est-ce
    qu'elle joue toujours du piano?
  I still don't understand why you left = je
    ne comprends toujours pas pourquoi tu
    es parti
• (*when referring to the future*) = encore
  she could still win = elle pourrait encore
    gagner

still²
1 *adverb*
  to sit still = se tenir tranquille
2 *adjective*
  = calme

sting *verb*
  = piquer

stir *verb*
  = remuer

stomach *noun* ▶ 201 |, ▶ 266 |
  the stomach = l'estomac (*masculine*)
  to have a pain in one's stomach = avoir
    mal au ventre

stone *noun*
  a stone = une pierre
  (*a pebble*) = un caillou

stop
1 *verb*
• (*to put an end to*) = arrêter
  to stop [smoking | laughing | working ...]
    = arrêter de [fumer | rire | travailler ...]
  stop it! = arrête!
• (*to prevent*)
  to stop someone from [leaving | winning |
    talking ...] = empêcher quelqu'un de
    [partir | gagner | parler ...]
• (*to come to a halt*) = s'arrêter (**!** + *être*)
  the bus didn't stop = le bus ne s'est pas
    arrêté
• (*when talking about machines, noise,
  weather*) = s'arrêter (**!** + *être*)
  suddenly the noise stopped = tout à
    coup, le bruit s'est arrêté
  it's stopped raining = il s'est arrêté de
    pleuvoir, la pluie s'est arrêtée
2 *noun*
  a (bus) stop = un arrêt (de bus)
  to miss one's stop = rater son arrêt

store *noun*
  a store = un magasin
  (*smaller*) = une boutique

storey (*British English*), **story** (*US
English*) *noun*
  a storey = un étage

storm *noun*
  a storm = une tempête
  (*with thunder*) = un orage

S

story noun
* a story = une histoire
  a true story = une histoire vécue
  a ghost story = une histoire de fantômes
* (in a newspaper)
  a story = un article
* (a rumour)
  a story = une rumeur
* (US English) ▶ **storey**

stove noun (US English)
  a stove = une cuisinière

straight
1 adjective
* straight = droit/droite
  a straight line = une ligne droite
* (not curly) = raide
  to have straight hair = avoir les cheveux
    raides
* (in the right position) = bien droit/droite
  the picture isn't straight = le tableau est
    de travers
* (honest) = honnête, droit/droite
2 adverb
* straight = droit
  to stand up straight = se tenir droit
  to go straight ahead = aller tout droit
* (without delay) = directement
  to go straight home = rentrer directement

strange adjective
* (odd) = bizarre
  it's strange that she doesn't come any
    more = il est bizarre qu'elle ne vienne
    plus

  ! Note that the subjunctive is used after il
  est bizarre que.

* (unknown) = inconnu/inconnue

stranger noun
  a stranger = un inconnu/une inconnue
  (a foreigner) = un étranger/une étrangère

straw noun
* (for feeding animals)
  straw = la paille
* (for drinking)
  a straw = une paille

strawberry noun
  a strawberry = une fraise

stream noun
  a stream = un ruisseau

street noun
  a street = une rue

streetlamp noun
  a streetlamp = un réverbère

strength noun
  strength = la force

stressful adjective
  = stressant/stressante

---

stretch verb
  = s'étirer (**!** + être)
  to stretch one's arms = s'étirer les bras

strict adjective
  = strict/stricte

strike noun
  a strike = une grève
  to go on strike = se mettre en grève

string noun
  string = la ficelle
  a piece of string = un bout de ficelle

striped adjective
  = rayé/rayée

stroke verb
  = caresser

stroller noun (US English)
  a stroller = une poussette

strong adjective
* (having physical, mental strength)
  = fort/forte
  she's strong = elle a de la force, elle est
    forte
* (not easily damaged) = solide
* (having force, power) = fort/forte
  a strong wind = un vent fort
  it's strong tea = c'est du thé fort
* (obvious, noticeable) = fort/forte (**!** before
  the noun)
  a strong German accent = un fort accent
    allemand
  a strong smell of garlic = une forte odeur
    d'ail
* (having military power)
  = puissant/puissante

stubborn adjective
  = entêté/entêtée

student noun ▶ 315 |
  a student (at university) = un étudiant/une
    étudiante
  (at school) = un élève/une élève

study
1 verb
  to study history = étudier l'histoire, faire
    des études d'histoire
  to study to be a teacher = faire des études
    pour être professeur
  to study for an exam = réviser pour un
    examen
2 noun
  a study = un bureau

stuff
1 noun
  stuff (things) = les choses (feminine plural)
  (belongings) = les affaires (feminine plural)
2 verb
  to stuff a suitcase with clothes = bourrer
    une valise de vêtements
  to stuff oneself = s'empiffrer**✱** (**!** + être)

stuffing noun
  a stuffing = une farce

---

stupid *adjective*
= bête, stupide

style *noun*
* (*a way of dressing, behaving*)
  style = la classe
  to have style = avoir de la classe
* (*a design, a type*)
  a style (*of car, garment*) = un modèle
  (*of building*) = un type
* (*a fashion*)
  a style = une mode

stylish *adjective*
= élégant/élégante

subject *noun*
* (*of a conversation*)
  a subject = un sujet
  to change the subject = parler d'autre
  chose
* (*being studied*)
  a subject (*at school, college*) = une
  matière
  (*for an essay, a report*) = un sujet

suburb *noun*
  the suburbs = la banlieue (*singular*)

subway *noun*
* (*US English*) (*the underground*)
  the subway = le métro
* (*British English*) (*an underground passage*)
  a subway = un passage souterrain

succeed *verb*
= réussir

success *noun*
  success = le succès, la réussite
  to be a success (*if it's a party*) = être
  réussi/réussie
  (*if it's a film, a book*) = avoir du succès

successful *adjective*
  to be successful (*in an attempt*) = réussir
  (*describing a film, a book*) = avoir du
  succès

such
1 *determiner*
  there's no such thing = ça n'existe pas
2 *adverb*
  they have such a lot of money = ils ont
  tant d'argent
  she's such a strange person = elle est si
  bizarre
  I've never seen such a mess = je n'ai
  jamais vu une pagaille✱ pareille

suddenly *adverb*
= tout à coup

suffer *verb* ▶ 266 ❙
= souffrir

sugar *noun*
  sugar = le sucre

suggestion *noun*
  a suggestion = une suggestion

suicide *noun*
  to commit suicide = se suicider (**!** + *être*)

suit
1 *noun*
  a suit (*a man's*) = un costume
  (*a woman's*) = un tailleur
2 *verb*
* (*to be convenient*) = convenir
  to suit someone = convenir à quelqu'un
  does Friday suit you? = est-ce que
  vendredi te convient?
* (*to look well on*)
  the hat suits you = le chapeau te va bien

suitable *adjective*
  a suitable present = un cadeau approprié
  to be suitable for children = convenir aux
  enfants

suitcase *noun*
  a suitcase = une valise

sum *noun*
* **a sum of money** = une somme d'argent
* **a sum** = un calcul
  to be good at sums = être bon/bonne en
  calcul
  sum up = récapituler

summer *noun*
  summer = l'été (*masculine*)
  in summer = en été

summer holiday (*British English*),
summer vacation (*US English*) *noun*
  the summer holiday = les vacances d'été
  (*from school*) = les grandes vacances
  ! *Note that* **vacances** *is feminine plural.*

sun *noun*
  the sun = le soleil
  to sit in the sun = s'asseoir au soleil

sunbathe *verb*
= se faire bronzer (**!** + *être*)

sunburn *noun*
  sunburn = un coup de soleil

sunburned *adjective*
  to get sunburned = attraper un coup de
  soleil

Sunday *noun* ▶ 222 ❙
  Sunday = dimanche (*masculine*)

sunglasses *noun*
  sunglasses = les lunettes de soleil
  ! *Note that* **lunettes** *is feminine plural.*

sunny *adjective*
= ensoleillé/ensoleillée
  it's going to be sunny = il va faire du soleil

sunset *noun*
  sunset = le coucher du soleil

sunshade *noun*
  a sunshade = un parasol

sunshine *noun*
  sunshine = le soleil

S

suntan *noun*
a suntan = un bronzage
to get a suntan = bronzer

suntan oil *noun*
a suntan oil = une huile solaire

supermarket *noun*
a supermarket = un supermarché

supper *noun*
a supper (*an evening meal*) = un dîner
(*after a show*) = un souper

support *verb*
• (*to agree with, to help*) = soutenir
  to support the strike = soutenir la grève
• (*to keep*)
  to support a family = subvenir aux besoins
    d'une famille
  to support oneself = subvenir à ses
    propres besoins
• (*to hold, to help physically*) = soutenir

supporter *noun*
a supporter (*of a team*) = un supporter
(*of a party*) = un sympathisant/une
  sympathisante

suppose *verb*
• (*to imagine*) = supposer
  I don't suppose you know yet? = je
    suppose que tu n'es pas encore au
    courant?
• (*to be meant to*)
  to be supposed to = être censé/censée
  I'm supposed to pay for the shopping = je
    suis censé payer les courses

sure *adjective*
• (*certain*) = sûr/sûre
  I'm sure he said nine o'clock = je suis sûr
    qu'il a dit neuf heures
  are you sure? = est-ce que tu en es sûr?
  I'm not sure if she's coming = je ne sais
    pas trop si elle vient
  to make sure that the door is closed
    = s'assurer que la porte est fermée
• (*bound*)
  he's sure to win = il va sûrement gagner
• sure of oneself = sûr/sûre de soi

  ! Note that soi *will change to* moi, lui, elle,
  eux *etc, depending on the person or
  people being described.*

  she's sure of herself = elle est sûre d'elle

surf *verb* ▶ 248 |
to go surfing = faire du surf

surface
1 *noun*
a surface = une surface
2 *verb*
= remonter à la surface

surfboard *noun*
a surfboard = une planche de surf

surgeon *noun* ▶ 315 |
a surgeon = un chirurgien

surgery *noun*
• to have surgery = se faire opérer (**!** + *être*)
• (*British English*) (*the place*)
  a surgery = un cabinet médical

surname *noun*
a surname = un nom de famille

surprise
1 *noun*
• (*an event, a gift*)
  a surprise = une surprise
• (*being amazed*)
  surprise = la surprise, l'étonnement
    (*masculine*)
  to take someone by surprise = prendre
    quelqu'un au dépourvu
2 *verb*
= surprendre

surprised *adjective*
= étonné/étonnée
I'm not surprised = ça ne m'étonne pas

surrender *verb*
= se rendre (**!** + *être*)

surround *verb*
= entourer
to be surrounded by trees = être
  entouré/entourée d'arbres

surroundings *noun*
the surroundings (*of a town*) = les
  environs (*masculine*)

survey *noun*
a survey = un sondage

survive *verb*
= survivre
to survive the winter = survivre à l'hiver
to survive an accident = réchapper d'un
  accident

suspect
1 *verb*
= soupçonner
she's suspected of stealing money = elle
  est soupçonnée d'avoir volé de l'argent
2 *noun*
a suspect = un suspect/une suspecte

suspicious *adjective*
= méfiant/méfiante
to be suspicious of someone = se méfier
  de quelqu'un

swan *noun*
a swan = un cygne

swap *verb*
= échanger

sweat *verb*
= transpirer

sweater *noun*
a sweater = un pull

sweatshirt *noun*
a sweatshirt = un sweatshirt

Sweden *noun* ▶ 218 |
  Sweden = la Suède

Swedish ▶ 275 |
1 *adjective*
  = suédois/suédoise
2 *noun*
  Swedish = le suédois

sweep *verb*
  = balayer

sweet
1 *adjective*
• sweet (*tasting of sugar*) = sucré/sucrée
  (*not bitter or dry*) = doux/douce
  to have a sweet tooth = aimer les
    sucreries
• (*describing a smell*) = bon/bonne (**!** *before
  the noun*)
• (*kind, gentle*) = gentil/gentille
• (*cute*) = mignon/mignonne
2 *noun* (*British English*)
  a sweet = un bonbon

swim
1 *verb*
  = nager
  to swim across a lake = traverser un lac à
    la nage
2 *noun*
  a swim = une baignade
  to go for a swim (*in the sea*) = aller se
    baigner (**!** + *être*)

swimming *noun* ▶ 248 |
  swimming = la natation

swimming pool *noun*
  a swimming pool = une piscine

swimsuit *noun*
  a swimsuit = un maillot de bain

swing
1 *verb*
• (*to move back and forth*) = se balancer
  (**!** + *être*)
  to swing on a gate = se balancer sur un
    portillon
• (*to move something back and forth*)
  = balancer
  to swing one's legs = balancer les jambes
2 *noun*
  a swing = une balançoire

Swiss ▶ 275 |
1 *adjective*
  = suisse
2 *noun*
  the Swiss = les Suisses (*masculine plural*)

switch
1 *noun*
  a switch (*for a light*) = un interrupteur
  (*on a radio, an appliance*) = un bouton
2 *verb*
  = changer
  to switch seats = changer de place
  to switch from English to French = passer
    de l'anglais au français

switch off = éteindre
  to switch off the light = éteindre la
    lumière
switch on = allumer
  to switch the radio on = allumer la radio

Switzerland *noun* ▶ 218 |
  Switzerland = la Suisse

sympathetic *adjective*
  (*showing pity*)
    = compatissant/compatissante
  (*showing understanding*)
    = compréhensif/compréhensive

syringe *noun*
  a syringe = une seringue

system *noun*
  a system = un système

Tt

table *noun*
  a table = une table

tablet *noun*
  a tablet = un comprimé

table tennis *noun* ▶ 248 |
  table tennis = le tennis de table, le ping-
    pong®

tail *noun*
  a tail = une queue

take *verb*
  ! *See the usage note on* **Talking about**
  time ▶ 356 | *for more information and*
  examples.

• (*to take hold of*) = prendre
  to take someone by the hand = prendre
    quelqu'un par la main
• (*to carry with one*) = emporter, prendre
  I took my umbrella = j'ai emporté mon
    parapluie
  I'll take the letters to Jack = je vais porter
    les lettres à Jack
• (*to accompany, to bring*) = emmener
  to take the children for a walk = emmener
    les enfants faire une promenade
  to take someone home = raccompagner
    quelqu'un
• (*to remove*) = prendre
  to take a book off the shelf = prendre un
    livre sur l'étagère
• (*to steal*) = prendre, voler
• (*to cope with, to bear*) = supporter
  he can't take the pain = il ne supporte pas
    la douleur
  I can't take any more = je n'en peux plus

T

- (*when talking about what is necessary*)
  it takes [**time** | **courage** | **patience** ...] = il faut [du temps | du courage | de la patience ...]
  it takes two hours to get to Paris = il faut deux heures pour aller à Paris
  to take a long time to do one's homework = mettre longtemps pour faire ses devoirs
  it won't take long = ça ne prendra pas longtemps
- (*to accept*) = accepter
- (*to react to*) = prendre
  he took the news badly = il a mal pris la nouvelle
- (*to use when travelling*) = prendre
  to take a taxi = prendre un taxi
  take the first turn on the right = prenez la première rue à droite
- (*to do*)
  to take exams = passer des examens
- (*to have*) = prendre
  to take [**a vacation** | **a shower** | **driving lessons** ...] = prendre [des vacances | une douche | des leçons de conduite ...]
  I don't take sugar = je ne prends pas de sucre
- (*to wear*)
  to take a size 10 (*in clothes*) = s'habiller en 38
  to take a size 5 (*in shoes*) = chausser du 38
take apart = démonter
take away
  to take away the rubbish = enlever les déchets
  to take someone away = emmener quelqu'un
take back = rapporter
  I had to take the dress back = j'ai dû rapporter la robe
take down
- (*to remove*)
  to take a poster down = enlever une affiche
  to take down a tent = démonter une tente
- (*to write down*) = noter
take hold of = prendre
take off
- (*from an airport*) = décoller
- (*to remove*) = enlever
  I took off my shoes = j'ai enlevé mes chaussures
  to take off one's clothes = se déshabiller (**!** + *être*)
take out
- (*from a box, a pocket, a bag*) = sortir
  he took a pen out of his pocket = il a sorti un stylo de sa poche
- (*from a bank account*) = retirer
  to take money out = retirer de l'argent
- (*to be nasty to*)
  to take it out on someone = s'en prendre à quelqu'un

take part
  to take part in a game = participer à un jeu
take place = avoir lieu
take up
- (*as a hobby*)
  to take up windsurfing = se mettre à faire de la planche à voile
- (*to use up*) = prendre
  to take up space = prendre de la place

talented *adjective*
= doué/douée

talk
1 *verb*
- (*to speak*) = parler
  to talk on the phone = parler au téléphone
  to talk in French = parler en français
  to talk to someone = parler à quelqu'un
  I talked to them about the trip = je leur ai parlé de la sortie
  they were talking about you = ils parlaient de toi
  to talk to oneself = parler tout seul/toute seule
- (*to chat*) = bavarder
2 *noun*
- (*a conversation*)
  a talk = une conversation
- (*about a special subject*)
  a talk (*in class*) = un exposé
  (*to a club, a group*) = une causerie
- (*discussions*)
  talks = les négociations (*feminine*)

talkative *adjective*
= bavard/bavarde

tall *adjective* ▶ 285 |
  (*describing a person*) = grand/grande
  (**!** *before the noun*)
  (*describing a building, a tree*) = haut/haute
  to be six feet tall ≈ mesurer un mètre quatre-vingts
  to get tall = grandir

tan *noun*
  a tan = un bronzage
  to get a tan = bronzer

tanned *adjective*
= bronzé/bronzée

tap
1 *noun* (*British English*)
  a tap = un robinet
  to turn the tap off = fermer le robinet
2 *verb*
  to tap on the door = frapper à la porte

tape
1 *noun*
- **a tape** (*for a tape recorder*) = une cassette
  (*for a video*) = une cassette vidéo
- (*for repairs, for sticking*)
  tape = le scotch®
2 *verb*
= enregistrer

tape recorder *noun*
a tape recorder = un magnétophone

target
1 *noun*
a target = une cible
2 *verb*
= viser

tart *noun* (*British English*)
a tart = une tarte
an apple tart = une tarte aux pommes

task *noun*
a task = une tâche

taste
1 *noun*
* (*when eating, drinking*)
a taste = un goût
* (*when talking about preferences*)
taste = le goût
to have good taste = avoir du goût
2 *verb*
* (*when describing a flavour*)
to taste good = être bon/bonne
to taste awful = avoir mauvais goût
it tastes like cabbage = ça a le goût du chou
* (*when eating, drinking*) = goûter

Taurus *noun*
Taurus = Taureau (*masculine*)

tax *noun*
a tax (*on income, profits*) = un impôt
(*on goods, property*) = une taxe

taxi *noun*
a taxi = un taxi

taxi rank (*British English*), **taxi stand**
(*US English*) *noun*
a taxi rank = une station de taxis

tea *noun*
* (*the product*)
tea = le thé
* (*a cup of tea*)
a tea = un thé
* (*British English*) (*a meal*)
tea (*in the afternoon*) = le thé
(*in the evening*) = le dîner

teach *verb*
* (*to help someone to learn skills*)
to teach someone [to read | to drive | to ride a horse ...] = apprendre à quelqu'un à [lire | conduire | monter à cheval ...]
* (*to work as a teacher*) = enseigner
to teach French to adults = enseigner le français à des adultes

teacher *noun* ▶ 315|
a teacher = un enseignant/une enseignante
(*in a primary school*) = un professeur des écoles, un instituteur/une institutrice
(*in a secondary school*) = un professeur

team *noun*
a team = une équipe

teapot *noun*
a teapot = une théière

tear¹ *verb*
* (*to cause damage to*) = déchirer
to tear a page out of a book = arracher une page d'un livre
* (*to get damaged*) = se déchirer (**!** + *être*)
tear off = détacher
tear up = déchirer

tear² *noun*
a tear = une larme
to burst into tears = fondre en larmes

tease *verb*
= taquiner

teaspoon *noun*
a teaspoon = une petite cuillère

technical *adjective*
= technique

teenager *noun*
a teenager = un adolescent/une adolescente

telephone *noun*
a telephone = un téléphone

telephone directory *noun*
a telephone directory = un annuaire

telescope *noun*
a telescope = un télescope

television *noun*
a television = un téléviseur
I saw the film on television = j'ai vu le film à la télévision

tell *verb*
* (*to say to*) = dire à
did you tell your parents? = est-ce que tu l'as dit à tes parents?
to tell someone about a problem = parler d'un problème à quelqu'un
* (*for interest, fun*) = raconter
to tell jokes = raconter des blagues✗
* (*when giving orders or instructions*)
to tell someone to leave the classroom = dire à quelqu'un de quitter la salle de classe
to tell someone not to smoke = interdire à quelqu'un de fumer
* (*to work out, to know*)
I can tell (that) she's disappointed = je vois bien qu'elle est déçue
you can tell he's lying = on voit bien qu'il ment
* (*when making distinctions*)
to tell the twin brothers apart = distinguer les jumeaux
I can't tell which is which = je n'arrive pas à les distinguer
* (*to reveal*) = répéter
don't tell anyone = ne le répète pas
tell off
to tell someone off = réprimander quelqu'un

T

temper *noun*
  to be in a temper = être en colère
  to lose one's temper = se mettre en colère

temperature *noun* ▶ **266** |
  the temperature = la température
  to have a temperature = avoir de la
    température, avoir de la fièvre

temporary *adjective*
  (*describing a job*) = temporaire
  (*describing accommodation*) = provisoire

ten *number* ▶ **187** |, ▶ **211** |
  ten = dix
  ten houses = dix maisons
  I've got ten (of them) = j'en ai dix

tennis *noun* ▶ **248** |
  tennis = le tennis

tennis court *noun*
  a tennis court = un court de tennis

tense *adjective*
  = tendu/tendue

tent *noun*
  a tent = une tente

tenth *number*
• (*in a series*) = dixième
• (*in dates*) ▶ **222** |
  the tenth of December = le dix décembre

term *noun*
  a term = un trimestre

terrible *adjective*
• (*expressing shock*) = épouvantable
• (*used for emphasis*) = affreux/affreuse

terrified *adjective*
  = terrifié/terrifiée

terror *noun*
  terror = la terreur

terrorist *noun*
  a terrorist = un terroriste/une terroriste

test
1 *verb*
• (*to try out*) = essayer, tester
• (*in exams*) = contrôler
2 *noun*
• a test = un test
  (*in school, college*) (*written*) = un contrôle
  (*oral*) = un contrôle oral
  a driving test = un examen du permis de
    conduire
• to have an eye test = se faire faire un
  examen de la vue

than
1 *preposition*
• (*in comparisons*) = que
  to be [stronger | more intelligent | faster …]
    than = être [plus fort | plus intelligent | plus
    rapide …] que
  I've got more money than you = j'ai plus
    d'argent que toi

• (*when talking about quantities*) ▶ **317** | = de
  more than half of the pupils are absent
    = plus de la moitié des élèves sont
    absents
  it's worth less than £100 = ça vaut moins
    de 100 livres
2 *conjunction*
  = que
  he's older than I am = il est plus âgé que
    moi

thank *verb*
  = remercier

thanks
1 *adverb* = merci
2 thanks to = grâce à

thank you *adverb*
  = merci
  thank you for coming = merci d'être venu
  'more wine?'—'thank you' = 'encore un
    peu de vin?'—'volontiers'

that *pronoun*
▶ **351** | *See the boxed note on* **that** *for more
information and examples.*
  what's that? = qu'est-ce que c'est?
  who's that? = qui est-ce?
  is that Louis? = c'est Louis?
  that's how they make butter = c'est
    comme ça qu'on fait le beurre
  that's not true = ce n'est pas vrai
  that's the kitchen = ça, c'est la cuisine

the *determiner*
▶ **352** | *See the boxed note on* **the** *for
detailed information and examples.*

theatre (*British English*), **theater** (*US
English*) *noun*
  a theatre = un théâtre

their *determiner*
  their = leur (+ *singular*)
  = leurs (+ *plural*)
  I don't like their house = je n'aime pas
    leur maison
  they're selling their CDs = ils vendent
    leurs disques compacts

theirs *pronoun*
  the new house is theirs = la nouvelle
    maison est à eux
  which car is theirs? = laquelle est leur
    voiture?
  my car is red but theirs is green = ma
    voiture est rouge mais la leur est verte
  our parents are younger than theirs = nos
    parents sont plus jeunes que les leurs

  ! *Note that, when comparing objects,
  people etc., one of the following
  translations—*le leur, la leur *or* les
  leurs—*will be used. To know which one to
  use, find out whether the object, person
  etc. being described is masculine
  singular, feminine singular or just plural.*

that

As a determiner

In French, determiners agree with the noun that follows; so **that** is translated as follows:

ce or **cet**	+	*masculine singular noun*	**ce** monsieur, **cet** homme
cette	+	*feminine singular noun*	**cette** femme
ces	+	*noun plural*	**ces** livres, **ces** histoires

Note, however, that the above translations are also used for the English **this** (plural *these*). So when it is necessary to insist on **that** as opposed to another or others of the same sort, the adverbial tag **-là** is added to the noun:

    *I prefer **that** colour*   = je préfère **cette** couleur**-là**

As a pronoun

- In French, pronouns reflect the gender and number of the noun they are standing for.

  So **that** (meaning *that one*) is translated by

celui-là	*for a masculine noun*
celle-là	*for a feminine noun*

  and **those** (meaning *those ones*) is translated by

ceux-là	*for a masculine noun*
celles-là	*for a feminine noun*

    all the dresses are nice but   = toutes les robes sont jolies mais
    *I like **that** best*   je préfère **celle-là**

- When used as a relative pronoun, **that** is translated by **qui** when it is the subject of the verb and by **que** when it is the object:

    *the man **that** stole the car*   = l'homme **qui** a volé la voiture
    *the film **that** I saw*   = le film **que** j'ai vu

  Remember that in the present perfect and past perfect tenses, the past participle agrees with the noun that **que** is referring back to:

    *the girl **that** I met*   = la fille **que** j'ai rencontrée
    *the apples **that** I bought* = les pommes **que** j'ai achetées

- When that is used as a relative pronoun with a preposition, it is translated by **lequel** when standing for a masculine singular noun, by **laquelle** when standing for a feminine singular noun, by **lesquels** when standing for a masculine plural noun, and by **lesquelles** when standing for a feminine plural noun:

    the chair that I was sitting on   = la chaise sur **laquelle** j'étais assis
    the children that I bought the   = les enfants pour **lesquels** j'ai acheté les livres
    books for

  If the preposition would normally be translated by **à** in French (**to**, **at** etc), the translation of the whole (*preposition + relative pronoun*) will be:

auquel	*for a masculine noun*
à laquelle	*for a feminine noun*
auxquels	*for a masculine plural noun*
auxquelles	*for a feminine plural noun*

    *the girls **that** I was talking to*   = les filles **auxquelles** je parlais

  If the preposition used would normally be translated by **de** in French (**of**, **from** etc), the translation of the whole (*preposition + relative pronoun*) will be **dont** in all cases:

    *the people **that** I've talked about* = les personnes **dont** j'ai parlé

As a conjunction

When used as a conjunction, **that** can almost always be translated by **que** (**qu'** before a vowel or mute h):

  *she said **that** she would do it*   = elle a dit **qu'**elle le ferait

T

the

- In French the definite article, like determiners, agrees with the noun that follows; so **the** is translated as follows:

le or **l'** +	*masculine singular noun*	**le** chien, **l'**ami
la or **l'** +	*feminine singular noun*	**la** chaise, **l'**amie
les +	*masculine plural noun*	**les** hommes, **les** avions
les +	*feminine plural noun*	**les** femmes, **les** autos

- When **the** is used after a preposition in English, the two words (*preposition* + **the**) are often translated by one word in French. If the preposition would normally be translated by **de** in French (**of**, **about**, **from** etc), the *preposition* + **the** is translated according to whether the noun is masculine or feminime, singular or plural:

	le or **l'** + *masculine singular noun*	**du** chien, **de l'**ami
de +	**la** or **l'** + *feminine singular noun*	**de la** chaise, **de l'**amie
	les + *masculine plural noun*	**des** hommes, **des** avions
	les + *feminine plural noun*	**des** femmes, **des** autos

If the preposition would usually be translated by **à** (**at**, **to** etc) the *preposition* + **the** is translated according to whether the noun is masculine or feminine, singular or plural:

	le or **l'** + *masculine singular noun*	**au** chien, **à l'**ami
à +	**la** or **l'** + *feminine singular noun*	**à la** chaise, **à l'**amie
	les + *masculine plural noun*	**aux** hommes, **aux** avions
	les + *feminine plural noun*	**aux** femmes, **aux** autos

- Other than this, there are few problems in translating **the** into French. The following cases are, however, worth remembering as not following exactly the pattern of the English:

the good, the poor, the unemployed	= **les** bons, **les** pauvres, **les** chômeurs
Charles the First, Elizabeth the Second	= Charles 1er (Premier), Elizabeth II (Deux)
she's the actress of the year	= c'est **la plus grande** actrice de l'année
the Tudors, the Batemans, the Kennedys	= **les** Tudor, **les** Bateman, **les** Kennedy
the sporting event of the year	= **le grand** événement sportif de l'année
it's the film to see	= c'est **le** film à voir

▶ This dictionary contains usage notes on such topics as **days of the week**, **illnesses**, **the human body**, and **musical instruments**, many of which use **the**; for the index to these notes see ▶ **400**].

---

them *pronoun*
▶ **353**] *See the boxed note on* them *for detailed information and examples.*

themselves *pronoun*
- (*when used as a reflexive pronoun*)
  they want to enjoy themselves = ils/elles veulent s'amuser
  they didn't hurt themselves = ils/elles ne se sont pas fait mal
- (*when used for emphasis*)
  they said it themselves = ils l'ont dit eux-mêmes/elles l'ont dit elles-mêmes
  they did it all by themselves = ils l'ont fait tout seuls/elles l'ont fait toutes seules

  ! *Remember that, when talking about mixed groups, the masculine form* eux-mêmes *is used to translate* themselves.

then *adverb*
- (*at that point in time*) = alors, à ce moment-là
  I was living in Paris then = j'habitais alors Paris

we saw each other a lot then = on se voyait beaucoup à ce moment-là
  from then on = à partir de ce moment-là
- (*after, next*) = puis, ensuite
  I went for a drink and then had dinner = je suis allé prendre un pot✳ et puis j'ai dîné

there
1 *pronoun*
  there is a problem = il y a un problème
  there aren't any shops = il n'y a pas de magasins
  there was no room = il n'y avait pas de place
  there will be a lot of people = il y aura beaucoup de monde
2 *adverb*
- (*when talking about location*) = là
  who's there? = qui est là?
  the train wasn't there = le train n'était pas là
  go over there = va là-bas
  when do we get there? = quand est-ce qu'on arrive?
  they don't go there very often = ils n'y vont pas très souvent

---

✳ *in informal situations*

them

- When used as a direct object pronoun, referring to people, animals or things, **them** is translated by **les**:

I know them	= je **les** connais
I don't know them	= je ne **les** connais pas
do I know them?	= est-ce que je **les** connais?

Note that the object pronoun normally comes before the verb in French and that, in tenses like the present perfect and past perfect, the past participle agrees with the direct object pronoun:

*he's seen **them***	= il **les** a vus
	(**them** *being masculine or of mixed gender*)
	= il **les** a vues
	(**them** *being all feminine gender*)
*he hasn't seen **them***	= il ne **les** a pas vus
	= il ne **les** a pas vues
*has he seen **them**?*	= est-ce qu'il **les** a vus?
	= est-ce qu'il **les** a vues?

- In imperatives, the direct object pronoun is translated by **les** and comes after the verb:

*catch **them**!*	= attrape-**les**!*
*take **them**!*	= prenez-**les**!*

But in negative commands, **les** comes before the verb:

*don't take **them**!*	= ne **les** prenez pas!
*don't hit **them**!*	= ne **les** frappe pas!

- When used as an indirect object pronoun, **them** is translated by **leur**:

*I gave it **to them***	= je le **leur** ai donné
*I didn't give it **to them***	= je ne le **leur** ai pas donné
*did I give it **to them**?*	= est-ce que je le **leur** ai donné?

- In imperatives, the indirect object pronoun is translated by **leur** and comes after the verb:

*write **to them**!*	= écris-**leur**!*
*say it **to them**!*	= dis-le-**leur**!*

But in negative commands, **leur** comes before the verb:

*don't show it **to them**!*	= ne le **leur** montre pas!

- After prepositions and the verb **to be**, the translation is **eux** for masculine or mixed gender and **elles** for feminine gender:

*he did it **for them***	= il l'a fait **pour eux**
	(**them** *being masculine or of mixed gender*)
	= il l'a fait pour **elles**
	(**them** *being all feminine gender*)
*it's **them***	= ce sont **eux**
	ce sont **elles**

* Note the hyphen(s).

Note that the entries for **her**, **him**, **me** and **us** are modelled in this note.

T

- (*when drawing attention*)
  there's [the sea | my watch | Natalie ...] = voilà [la mer | ma montre | Natalie ...]
  there they are = les voilà
  there you are, there you go = et voilà

therefore *adverb*
= donc, par conséquent

these
1 *determiner*
  these = ces

  these books aren't mine = ces livres ne sont pas à moi
2 *pronoun*
  what are these? = qu'est-ce que c'est?
  these are your things = ce sont tes affaires
  these are my friends = ce sont mes amis
  I prefer THESE = je préfère ceux-ci/celles-ci

  ! *See the note on* **this** *for further information about the use of* **-ci**.

they pronoun
  they = ils/elles
  they'll be there too = ils/elles seront là aussi
  there they are! = les voilà!
  they're intelligent girls = ce sont des filles intelligentes
  that's how they make yogurt = c'est comme ça qu'on fait le yaourt

  ! Note that on is used to translate they when talking in an impersonal or vague way about people.

thick adjective
  = épais/épaisse

thief noun
  a thief = un voleur/une voleuse

thigh noun ▶ 201 |
  the thigh = la cuisse

thin adjective
  = mince
  to get thin = maigrir

thing noun
• a thing = une chose, un truc
  I've got things to do = j'ai des choses à faire
  that was a stupid thing to do = c'était stupide de faire ça
  the best thing would be to call him = le mieux serait de l'appeler
  I can't hear a thing = je n'entends rien
• (belongings)
  things = les affaires (feminine)

think verb
• (when talking about opinions) = penser, croire
  what do you think of it? = qu'est-ce que tu en penses?
  I think it's unfair = je pense que c'est injuste
  'will they come?'—'I don't think so' = 'est-ce qu'ils vont venir?'—'je ne crois pas'
  who do you think will win? = qui va gagner à ton avis?
• (to concentrate on an idea) = réfléchir
  think hard before answering = réfléchis bien avant de répondre
• (to remember)
  I can't think of his name = je ne me rappelle plus son nom
• (to take into account, to have in mind)
  to think of someone = penser à quelqu'un
  I thought of you when I saw the dress = j'ai pensé à toi quand j'ai vu la robe
  we didn't think of closing the window = nous n'avons pas pensé à fermer la fenêtre
• (to have vague plans to)
  to be thinking of changing jobs = envisager de changer de travail
• (to have an idea about)
  to think of a solution = trouver une solution

third
1 adjective
  = troisième
2 noun
• (in a series)
  the third = le troisième/la troisième
• (in dates) ▶ 222 |
  the third of June = le trois juin
• (when talking about quantities) ▶ 317 |
  a third of the population = un tiers de la population
3 adverb
  = troisième
  to come third = arriver troisième

thirsty adjective
  to be thirsty = avoir soif
  I'm very thirsty = j'ai très soif

thirteen number ▶ 187 |, ▶ 211 |
  thirteen = treize

thirteenth number
• (in a series) = treizième
• (in dates) ▶ 222 |
  Friday the thirteenth = vendredi treize

thirty number ▶ 187 |, ▶ 211 |
  thirty = trente

this
1 determiner
  this = ce/cette (**!** cet + masculine + vowel or mute h)
  I like this garden = j'aime bien ce jardin
  do you know this place? = est-ce que tu connais cet endroit?
  who is this woman? = qui est cette femme?
  I prefer THIS hotel to the others = je préfère cet hôtel-ci aux autres

  ! Note that, since the translations for this and that are the same, the tag -ci must be added to the noun and pronoun if a clear distinction is to be made.

2 pronoun
  what's this? = qu'est-ce que c'est?
  who's this? = qui est-ce?
  this is the kitchen = voici la cuisine
  this is my sister = voici ma sœur
  this isn't the right address = ce n'est pas la bonne adresse
  how much is THIS? = combien coûte celui-ci/celle-ci?

those
1 determiner
  those = ces
  those books are yours = ces livres sont à toi
2 pronoun
  what are those? = qu'est-ce que c'est?
  those are my letters = ce sont mes lettres
  those are my cousins = ce sont mes cousins
  I prefer THOSE = je préfère ceux-là/celles-là
  ▶ 351 | See the boxed note on that for further information about the use of -là.

though conjunction
= bien que
though it's expensive, it's still a good buy
= bien que ce soit cher, ça reste un bon
achat
! Note that the subjunctive is used after
bien que.

thought noun
a thought = une pensée

thousand number
one thousand, a thousand = mille
four thousand pounds = quatre mille
livres
about a thousand people = un millier de
personnes

thread noun
thread = le fil

threat noun
a threat = une menace

threaten verb
= menacer

three number ▶ 187 ▮, ▶ 211 ▮
three = trois
three sisters = trois sœurs
I've got three (of them) = j'en ai trois

throat noun ▶ 201 ▮
the throat = la gorge

through
! Often through occurs in combinations
with verbs, for example: go through, let
through, read through etc. To find the
correct translations for this type of verb,
look up the separate dictionary entries at
go, let, read etc.

preposition
• (from one side to the other) = à travers
to see through the fog = voir à travers le
brouillard
to drive through the desert = traverser le
désert (en voiture)
• (via, by way of)
to go through the town centre = passer par
le centre-ville
to look through a window = regarder par
une fenêtre
• (past)
to go through a red light = brûler un feu
rouge
to go through customs = passer la douane
• (when talking about time)
right through the day = toute la journée
from Friday through to Sunday = de
vendredi jusqu'à dimanche
open April through September (US
English) = ouvert d'avril à fin septembre

throw verb
= lancer
to throw stones at someone = lancer des
pierres à quelqu'un
throw me the ball = lance-moi le ballon
to throw a book on the floor = jeter un
livre par terre

throw away, throw out = jeter

thumb noun ▶ 201 ▮
the thumb = le pouce

thunder noun
thunder = le tonnerre

thunderstorm noun
a thunderstorm = un orage

Thursday noun ▶ 222 ▮
Thursday = jeudi (masculine)

ticket noun
a ticket (for a plane, a train, a film, an
event) = un billet
(for a bus, the underground, a locker) = un
ticket

tickle verb
= chatouiller

tide noun
the tide = la marée
the tide is out = c'est la marée basse
the tide is coming in = la marée monte

tidy adjective
(describing a place, a desk) = bien
rangé/rangée
(describing a person) = ordonné/ordonnée
tidy up = ranger

tie
1 verb
= attacher
to tie a dog to a tree = attacher un chien à
un arbre
to tie a parcel (up) with string = ficeler un
paquet
2 noun
• (worn with a shirt)
a tie = une cravate
• (in sport)
a tie = un match nul
tie up = ligoter

tiger noun
a tiger = un tigre

tight adjective
= serré/serrée

tights noun (British English)
tights = un collant (singular)

till¹ ▶ until

till² noun
a till = une caisse

timber noun
timber = le bois (de construction)

time noun
• **time** = le temps
I don't have time to go there = je n'ai pas
le temps d'y aller
we haven't seen them for some time = ça
fait un moment qu'on ne les a pas vus
a long time ago = il y a longtemps

T

Talking about time

▶ For time by the clock, ▶ **211 |**; for days of the week, months, and dates, ▶ **222 |**.

How long?

Note the various ways of translating **take** into French:

how long does it take?	= combien de temps faut-il?
it took me a week	= il m'a fallu une semaine / cela m'a pris une semaine
it'll take at least a year	= il faudra au moins un an
it'll only take a minute	= ça ne prendra qu'une minute

Use **en** for **in** when expressing the time something took or will take:

*he did it **in** an hour*	= il l'a fait **en** une heure

The commonest translation of **for** in the 'how long' sense is **pendant**:

*I worked in a factory **for** a year*	= j'ai travaillé en usine **pendant** un an

But use **pour** to translate **for** when the length of time is seen as being still to come:

*we're here **for** a month*	= nous sommes là **pour** un mois

And use **depuis** to translate **for** when the action began in the past and is still going on:

*she has been here **for** a week*	= elle est ici **depuis** une semaine
*I haven't seen her **for** years*	= je ne l'ai pas vue **depuis** des années

When?

Use **dans** for **in** when something is seen as happening in the future:

*I'll be there **in** an hour*	= j'y serai **dans** une heure
***in** three weeks' time*	= **dans** trois semaines
when did it happen?	= quand est-ce que c'est arrivé?
a month ago	= il y a un mois
a week ago yesterday	= il y a eu huit jours hier
when will you see him?	= quand est-ce que tu le verras?
***in** a few days*	= **dans** quelques jours
a month from tomorrow	= **dans** un mois demain
when you see him, tell him to call me	= quand tu le verras,* dis-lui de m'appeler

How often?

how often does it happen?	= cela arrive tous les combien?
every year	= tous les ans
five times a day	= cinq fois par jour
once every three months	= une fois tous les trois mois

How much an hour (etc)?

*how much do you get **an** hour?*	= combien gagnez-vous **de** l'heure?
*to be paid $20 **an** hour*	= être payé 20 dollars **de** l'heure
*to be paid **by** the hour*	= être payé **à** l'heure
*how much do you get **a** week?*	= combien gagnez-vous **par** semaine?
*$3,000 **a** month*	= 3 000 dollars **par** mois

* Note that, when talking about future time, the future tense of the verb is used after **quand**.

• *(when talking about a specific hour or period of time)*
the time = l'heure *(feminine)*
what's the time?, what time is it? = quelle heure est-il?
what time does the film start? = à quelle heure commence le film?

to arrive on time = arriver à l'heure
in [five days' | a week's | six months' ...] **time** = dans [cinq jours | une semaine | six mois ...]
this time last year = il y a exactement un an
by this time next week = d'ici la semaine prochaine
it's time we left = il est temps de partir

- (*a moment*)
  a time = un moment
  at times = par moments
  at the right time = au bon moment
  this is no time to argue = ce n'est pas le
    moment de se disputer
  any time now = d'un moment à l'autre
  for the time being = pour le moment
- (*a period in the past*)
  a time = une époque
  they didn't know each other at the time
    = ils ne se connaissaient pas à l'époque
- (*an experience*)
  to have a good time = bien s'amuser
    (**!** + *être*)
  to have a hard time concentrating = avoir
    du mal à se concentrer
- (*an occasion*)
  the first time we met = la première fois
    que nous nous sommes rencontrés
  from time to time = de temps en temps
- (*when comparing*)
  three times more expensive = trois fois
    plus cher
  ten times quicker = dix fois plus rapide

timetable *noun*
- (*for trains, buses*)
  a timetable = un horaire
- (*in school, at work*)
  a timetable = un emploi du temps

tin *noun*
- (*the metal*)
  tin = l'étain (*masculine*)
- (*British English*) (*a can*)
  a tin = une boîte (de conserve)
  a tin of beans = une boîte de haricots

tin opener *noun* (*British English*)
  a tin opener = un ouvre-boîtes

tiny *adjective*
  = tout petit/toute petite

tip *noun*
- (*the point, the end*)
  the tip (*of a pen, a stick, a shoe*) = la
    pointe
  (*of the finger, nose, tongue*) = le bout
  on the tips of one's toes = sur la pointe
    des pieds
- (*given in a hotel, a restaurant*)
  a tip = un pourboire
- (*a piece of advice*)
  a tip = un conseil

tire *noun* (*US English*)
  a tire = un pneu

tired *adjective*
- (*needing rest*) = fatigué/fatiguée
  to get tired = se fatiguer (**!** + *être*)
- (*needing a change*)
  I'm tired of being a waitress = j'en ai assez
    d'être serveuse

tiring *adjective*
  = fatigant/fatigante

tissue *noun*
  a tissue = un mouchoir en papier

to *preposition* ▶ 211 |
▶ 358 | *See the boxed note on* **to**. *There are
many adjectives like* **mean**, **nice**, **rude** *etc
and verbs like* **belong**, **write** *etc which involve
the use of* **to**. *For translations, look up the
adjective entries at* **mean**, **nice**, **rude** *or the
verb entries at* **belong**, **write**.

toast *noun*
  toast = le pain grillé
  a piece of toast = une tranche de pain
    grillé

toaster *noun*
  a toaster = un grille-pain

today *adverb* ▶ 356 |
  = aujourd'hui

toe *noun* ▶ 201 |
  the toe = l'orteil (*masculine*)

toffee *noun*
  toffee = le caramel

together *adverb*
  = ensemble

toilet *noun*
  a toilet = des toilettes (*feminine plural*)

toilet paper *noun*
  toilet paper = le papier hygiénique

tomato *noun*
  a tomato = une tomate

tomorrow *adverb* ▶ 356 |
  = demain

tongue *noun* ▶ 201 |
  the tongue = la langue

tonight *adverb*
  (*this evening*) = ce soir
  (*during the night*) = cette nuit

too *adverb*
- (*also*) = aussi
  I'm going too = j'y vais aussi
- (*more than is necessary or desirable*)
  = trop
  it's too [big | dear | far ...] = c'est trop [grand |
    cher | loin ...]
  there were too many people = il y avait
    trop de monde
  I ate too much = j'ai trop mangé

tool *noun*
  a tool = un outil

tooth *noun* ▶ 201 |
  a tooth = une dent
  a set of false teeth = un dentier

toothache *noun* ▶ 266 |
  to have a toothache = avoir mal aux dents

toothbrush *noun*
  a toothbrush = une brosse à dents

toothpaste *noun*
  toothpaste = le dentifrice

T

to

▶ This dictionary contains usage notes on such topics as **The clock**, **Length and weight measurements**, **Games and sports** etc. Many of these use the preposition **to**. For the index to these notes **▶ 400 |**.

As a preposition

● When **to** is used as a preposition with verbs of movement (*go*, *travel* etc), it is often translated by **à** (*à Paris*, *à Londres*), but remember to use **en** with feminine countries (*en France*) and **au** with masculine countries (*au Portugal*).

Remember when using **à** in French that **à** + **le** always becomes **au**:

to the office	= **au** bureau

and **à** + **les** always becomes **aux**:

to the shops	= **aux** magasins

● When **to** is used as a preposition with verbs such as *speak*, *give*, *say* etc, it is usually translated by **à**:

give the book to Jane	= donne le livre **à** Jane
I'll speak to the headmistress	= je vais parler **à** la directrice
she said it to my father	= elle l'a dit **à** mon père
show it to the policeman	= montre-le **à** l'agent
I pointed it out to the stewardess	= je l'ai signalé **à** l'hôtesse
give the ball to the little boy	= donne le ballon **au*** petit garçon
we gave it to the children	= nous l'avons donné **aux*** enfants

* Remember that **à** + **le** = **au** and **à** + **les** = **aux**

● When **to** is used as a preposition with personal pronouns (*me*, *you*, *him*, *her*, *us*, *them*), the two words (*preposition* + *pronoun*) are translated by **me/te/lui/lui/nous/vous/leur**:

she gave it to them	= elle le **leur** a donné
I'll say it to her	= je vais le **lui** dire
will you lend it to me?	= est-ce que tu **me** le prêtes?

As part of an infinitive

● When **to** forms the infinitive of a verb taken alone, it needs no translation:

to go	= aller
to sing	= chanter

However, when **to** is used as part of an infinitive giving the meaning **in order to**, it is translated by **pour**:

he's gone into town to buy a shirt	= il est parti en ville **pour acheter** une chemise
I need it to do my homework	= j'en ai besoin **pour faire** mes devoirs

● **to** is also used as part of an infinitive after certain adjectives: **easy to read** etc. Here **to** is usually translated by **à**:

her writing is easy to read	= son écriture est facile **à** lire
his accent is difficult to understand	= son accent est dur **à** comprendre

However, when the infinitive has an object, **to** is usually translated by **de**:

it's easy to lose one's way	= il est facile **de** perdre son chemin
it's difficult to work at night	= c'est difficile **de** travailler la nuit

▶ **to** is also used as part of an infinitive after certain verbs: *she told me* **to** *wash my hands*, *I'll help him* **to** *tidy the room* etc. Here the translation, usually either **à** or **de**, depends on the verb used in French. To find the correct translation, consult the appropriate verb entry: **tell**, **help** etc.

---

top
1 *noun*
● (*the highest part*)
  the top of the hill = le sommet de la colline
  the top of the stairs = le haut de l'escalier

at the top of [the page | the stairs | street ...] = en haut [de la page | de l'escalier | de la rue ...]
● (*a cover, a lid*)
  a top (*on a bottle*) = un bouchon
  (*on a pan*) = un couvercle
  (*on a pen*) = un capuchon

- (*the highest level*)
  to get to the top = réussir
  to be at the top of the class = être premier/première de la classe
2 *adjective*
  the top [shelf | drawer | button ...] = [l'étagère | le tiroir | le bouton ...] du haut

torch *noun* (*British English*)
  a torch = une lampe de poche

torn *adjective*
  = déchiré/déchirée

tortoise *noun*
  a tortoise = une tortue

total
1 *noun*
  a total = un total
2 *adjective*
  = total/totale

touch
1 *verb*
- (*with one's hand*) = toucher
- (*to interfere with*) = toucher à
  don't touch my things = ne touche pas à mes affaires
2 *noun*
  to [be | get | stay ...] **in touch with someone** = [être | se mettre | rester ...] en contact avec quelqu'un

tough *adjective*
- (*not soft, not sensitive*) = coriace
- (*rough*) = dur/dure
  a tough area = un quartier dur
- (*difficult*) = difficile
- (*severe*)
  a tough law = une loi sévère

tour
1 *noun*
- (*by a team, a band, a theatre group*)
  a tour = une tournée
  on tour = en tournée
- (*by tourists, pupils, visitors*)
  a tour = une visite
  to go on a tour of the castle = visiter le château
2 *verb*
  to go touring = faire du tourisme
  to tour the United States = visiter les États-Unis

tourism *noun*
  tourism = le tourisme

tourist *noun*
  a tourist = un touriste/une touriste

tourist office *noun*
  a tourist office (*local*) = un syndicat d'initiative

toward(s) *preposition*
- (*when talking about place, time*) = vers

towards the east = vers l'est
  towards evening = vers le soir
- (*when talking about attitudes*) = envers
  to be friendly towards someone = se montrer cordial envers quelqu'un

towel *noun*
  a towel = une serviette

tower *noun*
  a tower = une tour

tower block *noun* (*British English*)
  a tower block = une tour d'habitation

town *noun*
  a town = une ville
  to go into town = aller en ville

town hall *noun*
  a town hall = une mairie

toy *noun*
  a toy = un jouet

track *noun*
- (*a path*)
  a track = un sentier, un chemin
- (*for sports*)
  a track = une piste
- (*the rails*)
  the track(s) = la voie ferrée
- (*left by a person, an animal, a car*)
  tracks = des traces (*feminine*)

tracksuit *noun*
  a tracksuit = un survêtement

trade *noun*
- **trade** = le commerce
- **a trade** = un métier

tradition *noun*
  a tradition = une tradition

traffic *noun*
  traffic = la circulation

traffic jam *noun*
  a traffic jam = un embouteillage, un bouchon

traffic lights *noun*
  traffic lights = les feux (*masculine*)

train
1 *noun*
  a train = un train
  the train to Paris = le train à destination de Paris
2 *verb*
- (*to teach, to prepare*)
  to train employees = former des employés
  to train athletes = entraîner des athlètes
- (*to learn a job*)
  to train as a doctor = suivre une formation de médecin
  she trained as a teacher = elle a reçu une formation d'enseignante
- (*for a sporting event*) = s'entraîner
  (**!** + *être*)

T

trainer noun (British English)
a trainer (high) = une basket
(low) = un tennis

training course noun
a training course = un stage de formation

tramp noun
a tramp = un clochard/une clocharde

translate verb
= traduire

translator noun ▶ 315
a translator = un traducteur/une
traductrice

transport, **transportation** (US
English) noun
transport = le transport
a means of transport = un moyen de
transport

trap noun
a trap = un piège
to set a trap for someone = tendre un
piège à quelqu'un

trash noun (US English)
trash = les ordures (feminine plural)

trash can noun (US English)
a trash can = une poubelle

travel verb
= voyager
to travel abroad = aller à l'étranger
to travel a long way = faire beaucoup de
chemin

travel agency noun ▶ 315
a travel agency = une agence de voyages

traveller (British English), **traveler** (US
English) noun
a traveller = un voyageur/une voyageuse

traveller's cheque (British English),
traveler's check (US English) noun
a traveller's cheque = un chèque-voyage

tray noun
a tray = un plateau

treat verb
• (to deal with, to behave with) = traiter
to treat someone badly = mal se conduire
envers quelqu'un
• (to pay for)
to treat someone to a glass of wine
= payer un verre de vin à quelqu'un

treatment noun
treatment = le traitement
to receive treatment = être sous
traitement

tree noun
a tree = un arbre

× in informal situations

tremble verb
= trembler

trendy adjective
= branché/branchée×

trial noun
a trial = un procès
to go on trial = passer en jugement

triangle noun
a triangle = un triangle

trick
1 noun
• (a joke)
a trick = un tour, une blague×
to play a trick on someone = jouer un
tour à quelqu'un
• (a means of deceiving)
a trick = une combine
• (to entertain)
a trick = un tour
2 verb
= duper, rouler×

trip
1 noun
a trip (abroad) = un voyage
(a day out) = une excursion, une sortie
to be on a business trip = être en voyage
d'affaires
2 verb
to trip (up) = trébucher
to trip someone (up) = faire trébucher
quelqu'un

trouble noun
• (difficulties)
trouble = les ennuis (masculine plural)
to be in trouble = avoir des ennuis
to get someone into trouble = créer des
ennuis à quelqu'un
to make trouble = faire des histoires×
• (an effort)
to take the trouble to check = se donner la
peine de vérifier
to go to a lot of trouble = se donner
beaucoup de mal

trousers noun
trousers = un pantalon (singular)

trout noun
a trout = une truite

truck noun
a truck = un camion

truck driver noun ▶ 315
a truck driver = un routier

true adjective
= vrai/vraie
is it true that he's leaving? = est-ce que
c'est vrai qu'il part?
to come true = se réaliser (! + être)

trumpet noun ▶ 290
a trumpet = une trompette

trunk *noun*
- (*of a tree*)
  a trunk = un tronc
- (*of an elephant*)
  a trunk = une trompe
- (*US English*) (*in a car*)
  the trunk = le coffre

trust *verb*
- (*to believe*) = se fier à (**!** + *être*)
  to trust a friend = se fier à un ami
  I don't trust them = je me méfie d'eux
- (*to rely on*) = faire confiance à
  you can't trust him = on ne peut pas lui faire confiance

truth *noun*
  the truth = la vérité

try
1 *verb*
- **to try** = essayer
  to try [to understand | to come | to forget …] = essayer [de comprendre | de venir | d'oublier …]
  try phoning him = essaie de lui téléphoner
- (*to test*) = essayer
  to try (out) a recipe = essayer une recette
  to try (on) a pair of jeans = essayer un jean
- (*to taste*) = goûter
- (*in court*) = juger
2 *noun*
  to score a try = marquer un essai

T-shirt *noun*
  a T-shirt = un T-shirt

tube *noun*
- **a tube** = un tube
- (*British English*) (*the underground*)
  the tube = le métro

Tuesday *noun* ▶ **222**
  Tuesday = mardi (*masculine*)

tuna *noun*
  tuna = le thon

tunnel *noun*
  a tunnel = un tunnel

turkey *noun*
  a turkey = une dinde

Turkey *noun* ▶ **218**
  Turkey = la Turquie

turn
1 *verb*
- (*to move one's body*) = se retourner
  (**!** + *être*)
  to turn one's face toward(s) the sun = tourner le visage vers le soleil
- (*to change direction*) = tourner
  to turn right = tourner à droite
  to turn the corner = tourner au coin de la rue
- (*to twist*) = tourner
  to turn the handle = tourner la poignée

- (*to change*)
  to turn the bedroom into an office = transformer la chambre en bureau
  to turn someone into a criminal = faire un criminel de quelqu'un
- (*to become*)
  to turn into a butterfly = se transformer en papillon
  to turn red = rougir
2 *noun*
- (*a bend*)
  a turn = un tournant, un virage
- (*in games*)
  a turn = un tour
  whose turn is it? = c'est à qui le tour?
turn around, turn round
- (*to face the other way*) (*if it's a person*) = se retourner (**!** + *être*)
  (*if it's a car*) = faire demi-tour
  to turn the table around = tourner la table dans l'autre sens
- (*to go round and round*) = tourner
turn away = se détourner (**!** + *être*)
turn back = faire demi-tour
turn down
- (*to lower*) = baisser
  to turn down the radio = baisser la radio
- (*to reject*) = refuser
  to turn someone down = refuser quelqu'un
turn off
  to turn the oven off = éteindre le four
  to turn off the light = éteindre la lumière
  to turn the tap off = fermer le robinet
turn on = allumer
  to turn on the TV = allumer la télévision
  to turn the tap on = ouvrir le robinet
turn out
  to turn out all right (in the end) = s'arranger (**!** + *être*)
  to turn out to be easy = se révéler facile
turn over
- (*to roll over*) = se retourner (**!** + *être*)
- **to turn over the page** = tourner la page
turn up
- (*to show up*) = arriver
- (*to increase*)
  to turn up the heating = augmenter le chauffage
  to turn the music up = mettre la musique plus fort

turtle *noun*
- **a (sea) turtle** = une tortue marine
- (*US English*) (*a tortoise*)
  a turtle = une tortue

TV *noun*
  a TV = une télévision, une télé✱

twelfth *number*
- (*in a series*) = douzième
- (*in dates*) ▶ **222**
  the twelfth of July = le douze juillet

twelve *number* ▶ **187**, ▶ **211**
  twelve = douze
  twelve pupils = douze élèves
  I've got twelve (of them) = j'en ai douze

twenty number ▶ 187 |, ▶ 211 |
twenty = vingt

twice adverb
= deux fois
twice as many people = deux fois plus de monde
twice as much time = deux fois plus de temps

twin
1 noun
a twin = un jumeau/une jumelle
2 adjective
a twin brother = un frère jumeau
a twin sister = une sœur jumelle

twist verb
• (to bend out of shape) = tordre
• (to injure) ▶ 266 |
to twist one's ankle = se tordre la cheville

two number ▶ 187 |, ▶ 211 |
two = deux
two brothers = deux frères
I've got two (of them) = j'en ai deux

type
1 noun
a type = un type, un genre
this type of [person | book | building …] = ce genre de [personne | livre | bâtiment …]
he's not my type = ce n'est pas mon genre
2 verb
= taper (à la machine)

typewriter noun
a typewriter = une machine à écrire

typical adjective
= typique

typist noun ▶ 315 |
a typist = un dactylo/une dactylo

tyre noun (British English)
a tyre = un pneu

U u

ugly adjective
= laid/laide

umbrella noun
an umbrella = un parapluie

unbelievable adjective
= incroyable

uncle noun
an uncle = un oncle

uncomfortable adjective
• (awkward) = pénible
to make someone (feel) uncomfortable = mettre quelqu'un mal à l'aise

• (describing shoes, seats) = inconfortable
(describing heat, conditions) = pénible

unconscious adjective
= sans connaissance
to knock someone unconscious = assommer quelqu'un

under preposition
• under = sous
to hide under the bed = se cacher sous le lit
I found the newspaper under it = j'ai trouvé le journal dessous
• (less than)
to earn under three pounds an hour = gagner moins de trois livres de l'heure
children under five = les enfants de moins de cinq ans

underground noun (British English)
the underground = le métro

underline verb
= souligner

underneath
1 adverb
= en dessous
I want to see what's underneath = je veux voir ce qu'il y a dessous
2 preposition
= au-dessous de, sous
underneath the building = au-dessous du bâtiment

underpants noun
underpants = un slip (singular)

understand verb
= comprendre
I can't understand what they're saying = je ne comprends pas ce qu'ils disent
to make oneself understood = se faire comprendre

understanding adjective
= compréhensif/compréhensive

underwater adverb
= sous l'eau

underwear noun
underwear = les sous-vêtements (masculine plural)

undo verb
= défaire
to undo a button = défaire un bouton

undress verb
= se déshabiller (**!** + être)

uneasy adjective
= inquiet/inquiète

unemployed adjective
to be unemployed = être au chômage, être sans emploi

unemployment noun
unemployment = le chômage

unfair *adjective*
= injuste

unfortunately *adverb*
= malheureusement

unfriendly *adjective*
(*describing a person*) = peu amical/peu
  amicale
(*describing a place*)
  = inhospitalier/inhospitalière

ungrateful *adjective*
= ingrat/ingrate

unhappy *adjective*
• (*sad*) = malheureux/malheureuse
• (*not satisfied*) = mécontent/mécontente

unhealthy *adjective*
(*describing a way of life, food*)
  = malsain/malsaine
(*describing a person*) = maladif/maladive
(*describing conditions*) = insalubre

uniform *noun*
a uniform = un uniforme

union *noun*
a union = un syndicat

unique *adjective*
= unique

United Kingdom *noun* ▶ 218|
the United Kingdom = le Royaume-Uni

United States (of America) *noun*
▶ 218|
the United States (of America) = les États-
  Unis (d'Amérique)
  ! *Note that* États *is masculine plural.*

universe *noun*
a universe = un univers

university *noun*
a university = une université

unkind *adjective*
to be unkind (*describing a person, an
  action*) = ne pas être très gentil/gentille
(*describing a remark*) = être
  désobligeant/désobligeante

unknown *adjective*
= inconnu/inconnue

unless *conjunction*
it won't work unless you plug it in = ça ne
  marchera pas si tu ne le branches pas
she can't work unless she finds an au pair
  = elle ne peut pas travailler à moins de
  trouver une jeune fille au pair
she can't work unless we find an au pair
  = elle ne peut pas travailler à moins
  qu'on ne lui trouve une jeune fille au
  pair
  ! *Note that the subjunctive is used after* à
  moins que.

unlock *verb*
= ouvrir

unlucky *adjective*
= malchanceux/malchanceuse
you were unlucky = tu n'as pas eu de chance

unpack *verb*
to unpack a suitcase = défaire une valise
to unpack one's belongings = déballer ses
  affaires

unsuitable *adjective*
= inapproprié/inappropriée

untidy *adjective*
(*in one's habits*)
  = désordonné/désordonnée
(*in how one looks*) = peu soigné/peu soignée

until
1 *preposition*
= jusqu'à
I'm staying until Thursday = je reste
  jusqu'à jeudi
until now = jusqu'à présent
I'm going to wait until after Christmas = je
  vais attendre que Noël soit passé
she won't get an answer until next week
  = elle n'aura pas de réponse avant la
  semaine prochaine
2 *conjunction*
I'll wait until I get back home = j'attendrai
  d'être rentré
we'll stay until they come = nous
  resterons jusqu'à ce qu'ils arrivent
don't look until it's ready = ne regarde pas
  avant que ce soit prêt
  ! *Note that the subjunctive is used after*
  jusqu'à ce que *and* avant que.

unusual *adjective*
• (*rare*) = peu commun/peu commune
it's unusual to see so few people = il est
  rare de voir si peu de monde
• (*different, out of the ordinary*)
  = original/originale

up
  ! *Often* up *occurs in combinations with
  verbs, for example:* blow up, give up, own
  up, *etc. To find the correct translations for
  this type of verb, look up the separate
  dictionary entries at* blow, give, own *etc.*

1 *preposition*
the cat's up the tree = le chat est dans
  l'arbre
to go up the street = remonter la rue
she ran up the stairs = elle a monté
  l'escalier en courant
the library is up those stairs = la
  bibliothèque se trouve en haut de cet
  escalier
2 *adverb*
up in the sky = dans le ciel
up on (top of) the wardrobe = sur l'armoire
to go up = monter (! + *être*)
to go up to Scotland = aller en Écosse
up there = là-haut
put the picture a bit further up = mets le
  tableau un peu plus haut
to climb all the way up = monter jusqu'en
  haut

U

3 *adjective*
* (*out of bed*)
  to be up = être debout
  to be up all night = veiller toute la nuit
* (*higher in amount, level*)
  to be up by 20% = avoir augmenté de 20%
4 up to
* (*well enough*)
  to be up to going out = avoir la force de
    sortir
  I'm not up to it = je n'en ai pas la force
* (*when talking about who is responsible*)
  it's up to [me | you | them …] to decide
    = c'est à [moi | toi | eux …] de décider
* (*until*) = jusqu'à
  up to now = jusqu'à présent
  up to 1996 = jusqu'en 1996

upset
1 *adjective*
  to be upset (*annoyed*) = être
    contrarié/contrariée
    (*distressed*) = être très affecté/affectée
  to get upset (*annoyed*) = se fâcher
    (**!** + *être*)
    (*distressed*) = se mettre dans tous ses états
    (**!** + *être*)
2 *verb*
* (*to make someone unhappy*) (*if it's an
  event*) = bouleverser
  (*if it's a person*) = faire de la peine à
* (*to annoy*) = contrarier

upside down *adverb*
  = à l'envers
  you're holding the book upside down = tu
    tiens le livre à l'envers

upstairs *adverb*
  = en haut
  to go upstairs = monter (l'escalier)
  to bring the cases upstairs = monter les
    valises

urgent *adjective*
  = urgent/urgente

us *pronoun*

  > **!** us *is always translated by* nous. *Note
  > that there is a boxed usage note at* them.
  > *The entries* me, him, her *and* us *are
  > modelled on this note where you will find
  > detailed grammatical information and
  > fuller explanations.*

* **they know us** = ils nous connaissent
  they don't know us = ils ne nous
    connaissent pas
  do they know us? = est-ce qu'ils nous
    connaissent?
* **he's seen us** = il nous a vus
  he hasn't seen us = il ne nous a pas vus
  has he seen us? = est-ce qu'il nous a vus?
* **help us!** = aide-nous!
  catch us! = attrape-nous!
  don't bother us! = ne nous embête pas!
  don't hit us! = ne nous frappe pas!

* **she gave the book to us** = elle nous a
  donné le livre
  she didn't give the book to us = elle ne
    nous a pas donné le livre
  did she give the book to us? = est-ce
    qu'elle nous a donné le livre?
* **write to us!** = écris-nous!
  say it to us! = dis-le-nous!
  don't show it to us! = ne nous le montre
    pas!
* **he did it for us** = il l'a fait pour nous
  it's us = c'est nous
  stand in front of us = mets-toi devant nous

USA *noun* ▶ **218|**
  the USA = les USA (*masculine plural*)

use
1 *verb*
* (*to make use of*) = se servir de (**!** + *être*)
  I use the car to go to work = je me sers de
    la voiture pour aller au travail
  he uses the room as an office = il se sert
    de la pièce comme bureau
  what is it used for? = ça sert à quoi?
  to use the opportunity to learn French
    = profiter de l'occasion pour apprendre
    le français
  to use a different word = employer un
    autre mot
* (*to operate on*)
  to use petrol = marcher à l'essence
  to use water = utiliser de l'eau
* (*to go through*) = consommer
  it uses a lot of petrol = ça consomme
    beaucoup d'essence
* (*to take advantage of*)
  to use someone = se servir de quelqu'un
2 *noun*
* **to make use of a room** = utiliser une pièce
  to have the use of a car = avoir l'usage
    d'une voiture
  to lose the use of one's legs = perdre
    l'usage de ses jambes
* (*when talking about what is useful*)
  to be of use to someone = être utile à
    quelqu'un, servir à quelqu'un
  to be no use = ne servir à rien
  the bike is no use any more = le vélo est
    hors d'usage
  what's the use of complaining? = à quoi
    bon se plaindre?

use up
  to use up all the money = dépenser tout
    l'argent
  to use up the milk = finir le lait

used
1 *verb*

  > **!** Note that the imperfect tense in French
  > is generally used to translate used to +
  > verb: she used to live in Toulouse = elle
  > habitait Toulouse.

  I used to read a lot = je lisais beaucoup
  you used not to smoke = tu ne fumais pas
    avant
  there used to be a castle here = il y avait
    un château ici dans le temps

2 *adjective*
to be used to [children | animals | tourists ...]
= avoir l'habitude des [enfants | animaux |
touristes ...]
he's not used to living on his own = il n'a
pas l'habitude de vivre seul
to get used to a new job = s'habituer à un
nouveau travail

useful *adjective*
= utile

useless *adjective*
• (*not working, having no use*) = inutilisable
• (*having no point or purpose*) = inutile
it's useless complaining = il est inutile de
se plaindre, ça ne sert à rien de se
plaindre
• (*describing a person*) = nul/nulle
to be useless at chemistry = être
nul/nulle en chimie

usually *adverb*
= d'habitude, normalement

vacant *adjective*
= libre

vacation *noun* (*US English*)
a vacation = des vacances (*feminine plural*)
to take a vacation = prendre des vacances

vacuum *verb*
to vacuum a room = passer l'aspirateur
dans une pièce

vacuum cleaner *noun*
a vacuum cleaner = un aspirateur

vague *adjective*
= vague

vain *adjective*
= vaniteux/vaniteuse

valid *adjective*
(*describing a licence, a passport*) = valide
(*describing a ticket, an offer*) = valable

valley *noun*
a valley = une vallée

valuable *adjective*
• (*very useful*) = précieux/précieuse
• (*worth a lot of money*)
to be valuable = avoir de la valeur

van *noun*
a van (*small*) = une camionnette
(*larger*) = un fourgon

vandalize *verb*
= vandaliser

vanilla *noun*
vanilla = la vanille

various *adjective*
= divers/diverses
there are various ways of saying it = on
peut le dire de diverses façons

vary *verb*
= varier
to vary from town to town = varier d'une
ville à l'autre

vase *noun*
a vase = un vase

veal *noun*
veal = le veau

vegetable *noun*
a vegetable = un légume

vegetarian *noun*
a vegetarian = un végétarien/une
végétarienne

vein *noun* ▶ **201**
a vein = une veine

velvet *noun*
velvet = le velours

versus *preposition*
= contre

very
1 *adverb*
very = très
I don't know him very well = je ne le
connais pas très bien
to eat very little = manger très peu
you haven't said very much = tu n'as pas
dit grand-chose
we like them very much = on les aime
beaucoup
for the very first time = pour la toute
première fois
they called me the very next day = ils
m'ont appelé dès le lendemain
2 *adjective*
at the very beginning = au tout début
to sit at the very front = s'asseoir tout
devant
to stay to the very end = rester jusqu'au
bout
you are the very person I need = tu es
exactement la personne qu'il me faut

vest *noun*
• (*British English*) (*a piece of underwear*)
a vest = un maillot de corps
• (*US English*) (*a waistcoat*)
a vest = un gilet

vet *noun* ▶ **315**
a vet = un vétérinaire/une vétérinaire

via *preposition*
(*on tickets, timetables*) = via
(*in general*) = en passant par
we came via Paris = nous sommes venus
en passant par Paris

vicious *adjective*
- (*violent*) = brutal/brutale
- (*nasty, meant to hurt*)
  = malveillant/malveillante

victory *noun*
  a victory = une victoire
  to win a victory = remporter une victoire

video
1 *noun*
- (*a recorded film, programme, event*)
  a video = une cassette vidéo
- ▶ **video cassette, video recorder**
2 *verb*
- (*to record*) = enregistrer
- (*to film*)
  to video a wedding = filmer un mariage
  en vidéo

video camera *noun*
  a video camera = une caméra vidéo

video cassette *noun*
  a video cassette = une cassette vidéo

video game *noun*
  a video game = un jeu vidéo

video recorder *noun*
  a video recorder = un magnétoscope

view *noun*
- a view = une vue
  you're blocking my view = tu me bouches
  la vue
  if you want to get a better view, come
  here = si tu veux mieux voir, viens ici
- (*an opinion, an attitude*)
  a view = un avis, une opinion
  a point of view = un point de vue

village *noun*
  a village = un village

vinegar *noun*
  vinegar = le vinaigre

vineyard *noun*
  a vineyard = un vignoble

violent *adjective*
  = violent/violente

violin *noun* ▶ **290 |**
  a violin = un violon

Virgo *noun*
  Virgo = Vierge (*feminine*)

visit
1 *verb*
  to visit Paris (*to see*) = visiter Paris
  (*to stay*) = faire un séjour à Paris
  to visit someone (*to call on*) = aller voir
    quelqu'un
  (*more formally*) = rendre visite à quelqu'un
  (*to stay with*) = aller passer quelques jours
    chez quelqu'un
2 *noun*
  a visit (*a call*) = une visite

(*a stay*) = un séjour
  to pay someone a visit = rendre visite à
  quelqu'un

visitor *noun*
- (*a guest*)
  a visitor = un invité/une invitée
  to have visitors = avoir de la visite
- (*a tourist*)
  a visitor = un visiteur/une visiteuse

vocabulary *noun*
  vocabulary = le vocabulaire

voice *noun*
  a voice = une voix
  to have a good voice = avoir une jolie
    voix
  to speak in a low voice = parler à voix
    basse
  to sing at the top of one's voice = chanter
    à tue-tête

volleyball *noun* ▶ **248 |**
  volleyball = le volley-ball

vomit *verb*
  = vomir

vote *verb*
  = voter

Ww

wages *noun*
  wages = le salaire (*singular*)

waist *noun* ▶ **201 |**
  the waist = la taille

waistcoat *noun* (*British English*)
  a waistcoat = un gilet

wait *verb*
- to wait = attendre
  to wait for someone = attendre quelqu'un
  I'm waiting to use the phone = j'attends de
  pouvoir téléphoner
  to wait for someone to leave = attendre
  que quelqu'un s'en aille
  let's have a beer while we're waiting for
  them = allons prendre une bière en
  attendant qu'ils arrivent

  ! *Note that the subjunctive is used after*
  attendre que.

  I can't wait to see them = j'ai hâte de les
  voir
- (*in a restaurant*)
  to wait on table, to wait table (*US English*)
  = travailler comme serveur/serveuse
wait up = veiller
  to wait up for someone = veiller jusqu'au
  retour de quelqu'un

waiter noun ▶ 315|
a waiter = un serveur

waiting room noun
a waiting room = une salle d'attente

waitress noun ▶ 315|
a waitress = une serveuse

wake verb
to wake someone = réveiller quelqu'un
wake up = se réveiller (**!** + être)

Wales noun ▶ 218|
Wales = le pays de Galles

walk
1 verb
(rather than run) = marcher
(rather than drive or ride) = aller à pied
(for pleasure) = se promener (**!** + être)
let's walk to the pool = allons à la piscine à pied
to walk down the street = descendre la rue
to walk the dog = promener le chien
2 noun
a walk = une promenade
to go for a walk = faire une promenade
it's five minutes' walk from here = c'est à cinq minutes à pied d'ici
walk around = se promener (**!** + être)
to walk around town = se promener en ville
to walk around the lake = faire le tour du lac
walk away = s'éloigner (**!** + être)
walk back = revenir à pied
to walk back home = rentrer à pied
walk by = passer (**!** + être)
walk in = entrer (**!** + être)
walk out = sortir (**!** + être)
to walk out of the room = sortir de la pièce
walk round = faire le tour
to walk round the exhibition = visiter l'exposition
walk up to = s'approcher de (**!** + être)

walkman® noun
a walkman = un baladeur, un walkman®

wall noun
a wall = un mur

wallet noun
a wallet = un portefeuille

wallpaper noun
wallpaper = le papier peint

walnut noun
a walnut = une noix

wander verb
to wander around town = se balader en ville
wander away, wander off = s'éloigner (**!** + être)

want verb
• to want = vouloir
do you want another coffee? = est-ce que tu veux un autre café?
he wants [to go out | to go home | to play …] = il veut [sortir | rentrer | jouer …]
she didn't want to stay = elle n'a pas voulu rester
do you want me to come with you? = est-ce que tu veux que je vienne avec toi?
! Note that the subjunctive is used after vouloir que.

• (to need) = avoir besoin de
do you want anything in town? = est-ce que tu as besoin de quelque chose en ville?

war noun
a war = une guerre

wardrobe noun
a wardrobe = une armoire

warm
1 adjective
= chaud/chaude
to be warm, to feel warm = avoir chaud
I'm very warm = j'ai très chaud
it's nice and warm in the classroom = il fait bon dans la salle de classe
to get warm = se réchauffer (**!** + être)
to keep warm = rester au chaud
to keep a meal warm = tenir un repas au chaud
2 verb
to warm the plates = chauffer les assiettes
to warm one's hands = se réchauffer les mains
warm up
• (to get warm) = se réchauffer (**!** + être)
• (for a sporting event) = s'échauffer (**!** + être)
• (to make warm) = réchauffer

warn verb
= avertir, prévenir
to warn someone about the risks = mettre quelqu'un en garde contre les risques
to warn someone to be careful = conseiller à quelqu'un de faire attention
I warned him not to take the car = je lui ai déconseillé de prendre la voiture

wash verb
• (to clean) = laver
to wash one's clothes = laver ses vêtements
to wash one's face = se laver le visage
• (to get clean) = se laver (**!** + être)
wash out
to wash out = partir au lavage
to wash a stain out = faire partir une tache au lavage
wash up
• (British English) (to do the dishes) = faire la vaisselle

- (US English) (to clean oneself) = se
  rafraîchir (**!** + être)

washbasin (British English), **wash-
hand basin** noun
  a washbasin = un lavabo

washing noun
  the washing = le linge
  to do the washing = faire la lessive

washing machine noun
  a washing machine = une machine à laver

washing-up noun (British English)
  the washing-up = la vaisselle
  to do the washing-up = faire la vaisselle

wasp noun
  a wasp = une guêpe

waste
1 verb
  = gaspiller
  to waste energy = gaspiller de l'énergie
  to waste one's time = perdre son temps
2 noun
- it's a waste of money = c'est de l'argent
  gaspillé
  a waste of time = une perte de temps
  it's a waste of time going there = y aller
    est une perte de temps
  to let food go to waste = gaspiller de la
    nourriture
- waste = les déchets (masculine plural)

watch
1 verb
- (to look at) = regarder
  to watch television = regarder la
    télévision
  she watched me making the meal = elle
    m'a regardé préparer le repas
- (to observe, to follow) = surveiller
  I feel I'm being watched = j'ai l'impression
    qu'on me surveille
- (to pay attention to)
  watch what you're doing = fais attention à
    ce que tu fais
  watch you don't fall = fais attention de ne
    pas tomber
2 noun
  a watch = une montre
watch out = faire attention

water
1 noun
  water = l'eau (feminine)
  drinking water = l'eau potable
  to let in water = prendre l'eau
2 verb
  = arroser

waterfall noun
  a waterfall = une cascade

water-skiing noun ▶ 248 |
  water-skiing = le ski nautique

wave
1 verb
- (to signal with one's hand)
  to wave to someone = saluer quelqu'un
    de la main
  to wave goodbye = faire au revoir de la
    main
- (to direct)
  to wave someone on = faire signe à
    quelqu'un d'avancer
- to wave flags = agiter des drapeaux
2 noun
  a wave = une vague

way
1 noun
- (a means, a method)
  a way = un moyen
  it's a way of earning money = c'est un
    moyen de gagner de l'argent
  it's a good way to make friends = c'est un
    bon moyen de se faire des amis
  he does it the wrong way = il s'y prend
    mal
  that's not the way to do it = ce n'est pas
    comme ça qu'on fait
- (how one does something)
  a way = une façon
  I like the way she dresses = j'aime sa
    façon de s'habiller
  I prefer to do it my way = je préfère le faire
    à ma façon
- (a route, a road)
  a way = un chemin
  I can't remember the way to the station
    = je ne me souviens plus du chemin
    pour aller à la gare
  we can buy something to eat along the
    way = on peut acheter quelque chose à
    manger en chemin
  on the way back = sur le chemin du
    retour
  I met them on the way back from town = je
    les ai rencontrés en revenant de la ville
  on the way to Paris = en allant à Paris
  where's the way out? = où est la sortie?
  to make one's way to the stairs = se
    diriger vers l'escalier
  to lose one's way = se perdre (**!** + être)
- (a direction)
  which way are you going? = dans quelle
    direction est-ce que tu vas?
  they went that way = ils sont partis par là
  come this way = venez par ici
- (someone's route)
  to be in someone's way = empêcher
    quelqu'un de passer, bloquer le passage
    à quelqu'un
  to be in the way = gêner le passage
  to get out of the way = s'écarter (**!** + être)
- (when talking about distances)
  it's a long way from here = c'est loin d'ici
  to go all the way to Portugal = aller
    jusqu'au Portugal

- (*what one wants*)
  she always wants her own way = elle ne
  veut en faire qu'à sa tête
  if I had my own way, I'd go alone = si cela
  ne tenait qu'à moi, j'irais tout seul
2 by the way
  what's his name, by the way? = comment
  s'appelle-t-il, au fait?

we *pronoun*

> ! *Note that* we *is generally translated by*
> nous *but that, in informal French,* on *is
> also very common:* we're going to the
> cinema = nous allons au cinéma, on va au
> cinéma.

  we = nous
  we saw her yesterday = nous l'avons vue
  hier, on l'a vue hier
  we didn't agree = nous, nous n'étions pas
  d'accord
  we all make mistakes = tout le monde
  peut se tromper

weak *adjective*
- (*not healthy*) = faible
  to have a weak heart = avoir le cœur
  fragile
- (*not good or able*) = faible
  to be weak at languages = être faible en
  langues
- (*easily damaged*) = fragile
- (*having very little power*) = faible
- (*describing tea or coffee*) = léger/légère

wealthy *adjective*
  = riche

wear *verb*
- (*to be dressed in*) = porter
  to be wearing jeans = porter un jean
  to wear black = s'habiller en noir
- (*to put on*) = mettre
  what will you wear? = qu'est-ce que tu vas
  mettre?
  I've got nothing to wear = je n'ai rien à me
  mettre
- (*to damage*) = user
  wear out
  to wear out = s'user (! + *être*)
  to wear one's shoes out = user ses
  chaussures
  to wear someone out = épuiser quelqu'un

weather *noun*
  the weather = le temps
  what's the weather like? = quel temps
  fait-il?
  the weather is [bad | nice | hot ...] = il fait
  [mauvais | bon | chaud ...]
  in [cold | warm | wet ...] weather = quand [il
  fait froid | il fait bon | il pleut ...]

weather forecast *noun*
  the weather forecast = les prévisions
  météorologiques, la météo

> ! *Note that* prévisions *is feminine plural.*

wedding *noun*
  a wedding = un mariage

Wednesday *noun* ▶ 222
  Wednesday = mercredi (*masculine*)

week *noun* ▶ 356
  a week = une semaine
  in two weeks' time = dans quinze jours

weekend *noun* ▶ 356
  a weekend = un week-end

weigh *verb* ▶ 285
  = peser
  what do you weigh? = combien pèses-tu?
  to weigh oneself = se peser (! + *être*)

weight *noun* ▶ 285
  weight = le poids
  to lose weight = maigrir

weird *adjective*
  = bizarre

welcome
1 *verb* ▶ 237
  to welcome someone = accueillir
  quelqu'un
2 *adjective*
- (*when receiving people*)
  to be welcome = être le bienvenu/la
  bienvenue
  welcome to the United States!
  = bienvenue aux États-Unis!
- (*when acknowledging thanks*)
  'thanks'—'you're welcome' = 'merci'—'de
  rien'
3 *noun*
  a welcome = un accueil

well
1 *adverb* ▶ 237
- **well** = bien
  he dresses well = il s'habille bien
  I'd like to speak French well = j'aimerais
  parler bien le français
  the [exam | interview | class ...] went well
  = [l'examen | l'entretien | le cours ...] s'est bien
  passé
  the work is well paid = le travail est bien
  payé
  she is well able to defend herself = elle est
  tout à fait capable de se défendre
  he's not eating well = il n'a pas d'appétit
- (*other uses*)
  we may as well go home = on ferait aussi
  bien de rentrer
  you may well be right = il se pourrait bien
  que tu aies raison

> ! *Note that the subjunctive is used after* il
> se pourrait bien que.

2 *adjective*
  to feel well = se sentir bien
  I hope everyone is well = j'espère que tout
  le monde va bien
  I'm very well = je vais très bien
  to get well = se rétablir (! + *être*)
3 as well = aussi

W

4 as well as = ainsi que

well-known *adjective*
= célèbre

Welsh ▶ 275 |
1 *adjective*
= gallois/galloise
2 *noun*
* (*the people*)
the Welsh = les Gallois (*masculine plural*)
* (*the language*)
Welsh = le gallois

west
1 *noun*
the west = l'ouest (*masculine*)
in the west of France = dans l'ouest de la
France
2 *adverb*
to go west = aller vers l'ouest
to live west of Paris = vivre à l'ouest de
Paris
3 *adjective*
= ouest (**!** *never changes*)
to work in west London = travailler dans
l'ouest de Londres

West Indies *noun* **▶ 218 |**
the West Indies = les Antilles (*feminine*)

wet
1 *adjective*
* (*damp*) = mouillé/mouillée
your hair is wet = tu as les cheveux
mouillés
to get wet = se faire mouiller (**!** + *être*)
she got her feet wet = elle s'est mouillé les
pieds
* (*when talking about weather*) = humide
in wet weather = par temps humide
on a wet day = quand il pleut
2 *verb*
= mouiller

what
▶ *See the boxed note on* what *for more
information and examples.*
1 *pronoun*
* (*used in questions*)
what's her phone number? = quel est son
numéro de téléphone?
what's that box? = qu'est-ce que c'est que
cette boîte?
what's this button for? = à quoi sert ce
bouton?
what's the French for 'boring'?
= comment dit-on 'boring' en français?
what does he look like? = il est comment?
* (*used as a relative pronoun*)
do what you want = faites ce que vous
voulez
what we need is a timetable = ce qu'il
nous faut c'est un horaire
2 *determiner*
do you know what train to take? = est-ce
que tu sais quel train il faut prendre?
what a great idea! = quelle bonne idée!

3 *exclamation*
= quoi!, comment!
4 what if = et si
what if I don't get there on time? = et si je
n'y suis pas à l'heure?

whatever *pronoun*
* (*when anything is possible*)
take whatever you want = prends tout ce
que tu veux
whatever you think is useful = tout ce qui
vous paraît utile
* (*when it doesn't matter*)
whatever they do, it won't change
anything = quoi qu'ils fassent, ça ne
changera rien

  ! *Note that the subjunctive is used after* quoi
que *(*quoi qu' *before vowel or mute h).*

wheat *noun*
wheat = le blé

wheel *noun*
a wheel = une roue

wheelchair *noun*
a wheelchair = un fauteuil roulant

when
1 *adverb*
= quand
when did she leave? = quand est-ce
qu'elle est partie?
when is your birthday? = c'est quand ton
anniversaire?
* I don't know when the film starts = je ne sais
pas à quelle heure le film commence

  ! *See the usage note on* The clock **▶ 356 |**
for further information on time expressions.

2 *conjunction*
= quand
I was asleep when the phone rang = je
dormais quand le téléphone a sonné
he didn't like French when he was at
school = il n'aimait pas le français
quand il était au collège
when I'm 18 I'll have my own car = quand
j'aurai 18 ans j'aurai ma propre voiture

  ! *Note that, when talking about future
time, the future tense is used after* quand.

3 *pronoun*
* (*used as a relative pronoun*) = où
in the days when there was no TV = à
l'époque où il n'y avait pas de télévision
* (*used in questions*) = quand

where
1 *adverb*
= où
where are you going? = où vas-tu?
where do they work? = où est-ce qu'ils
travaillent?
do you know where [he is | Tom is | we're
going ...]? = est-ce que tu sais où [il est | est
Tom | nous allons ...]?
I wonder where he lives = je me demande
où il habite
the village where we live = le village où
nous habitons

what

As a pronoun

In questions

- When used in questions as an object pronoun, **what** is translated by **qu'est-ce que** (**qu'est-ce qu'** in front of a vowel or mute h):

what is he doing?	= **qu'est-ce qu'**il fait?
what did you say?	= **qu'est-ce que** tu as dit?
what are we going to do?	= **qu'est-ce que** nous allons faire?

- Alternatively, you can use **que** (**qu'** before a vowel or mute h), but note that, after **que**, the order of subject and verb is reversed and a hyphen is inserted between them if the subject is a pronoun:

what is he doing?	= **que** fait-il?
what did you say?	= **qu'**as-tu dit?
what are we going to do?	= **qu'**allons-nous faire?

- When used in questions as a subject pronoun, what is translated by **qu'est-ce qui**:

what is happening?	= **qu'est-ce qui** se passe?
what happened?	= **qu'est-ce qui** s'est passé?
what is going to happen?	= **qu'est-ce qui** va se passer?

Again, if you use **que**, the order of subject and verb is reversed, the subject becomes **il** and a hyphen is inserted between them:

what is happening?	= **que** se passe-t-**il**?*
what happened?	= **que** s'est-**il** passé?
what is going to happen?	= **que** va-t-**il** se passer?

* In this case, an additional **-t-** is required for the liaison between the two vowels to be made.

To introduce a clause

- When used to introduce a clause as the object of the verb, **what** is translated by **ce que** (**ce qu'** before a vowel or mute h):

*I don't know **what** he wants*	= je ne sais pas **ce qu'**il veut
*did they have **what** you wanted?*	= est-ce qu'ils avaient **ce que** tu voulais?
***what** he said was that he didn't care*	= **ce qu'**il a dit c'est que ça lui était égal

- When **what** is the subject of the verb, it is translated by **ce qui**:

*tell me **what** happened*	= raconte-moi **ce qui** s'est passé
*I want to know **what**'s happening*	= je veux savoir **ce qui** se passe
***what** matters is that we won*	= **ce qui** compte, c'est que nous avons gagné

With prepositions

What, when it is used with a preposition in English, is translated by **quoi**. In French, however, the preposition always comes before **quoi**:

what are you thinking about?	= à **quoi** penses-tu?
*I don't know **what** he is talking about*	= je ne sais pas de **quoi** il parle

As a determiner

When **what** is used as a determiner, it is translated by **quel**, **quelle**, **quels** or **quelles**, according to whether the noun that follows is masculine or feminine, singular or plural:

what train did you catch?	= **quel** train as-tu pris?
what time is it?	= **quelle** heure est-il?
what books do you like?	= **quels** livres aimes-tu?
what colours do you like?	= **quelles** couleurs aimes-tu?

▶ For more examples, see the entry **what**.

2 *conjunction*

that's where she fell = c'est là qu'elle est tombée

I'll leave the key where you can see it = je laisserai la clé là où tu peux la voir

whether *conjunction*

= si

I don't know whether or not to accept = je ne sais pas si je dois accepter

which

▶ *See the boxed note on* which *for more information and examples.*

1 *pronoun*

the house which I told you about = la maison dont je t'ai parlé

2 *determiner*

which one of the nurses speaks French? = laquelle des infirmières parle français?

ask him which bus leaves first = demande-lui quel bus va partir le premier

while *conjunction*

= pendant que

I had a party while my parents were in Spain = j'ai fait une fête pendant que mes parents étaient en Espagne

she fell asleep while watching TV = elle s'est endormie en regardant la télévision

whisper *verb*

= chuchoter

whistle

1 *verb*

= siffler

2 *noun*

a whistle = un sifflet

white *adjective* ▶ **213**

= blanc/blanche

who *pronoun*

• (*used in questions*) = qui

who told you? = qui (est-ce qui) te l'a dit?

who did you invite? = qui est-ce que tu as invité?

who did he buy the book for? = pour qui a-t-il acheté le livre?

• (*used as a relative pronoun*)

my friend who lives in Paris = mon ami qui habite Paris

those who can't come by car = ceux/celles qui ne peuvent pas venir en voiture

a friend who I see at work = un ami que je vois au travail

whole

1 *noun*

the whole of [the country | London | August…] = tout [le pays | Londres | le mois d'août…]

2 *adjective*

a whole day = toute une journée, une journée entière

three whole weeks = trois semaines entières

I don't want to spend my whole life here = je ne veux pas passer toute ma vie ici

whom *pronoun*

• (*used in questions*) = qui

whom did you meet? = qui as-tu rencontré?

• (*used as a relative pronoun*)

the person to whom I spoke on the phone = la personne à qui j'ai parlé au téléphone

whose

1 *pronoun*

• (*used in questions*) = à qui

whose is the dog? = à qui est le chien?

• (*used as a relative pronoun*) = dont

the boy whose bike was stolen = le garçon dont le vélo a été volé

the woman whose house I'm buying = la femme dont j'achète la maison

2 *determiner*

whose car is that? = à qui est cette voiture?

whose pen did you borrow? = à qui as-tu emprunté un stylo?

why

1 *adverb*

• (*used in questions*) = pourquoi

why did you do that? = pourquoi est-ce que tu as fait ça?

why aren't they coming? = pourquoi est-ce qu'ils ne viennent pas?

why not? = pourquoi pas?

• (*when making suggestions*)

why don't we eat out tonight? = et si on allait au restaurant ce soir?

2 *conjunction*

= pour ça

that's why I can't stand him = c'est pour ça que je le déteste

wide *adjective* ▶ **285**

• (*in size*) = large

a wide garden = un jardin large

the room is ten metres wide = la pièce a dix mètres de large

• (*in range*)

a wide range of games = un très grand choix de jeux

width *noun* ▶ **285**

width = la largeur

wife *noun*

a wife = une femme

wild *adjective*

• (*describing animals, birds*) = sauvage

• (*noisy, out of control*) = fou/folle

to go wild = se déchaîner (**!** + *être*)

wildlife *noun*

wildlife = la faune

which

As a pronoun

In questions

When **which** (meaning *which one* or *which ones*) is used as a pronoun in questions, it is translated by **lequel**, **laquelle**, **lesquels** or **lesquelles**, according to whether the noun it is standing for is masculine or feminine, singular or plural:

there are three peaches, = il y a trois pêches,
which do you want? **laquelle** veux-tu?

When **which** is followed by a superlative adjective, then the translation is **quel**, **quelle**, **quels** or **quelles**, according to whether the noun it is standing for is masculine or feminine, singular or plural:

(of the apples) which is the biggest? = **quelle** est la plus grosse?
(of the books) which is the most useful? = **quel** est le plus utile?
(of the cars) which are the fastest? = **quelles** sont les plus rapides?
(of the computers) which are the cheapest? = **quels** sont les moins chers?

In relative clauses

When used as a pronoun, **which** is translated by **qui** when it is the subject of the verb, and by **que** when it is the object:

the book which is on the table = le livre **qui** est sur la table
the book which Tina is reading = le livre **que** lit Tina

Note the different word order of subject and verb; this is the case where the subject is a noun but not where the subject is a pronoun:

the book which I am reading = le livre **que** je lis
the book which he's writing = le livre **qu'**il écrit
the film which we're going to see = le film **que** nous allons voir

Remember that in the present perfect and past perfect tenses, the past participle agrees with the noun **que** is referring back to:

the film which we saw = le film **que** nous avous vu
the car which they stole = la voiture **qu'**ils ont volée
the books which I gave you = les livres **que** je t'ai donnés (*masculine plural*)
the dresses which she bought yesterday = les robes **qu'**elle a achetées hier (*feminine plural*)

As a determiner

When **which** is used as a determiner in questions, it is translated by **quel**, **quelle**, **quels** or **quelles** according to whether the noun that follows is masculine or feminine, singular or plural:

which car is yours? = **quelle** voiture est la vôtre?
which dress did she buy? = **quelle** robe a-t-elle achetée?*
which houses are for sale? = **quelles** maisons sont à vendre?
which computer doesn't work? = **quel** ordinateur ne marche pas?
which books did he borrow? = **quels** livres a-t-il empruntés?*

Note that, in the second and third examples, the object precedes the verb or auxiliary verb so that the past participle agrees with it.

* In this case, an additional -t- is required for the liaison between the two vowels to be made.

W

---

will *verb*

! *Note that, when referring to the future, French generally uses the future tense of the verb to translate* **will** + *verb:* I will sing = je chanterai. *When talking about something in the near future, the present tense of* **aller** + *verb is also possible:* je vais chanter.

• (*when talking about the future*)
she won't agree = elle ne sera pas d'accord
it will be sunny tomorrow = il va faire beau demain
what will we do? = qu'est-ce que nous allons faire?

- (when talking about intentions)
  I'll wait for you at the airport = je t'attendrai à l'aéroport
  we won't stay too long = nous ne resterons pas trop longtemps
- (in invitations and requests)
  will you have some coffee? = est-ce que vous voulez du café?, voulez-vous du café?
  will you ask him for me? = est-ce que tu peux lui demander de ma part?
- (when making assumptions)
  they won't know what's happened = ils ne doivent pas savoir ce qui s'est passé
- (in short questions and answers)
  you'll come again, won't you? = tu reviendras, n'est-ce pas?
  that will be cheaper, won't it? = ça sera moins cher, non?
  'he won't be ready'—'yes he will' = 'il ne sera pas prêt'—'si'

win verb
= gagner

wind noun
a wind = un vent

window noun
a window (in a house) = une fenêtre
(in a shop) = une vitrine
(in a car, a bus) = une vitre

windsurfing noun ▶ 248 |
windsurfing = la planche à voile

windy adjective
it's windy = il fait du vent

wine noun
wine = le vin

wing noun
a wing = une aile

winter noun
winter = l'hiver (masculine)
in winter = en hiver

wipe verb
= essuyer
to wipe one's feet = s'essuyer les pieds
to wipe one's nose = se moucher
(**!** + être)

wise adjective
(describing a person) = sage
(describing a decision, a choice)
= judicieux/judicieuse

wish
1 noun
- **a wish** = un souhait
  to make a wish = faire un vœu
- (in greetings)
  best wishes = meilleurs vœux
  (in a letter) = amicalement

2 verb
- (expressing what one would like)
  I wish they could come = si seulement ils pouvaient venir
  she wished she hadn't lied = elle regrettait d'avoir menti
- (in greetings) = souhaiter
  to wish someone a happy birthday = souhaiter un bon anniversaire à quelqu'un

with preposition
- **with** = avec
  to go away with friends = partir avec des amis
  I'm living with my parents = j'habite chez mes parents
  to be pleased with the house = être content/contente de la maison
- (when describing)
  a girl with black hair = une fille aux cheveux noirs
  the boy with the broken leg = le garçon à la jambe cassée
  his clothes were covered with mud = ses vêtements étaient couverts de boue
  he was walking along with his hands in his pockets = il se promenait les mains dans les poches
  she's married with two children = elle est mariée et mère de deux enfants

without preposition
= sans
we got in without paying = on est entré sans payer

wolf noun
a wolf = un loup

woman noun
a woman = une femme
a single woman = une célibataire

wonder verb
- (to ask oneself) = se demander (**!** + être)
  I wonder [how | why | who ...] = je me demande [comment | pourquoi | qui ...]
  I was wondering when you'd arrive = je me demandais quand tu arriverais
- (in polite requests)
  I wonder if you could help me? = pourriez-vous m'aider?

wonderful adjective
= merveilleux/merveilleuse

wood noun
- (timber)
  wood = le bois
  made of wood = en bois
- (a small forest)
  a wood = un bois

wool noun
wool = la laine

word noun
a word = un mot
what's the French word for 'break'? = comment dit-on 'break' en français?
in other words = autrement dit

work

1 *verb*
- (*to have or do a job*) = travailler
  to work at home = travailler à domicile
  to work as a doctor = être médecin
- (*to operate properly*) = marcher
  the TV isn't working = la télévision ne
  marche pas, la télévision est en panne
- (*to be successful*) (*if it's an idea, a trick*)
  = marcher
  (*if it's a plan*) = réussir
  (*if it's a medicine, a treatment*) = agir
- (*to use, to operate*) = se servir de (**!** + *être*)
  do you know how to work the computer?
  = est-ce que tu sais te servir de
  l'ordinateur?

2 *noun*
- **work** = le travail
  I've got work to do = j'ai du travail
  to be out of work = être au chômage
  the students' work = le travail des élèves
  it's hard work learning French = c'est dur
  d'apprendre le français
- (*for building, for repairs*)
  work(s) = les travaux (*masculine plural*)
  there are road works at the moment = il y
  a des travaux en ce moment
- (*by an artist, a musician*)
  a work = une œuvre

work out
- (*to find*) = trouver
  to work out the answer = trouver la
  réponse
- (*to understand*) = comprendre
- (*with figures*) = calculer
- (*to go well*) = marcher
- (*to take exercise*) = s'entraîner (**!** + *être*)

work up
  to get worked up = s'énerver (**!** + *être*)

worker *noun*
  a worker (*in a factory*) = un ouvrier/une
  ouvrière
  (*in an office, a bank*) = un employé/une
  employée

world *noun*
  the world = le monde
  all over the world = dans le monde entier
  the biggest city in the world = la plus
  grande ville du monde

World Cup *noun*
  the World Cup = la Coupe du Monde

worm *noun*
  a worm = un ver

worried *adjective*
  = inquiet/inquiète
  to be worried about someone = se faire du
  souci pour quelqu'un

worry *verb*
- (*to be worried*) = s'inquiéter (**!** + *être*)
  there's nothing to worry about = il n'y a
  pas de quoi s'inquiéter
- (*to make someone worried*) = inquiéter
  it's worrying me = ça m'inquiète

worse *adjective*
  = pire
  this book is worse than the others = ce
  livre est pire que les autres
  she's worse than me at sports = elle est
  pire que moi en sport
  the weather is going to get worse = le
  temps va empirer
  he's getting worse (*in health*) = il va plus
  mal

worst

1 *noun*
  the worst = le pire/la pire
  to be the worst at French = être le plus
  mauvais/la plus mauvaise en français

2 *adjective*
  = plus mauvais/plus mauvaise
  the worst hotel in town = le plus mauvais
  hôtel de la ville
  the worst film I've ever seen = le plus
  mauvais film que j'aie jamais vu

  ! *Note that the subjunctive is used after
  the superlative* le plus mauvais… que.

  his worst enemy = son pire ennemi
  the worst thing to do would be to tell him
  = le pire serait de le lui dire

worth *adjective*
  to be worth £100 = valoir 100 livres
  it's not worth the trouble = ça n'en vaut
  pas la peine

would *verb*

  ! *Note that French usually uses verbs in
  the conditional to translate* would + *verb:*
  I would buy = j'achèterais.

- (*when talking about hypothetical rather
  than real situations*)
  if I had more money, I would buy a car = si
  j'avais plus d'argent, j'achèterais une
  voiture
  **we would have missed the train if we'd
  left later** = nous aurions raté le train si
  nous étions partis plus tard
- (*in reported speech*)
  I thought you'd forget to come = je
  pensais que tu oublierais de venir
  we were sure she would like it = nous
  étions sûrs que ça lui plairait
- (*when making an assumption*)
  she'd be 30 now = elle doit avoir 30 ans
  maintenant
  it would have been about midday = il
  devait être à peu près midi
- (*to be prepared to*)
  he wouldn't listen to me = il ne voulait pas
  m'écouter
- (*when talking about one's wishes*)
  I'd like a beer = je voudrais une bière
  we would like to stay another night = nous
  aimerions rester une nuit de plus

• (when asking, offering or advising)
would you turn the TV off? = est-ce que tu veux bien éteindre la radio?
would you excuse me? = excusez-moi
would you like something to eat? = voulez-vous manger quelque chose?
you would do well to check = tu ferais mieux de vérifier

wrap verb
= envelopper
to wrap (up) a present = emballer un cadeau

wreck
1 verb
(if it's a person) = détruire
(if it's a fire, a bomb) = dévaster
2 noun
a wreck = une épave

wrestling noun ▶ 248 |
wrestling = le catch

wrist noun ▶ 201 |
the wrist = le poignet

write verb
= écrire
to write to someone, to write someone (US English) = écrire à quelqu'un
to write [an essay | a cheque | a note ...] = faire [une rédaction | un chèque | un mot ...]
write back = répondre
write down = noter
write out = écrire

writing noun
writing = l'écriture (feminine)
your writing is good = tu écris bien

writing pad noun
a writing pad = un bloc de papier à lettres

wrong adjective
• (not as it should be)
there's something wrong = il y a quelque chose qui ne va pas
what's wrong? = qu'est-ce qu'il y a?
what's wrong with you? (if ill, in pain) = qu'est-ce que tu as?
(if behaving oddly) = qu'est-ce qui t'arrive?
• (not proper or suitable)
= mauvais/mauvaise (**!** before the noun)
I took the wrong key = j'ai pris la mauvaise clé
to say the wrong thing = faire une gaffe
to go the wrong way = se tromper de chemin
• (not correct)
that's wrong = c'est faux
to dial the wrong number = faire un faux numéro, se tromper de numéro
it's the wrong answer = ce n'est pas la bonne réponse
to be wrong (if it's a person) = avoir tort, se tromper (**!** + être)

• (not honest, not good)
it's wrong to steal = c'est mal de voler
she hasn't done anything wrong = elle n'a rien fait de mal
there's nothing wrong with trying = il n'y a pas de mal à essayer

X-ray
1 noun
an X-ray = une radiographie, une radio
to have an X-ray = se faire radiographier
2 verb
= radiographier

yacht noun
a yacht = un yacht

yard noun
• (when measuring) ▶ 285 |
a yard ≈ un yard
! Note that a **yard** = 0.9144 m.

• (of a building)
a yard = une cour
• (US English) (a garden)
a yard = un jardin

yawn verb
= bâiller

year noun
! Note that **year** is usually translated by **an** in French. However it is sometimes translated by **année**, when there is an emphasis on the idea of duration.

• (when talking about time) ▶ 356 |
a year = un an
last year = l'an dernier, l'année dernière
two years ago = il y a deux ans
to work all year round = travailler toute l'année
he's lived there for years = il y habite depuis des années
that'll take years! = ça va prendre une éternité!
• (when talking about age) ▶ 187 |
a year = un an
to be 15 years old, to be 15 years of age = avoir 15 ans
a four-year old = un enfant/une enfant de quatre ans

- (*in a school system*)
  first year, year one ≈ la sixième
  to be in second year, to be in year two ≈ être en cinquième
  a first year ≈ un élève/une élève de sixième

yell
1 *verb*
= hurler
to yell at someone = crier après quelqu'un
2 *noun*
a yell = un hurlement

yellow *adjective* ▶ 213 |
= jaune
to go yellow = jaunir

yes *adverb*
yes = oui
'**are you coming with us?**'—'**yes I am**'
= 'est-ce que tu viens avec nous?'—'oui'
'**they don't know each other**'—'**yes they do**' = 'ils ne se connaissent pas'—'(mais) si'
'**didn't he tell you?**'—'**yes he did**' = 'il ne te l'a pas dit?'—'si'

yesterday *adverb*
= hier

yet
1 *adverb*
= encore
not yet = pas encore
it's not ready yet = ce n'est pas encore prêt
have they arrived yet? = est-ce qu'ils sont arrivés?
has she met them yet? = est-ce qu'elle les a déjà rencontrés?
2 *conjunction*
= pourtant

yogurt *noun*
yogurt = le yaourt

you *pronoun*
▶ 378 | *See the boxed note on* you *for detailed information and examples.*

young
1 *adjective*
= jeune
a young lady = une jeune femme
young people = les jeunes (*masculine*)
she is a year younger than me = elle a un an de moins que moi
a younger brother = un frère cadet
a younger sister = une sœur cadette
to look young = faire jeune
2 *noun*
the young (*of an animal*) = les petits (*masculine plural*)

your *determiner*
▶ 379 | *See the boxed note on* your *for detailed information and examples. See also the usage note on* The human body ▶ 201 |.

yours *pronoun*
▶ *See also the boxed notes on* you *and* your *for more information.*
the red car is yours (*informal*) = la voiture rouge est à toi
(*polite or to several people*) = la voiture rouge est à vous
my garden is bigger than yours (*informal*)
= mon jardin est plus grand que le tien
(*polite or to several people*) = mon jardin est plus grand que le vôtre
her children are older than yours
(*informal*) = ses enfants sont plus âgés que les tiens
(*polite or to several people*) = ses enfants sont plus âgés que les vôtres

! *Note that, when comparing objects, people, etc, one of the following translations—le tien, la tienne, les tiens/tiennes, le/la vôtre or les vôtres—will be used. To know which one to use, find out whether the object, person, etc being described is masculine or feminine, singular or plural and whether you are using the polite or the informal form of address.*

yourself *pronoun*
- (*when used as a reflexive pronoun*)
  you'll enjoy yourself (*informal*) = tu vas t'amuser
  (*polite*) = vous allez vous amuser
  did you hurt yourself? (*informal*) = est-ce que tu t'es fait mal?
  (*polite*) = est-ce que vous vous êtes blessé?
- (*when used for emphasis*)
  you did it yourself (*informal*) = tu l'as fait toi-même
  (*polite*) = vous l'avez fait vous-même

yourselves *pronoun*
- (*when used as a reflexive pronoun*)
  you'll enjoy yourselves = vous allez vous amuser
  did you hurt yourselves? = est-ce que vous vous êtes fait mal?
- (*when used for emphasis*)
  are you going to organize it yourselves?
  = est-ce que vous allez l'organiser vous-mêmes?
  you want to be by yourselves = vous voulez être seuls

youth *noun*
- (*a young man*)
  a youth = un jeune
- (*young people*)
  the youth = les jeunes (*masculine plural*)

youth club *noun*
a youth club = un club de jeunes

youth hostel *noun*
a youth hostel = une auberge de jeunesse

youth worker *noun*
a youth worker = un éducateur/une éducatrice

you

Used to address people

- In English **you** is used to address everybody, whereas French has two forms: **tu** and **vous**. The usual word to use when you are speaking to anyone you do not know very well is **vous**. This is sometimes called the polite form:

*where are **you** going?*	= où allez-**vous**?
*I'm thinking of **you***	= je pense à **vous**
*would **you** like some coffee?*	= voulez-**vous** du café?
*can I help **you**?*	= est-ce que je peux **vous** aider?
*what can I do for **you**?*	= qu'est-ce que je peux faire pour **vous**?

The more informal pronoun **tu** is used between close friends and family members, within groups of children and young people, by adults when talking to children and always when talking to animals; **tu** is the subject form, the direct and indirect object form is **te** (**t'** before a vowel or mute h) and the form for emphatic use or use after a preposition is **toi**:

*where are **you** going?*	= où vas-**tu**?
*I'm thinking of **you***	= je pense à **toi**
*would **you** like some coffee?*	= veux-**tu** du café?
*can I help **you**?*	= est-ce que je peux **t'**aider?
*there's a letter for **you***	= il y a une lettre pour **toi**

As a general rule, when talking to a French person use **vous**, wait to see how they address you and follow suit. It is safer to wait for the French person to suggest using **tu**.

Note that **tu** is only a singular pronoun and **vous** is its plural form.

Remember that in French the object and indirect object pronouns are always placed before the verb:

*she knows **you***	= elle **vous** connaît
	= elle **te** connaît
*I'll give **you** my address*	= je **vous** donnerai mon adresse
	je **te** donnerai mon adresse

- In tenses like the present perfect and the past perfect, the past participle agrees with the direct object:

*I saw **you** on Saturday*	
(to one male: polite form)	= je **vous** ai vu samedi
(to one female: polite form)	= je **vous** ai vue samedi
(to one male: informal form)	= je **t'**ai vu samedi
(to one female: informal form)	= je **t'**ai vue samedi
(to two or more people, male or mixed)	= je **vous** ai vus samedi
(to two or more females)	= je **vous** ai vues samedi

Used impersonally

When **you** is used impersonally as the more informal form of **one**, it is translated by **on** for the subject form and by **vous** or **te** for the object form, depending on whether the comment is being made amongst friends or in a more formal context:

***you** can do as **you** like here*	= **on** peut faire ce qu'**on** veut ici
***you** could easily lose your bag here*	= **on** pourrait facilement perdre son sac ici
***you** never know*	= **on** ne sait jamais
*these mushrooms can make **you** ill*	= ces champignons peuvent **vous** rendre malade
	= ces champignons peuvent **te** rendre malade

▶ For a guide to the correct verb forms with **vous**, **tu** and **on**, consult the verb in the French-English part of the dictionary and check the number in the box, which will refer you to the French verb tables at the back of the dictionary.

your

▶ For a full note on the use of the **vous** and **tu** forms in French, see the note on **you** ▶ 378⏋.

● In French, determiners agree with the noun that follows:

your + *masculine singular noun*
(to one person: polite form or to two or more people)   **votre** chien, **votre** ami
(to one person: informal form)   **ton** chien, **ton** ami

your + *feminine singular noun*
(to one person: polite form or to two or more people)   **votre** pomme, **votre** orange
(to one person: informal form)   **ta** pomme, **ton*** orange

* Note that **ton** is used with a feminine noun beginning with a vowel or mute h.

your + *plural noun*
(to one person: polite form or   **vos** chiens, **vos** amis,
to two or more people)   **vos** pommes, **vos** oranges
(to one person: informal form)   **tes** chiens, **tes** amis,
    tes pommes, **tes** oranges

When **your** is stressed, **à vous** or **à toi** is added after the noun:

(to one person: polite form) **your** house   = **votre** maison **à vous**
(to two or more people)   = **vos** maisons **à vous**
(to one person: informal form) **your** house   = **ta** maison **à toi**
(to one person: polite form) **your** parents   = **vos** parents **à vous**
(to two or more people)   = **vos** parents **à vous**
(to one person: informal form) **your** parents   = **tes** parents **à toi**

● When used impersonally to mean **one's**, **your** is translated by **son, sa** or **ses**, when **you** is translated by **on**:

*you pay **your** bills at the end of the week*   = on paie **ses** factures à la fin de la
    semaine
*you get good value for **your** money*   = on en a pour **son** argent

The translation after an impersonal verb in French is **son, sa, ses**:

*you have to buy **your** tickets at the door*   = il faut acheter **ses** billets à l'entrée

Note, however, the following:

*smoking is bad for **your** health*   = le tabac est mauvais pour **la** santé
***your** average student*   = **l'**étudiant moyen

▶ For **your** used with parts of the body, see the usage note on **The human body** ▶ 201⏋.

Zz

zap *verb*
● (*to destroy*) = détruire
● (*British English*) (*to switch channels*)
to zap from channel to channel = zapper**✱**
● (*to remove from a computer screen*)
= supprimer

zapper *noun* (*British English*)
a zapper = une télécommande

zebra *noun*
a zebra = un zèbre

zebra crossing *noun* (*British English*)
a zebra crossing = un passage pour
piétons

zero *number*
zero = zéro

zip (*British English*), **zipper** (*US English*)
noun
a zip = une fermeture éclair®
to undo a zip = ouvrir une fermeture
éclair®

zip code *noun* (*US English*)
a zip code = un code postal

zodiac *noun*
the zodiac = le zodiaque

zone *noun*
a zone = une zone

zoo *noun*
a zoo = un zoo

✱ in informal situations

French verbs

Present indicative
je chante = *I sing, I'm singing*

Future indicative
je chanterai = *I will sing*

Imperfect indicative
je chantais = *I was singing*

Perfect indicative
j'ai chanté = *I sang, I have sung*

Pluperfect indicative
j'avais chanté = *I had sung*

Present subjunctive
bien que je chante = *although I sing*

Present conditional
s'il y avait une chorale, je chanterais = *if there was a choir, I would sing*

Past participle
chanté/chantée = *sung*

1 chanter

Present indicative

je	chante
tu	chantes
il	chante
nous	chantons
vous	chantez
ils	chantent

Present subjunctive

(que)	je	chante
(que)	tu	chantes
(qu')	il	chante
(que)	nous	chantions
(que)	vous	chantiez
(qu')	ils	chantent

Future indicative

je	chanterai
tu	chanteras
il	chantera
nous	chanterons
vous	chanterez
ils	chanteront

Present conditional

je	chanterais
tu	chanterais
il	chanterait
nous	chanterions
vous	chanteriez
ils	chanteraient

Imperfect indicative

je	chantais
tu	chantais
il	chantait
nous	chantions
vous	chantiez
ils	chantaient

Past participle

chanté/chantée

Pluperfect indicative

j'	avais	chanté
tu	avais	chanté
il	avait	chanté
elle	avait	chanté
nous	avions	chanté
vous	aviez	chanté
ils	avaient	chanté
elles	avaient	chanté

Perfect indicative

j'	ai	chanté
tu	as	chanté
il	a	chanté
elle	a	chanté
nous	avons	chanté
vous	avez	chanté
ils	ont	chanté
elles	ont	chanté

2 oublier

Present indicative

j'	oublie
tu	oublies
il	oublie
nous	oublions
vous	oubliez
ils	oublient

Present subjunctive

(que)	j'	oublie
(que)	tu	oublies
(qu')	il	oublie
(que)	nous	oubliions
(que)	vous	oubliiez
(qu')	ils	oublient

Future indicative

j'	oublierai
tu	oublieras
il	oubliera
nous	oublierons
vous	oublierez
ils	oublieront

Present conditional

j'	oublierais
tu	oublierais
il	oublierait
nous	oublierions
vous	oublieriez
ils	oublieraient

Imperfect indicative

j'	oubliais
tu	oubliais
il	oubliait
nous	oubliions
vous	oubliiez
ils	oubliaient

Past participle

oublié/oubliée

Pluperfect indicative

j'	avais	oublié
tu	avais	oublié
il	avait	oublié
elle	avait	oublié
nous	avions	oublié
vous	aviez	oublié
ils	avaient	oublié
elles	avaient	oublié

Perfect indicative

j'	ai	oublié
tu	as	oublié
il	a	oublié
elle	a	oublié
nous	avons	oublié
vous	avez	oublié
ils	ont	oublié
elles	ont	oublié

3 finir

Present indicative

je	finis
tu	finis
il	finit
nous	finissons
vous	finissez
ils	finissent

Future indicative

je	finirai
tu	finiras
il	finira
nous	finirons
vous	finirez
ils	finiront

Imperfect indicative

je	finissais
tu	finissais
il	finissait
nous	finissions
vous	finissiez
ils	finissaient

Perfect indicative

j'	ai	fini
tu	as	fini
il	a	fini
elle	a	fini
nous	avons	fini
vous	avez	fini
ils	ont	fini
elles	ont	fini

Present subjunctive

(que)	je	finisse
(que)	tu	finisses
(qu')	il	finisse
(que)	nous	finissions
(que)	vous	finissiez
(qu')	ils	finissent

Present conditional

je	finirais
tu	finirais
il	finirait
nous	finirions
vous	finiriez
ils	finiraient

Past participle

fini/finie

Pluperfect indicative

j'	avais	fini
tu	avais	fini
il	avait	fini
elle	avait	fini
nous	avions	fini
vous	aviez	fini
ils	avaient	fini
elles	avaient	fini

5 apercevoir

Present indicative

j'	aperçois
tu	aperçois
il	aperçoit
nous	apercevons
vous	apercevez
ils	aperçoivent

Future indicative

j'	apercevrai
tu	apercevras
il	apercevra
nous	apercevrons
vous	apercevrez
ils	apercevront

Imperfect indicative

j'	apercevais
tu	apercevais
il	apercevait
nous	apercevions
vous	aperceviez
ils	apercevaient

Perfect indicative

j'	ai	aperçu
tu	as	aperçu
il	a	aperçu
elle	a	aperçu
nous	avons	aperçu
vous	avez	aperçu
ils	ont	aperçu
elles	ont	aperçu

Present subjunctive

(que)	j'	aperçoive
(que)	tu	aperçoives
(qu')	il	aperçoive
(que)	nous	apercevions
(que)	vous	aperceviez
(qu')	ils	aperçoivent

Present conditional

j'	apercevrais
tu	apercevrais
il	apercevrait
nous	apercevrions
vous	apercevriez
ils	apercevraient

Past participle

aperçu/aperçue

Pluperfect indicative

j'	avais	aperçu
tu	avais	aperçu
il	avait	aperçu
elle	avait	aperçu
nous	avions	aperçu
vous	aviez	aperçu
ils	avaient	aperçu
elles	avaient	aperçu

4 offrir

Present indicative

j'	offre
tu	offres
il	offre
nous	offrons
vous	offrez
ils	offrent

Future indicative

j'	offrirai
tu	offriras
il	offrira
nous	offrirons
vous	offrirez
ils	offriront

Imperfect indicative

j'	offrais
tu	offrais
il	offrait
nous	offrions
vous	offriez
ils	offraient

Perfect indicative

j'	ai	offert
tu	as	offert
il	a	offert
elle	a	offert
nous	avons	offert
vous	avez	offert
ils	ont	offert
elles	ont	offert

Present subjunctive

(que)	j'	offre
(que)	tu	offres
(qu')	il	offre
(que)	nous	offrions
(que)	vous	offriez
(qu')	ils	offrent

Present conditional

j'	offrirais
tu	offrirais
il	offrirait
nous	offririons
vous	offririez
ils	offriraient

Past participle

offert/
offerte

Pluperfect indicative

j'	avais	offert
tu	avais	offert
il	avait	offert
elle	avait	offert
nous	avions	offert
vous	aviez	offert
ils	avaient	offert
elles	avaient	offert

6 attendre

Present indicative

j'	attends
tu	attends
il	attend
nous	attendons
vous	attendez
ils	attendent

Future indicative

j'	attendrai
tu	attendras
il	attendra
nous	attendrons
vous	attendrez
ils	attendront

Imperfect indicative

j'	attendais
tu	attendais
il	attendait
nous	attendions
vous	attendiez
ils	attendaient

Perfect indicative

j'	ai	attendu
tu	as	attendu
il	a	attendu
elle	a	attendu
nous	avons	attendu
vous	avez	attendu
ils	ont	attendu
elles	ont	attendu

Present subjunctive

(que)	j'	attende
(que)	tu	attendes
(qu')	il	attende
(que)	nous	attendions
(que)	vous	attendiez
(qu')	ils	attendent

Present conditional

j'	attendrais
tu	attendrais
il	attendrait
nous	attendrions
vous	attendriez
ils	attendraient

Past participle

attendu/attendue

Pluperfect indicative

j'	avais	attendu
tu	avais	attendu
il	avait	attendu
elle	avait	attendu
nous	avions	attendu
vous	aviez	attendu
ils	avaient	attendu
elles	avaient	attendu

7 être

Present indicative

je	suis
tu	es
il	est
nous	sommes
vous	êtes
ils	sont

Present subjunctive

(que)	je	sois
(que)	tu	sois
(qu')	il	soit
(que)	nous	soyons
(que)	vous	soyez
(qu')	ils	soient

Future indicative

je	serai
tu	seras
il	sera
nous	serons
vous	serez
ils	seront

Present conditional

je	serais
tu	serais
il	serait
nous	serions
vous	seriez
ils	seraient

Imperfect indicative

j'	étais
tu	étais
il	était
nous	étions
vous	étiez
ils	étaient

Past participle

été (invariable)

Pluperfect indicative

j'	avais	été
tu	avais	été
il	avait	été
elle	avait	été
nous	avions	été
vous	aviez	été
ils	avaient	été
elles	avaient	été

Perfect indicative

j'	ai	été
tu	as	été
il	a	été
elle	a	été
nous	avons	été
vous	avez	été
ils	ont	été
elles	ont	été

8 avoir

Present indicative

j'	ai
tu	as
il	a
nous	avons
vous	avez
ils	ont

Present subjunctive

(que)	j'	aie
(que)	tu	aies
(qu')	il	ait
(que)	nous	ayons
(que)	vous	ayez
(qu')	ils	aient

Future indicative

j'	aurai
tu	auras
il	aura
nous	aurons
vous	aurez
ils	auront

Present conditional

j'	aurais
tu	aurais
il	aurait
nous	aurions
vous	auriez
ils	auraient

Imperfect indicative

j'	avais
tu	avais
il	avait
nous	avions
vous	aviez
ils	avaient

Past participle

eu/eue

Pluperfect indicative

j'	avais	eu
tu	avais	eu
il	avait	eu
elle	avait	eu
nous	avions	eu
vous	aviez	eu
ils	avaient	eu
elles	avaient	eu

Perfect indicative

j'	ai	eu
tu	as	eu
il	a	eu
elle	a	eu
nous	avons	eu
vous	avez	eu
ils	ont	eu
elles	ont	eu

9 aller

Present indicative

je	vais
tu	vas
il	va
nous	allons
vous	allez
ils	vont

Present subjunctive

(que)	j'	aille
(que)	tu	ailles
(qu')	il	aille
(que)	nous	allions
(que)	vous	alliez
(qu')	ils	aillent

Future indicative

j'	irai
tu	iras
il	ira
nous	irons
vous	irez
ils	iront

Present conditional

j'	irais
tu	irais
il	irait
nous	irions
vous	iriez
ils	iraient

Imperfect indicative

j'	allais
tu	allais
il	allait
nous	allions
vous	alliez
ils	allaient

Past participle

allé/allée

Pluperfect indicative

j'	étais	allé
tu	étais	allé
il	était	allé
elle	était	allée
nous	étions	allés
vous	étiez	allés
ils	étaient	allés
elles	étaient	allées

Perfect indicative

je	suis	allé
tu	es	allé
il	est	allé
elle	est	allée
nous	sommes	allés
vous	êtes	allés
ils	sont	allés
elles	sont	allées

10 faire

Present indicative

je	fais
tu	fais
il	fait
nous	faisons
vous	faites
ils	font

Present subjunctive

(que)	je	fasse
(que)	tu	fasses
(qu')	il	fasse
(que)	nous	fassions
(que)	vous	fassiez
(qu')	ils	fassent

Future indicative

je	ferai
tu	feras
il	fera
nous	ferons
vous	ferez
ils	feront

Present conditional

je	ferais
tu	ferais
il	ferait
nous	ferions
vous	feriez
ils	feraient

Imperfect indicative

je	faisais
tu	faisais
il	faisait
nous	faisions
vous	faisiez
ils	faisaient

Past participle

fait/faite

Pluperfect indicative

j'	avais	fait
tu	avais	fait
il	avait	fait
elle	avait	fait
nous	avions	fait
vous	aviez	fait
ils	avaient	fait
elles	avaient	fait

Perfect indicative

j'	ai	fait
tu	as	fait
il	a	fait
elle	a	fait
nous	avons	fait
vous	avez	fait
ils	ont	fait
elles	ont	fait

11 créer

Present indicative		Present subjunctive		
je	crée	(que)	je	crée
tu	crées	(que)	tu	crées
il	crée	(qu')	il	crée
nous	créons	(que)	nous	créions
vous	créez	(que)	vous	créiez
ils	créent	(qu')	ils	créent

Future indicative		Present conditional	
je	créerai	je	créerais
tu	créeras	tu	créerais
il	créera	il	créerait
nous	créerons	nous	créerions
vous	créerez	vous	créeriez
ils	créeront	ils	créeraient

Imperfect indicative		Past participle	
je	créais	créé/créée	
tu	créais		
il	créait		

Pluperfect indicative		
nous	créions	j'	avais	créé
vous	créiez	tu	avais	créé
ils	créaient	il	avait	créé
		elle	avait	créé

Perfect indicative			
j'	ai	créé	nous	avions	créé
tu	as	créé	vous	aviez	créé
il	a	créé	ils	avaient	créé
elle	a	créé	elles	avaient	créé
nous	avons	créé		
vous	avez	créé		
ils	ont	créé		
elles	ont	créé		

12 avancer

Present indicative		Present subjunctive		
j'	avance	(que)	j'	avance
tu	avances	(que)	tu	avances
il	avance	(qu')	il	avance
nous	avançons	(que)	nous	avancions
vous	avancez	(que)	vous	avanciez
ils	avancent	(qu')	ils	avancent

Future indicative		Present conditional	
j'	avancerai	j'	avancerais
tu	avanceras	tu	avancerais
il	avancera	il	avancerait
nous	avancerons	nous	avancerions
vous	avancerez	vous	avanceriez
ils	avanceront	ils	avanceraient

Imperfect indicative		Past participle	
j'	avançais	avancé/avancée	
tu	avançais		
il	avançait		

Pluperfect indicative		
nous	avancions	j'	avais	avancé
vous	avanciez	tu	avais	avancé
ils	avançaient	il	avait	avancé
		elle	avait	avancé

Perfect indicative			
j'	ai	avancé	nous	avions	avancé
tu	as	avancé	vous	aviez	avancé
il	a	avancé	ils	avaient	avancé
elle	a	avancé	elles	avaient	avancé
nous	avons	avancé		
vous	avez	avancé		
ils	ont	avancé		
elles	ont	avancé		

13 changer

Present indicative		Present subjunctive		
je	change	(que)	je	change
tu	changes	(que)	tu	changes
il	change	(qu')	il	change
nous	changeons	(que)	nous	changions
vous	changez	(que)	vous	changiez
ils	changent	(qu')	ils	changent

Future indicative		Present conditional	
je	changerai	je	changerais
tu	changeras	tu	changerais
il	changera	il	changerait
nous	changerons	nous	changerions
vous	changerez	vous	changeriez
ils	changeront	ils	changeraient

Imperfect indicative		Past participle	
je	changeais	changé/changée	
tu	changeais		
il	changeait		

Pluperfect indicative		
nous	changions	j'	avais	changé
vous	changiez	tu	avais	changé
ils	changeaient	il	avait	changé
		elle	avait	changé

Perfect indicative			
j'	ai	changé	nous	avions	changé
tu	as	changé	vous	aviez	changé
il	a	changé	ils	avaient	changé
elle	a	changé	elles	avaient	changé
nous	avons	changé		
vous	avez	changé		
ils	ont	changé		
elles	ont	changé		

14 espérer

Present indicative		Present subjunctive		
j'	espère	(que)	j'	espère
tu	espères	(que)	tu	espères
il	espère	(qu')	il	espère
nous	espérons	(que)	nous	espérions
vous	espérez	(que)	vous	espériez
ils	espèrent	(qu')	ils	espèrent

Future indicative		Present conditional	
j'	espérerai	j'	espérerais
tu	espéreras	tu	espérerais
il	espérera	il	espérerait
nous	espérerons	nous	espérerions
vous	espérerez	vous	espéreriez
ils	espéreront	ils	espéreraient

Imperfect indicative		Past participle	
j'	espérais	espéré/espérée	
tu	espérais		
il	espérait		

Pluperfect indicative		
nous	espérions	j'	avais	espéré
vous	espériez	tu	avais	espéré
ils	espéraient	il	avait	espéré
		elle	avait	espéré

Perfect indicative			
j'	ai	espéré	nous	avions	espéré
tu	as	espéré	vous	aviez	espéré
il	a	espéré	ils	avaient	espéré
elle	a	espéré	elles	avaient	espéré
nous	avons	espéré		
vous	avez	espéré		
ils	ont	espéré		
elles	ont	espéré		

15 protéger

Present indicative

je	protège
tu	protèges
il	protège
nous	protégeons
vous	protégez
ils	protègent

Present subjunctive

(que)	je	protège
(que)	tu	protèges
(qu')	il	protège
(que)	nous	protégions
(que)	vous	protégiez
(qu')	ils	protègent

Future indicative

je	protégerai
tu	protégeras
il	protégera
nous	protégerons
vous	protégerez
ils	protégeront

Present conditional

je	protégerais
tu	protégerais
il	protégerait
nous	protégerions
vous	protégeriez
ils	protégeraient

Imperfect indicative

je	protégeais
tu	protégeais
il	protégeait
nous	protégions
vous	protégiez
ils	protégeaient

Past participle

protégé/protégée

Pluperfect indicative

j'	avais	protégé
tu	avais	protégé
il	avait	protégé
elle	avait	protégé
nous	avions	protégé
vous	aviez	protégé
ils	avaient	protégé

Perfect indicative

j'	ai	protégé
tu	as	protégé
il	a	protégé
elle	a	protégé
nous	avons	protégé
vous	avez	protégé
ils	ont	protégé
elles	ont	protégé

17 peler

Present indicative

je	pèle
tu	pèles
il	pèle
nous	pelons
vous	pelez
ils	pèlent

Present subjunctive

(que)	je	pèle
(que)	tu	pèles
(qu')	il	pèle
(que)	nous	pelions
(que)	vous	peliez
(qu')	ils	pèlent

Future indicative

je	pèlerai
tu	pèleras
il	pèlera
nous	pèlerons
vous	pèlerez
ils	pèleront

Present conditional

je	pèlerais
tu	pèlerais
il	pèlerait
nous	pèlerions
vous	pèleriez
ils	pèleraient

Imperfect indicative

je	pelais
tu	pelais
il	pelait
nous	pelions
vous	peliez
ils	pelaient

Past participle

pelé/pelée

Pluperfect indicative

j'	avais	pelé
tu	avais	pelé
il	avait	pelé
elle	avait	pelé
nous	avions	pelé
vous	aviez	pelé
ils	avaient	pelé
elles	avaient	pelé

Perfect indicative

j'	ai	pelé
tu	as	pelé
il	a	pelé
elle	a	pelé
nous	avons	pelé
vous	avez	pelé
ils	ont	pelé
elles	ont	pelé

16 mener

Present indicative

je	mène
tu	mènes
il	mène
nous	menons
vous	menez
ils	mènent

Present subjunctive

(que)	je	mène
(que)	tu	mènes
(qu')	il	mène
(que)	nous	menions
(que)	vous	meniez
(qu')	ils	mènent

Future indicative

je	mènerai
tu	mèneras
il	mènera
nous	mènerons
vous	mènerez
ils	mèneront

Present conditional

je	mènerais
tu	mènerais
il	mènerait
nous	mènerions
vous	mèneriez
ils	mèneraient

Imperfect indicative

je	menais
tu	menais
il	menait
nous	menions
vous	meniez
ils	menaient

Past participle

mené/menée

Pluperfect indicative

j'	avais	mené
tu	avais	mené
il	avait	mené
elle	avait	mené
nous	avions	mené
vous	aviez	mené
ils	avaient	mené
elles	avaient	mené

Perfect indicative

j'	ai	mené
tu	as	mené
il	a	mené
elle	a	mené
nous	avons	mené
vous	avez	mené
ils	ont	mené
elles	ont	mené

18 acheter

Present indicative

j'	achète
tu	achètes
il	achète
nous	achetons
vous	achetez
ils	achètent

Present subjunctive

(que)	j'	achète
(que)	tu	achètes
(qu')	il	achète
(que)	nous	achetions
(que)	vous	achetiez
(qu')	ils	achètent

Future indicative

j'	achèterai
tu	achèteras
il	achètera
nous	achèterons
vous	achèterez
ils	achèteront

Present conditional

j'	achèterais
tu	achèterais
il	achèterait
nous	achèterions
vous	achèteriez
ils	achèteraient

Imperfect indicative

j'	achetais
tu	achetais
il	achetait
nous	achetions
vous	achetiez
ils	achetaient

Past participle

acheté/achetée

Pluperfect indicative

j'	avais	acheté
tu	avais	acheté
il	avait	acheté
elle	avait	acheté
nous	avions	acheté
vous	aviez	acheté
ils	avaient	acheté
elles	avaient	acheté

Perfect indicative

j'	ai	acheté
tu	as	acheté
il	a	acheté
elle	a	acheté
nous	avons	acheté
vous	avez	acheté
ils	ont	acheté
elles	ont	acheté

19 rappeler

Present indicative
je	rappelle
tu	rappelles
il	rappelle
nous	rappelons
vous	rappelez
ils	rappellent

Present subjunctive
(que)	je	rappelle
(que)	tu	rappelles
(qu')	il	rappelle
(que)	nous	rappelions
(que)	vous	rappeliez
(qu')	ils	rappellent

Future indicative
je	rappellerai
tu	rappelleras
il	rappellera
nous	rappellerons
vous	rappellerez
ils	rappelleront

Present conditional
je	rappellerais
tu	rappellerais
il	rappellerait
nous	rappellerions
vous	rappelleriez
ils	rappelleraient

Imperfect indicative
je	rappelais
tu	rappelais
il	rappelait
nous	rappelions
vous	rappeliez
ils	rappelaient

Past participle
rappelé/rappelée

Pluperfect indicative
j'	avais	rappelé
tu	avais	rappelé
il	avait	rappelé
elle	avait	rappelé
nous	avions	rappelé
vous	aviez	rappelé
ils	avaient	rappelé
elles	avaient	rappelé

Perfect indicative
j'	ai	rappelé
tu	as	rappelé
il	a	rappelé
elle	a	rappelé
nous	avons	rappelé
vous	avez	rappelé
ils	ont	rappelé
elles	ont	rappelé

20 jeter

Present indicative
je	jette
tu	jettes
il	jette
nous	jetons
vous	jetez
ils	jettent

Present subjunctive
(que)	je	jette
(que)	tu	jettes
(qu')	il	jette
(que)	nous	jetions
(que)	vous	jetiez
(qu')	ils	jettent

Future indicative
je	jetterai
tu	jetteras
il	jettera
nous	jetterons
vous	jetterez
ils	jetteront

Present conditional
je	jetterais
tu	jetterais
il	jetterait
nous	jetterions
vous	jetteriez
ils	jetteraient

Imperfect indicative
je	jetais
tu	jetais
il	jetait
nous	jetions
vous	jetiez
ils	jetaient

Past participle
jeté/jetée

Pluperfect indicative
j'	avais	jeté
tu	avais	jeté
il	avait	jeté
elle	avait	jeté
nous	avions	jeté
vous	aviez	jeté
ils	avaient	jeté
elles	avaient	jeté

Perfect indicative
j'	ai	jeté
tu	as	jeté
il	a	jeté
elle	a	jeté
nous	avons	jeté
vous	avez	jeté
ils	ont	jeté
elles	ont	jeté

21 essayer

Present indicative
j'	essaie
tu	essaies
il	essaie
nous	essayons
vous	essayez
ils	essaient

Present subjunctive
(que)	j'	essaie
(que)	tu	essaies
(qu')	il	essaie
(que)	nous	essayions
(que)	vous	essayiez
(qu')	ils	essaient

Future indicative
j'	essaierai
tu	essaieras
il	essaiera
nous	essaierons
vous	essaierez
ils	essaieront

Present conditional
j'	essaierais
tu	essaierais
il	essaierait
nous	essaierions
vous	essaieriez
ils	essaieraient

Imperfect indicative
j'	essayais
tu	essayais
il	essayait
nous	essayions
vous	essayiez
ils	essayaient

Past participle
essayé/essayée

Pluperfect indicative
j'	avais	essayé
tu	avais	essayé
il	avait	essayé
elle	avait	essayé
nous	avions	essayé
vous	aviez	essayé
ils	avaient	essayé
elles	avaient	essayé

Perfect indicative
j'	ai	essayé
tu	as	essayé
il	a	essayé
elle	a	essayé
nous	avons	essayé
vous	avez	essayé
ils	ont	essayé
elles	ont	essayé

22 appuyer

Present indicative
j'	appuie
tu	appuies
il	appuie
nous	appuyons
vous	appuyez
ils	appuient

Present subjunctive
(que)	j'	appuie
(que)	tu	appuies
(qu')	il	appuie
(que)	nous	appuyions
(que)	vous	appuyiez
(qu')	ils	appuient

Future indicative
j'	appuierai
tu	appuieras
il	appuiera
nous	appuierons
vous	appuierez
ils	appuieront

Present conditional
j'	appuierais
tu	appuierais
il	appuierait
nous	appuierions
vous	appuieriez
ils	appuieraient

Imperfect indicative
j'	appuyais
tu	appuyais
il	appuyait
nous	appuyions
vous	appuyiez
ils	appuyaient

Past participle
appuyé/appuyée

Pluperfect indicative
j'	avais	appuyé
tu	avais	appuyé
il	avait	appuyé
elle	avait	appuyé
nous	avions	appuyé
vous	aviez	appuyé
ils	avaient	appuyé
elles	avaient	appuyé

Perfect indicative
j'	ai	appuyé
tu	as	appuyé
il	a	appuyé
elle	a	appuyé
nous	avons	appuyé
vous	avez	appuyé
ils	ont	appuyé
elles	ont	appuyé

23 nettoyer

Present indicative		Present subjunctive		
je	nettoie	(que)	je	nettoie
tu	nettoies	(que)	tu	nettoies
il	nettoie	(qu')	il	nettoie
nous	nettoyons	(que)	nous	nettoyions
vous	nettoyez	(que)	vous	nettoyiez
ils	nettoient	(qu')	ils	nettoient

Future indicative		Present conditional	
je	nettoierai	je	nettoierais
tu	nettoieras	tu	nettoierais
il	nettoiera	il	nettoierait
nous	nettoierons	nous	nettoierions
vous	nettoierez	vous	nettoieriez
ils	nettoieront	ils	nettoieraient

Imperfect indicative

je	nettoyais
tu	nettoyais
il	nettoyait
nous	nettoyions
vous	nettoyiez
ils	nettoyaient

Past participle

nettoyé/nettoyée

Pluperfect indicative

j'	avais	nettoyé
tu	avais	nettoyé
il	avait	nettoyé
elle	avait	nettoyé
nous	avions	nettoyé
vous	aviez	nettoyé
ils	avaient	nettoyé
elles	avaient	nettoyé

Perfect indicative

j'	ai	nettoyé
tu	as	nettoyé
il	a	nettoyé
elle	a	nettoyé
nous	avons	nettoyé
vous	avez	nettoyé
ils	ont	nettoyé
elles	ont	nettoyé

25 mourir

Present indicative		Present subjunctive		
je	meurs	(que)	je	meure
tu	meurs	(que)	tu	meures
il	meurt	(qu')	il	meure
nous	mourons	(que)	nous	mourions
vous	mourez	(que)	vous	mouriez
ils	meurent	(qu')	ils	meurent

Future indicative		Present conditional	
je	mourrai	je	mourrais
tu	mourras	tu	mourrais
il	mourra	il	mourrait
nous	mourrons	nous	mourrions
vous	mourrez	vous	mourriez
ils	mourront	ils	mourraient

Imperfect indicative

je	mourais
tu	mourais
il	mourait
nous	mourions
vous	mouriez
ils	mouraient

Past participle

mort/morte

Pluperfect indicative

j'	étais	mort
tu	étais	mort
il	était	mort
elle	était	morte
nous	étions	morts
vous	étiez	morts
ils	étaient	morts
elles	étaient	mortes

Perfect indicative

je	suis	mort
tu	es	mort
il	est	mort
elle	est	morte
nous	sommes	morts
vous	êtes	morts
ils	sont	morts
elles	sont	mortes

24 envoyer

Present indicative		Present subjunctive		
j'	envoie	(que)	j'	envoie
tu	envoies	(que)	tu	envoies
il	envoie	(qu')	il	envoie
nous	envoyons	(que)	nous	envoyions
vous	envoyez	(que)	vous	envoyiez
ils	envoient	(qu')	ils	envoient

Future indicative		Present conditional	
j'	enverrai	j'	enverrais
tu	enverras	tu	enverrais
il	enverra	il	enverrait
nous	enverrons	nous	enverrions
vous	enverrez	vous	enverriez
ils	enverront	ils	enverraient

Imperfect indicative

j'	envoyais
tu	envoyais
il	envoyait
nous	envoyions
vous	envoyiez
ils	envoyaient

Past participle

envoyé/envoyée

Pluperfect indicative

j'	avais	envoyé
tu	avais	envoyé
il	avait	envoyé
elle	avait	envoyé
nous	avions	envoyé
vous	aviez	envoyé
ils	avaient	envoyé
elles	avaient	envoyé

Perfect indicative

j'	ai	envoyé
tu	as	envoyé
il	a	envoyé
elle	a	envoyé
nous	avons	envoyé
vous	avez	envoyé
ils	ont	envoyé
elles	ont	envoyé

26 courir

Present indicative		Present subjunctive		
je	cours	(que)	je	coure
tu	cours	(que)	tu	coures
il	court	(qu')	il	coure
nous	courons	(que)	nous	courions
vous	courez	(que)	vous	couriez
ils	courent	(qu')	ils	courent

Future indicative		Present conditional	
je	courrai	je	courrais
tu	courras	tu	courrais
il	courra	il	courrait
nous	courrons	nous	courrions
vous	courrez	vous	courriez
ils	courront	ils	courraient

Imperfect indicative

je	courais
tu	courais
il	courait
nous	courions
vous	couriez
ils	couraient

Past participle

couru/courue

Pluperfect indicative

j'	avais	couru
tu	avais	couru
il	avait	couru
elle	avait	couru
nous	avions	couru
vous	aviez	couru
ils	avaient	couru
elles	avaient	couru

Perfect indicative

j'	ai	couru
tu	as	couru
il	a	couru
elle	a	couru
nous	avons	couru
vous	avez	couru
ils	ont	couru
elles	ont	couru

27 cueillir

Present indicative		Present subjunctive		
je	cueille	(que)	je	cueille
tu	cueilles	(que)	tu	cueilles
il	cueille	(qu')	il	cueille
nous	cueillons	(que)	nous	cueillions
vous	cueillez	(que)	vous	cueilliez
ils	cueillent	(qu')	ils	cueillent

Future indicative		Present conditional	
je	cueillerai	je	cueillerais
tu	cueilleras	tu	cueillerais
il	cueillera	il	cueillerait
nous	cueillerons	nous	cueillerions
vous	cueillerez	vous	cueilleriez
ils	cueilleront	ils	cueilleraient

Imperfect indicative

je	cueillais
tu	cueillais
il	cueillait
nous	cueillions
vous	cueilliez
ils	cueillaient

Past participle

cueilli/cueillie

Pluperfect indicative

j'	avais	cueilli
tu	avais	cueilli
il	avait	cueilli
elle	avait	cueilli
nous	avions	cueilli
vous	aviez	cueilli
ils	avaient	cueilli
elles	avaient	cueilli

Perfect indicative

j'	ai	cueilli
tu	as	cueilli
il	a	cueilli
elle	a	cueilli
nous	avons	cueilli
vous	avez	cueilli
ils	ont	cueilli
elles	ont	cueilli

28 faillir

Perfect indicative

j'	ai	failli
tu	as	failli
il	a	failli
elle	a	failli
nous	avons	failli
vous	avez	failli
ils	ont	failli
elles	ont	failli

Past participle

failli

Pluperfect indicative

j'	avais	failli
tu	avais	failli
il	avait	failli
elle	avait	failli
nous	avions	failli
vous	aviez	failli
ils	avaient	failli
elles	avaient	failli

29 fuir

Present indicative		Present subjunctive		
je	fuis	(que)	je	fuie
tu	fuis	(que)	tu	fuies
il	fuit	(qu')	il	fuie
nous	fuyons	(que)	nous	fuyions
vous	fuyez	(que)	vous	fuyiez
ils	fuient	(qu')	ils	fuient

Future indicative		Present conditional	
je	fuirai	je	fuirais
tu	fuiras	tu	fuirais
il	fuira	il	fuirait
nous	fuirons	nous	fuirions
vous	fuirez	vous	fuiriez
ils	fuiront	ils	fuiraient

Imperfect indicative

je	fuyais
tu	fuyais
il	fuyait
nous	fuyions
vous	fuyiez
ils	fuyaient

Past participle

fui/fuie

Pluperfect indicative

j'	avais	fui
tu	avais	fui
il	avait	fui
elle	avait	fui
nous	avions	fui
vous	aviez	fui
ils	avaient	fui
elles	avaient	fui

Perfect indicative

j'	ai	fui
tu	as	fui
il	a	fui
elle	a	fui
nous	avons	fui
vous	avez	fui
ils	ont	fui
elles	ont	fui

30 sortir

Present indicative		Present subjunctive		
je	sors	(que)	je	sorte
tu	sors	(que)	tu	sortes
il	sort	(qu')	il	sorte
nous	sortons	(que)	nous	sortions
vous	sortez	(que)	vous	sortiez
ils	sortent	(qu')	ils	sortent

Future indicative		Present conditional	
je	sortirai	je	sortirais
tu	sortiras	tu	sortirais
il	sortira	il	sortirait
nous	sortirons	nous	sortirions
vous	sortirez	vous	sortiriez
ils	sortiront	ils	sortiraient

Imperfect indicative

je	sortais
tu	sortais
il	sortait
nous	sortions
vous	sortiez
ils	sortaient

Past participle

sorti/sortie

Pluperfect indicative

j'	étais	sorti
tu	étais	sorti
il	était	sorti
elle	était	sortie
nous	étions	sortis
vous	étiez	sortis
ils	étaient	sortis
elles	étaient	sorties

Perfect indicative

je	suis	sorti
tu	es	sorti
il	est	sorti
elle	est	sortie
nous	sommes	sortis
vous	êtes	sortis
ils	sont	sortis
elles	sont	sorties

31 bouillir

Present indicative

je	bous
tu	bous
il	bout
nous	bouillons
vous	bouillez
ils	bouillent

Future indicative

je	bouillirai
tu	bouilliras
il	bouillira
nous	bouillirons
vous	bouillirez
ils	bouilliront

Imperfect indicative

je	bouillais
tu	bouillais
il	bouillait
nous	bouillions
vous	bouilliez
ils	bouillaient

Perfect indicative

j'	ai	bouilli
tu	as	bouilli
il	a	bouilli
elle	a	bouilli
nous	avons	bouilli
vous	avez	bouilli
ils	ont	bouilli
elles	ont	bouilli

Present subjunctive

(que)	je	bouille
(que)	tu	bouilles
(qu')	il	bouille
(que)	nous	bouillions
(que)	vous	bouilliez
(qu')	ils	bouillent

Present conditional

je	bouillirais
tu	bouillirais
il	bouillirait
nous	bouillirions
vous	bouilliriez
ils	bouilliraient

Past participle

bouilli/bouillie

Pluperfect indicative

j'	avais	bouilli
tu	avais	bouilli
il	avait	bouilli
elle	avait	bouilli
nous	avions	bouilli
vous	aviez	bouilli
ils	avaient	bouilli
elles	avaient	bouilli

32 découvrir

Present indicative

je	découvre
tu	découvres
il	découvre
nous	découvrons
vous	découvrez
ils	découvrent

Future indicative

je	découvrirai
tu	découvriras
il	découvrira
nous	découvrirons
vous	découvrirez
ils	découvriront

Imperfect indicative

je	découvrais
tu	découvrais
il	découvrait
nous	découvrions
vous	découvriez
ils	découvraient

Perfect indicative

j'	ai	découvert
tu	as	découvert
il	a	découvert
elle	a	découvert
nous	avons	découvert
vous	avez	découvert
ils	ont	découvert
elles	ont	découvert

Present subjunctive

(que)	je	découvre
(que)	tu	découvres
(qu')	il	découvre
(que)	nous	découvrions
(que)	vous	découvriez
(qu')	ils	découvrent

Present conditional

je	découvrirais
tu	découvrirais
il	découvrirait
nous	découvririons
vous	découvririez
ils	découvriraient

Past participle

découvert/
découverte

Pluperfect indicative

j'	avais	découvert
tu	avais	découvert
il	avait	découvert
elle	avait	découvert
nous	avions	découvert
vous	aviez	découvert
ils	avaient	découvert
elles	avaient	découvert

33 pleuvoir

Present indicative

il	pleut
ils	pleuvent

Future indicative

il	pleuvra
ils	pleuvront

Imperfect indicative

il	pleuvait
ils	pleuvaient

Perfect indicative

il	a	plu
ils	ont	plu

Present subjunctive

(qu')	il	pleuve
(qu')	ils	pleuvent

Present conditional

il	pleuvrait
ils	pleuvraient

Past participle

plu

Pluperfect indicative

il	avait	plu
ils	avaient	plu

34 asseoir

Present indicative

j'	assieds
tu	assieds
il	assied
nous	asseyons
vous	asseyez
ils	asseyent

Future indicative

j'	assiérai
tu	assiéras
il	assiéra
nous	assiérons
vous	assiérez
ils	assiéront

Imperfect indicative

j'	asseyais
tu	asseyais
il	asseyait
nous	asseyions
vous	asseyiez
ils	asseyaient

Perfect indicative

j'	ai	assis
tu	as	assis
il	a	assis
elle	a	assis
nous	avons	assis
vous	avez	assis
ils	ont	assis
elles	ont	assis

Present subjunctive

(que)	j'	asseye
(que)	tu	asseyes
(qu')	il	asseye
(que)	nous	asseyions
(que)	vous	asseyiez
(qu')	ils	asseyent

Present conditional

j'	assiérais
tu	assiérais
il	assiérait
nous	assiérions
vous	assiériez
ils	assiéraient

Past participle

assis/assise

Pluperfect indicative

j'	avais	assis
tu	avais	assis
il	avait	assis
elle	avait	assis
nous	avions	assis
vous	aviez	assis
ils	avaient	assis
elles	avaient	assis

35 prévoir

Present indicative

je	prévois
tu	prévois
il	prévoit
nous	prévoyons
vous	prévoyez
ils	prévoient

Present subjunctive

(que)	je	prévoie
(que)	tu	prévoies
(qu')	il	prévoie
(que)	nous	prévoyions
(que)	vous	prévoyiez
(qu')	ils	prévoient

Future indicative

je	prévoirai
tu	prévoiras
il	prévoira
nous	prévoirons
vous	prévoirez
ils	prévoiront

Present conditional

je	prévoirais
tu	prévoirais
il	prévoirait
nous	prévoirions
vous	prévoiriez
ils	prévoiraient

Imperfect indicative

je	prévoyais
tu	prévoyais
il	prévoyait
nous	prévoyions
vous	prévoyiez
ils	prévoyaient

Past participle

prévu/prévue

Pluperfect indicative

j'	avais	prévu
tu	avais	prévu
il	avait	prévu
elle	avait	prévu
nous	avions	prévu
vous	aviez	prévu
ils	avaient	prévu
elles	avaient	prévu

Perfect indicative

j'	ai	prévu
tu	as	prévu
il	a	prévu
elle	a	prévu
nous	avons	prévu
vous	avez	prévu
ils	ont	prévu
elles	ont	prévu

36 devenir

Present indicative

je	deviens
tu	deviens
il	devient
nous	devenons
vous	devenez
ils	deviennent

Present subjunctive

(que)	je	devienne
(que)	tu	deviennes
(qu')	il	devienne
(que)	nous	devenions
(que)	vous	deveniez
(qu')	ils	deviennent

Future indicative

je	deviendrai
tu	deviendras
il	deviendra
nous	deviendrons
vous	deviendrez
ils	deviendront

Present conditional

je	deviendrais
tu	deviendrais
il	deviendrait
nous	deviendrions
vous	deviendriez
ils	deviendraient

Imperfect indicative

je	devenais
tu	devenais
il	devenait
nous	devenions
vous	deveniez
ils	devenaient

Past participle

devenu/devenue

Pluperfect indicative

j'	étais	devenu
tu	étais	devenu
il	était	devenu
elle	était	devenue
nous	étions	devenus
vous	étiez	devenus
ils	étaient	devenus
elles	étaient	devenues

Perfect indicative

je	suis	devenu
tu	es	devenu
il	est	devenu
elle	est	devenue
nous	sommes	devenus
vous	êtes	devenus
ils	sont	devenus
elles	sont	devenues

37 suivre

Present indicative

je	suis
tu	suis
il	suit
nous	suivons
vous	suivez
ils	suivent

Present subjunctive

(que)	je	suive
(que)	tu	suives
(qu')	il	suive
(que)	nous	suivions
(que)	vous	suiviez
(qu')	ils	suivent

Future indicative

je	suivrai
tu	suivras
il	suivra
nous	suivrons
vous	suivrez
ils	suivront

Present conditional

je	suivrais
tu	suivrais
il	suivrait
nous	suivrions
vous	suivriez
ils	suivraient

Imperfect indicative

je	suivais
tu	suivais
il	suivait
nous	suivions
vous	suiviez
ils	suivaient

Past participle

suivi/suivie

Pluperfect indicative

j'	avais	suivi
tu	avais	suivi
il	avait	suivi
elle	avait	suivi
nous	avions	suivi
vous	aviez	suivi
ils	avaient	suivi
elles	avaient	suivi

Perfect indicative

j'	ai	suivi
tu	as	suivi
il	a	suivi
elle	a	suivi
nous	avons	suivi
vous	avez	suivi
ils	ont	suivi
elles	ont	suivi

38 vivre

Present indicative

je	vis
tu	vis
il	vit
nous	vivons
vous	vivez
ils	vivent

Present subjunctive

(que)	je	vive
(que)	tu	vives
(qu')	il	vive
(que)	nous	vivions
(que)	vous	viviez
(qu')	ils	vivent

Future indicative

je	vivrai
tu	vivras
il	vivra
nous	vivrons
vous	vivrez
ils	vivront

Present conditional

je	vivrais
tu	vivrais
il	vivrait
nous	vivrions
vous	vivriez
ils	vivraient

Imperfect indicative

je	vivais
tu	vivais
il	vivait
nous	vivions
vous	viviez
ils	vivaient

Past participle

vécu/vécue

Pluperfect indicative

j'	avais	vécu
tu	avais	vécu
il	avait	vécu
elle	avait	vécu
nous	avions	vécu
vous	aviez	vécu
ils	avaient	vécu
elles	avaient	vécu

Perfect indicative

j'	ai	vécu
tu	as	vécu
il	a	vécu
elle	a	vécu
nous	avons	vécu
vous	avez	vécu
ils	ont	vécu
elles	ont	vécu

39 suffire

Present indicative
je	suffis
tu	suffis
il	suffit
nous	suffisons
vous	suffisez
ils	suffisent

Present subjunctive
(que)	je	suffise
(que)	tu	suffises
(qu')	il	suffise
(que)	nous	suffisions
(que)	vous	suffisiez
(qu')	ils	suffisent

Future indicative
je	suffirai
tu	suffiras
il	suffira
nous	suffirons
vous	suffirez
ils	suffiront

Present conditional
je	suffirais
tu	suffirais
il	suffirait
nous	suffirions
vous	suffiriez
ils	suffiraient

Imperfect indicative
je	suffisais
tu	suffisais
il	suffisait
nous	suffisions
vous	suffisiez
ils	suffisaient

Past participle
suffi

Pluperfect indicative
j'	avais	suffi
tu	avais	suffi
il	avait	suffi
elle	avait	suffi
nous	avions	suffi
vous	aviez	suffi
ils	avaient	suffi
elles	avaient	suffi

Perfect indicative
j'	ai	suffi
tu	as	suffi
il	a	suffi
elle	a	suffi
nous	avons	suffi
vous	avez	suffi
ils	ont	suffi
elles	ont	suffi

40 dire

Present indicative
je	dis
tu	dis
il	dit
nous	disons
vous	dites*
ils	disent

Present subjunctive
(que)	je	dise
(que)	tu	dises
(qu')	il	dise
(que)	nous	disions
(que)	vous	disiez
(qu')	ils	disent

Future indicative
je	dirai
tu	diras
il	dira
nous	dirons
vous	direz
ils	diront

Present conditional
je	dirais
tu	dirais
il	dirait
nous	dirions
vous	diriez
ils	diraient

Imperfect indicative
je	disais
tu	disais
il	disait
nous	disions
vous	disiez
ils	disaient

Past participle
dit/dite

Pluperfect indicative
j'	avais	dit
tu	avais	dit
il	avait	dit
elle	avait	dit
nous	avions	dit
vous	aviez	dit
ils	avaient	dit
elles	avaient	dit

Perfect indicative
j'	ai	dit
tu	as	dit
il	a	dit
elle	a	dit
nous	avons	dit
vous	avez	dit
ils	ont	dit
elles	ont	dit

* vous interdisez

41 lire

Present indicative
je	lis
tu	lis
il	lit
nous	lisons
vous	lisez
ils	lisent

Present subjunctive
(que)	je	lise
(que)	tu	lises
(qu')	il	lise
(que)	nous	lisions
(que)	vous	lisiez
(qu')	ils	lisent

Future indicative
je	lirai
tu	liras
il	lira
nous	lirons
vous	lirez
ils	liront

Present conditional
je	lirais
tu	lirais
il	lirait
nous	lirions
vous	liriez
ils	liraient

Imperfect indicative
je	lisais
tu	lisais
il	lisait
nous	lisions
vous	lisiez
ils	lisaient

Past participle
lu/lue

Pluperfect indicative
j'	avais	lu
tu	avais	lu
il	avait	lu
elle	avait	lu
nous	avions	lu
vous	aviez	lu
ils	avaient	lu
elles	avaient	lu

Perfect indicative
j'	ai	lu
tu	as	lu
il	a	lu
elle	a	lu
nous	avons	lu
vous	avez	lu
ils	ont	lu
elles	ont	lu

42 écrire

Present indicative
j'	écris
tu	écris
il	écrit
nous	écrivons
vous	écrivez
ils	écrivent

Present subjunctive
(que)	j'	écrive
(que)	tu	écrives
(qu')	il	écrive
(que)	nous	écrivions
(que)	vous	écriviez
(qu')	ils	écrivent

Future indicative
j'	écrirai
tu	écriras
il	écrira
nous	écrirons
vous	écrirez
ils	écriront

Present conditional
j'	écrirais
tu	écrirais
il	écrirait
nous	écririons
vous	écririez
ils	écriraient

Imperfect indicative
j'	écrivais
tu	écrivais
il	écrivait
nous	écrivions
vous	écriviez
ils	écrivaient

Past participle
écrit/écrite

Pluperfect indicative
j'	avais	écrit
tu	avais	écrit
il	avait	écrit
elle	avait	écrit
nous	avions	écrit
vous	aviez	écrit
ils	avaient	écrit
elles	avaient	écrit

Perfect indicative
j'	ai	écrit
tu	as	écrit
il	a	écrit
elle	a	écrit
nous	avons	écrit
vous	avez	écrit
ils	ont	écrit
elles	ont	écrit

43 rire

Present indicative
je	ris
tu	ris
il	rit
nous	rions
vous	riez
ils	rient

Present subjunctive
(que)	je	rie
(que)	tu	ries
(qu')	il	rie
(que)	nous	riions
(que)	vous	riiez
(qu')	ils	rient

Future indicative
je	rirai
tu	riras
il	rira
nous	rirons
vous	rirez
ils	riront

Present conditional
je	rirais
tu	rirais
il	rirait
nous	ririons
vous	ririez
ils	riraient

Imperfect indicative
je	riais
tu	riais
il	riait
nous	riions
vous	riiez
ils	riaient

Past participle
ri

Perfect indicative
j'	ai	ri
tu	as	ri
il	a	ri
elle	a	ri
nous	avons	ri
vous	avez	ri
ils	ont	ri
elles	ont	ri

Pluperfect indicative
j'	avais	ri
tu	avais	ri
il	avait	ri
elle	avait	ri
nous	avions	ri
vous	aviez	ri
ils	avaient	ri
elles	avaient	ri

45 valoir

Present indicative
je	vaux
tu	vaux
il	vaut
nous	valons
vous	valez
ils	valent

Present subjunctive
(que)	je	vaille
(que)	tu	vailles
(qu')	il	vaille
(que)	nous	valions
(que)	vous	valiez
(qu')	ils	vaillent

Future indicative
je	vaudrai
tu	vaudras
il	vaudra
nous	vaudrons
vous	vaudrez
ils	vaudront

Present conditional
je	vaudrais
tu	vaudrais
il	vaudrait
nous	vaudrions
vous	vaudriez
ils	vaudraient

Imperfect indicative
je	valais
tu	valais
il	valait
nous	valions
vous	valiez
ils	valaient

Past participle
valu/value

Perfect indicative
j'	ai	valu
tu	as	valu
il	a	valu
elle	a	valu
nous	avons	valu
vous	avez	valu
ils	ont	valu
elles	ont	valu

Pluperfect indicative
j'	avais	valu
tu	avais	valu
il	avait	valu
elle	avait	valu
nous	avions	valu
vous	aviez	valu
ils	avaient	valu
elles	avaient	valu

44 devoir

Present indicative
je	dois
tu	dois
il	doit
nous	devons
vous	devez
ils	doivent

Present subjunctive
(que)	je	doive
(que)	tu	doives
(qu')	il	doive
(que)	nous	devions
(que)	vous	deviez
(qu')	ils	doivent

Future indicative
je	devrai
tu	devras
il	devra
nous	devrons
vous	devrez
ils	devront

Present conditional
je	devrais
tu	devrais
il	devrait
nous	devrions
vous	devriez
ils	devraient

Imperfect indicative
je	devais
tu	devais
il	devait
nous	devions
vous	deviez
ils	devaient

Past participle
dû/due

Perfect indicative
j'	ai	dû
tu	as	dû
il	a	dû
elle	a	dû
nous	avons	dû
vous	avez	dû
ils	ont	dû
elles	ont	dû

Pluperfect indicative
j'	avais	dû
tu	avais	dû
il	avait	dû
elle	avait	dû
nous	avions	dû
vous	aviez	dû
ils	avaient	dû
elles	avaient	dû

46 voir

Present indicative
je	vois
tu	vois
il	voit
nous	voyons
vous	voyez
ils	voient

Present subjunctive
(que)	je	voie
(que)	tu	voies
(qu')	il	voie
(que)	nous	voyions
(que)	vous	voyiez
(qu')	ils	voient

Future indicative
je	verrai
tu	verras
il	verra
nous	verrons
vous	verrez
ils	verront

Present conditional
je	verrais
tu	verrais
il	verrait
nous	verrions
vous	verriez
ils	verraient

Imperfect indicative
je	voyais
tu	voyais
il	voyait
nous	voyions
vous	voyiez
ils	voyaient

Past participle
vu/vue

Perfect indicative
j'	ai	vu
tu	as	vu
il	a	vu
elle	a	vu
nous	avons	vu
vous	avez	vu
ils	ont	vu
elles	ont	vu

Pluperfect indicative
j'	avais	vu
tu	avais	vu
il	avait	vu
elle	avait	vu
nous	avions	vu
vous	aviez	vu
ils	avaient	vu
elles	avaient	vu

47 savoir

Present indicative

je	sais
tu	sais
il	sait
nous	savons
vous	savez
ils	savent

Present subjunctive

(que)	je	sache
(que)	tu	saches
(qu')	il	sache
(que)	nous	sachions
(que)	vous	sachiez
(qu')	ils	sachent

Future indicative

je	saurai
tu	sauras
il	saura
nous	saurons
vous	saurez
ils	sauront

Present conditional

je	saurais
tu	saurais
il	saurait
nous	saurions
vous	sauriez
ils	sauraient

Imperfect indicative

je	savais
tu	savais
il	savait
nous	savions
vous	saviez
ils	savaient

Past participle

su/sue

Pluperfect indicative

j'	avais	su
tu	avais	su
il	avait	su
elle	avait	su
nous	avions	su
vous	aviez	su
ils	avaient	su
elles	avaient	su

Perfect indicative

j'	ai	su
tu	as	su
il	a	su
elle	a	su
nous	avons	su
vous	avez	su
ils	ont	su
elles	ont	su

48 vouloir

Present indicative

je	veux
tu	veux
il	veut
nous	voulons
vous	voulez
ils	veulent

Present subjunctive

(que)	je	veuille
(que)	tu	veuilles
(qu')	il	veuille
(que)	nous	voulions
(que)	vous	vouliez
(qu')	ils	veuillent

Future indicative

je	voudrai
tu	voudras
il	voudra
nous	voudrons
vous	voudrez
ils	voudront

Present conditional

je	voudrais
tu	voudrais
il	voudrait
nous	voudrions
vous	voudriez
ils	voudraient

Imperfect indicative

je	voulais
tu	voulais
il	voulait
nous	voulions
vous	vouliez
ils	voulaient

Past participle

voulu/voulue

Pluperfect indicative

j'	avais	voulu
tu	avais	voulu
il	avait	voulu
elle	avait	voulu
nous	avions	voulu
vous	aviez	voulu
ils	avaient	voulu
elles	avaient	voulu

Perfect indicative

j'	ai	voulu
tu	as	voulu
il	a	voulu
elle	a	voulu
nous	avons	voulu
vous	avez	voulu
ils	ont	voulu
elles	ont	voulu

49 pouvoir

Present indicative

je	peux
tu	peux
il	peut
nous	pouvons
vous	pouvez
ils	peuvent

Present subjunctive

(que)	je	puisse
(que)	tu	puisses
(qu')	il	puisse
(que)	nous	puissions
(que)	vous	puissiez
(qu')	ils	puissent

Future indicative

je	pourrai
tu	pourras
il	pourra
nous	pourrons
vous	pourrez
ils	pourront

Present conditional

je	pourrais
tu	pourrais
il	pourrait
nous	pourrions
vous	pourriez
ils	pourraient

Imperfect indicative

je	pouvais
tu	pouvais
il	pouvait
nous	pouvions
vous	pouviez
ils	pouvaient

Past participle

pu

Pluperfect indicative

j'	avais	pu
tu	avais	pu
il	avait	pu
elle	avait	pu
nous	avions	pu
vous	aviez	pu
ils	avaient	pu
elles	avaient	pu

Perfect indicative

j'	ai	pu
tu	as	pu
il	a	pu
elle	a	pu
nous	avons	pu
vous	avez	pu
ils	ont	pu
elles	ont	pu

50 falloir

Present indicative

il	faut

Present subjunctive

(qu')	il	faille

Future indicative

il	faudra

Present conditional

il	faudrait

Imperfect indicative

il	fallait

Past participle

fallu

Perfect indicative

il	a	fallu

Pluperfect indicative

il	avait	fallu

51 boire

Present indicative		Present subjunctive		
je	bois	(que)	je	boive
tu	bois	(que)	tu	boives
il	boit	(qu')	il	boive
nous	buvons	(que)	nous	buvions
vous	buvez	(que)	vous	buviez
ils	boivent	(qu')	ils	boivent

Future indicative		Present conditional	
je	boirai	je	boirais
tu	boiras	tu	boirais
il	boira	il	boirait
nous	boirons	nous	boirions
vous	boirez	vous	boiriez
ils	boiront	ils	boiraient

Imperfect indicative		Past participle
je	buvais	bu/bue
tu	buvais	
il	buvait	

Pluperfect indicative

Imperfect indicative		
nous	buvions	
vous	buviez	
ils	buvaient	

j'	avais	bu
tu	avais	bu
il	avait	bu
elle	avait	bu

Perfect indicative

j'	ai	bu
tu	as	bu
il	a	bu
elle	a	bu
nous	avons	bu
vous	avez	bu
ils	ont	bu
elles	ont	bu

nous	avions	bu
vous	aviez	bu
ils	avaient	bu
elles	avaient	bu

53 croire

Present indicative		Present subjunctive		
je	crois	(que)	je	croie
tu	crois	(que)	tu	croies
il	croit	(qu')	il	croie
nous	croyons	(que)	nous	croyions
vous	croyez	(que)	vous	croyiez
ils	croient	(qu')	ils	croient

Future indicative		Present conditional	
je	croirai	je	croirais
tu	croiras	tu	croirais
il	croira	il	croirait
nous	croirons	nous	croirions
vous	croirez	vous	croiriez
ils	croiront	ils	croiraient

Imperfect indicative		Past participle
je	croyais	cru/crue
tu	croyais	
il	croyait	

Pluperfect indicative

Imperfect indicative		
nous	croyions	
vous	croyiez	
ils	croyaient	

j'	avais	cru
tu	avais	cru
il	avait	cru
elle	avait	cru

Perfect indicative

j'	ai	cru
tu	as	cru
il	a	cru
elle	a	cru
nous	avons	cru
vous	avez	cru
ils	ont	cru
elles	ont	cru

nous	avions	cru
vous	aviez	cru
ils	avaient	cru
elles	avaient	cru

52 comprendre

Present indicative		Present subjunctive		
je	comprends	(que)	je	comprenne
tu	comprends	(que)	tu	comprennes
il	comprend	(qu')	il	comprenne
nous	comprenons	(que)	nous	comprenions
vous	comprenez	(que)	vous	compreniez
ils	comprennent	(qu')	ils	comprennent

Future indicative		Present conditional	
je	comprendrai	je	comprendrais
tu	comprendras	tu	comprendrais
il	comprendra	il	comprendrait
nous	comprendrons	nous	comprendrions
vous	comprendrez	vous	comprendriez
ils	comprendront	ils	comprendraient

Imperfect indicative		Past participle
je	comprenais	compris/comprise
tu	comprenais	
il	comprenait	

Pluperfect indicative

Imperfect indicative		
nous	comprenions	
vous	compreniez	
ils	comprenaient	

j'	avais	compris
tu	avais	compris
il	avait	compris
elle	avait	compris

Perfect indicative

j'	ai	compris
tu	as	compris
il	a	compris
elle	a	compris
nous	avons	compris
vous	avez	compris
ils	ont	compris
elles	ont	compris

nous	avions	compris
vous	aviez	compris
ils	avaient	compris
elles	avaient	compris

54 plaindre

Present indicative		Present subjunctive		
je	plains	(que)	je	plaigne
tu	plains	(que)	tu	plaignes
il	plaint	(qu')	il	plaigne
nous	plaignons	(que)	nous	plaignions
vous	plaignez	(que)	vous	plaigniez
ils	plaignent	(qu')	ils	plaignent

Future indicative		Present conditional	
je	plaindrai	je	plaindrais
tu	plaindras	tu	plaindrais
il	plaindra	il	plaindrait
nous	plaindrons	nous	plaindrions
vous	plaindrez	vous	plaindriez
ils	plaindront	ils	plaindraient

Imperfect indicative		Past participle
je	plaignais	plaint/plainte
tu	plaignais	
il	plaignait	

Pluperfect indicative

Imperfect indicative		
nous	plaignions	
vous	plaigniez	
ils	plaignaient	

j'	avais	plaint
tu	avais	plaint
il	avait	plaint
elle	avait	plaint

Perfect indicative

j'	ai	plaint
tu	as	plaint
il	a	plaint
elle	a	plaint
nous	avons	plaint
vous	avez	plaint
ils	ont	plaint
elles	ont	plaint

nous	avions	plaint
vous	aviez	plaint
ils	avaient	plaint
elles	avaient	plaint

55 éteindre

Present indicative	
j'	éteins
tu	éteins
il	éteint
nous	éteignons
vous	éteignez
ils	éteignent

Present subjunctive		
(que)	j'	éteigne
(que)	tu	éteignes
(qu')	il	éteigne
(que)	nous	éteignions
(que)	vous	éteigniez
(qu')	ils	éteignent

Future indicative	
j'	éteindrai
tu	éteindras
il	éteindra
nous	éteindrons
vous	éteindrez
ils	éteindront

Present conditional	
j'	éteindrais
tu	éteindrais
il	éteindrait
nous	éteindrions
vous	éteindriez
ils	éteindraient

Imperfect indicative	
j'	éteignais
tu	éteignais
il	éteignait
nous	éteignions
vous	éteigniez
ils	éteignaient

Past participle
éteint/éteinte

Pluperfect indicative		
j'	avais	éteint
tu	avais	éteint
il	avait	éteint
elle	avait	éteint
nous	avions	éteint
vous	aviez	éteint
ils	avaient	éteint
elles	avaient	éteint

Perfect indicative		
j'	ai	éteint
tu	as	éteint
il	a	éteint
elle	a	éteint
nous	avons	éteint
vous	avez	éteint
ils	ont	éteint
elles	ont	éteint

57 vaincre

Present indicative	
je	vaincs
tu	vaincs
il	vainc
nous	vainquons
vous	vainquez
ils	vainquent

Present subjunctive		
(que)	je	vainque
(que)	tu	vainques
(qu')	il	vainque
(que)	nous	vainquions
(que)	vous	vainquiez
(qu')	ils	vainquent

Future indicative	
je	vaincrai
tu	vaincras
il	vaincra
nous	vaincrons
vous	vaincrez
ils	vaincront

Present conditional	
je	vaincrais
tu	vaincrais
il	vaincrait
nous	vaincrions
vous	vaincriez
ils	vaincraient

Imperfect indicative	
je	vainquais
tu	vainquais
il	vainquait
nous	vainquions
vous	vainquiez
ils	vainquaient

Past participle
vaincu/vaincue

Pluperfect indicative		
j'	avais	vaincu
tu	avais	vaincu
il	avait	vaincu
elle	avait	vaincu
nous	avions	vaincu
vous	aviez	vaincu
ils	avaient	vaincu
elles	avaient	vaincu

Perfect indicative		
j'	ai	vaincu
tu	as	vaincu
il	a	vaincu
elle	a	vaincu
nous	avons	vaincu
vous	avez	vaincu
ils	ont	vaincu
elles	ont	vaincu

56 joindre

Present indicative	
je	joins
tu	joins
il	joint
nous	joignons
vous	joignez
ils	joignent

Present subjunctive		
(que)	je	joigne
(que)	tu	joignes
(qu')	il	joigne
(que)	nous	joignions
(que)	vous	joigniez
(qu')	ils	joignent

Future indicative	
je	joindrai
tu	joindras
il	joindra
nous	joindrons
vous	joindrez
ils	joindront

Present conditional	
je	joindrais
tu	joindrais
il	joindrait
nous	joindrions
vous	joindriez
ils	joindraient

Imperfect indicative	
je	joignais
tu	joignais
il	joignait
nous	joignions
vous	joigniez
ils	joignaient

Past participle
joint/jointe

Pluperfect indicative		
j'	avais	joint
tu	avais	joint
il	avait	joint
elle	avait	joint
nous	avions	joint
vous	aviez	joint
ils	avaient	joint
elles	avaient	joint

Perfect indicative		
j'	ai	joint
tu	as	joint
il	a	joint
elle	a	joint
nous	avons	joint
vous	avez	joint
ils	ont	joint
elles	ont	joint

58 distraire

Present indicative	
je	distrais
tu	distrais
il	distrait
nous	distrayons
vous	distrayez
ils	distraient

Present subjunctive		
(que)	je	distraie
(que)	tu	distraies
(qu')	il	distraie
(que)	nous	distrayions
(que)	vous	distrayiez
(qu')	ils	distraient

Future indicative	
je	distrairai
tu	distrairas
il	distraira
nous	distrairons
vous	distrairez
ils	distrairont

Present conditional	
je	distrairais
tu	distrairais
il	distrairait
nous	distrairions
vous	distrairiez
ils	distrairaient

Imperfect indicative	
je	distrayais
tu	distrayais
il	distrayait
nous	distrayions
vous	distrayiez
ils	distrayaient

Past participle
distrait/distraite

Pluperfect indicative		
j'	avais	distrait
tu	avais	distrait
il	avait	distrait
elle	avait	distrait
nous	avions	distrait
vous	aviez	distrait
ils	avaient	distrait
elles	avaient	distrait

Perfect indicative		
j'	ai	distrait
tu	as	distrait
il	a	distrait
elle	a	distrait
nous	avons	distrait
vous	avez	distrait
ils	ont	distrait
elles	ont	distrait

59 plaire

Present indicative		Present subjunctive		
je	plais	(que)	je	plaise
tu	plais	(que)	tu	plaises
il	plaît	(qu')	il	plaise
nous	plaisons	(que)	nous	plaisions
vous	plaisez	(que)	vous	plaisiez
ils	plaisent	(qu')	ils	plaisent

Future indicative		Present conditional	
je	plairai	je	plairais
tu	plairas	tu	plairais
il	plaira	il	plairait
nous	plairons	nous	plairions
vous	plairez	vous	plairiez
ils	plairont	ils	plairaient

Imperfect indicative		Past participle	
je	plaisais	plu/plue	
tu	plaisais		
il	plaisait		

		Pluperfect indicative		
nous	plaisions	j'	avais	plu
vous	plaisiez	tu	avais	plu
ils	plaisaient	il	avait	plu
		elle	avait	plu

Perfect indicative					
j'	ai	plu	nous	avions	plu
tu	as	plu	vous	aviez	plu
il	a	plu	ils	avaient	plu
elle	a	plu	elles	avaient	plu
nous	avons	plu			
vous	avez	plu			
ils	ont	plu			
elles	ont	plu			

60 mettre

Present indicative		Present subjunctive		
je	mets	(que)	je	mette
tu	mets	(que)	tu	mettes
il	met	(qu')	il	mette
nous	mettons	(que)	nous	mettions
vous	mettez	(que)	vous	mettiez
ils	mettent	(qu')	ils	mettent

Future indicative		Present conditional	
je	mettrai	je	mettrais
tu	mettras	tu	mettrais
il	mettra	il	mettrait
nous	mettrons	nous	mettrions
vous	mettrez	vous	mettriez
ils	mettront	ils	mettraient

Imperfect indicative		Past participle	
je	mettais	mis/mise	
tu	mettais		
il	mettait		

		Pluperfect indicative		
nous	mettions	j'	avais	mis
vous	mettiez	tu	avais	mis
ils	mettaient	il	avait	mis
		elle	avait	mis

Perfect indicative					
j'	ai	mis	nous	avions	mis
tu	as	mis	vous	aviez	mis
il	a	mis	ils	avaient	mis
elle	a	mis	elles	avaient	mis
nous	avons	mis			
vous	avez	mis			
ils	ont	mis			
elles	ont	mis			

61 battre

Present indicative		Present subjunctive		
je	bats	(que)	je	batte
tu	bats	(que)	tu	battes
il	bat	(qu')	il	batte
nous	battons	(que)	nous	battions
vous	battez	(que)	vous	battiez
ils	battent	(qu')	ils	battent

Future indicative		Present conditional	
je	battrai	je	battrais
tu	battras	tu	battrais
il	battra	il	battrait
nous	battrons	nous	battrions
vous	battrez	vous	battriez
ils	battront	ils	battraient

Imperfect indicative		Past participle	
je	battais	battu/battue	
tu	battais		
il	battait		

		Pluperfect indicative		
nous	battions	j'	avais	battu
vous	battiez	tu	avais	battu
ils	battaient	il	avait	battu
		elle	avait	battu

Perfect indicative					
j'	ai	battu	nous	avions	battu
tu	as	battu	vous	aviez	battu
il	a	battu	ils	avaient	battu
elle	a	battu	elles	avaient	battu
nous	avons	battu			
vous	avez	battu			
ils	ont	battu			
elles	ont	battu			

62 traduire

Present indicative		Present subjunctive		
je	traduis	(que)	je	traduise
tu	traduis	(que)	tu	traduises
il	traduit	(qu')	il	traduise
nous	traduisons	(que)	nous	traduisions
vous	traduisez	(que)	vous	traduisiez
ils	traduisent	(qu')	ils	traduisent

Future indicative		Present conditional	
je	traduirai	je	traduirais
tu	traduiras	tu	traduirais
il	traduira	il	traduirait
nous	traduirons	nous	traduirions
vous	traduirez	vous	traduiriez
ils	traduiront	ils	traduiraient

Imperfect indicative		Past participle	
je	traduisais	traduit/traduite	
tu	traduisais		
il	traduisait		

		Pluperfect indicative		
nous	traduisions	j'	avais	traduit
vous	traduisiez	tu	avais	traduit
ils	traduisaient	il	avait	traduit
		elle	avait	traduit

Perfect indicative					
j'	ai	traduit	nous	avions	traduit
tu	as	traduit	vous	aviez	traduit
il	a	traduit	ils	avaient	traduit
elle	a	traduit	elles	avaient	traduit
nous	avons	traduit			
vous	avez	traduit			
ils	ont	traduit			
elles	ont	traduit			

63 connaître

Present indicative

je	connais
tu	connais
il	connaît
nous	connaissons
vous	connaissez
ils	connaissent

Present subjunctive

(que)	je	connaisse
(que)	tu	connaisses
(qu')	il	connaisse
(que)	nous	connaissions
(que)	vous	connaissiez
(qu')	ils	connaissent

Future indicative

je	connaîtrai
tu	connaîtras
il	connaîtra
nous	connaîtrons
vous	connaîtrez
ils	connaîtront

Present conditional

je	connaîtrais
tu	connaîtrais
il	connaîtrait
nous	connaîtrions
vous	connaîtriez
ils	connaîtraient

Imperfect indicative

je	connaissais
tu	connaissais
il	connaissait
nous	connaissions
vous	connaissiez
ils	connaissaient

Past participle

connu/connue

Pluperfect indicative

j'	avais	connu
tu	avais	connu
il	avait	connu
elle	avait	connu
nous	avions	connu
vous	aviez	connu
ils	avaient	connu
elles	avaient	connu

Perfect indicative

j'	ai	connu
tu	as	connu
il	a	connu
elle	a	connu
nous	avons	connu
vous	avez	connu
ils	ont	connu
elles	ont	connu

64 naître

Present indicative

je	nais
tu	nais
il	naît
nous	naissons
vous	naissez
ils	naissent

Present subjunctive

(que)	je	naisse
(que)	tu	naisses
(qu')	il	naisse
(que)	nous	naissions
(que)	vous	naissiez
(qu')	ils	naissent

Future indicative

je	naîtrai
tu	naîtras
il	naîtra
nous	naîtrons
vous	naîtrez
ils	naîtront

Present conditional

je	naîtrais
tu	naîtrais
il	naîtrait
nous	naîtrions
vous	naîtriez
ils	naîtraient

Imperfect indicative

je	naissais
tu	naissais
il	naissait
nous	naissions
vous	naissiez
ils	naissaient

Past participle

né/née

Pluperfect indicative

j'	étais	né
tu	étais	né
il	était	né
elle	était	née
nous	étions	nés
vous	étiez	nés
ils	étaient	nés
elles	étaient	nées

Perfect indicative

je	suis	né
tu	es	né
il	est	né
elle	est	née
nous	sommes	nés
vous	êtes	nés
ils	sont	nés
elles	sont	nées

65 résoudre

Present indicative

je	résous
tu	résous
il	résout
nous	résolvons
vous	résolvez
ils	résolvent

Present subjunctive

(que)	je	résolve
(que)	tu	résolves
(qu')	il	résolve
(que)	nous	résolvions
(que)	vous	résolviez
(qu')	ils	résolvent

Future indicative

je	résoudrai
tu	résoudras
il	résoudra
nous	résoudrons
vous	résoudrez
ils	résoudront

Present conditional

je	résoudrais
tu	résoudrais
il	résoudrait
nous	résoudrions
vous	résoudriez
ils	résoudraient

Imperfect indicative

je	résolvais
tu	résolvais
il	résolvait
nous	résolvions
vous	résolviez
ils	résolvaient

Past participle

résolu/résolue

Pluperfect indicative

j'	avais	résolu
tu	avais	résolu
il	avait	résolu
elle	avait	résolu
nous	avions	résolu
vous	aviez	résolu
ils	avaient	résolu
elles	avaient	résolu

Perfect indicative

j'	ai	résolu
tu	as	résolu
il	a	résolu
elle	a	résolu
nous	avons	résolu
vous	avez	résolu
ils	ont	résolu
elles	ont	résolu

66 coudre

Present indicative

je	couds
tu	couds
il	coud
nous	cousons
vous	cousez
ils	cousent

Present subjunctive

(que)	je	couse
(que)	tu	couses
(qu')	il	couse
(que)	nous	cousions
(que)	vous	cousiez
(qu')	ils	cousent

Future indicative

je	coudrai
tu	coudras
il	coudra
nous	coudrons
vous	coudrez
ils	coudront

Present conditional

je	coudrais
tu	coudrais
il	coudrait
nous	coudrions
vous	coudriez
ils	coudraient

Imperfect indicative

je	cousais
tu	cousais
il	cousait
nous	cousions
vous	cousiez
ils	cousaient

Past participle

cousu/cousue

Pluperfect indicative

j'	avais	cousu
tu	avais	cousu
il	avait	cousu
elle	avait	cousu
nous	avions	cousu
vous	aviez	cousu
ils	avaient	cousu
elles	avaient	cousu

Perfect indicative

j'	ai	cousu
tu	as	cousu
il	a	cousu
elle	a	cousu
nous	avons	cousu
vous	avez	cousu
ils	ont	cousu
elles	ont	cousu

Numbers

Cardinal numbers in French

0	zéro*	80	quatre-vingts‡§
1	un†	81	quatre-vingt-un¶
2	deux	82	quatre-vingt-deux
3	trois	90	quatre-vingt-dix‡
4	quatre	91	quatre-vingt-onze
5	cinq	92	quatre-vingt-douze
6	six	99	quatre-vingt-dix-neuf
7	sept	100	cent
8	huit	101	cent un†
9	neuf	102	cent deux
10	dix	110	cent dix
11	onze	187	cent quatre-vingt-sept
12	douze	200	deux cents
13	treize	250	deux cent◊ cinquante
14	quatorze	1 000¤	mille
15	quinze	1 001	mille un†
16	seize	1 002	mille deux
17	dix-sept	1 020	mille vingt
18	dix-huit	1 200	mille** deux cents
19	dix-neuf	2 000	deux mille††
20	vingt	10 000	dix mille
21	vingt et un	100 000	cent mille
22	vingt-deux	100 200	cent deux mille
30	trente	1 000 000	un million‡‡
40	quarante	1 264 932	un million deux cent
50	cinquante		soixante-quatre mille
60	soixante		neuf cent trente-deux
70	soixante-dix‡	1 000 000 000	un milliard‡‡
71	soixante et onze	1 000 000 000 000	un billion‡‡

* In English *0* may be called *nought*, *zero*, *nil* or even *nothing*; French is always *zéro*: **a nought = un zéro**.

† **one** is **une** in French when it agrees with a feminine noun, so **un crayon** but **une table, des tables, vingt et une tables**, etc.

‡ (70) Also **septante** in Belgium and Switzerland. (80) Also **octante** in Switzerland and Canada, **huitante** in Switzerland. (90) Also **nonante** in Belgium and Switzerland.

§ Note that when *80* is used as a page number it has no *s*: **page eighty = page quatre-vingt**.

¶ **vingt** has no *s* when it is in the middle of a number. The only exception to this rule is when *quatre-vingts* is followed by *millions, milliards* or *billions*, e.g. **quatre-vingts millions, quatre-vingts billions** etc.

◊ **cent** does not take an *s* when it is in the middle of a number. The only exception to this rule is when it is followed by *millions, milliards* or *billions*, e.g. **trois cents millions, six cents billions** etc. It has a normal plural when it modifies other nouns: **200 inhabitants = deux cents habitants**.

¤ Where English would have a comma, French has simply a space. A full stop (period) can be used, e.g. **1.000**. As in English, there is no separation in dates between thousands and hundreds: **in 1995 = en 1995**.

** In dates, the spelling **mil** is preferred to **mille**, i.e. **en 1200 = en mil deux cents**. However, when the year is a round number of thousands, the spelling is always **mille**, so **en l'an mille, en l'an deux mille** etc.

†† **mille** is invariable; it never takes an *s*.

‡‡ The French words **million, milliard** and **billion** are nouns, and when written out in full they take **de** before another noun, e.g. **a million inhabitants = un million d'habitants**. However, when written in figures, **1,000,000 inhabitants = 1 000 000 habitants**, but is still spoken as **un million d'habitants**. When **million** etc. is part of a complex number, **de** is not used before the nouns, e.g. **6,000,210 people = six millions deux cent dix personnes**.

Use of *en*

Note the use of **en** in the following examples:

there are six	= il y **en** a six
I've got a hundred	= j'**en** ai cent

en must be used when the thing you are talking about is not expressed (the French says literally *there of them are six, I of them have a hundred* etc.). However, **en** is not needed when the object is specified:

there are six apples	= il y a six pommes

Approximate numbers

When you want to say **about** ..., remember the French ending **-aine**:

***about* ten**	= une diz**aine**
***about* ten books**	= une diz**aine** de livres
***about* fifteen**	= une quinz**aine**
***about* fifteen people**	= une quinz**aine** de personnes

Similarly *une trentaine, une quarantaine, une cinquantaine, une soixantaine* and *une centaine* (and *une douzaine* means a *dozen*). For other numbers, use **environ** (*about*):

***about* thirty-five**	= **environ** trente-cinq
***about* four thousand pages**	= **environ** quatre mille pages

Note the use of *centaines* and *milliers* to express approximate quantities:

***hundreds* of books**	= **des centaines** de livres
***thousands* of books**	= **des milliers** de livres
*I've got **thousands***	= j'en ai **des milliers**

Phrases

numbers up to ten	= les nombres jusqu'à dix
to count up to ten	= compter jusqu'à dix
almost ten	= presque dix
less than ten	= moins de dix
more than ten	= plus de dix
all ten of them	= tous les dix
all ten boys	= les dix garçons

Note the French word order:

my last ten pounds	= mes dix dernières livres
the next twelve weeks	= les douze prochaines semaines
the other two	= les deux autres
the last four	= les quatre derniers

Calculations in French

10 + 3 = 13	dix et trois font *or* égale treize
10 − 3 = 7	trois ôté de dix il reste sept *or* dix moins trois égale sept
10 × 3 = 30	dix fois trois égale trente
30 : 3 = 10	(30 ÷ 3 = 10) trente divisé par trois égale dix

Note how the French division sign differs from the English.

5^2	cinq au carré
5^3	cinq puissance trois
5^{100}	cinq puissance cent
$\sqrt{2}$	racine carrée de deux
$\sqrt{25} = 5$	racine carrée de vingt-cinq égale cinq
B > A	B est plus grand que A
A < B	A est plus petit que B

Numbers

Decimals in French

Note that French uses a comma where English has a decimal point.

	say
0,25	zéro virgule vingt-cinq
0,05	zéro virgule zéro cinq
0,75	zéro virgule soixante-quinze
3,45	trois virgule quarante-cinq
8,195	huit virgule cent quatre-vingt-quinze
9,1567	neuf virgule quinze cent soixante-sept or
	neuf virgule mille cinq cent soixante-sept
9,3456	neuf virgule trois mille quatre cent cinquante-six

Percentages in French

	say
25%	vingt-cinq pour cent
50%	cinquante pour cent
100%	cent pour cent
200%	deux cents pour cent
365%	trois cent soixante cinq pour cent
4,25%	quatre virgule vingt-cinq pour cent

Fractions in French

	say
½	un demi*
⅓	un tiers
¼	un quart
⅕	un cinquième
⅙	un sixième
⅐	un septième
⅛	un huitième
⅑	un neuvième
⅒	un dixième
1/11	un onzième
1/12	un douzième (etc)
⅔	deux tiers†
⅖	deux cinquièmes
2/10	deux dixièmes (etc)
¾	trois quarts
⅗	trois cinquièmes
3/10	trois dixièmes (etc)
1½	un et demi
1⅓	un (et) un tiers
1¼	un (et) un quart
1⅕	un (et) un cinquième
1⅙	un (et) un sixième
1⅐	un (et) un septième (etc)
5⅔	cinq (et) deux tiers
5¾	cinq (et) trois quarts
5⅘	cinq (et) quatre cinquièmes

45/100ths of = quarante-cinq centièmes de seconde a second

Ordinal numbers in French§

1st	1er‡	premier (*fem.* première)
2nd	2e	second or deuxième
3rd	3e	troisième
4th	4e	quatrième
5th	5e	cinquième
6th	6e	sixième
7th	7e	septième
8th	8e	huitième
9th	9e	neuvième
10th	10e	dixième
11th	11e	onzième
12th	12e	douzième
13th	13e	treizième
14th	14e	quatorzième
15th	15e	quinzième
16th	16e	seizième
17th	17e	dix-septième
18th	18e	dix-huitième
19th	19e	dix-neuvième
20th	20e	vingtième
21st	21e	vingt et unième
22nd	22e	vingt-deuxième
23rd	23e	vingt-troisième
24th	24e	vingt-quatrième
25th	25e	vingt-cinquième
30th	30e	trentième
31st	31e	trente et unième
40th	40e	quarantième
50th	50e	cinquantième
60th	60e	soixantième
70th	70e	soixante-dixième¶
71st	71e	soixante et onzième
72nd	72e	soixante-douzième
73rd	73e	soixante-treizième
74th	74e	soixante-quartorzième
75th	75e	soixante-quinzième
79th	79e	soixante-dix-neuvième
80th	80e	quatre-vingtième¶
81st	81e	quatre-vingt-unième
90th	90e	quatre-vingt-dixième¶
91st	91e	quatre-vingt-onzième
99th	99e	quatre-vingt-dix-neuvième
100th	100e	centième
101st	101e	cent unième
102nd	102e	cent deuxième
196th	196e	cent quatre-vingt-seizième
200th	200e	deux centième
300th	300e	trois centième
400th	400e	quatre centième
1,000th	1 000e	millième
2,000th	2 000e	deux millième
1,000,000th	1 000 000e	millionième

Like English, French makes nouns by adding the definite article:

***the* first**	= **le** premier (or **la** première, or **les** premiers *m pl* or **les** premières *f pl*)
***the* second**	= **le** second (or **la** seconde etc)
***the* first three**	= **les** trois premiers or **les** trois premières

Note the French word order in:

***the* third richest country in the world**	= **le** troisième pays **le** plus riche du monde

* Note that **half**, when not a fraction, is translated by the noun **moitié** or the adjective **demi**; see the dictionary entry.

† Note the use of **les** and **d'entre** when these fractions are used about a group of people or things: **two-thirds of them = les deux tiers d'entre eux**.

‡ This is the masculine form; the feminine is **1re** and the plural **1ers** (*m*) or **1res** (*f*). All the other abbreviations of ordinal numbers are invariable.

§ All the ordinal numbers in French behave like ordinary adjectives and take normal plural endings where appropriate.

¶ (70e) Also **septantième** in Belgium and Switzerland. (80e) Also **huitantième** in Switzerland. (90e) Also **nonantième** in Belgium and Switzerland.

Index of lexical and grammar notes